Milestone Documents of World Religions

Exploring Traditions of Faith
Through Primary Sources

MILESTONE DOCUMENTS OF WORLD RELIGIONS

Exploring Traditions of Faith
Through Primary Sources

Volume 2
240 – 1570

David M. Fahey, Editor in Chief

Schlager Group
Dallas, Texas

Milestone Documents of World Religions
Copyright © 2011 by Schlager Group Inc.

All rights reserved. No part of this book may be reproduced or utilized in any form or by any means, electronic or mechanical, including photocopying, recording, or by any information storage or retrieval systems, without permission in writing from the publisher. For information, contact:

Schlager Group Inc.
2501 Oak Lawn Avenue, Suite 440
Dallas, Tex. 75219
USA

You can find Schlager Group on the World Wide Web at
http://www.schlagergroup.com
Text and cover design by Patricia Moritz

Printed in the United States of America

10 9 8 7 6 5 4 3 2 1

ISBN: 978-0-9797758-8-8

This book is printed on acid-free paper.

Contents

Editorial and Production Staff viii
Contributors ix
Acknowledgments xi
Reader's Guide xii
Introduction xiii

Volume 1: 2404 BCE–200 CE

Pyramid Texts 2
"Instructions of Ptahhotep" 14
"Hymn to the Nile" 28
Hymn of the Righteous Sufferer 40
Rig Veda 54
Egyptian Book of the Dead 72
Enuma Elish 86
Bible: Exodus 104
Bible: Genesis 118
"Great Hymn to the Aten" 138
Epic of Gilgamesh 148
Noble Eightfold Path 164
Jain Sutras 180
Upanishads 196
Confucius: Analects 212
Orphic Tablets and Hymns 226
Dao De Jing 240
Book of Enoch 264
Cleanthes: "Hymn to Zeus" 282
Han Feizi 292
Bhagavad Gita 304
Book of Rites 322
Laws of Manu 338
Pseudo-Sibylline Oracles 354
Lotus Sutra 372
Lucretius: *On the Nature of Things* 390

Gospel of Thomas	406
Bible: Revelation	424
Ptolemy: "Letter to Flora"	442
Pirke Avot	454
Sefer Yetzirah	468

Volume 2: 240–1570

Mani: Evangelium	484
Heart Sutra	496
Popol Vuh	506
Nicene Creed	518
Tirumular: "Atbudha Dance"	528
Dionysius the Areopagite: *The Celestial Hierarchy*	542
Book of the Cave of Treasures	558
Emerald Tablet	574
Qur'an	584
Shantideva: *Bodhicaryavatara*	602
The Voyage of Bran	616
Nihongi	630
Tibetan Book of the Dead	646
Sahih al-Bukhari	662
Usul al-kafi	678
Yengishiki	692
Vishnu Purana	706
Mishneh Torah	722
Book of the Bee	740
Ibn al-'Arabi: *The Meccan Illuminations*	754
Snorra Edda	768
Francis of Assisi: "Canticle of the Creatures"	786
Thomas Aquinas: *Summa theologiae*	796
gZi-brjid	816
Mohawk Thanksgiving Address	832
Henricus Institoris and Jacobas Sprenger: *Malleus maleficarum*	844
Martin Luther: *Ninety-five Theses*	860
The Key of Solomon the King	874
Paracelsus: *Concerning the Nature of Things*	890
Rig Veda Americanus	908
Canons and Decrees of the Council of Trent	924
The Life of St. Teresa of Jesus	942
Shulchan Arukh	958

Volume 3: 1604–2002

Raag Gond	974
Fama Fraternitatis	996
Westminster Confession	1014
John Bunyan: *Pilgrim's Progress*	1032
Kumulipo	1048
Hakuin Ekaku: "Song of Meditation"	1070
Ba'al Shem Tov: "The Holy Epistle"	1080
Emanuel Swedenborg: *Invitation to the New Church*	1090
Francis Barrett: *The Magus*	1112
Doctrine and Covenants of the Church of Jesus Christ of Latter-day Saints	1130
Bab: Persian Bayan	1150
Kitab al-Jilwah	1168
Allan Kardec: *The Spirits' Book*	1180
Baha'u'llah: Kitab-i-aqdas	1194
Mary Baker Eddy: *Science and Health with Key to the Scriptures*	1208
Pittsburgh Platform	1224
Helena Blavatsky: *The Secret Doctrine*	1234
Rufus M. Jones: "Essential Truths"	1252
Rudolf Steiner: *Theosophy*	1264
Emma Goldman: "The Philosophy of Atheism"	1278
Robert Athlyi Rogers: Holy Piby	1292
Humanist Manifesto	1306
Meher Baba: *Discourses*	1318
Gerald Gardner: *Book of Shadows*	1334
Vatican II	1352
Ayatollah Khomeini: Islamic Government: Governance of the Jurist	1372
Yoruba Praise Poem to Sango	1388
Li Hongzhi: *Zhuan falun*	1396
Ismar Schorsch: *The Sacred Cluster*	1414
Jose Trigueirinho: *Calling Humanity*	1430
List of Documents by Religious Tradition	1451
Subject Index	1455

MILESTONE DOCUMENTS OF WORLD RELIGIONS

Exploring Traditions of Faith
Through Primary Sources

The death of Mani, from a thirteenth-century history book
(Or Ms 161 fol.91r Death of Mani, from 'The Chronology of Ancient Nations' by Al-Biruni / Edinburgh University Library, Scotland / With kind permission of the University of Edinburgh / The Bridgeman Art Library International)

Mani: Evangelium

ca. 240 –270

"Welfare and blessing upon the children of well-being and on the speakers and hearers of the true word."

Overview

Written sometime in the latter half of the third century, Mani's Evangelium, or "Living Gospel," which survives only in fragmentary form, is thought to present the main features of the author's creation myth, the origin of his prophetic mission, and his experiences traveling among other religious cultures. It served as one of the main scriptural texts of the emerging Manichaean religion, which began in Mesopotamia (in the region of modern-day Iraq) and spread westward into Egypt, the rest of North Africa, and parts of southern Europe and eastward along the Silk Road into Central Asia and eventually medieval China. Evidence of the text's existence has been found in most of these geographic contexts, marking the Evangelium as one of the most widely read Manichaean texts.

Ironically, even though Mani intentionally wrote his own scriptures for his new religion, very little of this material has survived into modern times. In the case of the Evangelium, there remain only a few Greek quotations, some manuscript fragments in Middle Persian, and an as-yet unpublished Coptic manuscript from Egypt, which contains readings from Mani's gospel meant for the community's liturgy. In particular, a number of key passages from this work are quoted in a later Manichaean text called *On the Origin of His Body*, found in a miniature Greek manuscript that was probably worn as an amulet and which tells the story of Mani's early life.

Context

Mani "the Living" (*Mani hayya* in Aramaic), or Manichaeus, as he was known to Westerners, was a Persian prophet of the third century CE who lived in the early years of the Sassanian Empire and founded what might be called the first self-consciously world-oriented religion in history. Persia (modern-day Iran) at this time was home to a number of different religious groups, including Zoroastrians, Jews, and various Christians sects as well as Buddhists on the eastern frontiers. While Zoroastrianism was the traditional Persian religion, and Judaism had been present for many centuries, Christianity was rapidly expanding throughout the Persian Empire, which had only recently reestablished itself after a long period of decline. Some thought that this diversity of "foreign" religions was a threat to the traditional Zoroastrian priests, while others believed that the empire should be unified under a single faith. It was in this context that Mani was able to present himself as the culmination of all previous prophecies and revelations and as a unifying force within Persian society.

Mani harshly criticized the various religious communities of his time for, in his view, imperfectly preserving and thus distorting the revelations delivered by their founders. As such, one of the key aspects of his divine mission was to leave an authentic record of his own revelation written in his own hand. The first of these religious works was written in Middle Persian and was addressed to the Persian king Shapur I, from whom Mani sought and eventually received imperial support. The others were written in Aramaic, the common language of the ancient Near East at the time. In these works, Mani described his unique and highly imaginative religious vision of the world as a battleground between forces of light and darkness. Human beings, he taught, are at the center of this epic struggle and would ultimately be the key to its eventual resolution, as long as they heeded his divinely revealed wisdom.

About the Author

Born somewhere in Persia in 216 CE to members of the aristocracy, Mani must have had what can only be described as an unusual childhood for his time. Removed from his mother at an early age and taken by his father to live in an insulated sectarian religious community, Mani nevertheless seems to have been able to achieve a high degree of literacy and education, even honing his artistic skills. Evidence indicates that he was widely versed in stories and traditions from more than one religious group. His father, Pattik, seems to have been the ancient equivalent of a spiritual "seeker," as he joined a Judeo-Christian baptizing sect known as the Elchasaites after hearing a voice in a temple commanding him to refrain from consuming meat

Time Line

216	■ Mani is born in Mesopotamia.
CA. 240–270	■ Mani writes the Evangelium, or "Living Gospel."
276/277	■ Mani is executed by the Persian king Bahram II.
297	■ The Roman emperor Diocletian issues an edict against the Manichaeans.
373	■ Augustine of Hippo joins the Manichaean Church.
387	■ Augustine of Hippo converts to Christianity, to become a renowned theologian and a canonized saint after his death.
405	■ Further anti-Manichaean legislation is introduced in the Roman Empire.
CA. 675	■ Manichaeans enter China.
763	■ Manichaeanism becomes the official religion of the Turkish Uighur Empire.
843	■ Chinese Manichaean temples and monasteries are ordered closed.
1292	■ Marco Polo meets Manichaeans in Zaitun (now Quanzhou), China.

or wine. The exact nature of his religious orientation before that event remains unclear.

Mani, it would appear, was never quite comfortable in this religious setting and is portrayed by his biographers as having grown increasingly dissatisfied with the teachings of his elders in the community. While he was still a boy, he had a profound experience of the suffering experienced by the plants harvested by his coreligionists and began to receive divine messages from a being called the "Father of Truth" by means of his celestial "twin," who counselled him to remain patient. Eventually, the time arrived to break with his home community and fulfill his own destiny as a prophet and religious reformer.

After a series of journeys, including one to study the traditions of India, Mani began to formulate and express his own religious message based upon a complex myth about the creation of the world out of two eternally opposed principles—light and darkness. The conflict between these two principles, Mani taught, resulted in the creation of the world and the imprisonment of light particles within matter. Human beings, who symbolize this struggle on a microcosmic scale, can serve as engines of cosmic salvation by consuming foods thought to contain a high proportion of light substance, such as fruits and vegetables.

These teachings resulted in the development of the central Manichaean ritual, during which the elite members of the community, known as the elect, consume food prepared for them by the laity, known as the catechumens or hearers. Eventually, when enough light particles have been liberated, the matter of darkness will collapse inward upon itself and be burned in a "Great Fire" lasting 1,486 years. Sometimes referred to as the religion of the Two Principles and the Three Times, Manichaeanism saw the final separation of light and darkness as permanent. At the heart of Mani's myth is a trinitarian pattern of Father-Mother-Child in which God sacrifices a part of his essence for the liberation of all light-beings. This parallels in a highly mythologized sense the basic dynamic of early Christian salvation discourse and provides further evidence of the movement's fundamentally Christian origins.

After receiving a certain degree of official support from Shapur I, Mani was allowed to spread his message throughout the Persian Empire and to send missionaries to points beyond—into the Roman Empire and Central Asia. When the king died, however, jealousy among the traditional Zoroastrian priesthood led to Mani's arrest and execution in either 276 or 277, which his followers commemorated as his symbolic "crucifixion." In the wake of Mani's death, the Manichaean Church was scattered, although its missionaries continued to bring his message to the far corners of the world, translating Manichaean writings into a multitude of languages as they went. This dissemination explains the diverse linguistic profile of Manichaean source material, which is preserved in Latin, Greek, Coptic, Syriac, Middle Persian, Turkish, Arabic, and Chinese.

Explanation and Analysis of the Document

Even though a growing number of authentic Manichaean texts have been discovered, most consist of writings from later generations of disciples. Often, these works reflect the concerns of the later times and incorporate new developments in Manichaean teaching. Little remains from Mani's own "canonical" writings, meaning that scholars are at a distinct disadvantage in trying to reconstruct an accurate picture of his religious thought. Moreover, the variety of ancient languages in which the source material is found makes the study of Manichaeanism one of the most challenging theological research specializations. Nonetheless, a much clearer picture of Mani's motives and experiences as a religious leader has slowly begun to emerge.

The fragments included here represent all the passages from Mani's Evangelium that have been identified and published from a variety of different sources. Much more material remains unpublished, in particular, the passages found in the Coptic manuscript from Egypt. The extremely poor condition of this manuscript, along with a number of intervening historical circumstances, has delayed the publication of its contents. The few available passages from the Evangelium provide a glimpse into the tradition founded by one of the most important religious figures of late antiquity.

Owing to their age, the manuscripts in which these texts are found are badly damaged. The pages have often deteriorated, and therefore parts of the original text are missing. Sometimes the missing words can be reconstructed based on what is being said before or after the gap, especially if a few letters can be still seen. In this case the reconstructed words are marked by square brackets. Frequently, however, we cannot fill in the blanks, so the missing passage is marked with an ellipsis in square brackets. Finally, the fact that the grammar of the original ancient language can be difficult to translate into English means that the translator sometimes has to insert words not found in the original text, just so it will read more smoothly in English. These words are surrounded by parentheses. If the translator is unsure of the reconstruction, a question mark is used to indicate this uncertainty.

♦ **Fragment 1**

In this fragment from the Evangelium, Mani presents his prophetic credentials as an "apostle of Jesus Christ" sent on behalf of the "Father of Truth." The Father is described as an eternal being who exists before and after the creation of "everything." While this could be read simply as religious rhetoric in veneration of the Father, it nevertheless appears to contradict or at least mediate Mani's teaching that, as documented elsewhere, two eternally opposed principles lay at the foundation of the universe. Whether or not Mani was a cosmic dualist in the strictest sense has been debated by scholars, since he appears equally insistent on both the primacy of the Father, as lord of the light realm, and the reality of darkness and its material prison. Ultimately, however, it is the Father and his powers of light who will triumph at the end of time.

Mani also presents himself as the revealer of "truth." For Mani, this is a truth not found in other religious traditions, since their founders did not record their wisdom in writing and therefore allowed it to be distorted. He reveals this truth only to a select group of individuals, variously described as his "companions," the "children of peace," "the undying generation," and the chosen "elect." While Mani's religious vision was universal in tone, it was elitist in application. Only members of the Manichaean community had access to the core teachings. The word *hope* (written in Greek in this fragment) reflects a basic wordplay in Aramaic, the language of Mani and his earliest followers, by which the same root can mean both "hope" and "gospel." In this sense, there is a fundamental optimism in Mani's message, since the "[good] news" that he preaches in his "gos-

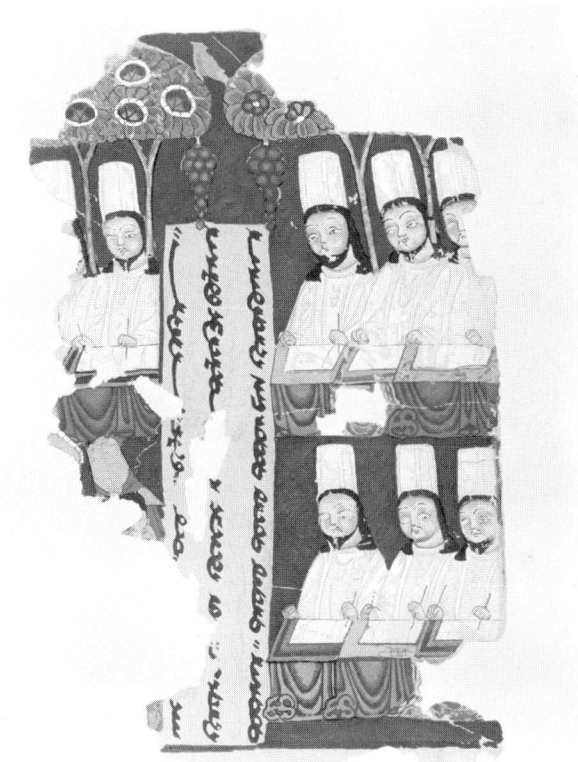

Fragment of manuscript from Turkestan, showing Manichaean priests
(Manichaean Priests, Manichaean miniature with text in Uigur (vellum), Turkestan School / Ruins of Idikut-Shahri, Turfan, Turkestan / Archives Charmet / The Bridgeman Art Library International)

pel" is the eventual triumph of light over darkness. In this way, Manichaeanism cannot be stereotyped with the same pessimistic outlook often attributed to Gnostic groups.

The passage also contains an argument that was commonplace in Mani's writings, namely, that he himself recorded the revelation given to him by the Father, thereby insulating his followers from any charges of corrupting and altering his words. Scholars have long suggested that because of this foundation, Manichaean teaching remained consistent through all the geographic areas and time periods in which it existed. Recent research, however, suggests that this was not the case and that certain aspects of Manichaean discourse were altered as the movement developed.

One puzzling aspect of this passage concerns the form used for Mani's name, which was normally rendered in Greek and Coptic as Manichaios or in Latin as Manichaeus but in this case occurs as *Mannichaeus*, with two *n*'s. This has been interpreted as Greek wordplay whereby Mani's Aramaic honorific *Mani hayya*, meaning "Mani the Living," comes to mean "source of Manna," that is, the bread that nourished the Hebrews during the Exodus, their legendary departure from ancient Egypt. It seems doubtful that Mani would have applied such Greek wordplay to himself. It is possible, then, that this citation from his gospel has experienced some light editorial coloring.

Essential Quotes

> "I Mannichaeus, apostle of Jesus Christ, through the will of God, the Father of Truth, from whom I also came into being."

> "For if [the whole] world and all men obeyed [him], I would be able, with this possession and advantage which my father has given me, to enrich them and render the wisdom sufficient for the whole world."

> "I have distinguished the light-gods from the archons."

> "Welfare and blessing upon the children of well-being and on the speakers and hearers of the true word."

♦ Fragment 2

This passage speaks to the issue of Mani's intended audience. Given the universalizing nature of his message, he presumably intended his message for the entire world, which he saw as languishing in sectarian error. Mani, however, was keenly aware of the hostility that his religious critique was likely to inspire; thus, the "secrets" of the Father are said to be reserved for the members of his religious community of believers, thereby reinforcing an esoteric tendency common among ancient Gnostic groups. Nevertheless, Mani does express his wish that the whole world might do the will of the Father.

The notion that Mani preached a universal message intended to complete and correct all previous prophecies provided a significant template for later Islamic ideas about the finality and supremacy of Muhammad's revelation. While there is evidence of a Manichaean presence in Arabia in late antiquity, just how widespread the religion's ideas would have then been remains uncertain.

♦ Fragment 3

In this passage, Mani expresses gratitude to the Father for sending him the "Syzygos," or "companion" (referred to as the "twin" in the tenth-century Islamic literary survey *Kitab al-fihrist*, or Book of the Index, by Muhammad ibn Ishaq ibn al-Nadim), who served as celestial messenger and agent of revelation. This being, he states, liberated him "from the error of those of that rule," meaning the erroneous doctrines of the sect in which he was brought up. Mani's break with the Elchasaites is central to the narrative of *On the Origin of His Body* in its surviving form, with the break portrayed as the springboard from which he then launches his missionary career.

♦ Fragment 4

This fragment is from the "First Discourse" of the Evangelium, known as the aleph chapter; some accounts suggest that Mani's original gospel was divided according to the letters of the Aramaic alphabet. In this passage, Mani affirms his dualistic vision of the cosmos, which divides beings into two camps: those derived from the light realm belonging to the Father and those who are the progeny of darkness. It also highlights the fact that Mani conceived of the light realm as existing in the lofty sphere of the heavens, while the kingdom of darkness was relegated to the depths of the abyss, where its "archons," or rulers, exist in a state of perpetual war and chaos. Mani alludes to the "light-gods" in the plural, because in Manichaean discourse the light realm is inhabited by a multiplicity of divine beings. Some of them have specific functions within the Manichaean creation myth, while others simply populate the Father's celestial court, of which he is ultimately sovereign. This, too, highlights the often perplexing nature of Manichaean theology. As mentioned, Mani is said to have taught the existence of two eternally opposed principles, yet he sometimes speaks of the Father in rather monotheistic tones. Similarly, even though the Father is the supreme ruler of the light realm and the source of divine power, his world is populated by a number of divine beings and essences, verging on polytheism. In this sense, Manichaeanism is a religion that is extremely difficult to classify.

♦ Fragments 5 and 6

In these fragmentary passages, Mani alludes to "the *dogma*," or sectarian teaching, and "the *nomos*," or religious law, of his home community, philosophies that he came to distrust and ultimately to reject. Both terms imply a certain degree of strictness and inflexibility, especially nomos, which was the Greek equivalent of *torah*—the Jewish law. Part of the Elchasaite teaching seems to have involved the classification of plants according to their worth and ritual purity. When Mani established his own religious community, the classification of plants according to their light content played a central role in ritual activities.

In Fragment 5, Mani makes repeated reference to his "body" and its origin, which resonates with the title of the work *On the Origin of His Body* from the miniature Greek manuscript. The term *body* is thought by some to represent the Manichaean community as a whole. Therefore, when the text refers to the origin of Mani's "body," it may carry the double meaning of both his early life and the beginnings of his movement.

◆ Fragment 7

In this passage, Mani recounts his travels to India, which he seems to have undertaken both to study the doctrines of the Brahmans and to spread his own religious message, although it is unclear how much he had formulated his message at this point. In India, which bordered on the Persian Empire, he found a country with a variety of ancient and well-established "sects" and "castes," although the Brahmans, in particular, he found too settled in their ways to accept any kind of new teaching. They, he claims, appear to listen only to their own teachers and forefathers. This insular and conservative religious perspective appeared to startle Mani, who was attempting to build a universal and transnational church for all of humanity.

Mani's missionary journey to India may have some sort of connection to the alleged missionary journey of the apostle Thomas to the same region. Scholars have noticed a number of significant points of contact between Manichaeanism and the literature associated with Thomas and the Christian traditions he inspired. At the very least, Manichaeans and Thomasine Christians were active in the same Mesopotamian environment, which appears to have lead to a certain degree of cross-fertilization.

◆ Fragment 8

In this fragment, Mani relates a peculiar bit of Jewish lore related to the Exodus story. This, in itself, is exceptional because it has often been assumed that Mani had little interest in mainstream Jewish traditions. Yet in this instance he explains that the name of "Mount Sinai" was derived from the type of thistle, *sina,* found in its vicinity. It is interesting to note that in this recounting of the episode from the Exodus story, no mention appears to be made of Moses, the central figure of the Jewish narrative. Rather, the "seed of Abraham" are described as "Babylonians" and "Chaldaeans," both peoples from Mani's homeland of Mesopotamia, although the motive for this identification remains unclear. Perhaps Mani was attempting to appeal to a common "Babylonian" origin for himself and the Jews. After all, Mani is elsewhere (in Abu Raihan Muhammad ibn Ahmad al-Beruni's eleventh-century cultural investigation *Kitab fi tahqiq ma li'l-Hind,* translated as *India*) quoted as identifying himself as the messenger of "the God of Truth to Babylonia."

◆ Fragment 9

This excerpt from the aleph chapter of the Evangelium is found in a Middle Persian liturgical text evoking the Maiden of Light, the being who in Manichaean cosmogony assists the First Man in his battle against the powers of darkness. It is important to note the unique mode of Trinitarian language employed here, which mentions the Maiden being praised by a Father, Mother, and Son. Each of these beings plays a central role in the unfolding of the Manichaean creation story, with the basic framework of that story and of early Manichaean theology in general apparently built upon the alternative notion of the Trinity found here and in other examples of Gnostic literature. This concept of the Trinity, based on an idea of Father, Mother, and Child, appears to have rivaled the proto-orthodox doctrine of Father, Son, and Holy Spirit—which is itself placed in remarkable juxtaposition with the Manichaean Trinity in the ensuing sentences. Thus, two different concepts of the Trinity underlie the same passage. In the fragment's last paragraph (which may, in fact, not form part of the original Evangelium), Mani reaffirms his status as an "apostle of Jesus the friend" and reiterates that he owes his wisdom to "the Father, the true God."

◆ Fragment 10

This bilingual passage, alternating versions of lines in Middle Persian and in Sogdian, resembles the previous fragment in that it constitutes a litany of praise, although this time Jesus, the Maiden of Light, the "holy church," and the "hearers of the true word" are venerated. Within the context of Central Asia, it appears as though Sogdian was the language most commonly understood by the merchant class, by which the religion was spread and took root. This explains the bilingualism of the manuscript fragment. The Sogdian version of the litany gives insight into Manichaean missionary practices, where the Father is equated with "Zurwan," or Zurvan, the Iranian high god favored by members of the Sassanian court. Unlike some of its religious rivals, Manichaeanism never placed great importance on one particular language as a sacred literary vehicle. Instead, Manichaeans used a multiplicity of dialects to transmit their message and disseminate their texts as widely as possible.

Audience

Like most religious literature, Mani's Evangelium was likely intended for consumption within the Manichaean tradition, unlike his first known work, *Shaburagan,* which was addressed specifically to the Persian court of King Shapur I. Still, it is entirely possible that portions of the gospel were used in or adapted to literature aimed at recruiting new members. While it is conceivable that a text such as *On the Origin of His Body* could have been read as a sort of introductory biography by outsiders interested in the movement, the passages from the Evangelium contained in the unedited Coptic manuscript were certainly intended for liturgical use within the community itself. Yet given the fragmentary nature of the text, it remains difficult to ascertain its full function and intended audience. Presumably that function parallels the purpose of other early Christian Gospels or at least Mani's idea of how those Gospels functioned, in that the Evangelium probably provided a primary vehicle for Mani to communicate the central narrative of his life and revelation, aspects that are essentially inseparable, much as they are in the mainstream Christian understanding of Jesus.

Still, given the range of primary Manichaean sources discovered so far and the fact that so little comes from Mani's own works, it is difficult to tell how the community's literature was used among its various hierarchies. For instance, it is possible that some literature was reserved for the elite members of the community, the elect, while other texts were read by the laity, known as catechumens or hearers. This is certainly the impression given by some recently discovered Manichaean personal letters from Egypt. A third possibility could be that later Manichaean tradition shaped the discourse in ways divergent from Mani's own writings and thus led to a deemphasis of the canonical writings. At the same time, the Evangelium itself appears to be one of the canonical texts that continued to be read with some regularity.

Thus, modern scholars can assume that the Evangelium was intended to be read by members of the Manichaean community, whether elect or catechumen, and that it was read in at least four known linguistic settings—the original Aramaic (no longer extant), Greek, Coptic, and Middle Persian. This means that the text was known and actively used in the liturgies of western, eastern, and central Manichaean communities.

While there are no known Manichaeans in the present day—at least none that can trace their origins to the ancient Manichaean Church—the Evangelium is an important witness to an alternative stream of Christianity that had a rich and varied history. Certainly many past Christian authorities would have been content to see the Manichaean tradition erased from historical memory, but there can be no denying the immense and widespread impact of this great rival to the mainstream church. Religious historians can only hope that the unedited portions of the Evangelium will be published in the near future, thereby giving a more complete picture of its content and message.

Impact

Although it initially escaped the attention of Roman officials, the Persian origins of Manichaeanism led to it being declared an illegal sect by Emperor Diocletian in 297. Nevertheless, the movement continued to grow, attracting new followers, such as, most notably, Augustine of Hippo, who

---

Questions for Further Study

1. Why do you think the Evangelium and the Manichaean religion essentially disappeared but Islam developed into a major world religion—this despite the fact that both Mani and Muhammad based their religions on personal revelations and neither broke entirely with earlier established faiths? For reference, see the entry on the Sahih al-Bukhari.

2. Mani's vision is described as being one of an epic battle between the forces of light and darkness. Compare his vision with that found in Dionysius the Areopagite: *The Celestial Hierarchy*. Why do you think images of light (and darkness) are used frequently in writing about spiritual matters?

3. The following statement is made about Mani: "While he was still a boy, he had a profound experience of the suffering experienced by the plants harvested by his coreligionists and began to receive divine messages from a being called the 'Father of Truth' by means of his celestial 'twin,' who counselled him to remain patient." Mani went on to become a religious leader, and his work is being read some seventeen centuries later. What do you think the response might be if Mani lived today and had similar views? What, in your opinion, accounts for the difference?

4. What is Manichaeanism? Why was it considered a threat? What was the reaction of the Catholic Church to Manichaeanism and why? Why, "among Muslim scholars," were Manichaeans "not accorded the same degree of tolerance as was granted to Jews and Christians as 'peoples of the book'"?

5. The Near East during this time was a swirl of cultures and religions: Christianity and various offshoots of Christianity, Judaism, the Roman Empire, Greeks, Persians, Zoroastrians, Arabs, and others. How would you describe the position of Manichaeanism in this swirl of contending cultures and beliefs?

after nearly a decade with the sect would go on to become one of the most influential Christian theologians of all time and a canonized saint.

After the seventh century, the situation of Manichaeans in the Islamic world was equally precarious. Although they generated a great deal of curiosity among Muslim scholars, Manichaeans were not accorded the same degree of tolerance as was granted to Jews and Christians as "peoples of the book." Sogdian traders carried the religion eastward along the Silk Road, where it adapted to local Iranian and Buddhist terminology. Although it was greeted with suspicion by many, Manichaeanism would briefly be adopted as the official religion of the Uighur Turks of Central Asia during the eighth and ninth centuries. Gradually, the Manichaean Church fades from the historical record, suppressed in the west and disappearing once and for all in the late medieval period along the southern coast of China. All that exists of its fascinating history are the scattered literary remains that include the Evangelium. Rumors of a small number of Manichaean families in China persisted until recent times.

It is difficult to gauge the specific impact of Mani's Evangelium other than to say that it represents one of the core scriptural texts—if not the core text—of one of late antiquity's most widespread and influential religious movements. From the fourth-century pages of Augustine's *Confessions* to the tenth-century *Fihrist* of the Muslim encyclopedist Ibn al-Nadim, Manichaeans are a persistent and inescapable presence within late antique and early-medieval religious discourse. Highly effective religious organizers and prolific publishers of religious literature, Manichaeans left an indelible mark on the cultural landscape of both Eastern and Western religious cultures. More important, however, is where Mani and his message stand in the chain of the great revealed religions. After all, Mani proclaimed himself "Seal of the Prophets" long before the age of the Prophet of Mecca, Muhammad. This and other parallels point to Manichaeanism as a pivotal and all-too-often neglected link in the chain of religious ideas formed by the great Abrahamic traditions.

Further Reading

■ Books

Burkitt, Francis C. *The Religion of the Manichees*. Cambridge, U.K.: Cambridge University Press, 1925.

Funk, Wolf-Peter. "Mani's Account of Other Religions according to the Coptic Synaxeis Codex." In *New Light on Manichaeism: Papers from the Sixth International Congress on Manichaeism*, ed. Jason David BeDuhn. Leiden, Netherlands: Brill, 2009.

Gardner, Iain, and Samuel N. C. Lieu, eds. *Manichaean Texts from the Roman Empire*. Cambridge, U.K.: Cambridge University Press, 2004.

Klimkeit, Hans-Joachim, ed. and trans. *Gnosis on the Silk Road: Gnostic Texts from Central Asia*. New York: HarperCollins, 1993.

Lieu, Samuel N. C. *Manichaeism in the Later Roman Empire and Medieval China*. Tübingen, Germany: J. C. B. Mohr, 1992.

Tardieu, Michel. *Manichaeism*, trans. M. B. DeBevoise. Urbana: University of Illinois Press, 2008.

—Timothy Pettipiece

MANI: EVANGELIUM

♦ **Fragment 1**
(from the Greek Cologne Mani Codex 66–68)

He wrote [again and] said in the gospel of his most holy hope: "I Mannichaeus, apostle of Jesus Christ, through the will of God, the Father of Truth, from whom I also came into being. He lives and abides for all eternity. Before everything he is, and he remains after everything. Everything which has happened and will happen, is established through his power. From him I have my being, and I exist also according to his will. And from him all that is true was revealed to me and from [his] truth I exist. I have seen [the truth of eternity which he revealed.] And I declared the truth to my companions; I preached peace to the children of peace; I proclaimed hope to the undying generation; I chose the elect and showed the path leading to the height to those who will go up according to this truth. I have proclaimed hope and revealed this revelation; and have written this immortal gospel, in which I have put down these pre-eminent secret rites and declared great deeds, indeed the greatest and holiest of supreme deeds of power. [And] these things which [he revealed] I have made known [to those who live in accordance with] the vision of supreme truth which I have seen, and the most glorious revelation which was revealed to me."

♦ **Fragment 2**
(from the Greek Cologne Mani Codex 68–69)

Yet again he said: "All the secrets which my father gave me, I have hidden and sheltered from the sects and gentiles and indeed the world, but to you I have revealed them in accordance with the will of my most blessed father. And if he should wish me to once more, I will reveal them to you. For the gift which was given to me by my father is very great and [rich]. For if [the whole] world and all men obeyed [him], I would be able, with this possession and advantage which my father has given me, to enrich them and render the wisdom sufficient for the whole world."

♦ **Fragment 3**
(from the Greek Cologne Mani Codex 69–70)

Again he said: "When my father showed favour and treated me with pity and solicitude, he sent from there my never-failing Syzygos, the complete fruit of immortality, who might ransom and redeem me from the error of those of that rule. He came to [me and] brought to me [the] noblest hope, the [redemption] of immortality, true instructions and the laying on of hands from my father. He came and chose me in preference to others and set me aside, drawing me away from the midst of those of that rule in which I was brought up."

♦ **Fragment 4**
(from the unpublished Coptic Synaxeis Codex)

(I have set apart,) … [the living] offspring [… from] what is dead, the children of the light from [the] offspring of darkness. I have separated the children of the height from the offspring of the abyss, the children of God from the children of the enemy. I have distinguished the light-gods from the archons …

♦ **Fragment 5**
(from the unpublished Coptic Synaxeis Codex)

… the *dogma* and … in the *nomos* … among them … and the birth/generation of the body … they nourished my body alone … in that *dogma* … and its presbyters … my body … that I should do … thus I did not trust them when I was small …

♦ **Fragment 6**
(from the unpublished Coptic Synaxeis Codex)

… in a … way, according to individual *nomoi*. They did … They separated plant from plant, vegetable from vegetable, [herb] from herb (?). And so did I. I separated (?) … their outrage, according to their *nomos* … I took it from them, they being … consideration. In this way, I chanced upon (?) … they … by his/its *schema*, by his/its *typos*, thus … outside. I went into the monasteries [which belonged [?]) to them. They (?) desired … outside and [inside (?) …] … in it.

♦ **Fragment 7**
(from the unpublished Coptic Synaxeis Codex)

… little by little … the error of their *nomos*. But … error … They have already dissolved [and …] them in/by the bond of the *nomos*, by way of the … They were … away on account of its error. Thus [I …] little by little and I drew many away from the error [of the]

Document Text

nomos. I led them from death to life, for I [am ...] against them (?) ... according to their ... for a time.

I ... their (?) ... in the countries of the land (?) of the east, of [India]. In that place [I encountered (?)] many sects (*dogma*) and castes [which (?) ...] except for [their] *nomos*, while the ... through one another, according to the ... that place, the ones that I distinguished—caste by caste, *dogma* by *dogma*. In that place I took a close look at the caste of the Brahmans (and found out) that they were strong and settled in their ... in the land of the east. They are respected in their [caste (?) ...] ... other *dogma(ta)*. Now, their *nomos* is the following. I took a close look at their *nomos* and found that (?) the leaders and teachers ... in prophecy and ascesis, in special skills ... the hair of their head. It is to their own teachers that they listen—ever since (?) [their] prophets, their fathers.

When I saw myself that they were in such a manner opposed and incapable of listening to any but their own ... and their *nomos*, that they are lined up and are ... their caste and did not search outside of ... their *nomos*. As soon as [I ...] ... my head, I sought after ... I travelled around in their countries ... I ... the disposition which ... their places which ... I (?) said (?), "Your *nomos*, which ... which ..."

♦ **Fragment 8**
(from the unpublished Coptic Synaxeis Codex)
... [he] chose the tribe ... [the] entire [country] ... [He] ... their ... so that they ... godhead. Later on, [he] ... in order to [...], that is (?), the *skhina* ... , in order to seize ... set free (?) her army. Finally, then, after having ... the seed of Abraham, she (?) ... them off. They ... and they ... the slavery and the humiliation ... (forced?) labor. So they departed from Egypt [and passed through (?)] the field of the mountain of *sina* (that is, Mount Sinai). There were great [quantities of] thistles [growing (?)] in that [place (?)]. Now, the thistle is called *sina* in the language of that place ... ... *skhina*, after the name of the thorn-tree with which [the whole place (?)] is filled. ... These Babylonians released ... and they ... in it. They seized [the land (?) of] ... and became kings in it ... Euphrates ... these Chal[daeans (?)] ... in Hebrew ... in Babylon ...

♦ **Fragment 9**
(from Middle Persian M17)
He teaches in the Gospel Aleph.

[She was praised and be praised), the Maiden of Light, head of all wisdoms. It was praised and is praised, the holy church, by the power of the Father,

Glossary

Aleph	the prototypical first letter in various alphabets, including that of Hebrew, Arabic, and the Phoenician
archons	maleficent, world-governing powers created with the material world by a subordinate god called the Demiurge, or creator
Brahmans	the priestly caste in India
Chaldaea	a region in the southern part of modern-day Iraq, frequently used at the time as a synonym for Babylonia
dogma	here, sectarian teachings
Euphrates	a major river in modern-day Iraq
nomoi	plural of nomos
nomos	religious law
presbyters	church elders
Ramratrux	a Sogdian version of "Mother of Life," possibly meaning "liberal with joy"
skhina	probably a reference to a dish eaten by Jews, especially in Morocco
Sogdian	pertaining to Sogdiana, an ancient Iranian civilization
Syzygos	"companion"
Zurwan	or Zurvan, the Iranian high god favored by members of the Sassanian court

Document Text

by the praise of the Mother, and [by the wisdom of the Son], and on the speakers and hearers of the true word. [8 *lines blank*] Let there be praise and honour to the Father and to the Son and to the Holy Ghost and [to the holy book.][... *ca. 15 lines lost* ... which instructs the eye and] ear, and teaches the fruit of truth. [8 *lines left blank*]

I Mani, apostle of Jesus the friend, by the will of the Father, the true God, he from whom I came to be, ... is after all [things], and everything which has been and will be stands by his power. The fortunate receive this [good] news, the wise recognize [it], the strong don [it] (as their armour), the learned [consider(?)] (it to be) better ...

♦ **Fragment 10
(from bilingual Middle Persian [Pe.] and Sogdian [Sogd.] M172)**

... [Pe.] and the understanding of the wise. [Sogd.] *He has been praised and will be praised, the dearest-of-the-dear son, the life-giving [saviour] Jesus, head of all giving, support of the pure and perception of the wise.* [Pe.] She was praised and be praised the Maiden of Light, head of all wisdoms. [Sogh.] *She has been praised and will be praised, the wonder-working Kanigrosan [Maiden of Light], who is head of all wisdom.* [Pe.] It was praised and is praised, the holy church, by the power of the Father, by the praise of the Mother, and by the wisdom of the Son. [Sogd.] *It has been praised and will be praised, the holy church, righteousness, by the power of the Father, god Zurwan, by the praise of the Mother [of Life], god Ramratrux, and by the wisdom of the Son Jesus.* [Pe.] Welfare and blessing upon the children of well-being and on the speakers and hearers of the true word. [Sogd.] *Welfare and blessing upon the children of well-being and on the speakers and hearers of the trustworthy holy word.* [Pe.]

Let there be praise and honour to the Father and to the Son and to the Holy Ghost and to the holy book. [Sogd.] *Likewise let there be praise and reverence to the Father and to the Son and to the Holy Spirit, and to the living scripture.* [Pe.] The saying of the living Gospel, which instructs eye and ear, and teaches the fruit of truth.

The Buddha preaching on Vulture Peak
(Shaka, the Historical Buddha, Preaching on Vulture Peak, Japanese School [8th century] / Museum of Fine Arts, Boston, Massachusetts, USA / William Sturgis Bigelow Collection / The Bridgeman Art Library International)

Heart Sutra

ca. 250–400 CE

"Form does not differ from emptiness; emptiness does not differ from form."

Overview

The Heart Sutra is one of several texts that are classed as Prajnaparamita Sutras, or "Perfection of Wisdom" texts. Perfection of Wisdom scriptures are associated with the first expression of the ideas related to a radical shift in the focus of Buddhism that arose in India around the beginning of the first millennium. Adherents promoted this new perspective by calling it Mahayana (translated as "great vehicle") as a way to express their sense of the superiority of their views over earlier forms of Buddhism. Perfection of Wisdom scriptures are the hallmark of the Mahayana movement. Mahayana Buddhists took their texts and teachings outside India to China, where this form of Buddhism eventually spread across Asia. Devoted followers of Mahayana Buddhism attribute all Perfection of Wisdom scriptures to Nagarjuna (ca. 150–250 CE). Nagarjuna is regarded as a second Buddha by most East Asian Mahayana Buddhists. The Heart Sutra concisely summarizes key principles that are representative of longer Perfection of Wisdom texts.

The Perfection of Wisdom scriptures are ordered by length. The Perfection of Wisdom in Eight Thousand Lines is the oldest, dating to around 250 CE, but the first Perfection of Wisdom scripture may have been written as early as 100 BCE. The Heart Sutra is among the shortest of the Perfection of Wisdom scriptures. The only shorter version is the Perfection of Wisdom in One Letter. These shorter versions and verse summaries were written between 250 and 500 CE. The oldest known copy of the Heart Sutra was written in Chinese around 400 CE and is attributed to the Indian philosopher Kumarajiva (344–413 CE). India is the source of most Perfection of Wisdom scriptures. The oldest Sanskrit version of the Heart Sutra dates to the mid-seventh century CE. It may be that the Heart Sutra was originally written in Chinese and then translated into Sanskrit in an attempt to make it appear to have originated in India.

Context

Describing the historical context behind the Heart Sutra involves more than one perspective. We must consider the historical milieu that gave rise to its writing and also take into account how adherents understand its origins. The Buddha was born as a prince with the name Siddhartha Gautama. According to Buddhist legends, at the age of twenty-nine he reached enlightenment, becoming Shakyamuni Buddha, and was persuaded to teach others the process he had used to reach this state of liberation. The summary of his teaching is called the Four Noble Truths. Buddhists refer to the moment that he delivered this first teaching as the First Turning of the Wheel. It is understood to have taken place at a deer park in Sarnath near Varanasi in northern India (near modern-day Nepal) to an audience of his close associates.

Most Mahayana traditions claim that the Buddha spoke the Perfection of Wisdom and other Mahayana scriptures at a subsequent event referred to as the Second Turning of the Wheel. According to legend, this event took place before an audience of bodhisattvas on Vulture Peak, located in Bihar, India. (Bodhisattvas are beings who have reached a high level of understanding and who are on their way to becoming fully enlightened buddhas.) The event has no historic authenticity in any ordinary sense: Mahayana devotees believe that this gathering took place on a higher plane, accessible only by supernatural means. Moreover, the Buddha was able to deliver several scriptures simultaneously at a multiplicity of locations. Mahayana adherents agree that it requires considerable mind stretching to accept and understand this possibility.

Mahayana Buddhists believe that at the time the Perfection of Wisdom and other Mahayana scriptures were first delivered, there was no one on earth who was capable of hearing their wisdom or even accessing the higher plane where the Buddha first spoke them. For this reason, the Buddha hid these teachings in the land of the Nagas for a later time, when humanity would have matured sufficiently to grasp their meaning. Legends claim that the Indian philosopher Nagarjuna, considered the second Buddha by most East Asian Mahayana Buddhists, retrieved many of these scriptures from the land of the Nagas.

Grasping the central tenets of Mahayana Buddhist philosophy requires some background knowledge of early Indian Buddhism, which traces its origins to the Buddha's first teaching of the Four Noble Truths. These teachings

Time Line

CA. 480 BCE	Using eighty years as the estimated length of his life, this is the date accepted for the birth of Siddhartha Gautama.
CA. 451 BCE	According to legend, at the age of twenty-nine Siddhartha Gautama reaches enlightenment, becoming Shakyamuni Buddha.
CA. 451–400 BCE	According to Mahayana devotees, the Second Turning of the Wheel takes place during the Buddha's lifetime.
CA. 420–380 BCE	The Buddha dies.
CA. 300 BCE	The earliest materials found in the Abhidharma are composed.
25 BCE	The Theravadins hold a council in Anuradhapura, the ancient capital of Sri Lanka, establishing the contents of the set of scriptures referred to today as the Pali canon.
CA. 150 CE	Nagarjuna, regarded as the founder of East Asian Mahayana Buddhism and revered as a second Buddha, is born.
CA. 250-500	The Perfection of Wisdom in the form of short sutras and verse summaries appears.
CA. 400	The earliest extant translation of the Heart Sutra appears, written in Chinese and attributed to the Indian philosopher Kumarajiva but possibly produced by one of his followers.
649	Xuanzang translates the Heart Sutra into Chinese.
CA. 750	The first Tibetan translation of the Heart Sutra appears.

focus on suffering and how to overcome it—a process explained in terms of the Buddhist concept of the "chain of dependent origination." Thoroughly understanding the interrelationship of all things is fundamental to understanding the concept of emptiness. Understanding the concept of emptiness, in turn, is the key to overcoming suffering.

The way early Indian Buddhists thought about these concepts is presented in the Abhidharma. The Abhidharma is one of the three "baskets" of scriptures that, as a set, form the Pali canon. In 25 BCE, the Theravadin Buddhists held a council in Anuradhapura, the ancient capital of Sri Lanka. This council established the contents of the Tripitaka, the "three baskets" of texts that make up their version of the Buddhist canon. The other two baskets are the sutras (words of the Buddha) and the *vinaya* (rules for monks and nuns). The texts in the Abhidharma classify and analyze the teachings of the Buddha collected in the sutras. According to early Buddhist legends, the Buddha taught the Abhidharma to his mother shortly after he attained enlightenment. However, unlike the scriptures collected in the other two baskets, the texts of the Abhidharma are understood to have been composed by learned followers of the Buddha. Nevertheless, adherents understand the learning contained in the Abhidharma as expressing the teaching of the Buddha.

According to the Abhidharma system, elements called dharmas are the most fundamental factors of existence. These dharmas form clusters that determine the quality of material and psychological aspects of all entities, both animate and inanimate. The composition of these clusters changes from moment to moment in accordance with the concept of the chain of dependent origination. The Buddha explained the chain of dependent origination in his first teaching of the Four Noble Truths. The term *skandha* refers to a particular set of clusters of dharmas. The five *skandhas* are form, feeling, cognition, formation, and consciousness.

The scriptures associated with the Perfection of Wisdom challenge how earlier Buddhists explained the process of enlightenment and also the nature of what is attained when enlightenment is reached. Mahayana Buddhist philosophy explicates a more nuanced understanding of the concept of emptiness than earlier Buddhism and promotes the value of the path of the bodhisattva as key to the attainment of perfect wisdom. The Perfection of Wisdom is the first set of scriptures to promote these ideas. This shift in thinking marks a turn in Buddhist philosophy from the early Indian Buddhism that is associated with the Pali canon. According to Mahayana Buddhist philosophy, to become enlightened a person must realize that not only the *skandhas* but even the content of the dharmas themselves are contingent and unstable and subject to the chain of dependent origination.

Mahayana Buddhist philosophy explains that even emptiness itself is empty, a concept difficult to understand in human intellectual terms. Nevertheless, realizing the utter emptiness of emptiness itself is key to conquering the problem of suffering and attaining enlightenment. The Mahayana Buddhists note that it is only through the path of the bodhisattva that individuals can reach this understanding. Bodhisattvas are beings who are dedicated to helping others share the same level of wisdom that they themselves have attained. The Heart Sutra summarizes the relationship between completely understanding the concept of emptiness and the work of bodhisattvas.

As noted, the Heart Sutra is among the shortest of the Perfection of Wisdom scriptures, and the oldest-known copy is believed to have been written around 400 CE. In 649 CE, the Chinese monk, explorer, and translator Xuanzang translated the Heart Sutra into Chinese. This is the first version that refers to the words of the Heart Sutra as a sutra rather than simply a set of powerful words for chanting. Xuanzang's version was instrumental in popularizing the Heart Sutra throughout Asia. One of Xuanzang's students wrote a commentary on the Heart Sutra that became very important in the evolution of Tibetan Buddhism. In the mid-eighth century, the Heart Sutra was translated into Tibetan. In the mid-eighteenth century, an important version of the Tibetan Buddhist canon included the Heart Sutra in two sections: It appears with other Perfection of Wisdom scriptures and with collections of tantric, or explanatory, texts. The double posting speaks both to the significance of the Heart Sutra for Tibetan Buddhism and to an understanding of the potency of the words of the scripture.

The Heart Sutra was first translated into English in 1894. More than six decades later, in 1958, Edward Conze published what became a standard translation of the Heart Sutra, as well other longer Perfection of Wisdom texts, in English. The fourteenth Dalai Lama published an English commentary on the Heart Sutra in 2002.

About the Author

Reflecting on who wrote the Heart Sutra and assessing its authenticity raises a number of concerns with respect to the dating of particular Heart Sutra texts; additionally, different Buddhist traditions use varying criteria to determine the authenticity of scriptures. Mahayana Buddhists understand all Perfection of Wisdom texts to be the words of the Buddha. By contrast, non-Mahayana Buddhists consider the Heart Sutra and other Mahayana scriptures as the work of poets.

Putting aside devotional notions about the origin of this text, scholars also have many questions concerning where the Heart Sutra was first written as well as who wrote it. Chinese Heart Sutra texts purport to have been translated from earlier Indian Sanskrit originals. However, scholars have been unable to verify the authenticity of the supposed earlier texts. In particular, the Buddhist scholar Janice Nattier has raised important questions regarding the nature of the oldest-known Sanskrit copy of the *Heart Sutra*. Using sophisticated linguistic analysis, Nattier has proposed that this early Sanskrit version was first written in Chinese and then translated into Sanskrit.

Most scholars accept Nattier's argument. However, it is still possible that there was a Sanskrit original that was destroyed when Buddhism was suppressed in India in the thirteenth century. In support of this theory, scholars have noted that a commentary on the Heart Sutra written by the

Time Line	
1729–1744	■ The Heart Sutra appears twice in two places in the Tibetan canon.
1894	■ The Heart Sutra is first translated into English.
1958	■ Edward Conze publishes an English translation of the Heart Sutra, along with other Perfection of Wisdom texts.
2002	■ The fourteenth Dalai Lama publishes a commentary on the Heart Sutra.

Korean scholar-monk and translator Wonch'uk (613–696) intimates that he had access to a Sanskrit original that may have been written even earlier than the Chinese translation attributed to the Indian Buddhist scholar-monk Kumarajiva. This is an important counterargument. Tibetan scholars, in particular, have long admired the exegetical work of Wonch'uk, and his work continues to be respected by modern-day scholars. Unfortunately, the text to which Wonch'uk refers is no longer extant. Nevertheless, it is possible that such a text may have existed and that someday it, or another earlier Sanskrit text, may be found.

Explanation and Analysis of the Document

The Heart Sutra is spoken by Avalokiteshvara, the bodhisattva of infinite compassion, to the arhat Shariputra. Shariputra was an early follower of the Buddha who attained the status of arhat, which, according to non-Mahayana tradition, is a fully human person who has reached a state of enlightenment that is nearly equal to that of a buddha. Early Buddhist scriptures describe him as a well-educated, philosophically inclined individual who was a bit older than the Buddha and died before him. Shariputra is associated with the compilation of the Abhidharma.

Despite the brevity of the Heart Sutra, Buddhist teachers and scholars continue to puzzle over the many ways it can be interpreted, used, and understood. Readers should bear in mind that even the way in which the Heart Sutra has been translated into English is a form of interpretation. The outline given here provides a basic overview of its structure and the ideas that it presents.

The title of the Heart Sutra can be interpreted in more than one way; in fact, the earliest versions do not refer to it as a sutra at all. Recall that it was not until Xuanzang's Chinese translation that the Heart Sutra was first considered a sutra rather than simply a set of powerful words for chanting. One way to read the title is as an announcement

Essential Quotes

> "Form does not differ from emptiness; emptiness does not differ from form. Form itself is emptiness; emptiness itself is form."

> "Gaté Gaté Paragaté Parasamgaté."

that the text will provide the essence, or heart, of what is elaborated in much longer versions of the Prajnaparamita. On the other hand, presented simply as the "Heart Sutra," it conveys a sense that what is offered here is intended for the heart. The Heart Sutra does both. It provides guidance for removing wrong ideas from the heart and a concise summary of the wisdom of the Prajnaparamita.

The opening line of the Heart Sutra tells us that the implied speaker is the bodhisattva Avalokiteshvara. In later Buddhist traditions, Avalokiteshvara is understood to be a manifestation of the Buddha. It is according to this perspective that later Mahayana traditions consider the Heart Sutra to be the word of the Buddha, which was spoken by the Buddha in his manifestation as Avalokiteshvara. The presence of the bodhisattva Avalokiteshvara is unusual. Avalokiteshvara does not appear in any of the other Perfection of Wisdom scriptures but was a very popular deity in early Chinese Buddhism. Mention of Avalokiteshvara is one thing scholars point to in support of the theory that the Heart Sutra was written first in Chinese and then back-translated into Sanskrit.

This first line also gives us a clue that the venue is extraordinary. We are told that the event takes place just after Avalokiteshvara was meditating on the wisdom of Prajnaparamita. In Buddhism, when a particularly skilled person enters into a deep state of meditation, that person has access to states that are not normally accessible to average people. This understanding is used by Mahayana adherents to support their beliefs that the Heart Sutra was delivered during the lifetime of the Buddha. According to this view, it was not heard by living humans at the time because no one on earth had the capacity to hear what was said or possessed the meditative skills to reach the plane where it could be heard.

In addition, the opening sentence of the Heart Sutra summarizes the process that allowed Avalokiteshvara to reach the high level from which he was able to convey the wisdom he was about to deliver. Avalokiteshvara was meditating on the Prajnaparamita. This is important because the Prajnaparamita is understood as both the embodiment of Perfect Wisdom and as a reference to the text itself. This sort of self-referential statement is a characteristic of many Mahayana texts and sets them apart from earlier Buddhist literature. Such an assertion also alerts us to the incredible potency of the text. Stating that the text is an embodiment of Perfect Wisdom is a way of affirming that it should be revered as a relic of the Buddha. Relics of the Buddha evoke the presence of the Buddha. If the Heart Sutra is understood as itself a relic of the Buddha, then it has the capacity to evoke the presence of the Buddha. Understanding how it is that the Heart Sutra can be a relic of the Buddha points to an important transformation in the history of Buddhist philosophy that was ushered in with Mahayana thinking.

The second paragraph introduces Shariputra. It appears that Avalokiteshvara is telling Shariputra about the power of the Heart Sutra. The presence of Shariputra is unusual, as most Perfection of Wisdom texts are delivered in response to a different arhat by the name of Subhuti. This may be another clue that the Heart Sutra was not originally written in India.

In the third paragraph, Avalokiteshvara explains to Shariputra that the five *skandhas* are "empty." This is the central statement of the Heart Sutra. The text here concisely summarizes the Mahayana concept of emptiness. Because this concept is presented in a series of negations, it is all too easy to understand emptiness as being nihilistic. The challenge is to realize that truly understanding emptiness calls for service to others and is anything but a retreat into nihilism.

In the fourth paragraph, we learn more about the powerful insights that are available to anyone who follows the bodhisattva path and relies on the wisdom contained in the Prajnaparamita. Nirvana is state of being that entails peace and calm beyond the normal range of human experience. This state is reserved for those liberated from the cycle of death and rebirth, called samsara. The precise nature of nirvana is understood differently in various Buddhist philosophic systems. Early Buddhist philosophy gives the impression that nirvana is a faraway place. The suggestion here is that nirvana is closer than we expect and that once we are able to attain the crystal-clear mental state promised by the Perfection of Wisdom, we will have access to it.

"Anuttara-samyak-sambodhi" is a Sanskrit phrase that can be translated as "Perfect Enlightenment that cannot be surpassed by wisdom of any other kind." A buddha is some-

View of the ruined city of Anuradhapura
(View of the ruined city [photo], / Anuradhapura, Sri Lanka / © World Religions Photo Library / The Bridgeman Art Library International)

one who realizes the fullest meaning of emptiness, and this entails the ability to understand the ultimate nature of things. The buddhas of the three periods are buddhas of the past, the present, and the future. Early Indian Buddhism recognizes only the historical Buddha, Shakyamuni. By contrast, Mahayana Buddhism recognizes many buddhas who came before and will come after Shakyamuni.

Early Buddhist philosophy equates reaching enlightenment with liberation from the cycle of existence. Later Buddhist philosophy developed ideas concerning various levels of enlightenment. Avalokiteshvara tells Shariputra that the Prajnaparamita provides a method for reaching the highest possibly enlightenment. The suggestion is that Mahayana teachings offers the potential to reach a higher level of enlightenment than is possible by following the teachings of earlier Buddhist scriptures.

At the end of paragraph 4, we are told that the entire Prajnaparamita has the potency of a mantra. Because the Heart Sutra summarizes the Prajnaparamita, it also has the potency of a mantra. There is a long tradition associated with chanting the Heart Sutra as a means to assure a variety of good outcomes. This understanding is behind the daily practice of chanting the Heart Sutra carried out in Buddhist monasteries around the world. Indeed, it was not for several centuries that the word *sutra* was added to the title of the Heart Sutra, allowing it to be appreciated as the oral teachings of the Buddha.

In the Mahayana tradition, there is some debate over how to classify the Heart Sutra within the Buddhist canon. As noted, in the Tibetan Buddhist canon, a copy of the Heart Sutra appears in two different sections of the Kanjur—the collection of scriptures that are understood to be the words of the Buddha. One section of the Kanjur holds all the accepted versions of the Perfection of Wisdom texts that have been translated into Tibetan. As expected, the Heart Sutra is among these texts. However, a version of the Heart Sutra is included in the tantra section of the Kanjur as well. Compilers included the Heart Sutra in the tantra section because they recognized the text as having the potency of a mantra.

The text ends with the mantra of the Heart Sutra. This mantra is usually not translated. The grammar of the original Sanskrit does not convey a clear meaning. Also, as is typical of mantras, the actual sound of the original Sanskrit words is understood to have considerable potency: Translating the words into any other language would lessen that potency. When this final set of words is translated, commentators have various opinions about how to interpret them. A common translation in English is "Gone, gone, gone beyond, gone completely beyond; enlightenment; hail." Some commentators understand the reference in the Heart Sutra to the "Great Spiritual Mantra" as referring to the Prajnaparamita itself and not just to the set of words in Sanskrit. In this interpretation, the Prajnaparamita is seen as pointing to something beyond the grasp of normal human intellect. Nevertheless, the human intellect is still considered useful and necessary. For some observers, then, the final set of words can be understood as an exhortation to use one's intellect but to keep going—and go beyond intellectual understanding in order to reach ultimate enlightenment.

Audience

The Heart Sutra was delivered by the Buddha as part of the teachings associated with the extraordinary event known as the Second Turning of the Wheel. Only very advanced individuals could access the plane upon which it was delivered. At the initial time of its delivery, no human being had this capacity. Sometime around 100 BCE, ideas associated with the emerging Mahayana movement began to appear. Versions of the Perfection of Wisdom are considered the earliest expression of these ideas. Scholars associate these texts with the ancient Indian Buddhist monastery known as Mahasanghika, a place associated with the first spreading of Mahayana ideas. As such, the initial audience for the Perfection of Wisdom ideas was the monastic community. The Heart Sutra summarizes ideas associated with this movement. Significantly, the important Chinese monk-scholar and translator Xuanzang visited this monastery in the seventh century.

The Heart Sutra's succinct expression of Mahayana Buddhist ideas continues to captivate Buddhist and non-Buddhists throughout the world. Devotees repeat it for inspiration, monastics chant it as part of daily rituals, and scholars still puzzle over how to interpret it with precision.

Impact

The Heart Sutra, or Heart of Wisdom Sutra, is one of the most popular Buddhist texts in the world. For centuries, Buddhists across Asia—and now across the globe—have chanted the words of the Heart Sutra as sacred text. Many devotees believe that the words of the Heart Sutra have protective quality in themselves. Meditators repeat it as a way to focus their minds. Copying the Heart Sutra can form the basis of meditation. In Japan, in particular, scholars have noted the ubiquity of impressions of the Heart Sutra on various goods, including teacups, hand towels, neckties, and even taxicab windows. Some experts have suggested that reflecting on the various ways Buddhists venerate the Heart Sutra provides a measure of both the extent of its popularity and the breadth of the Buddhist tradition.

Scholars today and throughout history have studied copies of the Heart Sutra for linguistic, historical, and cultural insight. The number of commentaries written on the text throughout history shows how deeply it has been admired by generations of scholars from many Buddhist traditions. The discovery of early copies and textual fragments of the Heart Sutra and other Mahayana texts have forced scholars to rethink the history of Buddhism.

Questions for Further Study

1. Why do you think the phrase "Turning of the Wheel" was used to refer to the act of teaching by the Buddha? What meaning does this phrase suggest?

2. The entry states that in 25 BCE, the Theravadin Buddhists held a council in Anuradhapura that established the contents of the Tripitaka, the "three baskets" of texts that make up their version of the Buddhist canon. Compare this with the entry "Canons and Decrees of the Council of Trent," a Catholic Church council held in the sixteenth century. What similar goals did the councils have? How did they differ? How did each council reflect its culture and time?

3. Eastern religions place considerable emphasis on such concepts as wisdom and enlightenment. How is the Buddhist conception of these matters similar to and different from the Hindu conception as outlined in the entry on the Bhagavad Gita?

4. Why is this sutra called the *Heart* Sutra?

5. What problems do translators of such documents as the Heart Sutra face? Why might different translations of the text differ in important ways? What impact might these differences have for the reader's understanding of the text?

According to Buddhist tradition, shortly after the Buddha died, his close followers held a council in the ancient capital city of Rajagriha (present-day Rajgir, India) to determine how to preserve the Buddha's teachings. Although details embellishing this event were likely added later, many historians agree that this meeting did indeed take place. All we know for certain is that it happened during the first rainy season following the Buddha's death. Most modern scholars accept the date of the Buddha's death as occurring within a few decades of 400 BCE. The Buddha's teachings were preserved orally for several centuries. As Buddhism spread, various schools formed. Each of these schools had its own ideas about the authenticity of scriptures that were spoken by the Buddha.

Theravadin Buddhism flourishes today most notably in Southeast Asia. Theravadin Buddhists promote the Pali canon as both the oldest collection of Buddhist scriptures and the most authentic version of what the Buddha taught. They also claim that the Buddhist canon was closed with the writing of the Pali canon. In their view, texts that are not included in the Pali canon or were written down after the time of the Pali canon cannot be authentic. Modern scholarship challenges these claims. Scholars today realize that other Buddhist schools maintained oral scriptural traditions that continued after the closing of the Pali canon. Moreover, recent discoveries of ancient Buddhist texts suggest the possibility of an earlier version of the Buddhist canon that follows a different oral tradition than the one reflected in the Pali canon. The destruction of Buddhist sites in India by Muslim invasions beginning in the thirteenth century wiped out traces of Sanskrit Buddhist texts that may have formed a Sanskrit canon—one that served as an alternative to the Pali canon. Textual fragments of the Heart Sutra and other Mahayana texts support arguments concerning the possibility that scriptural traditions existed in India that both predate and persisted after the writing of the Pali canon.

Various Buddhist traditions use different standards to determine whether particular texts can be accepted as expressing the words of the Buddha. The Heart Sutra challenges some of the criteria used by some Buddhist traditions. Whether or not one accepts the legends associated with the Heart Sutra, the wisdom it delivers continues to have relevance today. In more recent times, the Heart Sutra has come to be revered by traditions that are more closely associated with earlier Buddhism and the Pali canon. Even the Thai monk Thich Nhat Hanh, who follows the Theravadin tradition, has written a commentary on the Heart Sutra.

Further Reading

■ Books

Tenzin Gyatso. *The Essence of the Heart Sutra: The Dalai Lama's Heart of Wisdom Teachings*. Boston, Mass.: Wisdom Publications, 2005.

Thich Nhat Hanh. *The Heart of Understanding: Commentaries on the Prajnaparamita Heart Sutra*. Berkeley, Calif.: Parallax Press, 1987.

Prebish, Charles S. "Councils: Buddhist Councils." In *Encyclopedia of Religion*, ed. Lindsay Jones. Detroit, Mich.: Macmillan Reference, 2005.

■ Journals

Nattier, Janice J. "The Heart Sutra: A Chinese Apocryphal Text?" *Journal of the International Association of Buddhist Studies* 15, no. 2 (1992): 153–223.

■ Web Sites

"Buddhism." The Schøyen Collection Web site.
    http://www.schoyencollection.com/Buddhism.htm

—Cynthia Col

Heart Sutra

When Bodhisattva Avalokiteshvara was practicing the profound Prajna Paramita, he illuminated the Five Skandhas and saw that they are all empty, and he crossed beyond all suffering and difficulty.

Shariputra, form does not differ from emptiness; emptiness does not differ from form. Form itself is emptiness; emptiness itself is form. So too are feeling, cognition, formation, and consciousness.

Shariputra, all Dharmas are empty of characteristics. They are not produced, not destroyed, not defiled, not pure; and they neither increase nor diminish. Therefore, in emptiness there is no form, feeling, cognition, formation, or consciousness; no eyes, ears, nose, tongue, body, or mind; no sights, sounds, smells, tastes, objects of touch, or Dharmas; no field of the eyes up to and including no field of mind consciousness; and no ignorance or ending of ignorance, up to and including no old age and death or ending of old age and death. There is no suffering, no accumulating, no extinction, and no Way, and no understanding and no attaining.

Because nothing is attained, the Bodhisattva through reliance on Prajna Paramita is unimpeded in his mind. Because there is no impediment, he is not afraid, and he leaves distorted dream-thinking far behind. Ultimately Nirvana! All Buddhas of the three periods of time attain Anuttara-samyak-sambodhi through reliance on Prajna Paramita. Therefore know that Prajna Paramita is a Great Spiritual Mantra, a Great Bright Mantra, a Supreme Mantra, an Unequalled Mantra. It can remove all suffering; it is genuine and not false. That is why the Mantra of Prajna Paramita was spoken. Recite it like this:

Gaté Gaté Paragaté Parasamgaté

Bodhi Svaha!

Glossary

Anuttara-samyak-sambodhi	perfect enlightenment
bodhisattva	any enlightened person who seeks enlightenment for others
Prajna Paramita	the central concept of Mahayana Buddhism as expressed in the sutras
Shariputra	a disciple of the Buddha
skandhas	aggregates of mental and physical characteristics that come together to create an individual

Polychrome ceramic vase depicting a Mayan lord receiving tribute
(© Trustees of the British Museum)

Popol Vuh

ca. 250–925

"Name now our names, praise us. We are your mother, we are your father."

Overview

The Popol Vuh is one of the most important examples of pre-Columbian literature to survive the Spanish conquest of the Americas. It is a work of epic poetry that tells the origin story of the Maya and, more specifically, the Quiché, a Mayan ethnic group that dominated the highlands of modern-day Guatemala during the postclassic period of Mayan history (925–1530 CE). The Popol Vuh begins by explaining how the world came into existence and speaks of the exploits of the Hero Twins, important figures in Mayan mythology. Finally, the book ends with the creation of humans, the foundation of the Quiché people, and their history from their migration into their homeland to the Spanish conquest.

The Popol Vuh has a long and complex history. The oldest known written copy of the work dates to about 1701–1703; however, it is much older. The modern form of the Popol Vuh took shape sometime in the 1550s when anonymous authors drew upon ancient sources to record the story. The authors spoke of an original manuscript upon which their work was based, presumably a book or documents that recorded religious and historical information written in Mayan glyphs. That source is lost to us today. The authors almost certainly also drew from oral tradition: stories, myths, and histories of the Quiché people. The story line of the Popol Vuh was well known during the classic Maya period (250–925 CE); archaeologists have identified the Hero Twins and other characters from the Popol Vuh on vases and monuments. It is likely that the sources consulted by the authors of the Popol Vuh date to this era or perhaps even earlier, to the preclassic Maya period (ca. 1800 BCE–250 CE).

After having recorded the Popol Vuh, the authors hid the manuscript from the Spanish out of fear that the conquerors would destroy it; the Spanish had destroyed countless other Mayan codices (manuscripts). After 150 years, the work finally came to light around 1701–1703, when a Dominican monk named Francisco Ximénez obtained the manuscript. Ximénez wrote out a copy and added a Spanish translation of his own alongside the Quiché. This manuscript is the earliest known copy of the Popol Vuh; no one knows what became of the original Quiché text.

Context

Around 1250 CE a group of Toltec migrants from central Mexico entered the highlands of Guatemala and intermarried with the local Mayan people. The Quiché people came from the fusion of these two traditions. They established their capitol at Q'umarkaj and launched a series of military expeditions, conquering many other Mayan ethnic groups. They thus became the dominant people of the highlands.

On December 6, 1523, the Spanish conquistador Pedro de Alvarado set out from the recently conquered Aztec capital of Tenochtitlán (ancient Mexico City) in the hope of discovering gold and with orders from Hernán Cortés to verify reports of rich lands and new races of people. Alvarado led one hundred and twenty horsemen, three hundred foot soldiers, and many native allies from the nearby cities of Cholula and Tlaxcala. As the Spanish approached Q'umarkaj, the Quiché raised an army led by the warrior Tecún Umán. The two armies met in February 1524 at the plain of Xelaju, where the Quiché were defeated.

After the Battle of Xelaju, the Quiché invited the Spanish to their capital city, ostensibly to discuss peace terms. However, the Quiché planned to trap the Spanish in the newly deserted city; they intended to remove the causeways that were the main roads into Q'umarkaj and set the city afire. The Spanish detected the trap, and Alvarado ordered his men to lay waste to the city and the Quiché themselves. After the sacking of Q'umarkaj, the Quiché nation fell.

The Spanish conquest of Guatemala was lengthy, continuing until 1548. Alvarado ruled Guatemala as captain general of the region from 1527 until his death in 1541. The Spanish conquest of Guatemala and the New World in general was not just a military one. The Spanish sought to convert native populations to Christianity and to Hispanicize their culture and way of life, thus better integrating them into the Spanish Empire through cultural transformation. The second wave of Spaniards arrived in Quiché lands soon after Alvarado's death. In the late 1540s, the Maya were gathered together into villages to be taught the catechism under the Spanish policy of *congregación*, or missionization. Missionization sought to change the religious beliefs of the Maya through teach-

Time Line

CA. 1800 BCE
- The preclassic Mayan period begins, lasting until 250 CE; this is the probable era of the formation of Mayan mythology and foundational religious beliefs.

250 CE
- The classic Mayan period begins, lasting until 925; the ancient source of the Popol Vuh might date to this era.

CA. 1250 CE
- The Toltecs arrive in the Guatemalan highlands and found the Quiché ruling dynasty.

1524
- **February**
  Pedro de Alvarado's troops meet the Quiché army led by the warrior Tecún Umán and defeat them.

CA. 1554
- The Popol Vuh is redacted from its possible original source and oral traditions.

1562
- **July 12**
  Diego de Landa burns Mayan codices; Landa admits to burning twenty-seven books, while other sources maintain that thousands of texts went into the fire.

CA. 1701
- The Dominican friar Francisco Ximénez obtains the original 1550s document, transcribes the Quiché, and makes a side-by-side translation into Spanish.

1854
- Carl Scherzer finds Ximénez's book at the University of San Carlos in Guatemala City and commissions a copy.

1856
- Scherzer publishes the Spanish version of the Popol Vuh for the first time, and it is widely acclaimed in Europe.

1861
- The Quiché version of the Popol Vuh is published for the first time, with an accompanying French translation by Father Charles-Étienne Brasseur de Bourbourg.

1930s
- Epigraphers begin work to break the Mayan code and thus decipher the Mayan glyphs.

---

ing Roman Catholic doctrine. Spanish missionaries overtly and symbolically dominated Mayan religious sites by building churches nearby or on top of them and through punishing, verbally and sometimes physically, those individuals who disobeyed.

The early experiences of the Quiché with the Roman Catholic Church occurred at a crucial and turbulent time in the Yucatán Peninsula. In 1562 the Franciscan friar Diego de Landa, prelate of Yucatán, was informed that friars in the region had found caches of human skulls and figures depicting Mayan gods among missionized and, the friars presumed, Catholic Mayan Indians. Landa was outraged and ordered an Inquisition to unearth idolaters and idolatrous materials. During the Inquisition, more than 4,500 Maya were tortured. Records show that 158 people died as a result of the torture, and many others were permanently injured. On July 12, 1562, Landa oversaw a ceremony known as an auto-da-fé (act of faith), during which more than five thousand Mayan figures were burned. Additionally, Landa burned Mayan codices. The anthropologist Inga Clendinnen records that Landa characterized the books as being nothing but "superstition and lies of the devil." Landa later admitted to burning twenty-seven codices; other sources claim that thousands of books were destroyed. These codices contained invaluable Mayan knowledge and records. Today, only four known Mayan codices remain. Diego de Landa was sent back to Spain to stand before the Council of the Indies, one of the ruling bodies of the Spanish American empire. The council condemned his actions as a false Inquisition. Ultimately, Landa was absolved of his crimes in 1569 and sent back to Yucatán as bishop in 1571.

It is in this context that the Popol Vuh was produced in the early 1550s. The authors were driven by two equally pressing needs: to preserve their heritage and to protect their identity. Although Diego de Landa's Inquisition had not yet begun, Maya in the Yucatán and in the lands of the Quiché understood the need for secrecy in continuing to practice their old beliefs and customs. While colonial Spaniards might have considered many of these practices innocuous, other practices, such as human sacrifice, shocked and horrified them. Human sacrifice and the shedding of their own blood by elite Mayan individuals (a practice called autosacrifice), however, were integral to the Mayan religious system. There is evidence that both practices continued, largely in secret, for well over forty years after the Spanish arrived in Mayan lands.

By the early 1700s, more than one hundred fifty years later, the situation had changed considerably. Many traditional Mayan religious beliefs had merged with Catholicism in a process known as syncretism. The Quiché considered themselves to be, by and large, Catholics. Yet ancient knowledge and many traditional beliefs were still held in high esteem, and many Mayan gods were still known and spoken of, if not venerated. In this atmosphere, the Dominican Francisco Ximénez obtained and copied the 1550s document.

The archaeologist Richard Hansen shows a limestone frieze depicting the Hero Twins, from northern Guatemala.
(AP/Wide World Photos)

About the Author

There are few straightforward answers about the authors of the Popol Vuh. The authors of the 1550s manuscript chose anonymity, almost certainly to protect themselves from the anger of the Spanish. Modern historians and anthropologists have been able to speculate as to the identity of the authors based on clues within the Popol Vuh and Spanish documents preserved in the national and other archives of Guatemala and Spain.

The Popol Vuh was most likely produced in the village of Santa Cruz del Quiché. In the conclusion of the book, the authors refer to "Quiché, which is now called Santa Cruz." The text itself hints at the identities of the authors. The end of the work provides a genealogy of the Quiché, which names their great families and their rulers and their offices. The final passages of the genealogy name the minister installed in 1554 and list the current offices held. Finally, in the next-to-last passage of the work, the authors write, "And there are three Masters of Ceremonies in all.... They are the givers of birth, they are the Mothers of the Word, they are the Fathers of the Word." The passage goes on to state that the three Masters of Ceremonies represent three of the noble families of the Quiché. In *The Popol Vuh: Sacred Book of the Maya*, Allen J. Christenson contends that the phrase *the Word* is used throughout the text to refer to the Popol Vuh itself. Thus, the three Masters of Ceremonies, all members of Quiché nobility, wrote the Popol Vuh. Christenson further deduces that one of the authors was named Don Cristóbal Velasco, who signed a contemporary document with the title Nim Chocoh Cavec, Master of Ceremonies for the "Cauec" (the spelling of "Cavec" in Maya) family. We know nothing more about Velasco.

Explanation and Analysis of the Document

The Popol Vuh expresses many foundational ideas of the ancient Maya. One of the most important ideas is that the natural rhythm of the world, life, and time itself is cyclical, repeating itself endlessly in varying forms. A second theme is the struggle between order and chaos. Humans and gods alike struggle to create order from chaos, to shape the world into a form that they find pleasing. Inevitably, however, chaos disturbs this ordered plan. Ultimately, the force of chaos is the most powerful in the universe; even the gods themselves fight against it and in the end are conquered by it, only to begin the process of creation again. In this way, the two themes overlap and interplay; the battle between chaos and order is a never-ending cycle itself.

Essential Quotes

"Name now our names, praise us. We are your mother, we are your father. Speak now."

"The time for the planting and dawning is nearing. For this we must make a provider and nurturer. How else can we be invoked and remembered on the face of the earth? We have already made our first try at our work and design, but it turned out that they didn't keep our days, nor did they glorify us."

"They came into being, they multiplied, they had daughters, they had sons, these manikins, woodcarvings. But there was nothing in their hearts and nothing in their minds, no memory of their mason and builder. They just went and walked wherever they wanted. Nor did they remember the Heart of Sky."

"Such was the scattering of the human work, the human design. The people were ground down, overthrown. The mouths and faces of all of them were destroyed and crushed. And it used to be said that the monkeys in the forests today are a sign of this. They were left as a sign because wood alone was used for their flesh by the builder and sculptor."

In the first section of the Popol Vuh, the gods create the earth out of nothingness, thus forming order out of chaos. The gods then turn their hands to the creation of humans. It is here that the excerpt from the document begins. Among the gods assembled are the Sovereign Plumed Serpent, Heart of Earth, Heart of Sky, and Hurricane. The Popol Vuh refers to them as creators, repeatedly calling them "Maker, Modeler, Bearer, Begetter," or some combination of these titles. By emphasizing the action of creation and through the repetition of the titles associated with creation, the Popol Vuh stresses the importance and significance of the struggle to bring order from chaos. Moreover, the repetition of titles in sequence, always using more than one title, is rhythmic and chantlike. The Popol Vuh's roots lie in oral history and storytelling; its use of language is deeply tied to methods of storytelling.

The excerpt from the Popol Vuh begins with the first attempt of the gods to create sentient beings who can walk and talk, reproduce and survive, and worship and make offerings. Their creation must be "a giver of praise, giver of respect." Just as important, this being must be able to be a "keeper of days." This refers to an important part of Mayan religious beliefs; *ajq'ij*, or "daykeepers," have been an important part of Mayan religion for thousands of years. Daykeepers were diviners and keepers of the Mayan calendar. The Mayan calendar was extremely complex and also very accurate—more accurate, in fact, than the calendar we follow today. It consisted of two calendars used for different purposes. The Haab was a solar calendar that tracked day-to-day events; the Tzolkin was a lunar calendar used for ritual purposes. These two calendars intersected to give a different day name for every day in a fifty-two-year cycle. It was the job of the daykeeper to keep track of the calendar and read the auguries associated with each day's name. Daykeepers ensured that humans kept track of ritual days and knew where they were in the cycle of the calendar and what kinds of auguries the gods had made for each day name. The daykeepers provided a vital connection between humans and the gods. They kept order in the passage of time and provided a constant reminder that time itself is cyclical, that an end is coming and a new cycle will be reborn from the death of the old cycle.

In their quest to fashion a keeper of days, the gods first create the animals: jaguars, rattlesnakes, deer, birds, and others. The gods then order the animals to worship them, commanding them to "name our names, praise us." Yet the animals cannot, and the gods conclude that their creations must be changed and brought down in the order of beings. The gods advise the animals to "just accept your service, just let your flesh be eaten. . . . This must be your service." This first failure in the gods' quest to create sentient beings that are able to worship them shows us two things. First, even the gods are imperfect and subject to the forces of chaos, which destroy their carefully planned order. Second, like all origin stories, it informs us about the beliefs and worldview of its culture: Animals are created to serve humans (and more specifically, the Maya) by nourishing them with their flesh.

In their second attempt, the gods make a being of earth and mud. This attempt, too, proves to be unsatisfactory. Its body and face are malformed and soft. It is able to talk but speaks senselessly. It is crumbling and disintegrating, and even the gods cannot keep this being together; their creation breaks down before their very eyes. The gods conclude that this being was a failure. Chaos triumphs again.

Before their next attempt, the gods consult two ancient mythical daykeepers named Xpiyacoc and Xmucane. These diviners are older even than the gods themselves; the gods address them respectfully as "grandmother" and "grandfather." The gods seek advice on how to create a being that can worship them, and they are told that they should proceed with their plan to create new beings out of wood. The wood beings, or "manikins," are more successful than the gods' two attempts. They are "human in looks and human in speech" and are able to multiply and have daughters and sons. The manikins build houses, keep domesticated animals, and cook tortillas, but they have "nothing in their hearts and nothing in their minds, no memory of their mason and builder." They do not worship the gods.

The gods, realizing that they have failed a third time, send a flood to destroy the wooden humans; they also send beings who gouge out the manikins' eyeballs and eat their flesh. All of creation turns against the manikins, the beings who neglected the gods. The domesticated animals who fed the manikins, the dogs and turkeys, tell them "now it is *you* whom *we* shall eat." Their grinding stones, tortilla griddles, and cooking pots rebuke them as well, threatening to "pound and grind [their] flesh" and "burn [them]." As the wooden humans try to flee, other creations turn on them: Houses collapse beneath them, and caves deny them refuge. And so this cycle of creation comes to an end.

This creation cycle reflects the recurring sequence of chaos and order. There may be some initial success, but ultimately chaos destroys whatever order has been imposed. Then the cycle begins again. The saga of the creation of humans is taken up again toward the middle of the Popol Vuh, when the gods fashion humans from corn, the sacred food of the Maya. This was the successful creation of humans; the birth of the Maya. Humans are created, and they finally are able to worship the gods, praise them, give thanks, and keep their days. In the traditional Mayan worldview, today's humans are the descendants of the people of corn. Although the gods have been successful in their creation, the world and creation and humanity will end, and chaos will once again reign. And the gods will have to create order from chaos yet again.

Audience

The Quiché themselves were the initial audience of the Popol Vuh. The authors produced the document as a lasting testament and record of the origins of their people, preserving the words and beliefs of the ancestors and connecting the living population with them.

The recorded form of the Popol Vuh reflects an enormous shift in the technology and knowledge of its audience. Before Spanish contact, the Maya had been the most literate people in the Americas, and they had developed the most advanced form of writing in the Western Hemisphere. All of this changed after the collapse of the Mayan civilization and the missionization of the Maya. Knowledge of how to read the glyphs had begun to slowly fade and ultimately was lost. The authors of the Popol Vuh based the text on one or more ancient documents, which would have been written in glyphs. Yet Francisco Ximénez records that he transcribed the document from Quiché written in the Latin alphabet. The authors made this switch partly as a reflection of the changing technologies; they also might have intended to hide the document in plain sight by disguising it in the Latin alphabet.

When Ximénez transcribed the document sometime around 1701, he had its second audience and second purpose in mind. As a Dominican, he sought not only to convert the Maya but also to study them in order to better understand their language and culture. Monastic orders such as the Dominicans were inveterate producers of documents detailing the beliefs, customs, rituals, language, and culture of their parishioners. They produced these documents for several reasons. First, they wanted to understand the culture and beliefs of the Maya so that they could better convert them to Christianity. Second, they recorded their knowledge so that the monks who came after them could read and learn about the culture quickly upon arrival.

Finally, they observed and recorded because the Spanish crown commanded it in order to better understand new and faraway subjects of the crown. Thus, for Ximénez, the Popol Vuh provided great insight into the Quiché. Finally, the Popol Vuh has a large modern audience. Historians, epigraphers, and anthropologists value it as an invaluable source about the ancient Maya. But modern Mayan peoples, Quiché among them, turn to the Popol Vuh for the same reason their forefathers in the 1550s did: to better understand their ancestors and to feel a connection with them.

Impact

Because the Popol Vuh was kept hidden by the Quiché for nearly one hundred fifty years, it is nearly impossible to truly understand and measure its impact during that era. It is certain that it did have great influence on Quiché society. Allen Christenson records that Francisco Ximénez called the Popol Vuh "the doctrine which they first imbibed with their mother's milk" and said that "all of them knew it almost by heart." For the colonial Quiché, the Popol Vuh provided an alternative to the Catholic view of the universe. Both the Popol Vuh and the Bible in part function as origin stories and try to answer questions about cultural identity and divine purpose. Who are we? Where did we come from? What kind of relationship do we have with God/the gods? What place do we hold in the universe? Why were we created? The Popol Vuh furnishes very different answers to these questions than the Bible and thus helped the colonial Quiché preserve their identity.

The impact of the Popol Vuh today is much easier to explore and appreciate, though it remains largely the same: It gives us an invaluable look into the culture and beliefs of the ancient Maya. For modern epigraphers working to decipher the Mayan glyphs, the Popol Vuh may furnish suggestions of the meanings of untranslated glyphs. As knowledge of the glyphs increases, our understanding of the Popol Vuh grows, and the translation more closely approaches the authors' original intent.

For the modern Maya, the Popol Vuh offers the same thing that it did for their ancestors: answers to questions about their origins and stories about important mythical figures and gods. This knowledge was especially important for the Maya during the Guatemalan Civil War of 1960–1996. During this war, thousands of human rights violations were committed against the Mayan peoples by their government. Some two hundred thousand people died during the war, most of them Mayan. In the 1980s government death squads massacred entire villages, deeming the inhabitants poor, stupid Indians who were inferior to the city mestizo populations. Mayan peoples reacted by actively embracing their identity and culture, starting a Mayan resurgence movement. The Popol Vuh played an integral part in this movement as a foundational document of Mayan culture.

Further Reading

■ Books

Bassie-Sweet, Karen. *Maya Sacred Geography and the Creator Deities*. Norman: University of Oklahoma Press, 2008.

Christenson, Allen J. *Popol Vuh: The Sacred Book of the Maya*. Norman: University of Oklahoma Press, 2007.

Clendinnen, Inga. *Ambivalent Conquests: Maya and Spaniard in Yucatan, 1517–1570*. London: Cambridge University Press, 1987.

Menchu, Rigoberta. *I, Rigoberta Menchu: An Indian Woman in Guatemala*, ed. Elisabeth Burgos-Debray and trans. Ann Wright. London: Verso, 1984.

Tedlock, Dennis. *Popol Vuh: The Definitive Edition of the Mayan Book of the Dawn of Life and the Glories of Gods and Kings*. New York: Touchstone, 1996.

Questions for Further Study

1. What motives prompted the writing of the Popol Vuh?

2. Discuss the extent to which the Popol Vuh can be regarded as history, as mythology, and as sacred scripture.

3. The Popol Vuh consists largely of an examination of the origins of the world and of the Mayan people. In what ways are these accounts similar to—and how do they differ from—similar accounts in another religious tradition with which you might be familiar, such as the Judeo-Christian account in the biblical book of Genesis or Native American accounts contained in a variety of sources, depending on the tribe?

4. What short-term and long-term effects did Spanish conquest have on the peoples of Central America?

■ **Journals**

Carlsen, Robert S., and Martin Prechtel. "The Flowering of the Dead: An Interpretation of Highland Maya Culture." *Man* New Series 26, no. 1 (March 1991): 23–42.

Himelblau, Jack. "The Popol Vuh of the Quiché Maya of Guatemala: Text, Copyist, and Time Frame of Transcription." *Hispania* 72, no. 1 (March 1989): 97–122.

Houston, Stephen, et al. "The Language of Classic Maya Inscriptions." *Current Anthropology* 41, no. 3 (June 2000): 321–356.

■ **Web Sites**

"Popol Wuj Online" The Ohio State University Libraries Web Site. http://library.osu.edu/sites/popolwuj/folios_eng/index.php.

"The Popol Vuh at the Newberry Library" Newberry Library Web site. http://www.newberry.org/collections/PopolVuh.html.

—Tamara Shircliff Spike

Popol Vuh

Then the mountains were separated from the water, all at once the great mountains came forth. By their genius alone, by their cutting edge alone they carried out the conception of the mountain-plain, whose face grew instant groves of cypress and pine.

And the Plumed Serpent was pleased with this:

"It was good that you came, Heart of Sky, Hurricane, and Newborn Thunderbolt, Sudden Thunderbolt. Our work, our design will turn out well," they said.

And the earth was formed first, the mountain-plain. The channels of water were separated; their branches wound their ways among the mountains. The waters were divided when the great mountains appeared.

Such was the formation of the earth when it was brought forth by the Heart of Sky, Heart of Earth, as they are called, since they were the first to think of it. The sky was set apart, and the earth was set apart in the midst of the waters.

Such was their plan when they thought, when they worried about the completion of their work.

Now they planned the animals of the mountains, all the guardians of the forests, creatures of the mountains: the deer, birds, pumas, jaguars, serpents, rattlesnakes, fer-de-lances, guardians of the bushes.

A Bearer, Begetter speaks:

"Why this pointless humming? Why should there merely be rustling beneath the trees and bushes?"

"Indeed—they had better have guardians," the others replied. As soon as they thought it and said it, deer and birds came forth.

And then they gave out homes to the deer and birds:

"You, the deer: sleep along the rivers, in the canyons. Be here in the meadows, in the thickets, in the forests, multiply yourselves. You will stand and walk on all fours," they were told.

So then they established the nests of the birds, small and great:

"You, precious birds: your nests, your houses are in the trees, in the bushes. Multiply there, scatter there, in the branches of trees, the branches of bushes," the deer and birds were told.

When this deed had been done, all of them had received a place to sleep and a place to stay. So it is that the nests of the animals are on the earth, given by the Bearer, Begetter. Now the arrangement of the deer and birds was complete.

And then the deer and birds were told by the Maker, Modeler, Bearer, Begetter:

"Talk, speak out. Don't moan, don't cry out. Please talk, each to each, within each kind, within each group," they were told—the deer, birds, puma, jaguar, serpent.

"Name now our names, praise us. We are your mother, we are your father. Speak now:

'Hurricane,
Newborn Thunderbolt, Sudden Thunderbolt,
Heart of Sky, Heart of Earth,
Maker, Modeler,
Bearer, Begetter,'

speak pray to us, keep our days," they were told. But it didn't turn out that they spoke like people: they just squawked, they just chattered, they just howled. It wasn't apparent what language they spoke; each one gave a different cry. When the Maker, Modeler heard this:

"It hasn't turned out well, they haven't spoken," they said among themselves. "It hasn't turned out that our names have been named. Since we are their mason and sculptor, this will not do," the Bearers and Begetters said among themselves. So they told them:

"You will simply have to be transformed. Since it hasn't turned out well and you haven't spoken, we have changed our word:

"What you feed on, what you eat, the places where you sleep, the places where you stay, whatever is yours will remain in the canyons, the forests. Although it turned out that our days were not kept, nor did you pray to us, there may yet be strength in the keeper of days, the giver of praise whom we have yet to make. Just accept your service, just let your flesh be eaten.

"So be it, this must be your service," they were told when they were instructed—the animals, small and great, on the face of the earth.

And then they wanted to test their timing again, they wanted to experiment again, and they wanted to prepare for the keeping of days again. They had not heard their speech among the animals; it did not come to fruition and it was not complete.

And so their flesh was brought low: they served, they were eaten, they were killed—the animals on the face of the earth.

Again there comes an experiment with the human work, the human design, by the Maker, Modeler, Bearer, Begetter:

"It must simply be tried again. The time for the planting and dawning is nearing. For this we must make a provider and nurturer. How else can we be invoked and remembered on the face of the earth? We have already made our first try at our work and design, but it turned out that they didn't keep our days, nor did they glorify us.

"So now let's try to make a giver of praise, giver of respect, provider, nurturer," they said.

So then comes the building and working with earth and mud. They made a body, but it didn't look good to them. It was just separating, just crumbling, just loosening, just softening, just disintegrating, and just dissolving. Its head wouldn't turn, either. Its face was just lopsided, its face was just twisted. It couldn't look around. It talked at first, but senselessly. It was quickly dissolving in the water.

"It won't last," the mason and sculptor said then. "It seems to be dwindling away, so let it just dwindle. It can't walk and it can't multiply, so let it be merely a thought," they said.

So then they dismantled, again they brought down their work and design. Again they talked:

"What is there for us to make that would turn out well, that would succeed in keeping our days and praying to us?" they said. Then they planned again:

"We'll just tell Xpiyacoc, Xmucane, Hunahpu Possum, Hunahpu Coyote, to try a counting of days, a counting of lots," the mason and sculptor said to themselves. Then they invoked Xpiyacoc, Xmucane.

Then comes the naming of those who are the midmost seers: the "Grandmother of Day, Grandmother of Light," as the Maker, Modeler called them. These are names of Xpiyacoc and Xmucane.

When Hurricane had spoken with the Sovereign Plumed Serpent, they invoked the daykeepers, diviners, the midmost seers:

"There is yet to find, yet to discover how we are to model a person, construct a person again, a provider, nurturer, so that we are called upon and we are recognized: our recompense is in words.

Midwife, matchmaker,
our grandmother, our grandfather,
Xpiyacoc, Xmucane,
let there be planting, let there be the dawning
of our invocation, our sustenance, our recognition
by the human work, the human design,
the human figure, the human form.
So be it, fulfill your names;
Hunahpu Possum, Hunahpu Coyote,
Bearer twice over, Begetter twice over,
Great Peccary, Great Coati,
lapidary, jeweler,
sawyer, carpenter,
plate shaper, bowl shaper,
incense maker, master craftsman,
Grandmother of Day, Grandmother of Light.

"You have been called upon because of our work, our design. Run your hands over the kernels of corn, over the seeds of the coral tree, just get it done, just let it come out whether we should carve and gouge a mouth, a face in wood," they told the daykeepers.

And then comes the borrowing, the counting of days; the hand is moved over the corn kernels, over the coral seeds, the days, the lots.

Then they spoke to them, one of them a grandmother, the other a grandfather.

This is the grandfather, this is the master of the coral seeds: Xpiyacoc is his name.

And this is the grandmother, the daykeeper, diviner who stands behind others: Xmucane is her name.

And they said, as they set out the days:

"Just let it be found, just let it be discovered,
say it, our ear is listening,
may you talk, may you speak,
just find the wood for the carving and sculpting
by the builder, sculptor.
Is this to be the provider, the nurturer
when it comes to the planting, the dawning?
You corn kernels, you coral seeds,
you days, you lots:
may you succeed, may you be accurate,"

they said to the corn kernels, coral seeds, days, lots. "Have shame, you up there, Heart of Sky: attempt no deception before the mouth and face of Sovereign Plumed Serpent," they said. Then they spoke straight to the point:

"It is well that there be your manikins, woodcarvings, talking, speaking, there on the face of the earth."

"So be it," they replied. The moment they spoke it was done: the manikins, woodcarvings, human in looks and human in speech.

This was the peopling of the face of the earth:

They came into being, they multiplied, they had daughters, they had sons, these manikins, woodcarvings. But there was nothing in their hearts and nothing in their minds, no memory of their mason and builder. They just went and walked wherever they wanted. Now they did not remember the Heart of Sky.

And so they fell, just an experiment and just a cutout for humankind. They were talking at first but their faces were dry. They were not yet developed in the legs and arms. They had no blood, no lymph. They had no sweat, no fat. Their complexions were dry, their faces were crusty. They flailed their legs and arms, their bodies were deformed.

And so they accomplished nothing before the Maker, Modeler who gave them birth, gave them heart. They became the first numerous people here on the face of the earth.

Again there comes a humiliation, destruction, and demolition. The manikins, woodcarvings were killed when the Heart of Sky devised a flood for them. A great flood was made; it came down on the heads of the manikins, woodcarvings.

The man's body was carved from the wood of the coral tree by the Maker, Modeler. And as for the woman, the Maker, Modeler needed the hearts of bulrushes for the woman's body. They were not competent, nor did they speak before the builder and sculptor who made them and brought them forth, and so they were killed, done in by a flood: There came a rain of resin from the sky.

There came the one named Gouger of Faces: he gouged out their eyeballs. There came Sudden Bloodletter: he snapped off their heads.

There came Crunching Jaguar: he ate their flesh.

There came Tearing Jaguar: he tore them open.

They were pounded down to the bones and tendons, smashed and pulverized even to the bones. Their faces were smashed because they were incompetent before their mother and their father, the Heart of Sky, named Hurricane. The earth was blackened because of this; the black rainstorm began, rain all day and rain all night. Into their houses came the animals, small and great. Their faces were crushed by things of wood and stone. Everything spoke: their water jars, their tortilla griddles, their plates, their cooking pots, their dogs, their grinding stones, each and every thing crushed their faces. Their dogs and turkeys told them:

"You caused us pain, you ate us, but now it is you whom we shall eat." And this is the grinding stone:

Document Text

"We were undone because of you.

Every day, every day,
in the dark, in the dawn, forever,
r-r-rip, r-r-rip,
r-r-rub, r-r-rub,
right in our faces, because of you.

"This was the service we gave you at first, when you were still people, but today you will learn of our power. We shall pound and we shall grind your flesh," their grinding stones told them.

And this is what their dogs said, when they spoke in their turn:

"Why is it you can't seem to give us our food? We just watch and you just keep us down, and you throw us around. You keep a stick ready when you eat, just so you can hit us. We don't talk, so we've received nothing from you. How could you not have known? You did know that we were wasting away there, behind you.

"So, this very day you will taste the teeth in our mouths. We shall eat you," their dogs told them, and their faces were crushed.

And then their tortilla griddles and cooking pots spoke to them in turn:

"Pain! That's all you've done for us. Our mouths are sooty, our faces are sooty. By setting us on the fire all the time, you burn us. Since we felt no pain, you try it. We shall burn you," all their cooking pots said, crushing their faces.

The stones, their hearthstones were shooting out, coming right out of the fire, going for their heads, causing them pain. Now they run for it, helter-skelter.

They want to climb up on the houses, but they fall as the houses collapse.

They want to climb the trees; they're thrown off by the trees.

They want to get inside caves, but the caves slam shut in their faces.

Such was the scattering of the human work, the human design. The people were ground down, overthrown. The mouths and faces of all of them were destroyed and crushed. And it used to be said that the monkeys in the forests today are a sign of this. They were left as a sign because wood alone was used for their flesh by the builder and sculptor.

So this is why monkeys look like people: they are a sign of a previous human work, human design—mere manikins, mere woodcarvings.

Glossary

Newborn Thunderbolt	a god who came down from the sky along with Heart of Sky and Hurricane
Sudden Thunderbolt	the god from the sky who followed Newborn Thunderbolt

Athanasius of Alexandria
(St. Athanasius of Alexandria, from 'Crabbes Historical Dictionary', published in 1825 (litho), English School (19th century) / Private Collection / Ken Welsh / The Bridgeman Art Library International)

Nicene Creed

325

"True God from true God, begotten, not made, of the same being as the Father, through whom all things came to be."

Overview

The Nicene Creed is the first official formulation of the doctrine of the Trinity by the universal Christian congregation, which identifies itself therein as "the Catholic and Apostolic Church." The creed was codified in 325 by the Council of Nicaea, the Church's premier ecumenical—literally, "representing the entire inhabited world"—council, composed of 318 bishops from all regions where the Christian faith had spread. Since its development, the Nicene Creed has been embraced by all mainstream forms of Christianity, and its contents are therefore dogma in contemporary Roman Catholicism, Eastern Orthodoxy, and Protestantism. The creed became necessary soon after Christianity received toleration in 313 from the Roman Empire, which had persecuted the Church, sometimes regularly and sometimes sporadically, from the time of its first-century inception. While it was concerned with the fundamental matter of the survival of its adherents, the Church originally lacked the energy and leisure to resolve the theological question of precisely how the Father, Son, and Holy Spirit, each of whom the New Testament calls "God," could comprise the one monotheistic God.

By the late second century, the word *trinity* (from the Latin *trinitas*, from *tri-unitas*, meaning "tri-unity") had come to designate the notion that somehow God was a composite unity of three parts. But the issue of explaining if and how this notion could be true grew acute when Arius (ca. 250–336), a popular presbyter in Alexandria, Egypt, attacked the Trinity as undermining monotheism and substituted the much simpler ideas that the Father alone is God, the Father created the Son, and the Son created the Holy Spirit. After Arius was excommunicated by his overseeing bishop, Alexander, in 321, riots led by Arius's supporters broke out in the streets of Alexandria, and soon all Egypt was torn by strife over the issue of whether Jesus was Creator or creature. This situation outraged the Roman emperor Constantine I, who had legalized Christianity eight years earlier precisely for its promise to unify his already fractious empire. A politician indifferent toward theological issues, Constantine sent letters to Alexander and Arius in 323 accusing them of merely disputing over trivialities and ordering them to reconcile their differences. Upon finding that his letters just made matters worse, in 325 Constantine called for a council of all the Church's bishops, which he presumed to moderate, at Nicaea, in Bithynia (present-day Iznik, Turkey) to work out a solution to the dispute. That solution, the Nicene Creed, not only furnished a sophisticated theology of Jesus's status as God and Creator but also set the stage for state involvemenm in Church affairs over the next millennium.

Context

At the center of the controversy leading up to the Council of Nicaea stood Arius's doctrine of Jesus, rooted in the presuppositions of unitarianism and the distinctiveness of the Logos—Greek for "word," signifying the divine mind personified by Jesus. On the one hand, unitarianism stipulated that the only way God could be a single being was for him to be a single person, namely, the Father. On the other hand, the doctrine of distinctiveness held that the Logos, which became flesh in Jesus (as recorded in John 1:14), was an immaterial being independent of God. Together, these two presuppositions ruled out the modalistic doctrine, widespread among many Christian laity, that God was a single person who played three different roles (that is, assumed three different modes) throughout salvation history: the role of the Father in the Old Testament, the role of the Son in the New Testament, and the role of the Holy Spirit in the age of the Christian Church. Instead, Arius argued that the Logos was the first and greatest creation of God the Father, through whom God made all other things invisible (as with the Holy Spirit and the angels) or visible (as with the universe). In philosophical terms, the Logos and God the Father were not of the same *ousia*, a Greek word meaning "essence," "substance," "being," and "nature." For this reason, Arius wrote that the Logos is "different from and unlike the essence"—in Greek, *heteroousios*—of the Father in all respects."

As a creature, the Logos is mutable by nature and possesses free will and so could choose either to sin or not to sin. At the virginal conception, God produced Jesus by

Time Line

313
- Emperor Constantine issues the Edict of Milan, granting Christianity legal toleration in the Roman Empire.

318
- Arius denounces the doctrine of the Trinity as polytheistic and claims that Christ is the first and greatest creation of God.

319
- Athanasius writes *De incarnatione verbi Dei* (*Treatise on the Incarnation of the Word*), defending the notion that Christ is the Creator, God.

321
- Alexander convokes a local council in Alexandria and there has Arius declared a heretic. Afterward, Arius's supporters start riots in Alexandria and other major Egyptian cities.

322
- Arius composes "Thaleia," a catchy song asserting that "there was once when he was not," to popularize his doctrine that Christ was a creature of God.

323
- Constantine sends letters to Alexander and Arius ordering them to stop their dispute; the letters only exacerbate the situation.

325
- Constantine calls the Catholic Church's First Ecumenical Council in the Bithynian city of Nicaea. The 318 assembled bishops draw up the Nicene Creed, which proclaims the doctrine of the Trinity in precise philosophical language and condemns Arius and his followers.

326
- Athanasius is made bishop of Alexandria by both public and ecclesiastical acclamation.

336
- Constantine, now favoring the Arians, exiles Athanasius to the southwest German city of Treves (now Trier).

337
- Constantine dies, having received baptism on his deathbed.

---

conjoining the Logos, which stood in for a human soul, with a human body derived from Mary. Hence for Arius, Jesus was neither truly human—that is, of human body and human soul—nor truly God; rather, Jesus was a superhuman hybrid, a human body without a human soul but with the supernatural though less-than-divine Logos taking its place. However, because Jesus freely chose to unify his will with the Father's will and so received God's favor, the New Testament could metaphorically call Jesus "God" and "Son of God." Seeking popular appeal, Arius set his doctrine of Jesus to music in the catchy song "Thaleia" (Banquet), which contained the ensuingly infamous line regarding the Logos, "There was once when he was not"—meaning that there was a time when the Logos did not exist.

Arius's chief opponent proved to be not Bishop Alexander but the young theologian and presbyter Athanasius, who in 319 composed the influential treatise *De incarnatione verbi Dei*, or *Treatise on the Incarnation of the Word*. This treatise held that the Logos had existed from all eternity with the Father and was of the same essence—in Greek, *homoousios*—as the Father, though he was an individual distinct from the Father. Just as a river springing from a lake is different from the lake but identical in substance to the lake, as both are water, Athanasius claimed that the Son is different from the Father but identical in substance to the Father, as both are God. This insistence on the Logos being deity prevailed for reasons concerning human salvation: If the Logos were less than God, believed Athanasius, he could not be the savior of humankind. How, Athanasius rhetorically queried, could a mere creature, however exalted, save humanity from its sins?

Contrary to Arius's view that the Logos was created by the Father at a point in time, Athanasius posited that the Logos was begotten of the Father, or eternally and automatically generated from the essence of the Father. To illustrate, Athanasius furnished an analogy with the human mind. The human mind does not choose to generate reason but automatically does so; moreover, it is self-evident that the mind and reason always coexist and are equally human. Similarly, the eternal Father did not choose to generate the Logos but necessarily did so, rendering the Logos coeternal with and equal to the Father. Never occupying himself with the seemingly esoteric question of Jesus's composition, Athanasius felt that Jesus's full humanity was so obvious as to require no justification, and the Logos's becoming flesh as Jesus made Jesus fully God as well.

The dispute between Arius and his opponents was the primary reason why the Council of Nicaea was called. The Nicene Creed was therefore composed to permanently settle the dispute, providing a doctrine of Christ's relationship to the Father that could be affirmed by all the faithful. At the council, Eusebius, Athanasius, and Arius emerged as the leaders of three respective parties, with the Eusebian party largest, the Athanasian party second largest, and the Arian party smallest. The Eusebians, convinced that Jesus was God, were horrified at the Arian claim that the Logos was the first and greatest creature of God. However, as pastors and not philosophers, the Eusebians were very reluctant to use extrabiblical philosophical concepts like *ousia*, which they had difficulty understanding, to explain Jesus's relationship to the Father. They were content to simply condemn Arianism as heresy and then return to their local churches. When it quickly became apparent that Arianism could not be pronounced false without a positive statement of doctrinal truth to serve as a frame of reference, Eusebius proposed the following statement: "We believe in one God, the Father Almighty, Maker of all things seen and unseen. And in one Lord Jesus Christ, the *Logos* of God, God from God, Light from Light, life from life, the unique Son, the firstborn of all creation, begotten of the Father before all ages, by whom also all things were made; who for our salvation was made flesh, and lived among humans, and suffered, and rose again the third day, and ascended to the Father, and shall come again in glory to judge the living and the dead. And in the Holy Spirit." This statement contains no technical terms but only draws on vocabulary used in scripture, a strategy that initially, for the majority of bishops, seemed to safeguard the sufficiency of scripture in theological matters.

To this assessment, Athanasius replied that the sufficiency of scripture did not indicate that extrabiblical terminology should be avoided in expressing doctrinal truth; if that were the case, scripture could never be validly translated into foreign languages. Rather, the sufficiency of scripture indicated that the meaning of its vocabulary contained the sum total of doctrinal truth, to which nothing could either be added or subtracted. So, as Athanasius insisted, when persons such as the Arians misconstrue what biblical vocabulary means, it is not merely proper but mandatory to use extrabiblical terminology—the more precise, the better—to unequivocally state scripture's meaning. To illustrate, Athanasius pointed out that the Arians interpreted Eusebius's identification of Jesus as "the firstborn of all creation" (from Colossians 1:15) as denoting Jesus's status as the first creation of God, despite the intended meaning of Eusebius (and the apostle Paul, who was considered to be the author of Colossians) that Jesus was the anointed ruler of all creation.

At this juncture, the Eusebians perceived that *ousia* language, notwithstanding their aversion, would be unavoidable in any declarative creed. Denouncing the Arian phrasing "of a different being than the Father" (*heteroousios*) as a rank denial of Jesus's status as deity but unsure whether his divinity implied the Athanasian phrasing "of the same being as the Father" (*homoousios*), the Eusebians proposed the compromise language that Jesus was "of a similar nature to the Father" (*homoiousios*). The debate between *homoousios* and *homoiousios* grew so intense that, according to Eusebius, a frustrated Constantine, who perceived no difference between the two, scornfully exclaimed, "The whole Christian world is convulsed over a diphthong!" But when it became apparent, after a few weeks of wrangling, that the Arians were willing to adopt the phrasing "of a similar nature to the Father," since they could reinterpret this vague phrase in agreement with their own theology, the Eusebians were driven by their sheer disgust toward Arian theology to abandon

Time Line

341
- Macedonius, the bishop of Constantinople, declares that the Holy Spirit was either a creature subordinate to the Father and the Son or an impersonal force used by the Father and the Son.

357
- Arians meet in the Bohemian city of Sirmium (in modern-day Serbia) to write their own creed affirming that Christ and the Holy Spirit are *heteroousios* (of a different substance) with God and not *homoousios* (of the same substance) with God.

381
- The Roman emperor Theodosius I convenes the Church's Second Ecumenical Council in Constantinople; there, 186 bishops form the Niceno-Constantinopolitan Creed, a revision of the Nicene Creed affirming the divinity of the Holy Spirit. Afterward, Theodosius declares Christianity the official religion of the Roman Empire.

their phrasing and concur with Athanasius on the language "of the same being as the Father." With this critical matter resolved, the Nicene Creed was officially codified.

About the Author

The two major architects of the Nicene Creed were Eusebius of Caesarea (ca. 260–340), who produced what would become its preliminary draft, and Athanasius (296–373), who revised that draft to yield the form accepted by the council at large. Eusebius was born in 260 in Caesarea, in Palestine, where he studied under the Alexandrian scholar Pamphilius. After Pamphilius's martyrdom in 310, his library, containing copies of the scriptures, biblical commentaries, and writings of second- and third-century church fathers, provided the foundation of Eusebius's scholarship. Because Eusebius had lived through horrific persecution, Constantine's legalization of Christianity in 313 earned him Eusebius's undying support—support that would in hindsight prove naive, in light of the moral and social problems that would come to the Church through its fusion with politics. That same year Eusebius was ordained as bishop of Caesarea and, upon endearing himself to Constantine, became the emperor's official chronicler. Although he went on to write three aretologies (tributes to the virtues) of Constantine, Eusebius became best known for his ten-volume *Historia ecclesiastica*, or *Church History* (written from 315 to

Emperor Constantine I
(Emperor Constantine I [c.274-337] the Great [mosaic], Byzantine / San Marco, Venice, Italy / Giraudon / The Bridgeman Art Library International)

326), the first work of its kind. Since it meticulously traced the history of Christianity from the time of Jesus to the cessation of Roman persecution, Eusebius is known to posterity as the "Father of Church History."

Athanasius was born in 296 in Alexandria and received training for the Christian ministry from a young age. Showing considerable promise as a theologian in his teenage years, Athanasius was taken under the wing of Bishop Alexander in 315. In 318 Athanasius was ordained as a presbyter in Alexandria, gaining acclamation among the laity for his learned preaching and his dedication to fasting and other spiritual disciplines. Athanasius's lifelong theological program constituted the vindication of the full divinity of Christ, which he regarded as the cornerstone of the Christian faith. In attempting to safeguard Christ's status as deity from the Arians, Athanasius showed such fearless independence at Nicaea in pushing for the affirmation of *homoousios* that his opponents coined the now-famous Latin phrase *"Athanasius contra mundum, et mundus contra Athanasium"* (Athanasius against the world, and the world against Athanasius). When Alexander died in 326, Athanasius succeeded him as bishop of Alexandria, a position that brought him much hardship. Depending on whether or not the sitting Roman emperor sympathized with the Arians, Athanasius was either banished from or recalled to the empire. Athanasius thus spent twenty of his forty-six years as bishop in exile. Unflinching in his fidelity to his theological convictions, Athanasius was named by the fifth-century Church as the "Father of Orthodoxy."

Explanation and Analysis of the Document

Every clause in the Nicene Creed deals with an actual or potential matter of controversy. Every clause is designed either to indicate the orthodox alternative to an ostensibly heretical idea taught by some existing school of thought or to preclude later misunderstanding about what the Catholic Church officially taught. Noncontroversial matters, by contrast, are not addressed, for the Church had no need to do so.

♦ Paragraph 1

The creed begins with the affirmation that Christians believe in only one God (monotheism), not three gods (tritheism). This emphatic remark was aimed at assuaging the fear shared by Arius and many of his ecclesiastical and popular supporters that the Trinity entailed belief in three gods. The creed proceeds to designate that, within the administrative operation (or economy) of the Trinity, the Father occupies the highest position. The assertion of different positions necessitates different individuals to fill those positions, thereby excluding the possibility of modalism, the popular view that the Father, Son, and Holy Spirit are merely names for three different roles that one and the same individual plays. (Modalism is still alive and well among Christian laity in the form of the "water analogy," which holds that, just as water can be solid, liquid, or gas under different conditions, so a unitarian God can be Father, Son, or Holy Spirit under different conditions.)

The Father is described as "almighty," meaning omnipotent or all-powerful. This seemingly innocuous comment introduces one of two underlying arguments against Arianism to be gradually unfolded throughout the creed. God's omnipotence logically necessitates that no other being besides God can be omnipotent, since in that case God would not have all power. So, the question is implicitly raised: Is Jesus also almighty? The second underlying argument is introduced by the statement that the Father is the Creator of all things, both what is seen, or the physical universe, and the unseen spiritual realm, including various invisible entities like time, angels, and abstractions. So, the question is implicitly raised: Is Jesus also the Creator of all things, or is Jesus one of the invisible entities the Father created?

♦ Paragraph 2

The answers to the two implicit questions come immediately, as Jesus is called the "one Lord." This is a quotation from the fundamental Jewish confession of monotheism known as the Shema (Deuteronomy 6:4–5), which describes the sole creator God as "one Lord." Hence Jesus, every bit as much as the Father, is the omnipotent Creator of all things, not merely the greatest temporal creature. Up to this point, the creed has followed Eusebius's initial draft. Now comes the first revision of Eusebius's wording, as Jesus's description is changed from the "Logos of God" to the "Son of God." Proposed by Athanasius, this change was made for two reasons. First, Arius used the term *Logos* so frequently that when laypeople heard

Essential Quotes

> "We believe in . . . one Lord, Jesus Christ the Son of God, begotten of the Father, the only-begotten, that is, of the essence of the Father."

> "True God from true God, begotten, not made, of the same being as the Father, through whom all things came to be, both the things in heaven and on earth, who for us humans and for our salvation came down and was made flesh, becoming human, who suffered and rose again on the third day."

> "But those who say that . . . the Son of God is of a different essence or created or subject to moral change or alteration—these doth the Catholic and Apostolic Church anathematize."

it, they immediately associated it with Arius's teaching that the Logos was the first and greatest creation of God. By using "Son" instead, the complete humanity of Jesus could be affirmed without suggesting Jesus's creation; the New Testament calls Jesus "Son of God" because he had no human father but was miraculously conceived by the Virgin Mary (Luke 1:34–35). Second, "Son of God" had long been a title for the Roman emperor, from Augustus on, identifying the divinely anointed ruler of the world. Even though Constantine was sitting among the bishops as their moderator, Athanasius wanted not too subtly to remind Constantine and all future political leaders that they were not divinely anointed rulers of the world; Jesus alone held that status.

A full-scale attack on Arianism comes next in the creed's discussion of Jesus's relationship to the Father. Shortening and then reordering Eusebius's phrase "begotten of the Father before all ages," Athanasius described Jesus as "begotten of the Father," or automatically generated by the Father as a result not of the Father's will but of the divine essence. Just as the mind generates reason without choosing to do so by virtue of human nature itself, so the Father generated the Son without choosing to do so by virtue of the divine nature itself. Since the Father is the timeless creator of the world who never came into being, it follows that the Son is also timeless and never came into being but rather always existed. Athanasius insisted on dropping the ambiguous phrase "before all ages," since it could be taken to mean by the Arians that the Son, though preexisting vis-à-vis human history, was still created, rather than being taken as a synonym for "eternal," as Eusebius intended.

Again following Eusebius, the next term, which in English has been traditionally yet wrongfully translated "only-begotten," is *monogenes*, which did not designate begetting but a quite different idea. The reason why *monogenes* has historically been rendered "only-begotten" goes back to the King James Version of the Bible of 1611. The translators, with no knowledge of the type of Greek in which the New Testament was written, were forced to guess at the meaning of the biblical term *monogenes*. They concluded wrongfully that it meant "only-begotten." However, it is now known by Greek scholars that *monogenes* meant "the only one of its kind, the only one of its class." Hence Jesus is the only Son of his kind or class, namely, the "unique Son" (as formulated by Eusebius) of God. This is because, unlike Christian believers who are the Father's adopted sons and daughters and thus do not share the essence of the Father, Jesus is the only Son who is deity and thus shares the essence of the Father. Hence, Athanasius added the unambiguous clarification to *monogenes*, "that is, of the essence of the Father."

The next two phrases, "God from God, Light from Light," come directly from Eusebius and are followed by several explanatory phrases from Athanasius that categorically exclude Arianism. Here "God" and "Light" are nonexclusively assigned to Son and Father rather than exclusively equated with the Father and the Son, respectively. In other words, "God" and "Light" are used in the same way as "red" in the statement "The coat and its thread are red; red from red" (which does not negate there being only one color red) and not in the same way as "cat" in the statement "Fluffy gave birth to Tiger; cat from cat" (which negates there being only one cat). Both the Eusebian and Athanasian schools interpreted "God from God" as the Son's timeless generation from the Father in accord with the analogies of human reason's instantaneous generation from the human mind and of light in an empty room of a house being instantaneously generated from a lit candle in an adjacent room—as in "Light from Light."

But Athanasius knew full well that, if left alone, Arians would interpret "God" and "Light" in the same way as "cat" in the aforementioned example, thus affirming that the one true God produced a lesser god and the one great Light produced a lesser light. To preclude this interpretation, Athanasius added the univocal "true God from true God," emphasizing that the Son and the Father constitute the one true God. To sharply differentiate between Jesus's "begottenness," or timeless generation from the Father, and Jesus's temporal creation by the Father, Athanasius explicitly added the declaration, "begotten, not made." If Jesus was not made, then Jesus can only be the Creator. Consequently, Jesus and the Father are parts of the same being, or *homoousios*: "of the same being as the Father." It is through Jesus that "all things came to be, both the things in heaven and on earth" (that is, both the invisible and visible things), not, as Arius insisted, that "all other things in heaven"—that is, all things except Jesus, who was himself a created thing—"and all things on earth came to be."

Afterward, Eusebius's wording is followed with only light revision. As the Eusebians and Athanasians concurred, Jesus's status as deity was of crucial importance for human salvation, since only God could save humanity. All this is expressed in the phrase "who for us humans and for our salvation came down and was made flesh." Because the Arians could also say that the Logos was made flesh (as he assumed a hominid body) and, as in Eusebius's proposal, "lived among humans," Athanasius replaced this phrase with "becoming human," which could not be said about Arius's superhuman yet created Jesus. The paragraph's final three clauses discredit Gnosticism, a popular movement in competition with Christianity to which Arians, Eusebians, and Athanasians alike were opposed. Most Gnostics held to a spiritualistic view of Jesus, according to which a purely immaterial Jesus only seemed to have a body, die, rise from the dead, and ascend into heaven. In contrast, the creed affirms that Jesus indeed "suffered and rose again on the third day" and "ascended into heaven." Since the Gnostics did not believe in either sin or objective morality, they denied any future judgment. Accordingly, the creed counters that Jesus "is coming to judge the living and the dead."

♦ **Paragraph 3**

At this point in Christian history, no developed theology of the Holy Spirit had been devised by any school of thought. However, by listing the Holy Spirit along with the divine Father and the divine Son, the creed implicitly affirms that the Spirit possesses the same essential attributes as the Father and the Son. In other words, the Spirit is an individual and is God in the same way that the Father and the Son are divine individuals.

♦ **Appendix**

While it is not part of the Nicene Creed proper, the council, by a final vote of 316 to 2, appended an anathema of Arianism. An *anathema* is the strongest possible religious curse, reserved for those judged in word or deed to proclaim a gospel different from the Gospel of Christ (Galatians 1:8). It signifies that if persons continue to believe in that for which they have been cursed up to the moment of death without repentance, they will be eternally condemned. The anathema cites several quotes from Arius's writings and states that all who believe that Christ was created by and is different from the Father will be damned.

Audience

As dogma, or official doctrine, produced by an ecumenical council, the creed's audience consisted of the entire Christian world, at that time stretching throughout the Roman Empire and parts of the Sassanid Empire. Thus Christians in Europe, North Africa, and the Middle East had this creed promulgated as essential doctrine in their churches by their returning bishops. Moreover, after emperor Theodosius I made Christianity the state religion of the Roman Empire in 381, it became illegal in the empire to believe anything contrary to the creed, on pain of banishment.

Impact

For more than half a century after its codification, the Nicene Creed provoked reaction from Arians, who employed political intrigue to gain the favor of the sitting Roman emperor and called several of their own councils to undermine the concept of Jesus as uncreated God. By 336, the Arians had convinced Constantine of their views, who proceeded to exile Athanasius to the Germanic city of Treves (now Trier). Although Athanasius returned to Alexandria after Constantine's death, the theologian would be banished from the empire four more times under successive pro-Arian emperors, returning after the death of each one. The most important Arian council assembled in 357 at Sirmium, a Bohemian (now Serbian) city, formulating its own creed asserting that Christ and the Holy Spirit are *heteroousios* with God and not *homoousios* with God. Moreover, the Nicene Creed's ambiguity concerning the Holy Spirit led Bishop Macedonius of Constantinople to propose, in 341, that the Spirit is not God. Rather, the Holy Spirit is either a being subordinate to the Father and the Son or else an impersonal force used by the Father and the Son. The renewed controversy over Christ and the new controversy over the Holy Spirit led Theodosius I to convoke the Second Ecumenical Council at Constantinople in 381, the same year he adopted Christianity as Roman law.

The Council of Constantinople made several additions to the Nicene Creed, the result of which was the Niceno-Constantinopolitan Creed. These additions were of three types: further anti-Arian and anti-Gnostic remarks concerning Christ, an explicit doctrine of the Holy Spirit, and a statement of the Catholic Church's worldwide unity, authority, and ultimate victory over death. Supplementary text concerning Christ included the phrasing "eternally" (as in, "eternally begotten of the Father"), "was incarnate by the Holy Spirit of the Virgin Mary" (stressing Jesus's humanity), "was crucified also for us under Pontius Pilate" (stressing the reality of Jesus's death), and "according to the Scriptures" (stressing the truth of Jesus's Resurrection). The paragraph-long affirmation on the Holy Spirit insists that the Spirit is Lord (that is, God), an individual who proceeds from the Father just as Christ does, the object of worship, and the inspirer of scripture: "And we believe in the Holy Spirit, the Lord and Giver of life, who proceeded from the Father, who with the Father and the Son together is worshiped and glorified, who spoke by the prophets." The declaration on the Church avows, "And we believe in one holy catholic and apostolic church. We acknowledge one baptism for the remission of sins. And we look for the resurrection of the dead, and the life of the world to come. Amen." Following the Second Ecumenical Council, its Niceno-Constantinopolitan Creed immediately displaced the original Nicene Creed in all Christian churches and so, despite the name's technical inaccuracy, assumed the old moniker "Nicene Creed."

The Niceno-Constantinopolitan Creed is therefore the "Nicene Creed" recited throughout the contemporary Christian world. One small difference, springing from the Third Synod of Toledo, held in Spain in 589, separates the text used in Catholic and Protestant churches from the text used in Eastern Orthodox churches. The synod added the word *filioque*, "and the Son," to the clause on the Holy Spirit's procession, thus yielding "who proceeded from the Father and the Son." Recognized by Western-descended churches but not by Eastern-descended churches, the *filioque* clause is today part of the Catholic and Protestant text but not part of the Eastern Orthodox text.

Further Reading

■ Books

Ayres, Lewis. *Nicaea and Its Legacy: An Approach to Fourth-Century Trinitarian Theology*. Oxford, U.K.: Oxford University Press, 2006.

Cairns, Earle E. *Christianity through the Centuries: A History of the Christian Church*. 3rd. ed. Grand Rapids, Mich.: Zondervan, 1996.

González, Justo L. *A History of Christian Thought*. Vol. 1: *From the Beginnings to the Council of Chalcedon*. Rev. ed. Nashville, Tenn.: Abingdon, 1987.

Keen, Ralph. *The Christian Tradition*. Upper Saddle River, N.J.: Prentice Hall, 2004.

McGrath, Alister E. *Historical Theology: An Introduction to the History of Christian Thought*. Malden, Mass.: Blackwell, 1998.

McGrath, Alister E. *Christian Theology: An Introduction*. 3rd. ed. Malden, Mass.: Blackwell, 2001.

Questions for Further Study

1. Compare the Christian concept of the Trinity with the notion of God as a unity as explicated in Moses Ben Maimon's *Mishneh Torah*. Are the views inconsistent?

2. Explain the fundamental controversy that made the Council of Nicaea, and the Nicene Creed, necessary in the view of church leaders.

3. At the time of the Council of Nicaea—and beyond—the early Christian Church was deeply concerned with heresy. Why do you think heretical beliefs were of such concern to the Church hierarchy? What difference did it make if a branch of the Christian Church adopted a slightly differing view of, for example, the relationship between God the Father and Jesus Christ?

4. Summarize the intersections between religion and politics at the time of the Council of Nicaea and the years following.

5. What did Emperor Constantine mean when he exclaimed, "The whole Christian world is convulsed over a diphthong!" What was the diphthong, and why was it considered important?

Olson, Roger E. *The Story of Christian Theology: Twenty Centuries of Tradition and Reform*. Downers Grove, Ill.: InterVarsity Press, 1999.

■ Web Sites

Bratcher, Dennis. "Christian Creeds, Confessions, and Catechisms." The Voice Web site.
http://www.crivoice.org/creeds.html

—Kirk R. MacGregor

Nicene Creed

We believe in one God, the Father Almighty, Maker of all things seen and unseen.

And in one Lord, Jesus Christ the Son of God, begotten of the Father, the only-begotten, that is, of the essence of the Father, God from God, Light from Light, true God from true God, begotten, not made, of the same being as the Father, through whom all things came to be, both the things in heaven and on earth, who for us humans and for our salvation came down and was made flesh, becoming human, who suffered and rose again on the third day, ascended into heaven, who is coming to judge the living and the dead.

And in the Holy Spirit.

But those who say that "there was once when he was not" and "before he was begotten he was not" and "he was made out of things that were not" or maintain that the Son of God is of a different essence or created or subject to moral change or alteration—these doth the Catholic and Apostolic Church anathematize.

Glossary

anathematize	denounce, curse as evil, threaten with divine punishment

Shiva Nataraja
(Shiva Nataraja [bronze], Indian School [11th century] / Government Museum and National Art Gallery, Madras, India / Giraudon / The Bridgeman Art Library International)

Tirumular: "Atbudha Dance"

ca. 400–700

"When the Creator dances / The World He created dances."

Overview

The Tamil poem "Atbudha Dance" extols the wonder and awe of the Cosmic Dance of the King of the Dance. It is excerpted from an ancient South Indian Tamil devotional poem or hymn called "Tirumantiram" (Sacred Mantra or Prayer), composed by the legendary Tamil sage Tirumular. The dates most commonly given for the Tirumantiram and the "Atbudha Dance" are between 400 and 700 CE. Tirumular, its author, is an almost-mythical figure in the Tamil Shaivite (Shiva worshipper) tradition. Many fundamental concepts of this tradition were first found in his innovative text. One such example is the work's emphasis on worship of the Hindu god Shiva (or Siva) as the Cosmic Dancer, Shiva Nataraja. The Tirumantiram consists of some three thousand verses and is one of the four central texts of the main book for the Tamil sect of the Hindu god Shiva as Nataraja, Shaiva Siddhanta (Doctrine of Shiva); this main book is called Tirumarai (Sacred Book).

Shaiva Siddhanta is a Hindu school of Shiva worshipers with tens of millions of followers and thousands of active temples found primarily in the South Indian state of Tamil Nadu and to a much lesser degree in Sri Lanka, where Tamil speakers also live. Many of its core concepts stem from the Tirumantiram. For this reason a study of the poem's emphasis on the Dance of Shiva sheds unique insight into the origins and worship of Shiva Nataraja. In modern times, owing to the widespread notoriety of the celebrated South Indian bronze images (ca. 600–850) of Shiva dancing encircled by fire, Shiva Nataraja, king of the dance, has come to be viewed as the face of Hinduism.

Context

It is believed that the school of Shaiva Siddhanta, which gave rise to the popular worship of the Hindu god Shiva as Nataraja, developed first in North India, borrowing heavily from its predecessor, the ascetic Pashupata tradition of devotional (bhakti) Shiva worship. The Pashupatas no longer exist but are believed to be the earliest representatives of Shaivism, first appearing somewhere between the first and second centuries CE. Shaivism began to flourish during the Gupta Empire (330–550 CE), a time of revival for all forms of Hinduism. It was during this period that the intensely devotional Shaivism of the Pashupatas entered South India, eventually displacing the more prevalent religions of Buddhism and Jainism by about 700.

Between 600 and 800, the great Tamil saint-poets (Nayanars) of Shaiva Siddhanta, such as Tirumular, Campantar, Appar, Cuntarar, and Manikkavacakar, used the power of their devotional songs (bhajans) to assert a devotion missing in Buddhism and Jainism venerating and exalting the glory of divine love to be gained from worship of Shiva. Their songs would later form part of the compendium Tirumurai, which is one of four major texts, along with the Vedas (foundational texts of Hinduism), Shaiva Agamas (twenty-eight authoritative scriptures), and Meykanda or Siddhanta Shastras, constituting the scriptural basis of the Tamil Shaiva Siddhanta canon.

In the north of India in the twelfth century, Shaiva Siddhantia developed a broad theology producing its own exegetical works. Many of these works were appropriated by influential South Indian Tamil Shaiva Siddhanta twelfth-century authors and poets, such as Aghorasiva and Trilocanasiva. But while the influence and prestige of Shaiva Siddhanta was increasing in South India, it was decreasing and dying out in other parts of India, so that after the twelfth century, Shaiva Siddhanta came to be associated exclusively with Tamil-speaking South India.

Although the scriptural canon of Tamil Shaiva Siddhanta consists of four important *shastras* (sacred works), the *shastra* relevant to the subject of Shiva Nataraja is the Tirumurai, a twelve-volume anthology of Tamil devotional poems and songs from the leading Nayanars (poet-saints). The Nayanars were sixty-three Shaivite devotional poets who traveled throughout Tamil Nadu singing the praises of Shiva. Their heartfelt *bhajans* were instrumental in raising awareness and popularizing the Shaiva Siddhanta religion throughout Tamil Nadu.

The tenth volume of the Tirumurai is the Tirumantiram (sometimes written Thirumanthiram or Tirumandhiram) by Tirumular (also Tirumoolar), who is credited with being the earliest or first of the Nayanars to sing the praises

Time Line	
CA. 100 CE	■ The Pashupata tradition, the earliest form of Shaivism, first appears in North India.
330–550	■ Shaivism begins to flourish during the era of the Gupta Empire; Pashupatas enter South India.
CA. 400–700	■ Tirumular writes the Tirumantiram using the term *Shaiva Siddhanta* for the first time, laying the groundwork for the later system of Shaiva Siddhanta and the first exposition of the Shaiva Agamas in Tamil.
600–700	■ Pashupata-based (bhakti) devotional worship of Shiva supplants Buddhism and Jainism as the dominant religion of South India. ■ Tamil Nayanars (poet-saints or devotional poets) travel throughout South India singing devotional songs (*bhajans*) that refute concepts of Buddhism and Jainism and venerate Shiva. ■ South Indian Shaiva Siddhanta emerges. ■ Worship of Shiva Nataraja begins with repeated emphasis in the Tirumantiram.
1100–1200	■ North Indian Shaiva Siddhanta develops theology and exegetical works, and South Indian Tamil Shaiva Siddhanta writer-poets usurp them for their own.
1300–1400	■ Shaiva Siddhanta dies out in the rest of India, becoming exclusively associated with Tamil-speaking South India.

of Shiva in Tamil Nadu. This work, originally called the Mantra Mala (Garland of Prayer), is an influential and innovative work consisting of about three thousand verses in nine chapters dealing with various aspects of spirituality and ethics, laying down much of the groundwork for the later system of Tamil Shaiva Siddhanta. It was the first book to use the term *Shaiva Siddhanta* and provides the earliest known exposition of the Shaiva Agamas in Tamil. Many of its phrases and verses became the later Mahavakyas (Great Sayings) of Shaiva Siddhanta. Its poetry is uniquely composed in an unusual metrical structure with each line consisting of eleven or twelve syllables.

Although the Dance of Shiva is referred to throughout the book, an entire section of the ninth chapter describes Shiva's Dance in detail as blissful, beautiful, graceful, rapturous, and full of wonder. Shiva is depicted dancing with his consort, Shakti (or Sakti), performing the Dance of the Seven Melodies and the Primal Dance at the Golden Temple, dancing in space and inside the heart of the devotee. This section, called "Darshan (Grace) of the Sacred Dance," is divided further into five subsections, the last of which is the "Atbudha Dance."

Legend says that after Tirumular received the precepts of the Shiva Agama, he reached Thillai (also known as Chidambaram) and witnessed Shiva's great Cosmic Dance. Lord Shiva had come to punish a group of wayward *rishis* (seers, saints). Shiva, the patron of ascetics, heard that the *rishis* had become corrupted by the potent powers they had gained through their religious austerities.

Deciding to teach them a lesson, Shiva visited their hermitage disguised as an irresistibly handsome young mendicant seeking alms. He was accompanied by the god Vishnu feigning to be his exquisitely beautiful wife, Mohini. Both gods had their fun tricking the infatuated *rishis* and their wives. But the *rishis*, upon seeing their wives captivated by the young ascetic, became enraged with jealousy and anger. Calling upon their powers, they summoned a fierce tiger from the sacrificial fires. The ferocious carnivore raced toward Shiva, who simply caught it by the neck, skinning it alive and wrapping its fur skin about him like a silken cloth. Mustering their powers once again, the *rishis* conjured up a monstrous hissing snake, which lunged savagely at Shiva, who crushed it with the twist of his hands and wrapped it easily around his neck like a garland. One last time the *rishis* summoned the entire strength of all their powers, invoking a dark and hideously grotesque monster-like dwarf, called Muyalaka. Snarling viciously, he leaped at Shiva, who deftly pressed the tip of his foot down, breaking the wailing beast's back. Turning toward the stunned *rishis*, Shiva began blissfully dancing the Ananda Tandava Dance. Realizing their folly, the *rishis* surrendered willingly at his feet.

The eternal Ananda (blissful) Tandava (vigorous) Dance perpetuates the cycles of creation and destruction. Shiva's dance encompasses his five acts: creation, preservation, destruction, concealing, and liberation. Although images of Nataraja performing his Cosmic Dance are worshipped in thousands of temples throughout Tamil Nadu, only the Chidambaram Temple near Pondicherry is solely dedicated to the worship of Nataraja.

Nataraja is typically portrayed as a statue. This celebrated image of the dancing four-armed Shiva Nataraja stands on his right leg upon the crushed dwarf, whirling about with his matted hair spread out on all sides. He is encircled by a ring of fire like the endless cycle of creation, and a cobra uncoils from his lower right forearm. His back right hand carries an hourglass-shaped damaru drum, from whose continuous beat, creation arises. His right front hand with the raised palm gives the gesture of protection, while his rear left hand holds a pot of fire from which proceeds all destruction. Pointing delicately with the fingers of

Dancers performing at the Chidambaram Temple
(Kathak dancers performing at the Chidambaram Temple [photo], / Tamil Nadu, India / © World Religions Photo Library / The Bridgeman Art Library International)

his front left hand in a sweeping gesture across his chest toward a left foot gracefully raised in a dancing posture, he expresses compassion and refuge for the individual soul.

About the Author

Tirumular was a legendary Tamil Shaivite religious figure, mystic, and writer. Most scholars estimate that he lived somewhere between 400 and 700 CE. There are two legends regarding the life of Tirumular. The first says that Tirumular was a great yogi named Sundara who lived on Mount Kailash. One day he journeyed to the south. While on the outskirts of Sathanur village, he heard a group of cows lowing pathetically as they circled the dead body of their cowherd, Mulan. Overcome by pity, Tirumular used his yogic powers to enter the body of the dead cowherd while hiding his own body inside a tree. He led the cows home, but upon returning he could not find his own body. Deciding it was Shiva's will, he accepted his destiny and continued to remain in Mulan's body. Immersing himself in meditation under a sacred pipal tree, he came to be known as Tirumular (with *tiru* meaning "sacred" and Mulan changed to Mular out of reverence). Every once in a while he would utter a verse or two. These were recorded and became the verses of the Tirumantiram. Another legend says that after Tirumular received the precepts of Shiva Agamas and witnessed Shiva's Cosmic Dance, Tirumular stayed in devotional meditation for an indefinite length of time. During this period, he realized he was chosen for the great purpose of rendering the Agamic truths into Tamil. Inspired, he wrote the Tirumantiram.

Explanation and Analysis of the Document

The "Atbudha Dance" is a devotional poem excerpted from the last chapter of Tirumular's Tirumantiram. This poem reflects the outpourings of the heart of the legendary yogi Tirumular as he witnesses Nataraja performing the Cosmic Dance of Creation and Destruction. Each verse conveys with emotional intensity the awe, wonder, and ecstasy experienced in the presence of the great Cosmic Dancer. The theology of Shaiva Siddhanta is poignantly couched in the devotional lines of the poetry. Nataraja is the eternal, enlightened guru who dances within the heart of the devotee in the temple of the body. His blissful formless form transcends the dualities of male and female, destruction and creation. Through his blessings, his won-

Essential Quotes

> "The Form that dances there / Is the Form of Guru within, / They who full know, / He is Form-Formless / They receive His Grace Divine."

> "At the sight of tamarind / Water in mouth wells up; /As like it, / Are all those who witness the Holy Dance; / They shed tears of joy; / They melt in love of Lord; / In their hearts, / Ambrosial bliss of Divine Light wells up."

> "When the Creator dances / The World He created dances; / To the measure He dances in our knowledge, / Our thoughts too dance; / When He in heart endearing dances, / The elements several too dance."

drous dance, revealed in the heart of the devotee, confers ultimate wisdom, truth, and liberation.

The first stanza, called the "Dance of the Form-Formless," declares Nataraja the supreme guru, or spiritual teacher. His formless dance is performed to enlighten the devotee and reveal that the Ultimate Reality of Unity transcends all duality of opposites. The formless Shiva includes both forms of Shiva and Shakti, his male and female aspects. Shakti is symbolized in the verse by the Tamil goddess Tiripurai, a manifestation of Uma, one of Shiva's many consorts. Nataraja's Cosmic Dance, like the formless Shiva, expresses the duality of creation and destruction simultaneously in the unity of the one dance. The dichotomy of opposites in unity is used by Tirumular to illustrate that what we see as form is merely superimposed on an underlying reality of unity and is not the true reality. Human beings may need form to aid them in focusing their attention during worship, but in reality the unity of Shiva transcends all forms.

The holy temple of Chittambara (or Chidambaram) in Tamil Nadu is the only temple in the world dedicated solely to Shiva Nataraja. Tirumular warns that when visiting the temple, the devotee must not be overshadowed by its magnificent grandeur or forget that the true dance of the dancer takes place only in the heart of each devotee. Whether Shiva is visualized in the form of the dancer or the formless guru within, his wisdom guides the aspirant on the path to ultimate liberation.

Spiritual liberation, according to the Tamil Siddhars—Shiva worshipers who were revered as saints and mystics—requires the rise of spiritual energy (*prana*) up the spine through the head to the crown of the head for full awakening. This sacred spot, the *sahasrara* chakra (energy vortex), at the tip of the head, is measured by the width of twelve fingers from the neck. When *prana* reaches the *sahasrara* chakra and full awakening takes place, then the Cosmic Dance of Nataraja is revealed to the devotee in the sacred temple of the body. This is the goal of the Shaiva Siddhanta.

In "Light-Form of the Divine Dancer," Tirumular compares the outer elements such as the clouds, lightning, rainbows, sky, and thunder, to the power and light of Shiva, concealed as *prana*, or spiritual energy, within our bodies. This divine energy arises within, without, and separately from six spiritual energy vortexes hidden within the body, called chakras or, as here, Adharas. These are the *muladhara* at the base of the spine, the *svadhisthana* just below the navel, the *manipura* at the solar plexus, the *anahata* at the heart, the *vishuddha* at the throat, and the *ajna* at the forehead. All of these chakras culminate in the seventh, the *sahasrara*, at the crown of the head.

In the stanza "Dance Witnessed by Those Who Transcend Maya and Mamaya," Tirumular describes the divine bliss of Shiva as beyond everything, including the five elements of space, wind, fire, water, and earth and the eight directions of north, northeast, east, southeast, south, southwest, west, and northwest—beyond all that is above and below and our five senses. To witness or experience divine bliss is to experience a unity beyond the duality of *maya* (impurity of the world) and *mamaya* (purity of the world). We become one in the resplendent beauty and purity of the eternal Dance of Shiva.

In the next three stanzas, Tirumular explains that the male and female forms of Nataraja, Shiva, and Shakti are two aspects of one reality. When they are acting or dancing separately, they are like the countless individual souls who have forgotten the unity of their divine heritage owing to the overbearing charm and illusion of the material world. To have the vision or experience of Shiva's Divine Dance within surpasses the seeming delights of the world and returns the soul to the beauty of divine unity within. Shakti, the female, represents the energy aspect of Shiva. Just as heat cannot be separated from fire, so Shakti is intrinsic to Shiva. Merged, they are one, one dance, the peerless "Dance of Divine Bliss."

Tirumular praises the third eye, or *ajna* chakra, in "Ajna Centre Is Astral Temple of Lord." He says if one looks deeply within the third eye, the *ajna* chakra, the vortex of energy at the forehead, one will find the vast space of the beginnings of time and creation, the primordial hum or hallowed sound of creation, the sacred mantra Aum. One will find the spiritual goal of one's heart's yearning. There is housed the temple of the Sacred Dance, and there is where Nataraja resides and where liberation is attained.

Tirumular in "Seven Pedestals of Shiva's Dance" is naming aspects of Shiva, or the spiritual experience, related to the awakening of the seven spiritual vortexes, or chakras, referred to earlier. The *sahasrara*, at the crown of the head, represents unbounded liberation, the vastness of the universe; *ajna*, at the forehead, brings knowledge of everything (Tattvas); *vishuddha*, at the throat, gives transcendental truth (Sadashiva); anahata, at the heart, bestows unity (Sushumna); *manipura*, at the solar plexus, grants spiritual power (Shakti Shakthavi); *svadhisthana*, below the navel, confers spiritual balance and stability (Shakti Sambhavi); *muladhara*, at the base of the spine, provides spiritual confidence and potential (Shakti Kundalini). These are the seven spiritual stages, or pedestals, that unfold or open as one advances toward complete liberation, Shiva Consciousness, gained with the final awakening at the *sahasrara*.

The flowering of spirituality, like the light of the "Astral Flower," awakens the soul, illuminating the arena in which Shiva dances within the individual. Each chakra is symbolized by a lotus flower. The gaining of spiritual bliss starts with the rising of *prana* through the four-petaled lotus of the *muladhara* chakra at the base of the spine and culminates at the *sahasrara*, or thousand-petaled lotus, at the crown of the head. Once the aspirant is liberated, the experience of the bliss of Shiva is realized as unlimited, like the vastness of space. The magnitude of this awakening or liberation, in "Septenary Centres of Cosmic Dance," is described as encompassing seventy million universes (where one Crore equals ten million), with seventy million different forms of life and seventy million continents and seventy million religious statues of Shiva, or Lingas, in all the eight directions. Shiva's body is the Cosmic Body. Its expanse is the unbounded space of the universe; the eight directions are his spreading hands; sun, moon, and fire are his loving eyes; Muyalaka, the demon Nataraja stands upon, is the darkness. There is nowhere that Shiva's Sacred Dance is not found: It is all creatures, all water and fire, all of the five elements comprising creation.

The "Pandaranga Dance" invokes an epithet for the ancient Vedic god Rudra, the precursor to Shiva. In Sanskrit, *Pandaranga* literally means "white-limbed," referring to Shiva smeared with white ash. Pandaranga is Shiva as the "Primal Lord," both fearsome and destructive. Residing in cremation grounds and surrounded by ghosts, goblins, and ghouls, wearing skulls around his neck and smeared with ash, he dances the Dance of the Dissolution of Creation.

Only the liberated, the saints, the heavenly beings, and the gods have witnessed Shiva's Dance. At the sight of the Holy Dance, they cry out from their "Rapturous Experience," reacting emotionally and uncontrollably like people spontaneously salivating from bitter fruit. Even those who merely hear Shiva's Dance experience a divine rapture that causes them to lose themselves like drunkards. Or, if they do retain their senses, they become frenzied. "Inside and outside the Heart," the Great Dancer is accompanied by the eleven beats of the sacred sound, which reaches the Holiest of Holies in the Highest Heaven. Shiva's sacred and constant companion, his bull Nandi, also dances the sacred Dance.

The "Dance of Divine Bliss" is joined by the nine spiritual centers of the human body, the sixteen types of time, the six major religions, the seven musical notes, the twenty-eight musical rhythms, the divine consort Shakti, and Shiva himself. The Cosmic music is a perfect harmony, or blending of seven melodies articulated by seven notes. In this Perfect Pitch, supreme knowledge, or Jnana yoga, is gained in the seventh state beyond the six chakras, at the *sahasrara*, the state of Liberation, the highest state of Enlightenment.

In the "Dance of Triple Pasha—Riddance—Mohanta Dance," Tirumular describes the basic philosophy of Shaiva Siddhanta: Liberation is gained by ridding oneself of all attachment to the world, or *pasha*, the soul's bondage. This liberation brings about the end of believing in the world as the ultimate source of fulfillment. The end of this illusion is called *mohanta*. Tirumular says the aspirant should repeat the sacred prayer "Aum nama Shivaya," or "Aum, I bow down to Shiva," for one year (360 rays) and raise *prana* up the spine through the three spheres or channels—*ida* (moon), *pingala* (sun), and *sushumna* (fire)—and through the six chakras. The "triple Karanas," or three actions of *pasha*, are the veiling of the soul from Shiva (*anava*), the illusionary allure of the material world (*maya*), and the burden of cause and effect (*karma*). It is said that *pasha*, with its three effects, is like the tether that Shiva, envisioned as a cowherd, uses to lead souls or *pasus*, cows, along the path to truth. The Triple Pasha Dance by Shiva brings about the end of illusion in the form of the Mohanta Dance, a dance of liberation.

For his devotees, Shiva is the wish-fulfilling Kalpaka Tree of paradise, which Tirumular calls the Kalpaka Tharu. Shiva adorns the hearts of his devotees. Witnessing the Dance of Shiva, the devotee realizes that "All Creation Dances" his Cosmic Dance, because the Creator himself dances. To the extent that they are aware of him, he dances in their thoughts. They watch in rapture as even the five elements of space, wind, fire, water, and earth dance his Dance. The saints have said Shiva was dancing the "Primal Dance" long ago, even though no one saw him dance it. And now, if the Dance is witnessed, it is through the blessing of Shiva's Shakti.

In the verse "He Danced in Asi-Pada State"—where Asi-Pada means "You Are That (Supreme)"—the liberated soul, having gained the state of Turiyatita, or Pure Consciousness, attains oneness with the Supreme Soul of Shiva by the movement of *prana* through the nine spiritual centers within. His two feet dance as one, representing the two aspects of Shiva and Shakti becoming one in the state of love. An "anguished Shakti," feeling the pain of separation from Shiva, becomes blissful once united. In the Cosmic "Dance of Ananda" everything and everyone dances. Tirumular goes on to sing the praises of two legendary sages, Patanjali and Vyaghrapada, whose great devotion was able to bring Shiva back to Thillai Hill (site of Chidambaram) to dance the Ananda Tandava Dance for a second time. He danced as Shakti. Spiritually accomplished (Siddha) and blissful, he danced as the embodiment of Supreme Grace.

Shiva dances the Vedanta-Siddhanta Truth. In "Shiva Natana" he is called the lord of the whole sound of creation (Nada), and his dance is the culmination of creation. In the "Jnana Dance," or wisdom dance, just as in prayer, all perplexities and bondage of the soul end. Shiva is the end and the beginning of the Vedas. Without realizing this truth, souls are seduced by the pleasures of the world. But Shiva is the beginning, middle, and the end of all life. He is each, every, and all. To superficially sing the praises of Bliss is not the same as the profundity experienced by the soul witnessing the "Dance of Bliss," which is "Union in Shiva."

In "Signification of Five-Lettered Mantra in Shiva Dance," the prayer "Shivaya nama," meaning "I bow to Shiva," is so sacred that each syllable is potent. Each soul is enshrouded with many minute impurities. In "Symbolism of Shiva Dance," Shiva dances as Hara, who takes away the impurities and distress of his devotees. Each gesture, movement, and posture of his dance has meaning. His drum is the sound of creation; his hands protect and preserve; his fire is dissolution. His foot planted firmly down pacifies all. His raised foot grants redemption. In his "Para Sundara [Supremely Beautiful] Dance in the Beyond," the dance transcends even the sacred syllable "Aum." Its beauty is unsurpassed, indescribable.

The "Form of Shiva," guru par excellence, dances in the temple of the heart of the devotee. To see his blazing form is to reach the "haven of Refuge." His body is blazing fiery red (as a result of his practice of spiritual austerities) and also smeared white with ash, signifying victory over desire and the senses. Shiva's Shakti is his highest form, forging the bond between him and his devotee. Representing desire, wisdom, and action, Shakti moves the world. Through her grace, the devotee reaches the loving feet of his Lord.

Audience

The audience for this book has always been the Tamil people themselves, an ethnolinguistic group native to South India and northeast Sri Lanka. The poems of the Tirumantiram, including "Atbudha Dance," are powerful and defining monuments for this people and their culture. At the time this piece was written, the Tamil Shaivite Siddhan-

---

Questions for Further Study

1. The Sefer Yetzirah, a document in Jewish mysticism, conceives of creation in terms of sound, particularly the sound of the letters of the Hebrew alphabet. The "Atbudha Dance" conceives of creation in terms of a cosmic dance. Why do you think these two religious traditions used these physical concepts to explain creation?

2. The vision of Shiva, along with many elements of Hindu religion, is likely to be unfamiliar to most people in the West, and indeed most would probably find the concepts surrounding Shiva and other Hindu gods to be strange and inexplicable. Why do you think the religious traditions of Asia, including India, developed in such a dramatically different direction from those in the West?

3. Compare this document with the Vishnu Purana. Both deal with the concept of opposites, or opposing forces of good and evil, creation and destruction, and the like. What fundamental views do the two documents share? How do they differ?

4. Compare this document with Li Hongzhi's *Zhuan falun*, which discusses the *qigong* movement in modern China. How does the *Zhuan falun* update *qigong* as outlined in the "Atbudha Dance"?

5. The concept of chakras is popular in a number of modern religious/philosophical movements, including New Age, Theosophy, Kundalini yoga, and others, and it has become a mainstay in alternative medical therapy because chakras are thought to provide the physical body with its vitality and are associated with interactions of body, mind, and emotions. What do you think the appeal of chakras is for people in the contemporary world?

ta religion was just taking shape. The poems in this work were a major part of that process. The powerful depiction of Shiva as Nataraja was instrumental in making worship of Nataraja the worship of choice. The tantric elements of "Atbudha Dance" have become embodied in the image of Shiva Nataraja, a symbol of Indian spiritual culture to the rest of the world.

Impact

The "Atbudha Dance" illustrates the intensely emotional approach of the early Nayanars, whose philosophy shaped the destiny of the Tamil culture. Its author, Tirumular, is considered by Shaivite Siddhantins and scholars alike to be the most influential poet-saint in early Tamil Shaiva Siddhanta history. His influence continues today, as his poems continue to be read avidly by young Tamils. The impact of the Tirumantiram, as exemplified by the excerpted poem "Atbudha Dance," was to galvanize an entire culture and its religious views around a devotional form of worship centering on the god Shiva as Nataraja. The Tirumantiram, which is the seminal text of Shaiva Siddhanta, has powerfully influenced the daily life of millions in South India for generations.

Further Reading

■ Books

Ganapathy, T. N. *The Philosophy of the Tamil Siddhas*. New Delhi: Indian Council of Philosophical Research, 1993.

Hart, George L., III. *The Poems of Ancient Tamil*. Berkeley: University of California Press, 1975.

Minatchisuntharan [Meenakshisundaran], T. P. *History of Tamil Literature*. Chidambaram, India: Annamalai University Publications, 1965.

Pillai, Vaiyapuri [Vaiyapurip Pillai]. *A History of Tamil Language and Literature*. Madras, India: New Century Book House, 1988.

Samuel, Geoffrey. *The Origins of Yoga and Tantra: Indic Religions to the Thirteenth Century*. Cambridge, U.K.: Cambridge University Press, 2008.

White, David Gordon. *The Alchemical Body: Siddha Traditions in Medieval India*. Chicago: University of Chicago Press, 1996.

Zvelebil, Kamil V. *The Poets of the Powers: Freedom, Magic, and Renewal*. Lower Lake, Calif.: Integral Publishing, 1993.

■ Journals

Yocum, Glenn. "The Ripening of Tamil Bhakti." *Journal of American Academy of Religion* 62 (1994): 151–162.

—Prudence F. Bruns

Tirumular: "Atbudha Dance"

- **Dance of the Form-Formless (Sadashiva)**

The Form that dances
Is Guru's Form,
It is in sooth Formless;
That Formless One shines
As Shakti Tiripurai as well;
She verily is Uma
That is Form-Formless.

- **The Form-Formless Dancer Is Gurupara**

The Holy Way is Form-Formless
In the Holy Temple of Chittambara,
The Form that dances there
Is the Form of Guru within,
They who full know,
He is Form-Formless
They receive His Grace Divine
That Jnana Way.

- **Nadanta Dance in Prana Source**

From within the head
In twelve finger-measure
The Prana breath rises high,
That highway you seek;
That is the Place where
Our Lord of Nadanta dances;
That verily is the Holy Temple.

- **Light-Form of the Divine Dancer**

The wind, the cloud, lightning, rainbow, sky and thunder
All these in space arise;
Like it,
Within the rapturous rays blended of Adharas six,
And without them too, separate,
He as Form of Light stands,
In body concealed.

- **Dance Witnessed by Those Who Transcend Maya and Mamaya**

In the elements five, and directions eight,
And above and below,
Beyond the intelligent senses
Is Bliss Divine;
For them to witness
That transcends Maya and Mamaya
The Lord stands and ever dances.

- **In Dance Shiva Blends**

The Dancer blends in Shakti of charming bracelets,
The Dancer blends in blemishless Bliss,
The Dancer blends in blemishless Jnana,
The Dancer and His Consort in Dance Blend.

- **Dance for Jiva's Redemption**

My Lord and His Shakti
That His Half took
Stood dancing;
That I witnessed;
For the countless Jivas
That are veiled by Maya;

Glossary

Adharas	the chakras
Ajna	the chakra at the forehead
Asi-Pada	"You Are That (Supreme)"
Bhootas	the five principles or elements of the universe
Bodha	knowing, spiritual knowledge, teaching
Chittambara	city in Tamil Nadu known for its holy temple to Shiva Nataraja
Crore	ten million
Ganas	Shiva's demigod attendants
Hara	a name for Shiva

Document Text

As Redemption He stands,
Dancing, dancing eternal.

♦ Bliss of Shiva-Shakti Pair Dance
The Form of Shakti is Bliss-All;
Of equal Bliss is Uma's Form;
Shakti's Form rising in Shiva's Form
As one merged and one dance performed;
That peerless dance is bliss Perfect.

♦ Ajna Centre Is Astral Temple of Lord
Straight within the fore-head
Between the eye-brows
Is the astral space vast;
Peer, peer within there
The luminous Mantra (Aum) will be;
The place where they in yearning sought Him
Is the place where He in yearning is;
That verily is the Holy Temple of Chittambara
And there did I firm sit.

♦ Seven Pedestals of Shiva's Dance
The universe vast,
The Tattvas numerous,
The Sadashiva,
The Sushumna central,
The Shakti Shakthavi,
The Shakti Shambhavi
The Shakti Kundalini
(That in Muladhara Plexus is)
—These seven are Shiva's pedestals;
On them He dances
He, the Being Transcendental.

♦ The Light of Astral Flower in the Dance Theatre
The shedding light
Of that Astral Flower Within,
Illumines the Dance Arena entire;
Wondrous indeed that Flower is;
Its petals four (in Muladhara)
Into a hundred petals blossomed (in Sahasrathala)
And into ten and two hundred worlds expanded,
In the interminable spaces vast.

♦ Septenary Centres of Cosmic Dance
Seven Crores are the universes vast,
Seven Crores are the life forms varied,
Seven Crores the continents of the sea-girt world,
Seven Crores the Lingas in directions eight
These the Temples where His Cosmic Dance performed are.

♦ Dance in Space
The Space is His Body;
The Muyalaka (Demon) is the Darkness in that space
The Directions eight are His spreading Hands,
The loving eyes three
Are the lights three (Sun, Moon and Fire);
Thus He dances
In the space arena,
That is Body Cosmic.

♦ Holy Dance Theatre
The Holy Dance arena is the creation countless;
The Holy Dance arena is the Holy Feet of Lord;
The Holy Dance arena is the sphere of Water and Fire,
The Holy Dance arena is the Letter-Five, verily.

Glossary

Iccha	will or desire
Jiva	the immortal essence or soul of a living being
Jnana	knowledge or wisdom
Kriya	action
Kundalini	a form of psycho-spiritual energy, the energy of the consciousness (which moves up the spine in spiritual awakening)
Lingas	representations of Shiva
Lord of Nadanta	Shiva as the Transcendental Lord beyond creation
Mamaya	purity of the world
Maya	impurity of the world

Document Text

♦ Pandaranga Dance at the End of Dissolution
The drums beat, the pipes played,
"Aum," they hummed;
The men danced,
"My Primal Lord!" they said;
The crowd of Ganas in serried ranks praised;
The numerous Bhootas sang
—Thus He danced the Pandaranga,
—The Dance of Dissolution
At end of Tiripurai conflagration.

♦ Who Witnesses Golden Temple Dance
The Celestials in the universe
And the Celestials Beyond,
And the holy ones in the sea-girt world
All, all, witnessed the Golden Temple dance
Of the Lord of Lotus Feet,
And that adoring
Reached. Shiva-State.

♦ Rapturous Experience Flowing from Witnessing Holy Dance
At the sight of tamarind
Water in mouth wells up;
As like it,
Are all those who witness the Holy Dance;
They shed tears of joy;
They melt in love of Lord;
In their hearts,
Ambrosial bliss of Divine Light wells up.

♦ So Too: They Who Hear of It
They stagger, their sense lost,
Drunk of Shivananda Bliss;
They who still retain their senses,
Frenzied become;
Thus are they,
Who the Divine Dance witnessed,
In the Holy Arena praised by all;
Even those who hear of it
Are like those who witness it;
—All rapture is theirs too.

♦ He Dances with Shakti
With fire and drum,
With Rudraksha garland and noose cord,
With elephant's goad, trident and skull,
With frightening blue throat where Jnana is,
With Shakti for His inseparate partner,
He dances the Dance Mighty.

♦ He Dances inside and outside the Heart
With the accompaniments eleven
That dance has,
With anklet feet and drum in hand,
The Nada reverberated,
And reached like Para-Para in High Heaven;
The Holy Nandi that thus danced,
Is verily inside your heart and outside too.

♦ Dance of Divine Bliss
The nine danced,
The sixteen danced,
The loving Faiths six danced,
The seven melodies danced;
The twenty and eight rhythmic beats danced;

Glossary

Mohanta	the end of the illusion of the world as the source of true fulfillment
Muladhara	the chakra at the base of the spine
Nada	sound
Pandaranga	"white-limbed," an epithet for Shiva representing destruction, as Rudra, smeared with white ash
Para-Para	"beyond," "supreme"
Para Sundara	"supremely beautiful"
Prana	spiritual energy
Rishis Patanjali and Vyaghrapada	two legendary sages
Rudraksha	a tree whose seeds are used for prayer beads

Document Text

The Love (Shakti) too danced;
He danced the Dance of Divine Bliss.

◆ Dance of Seven Melodies
As seven subtle melodies within the seven articulated,
As the seven letters they denote,
As one harmony in the seven musical notes,
He descended and pervaded;
In the seventh state beyond the six adharas
That Jnana yoga crosses
Is Aum Paranjothi, (the Divine Light)
In the dance of seven melodies He danced.

◆ Dance of Triple Pasha—Riddance—Mohanta Dance
The three letters A, U and M (Aum)
The five letters Na, Ma, Si, Va, Ya became;
And as three hundred and sixty rays they became;
Commencing from Muladhara that the waters hold
In through the centres six (Adharas) and spheres three (Sun, Moon, Fire)
That the triple Karanas their end may see,
He in ancient Pashas Triple danced
The Dance of Mohanta (Impurity-riddance).

◆ He Is Kalpaka Tree That Grants All Wishes
Above jewelled crowned heads of Celestials,
Are the flowery Feet of Lord,
A precious Jewel is He;
He adorns the rising heart of His loving devotees;
He is Tree Divine (Kalpaka Tharu)
Of Heavenly glades;
He transcends worlds all.

◆ When Creator Dances All Creation Dances
When the Creator dances
The World He created dances;
To the measure He dances in our knowledge,
Our thoughts too dance;
When He in heart endearing dances,
The elements several too dance;
Flaming as Divine Fire He dances,
That we witnessed in rapture surpassing.

◆ Primal Dance
"The Primal Dance He danced"
Thus say the holy ones;
None saw Him dance
That Primal Dance of yore;
When that Primal Dance they witness,
They dance indeed in the Grace
Of that Primal Shakti.

◆ He Danced in Asi-Pada State
In the nine centres mystic within
The ninth state (Turiyatita) attained;
In the centre that is love
His twin feet in Asi-Pada danced;
And as the anguished Shakti within Him danced,
My loving Father together with Her in rapture danced.

Glossary

Sadashiva	ever-auspicious form of Shiva, conferring grace
Shakti	the female principle, paired with Shiva as the male principle
Shivananda	bliss of Shiva
Sushumna	central channel of energy through which kundalini passes within the subtle body
Tapasvins	those who undertake *tapas,* or austerities
Tattva	Truth or Reality
Tiripurai	a manifestation of Uma
triple Karanas	three actions of *pasha*—the veiling of the soul from Shiva (*anava*), the illusionary allure of the material world (*maya*), and the burden of cause and effect (*karma*).
Uma	one of Shiva's consorts
Vedanta-Siddhanta	philosophy expounded by Tirumular in his Tirumantiram; it brings together the Vedas and the Agamas, reconciling monism and dualism.

Document Text

- **Dance of Ananda (Bliss)**

The Tattvas danced; Sadashiva danced;
The Thought danced; Shiva-Shakti danced;
The creation vast danced; the Vedas danced;
The Lord too danced,
The Dance of Ananda (Divine Bliss).

- **He Danced for Rishis Patanjali and Vyaghrapada**

In the splendorous Temple (of Chidambaram)
He danced,
For the two Rishis to witness
He danced, Form, Formless and as Cosmic Form,
Within the Divine Grace of Shakti
He danced,
He the Siddha, the Ananda;
As Form of Grace
He stood and danced.

- **He Danced in Vedanta-Siddhanta Truth**

Shiva danced, Shakti danced,
The worldly desires danced;
The space that dances not danced;
The Tattva-Nadanta wondrous danced;
When Shiva danced inside of Truth,
That indeed is Vedanta-Siddhanta.

- **Shiva Natana**

Nadanta that is end of Nada, (Principle of Sound)
Bodhanta that is end of Bodha (Jnana)
Vedanta that is end of Vedas
Shivananda that is Bliss of Shiva,
Sadashivananda that is without end,
In all these, He dances the Shiva Natana
He that is Nada Brahmam (Lord within the Sound-Principle).

- **Jnana Dance**

The perplexities of the Five Gods
Rudra and the rest to end,
The Jiva bonds standing afar,
In prayer to depart
The Holy Para by Himself dances everywhere;
Holy indeed is the Jnana Dance
That Shivananda Bliss fills.

- **Dance in the Three Lights**

As One Supreme He stood in times of yore,
Redeeming the Celestials countless,
He earned the name of Lord (Vikirtha)
He danced in the luminous Lights Three,
He accepted me in His Grace.

- **He Is Tattvas and Their Goal**

The Lord is the beginning of Vedas
He is beyond Nada Tattvas;
(Knowing this not,)
They sought the pleasures of this world
And in them revelled;
He is the Tattvas in order placed
And their Lord too at once;
In that in separateness
He commingling stood.

- **Dance of Bliss Is Union in Shiva**

"Bliss Bliss," they say;
Witless are they;
None know the Dance of Bliss;
Having witnessed the Dance of Bliss,
The Jiva its separateness ends,
And in Divine Bliss unites.

- **Signification of Five-Lettered Mantra in Shiva Dance**

"Leave this, be reformed,"
—Thus to Jivas gestures one hand in letter "Shi";
"Come like me, Be united in me"
—Thus to Tapasvins gestures another flower-like hand in letter "Va";
"Be in, Deva, fear not."
Thus to Celestials gestures the golden hand in letter "Ya."
The hand that holds fire
Gestures the letter "Na";
The foot on earth planted in dance
Gestures the letter "Ma"'
(Thus is the entire Five-Letter Mantra "Shi Va Ya Na Ma"
Is Divine Dance denoted.)

- **Further Signification of Dance-Form in Relation to Five Letter Mantra**

The hand that holds the drum, (Shi)
The hand that sways, (Va)
The hand that offers Refuge, (Ya)
The hand that holds the blazing Fire, (Na)
The lotus-foot, firm, on Anava Mala planted, (Ma)
—Thus of the Divine Dance Form
Shi Va Ya Na Ma denotes.

- **Symbolism of Shiva Dance**

Hara's drum is creation;
Hara's hand gesturing protection is preservation;
Hara's fire is dissolution;
Hara's foot planted down is Obfuscation (Tirodhayi)

Document Text

Hara's foot, raised in dance, is Grace (Redemption) abiding.

♦ Shakti Witnesses Trinity Dance of Shiva
The flaming fire is He;
The sparkling light within is He;
The Shakti of youthful eyes saw Him dance;
She saw the Three Gods merge
Into the One Primal Being;
In rapture She sang Vedas all.

♦ Para Sundara Dance in the Beyond
Nandi, My Father, Lord of Jnana,
In the one-letter mantra Aum, He entered,
Transcending it,
In the spaces beyond He dances,
In comeliness surpassing,
How shall I describe that Para Sundara Dance!

♦ Form of Shiva
A lion-hearted Guru is Nandi,
In the Holy Temple He does dance;
None know His Form divine;
Fiery red smeared white it is;
They who see His Form
Reach the haven of Refuge.

♦ Shakti's Grace Dance
Shakti in the Lord
Stands as Tat-Parai;
She forges the bond between Para and Jiva:
Standing as Iccha, Jnana and Kriya
She many acts performs;
And when She, Her Grace lends
You reach Hara's loving feet.

Dionysius the Areopagite converting the pagan philosophers
(Dionysius the Areopagite Converting the Pagan Philosophers, 1570s (oil on canvas), Caron, Antoine [1520-99] / J. Paul Getty Museum, Los Angeles, USA / The Bridgeman Art Library International)

Dionysius the Areopagite: *The Celestial Hierarchy*

ca. 500

"The angels complete the entire ranking of the heavenly intelligences. Among the heavenly beings it is they who possess the final quality of being an angel."

Overview

The Celestial Hierarchy is part of a late-fifth-century or early-sixth-century body of Greek literature that would later become known (in Latin) as the *Corpus Areopagiticum*, that is, the body of writings from (Dionysius) the Areopagite. These texts, likely composed in the area around Syria, reflect elements of Neoplatonic philosophy, controversial issues of Christian theology, along with components of mysticism. The *Corpus* survives in the form of four treatises (*The Celestial Hierarchy, The Ecclesiastical Hierarchy, The Divine Names,* and *The Mystical Theology*) along with ten letters supposedly written in the first century by Dionysius the Areopagite. The actual authorship is a problem of some complexity, and the author has long been known as Pseudo-Dionysius.

The Celestial Hierarchy traditionally comes first in the Dionysian corpus. Its initial chapters, excerpted here, link this treatise to themes, theology, and methodology of the other major Dionysian works and thus serve as a way of introducing all segments. This first treatise also creates a descriptive framework for later Christian understanding of the angels (the main topic of *The Celestial Hierarchy*). It deals with symbols in the Judeo-Christian scriptures that eventually came to shape the medieval theory of angels while at the same time cautioning against an overly literal interpretation of these symbols. In describing the beings of the heavens, Dionysius includes three classes, three functions, and three levels. This triad is further divided into three orders, which are then divided into three intelligences. All this exists within the framework of a perfect union.

Context

The world of Pseudo-Dionysius was one of an emerging Christian theology and faith that was being influenced by secular Neoplatonism in the eastern part of the Roman Empire. The Neoplatonists were reviving the ideas from Plato's school of thought (originating after 400 BCE) during the third to sixth centuries of the Common Era. Among the major driving forces within Neoplatonism was an attempt to understand the "One," which was believed to be beyond all human experience. Blending of the Neoplatonist philosophies and Christian theologies resulted, and this combination is particularly noteworthy in the Christian writer who identified himself as Dionysius.

During this period there was also a decline, if not a break, in Roman imperial authority and an eventual legitimization of Christianity as an officially recognized faith. However, Christianity, especially in the eastern part of the empire, continued to be swayed by a number of conflicting theological notions; these notions were called *heterodox* when they varied from the traditional understanding and *heretical* if formally condemned by one of the first seven ecumenical councils (325–787). These early assemblies of Christian bishops and theologians were pivotal in steering doctrine and practice within the faith. This was the period of the great Trinitarian controversies—prolonged and bitter debates over the nature and origin of Christ and the Holy Spirit. Ideas were in flux; depending upon the decade in which one was writing or teaching (and who was in authority), ideas could be ground for fertile debate or for exile and excommunication. Neoplatonism as studied outside of Christianity was also coming to an end during this time. Byzantine emperors such as Justinian (482–565), along with staunch supporters of the orthodox Christian faith, were closing down Neoplatonist schools like the one formerly led by Proclus in the city of Athens. A number of modern scholars have suggested that Dionysius may have studied at that school.

There were stretches of time during this tumultuous period when heterodoxy was tolerated. But eventually many of the Christian heretics or secular philosophers of the period (as well as their adherents) were forced to flee and find new homes in places like Persia. While the original Greek Dionysian corpus clearly pushed the envelope of orthodoxy, its heterodox ideas (including versions of Neoplatonism) could be seen as more or less acceptable at various times and places. It is not apparent that our author was ever displaced by persecution. His writings may have been accepted during his own time or deemed sufficiently ambiguous as to not offend, or he may have received some level of protection in the circle to which he belonged. The anonymity of authorship of the Dionysian corpus (claiming the work to

Time Line

CA. 50	■ The Athenian Dionysius the Areopagite is possibly converted to Christianity by Saint Paul.
CA. 96	■ Bishop Dionysius of Athens (traditionally associated with Paul's convert) dies.
CA. 250	■ Saint Denis (Denys), bishop of Paris and falsely alleged author of the Dionysian corpus, dies.
381	■ Gregory of Nazianzus attends the First Council of Constantinople and intimates the notion shared by the other Cappadocian fathers that God's nature is basically unknowable to humans.
CA. 410	■ Saint Augustine of Hippo writes *The City of God*, one of the most important theological works to incorporate elements of Greek philosophy.
451	■ The Council of Chalcedon, in Asia Minor, affirms that Christ had both a human and a divine nature, definitively rejecting the Monophysite (one nature) position.
485	■ The Neoplatonic philosopher Proclus, a significant influence on Pseudo-Dionysius, dies in Athens.
491	■ Peter the Iberian, a Georgian bishop and a possible author of the Dionysian corpus, dies in Palestine.
527	■ Theodora, a supporter of the Monophysites, becomes Byzantine empress with the elevation of her husband Justinian to the throne. They begin to allow for certain toleration of the Monophysite position.
538	■ Severus, an influential Monophysite patriarch, dies at Antioch.

be from Dionysius the Areopagite, a first-century convert of Saint Paul's), while giving legitimacy to the work, may also have served to protect the writer. Another reason for the survival of these texts may have been that Pseudo-Dionysius lived during a window of time when the bitter Trinitarian debates were relatively calm. Of course, since we do not know exactly who the author was or exactly when he wrote, theories as to the context of the Dionysian corpus have varied considerably.

About the Author

The *Corpus Areopagiticum* is a body of work most likely written by a Neoplatonic Christian cleric or mystic in Syria around the years 480–530 of the Common Era. The author calls himself Dionysius the Areopagite after the Dionysius mentioned in Acts 17:34, a member of the Athenian law court (the Areopagus) who was converted to Christianity by Saint Paul. Tradition suggested that this Dionysius later became the bishop of Athens and Corinth and died around 96 CE. Treatises and letters in the *Corpus Areopagiticum* are addressed by Dionysius to such first-century Christian figures as Timothy, Titus, Polycarp, and John the Evangelist. This Dionysius was long regarded as one of the apostolic fathers (prominent figures whose works have survived from the age immediately following the New Testament). Therefore, the corpus was treated in the early medieval period as being one step removed from the scriptures themselves. In addition, a French legend claimed authorship for an early bishop of Paris, Saint Denis (Denys), who died around 250. The twelfth-century scholar Peter Abelard was the first to disentangle authorship of the literature from these legendary sources, rejecting Saint Denis as author and questioning Saint Paul's Dionysius. By the Renaissance, the Florentine humanist Lorenzo Valla pointed out that the texts were very unlikely to have been written by the biblical Dionysius or anybody else in the first Christian centuries, since the earliest known citations were from the time of Pope Gregory the Great (ca. 540–604); other scholars subsequently bolstered Valla's contention. Arguments about Dionysius continued for some time, as the traditional authorship was supported by elements within the Catholic Church. It is now understood that these writings belong to the venerable ancient and medieval tradition of pseudepigraphy, the attribution of one's work to a figure of greater authority.

The work of Pseudo-Dionysius was apparently strongly influenced by the Athenian Neoplatonist Proclus (412–485). The latter's *Elements of Theology* contains 211 propositions and proofs for the existence of the One, who he claimed to be the First Principle of all things. In another work, the *Platonic Theology*, Proclus had unfolded a system of monistic (unitary) characteristics for the order of the Divine. Proclus proposed a universe that was inhabited by hierarchic beings that are distinct from, yet also emanate from, the One. This theological perspective is clearly embedded in the Dionysian corpus. Some have even suggested that Proclus himself wrote under the name Dionysius.

Modern scholarly investigation, however, has demonstrated that some of the heterodox theology of Pseudo-Dionysius belongs to a later period of turmoil and doctrinal tension in the church.

Several modern theorists have attempted to connect the Dionysian corpus with a writer named Peter the Iberian (411–491), a Georgian prince who later became a monk and bishop of Majuma (near Gaza). Others suggest the writer may have been a Monophysite cleric, possibly Sergius of Reshaina (d. 536), a Syrian priest and physician. The Monophysites (from a word meaning "one nature") rejected the teachings of the Council of Chalcedon (451), which insisted that Christ had two natures (human and divine). The council defined these natures as unchangeable, indivisible, and inseparable. Chalcedon caused a serious splintering of fifth-century Christian groups over this issue and related concerns regarding church leadership and authority. Pseudo-Dionysius dedicated an entire treatise, the *Ecclesiastical Hierarchy*, to demonstrating how these offices flow not from the institutions of man but from the plan of the Divine. If the writer of Pseudo-Dionysius was indeed a Monophysite or a member of some other heterodox group, there is little wonder why he would have kept his identity secret. Indeed, the *Corpus Areopagiticum* may have survived into the Middle Ages precisely because it was not identified with a heretical writer.

Explanation and Analysis of the Document

These excerpts constitute about one-third of the original treatise, chosen to provide an overview of the sensibilities of Dionysian theology and the corpus. Note that (in this presentation) the generic term *angels* refers to all of the nine classifications of the celestial hierarchs. In the Dionysian scheme, "Angels" (capitalized) signifies the lowest of celestial entities, below the Principalities and Archangels and closest to humans.

♦ Chapter 1

The treatise begins with the salutation from Dionysius (an elder) writing to Timothy (a fellow elder). This obviously is an attempt to set the tone of the work as one of instruction and wisdom. It legitimizes its theology as stemming from the apostolic tradition and authority of the biblical leaders Paul, Timothy, and Dionysius (despite the fact that it was written four centuries later). Interestingly the title "elder" is not used in the *Ecclesiastical Hierarchy* or other Dionysian treatises, suggesting that the titles may have been changed at a later date by translators or copyists of the manuscript. The text itself begins with a series of New Testament quotations (James 1:17; Romans 11:36) that indicate the procession of all things from God and their ultimate return to God. While the Divine remains immanent—that is, all-present, throughout and within all aspects of the world, yet somehow distinct—those things that God effects are connected to him as cause (both proceeding from him and returning to him). This eliminates the notion

Time Line

CA. 600
- Pope Gregory the Great endorses the Dionysian corpus and encourages its reception in the West.

1457
- The Florentine humanist Lorenzo Valla demonstrates that the Dionysian corpus cannot have been written in the first century.

of sequence and time when it comes to our relationship with the Divine. We see similar ideas of cause and effect in the fifth-century philosopher Proclus and in the thirteenth-century theologian Thomas Aquinas. For Dionysius, God's unity remains, and the process of the outpouring of God's goodness, which is part of God's revelation, affects those who are able to be enlightened by the Divine light.

♦ Chapter 2

In the second chapter Dionysius addresses the notion of scriptural symbols that represent the angels and God—images like multicolored horses (Zechariah 1:8, 6:2; Revelation 6:1–9), fiery thrones (Daniel 7:9), and weapon-bearing officers (Joshua 5:13). He suggests that while some of these images may be obscure, they should not be understood in an overly literal fashion. The images are meant to inspire, but they can both reveal and conceal. Human perceptions are limited by space and time, but scriptural images can give us a grasp of the infinite and invisible. If the images cannot show explicitly what the heavenly beings are, they may possibly indicate what they are not. So the scriptures must resort to lowly human images and ideas merely in order to begin to lift our senses to heavenly realms. Dionysius suggests that care must be taken when reading these treatises to go beyond the descriptions to approach what cannot be grasped in terms of this world.

♦ Chapter 4

The fourth chapter begins with a bit of recapitulation about all things relating to God, the Creator and the source of all existence, but quickly moves to the question of the angels. Since the angels participate in God in a closer fashion than humans and are nearer communicants of God's greatness and generosity, they have gifts of reason and intelligence much higher than those of humans. It is their job as messengers (the original meaning of *angel*) to impart on humanity a sense of their fullness of the Divine. According to Dionysius, the angels have given humans the Law so that God's order might be demonstrated and we might be uplifted. Dionysius thus felt that the angels were responsible for the revelations (Acts 7:38, Galatians 3:19, Hebrews 2:2). Some scholars have suggested that Moses himself might be considered "angelic" and that direct communication to him by God was possible only because

Angel of the Annunciation
(The Annunciation, c.1330 (oil on panel), Master of Cologne, [fl.1300-50] / Wallraf-Richartz Museum, Cologne, Germany / The Bridgeman Art Library International)

of his angelic state as an announcer or messenger. Higher angels also pass on information to lower angels, revealing both the commonalities and the differences among the orders (explored further in subsequent chapters). Chapter 4 goes on to give specific examples of particular angels who have acted as messengers to humans as recounted in the sacred scriptures. It also addresses the relationship of the angels to Christ, particularly the scriptural instances of angelic interaction with Jesus in his humanity. In the last paragraph here, Dionysius closely approaches the Monophysite notion that Christ took human form but did not change his essential divine nature. The phrase "angel of great counsel" evokes Isaiah 9:6, which notes that "a son is given to us and dominion is laid on his shoulders; and this is the name they might give him: Wonder Counselor."

♦ **Chapter 6**

The sixth chapter recounts the nine names for the celestial beings, which are largely found in the Bible: Seraphim, Cherubim, Thrones, Dominions, Powers, Authorities, Principalities, Archangels, and Angels. Dionysius says that while we cannot know the mystery of the minds of the angels, God has granted us some information about them. This also affirms the underlying theme of the Dionysian corpus that the *Thearchy* (Trinity) is always before us yet always beyond us. A sense of both wonder and praise connects his theological discourse.

It is clear that Dionysius arranged the angels in threefold triads (three groups of three) out of some Trinitarian connection or ciphering. They are not described as connected in this way in the scriptures. He gives credit to "my own sacred-initiator," understood to be Hierotheus, for this insight or inspiration regarding the arrangement. Hierotheus, possibly a teacher, appears in other treatises of the *Corpus Areopagiticum* as a figure connected with both Saint Paul and Dionysius. In several passages throughout his corpus Dionysius credits Hierotheus with a work entitled *The Elements of Theology*. This actually was the name of a treatise written by the fifth-century Neoplatonist (and non-Christian) philosopher Proclus. Was Hierotheus, then, in reality Dionysius's mentor Proclus? Triadic formulas were common Neoplatonist devices to symbolize degrees or extremes in virtue and character, and their presence in both Proclus and Dionysius need not indicate a direct connection. Proclus, in particular, tells of three triads of intelligible gods belonging to the higher realm of the *nous* (divine mind). Intermediary beings permeated certain areas of ancient thought, as written about by Plutarch and Plato in his *Symposium*.

The first triad, Dionysius tells us, is the one nearest to the Divine. It includes Seraphim, Cherubim, and Thrones. No being is closer or more akin to God or receives more enlightenment than these. Dionysius adds information from biblical religious symbolism, noting that the Cherubim and Seraphim are "said to possess many eyes and many wings" (Ezekiel 1:6, 1:18; Isaiah 6:2). The second triad consists of Authorities, Dominions, and Powers. At the end of the heavenly hierarchy come Angels, Archangels, and Principalities. In the remaining chapters Dionysius goes on to explain in further detail the duties of these creatures and the primary attributes of the first triad.

♦ **Chapter 7**

The seventh chapter headline points to "the first hierarchy" of Seraphim, Cherubim, and Thrones. It explains in some detail the biblical origins of the angelic names, their relationship to God, and their similarity to God. Dionysius was not expert in Hebrew, as deduced from his poor use of Hebrew words and phrases, but he attempts to unfold the meaning of the names. The Seraphim, "fire-makers" or "carriers of warmth," are presented as bright, flaming, uplifting, banishing of shadow, and purifying (later described as having six wings). The Cherubim are "outpouring of wisdom" or "fullness of knowledge," filled with the gifts of wisdom and capable of sharing these gifts. The Thrones are literally near the throne of God, or on their own thrones, proximate to the Most High. They transcend earthly defects—"separated from what is inferior," free from passion and material need and content to remain forever in the presence of God. Dionysius draws many of his symbols from the Old Testament (Genesis 3:24; Exodus 25:18–22, 37:6–9; Numbers 7:89; 1 Samuel 4:4; 1 Kings 6:23–28, 8:6–7; Psalms 18:10, 80:1, 99:1; Isaiah 37:16; Ezekiel 1:4–28, 10:3–22).

Essential Quotes

"We must lift up the immaterial and steady eyes of our minds to that outpouring of Light which is so primal, indeed much more so, and which comes from that source of divinity, I mean the Father. This is the Light which, by way of representative symbols, makes known to us the most blessed hierarchies among the angels."

"Jesus himself, the transcendent Cause of those beings which live beyond the world, came to take on human form without in any way changing his own essential nature. But I observe that never once did he abandon that human form which he had established and chosen, and he obediently submitted to the wishes of God the Father as arranged by the angels."

"The first group is forever around God and is said to be permanently united with him ahead of any of the others and with no intermediary. Here, then, are the most holy 'thrones' and the orders said to possess many eyes and many wings, called in Hebrew the 'cherubim' and 'seraphim.' Following the tradition of scripture, he says that they are found immediately around God and in a proximity enjoyed by no other."

"The second group, he says, is made up of 'authorities,' 'dominions,' and 'powers.' And the third, at the end of the heavenly hierarchies, is the group of 'angels,' 'archangels,' and 'principalities.'"

"As I have already said, the angels complete the entire ranking of the heavenly intelligences. Among the heavenly beings it is they who possess the final quality of being an angel. For being closer to us, they, more appropriately than the previous ones, are named 'angels' insofar as their hierarchy is more concerned with revelation and is closer to the world."

Dionysius moves on to extol the three virtues of the three ranks of the angels (treating the lower orders in the following chapters) as they exhibit elements of purification, illumination, and perfection. In *The Ecclesiastical Hierarchy* there are also three states of spiritual potency that will apply to humans. He says that the highest order of angels has the ability to pass on an undiluted purity, perfection, and light that comes from the Godhead. Purified of ignorance, contemplative, they are filled with light and in communion with the Son: "It is Jesus himself who is their instructor." Thus the order of Seraphim "achieves perfection . . . of primary knowledge and understanding." They can also grow in their enlightenment relationally to God. They have the ability to channel some of these gifts to the lesser angels and even to humans. Dionysius characterizes such revelations as being responsible for our understanding of God as "monad," "one in three persons," handing down from the loftiest angel to the most lowly of humans some emanation of himself.

♦ **Chapter 8**

Dominions, Powers, and Authorities are discussed in chapter 8. All three are said to have equal influence. There is little biblical evidence to support specific names of this middle group of angels, and so it has been suggested that this triad comes from the author's own inventive understanding of the scriptures. Dionysius does cite Zechariah 1, where we see a message from God being mediated first from an angel of a higher rank and then from one of a lower rank down to the prophet (or "theologian") Zechariah. A similar scenario appears in Ezekiel 9, where an angel in a white cloak (of lower rank than the Cherubim) passes on a revelation to even lower angels, who in turn bring the message to the people of Jerusalem. Other examples of this angelic chain of command appear in the book of Daniel.

The Dominions are seen as unearthly, or unlike those in positions of influence among men. The Dominions are benevolent, reject appearances, and constantly return to the one true Lord to share "in that everlasting and divine source of all dominion." The Powers are seen as having "masculine" characteristics, a courage that is quite the opposite of those humans who are lazy and soft. It is in this exceptional fortitude that they imitate God. The Authorities make the authority of God evident, and they harmonize both with the Divine and the other angels in a clear and uplifting way to manifest their "conformity to God."

♦ **Chapter 9**

This final chapter of the selection focuses on Principalities, Archangels, and Angels—the third and lowest grouping of the hierarchy. Like the other celestial hierarchies, these angels also reflect attributes of the Divine, though to a lesser degree. There are instances where the scriptures refer to angelic or celestial beings without specific reference to type (Seraphim, Cherubim, and so on); Dionysius puts them in the lowest order, that of Angels. Within the last triad, Dionysius creates an internal hierarchy. Angels occupy the lowest rank and seem to be the most immediate messengers to humans. Michael, for example, has been assigned to the nation of Israel, and, according to Daniel 10 and Deuteronomy 32:8, the other nations also have their own angels. Dionysius says it would be unfair of God to communicate to Israel himself and not the other nations. For that reason each nation has a messenger. But it was only Israel that returned to the Divine Light and accepted the angelic message. In the middle of this third group are the Archangels, mediators in the chain of communication. Highest are the Principalities, who also mediate between the Angels and Archangels, maintain order, and are like princes of the heavens. Dionysius clearly indicates that all three ranks of the lowest order answer to the Dominions, Powers, and Authorities.

Audience

While Dionysius's original audience may have been the ideologically divided Christians of his own time, we are still not sure exactly when his time was. The earliest reference to his texts is found in a body of Monophysite writings from around 533 linked to the patriarch Severus of Antioch. It is important to note that there were a variety of degrees to the Monophysite position and a number of contending branches of Monophysites. Severus used some of Dionysius's writings to support his anti-Chalcedonian teachings upholding the notion that there is only one nature of God. An early-twentieth-century scholarly theory by Joseph Stiglmayr posited that Pseudo-Dionysius was in fact Severus. The Severian Monophysites did indeed escape persecution after the Chalcedonian condemnation of Monophysitism. Their clever use of the ambiguous Dionysian texts may have been a factor in their success.

A sixth-century defender of Severus, Patriarch Theodosius I of Alexandria, also draws upon the work. In the same century, an opponent of Severus named John, a bishop of Scythopolis in Palestine, annotated (or glossed) the writings of Dionysius the Areopagite to make them "more" orthodox. Another Chalcedonian supporter, Maximus the Confessor, in his *Ambigua* and *Mystagogy*, accepted the Dionysian texts and treated them as orthodox. Maximus was such an important voice in Trinitarian and Christological orthodoxy that the Lateran Council at Rome in 649 accepted the Dionysian corpus into the mainstream of tradition. Jacob of Edessa used *The Celestial Hierarchy* as a reference to reflect upon the ranks of the angelic hosts. This Syrian bishop was one of the most respected seventh-century writers, although he did have some Monophysite leanings. Thanks to John of Scythopolis, the glossed translations of Dionysius (now free from obvious heresy) had begun to be embraced by the Latin West. Called the *Corpus Areopagiticum* by medieval scholars, the writings were endorsed by a number of popes. Pope Gregory the Great referred to Dionysius as an "ancient and venerable father." He was familiar with the doctrine of the celestial hierarchy and quoted Dionysius quite freely on the topic of the angelic hosts. By the medieval period Dionysius began to be included among the doctors (teachers) of the church.

Impact

The Dionysian corpus influenced the religious and scholarly communities from the sixth century onward, at first chiefly among the Greek-speaking theologians of the Eastern (Byzantine) empire. Its influence spread early to the Latin West, where the writings became an accepted part of the canon of important Christian texts, with *The Celestial Hierarachy* receiving the most commentary of all these works. The *Corpus Areopagiticum* went on to influence later medieval and Renaissance spirituality, literature, and to some degree even theology. Its appeal may have derived from the author's ability to communicate through images and symbols a spiritual understanding of things that defied rational expression.

The impact on scholarly religious circles lasted for centuries. During the ninth century in France it began to be circulated that Saint Denis, a third-century bishop of Paris, was the real author of the Dionysian corpus. A Greek manuscript of the corpus had made it to France in the late eighth century, and a (very poor) Latin translation of the work was completed at the important abbey of Saint Denis, near Paris, in 835. In a biography accompanying the translation, an abbot named Hildun alluded to the notion that his church's patron and Dionysius (Denys) were the same person. Through the early twentieth century, periodic attempts were made by French scholars to link the patron saint of Paris with the author of the Dionysian corpus.

John Scotus Eriugena, a ninth-century Irish theologian, philosopher, and expert in Greek, made another Latin translation and commentary. Since Eriugena also translated the authoritative Greek works of several fourth-century Cappadocian fathers (including Saints Basil of Caesarea, Gregory of Nyssa, and Gregory Nazianzus), his acceptance of the Dionysian corpus had an inestimable influence. By referencing Dionysius in both his writings and homilies and making doctrinal and spiritual connections to several established saints, Eriugena helped legitimize Pseudo-Dionysian theology in the Latin West. A clear indication of these mystical perceptions can be found in many of the Dionysian letters. Excursions into mysticism and exploration of Greek monastic writings by Western Latin religious figures became even more prevalent in the later Middle Ages.

Anastasius, a papal librarian, revised Eriugena's translation in 875 and added numerous remarks. By the early twelfth century the cathedral school at Laon, France, began to use excerpts from the Dionysian corpus in their sentences and glosses (philosophical and theological commentaries). Through these texts, Dionysian concepts found their way into the work of the twelfth-century philosopher Peter Lombard and the famous Abbot Suger of Saint Denis, who used the Dionysian symbolism of light to physically enhance and figuratively explain sacred space in his architectural work. (Suger's extension of the abbey church is regarded as the fountainhead of Gothic architecture.)

Hugh of Saint Victor edited two commentaries on *The Celestial Hierarchy* between 1125 and 1137, helping to ensure the influence of the *Corpus Areopagiticum* on the development of Scholasticism, the dialectical academic method that would dominate Catholic thought for centuries to come. By this time the Dionysian corpus was generally interpreted as exhibiting Trinitarian orthodoxy. Some of its ideas on the nature of the Trinity were now linked to the supremely influential theology of Saint Augustine of Hippo. This interpretation is particularly elucidated in the work of the thirteenth-century Franciscan scholar Saint Bonaventure. The tendency to overlook Dionysius's Monophysite leaning may have been aided by the Latin medieval fascination with his supposed antiquity and direct connection with early apostles such as Paul.

The English Franciscan Robert Grosseteste, the Dominican Saint Albert the Great, and his pupil and the greatest of all medieval philosophers, Saint Thomas Aquinas, all wrote treaties on the Dionysian writings. The angelology of Thomas's *Summa theologiae* pivotally rests on *The Celestial Hierarchy*. Even the Italian poetry of Dante Alighieri's *Divine Comedy* precisely mirrors Dionysius's order and description of the heavenly angelic hierarchies. Dante credits Dionysius in his *Paradiso* (28.130) for the use of his angelology. The work also greatly influenced the art and architecture of the High Middle Ages and the Renaissance. For example, the

Questions for Further Study

1. What was Neoplatonism, and why was it opposed by many early Christian theologians and the Church itself?

2. The early centuries of Christianity were marked by considerable turmoil, as various sects and heterodox views contended for authenticity. How did *The Celestial Hierarchy* contribute to that turmoil? How is that turmoil suggested by other documents such as the Book of Enoch, the Book of the Bee, Ptolemy's "Letter to Flora," and the Gospel of Thomas?

3. Do you believe in the existence of angels? Do you believe they have literal existence or that they are symbolic? Explain your view.

4. Why do you think the author of *The Celestial Hierarchy* was so interested in establishing such a hierarchy—that is, an ordered conception of supernatural beings? Does this concern with order and hierarchy tell you anything about preoccupations of the early Christian Church?

5. What did Saint Bonaventure mean when he called Dionysius "a prince among the mystics"? Why do you think he gave Dionysius that accolade?

south portal of Chartres cathedral portrays the nine ranks of angels in Dionysian order, along with all their elements.

Saint Bonaventure had once called Dionysius "a prince among the mystics." Dionysius exerted considerable influence on fourteenth- and fifteenth-century schools of mysticism. German mystical theologians like Meister Eckhardt, Johannes Tauler, and Willem van Ruysbroeck all incorporate Dionysian elements of spiritual understanding. Nicholas of Cusa, Johannes Heidenberg, and Jean Gerson attempted to blend both the intellectual and the spiritual elements of the Dionysian corpus with their studies. Denis the Carthusian wrote a very famous commentary on the works of Dionysius. The Renaissance humanists Pico della Mirandola and Marsilio Ficino undertook rigorous Italian translations of the Dionysian works, which became an important vehicle to understanding elements of Greek philosophy. The English humanists, such as John Colet, were most interested in the intersection of Christian and Greek philosophical elements of the work, but some of Colet's sixteenth-century pupils, including Thomas More and John Fisher, used the corpus to criticize certain early Reformation ideas proposed by Martin Luther. Spanish Renaissance mystics such as Abbot García de Cisneros, Francisco de Osuna, and John of the Cross were equally inspired by the *Corpus Areopagiticum*.

Interest continued into the sixteenth century, particularly as Greek versions were again read directly. However, some of this enthusiasm involved detraction and criticism, as more scholars and Protestant reformers began to discover that Pseudo-Dionysius was not actually a church father. Through the 1500s respect for the corpus began to slip. Nevertheless, the English Protestant poets Edmund Spenser in *The Faerie Queene* and John Milton in *Paradise Lost* curiously follow in rather close fashion the Dionysian order of the angels. Mixed reception continued through the early-modern period, with some interest particularly among Roman Catholics. While Dionysius was not completely ignored by seventeenth-century scholars, the significance of the Dionysian corpus had by then waned among Western Christians, and some later scholars became quite interested in attacking the Dionysian corpus.

Further Reading

■ Books

Arthur, Rosemary. *Pseudo-Dionysius as Polemicist: The Development and Purpose of the Angelic Hierarchy in Sixth-Century Syria*. London: Ashgate, 2008.

Coakley, Sarah, and Charles Stang, eds. *Re-thinking Dionysius the Areopagite*. Chichester, U.K.: Wiley-Blackwell, 2009.

La Porta, Sergio, ed. and trans. *Two Anonymous Sets of Scholia on Dionysius the Areopagite's Heavenly Hierarchy*. Louvain, Belgium: Peeters, 2008.

Louth, Andrew. *Denys the Areopagite*. 1989. Reprint. New York: Continuum, 2001.

Pseudo-Dionysius: The Complete Works, trans. Colm Luibheid. New York: Paulist Press, 1987.

Riordan, William. *Divine Light: The Theology of Denys the Areopagite*. San Francisco: Ignatius Press, 2008.

Rorem, Paul. *Pseudo-Dionysius: A Commentary on the Texts and an Introduction to Their Influence*. New York: Oxford University Press, 1993.

—Tim Davis

Dionysius the Areopagite: *The Celestial Hierarchy*

CHAPTER 1

Dionysius the Elder to Timothy the Fellow-Elder: Even though in various ways every divine enlightenment proceeds, out of its goodness, toward those provided for, it not only remains simple in itself but also unifies those it enlightens.

1. "Every good endowment and every perfect gift is from above, coming down from the Father of lights." But there is something more. Inspired by the Father, each procession of the Light spreads itself generously toward us, and, in its power to unify, it stirs us by lifting us up. It returns us back to the oneness and deifying simplicity of the Father who gathers us in. For, as the sacred Word says, "from him and to him are all things."

2. *Let* us, then, call upon Jesus, the Light of the Father, the "true light enlightening every man coming into the world," "through whom we have obtained access" to the Father, the light which is the source of all light. To the best of our abilities, we should raise our eyes to the paternally transmitted enlightenment coming from sacred scripture and, as far as we can, we should behold the intelligent hierarchies of heaven and we should do so in accordance with what scripture has revealed to us in symbolic and uplifting fashion. We must lift up the immaterial and steady eyes of our minds to that outpouring of Light which is so primal, indeed much more so, and which comes from that source of divinity, I mean the Father. This is the Light which, by way of representative symbols, makes known to us the most blessed hierarchies among the angels. . . .

CHAPTER 2

That divine and heavenly things are appropriately revealed even through dissimilar symbols. . . .

We cannot, as mad people do, profanely visualize these heavenly and godlike intelligences as actually having numerous feet and faces. They are not shaped to resemble the brutishness of oxen or to display the wildness of lions. They do not have the curved beak of the eagle or the wings and feathers of birds. We must not have pictures of flaming wheels whirling in the skies, of material thrones made ready to provide a reception for the Deity, of multicolored horses, or of spear-carrying lieutenants, or any of those shapes handed on to us amid all the variety of the revealing symbols of scripture. The Word of God makes use of poetic imagery when discussing these formless intelligences but, as I have already said, it does so not for the sake of art, but as a concession to the nature of our own mind. It uses scriptural passages in an uplifting fashion as a way, provided for us from the first, to uplift our mind in a manner suitable to our nature.

2. These pictures have to do with beings so simple that we can neither know nor contemplate them. What if someone therefore thinks that the scriptural imagery for these minds is incongruous and that the names given to the angels have the inadequacy of a pretense? Indeed, it could be argued that if the theologians wanted to give corporeal form to what is purely incorporeal, they should have resorted to a more appropriate and related fashioning, that they should have begun with what we would hold to be noblest, immaterial and transcendent beings, instead of drawing upon a multiplicity of the earthiest forms and applying these to godlike realities which are utterly simple and heavenly. Now perhaps this intends to lift us upward and not lead the celestial appearances down into incongruous dissimilarities. . . .

CHAPTER 4

What the designation "angel" signifies.

1. I think I have now explained what I mean by hierarchy itself and I must, accordingly, lift up a song of praise to the angelic hierarchy. With eyes that look beyond the world I must behold the sacred forms attributed to it by the scriptures, so that we may be uplifted by way of these mysterious representations to their divine simplicity. Then with due worship and thanksgiving we will glorify God, the source of everything we understand concerning the hierarchy.

One truth must be affirmed above all else. It is that the transcendent Deity has out of goodness established the existence of everything and brought it into being. It is characteristic of the universal Cause, of this goodness beyond all, to summon everything to communion with him to the extent that this is possible. Hence everything in some way partakes of the providence flowing out of this transcendent Deity which is the originator of all that is. Indeed nothing could exist without some share in the being and source of everything. Even the things which have no life participate in this, for it is the transcendent Deity which is the existence of every being. The living, in their turn, have a share in that power which gives life and which surpasses all life.

Beings endowed with reason and intelligence have a share in that absolutely perfect, primordially perfect wisdom which surpasses all reason and all intelligence. And, clearly, these latter beings are nearer to God, since their participation in him takes so many forms.

2. Compared with the things which merely are, with irrational forms of life and indeed with our own rational natures, the holy ranks of heavenly beings are obviously superior in what they have received of God's largess. Their thinking processes imitate the divine. They look on the divine likeness with a transcendent eye. They model their intellects on him. Hence it is natural for them to enter into a more generous communion with the Deity, because they are forever marching towards the heights, because, as permitted, they are drawn to a concentration of an unfailing love for God, because they immaterially receive undiluted the original enlightenment, and because, ordered by such enlightenment, theirs is a life of total intelligence. They have the first and the most diverse participation in the divine and they, in turn, provide the first and the most diverse revelations of the divine hiddenness. That is why they have a preeminent right to the title of angel or messenger, since it is they who first are granted the divine enlightenment and it is they who pass on to us these revelations which are so far beyond us. Indeed the Word of God teaches us that the Law was given to us by the angels. Before the days of the Law and after it had come, it was the angels who uplifted our illustrious ancestors toward the divine and they did so by prescribing roles of conduct, by turning them from wandering and sin to the right way of truth, or by coming to announce and explain sacred orders, hidden visions, or transcendent mysteries, or divine prophecies.

3. Someone might claim that God has appeared himself and without intermediaries to some of the saints. But in fact it should be realized that scripture has clearly shown that "no one ever has seen" or ever will see the being of God in all its hiddenness. Of course God has appeared to certain pious men in ways which were in keeping with his divinity. He has come in certain sacred visions fashioned to suit the beholders. This kind of vision, that is to say, where the formless God is represented in forms, is rightly described by theological discourse as a theophany. The recipients of such visions are lifted up to the divine. They are granted divine enlightenment and are somehow initiated in the divine things themselves. Yet it was the heavenly powers which initiated our venerable ancestors to these divine visions.

It could be argued that in the scriptural tradition the sacred ordinances of the Law were given directly by God himself to Moses, so that he might truly teach us that these ordinances are themselves a copy of the divine and the sacred. Yet theology quite clearly teaches that these ordinances were mediated to us by angels so that God's order might show us how it is that secondary beings are uplifted through the primary beings. Now the Law which was laid down by the transcendent source of all order has prescriptions affecting not only the highest and the lowest groups of intelligent beings but also those of equal order and it establishes that in every hierarchy appropriate order and power must be distributed within the primary, middle, and lowest strata and that those closer to God should be the initiators of those less close by guiding them to the divine access, enlightenment, and communion.

4. I note that the mystery of Jesus' love for humanity was first revealed to the angels and that the gift of this knowledge was granted by the angels to us. It was the most divine Gabriel who guided Zechariah the hierarch into the mystery that, contrary to all hope and by God's favor, he would have a son who would be a prophet of the divine and human work of Jesus, who was beneficently about to appear for the salvation of the world. Gabriel revealed to Mary how in her would be born the divine mystery of the ineffable form of God. Another angel forecast to Joseph the true fulfillment of the divine promises made to his ancestor David. Yet another angel brought the good news to the shepherds who, because of their quiet life withdrawn from the crowd, had somehow been purified. And with him "a multitude of the heavenly host" passed on to those on earth that famous song of jubilation.

But let us lift our eyes now to the most exalted revelations of scripture. Jesus himself, the transcendent Cause of those beings which live beyond the world, came to take on human form without in any way changing his own essential nature. But I observe that never once did he abandon that human form which he had established and chosen, and he obediently submitted to the wishes of God the Father as arranged by the angels. It was the angels who announced to Joseph the Father's arrangements regarding the withdrawal into Egypt and the return to Judaea. The commands of the Father were given to Jesus himself by the angels. I do not need to remind you of the sacred tradition concerning the angel who comforted Jesus or of the fact that because of his generous work for our salvation he himself entered the order of revealers and is called the "angel of great counsel." Indeed, when he announced what he knew of the Father, was it not as an angel? . . .

CHAPTER 6

What is the first rank of the heavenly beings, what is the middle, and what is the last?

1. How many ranks are there among the heavenly beings? What kind are they? How does each hierarchy achieve perfection?

Only the divine source of their perfection could really answer this, but at least they know what they have by way of power and enlightenment and they know their place in this sacred, transcendent order. As far as we are concerned, it is not possible to know the mystery of these celestial minds or to understand how they arrive at most holy perfection. We can know only what the Deity has mysteriously granted to us through them, for they know their own properties well. I have therefore nothing of my own to say about all this and I am content merely to set down, as well as I can, what it was that the sacred theologians contemplated of the angelic sights and what they shared with us about it.

2. The word of God has provided nine explanatory designations for the heavenly beings, and my own sacred-initiator has divided these into three threefold groups. According to him, the first group is forever around God and is said to be permanently united with him ahead of any of the others and with no intermediary. Here, then, are the most holy "thrones" and the orders said to possess many eyes and many wings, called in Hebrew the "cherubim" and "seraphim." Following the tradition of scripture, he says that they are found immediately around God and in a proximity enjoyed by no other. This threefold group, says my famous teacher, forms a single hierarchy which is truly first and whose members are of equal status. No other is more like the divine or receives more directly the first enlightenments from the Deity.

The second group, he says, is made up of "authorities," "dominions," and "powers." And the third, at the end of the heavenly hierarchies, is the group of "angels," "archangels," and "principalities."

CHAPTER 7

Concerning the seraphim, cherubim, and thrones, and theirs, the first hierarchy.

1. We accept that this is how the holy hierarchies are ordered and we agree that the designations given to these heavenly intelligences signify the mode in which they take on the imprint of God. Those with a knowledge of Hebrew are aware of the fact that the holy name "seraphim" means "fire-makers," that is to say, "carriers of warmth." The name "cherubim" means "fullness of knowledge" or "outpouring of wisdom." This first of the hierarchies is hierarchically ordered by truly superior beings, for this hierarchy possesses the highest order as God's immediate neighbor, being grounded directly around God and receiving the primal theophanies and perfections. Hence the descriptions "carriers of warmth" and "thrones." Hence, also, the title "outpouring of wisdom." These names indicate their similarity to what God is.

For the designation seraphim really teaches this—a perennial circling around the divine things, penetrating warmth, the overflowing heat of a movement which never falters and never fails, a capacity to stamp their own image on subordinates by arousing and uplifting in them too a like flame, the same warmth. It means also the power to purify by means of the lightning flash and the flame. It means the ability to hold unveiled and undiminished both the light they have and the illumination they give out. It means the capacity to push aside and to do away with every obscuring shadow.

The name cherubim signifies the power to know and to see God, to receive the greatest gifts of his light, to contemplate the divine splendor in primordial power, to be filled with the gifts that bring wisdom and to share these generously with subordinates as a part of the beneficent outpouring of wisdom.

The title of the most sublime and exalted thrones conveys that in them there is a transcendence over every earthly defect, as shown by their upward-bearing toward the ultimate heights, that they are forever separated from what is inferior, that they are completely intent upon remaining always and forever in the presence of him who is truly the most high, that, free of all passion and material concern, they are utterly available to receive the divine visitation, that they bear God and are ever open, like servants, to welcome God. . . .

. . . As those who are the first around God and who are hierarchically directed in a supreme way, they are initiated into the understandable explanations of the divine works by the very source of perfection.

3. The theologians have clearly shown that the lower ranks of heavenly beings have harmoniously received from their superiors whatever understanding they have of the operations of God, whereas the higher ranks have been enlightened in initiations, so far as permitted, by the very Godhead. For they tell us, that some of them are sacredly initiated by those of higher rank. Some learn that the "King of Glory," the one raised up into the heavens in a human form, is the "Lord of the heavenly powers." Others, as they puzzle over the nature of Jesus, acquire an understanding of his divine work on our behalf and it is Jesus himself who is their instructor, teaching them directly about the kindly work he has undertaken out of love for man. "I speak of righteousness and of saving judgment." . . .

So, then, the first hierarchy of the heavenly minds is hierarchically directed by the source of all perfection, because of its own capacity to be raised up directly to this source. It is filled with its due measure of utter purification, of infinite light, of complete perfection. It becomes purified, illuminated and perfected in that it is unmixed with any weakness, filled with the first of all light, and achieves perfection as a partaker of primary knowledge and understanding.

In summary, we can reasonably say that purification, illumination, and perfection are all three the reception of an understanding of the Godhead, namely, being completely purified of ignorance by the proportionately granted knowledge of the more perfect initiations, being illuminated by this same divine knowledge (through which it also purifies whatever was not previously beheld but is now revealed through the more lofty enlightenment), and being also perfected by this light in the understanding of the most lustrous initiations.

4. This, so far as I know, is the first rank of heavenly beings. It circles in immediate proximity to God. Simply and ceaselessly it dances around an eternal knowledge of him. It is forever and totally thus, as befits angels. In a pure vision it can not only look upon a host of blessed contemplations but it can also be enlightened in simple and direct beams. It is filled with divine nourishment which is abundant, because it comes from the initial stream, and nevertheless single, because the nourishing gifts of God bring oneness in a unity without diversity.

This first group is particularly worthy of communing with God and of sharing in his work. It imitates, as far as possible, the beauty of God's condition and activity. Knowing many divine things in so superior a fashion it can have a proper share of the divine knowledge and understanding. Hence, theology has transmitted to the men of earth those hymns sung by the first ranks of the angels whose gloriously transcendent enlightenment is thereby made manifest. Some of these hymns, if one may use perceptible images, are like the "sound of many waters" as they proclaim: "Blessed be the glory of the Lord from his place." Others thunder out that famous and venerable song, telling of God: "Holy, holy, holy is the Lord of hosts. The whole earth is full of his glory." . . .

. . . And this first group passes on the word that the Godhead is a monad, that it is one in three persons, that its splendid providence for all reaches from the most exalted beings in heaven above to the lowliest creatures of earth. It is the Cause and source beyond every source for every being and it transcendently draws everything into its perennial embrace.

CHAPTER 8

Concerning the dominions, powers, and authorities, and theirs, the middle hierarchy.

1. I must turn now to the middle rank of the heavenly intelligences and, with eyes that look beyond the world, I must behold, as far as possible, the dominions and the astonishing sights of the divine authorities and powers. Each designation of the beings far superior to us indicate ways in which God is imitated and conformed to.

The revealing name "dominions" signifies, in my view, a lifting up which is free, unfettered by earthly tendencies and uninclined toward any of those tyrannical dissimilarities which characterize a harsh dominion. Because it does not give way to any defect, it is above any abject creation of slaves, and, innocent of any dissimilarity, it is forever striving mightily toward the true dominion and the true source of all dominion. Benevolently and in accordance with capacity, it receives—as does its subordinates—the semblance of that domination. It rejects empty appearances, returns completely to the true Lord, and shares as far as it can in that everlasting and divine source of all dominion.

As for the holy "powers," the title refers to a kind of masculine and unshakable courage in all its godlike activities. It is a courage which abandons all laziness and softness during the reception of the divine enlightenments granted to it, and is powerfully uplifted to imitate God. Far from abandoning its godlike movement out of cowardice, it looks undeviatingly to that transcendent power which is the source of all power. Indeed this courage becomes, so far as possible, the very image of that power to which it shapes itself, being powerfully returned to it because it is the source of all power. And at the same time, it transmits to its own inferiors its dynamic and divinizing power.

The holy "authorities," as their name indicates, have an equal order with the divine dominions and powers. They are so placed that they can receive God in a harmonious and unconfused way and indicate the ordered nature of the celestial and intellectual authority. Far from employing their authoritative powers to do tyrannous harm to the inferiors, they are harmoniously and unfailingly uplifted toward the things of God and, in their goodness, they lift up with them the ranks of those inferior to them. They are likened, insofar as they can be, to that authority which is the source of all authority and creates all authority; and they make that authority evident, to the extent that angels can, in their harmonious orders of authoritative power.

Hence the middle rank of the heavenly intelligences manifests its conformity to God. This, as has been said, is how it achieves purification, illumination, and perfection, at second hand from the divine enlightenments by way of the first hierarchical rank, and passed on secondarily through that mediating rank.

2. This process of handing on from angel to angel can be a symbol for us of that perfection which comes complete from afar and grows dimmer as it proceeds from the first to the second group. Our holy instructors in the sacred sacraments have taught us that the directly revealed fulfillments of divine reality are superior to that participation in the divine visions which comes by way of others. Similarly, it seems to me, the immediate participation in God of those angels first raised up to him is more direct than that of those perfected through a mediator. Hence—to use the terminology handed down to us—the first intelligences perfect, illuminate, and purify those of inferior status in such a fashion that the latter, having been lifted up through them to the universal and transcendent source, thereby acquire their due share of the purification, illumination, and perfection of the One who is the source of all perfection.

The divine source of all order has established the all-embracing principle that beings of the second rank receive enlightenment from the Godhead through the beings of the first rank. This has been asserted frequently by the scripture writers, as you may discover.

Now God, out of his fatherly love for humanity, chastised Israel so as to return it to the road of sacred salvation. In order to cause a change of heart he handed Israel over to the vengeance of the barbarian nations. This was to ensure that the men who were under his special providence would be transformed for the better. Later, in his kindness, he released Israel from captivity and restored it to its former state of contentment. Zechariah, a theologian, had a vision concerning this. It was an angel of the first group, one of those in the immediate entourage of God, who was learning from God himself what scripture calls the "comforting words." (Incidentally, the term "angel," as already stated, refers to all of the heavenly beings without distinction.) An angel of an inferior rank met the first and received enlightenment from him. Instructed thus by him as by a hierarch in the matter of what God willed, he, in turn, was entrusted to initiate the theologian that "Jerusalem will be fully inhabited once again with crowds of people."

Ezekiel, another theologian, says that all this was sacredly ordained by God himself who in his supreme glory stands over the cherubim. God, out of fatherly love for humanity, willed correction for the sake of Israel's improvement and in an act of righteousness appropriately divine he commanded the innocent to be separated from the guilty. The one first initiated in this, after the cherubim, was the one whose loins were girt in sapphire and who wore a full-length cloak as a symbol of the hierarch. He in turn announced the divine decision to other angels, those who carry the axes, and he did so on the instructions of the Deity who is the source of order. To the one, the orders were to traverse all of Jerusalem and to put a mark on the foreheads of the innocent. The others were told: "Follow him into the city, lay about you and do not spare your eyes. But do not go near any of those who have been given the sign."

And what is one to say about the angel who said to Daniel, "The word went forth"? or about the first who took the fire from the midst of the cherubim? or of the cherubim who gave the fire into the hands of the one wearing "the holy stole," something which shows in particular the good order existing among the angels? What is to be said regarding the one who summoned the most divine Gabriel and declared, "Make him understand the vision"? And are there not other examples, given by the sacred theologians, of the divine and harmonious arrangement befitting the heavenly hierarchy? This arrangement is copied by our own hierarchy which tries to imitate angelic beauty as far as possible, to be shaped by it, as in images, and to be uplifted to the transcendent source of all order and of all hierarchy.

CHAPTER 9

Concerning the principalities, archangels, and angels, and theirs, the final hierarchy.

Document Text

1. It remains now to contemplate that final rank in the hierarchy of angels, I mean the godlike principalities, archangels, and angels. However, I think I should first explain, as best I can, the significance of these holy designations. The term "heavenly principalities" refers to those who possess a godlike and princely hegemony, with a sacred order most suited to princely powers, the ability to be returned completely toward that principle which is above all principles and to lead others to him like a prince, the power to receive to the full the mark of the Principle of principles and, by their harmonious exercise of princely powers, to make manifest this transcendent principle of all order. . . .

As I have already said, the angels complete the entire ranking of the heavenly intelligences. Among the heavenly beings it is they who possess the final quality of being an angel. For being closer to us, they, more appropriately than the previous ones, are named "angels" insofar as their hierarchy is more concerned with revelation and is closer to the world. Now I have already said that the superior rank—superior because it is closer to what is hidden—hierarchically directs the second group. This second group, made up of holy dominions, powers, and authorities, is in charge of the hierarchy of principalities, archangels, and angels. Its revelations are clearer than those of the first hierarchy, more hidden than those of the one after it. The revealing rank of principalities, archangels, and angels presides among themselves over the human hierarchies, in order that the uplifting and return toward God, and the communion and union, might occur according to proper order, and indeed so that the procession might be benignly given by God to all hierarchies and might arrive at each one in a shared way in sacred harmony. So, then, it is the angels who take care of our own hierarchy, or so the Word of God tells us. Michael is called the ruler of the Jewish people, and other angels are described as rulers of other nations, for "the Most High has established the boundaries of the nations by the number of his angels."

3. Someone might ask why it was that only the Hebrew people were lifted up to the divine enlightenment. The answer to this is that the angels have fully done their work of guardianship and that it is no fault of theirs if other nations wandered off into the cult of false gods. Indeed it was on their own initiative that these others abandoned the good uplifting toward the divine. Their irrational worship of what they took to be god-pleasing was an index of selfishness and presumption, and this can be proved by what happened to the Hebrew people. "You rejected the knowledge" of God, it says, and you followed the call of your heart. Our way of life is not predetermined and the free will of those benefiting from the gift of divine Light does not take away from such light its attribute of being a providential source of enlightenment. . . .

All this can be said of the other nations, those peoples from whom we ourselves are come so that we too might raise our gaze up to the limitless and bounteous ocean of divine Light, that Light which forever unfolds and bestows its gifts upon all beings. No strange gods were in command here. There is one universal source and it is toward this source that the angels, charged

Glossary

Blessed be the glory of the Lord from his place	quotation from the book of Ezekiel, chapter 3, verse 12
David	the second king of the Israelites and the first in the royal line from which Christ descended
good news to the shepherds	a reference to the birth of Christ
He became the portion of the Lord	quotation from the book of Deuteronomy, chapter 32, verse 9
Holy, holy, holy is the Lord of hosts	quotation from the book of Isaiah, chapter 6, verse 3
holy stole	a reference to events recorded in Ezekiel, chapter 10, verses 6–8
Joseph	the son of Jacob and an Old Testament hero

Document Text

with the sacred and hierarchical direction of each nation, led those willing to follow them. . . .

4. And here is another item for your understanding of the hierarchy. It was revealed to Pharaoh by the angel presiding over the Egyptians and to the ruler of the Babylonians by their angel that there is a concerned and authoritative Providence and Lordship over all things. Servants of the true God were established as leaders for those nations, and the manifestation of things represented by the angelic visions were revealed by God through the angels to certain sacred men near the angels, namely Joseph and Daniel. For there is only one ruling source and Providence in the world, and we must not imagine that the Deity took charge of the Jewish people alone and that angels or gods, on an equal footing with him or even hostile to him, had charge of the other peoples. The passage which might suggest this notion must be understood in this sacred sense, for it could not mean that God shared the government of mankind with other gods or angels or that he reigned in Israel as a local prince or chieftain. The single Providence of the Most High for all commanded angels to bring all peoples to salvation, but it was Israel alone which returned to the Light and proclaimed the true Lord, That is why the word of God indicates that Israel chose itself for special devotion to the true God by saying: "He became the portion of the Lord." But the theologians also say that Michael presides over the government of the Jewish people and that this is in order to make clear that Israel, like the other nations, was assigned to one of the angels, to recognize through him the one universal ruling source. For there is only one Providence over all the world, a supra-being transcending all power visible and invisible; and over every nation there are presiding angels entrusted with the task of raising up toward that Providence, as their own source, everyone willing to follow, as far as possible.

Excerpts from *Pseudo Dionysius: The Complete Works*; translation by Colm Luibheid. Copyright (c) 1987 by Colm Luibheid. Paulist Press, Inc., New York/Mahwah, NJ. Reprinted by permission of Paulist Press, Inc. www.paulistpress.com.

Glossary

Make him understand the vision	quotation from the book of Daniel, chapter 8, verse 16
Mary	the mother of Christ
Moses	the biblical patriarch to whom God revealed his laws in the Ten Commandments on Mount Sinai
the Most High has established the boundaries of the nations by the number of his angels	quotation from the book of Deuteronomy, chapter 32, verse 8
multitude of the heavenly host	quotation from the Gospel of Luke, chapter 2, verse 13
withdrawal into Egypt and the return to Judaea	a reference to the Israelites' bondage in and exodus from Egypt, as recorded in the book of Exodus
The word went forth	quotation from the book of Daniel, chapter 9, verse 23
Zechariah	an Old Testament prophet whose prophecies are recorded in the book of Zechariah

Stained glass windows depicting Jared and Methuselah, part of a genealogical set
(Window depicting a genealogical figure: Jared and Methuselah (stained glass), English School / Canterbury Cathedral, Kent, UK / The Bridgeman Art Library International)

Book of the Cave of Treasures

ca. 500–600

"When I die, embalm me with myrrh, and cassia, and stakte, and deposit my body in the Cave of Treasures."

Overview

The Book of the Cave of Treasures is an example of New Testament Apocrypha chronicling human history from Creation to the Resurrection of Jesus Christ. The title by which the book is known suggests that it is the story of a cave, while an alternate title provided in the text itself, "Book of the Succession of the Generations," implies that it is a book of genealogical records. But neither title is strictly accurate; the Cave of Treasures itself is described only vaguely, and the book is more than a simple outline of family trees and listings of ancestors and descendants. The purpose of the Book of the Cave of Treasures is to illustrate the continuity of a plan of salvation across the millennia of human history. It is the history presented in the Hebrew Bible, also known as the Old Testament, refocused through the lens of early Mesopotamian Christianity. From the religion's beginnings, Christian thinkers and writers asserted that continuity existed between the Hebrew Bible and Christian belief. Christian writers studied the words of Hebrew prophets and saw foreshadowings of the birth, ministry, Crucifixion, and Resurrection of Jesus of Nazareth.

The Book of the Cave of Treasures, which scholars believe was written in the sixth century by a Syriac-speaking Christian living in Edessa or Nisibis, represents part of this tradition of reinterpretation. It relates the events of the Hebrew Bible as part of a continuous narrative of God's plan for the salvation of humankind. Along the way it attempts to more fully explain events in the Hebrew Bible in light of Christian thought and theology. Throughout the work, events from the Hebrew Bible are presented in terms of their relevance to events in Christian history or theology. For example, the Garden of Eden is explained as symbolic of the institution of the Church—a place of comfort and refuge for a fallen humanity. In this way, the Book of the Cave of Treasures retrospectively expands the history and scope of Christianity—which at the time of the book's writing was a relatively young faith—back to the dawn of creation.

Context

After its advent in the Roman province of Judea, Christianity spread rapidly, not only west toward the Mediterranean world, Rome, and Europe but also east into the lands of the Sassanian Persian Empire. Numerous trade routes and other roads, such as the Persian Royal Road, provided avenues for Christian evangelists to travel and spread word of their faith. Geographically, the lands to the east were more accessible for Christian missionaries than were the far-flung lands of Europe. Since the Book of the Cave of Treasures originated in the world of Eastern Christianity, it was written in the Syriac language rather than the more commonly known languages of Latin or Greek.

Unlike with Western Christianity after the time of Constantine I, whose Edict of Milan of 313 extended recognition to the religion in the Roman Empire, in the lands of the Sassanian Persian Empire there was no widespread acceptance of Christianity. Persecutions were common; the Persians killed some sixteen thousand Christians in just forty years during the fourth century. Despite this hostility, Persian lands were attractive to those Christians whose theological views were not in line with the official doctrine of the bishops of Rome, whose influence was becoming dominant in western Christianity. Numerous councils met in these early centuries of the Christian Church, attempting to reach uniformity of thought on divisive issues such as the exact nature of the divinity of Jesus of Nazareth. Although these councils often declared a "solution" to such issues, they rarely achieved unity. Groups left on the outside by these councils, such as the Jacobites and Nestorians, migrated to lands beyond the bounds of Rome, where they were able to establish churches free of outside control.

One of the most significant geographical centers of eastern Christianity was northern Mesopotamia. Cities such as Nisibis (modern-day Nusaybin, Turkey), on the trade route between Asia Minor and the Near East, were important centers of church governance and culture. As many as a hundred monasteries once flourished in this area. Nisibis, in particular, was important as a refuge for scholars from Edessa (modern-day Urfa), one hundred miles to the west, after Roman church officials closed the Nestorian university there. As the religious world of the West was becoming

Time Line

20 BCE	A treaty between Rome and Persia fixes the boundary between the two empires along the Euphrates River, flowing from Asia Minor southeast toward the Persian Gulf.
150 CE	Christians are first recorded as present in Edessa.
177–212	Abgar VIII of Edessa, traditionally considered the first Christian monarch as of his conversion around 200, reigns.
196	Christians are recorded as subsisting among the Parthians, Bactrians, and other peoples throughout the Persian Empire. This is the first evidence of widespread Christianity in the Persian Empire.
214	Edessa becomes a Roman colony.
306	Ephraem the Syrian, who would be recognized by some traditions as author of the Book of the Cave of Treasures, is born in Nisibis.
330	The first monastery in Syria is established north of Nisibis.
431	The First Council of Ephesus, held in Ionia, condemns the teachings of Nestorius. His followers, known as Nestorians, begin migrating east to the lands of the Sassanian Persian Empire.
CA. 500–600	The Book of the Cave of Treasures is thought to have been composed.
CA. 600s–700s	Arabic translations of the Book of the Cave of Treasures appear.

more homogeneous by the year, in the eastern Persian lands Nestorian and Jacobite Christianity coexisted with Judaism, Zoroastrianism, and—by the seventh century—Islam.

Beginning in the sixth century, at about the time scholars believe that the Book of the Cave of Treasures was written, a common concern among educated Christians revolved around the genealogies of Jesus circulated by religious leaders. This concern stemmed from the theory that the original documents recording the genealogy of the patriarchs had probably been destroyed during the Babylonian Captivity, the period during the sixth and seventh centuries BCE when the Hebrew people were deported to Babylon by the Neo-Assyrian Empire. Subsequently constructed genealogical records were believed to be faulty—either out of error or a conspiracy by Jews to hide the true ancestry of Jesus. Thus, a demand existed for "correct" studies of the ancestry of Jesus and the history of the Old Testament. Additionally, Arabian adherents of Islam, as descendants of Abraham and his concubine Hagar, shared this desire for an accurate account of the ancient past. Syrians, Ethiopians, and Egyptians had similar interests in ancient genealogy at this time.

Thus, the Book of the Cave of Treasures was written in an environment dominated by many competing religious traditions that yet had common historical and geographical roots. By presenting the Christian story of salvation as an integral part of the stories of the lands and peoples of the region, the Book of the Cave of Treasures served as a way for the Christians of Mesopotamia to stake a claim to legitimacy in an increasingly crowded marketplace of faiths.

About the Author

The author of the Book of the Cave of Treasures is ultimately unknown. Traditionally, the Syriac Church and other Eastern churches attributed it to Ephraem the Syrian, as he is the author named in the preface to the work. Ephraem was a fourth-century theologian and hymnist who wrote in the Syriac language. Born in 306 CE, Ephraem died in 373; thus, if he was the author of the Book of the Cave of Treasures, it is a fourth-century work. However, when the text was studied in the nineteenth century, scholars such as E. A. Wallis Budge concluded that it owed too much to similar texts (such as the Book of Adam and Eve) to have appeared before the sixth century. Although it is unlikely that Ephraem himself is the author of the Book of the Cave of Treasures, it was originally written in his language of Syriac, and experts such as Budge have asserted that in invoking the name of this well-known Syriac thinker and writer, the true author may have wished to express a continuity and solidarity with his earlier, illustrious coreligionist.

Explanation and Analysis of the Document

This initial section of the Book of the Cave of Treasures, the first of six, details the history of earth from its creation to the death of Yared (Jared), understood as the first thousand years of the earth's history. This section introduces several key concepts that appear throughout the text, including the Creation and Fall of humanity, the exile of Cain, and the nature and purpose of the Cave of Treasures.

Bracketing in the document text indicates items for which the translator could find no direct translation or terms that needed clarification for the reader. The translator's rewording is placed in brackets to make the reader aware that the bracketed phrase is not a direct translation but a paraphrase to enhance reading.

♦ **The Title of the Work: The Scribe's Prayer**

Although this document is commonly referred to as the Book of the Cave of Treasures, the brief preface provides a much more descriptive title, the "Book of the Succession of the Generations." This may indeed be a better title, as the contents of the book are focused much more on the description of the generations leading to the birth of Christ than they are on the actual contents of the treasure cave or the activities that may have taken place there. The preface also asserts the traditional authorship of Saint Mar Aphrem, or Ephraem the Syrian, an assertion now considered spurious by scholars.

♦ **The Creation. First Day.**

This opening section of the text details the Christian version of the first day of Creation in more detail than the better-known account in Genesis. In particular, several examples of later Christian theology appear in this section. God is said to have created the foundations of existence and then the "hosts which are invisible"—the hierarchy of heavenly beings—as well as light, day, and night.

The Christian concept of the triune God—Father, Son, and Holy Spirit—appears next, with the "Spirit of holiness" hovering over the waters of the earth, providing the blessing that enabled the earth to warm and produce life. The author describes this activity as similar to the nurturing of baby birds by their mother. The text indicates that this life-giving essence was "united to the waters," acknowledging the life-giving nature of water and imbuing it with a theological purpose. The author uses the term "Paraclete," a Koine Greek word meaning "advocate," in reference to the Spirit. This term does not appear in the Hebrew Old Testament; it does appear in the New Testament, but only in the writings of Saint John.

♦ **The Creation. Second Day.**

This section details the creation of the "Lower Heaven," or the sky, and explains the layers of Heaven, where the uppermost level is of fire and the second is of light. The lower sky is described as dense with water and dark clouds, which are motionless in the sky. In the Genesis account of Creation, much less detail about the nature of the heavens appears. The motionless cloud of water that hangs in the sky will burst forth with water, being one of the sources of the Great Flood, which the Book of the Cave of Treasures discusses in a later section. Thus, the extended discussion of the location and nature of the water stored in the sky may represent a foreshadowing of the Flood.

♦ **The Creation. Third Day.**

On the third day, God separates the waters of the earth into one location, exposing the land below and giving the earth a dry surface. This surface is, however, fairly moist

Fall of Satan and the rebel angels
(Fall of Satan and the rebel angels from Heaven [oil on silvered copper], Swanenburgh, Jakob Isaaksz [1571-1638] / Rafael Valls Gallery, London, UK / The Bridgeman Art Library International)

and soft. The author explains how the waters are pooled not only on the surface but also beneath it, reaching the surface of the earth through a system of tunnels. Like the waters held above in the sky, these collected subsurface waters will rise to cause the Great Flood later in the story of humanity. As with the account of the second day, this appears to be an instance of foreshadowing. The tunnels also provide passage for currents of air, allowing wind to reach the surface of the earth and produce hot and cold weather.

♦ **The Creation. Fourth Day**

As with the previous days of Creation, the author here makes an effort to explain details omitted from earlier accounts. In this case, the author uses the creation of the sun, moon, and stars to explain the presence of hard, dry ground in view of the previous section's description of moist, soft ground. In keeping with the previous days' accounts, the author offers much more detail than is found in the more familiar Genesis story; contrary to the foreshadowing of the Great Flood, there is no apparent theological reason for the extended description here. The appearance of the sun draws the moisture out of the ground, hardening it. God gives the stars and moon water and air and then lights them. Picking up another lead from the third day, the heat of the sun causes the "conceived" plants and trees to sprout and grow.

BOOK OF THE CAVE OF TREASURES

Essential Quotes

> "And when he rose at full length and stood upright in the centre of the earth, he planted his two feet on that spot whereon was set up the Cross of our Redeemer; for Adam was created in Jerusalem."

> "Eden is the Holy Church, and the Paradise which was in it is the land of rest, and the inheritance of life, which God hath prepared for all the holy children of men."

> "And he commanded his son Seth, and said unto him, '. . . when I die, embalm me with myrrh, and cassia, and stakte, and deposit my body in the Cave of Treasures. And whosoever shall be left of your generations in that day . . . shall carry my body with him, and shall take it and deposit it in the centre of the earth, for in that place shall redemption be effected for me and for all my children.'"

> "And in the days of Yared, in the five hundredth year of his life, the children of Seth broke the oaths which their fathers had made them to swear. And they began to go down from that holy mountain to the encampment of iniquity of the children of Cain, the murderer, and in this way the fall of the children of Seth took place."

♦ **The Creation. Fifth Day.**

In this section, sea creatures appear, as God commands the oceans to produce fish, water serpents, and Leviathan—a sea monster that appears prominently in the book of Job in the Hebrew Bible. Sea monsters such as Leviathan and stories about them were popular in ancient Near Eastern mythology, with appearances dating back to ancient Sumeria. Additionally, on this day, God creates birds, serpents, cattle, and wild animals.

♦ **The Creation. Sixth and Seventh Days.**

The author's description of the sixth and seventh days is brief. On the sixth day God created Adam from the dust of the earth and Eve out of Adam's rib. This brief mention of the creation of humanity followed by a more detailed description mirrors the account in Genesis. Thus, the author of the Book of the Cave of Treasures is not only recounting the story of the Hebrew Bible but is also carefully echoing the structure and style of the original. The use of the term *Sabbath* to refer to the seventh day of the week is a variation on the account in Genesis 2:3, which states "And God blessed the seventh day, and sanctified it: because that in it he had rested from all his work which God created and made."

♦ **The Creation of Adam**

God made Adam on the sixth day of creation, during the first hour of the day. As in earlier sections of the Book of the Cave of Treasures, here the author incorporates into the Creation story aspects of first-millennium doctrine and thoughts that were not present in the Genesis account. God's words "let Us make man in Our image, and according to Our likeness" echo the more familiar account of Genesis 1:26. The author of this book, however, explains the use of the plural pronoun as a means by which God makes known the presence of the Trinity. The angels hear God's announcement about the creation of the human being and are awed with the magnitude of the miracle.

The author explains that God formed a living being from inert elements in order to demonstrate that all of creation is under his control. As Adam rises, he stands on the exact spot where the cross of Jesus's Crucifixion is to be planted millennia later in Jerusalem. God makes Adam "king, and priest, and prophet," giving him control over everything that is created.

♦ **The Revolt of Satan, and the Battle in Heaven.**

On the sixth day, one of the lower-order angels is envious of the adoration shown to Adam and does not wish to participate in the veneration. The rebellious angel divorces himself from the presence of God and, along with followers, is stripped of his celestial glory. This fallen angel is given the name Satana, or Satan. The motif of Satan undergoing a "fall" from Heaven does not appear in the Genesis account but is referred to in the Hebrew books of Isaiah and Ezekiel as well as the New Testament book of Luke. As Satan is exiled from Heaven, Adam ascends on a chariot of fire. Entering Heaven, Adam is commanded by God not to eat of "a [certain] tree." Unlike in the Genesis account, no explanation is given here as to the nature of the forbidden tree.

♦ **The Making of Eve.**

While Adam is in the heavenly Paradise, God puts him to sleep. Using a rib removed from Adam's right side, God creates Eve, introduced here as Khawa. The new couple spend three hours in Paradise, which, according to the author, is located on a high mountain encompassing the earth. The author refers to the Hebrew Bible, noting that, according to Moses, Adam is then moved to Eden.

♦ **The Symbolism of Eden.**

At this point, the author of the Book of the Cave of Treasures pauses the narrative to explicate the meaning of Eden and its relevance to the reader. Eden, the author explains, is a metaphor for the church, which is an expression of God's mercy and compassion. The author cites several examples from the Hebrew Bible that illustrate God's compassion. Knowing that Satan has plans for the downfall of humanity, God also develops a plan to save humanity. Adam, the first man, as priest, king, and prophet will minister God's redemption to humankind. Additionally, the author explains that the Tree of Life, which existed in Paradise, served to foreshadow the cross of Christ's Crucifixion. In this way, the author is explicitly illustrating a connection between Eden and Calvary (the Christian name for the site of the Crucifixion).

♦ **Satan's Attack on Adam and Eve.**

Satan persuades Eve with "lying words" and, although the author does not relate Satan's message to Eve, they persuade her to eat the fruit of the forbidden tree. Another variation on the more familiar Genesis account is the attribution of Eve's eating of the fruit to her "soft" nature as a woman.

♦ **Adam's Stay in Paradise.**

In the ninth hour of the sixth day, God exiles Adam and Eve from Paradise. At the same time, God provides encouragement to Adam, explaining that the son of God will one day descend to earth in human form in order to redeem Adam and all humankind. God also explains that Adam and Eve's descendants must embalm Adam's body after his death "with myrrh, cassia, and stakte" and entomb it within a cave but later move it to a spot "in the centre of the earth." These embalming materials are mentioned in various places in the Hebrew Bible, such as Psalm 45. In nonbiblical literature, the Greek historian Herodotus reports that many peoples of the Near East, including the Egyptians, used myrrh, a gum resin derived from a tree, and cassia, dried cinnamon bark, in their embalming methods. The author is thus familiar with the traditional burial techniques of the time and region. The spot at the earth's center, to be shown to humanity at a future time, will be the location at which humanity's redemption will occur. God also relates to Adam "everything which the Son would suffer on behalf of him."

♦ **Adam's Expulsion from Paradise.**

The gold, frankincense, and myrrh used by Adam to consecrate his and Eve's cave are the same as the gifts given by the three Magi to the infant Jesus in the New Testament. These materials, particularly the gold and frankincense, an aromatic resin, were materials strongly identified with royalty in the ancient Near East. Thus, where in the nativity story their presence is an indicator of the kingship of the infant Jesus, here they are used to illustrate the connections between Adam and Jesus, the former foreshadowing the latter. This is the Cave of Treasures, which will serve as a center of worship for Adam and his descendants.

Adam and Eve have sex for the first time—according to margin notes in the original manuscript, this may have been thirty years after their expulsion—and Eve subsequently bears twins: Cain, a boy, and Lebhudha, a girl. Later, the boy Abel and his twin sister, Kelimath, are born. Adam intends for his two sons to marry each other's twin sisters, but Cain objects, wishing to marry his own twin. Adam forbids such a marriage and commands his sons to make a sacrifice in the Cave of Treasures and start their married lives. But Satan "entered into" Cain and persuades him to kill his brother and take Lebhudha for himself. Cain's jealousy of Abel grows when Abel's sacrifice to God is accepted, while Cain's is not. Cain kills his brother with a piece of flint and is exiled to the "forest of Nodh" with his twin sister/wife. This account is significantly different from the Genesis account, but it is not unique. The romantic motivation for Cain's murder of Abel is also described in Conflict of Adam and Eve with Satan, an apocryphal work dating from the same time period as the Book of the Cave of Treasures. This story involving twin sisters of Cain and Abel also appears in the Jewish rabbinical literature as well as in some Islamic folklore. There is currently no way to know which works might have influenced the others. As for the reasons for the expanded story in the Book of the Cave of Treasures and these other works, scholars can only speculate. One aspect that this version illuminates is the source of the first marriages in human history. Although the Genesis myth implies that Cain would have to marry a sister to carry on his line, these apocryphal sources make it more explicit.

♦ **The Birth of Seth.—The Posterity of Seth.**

After a century of grief, Adam and Eve have a third son, Seth. Seth becomes "the father of the mighty men who lived before the Flood." Seth's son, Anosh; grandson, Kainan; and great-grandson, Mahlalail, become the first great patriarchs.

- **The Death of Adam.**

Adam dies at the age of 930. Genesis 4 mentions that Adam dies at this age but provides no details of his last days. The Book of the Cave of Treasures gives much more detail, providing a template for the subsequent sections. Before his death, he calls Seth, Anosh, Kainan, and Mahlalail to him and gives them the instructions for his burial, handed down by God when Adam was in Paradise.

The author points out that Adam dies on the exact date and at the exact time that "the Son of Man" would later die on the Cross. Like the presence of the gold, frankincense, and myrrh, this is another example of the author's drawing obvious parallels between Adam and Jesus. It also demonstrates the common narrative thread stretching from the earliest days of humanity to the days of Christ and his disciples.

- **The Burial of Adam.**

The account in Genesis 4 does not discuss Adam's burial, but Jewish tradition states that both Adam and Eve were buried in the Cave of the Patriarchs. Here, Seth embalms Adam according to the instructions; after 140 days of mourning, his body is taken to the Cave of Treasures and buried. At this time, the followers of Seth separate themselves from Cain and his descendants, as ordered by Adam. Seth and his people live on the "glorious mountain," while Cain and his people live on the plain.

- **The Rule of Seth.—The Rule of Anosh.— The Rule of Kainan.—The Rule of Mahlalail.**

These four sections contain a high degree of repetition and can be discussed collectively. Like many aspects of the Book of the Cave of Treasures, the material is an expansion of the more well-known stories in the Genesis myth. The closing sections of "The First Thousand Years" provide a description of the world in which Adam and Eve's descendants lived. One of the most significant differences from the Genesis account is the revelation that these "sons of God" took the place of those who rebelled and fell from Heaven, living in peace and leisure. In the Genesis account, toil and trouble emerged as soon as Adam and Eve ate the forbidden fruit. In this account, an idyllic existence, lived in harmony with God's law, persisted long after the tasting of the fruit.

Another noticeable motif in these sections is the continuing separation of the descendants of Seth from those of Cain. This alienation of Cain's descendants is one of the few rules imposed on the descendants of Adam from generation to generation. The author places emphasis on the moral chasm that exists between the two groups, with Seth and his children living in holiness and Cain's progeny existing in "enmity" with them.

- **The Rule of Yared.**

Yared, son of Mahlalail, serves well and is "complete in all the virtues." However, it is during the rule of Yared that the children of Seth disobey and mingle with the children of Cain and move to the "encampment of iniquity." This is the manner in which the "fall of the children of Seth" takes place. The followers of Satan, referred to by the author as "the handicraftsmen of sin," then appear on earth. Thus, after generations of living in harmony with God's law, the descendants of Seth very quickly fall into sinful ways, mingling with the descendants of Cain. Unlike the account in Genesis, this descent into iniquity occurs within a generation. The fifth chapter of Genesis, which contains the listing of Seth's descendants, makes no mention of these events. However, the beginning of the Flood narrative of Genesis 6 opens with God's displeasure at humanity's sinfulness, providing a slight parallel with the Cave of Treasures account.

Audience

The Book of the Cave of Treasures was targeted at the Syriac-speaking peoples—Christian and non-Christian—living in Mesopotamia from the sixth century onward. The Near East in the first millennium was a region with a wide variety of competing religious worldviews. By presenting a unified narrative of Christian history, the text would have strengthened the case of Christians attempting to proselytize their non-Christian neighbors. Seen through the lens of the Book of the Cave of Treasures, the Christian faith was not new but rather was a belief system with roots stretching back to the dawn of time, making it equivalent, in terms of longevity, to other religious faiths prominent in the Near East at the time. For modern readers and students, the Book of the Cave of Treasures provides a valuable glimpse into a Christian world that has faded into the mists of time. While history books focus on the rise of Christianity in the West—centered on Rome and the expansion of the faith into Europe—this book and others from the Near East provide a broader perspective on the faith's history in the first millennium.

Impact

As the history of the Book of the Cave of Treasures is largely unknown, scholars can only speculate as to its impact at the time it was written. We can assume that, at least for a time, it was a well-known work, as—according to Budge—it was translated into Arabic in the seventh or eighth century. The story of how the Book of the Cave of Treasures came to Western audiences begins with Joseph Simonius Assemani. Assemani was a scholar of eastern Christianity and languages such as ancient Syriac. In the first half of the eighteenth century he undertook a series of expeditions into Syria and Egypt, searching for ancient texts. One of the more than one hundred texts he brought back was the Book of the Cave of Treasures. While Assemani made some notes on the book for his *Bibliotheca Orientalis Clementino-Vaticana* (1719), a catalog of ancient manuscripts, the book itself was not published. Aside from these notes, scholars largely ignored the book until the nineteenth-century German scholar August Dillman noted the similarities between it and the Book of Adam and Eve, an Ethiopian text he was translating, and published discussion of these similarities in 1853.

Dillman's work on Ethiopic and other ancient texts was one of the factors contributing to increasing scholarly interest in texts from Africa and the Near East in the nineteenth century. In 1883, Carl Bezold published a German translation of the Book of the Cave of Treasures.

The book made its way into English through the work of the British Museum scholar E. A. Wallis Budge, who in 1927 translated the work in the course of his study of the *Book of the Bee*, a thirteenth-century Nestorian work by Bishop Solomon of Basra (in modern-day Iraq). Budge asserted that the *Book of the Bee* borrowed heavily from the Book of the Cave of Treasures. This modern scholarship indicates that the latter book may have served as the basis for many apocryphal works through the years, meaning that the myths and legends it contains may be some of the earliest forms of these stories.

Further Reading

■ Books

Chadwick, Henry. *The Early Church*. New York: Penguin, 1993.

Foltz, Richard. *Religions of the Silk Road: Overland Trade and Cultural Exchange from Antiquity to the Fifteenth Century*. New York: Palgrave Macmillan, 2000.

Frend, W. H. C. *The Rise of Christianity*. Minneapolis: Fortress Press, 1984.

Jenkins, Philip. *The Lost History of Christianity: The Thousand-Year Golden Age of the Church in the Middle East, Africa, and Asia—and How It Died*. New York: HarperOne, 2008.

Johnson, Paul. *History of Christianity*. New York: Touchstone, 1979.

Moffett, Samuel Hugh. *A History of Christianity in Asia*. Vol. 1: *Beginnings to 1500*. Maryknoll, N.Y.: Orbis, 1998.

■ Web Sites

Dickens, Mark. "The Church of the East." Oxus Communications Web site.
   http://www.oxuscom.com/Church_of_the_East.pdf

—Aaron J. Gulyas

Questions for Further Study

1. What, in your opinion, is the significance of the title, specifically "Cave of Treasures"? Why "cave," and what are the "treasures"?

2. Why was the concept of "continuity" important in early Christian belief? What difference would it have made if there had been some sort of gap in the historical record that early Christian (and Jewish) thinkers and historians were unable to fill? Why was it considered necessary to establish the genealogy of Christ?

3. The entry draws a distinction between Eastern Christianity and Western Christianity. How were the two versions of Christian thinking different? What factors—economic, historical, political, even geographical—might have accounted for the differing visions of Christianity?

4. The Book of the Cave of Treasures invites comparison with the Nestorian Book of the Bee, written some six centuries later. How are the two works similar? How do they differ? What impact might the passage of time have had on interpretation of biblical history?

5. How does the story of Cain and Abel in the Book of the Cave of Treasures differ from the account in the biblical book of Genesis? What factors do you think might have caused the author of the Book of the Cave of Treasures to interpret the story of Cain and Abel as he does?

Book of the Cave of Treasures

[THE TITLE OF THE WORK: THE SCRIBE'S PRAYER]

By the might of our Lord Jesus Christ we begin to write the "Book of the Succession of the Generations," that is to say, ME'ARATH GAZZE, which was composed by SAINT MAR APHREM. O our Lord, help Thou me in Thy Mercy. Amen.

[THE FIRST THOUSAND YEARS: ADAM TO YARED [Jared]]

♦ **[The Creation. First Day.]**

In the beginning, on the First Day, which was the holy First Day of the Week, the chief and firstborn of all the days, God created the heavens, and the earth, and the waters, and the air, and the fire, and the hosts which are invisible (that is to say, the Angels, Archangels, Thrones, Lords, Principalities, Powers, Cherubim and Seraphim), and all the ranks and companies of Spiritual beings, and the Light, and the Night, and the Day-time, and the gentle winds and the strong winds [i.e. storms]. All these were created on the First Day. And on the First Day of the Week the Spirit of holiness, one of the Persons of the Trinity, hovered over the waters, and through the hovering thereof over the face of the waters, the waters were blessed so that they might become producers of offspring, and they became hot, and the whole nature of the waters glowed with heat, and the leaven of creation was united to them. As the mother-bird maketh warm her young by the embrace of her closely covering wings, and the young birds acquire form through the warmth of the heat which [they derive] from her, so through the operation of the Spirit of holiness, the Spirit, the Paraclete, the leaven of the breath of life was united to the waters when He hovered over them.

♦ **[The Creation. Second Day.]**

And on the Second Day God made the Lower Heaven, and called it REKI'A [that is to say, "what is solid and fixed," or "firmament"]. This He did that He might make known that the Lower Heaven doth not possess the nature of the heaven which is above it, and that it is different in appearance from that heaven which is above it, for the heaven above it is of fire. And that second heaven is NUHRA [i.e. Light], and this lower heaven is, and because it hath the dense nature of water, it hath been called "Reki'a." And on the Second Day God made a separation between the waters and the waters, that is to say, between the waters which were above [Reki'a] and the waters which were below. And the ascent of these waters which were above heaven took place on the Second Day, and they were like unto a dense black cloud of thick darkness. Thus were they raised up there, and they mounted up, and behold, they stand above the Reki'a in the air; and they do not spread, and they make no motion to any side.

♦ **[The Creation. Third Day.]**

And on the Third Day God commanded the waters that were below the firmament [Reki'a] to be gathered together in one place, and the dry land to appear. And when the covering of water had been rolled up from the face of the earth, the earth showed itself to be in an unsettled and unstable state, that is to say, it was of a damp [or moist] and yielding nature. And the waters were gathered together into seas that were under the earth and within it, and upon it. And God made in the earth from below, corridors, and shafts, and channels for the passage of the waters; and the winds which come from within the earth ascend by means of these corridors and channels, and also the heat and the cold for the service of the earth. Now, as for the earth, the lower part of it is like unto a thick sponge, for it resteth on the waters. And on this Third Day God commanded the earth, and it brought forth herbs and vegetables, and it conceived in its interior trees, and seeds, and plants and roots.

♦ **[The Creation. Fourth Day.]**

And on the Fourth Day God made the sun, and the moon, and the stars. And as soon as the heat of the sun was diffused over the surface of the earth, the earth became hard and rigid, and lost its flaccidity, because the humidity and the dampness [caused by] the waters were taken away from it. The Creator made the sphere of the sun of fire and filled it with light. And God gave unto the sphere of the moon and the stars bodies of water and air, and filled them with light. And when the dust of the earth became hot, it brought forth all the trees], and plants, and seeds, and roots which had been conceived inside it on the Third Day.

♦ [The Creation. Fifth Day.]

And on the Fifth Day God commanded the waters, and they brought forth all kind of fish of divers appearances, and creatures which move about, and twist themselves and wriggle in the waters, and serpents, and Leviathan, and beasts of terrible aspects, and feathered fowl of the air and of the waters. And on this same day God made from the earth all the cattle and wild beasts, and all the reptiles which creep about upon the earth.

♦ [The Creation. Sixth Day.]

And on the Sixth Day, which is the Eve of the Sabbath, God formed man out of the dust, and Eve from his rib.

And on the Seventh Day God rested from His labours, and it is called "Sabbath."

♦ [The Creation of Adam.]

Now the formation of Adam took place in this wise: On the Sixth Day, which is the Eve of the Sabbath, at the first hour of the day, when quietness was reigning over all the Ranks [of the Angels], and the hosts [of heaven], God said, "Come ye, let Us make man in Our image, and according to Our likeness." Now by this word "Us" He maketh known concerning the Glorious Persons [of the Trinity]. And when the angels heard this utterance, they fell into a state of fear and trembling, and they said to one another, "A mighty miracle will be made manifest to us this day [that is to say], the likeness of God, our Maker." And they saw the right hand of God opened out flat, and stretched out over the whole world; and all creatures were collected in the palm of His right hand. And they saw that He took from the whole mass of the earth one grain of dust, and from the whole nature of water one drop of water, and from all the air which is above one puff of wind, and from the whole nature of fire a little of its heat and warmth. And the angels saw that when these four feeble [or inert] materials were placed in the palm of His right hand, that is to say, cold, and heat, and dryness, and moisture, God formed Adam. Now, for what reason did God make Adam out of these four materials unless it were [to show] that everything which is in the world should be in subordination to him through them? He took a grain from the earth in order that everything in nature which is formed of earth should be subject unto him; and a drop of water in order that everything which is in the seas and rivers should be his; and a puff of air so that all kinds [of creatures] which fly in the air might be given unto him; and the heat of fire so that all the beings that are fiery in nature, and the celestial hosts, might be his helpers.

God formed Adam with His holy hands, in His own Image and Likeness, and when the angels saw Adam's glorious appearance they were greatly moved by the beauty thereof. For they saw the image of his face burning with glorious splendour like the orb of the sun, and the light of his eyes was like the light of the sun, and the image of his body was like unto the sparkling of crystal. And when he rose at full length and stood upright in the centre of the earth, he planted his two feet on that spot whereon was set up the Cross of our Redeemer; for Adam was created in Jerusalem. There he was arrayed in the apparel of sovereignty, and there was the crown of glory set upon his head, there was he made king, and priest, and prophet, there did God make him to sit upon his honourable throne, and there did God give him dominion over all creatures and things. And all the wild beasts, and all the cattle, and the feathered fowl were gathered together, and they passed before Adam and he assigned names to them; and they bowed their heads before him; and everything in nature worshipped him, and submitted themselves unto him. And the angels and the hosts of heaven heard the Voice of God saying unto him, "Adam, behold; I have made thee king, and priest, and prophet, and lord, and head, and governor of everything which hath been made and created; and they shall be in subjection unto thee, and they shall be thine, and I have given unto thee power over everything which I have created." And when the angels heard this speech they all bowed the knee and worshipped Him.

♦ [The Revolt of Satan, and the Battle in Heaven.]

And when the prince of the lower order of angels saw what great majesty had been given unto Adam, he was jealous of him from that day, and he did not wish to worship him. And he said unto his hosts, "Ye shall not worship him, and ye shall not praise him with the angels. It is meet that ye should worship me, because I am fire and spirit; and not that I should worship a thing of dust, which hath been fashioned of fine dust." And the Rebel meditating these things would not render obedience to God, and of his own free will he asserted his independence and separated himself from God. But he was swept away out of heaven and fell, and the fall of himself and of all his company from heaven took place on the Sixth Day, at the second hour of the day. And the apparel of their glorious state was stripped off them. And his name was called "Satana" because he turned aside [from the right way], and "Sheda" because he was cast out, and "Daiwa" because he lost the apparel of his glory. And behold, from that time until the present day, he and all his hosts have been stripped of their apparel, and they go naked and have horrible faces. And when Satana was cast out from heaven, Adam was raised up so that he might ascend to Paradise in a chariot of fire. And the angels went before him, singing praises, and the Seraphim ascribed holiness unto him, and the Cherubim ascribed blessing; and amid cries of joy and praises Adam went into Paradise. And as soon as Adam entered Paradise he was commanded not to eat of a [certain] tree; his entrance into heaven took place at the third hour of the Eve of the Sabbath [i.e. on Friday morning].

♦ **[The Making of Eve.]**

And God cast a sleep upon Adam and he slept. And God took a rib from the loins on the right side of Adam, and He made Khawa [i.e. Eve] from it; and when Adam woke up, and saw Eve, he rejoiced in her greatly. And Adam and Eve were in Paradise, and clothed with glory and shining with praise for three hours. Now this Paradise was situated on a high range of hills, and it was thirty spans—according to the measurement of the spirit—higher than all the high mountains, and it surrounded the whole earth.

Now Moses the prophet said that God planted Paradise in Eden and placed Adam there.

♦ **[The Symbolism of Eden.]**

Now Eden is the Holy Church, and the Church is the compassion of God, which He was about to extend to the children of men. For God, according to His foreknowledge, knew what Satan had devised against Adam, and therefore He set Adam beforehand in the bosom of His compassion, even as the blessed David singeth concerning Him in the Psalm, saying, "Lord, Thou hast been an abiding place for us throughout all generations," that is to say, "Thou hast made us to have our abiding place in Thy compassion." And, when entreating God on behalf of the redemption of the children of men, David said, "Remember Thy Church, which Thou didst acquire in olden time" that is to say, "[Remember] Thy compassion, which Thou art about to spread over our feeble race." Eden is the Holy Church, and the Paradise which was in it is the land of rest, and the inheritance of life, which God hath prepared for all the holy children of men. And because Adam was priest, and king, and prophet, God brought him into Paradise that he might minister in Eden, the Holy Church, even as the blessed man Moses testifieth concerning him, saying, "That he might serve God by means of priestly ministration with praise, and that he might keep that commandment which had been entrusted to him by the compassion of God." And God made Adam and Eve to dwell in Paradise. True is this word, and it proclaimeth the truth: That Tree of Life which was in the midst of Paradise prefigured the Redeeming Cross, which is the veritable Tree of Life, and this it was that was fixed in the middle of the earth.

♦ **[Satan's Attack on Adam and Eve.]**

And when Satan saw that Adam and Eve were happy and joyful in Paradise, that Rebel was smitten sorely with jealousy, and he became filled with wrath. And he went and took up his abode in the serpent, and he raised him up, and made him to fly through the air to the skirts of Mount [Eden] whereon was Paradise. Now, why did Satan enter the body of the serpent and hide himself therein? Because he knew that his appearance was foul, and that if Eve saw his form, she would betake herself to flight straightway before him. Now, the man who wished to teach the Greek language to a bird—now the bird that can learn the speech of men is called "babbaghah" [i.e. parrot]—first bringeth a large mirror and placeth between himself and the bird. He then beginneth to talk to the bird, and immediately the parrot heareth the voice of the man, it turneth round, and when it seeth its own form [reflected] in the mirror, it becometh pleased straightway, because it imagineth that a fellow parrot is talking to it. Then it inclineth its ear with pleasure, and listeneth to the words of the man who is talking to it, and it becometh eager to learn, and to speak Greek. In this manner [i.e. with the object of making Eve believe that it was the serpent that spoke to her] did Satan enter in and dwell in the serpent, and he watched for the opportunity, and [when] he saw Eve by herself, he called her by her name. And when she turned round towards him, she saw her own form [reflected] in him, and she talked to him; and Satan led her astray with his lying words, because the nature of woman is soft [or, yielding].

And when Eve had heard from him concerning that tree, straightway she ran quickly to it, and she plucked the fruit of disobedience from the tree of transgression of the command, and she ate. Then immediately she found herself stripped naked, and she saw the hatefulness of her shame, and she ran away naked, and hid herself in another tree, and covered her nakedness with the leaves thereof. And she cried out to Adam, and he came to her, and she handed to him some of the fruit of which she had eaten, and he also did eat thereof. And when he had eaten he also became naked, and he and Eve made girdles for their loins of the leaves of the fig-trees; and they were arrayed in these girdles of ignominy for three hours. At mid-day they received [their] sentence of doom. And God made for them tunics of skin which was stripped from the trees, that is to say, of the bark of the trees, because the trees that were in Paradise had soft barks, and they were softer than the byssus and silk wherefrom the garments worn by kings are made. And God dressed them in this soft skin, which was thus spread over a body of infirmities.

♦ **[Adam's stay in Paradise.]**

At the third hour of the day Adam and Eve ascended into Paradise, and for three hours they enjoyed the good things thereof; for three hours they were in shame and disgrace, and at the ninth hour their expulsion from Paradise took place. And as they were going forth sorrowfully, God spake unto Adam, and heartened him, and said unto him, "Be not sorrowful, O Adam, for I will restore unto thee thine inheritance. Behold, see how greatly I have loved thee, for though I have cursed the earth for thy sake, yet have I withdrawn thee from the operation of the curse. As for the serpent, I have fettered his legs in his belly, and I have given him the dust of the earth for food; and Eve have I bound under the yoke of servitude. Inasmuch as thou hast transgressed my commandments get thee forth, but be not sad. After the fulfilment of the times which I have allotted that you shall be in exile outside [Paradise], in the land which is under the curse, behold, I will send my Son. And He shall go down [from heaven] for thy redemption, and He shall sojourn in a Virgin, and shall put on a body [of flesh], and through Him redemption and a return shall be effected for thee. But command thy sons, and order them to embalm thy body after thy death with myrrh, cassia, and stakte. And they shall place thee in this cave, wherein I am making you to dwell this day, until the time when your expulsion shall take place from the regions of Paradise to that earth which is outside it. And whosoever shall be left in those days shall take thy body with him, and shall deposit it on the spot which I shall show him, in the centre of the earth; for in that place shall redemption be effected for thee and for all thy children." And God revealed unto Adam everything which the Son would suffer on behalf of him.

♦ **[Adam's expulsion from Paradise.]**

And when Adam and Eve had gone forth from Paradise, the door of Paradise was shut, and a cherub bearing a two-edged sword stood by it. . . .

Now Adam and Eve were virgins, and Adam wished to know Eve his wife. And Adam took from the skirts of the mountain of Paradise, gold, and myrrh, and frankincense, and he placed them in the cave, and he blessed the cave, and consecrated it that it might be the house of prayer for himself and his sons. And he called the cave "ME'ARATH GAZZE" [*i.e.* "CAVE OF TREASURES"]. So Adam and Eve went down from that holy mountain [of Eden] to the slopes which were below it, and there Adam knew Eve his wife. And Eve conceived and brought forth Cain and Lebhudha, his sister, with him; and Eve conceived again and she brought forth Habhil [Abel] and Kelimath, his sister, with him. And when the children grew up, Adam said unto Eve, "Let Cain take to wife Kelimath, who was brought forth with Abel, and let Abel take to wife Lebhudha, who was brought forth with Cain." And Cain said unto Eve his mother, "I will take to wife my twin sister Lebhudha, and let Abel take to wife his twin sister Kelimath"; now Lebhudha was beautiful. When Adam heard these words, which were exceedingly displeasing unto him, he said, "It will be a transgression of the commandment for thee to take [to wife] thy sister, who was born with thee. Nevertheless, take ye to yourselves fruits of trees, and the young of sheep, and get ye up to the top of this holy mountain. Then go ye into the Cave of Treasures, and offer ye up your offerings, and make your prayers, and then ye shall consort with your wives." And it came to pass that when Adam, the first priest, and Cain and Abel, his sons, were going up to the top of the mountain, Satan entered into Cain [and persuaded him] to kill Abel, his brother, because of Lebhudha; and because his offering was rejected and was not accepted before God, whilst the offering of Abel was accepted, Cain's jealousy of his brother Abel was increased. And when they came down to the plain, Cain rose up against his brother Abel, and he killed him with a blow from a stone of flint. Then straightway Cain received the doom of death, instead of curses, and he became a fugitive and a wanderer all the days of his life. And God drove him forth into exile in a certain part of the forest of Nodh, and Cain took to wife his twin sister and made the place of his abode there.

Document Text

♦ **[The Birth of Seth.]**

And Adam and Eve mourned for Abel one hundred years. And then Adam knew his wife again, and she brought forth Seth, the Beautiful, a man mighty and perfect like unto Adam, and he became the father of the mighty men who lived before the Flood.

♦ **[The Posterity of Seth.]**

And to Seth was born Anosh [Enos], and Anosh begot Kainan [Cainan], and Kainan begot Mahlalail [Mahalaleel]; these [are] the Patriarchs who were born in the days of Adam.

♦ **[The Death of Adam.]**

And when Adam had lived nine hundred and thirty years, that is to say, until the one hundred and thirty-fifth year of Mahlalail, the day of his death drew nigh and came. And Seth, his son, and Anosh, and Kainan, and Mahlalail gathered themselves together and came to him. And they were blessed by him, and he prayed over them. And he commanded his son Seth, and said unto him, "Observe, my son Seth, that which I command thee this day, and do thou on the day of thy death give my command to Anosh, and repeat it to him, and let him repeat it to Kainan, and Kainan shall repeat it to Mahlalail, and let this [my] command be handed on to all your generations. And when I die, embalm me with myrrh, and cassia, and stakte, and deposit my body in the Cave of Treasures. And whosoever shall be left of your generations in that day, when your going forth from this country, which is round about Paradise, shall take place, shall carry my body with him, and shall take it and deposit it in the centre of the earth, for in that place shall redemption be effected for me and for all my children. And be thou, O my son Seth, governor of the sons of thy people. And thou shalt rule them purely and holily in the fear of God. And keep ye your offspring separate from the offspring of Cain, the murderer."

And when the report "Adam is dying" was known generally, all his offspring gathered together, and came to him, that is to say, Seth, his son, and Anosh, and Kainan and Mahlalail, they and their wives, and their sons, and their daughters; and Adam blessed them. And the departure of Adam from this world took place in the nine hundred and thirtieth year—according to the reckoning from the beginning—on the fourteenth day of the moon, on the sixth day of the month of Nisan [April], at the ninth hour, on the day of the Eve of the Sabbath [*i.e.* Friday]. At the same hour in which the Son of Man delivered up his soul to His Father on the Cross, did our father Adam deliver up his soul to Him that fashioned him; and he departed from this world.

♦ **[The Burial of Adam.]**

And when Adam was dead his son Seth embalmed him, according as Adam had commanded him, with myrrh, and cassia, and stakte; now Adam's dead body was the first [body buried] in the earth. And grief for him was exceedingly sore, and Seth [and his sons] mourned for his death one hundred and forty days; and they took Adam's body up to the top of the mountain, and buried it in the Cave of Treasures. And after the families and peoples of the children of Seth had buried Adam, they separated themselves from the children of Cain, the murderer. And Seth took Anosh, his firstborn, and Kainan, and Mahlalail, and their wives and children, and led them up into the glorious mountain where Adam was buried; and Cain and all his descendants remained below on the plain where Cain slew Abel.

♦ **[The Rule of Seth.]**

And Seth became the governor of the children of his people, and he ruled them in purity and holiness. And because of their purity they received the name, which is the best of all names, and were called "the sons of God," they and their wives and their sons. Thus they lived in that mountain in all purity and holiness and in the fear of God. And they went up on the skirts of [the mountain] of Paradise, and they became praisers and glorifiers of God in the place of that host of devils who fell from heaven. There they dwelt in peace and happiness: there was nothing about which they needed to feel anxiety, they had nothing to weary or trouble them and they had nothing to do except to praise and glorify God, with the angels. For they heard continually the voices of the angels who were singing praises in Paradise, which was situated at no great height above them—in fact, only about thirty spans—according to the measure of the spirit. They suffered neither toil nor fatigue, they had neither seed [time] nor harvest, but they fed themselves with the delectable fruits of glorious trees of all kinds, and they enjoyed the sweet scent and perfume of the breezes which were wafted forth to them from Paradise. [Thus lived] those holy men, who were indeed holy, and their wives were pure, and their sons were virtuous, and their daughters were chaste and undefiled. In them there was no rebellious thought, no envy, no anger, no enmity. In their wives and daughters there was no impure longing, and neither lasciviousness, nor cursing, nor lying was heard among them. The only oath which they used in swearing was, "By the blood of Abel." And they, and their wives, and their children used to rise up early in the morning, and go up to the top of that holy mountain, and worship there before God. And they were blessed by the body of Adam their father, and they lifted up their eyes to Paradise, and praised God; and thus they did all the days of their life.

And when Seth had lived nine hundred and thirteen years he became sick unto death. And Anosh his son, and Kainan, and Mahlalail, and Yared [Jared], and Henokh [Enoch], and their wives and their sons, gathered together and came unto him, and they were blessed by him. And he prayed over them, and commanded them, and made them to take an oath, and said unto them, "I will make you to take an oath, and to swear by the holy blood of Abel, that none of you will go down from this holy mountain to the children of Cain, the murderer. For ye know well the enmity which hath existed between us and Cain from the day whereon he slew Abel." And Seth blessed Anosh, his son; and gave him commands concerning the body of Adam, and he made him ruler over the children of his people. And Seth ruled them in purity and in holiness, and he ministered diligently before the body of Adam. And Seth died when he was nine hundred and twelve years old, on the seven-and-twentieth day of the blessed month of Abh [August], on the second day of the week [Monday], at the third hour, in the twentieth year of the life of Enoch. And Anosh, Seth's first-born son, embalmed his body and buried him in the Cave of Treasures, with his father Adam; and they made a mourning for him forty days.

◆ [The Rule of Anosh.]

And Anosh rose up to minister before God in the Cave of Treasures. And he became the governor of the children of his people, and he kept all the commandments which his father Seth had commanded him, and he urged them to be constant in prayer.

And in the days of Anosh, in his eight hundred and twentieth year, Lamech, the blind man, killed Cain, the murderer, in the Forest of Nodh. Now this killing took place in the following manner. As Lamech was leaning on the youth, his son [Tubal-Cain], and the youth was setting straight his father's arm in the direction in which he saw the quarry, he heard the sound of Cain moving about, backwards and forwards, in the forest. Now Cain was unable to stand still in one place and to hold his peace. And Lamech, thinking that it was a wild beast that was making a movement in the forest, raised his arm, and, having made ready, drew his bow and shot an arrow towards that spot, and the arrow smote Cain between his eyes, and he fell down and died. And Lamech, thinking that he had shot game, spake to the youth, saying, "Make haste, and let us see what game we have shot." And when they went to the spot, and the boy on whom Lamech leaned had looked, he said unto him, "O my lord, thou hast killed Cain." And Lamech moved his hands to smite them together, and as he did so he smote the youth and killed him also.

And when Anosh had lived nine hundred and five years, and was sick unto death, all the patriarchs gathered themselves together, and came unto him, viz. Kainan, his first-born son, and Mahlalail, and Yared, and Enoch, and Matushlah [Methuselah], they, and their wives, and their sons. And they were blessed by him, and he prayed over them and commanded them, and spake unto them, saying, "I will make you to swear by the holy blood of Abel that not one of you shall go down from this mountain to the plain, nor into the encampment of the children of Cain, the murderer; and ye shall not mingle yourselves among them. Take ye good heed unto this matter, for ye well know what enmity hath existed between us and them from the day whereon Cain slew Abel." And he blessed Kainan, his son, and commanded him concerning the body of Adam, that he should minister before it all the days of his life, and that he should rule over the children of his people in purity and holiness. And Anosh died at the age of nine hundred and five years, on the third day of the month of the First Teshrin [October], on the day of the Sabbath, in the fifty-third year of the life of Methuselah. And Kainan, his first-born, embalmed him and buried him in the Cave of Treasures, with Adam and Seth, his father. And they made a mourning for him forty days.

◆ [The Rule of Kainan.]

And Kainan stood up before God to minister in the Cave of Treasures. He was an honourable and pure man, and he governed the children of his people in the complete fear of God, and he fulfilled all the commandments of Anosh his father. And when Kainan had lived nine hundred and twenty years, and was sick unto death, all the Patriarchs gathered together and came unto him, viz. Mahlalail his son, and Yared, and Enoch and Methuselah and Lamech, they and their wives and their children, and were blessed by him. And he prayed over them and commanded them, saying, "I will make you swear by the holy blood of Abel that not one of you shall go down from this holy

Document Text

mountain into the camp of the children of Cain, the murderer, for ye all know well what enmity hath existed between us and them since the day whereon he killed Abel." And he blessed his son Mahlalail, and admonished him concerning the body of Adam, and said unto him, "Behold, O my son Mahlalail, minister thou before God in purity and holiness in the Cave of Treasures, and depart not thou from the presence of the body of Adam all the days of thy life. And be thou the governor of the children of thy people, and rule thou them purely and holily." Kainan died, being nine hundred and twenty years old, on the thirteenth day of the month of Hezeran [June], on the fourth day of the week [Wednesday], at mid-day, in the five and sixtieth year of [the life of] Lamech, the father of Noah. And Mahlalail, his son, embalmed him, and buried him in the Cave of Treasures; and they made mourning for him forty days.

♦ **[The Rule of Mahlalail.]**

And Mahlalail rose up and ministered before God in the place of Kainan his father. He was constant in prayer by day and by night, and he urged earnestly the children of his people to observe holiness and purity, and to pray without ceasing. And when Mahlalail had lived eight hundred and ninety-five years, and the day of his departure drew nigh, and he was sick unto death, all the Patriarchs gathered together and came unto him, viz. Yared, his first-born, and Enoch and Methuselah, and Lamech, and Noah, they and their wives and their children, and were blessed by him. And he prayed over them, and commanded them, saying, "I will make you to swear by the holy blood of Abel, that not one of you shall go down from this holy mountain. And ye shall not permit any one of your descendants to go down to the plain, to the children of Cain, the murderer, for ye all well know what enmity hath existed between us and them from the day whereon he slew Abel." And he blessed Yared, his first-born, and he commanded him concerning the body of Adam, and revealed unto him the place whereto he should make ready to go. And he also commanded him, and made him to swear an oath, saying, "Thou shalt not depart from the body of our father Adam all the days of thy life, and thou shalt be the governor of the children of thy people, and shalt rule them in chastity and holiness." And Mahlalail died, [being] eight hundred and ninety-five years old, on the second day of the month Nisan [April], on the first day of the week [Sunday], at the third hour of the day, in the four and thirtieth year of the life of Noah. And Yared, his first-born, embalmed him, and buried him in the Cave of Treasures; and the people made a mourning for him forty days.

Glossary

byssus	a silky fabric
cassia	a tree of shrub used for its aromatic bark
Cross of our Redeemer	the crucifix on which Christ would die
David	Israel's second king and the founder of the royal line from which Christ descended
frankincense	a sweet-smelling gum resin used chiefly as incense but also in embalming
Moses	a major Hebrew patriarch who led the Israelites out of bondage in Egypt and brought to them God's law in the form of the Ten Commandments
myrrh	an aromatic resin burned as incense and used in perfume
Noah	the biblical patriarch who survived with his family in an ark during a worldwide flood God sent to punish humankind
Nodh	or Nod ("wandering"), the place east of Eden to which Cain fled after murdering his brother, Abel
SAINT MAR APHREM	that is, Ephraem, the putative author of the text
stakte	a type of incense

♦ [The Rule of Yared.]

And Yared his son rose up and ministered before God [in the Cave of Treasures]. He was a perfect man, and was complete in all the virtues, and he was constant in prayer by day and by night. And because of the excellence of his life and conversation, his days were longer than those of all the children of his people. And in the days of Yared, in the five hundredth year of his life, the children of Seth broke the oaths which their fathers had made them to swear. And they began to go down from that holy mountain to the encampment of iniquity of the children of Cain, the murderer, and in this way the fall of the children of Seth took place.

AND IN THE FORTIETH YEAR OF YARED THE FIRST THOUSAND YEARS, FROM ADAM TO YARED, CAME TO AN END.

And in these years the handicraftsmen of sin, and the disciples of Satan, appeared, for he was their teacher, and he entered in and dwelt in them, and he poured into them the spirit of the operation of error, through which the fall of the children of Seth was to take place.

Hermes Trismegistus
(Ideal figure of Hermes Trismegistus, copy of illustration from 'De Divinatione et Magicis Praestigiis' by Jean-Jacques Boissard, 1605 [engraving] /Private Collection / The Stapleton Collection / The Bridgeman Art Library International)

Emerald Tablet

ca. 500–700

"And as all things have been arose from one by the mediation of one: so all things have their birth from this one thing by adaptation."

Overview

The Emerald Tablet, frequently known by its Latin title, Tabula smaragdina, is one of the most important documents in the history of alchemy. While most alchemical texts are centered on the actual work of the alchemist in the laboratory, the Emerald Tablet makes a theoretical, even theological, statement of the basic principles of alchemy. Composed anonymously at the end of the Greek alchemical tradition in Egypt sometime between the years 500 and 700 CE, the Emerald Tablet was translated into Arabic in the early ninth century and became a foundational document of Islamic alchemy during the Middle Ages. Part of the Emerald Tablet's appeal came from its attribution to Hermes Trismegistus, a mythical Egyptian philosopher who supposedly lived before the biblical Flood and whose writings carried immense authority in late antiquity and the Middle Ages; at the end of the Renaissance, however, in 1614, the humanist Isaac Casaubon proved these writings to be much later pseudepigrapha. The Emerald Tablet was next translated into Latin in twelfth-century Spain, together with the greater bulk of Arabic scholarship and ancient Greek texts known in the Muslim world, and it again became a key text for the development of alchemy, this time in western Europe. In this case alchemy finally led to the development of scientific chemistry, and in the seventeenth century the doctrine of occult sympathy taught by the Emerald Tablet gave Isaac Newton an imaginative basis for conceiving of the operation of force at a distance, allowing him to develop the theory of gravity.

Context

Alchemy is generally said to have been invented by Bolus of Mendes, a Greek philosopher who lived in Hellenistic Egypt around 200 BCE. His works recorded in Greek for the first time a number of traditional Egyptian physical techniques for simulating expensive materials such as silver, gold, gems, and purple murex dye, which were highly prized throughout antiquity. These techniques aimed at, rather than actually making silver or gold, for example, making a metal that was white or yellow in color, as with other substitutes that would pass a cursory inspection. The purpose was similar to that of modern costume jewelry: to fool the undiscerning into thinking that an ostentatious display is being made. However, this kind of simple laboratory-based work quickly evolved into a form of religious mysticism concerned with the salvation of the human soul.

One important idea came from folklore common in the ancient world holding that metals grow in the earth just as a fetus grows in the womb and that the various metals, such as lead, iron, copper, silver, and gold, are developmental stages that every vein of metallic ore passes through. If such were the case, transmutation of a metal from one stage to another would only be the hastening of a natural process. The philosophy of Aristotle further suggested that the physical substance of metals was essentially the same lifeless substrate and that the differences between them could be accounted for by different qualities of soul, which gave the metals individual forms such as gold or silver. Once alchemists believed that they were transforming the souls of metals, it was easy for them to believe that at the same time they were purifying their own souls and that the hypothetical philosopher's stone, which would transmute base metals into gold, would also, and more importantly, bring about their own salvation or divinization.

Apart from a few authors who wrote under their own names, like Zosimos of Panopolis (fl. ca. 300 CE), from the very beginning alchemical books were attributed either to famous philosophers of the past, such as Democritus (fl. ca. 400 BCE), or to legendary figures. The basic idea was that the full truth had been revealed to humankind by the gods in the remote past and had degenerated into ignorance since then, but it could be restored by recourse to ancient writers. Hermes Trismegistus—meaning "thrice-great"—quickly became the most important figure used in this way, both because of his supposed status as the revealer of the human arts and sciences and because of his prestige in the philosophical environment of alchemy: Greek-speaking intellectuals of native origin in Greco-Roman Egypt. (Alexander the Great conquered Egypt in 332 BCE, leading to its governance as a Hellenistic state by the self-proclaimed pharaoh Ptolemy I; the Roman Empire annexed Egypt as

Time Line

CA. 3000 BCE	■ The mythological figure Hermes Trismegistus is held to have flourished.
CA. 2650 BCE	■ Imhotep, a historical basis for Hermes Trismegistus, serves as chancellor of Egypt, to become known as the "first inventor" of the arts and sciences.
CA. 2000 –200 BCE	■ Egyptian priests develop proto-alchemical techniques and practices.
CA. 200 BCE	■ Bolus of Mendes writes the first alchemical book.
CA. 300 CE	■ Greco-Egyptian alchemy reaches its height in the generation of Zosimos of Panopolis and Maria the Jewess.
CA. 500–700	■ The Emerald Tablet is anonymously composed, probably in Greek.
CA. 800	■ Abu Musa Jabir ibn Hayyan rationalizes alchemy as a tool for the investigation of natural philosophy—science—creating a pool opposite that of magic, between which alchemy will oscillate for the next thousand years.
CA. 813–833	■ The *Sirr al-khaliqa* (Secret of Creation), containing the oldest surviving text of the Emerald Tablet, is anonymously composed.
CA. 1150	■ The Emerald Tablet is translated into Latin by John of Seville as part of a medico-alchemical compilation called the *Secretum secretorum* (Secret of Secrets)
1267	■ Roger Bacon publishes his *Opus majus* (Great Work), the first European advance on received Arabic alchemy; it contains the first European formula for gunpowder.
1661	■ Robert Boyle publishes the *Sceptical Chymist*, transmuting alchemy into modern scientific chemistry.

a province in 30 BCE.) Throughout late antiquity, alchemy became less practical and laboratory-based and more theological. The Emerald Tablet reflects this tendency inasmuch as it states the most abstract philosophical beliefs of alchemy in metaphorical language based on the physical properties of alchemical experiments. Precisely because of its theoretical nature, the Emerald Tablet became a key text in the legitimization of alchemy as it was received into Islamic and then into medieval culture, even as experimental work again became increasingly important.

The Emerald Tablet was composed, most likely in Greek, sometime between 500 and 700 CE, since its intellectual framework depends on Greek and alchemical literature from the immediately preceding period. The text is attributed to Hermes Trismegistus both by the text itself, in line 13, and by the framing story that introduces it in the ninth-century *Kitab sirr al-khaliqa wa san'at al-tabi'a* (Book of the Secret of Creation and the Art of Nature), known in short as the *Sirr al-khaliqa* (Secret of Creation), the first historically preserved document in which the text occurs. In the Greco-Egyptian tradition, Hermes Trismegistus was the discoverer of all human knowledge, an updating of the ancient Egyptian god Thoth. But certain Islamic intellectuals, the earliest being the astrologer Abu Ma'shar in his *Kitab al-uluf* (Book of Thousands), built a new version of Hermes Trismegistus on the Hellenistic foundation. They interpreted Trismegistus as "triplicate in wisdom" and believed that it was a title referring to three different individuals named Hermes who lived at various periods of history. The first Hermes they identified with Idris, an obscure ancient prophet mentioned in the Qur'an (19:56–57 and 21:85–86), and with the biblical patriarch Enoch, who "walked with god" (Genesis 5:24). The Islamic myth of Hermes also adapted traditions from the book of Enoch, a Hellenistic apocalyptic text that was never incorporated into the Bible.

The first Hermes, then, was the grandson of Adam and lived before the Great Flood. God allowed this Hermes to ascend into the heavens, and from understanding the workings of the divine world he saw firsthand, he came to understand all of the arts and sciences, which he passed on to humanity. He constructed the pyramids, invented medicine and all other wisdom, and became the prophet of a monotheistic paganism that was supposedly the original religion of the human race. This element of the myth was important because it legitimized Greek philosophy as coming from a prophetic source, so it could therefore be used by Muslim scholars. With his knowledge of astrology, this Hermes was able to predict that the Flood would come and wipe out humanity and all the wisdom of his revelation. So he invented writing, in the form of hieroglyphs, which he used to carve the totality of his philosophy onto the walls of Egyptian temples, where it would survive the universal inundation.

After the Flood, there were two further Hermeses, one in Babylon and one in Egypt, who were responsible for recovering the knowledge of the original Hermes and using it to found the Mesopotamian and Egyptian civilizations, respectively. The Babylonian Hermes took as his disciple the Greek philosopher Pythagoras, while the Egyptian Hermes instructed the Greek philosopher Asclepius, who was conflated with Apollonius of Tyana. This mythical framework not only established a genealogy of human knowledge and especially philosophy going back to divine revelation but also made philosophy something that originated in the East, in the person of Hermes Trismegistus, but for which the West wrongly took credit. This notion occurred both in the Hermetica—the body of works featuring or attributed to Hermes Trismegistus—and in philosophical literature of the Roman-era Iranian Empire, and it was taken up by Islamic civilization.

Written in the first few decades of the ninth century, the *Sirr al-khaliqa* integrated the Emerald Tablet into the Arab myth of Hermes Trismegistus. According to the *Sirr al-khaliqa*, Apollonius of Tyana descended into the depths of the labyrinth beneath the Egyptian temple complex of Akhmim (later Panopolis) seeking to discover the secrets of wisdom. He found the mummified body of Hermes Trismegistus holding a tablet of emerald; the text known as the Emerald Tablet was inscribed on it. This document was then used as the basis for Arab alchemical science. The Emerald Tablet thus stands for an expansive alchemical tradition, according to which knowledge of the arts and sciences was in some primordial time given to humanity in perfect form but has consistently degenerated and can be renewed only through older, uncorrupted sources of information. The very nature of alchemical research as laboratory work, however, militates against that paradigm, giving rise to new discoveries that can be demonstrated by experiment rather than merely validated through tradition. This dual nature of alchemy allowed Islamic culture to move briefly in the direction of a scientific paradigm of knowledge, a breakthrough that would finally come in western Europe and in which the Emerald Tablet would again play a role.

Time Line

CA. 1680
- Isaac Newton translates the *Emerald Tablet* into English.

1687
- Newton publishes the *Principia mathematica*, which includes the law of gravitational attraction.

served to legitimize Egyptian wisdom as superior to, and as a putative source of, Greek philosophy. He was based on the Egyptian god Thoth (Hermes in the Greek pantheon), the patron of wisdom, and to a lesser extent on Imhotep, who was the historical chancellor to the First Dynasty pharaoh Djoser (ca. 2650 BCE) and is celebrated in Egyptian tradition as the "first inventor" of the arts and sciences. Accordingly, Hermes Trismegistus was hailed as the discoverer of architecture, medicine, poetry, and philosophy, as well as other disciplines. Hermes Trismegistus figures in a number of philosophical dialogues and was appropriated by alchemists, astrologers, and magicians as the pseudepigraphic author for their treatises, which are specifically referred to as the technical Hermetica.

The frame story for the Emerald Tablet in the *Sirr al-khaliqa* describes it as having been discovered by Balinas, the Arabic name for Apollonius of Tyana, an obscure first-century Neopythagorean philosopher (none of whose works survive), whose biography by Philostratus the Athenian, *Life of Apollonius of Tyana*, suggests that he was a magician. Apollonius assumed an exaggerated role in Muslim philosophy and was confused with Asclepius, a disciple of Hermes Trismegistus in the Hermetica and in Greek mythical history the first physician.

About the Author

The authorship and even the original language of composition of the Emerald Tablet are matters of controversy. The earliest version of the text is found in the *Sirr al-khaliqa*, an anonymous Arabic alchemical work of the early ninth century (before 833). The document summarizes ideas of Greek alchemy and makes the most sense as part of that tradition. But there is no definite way of determining whether the Muslim alchemist has produced an original composition summarizing ideas he found in Greek texts or has translated a Greek original by some other unknown alchemist of a slightly earlier period. Islamic scholars generally received Greek alchemy through Syriac or Aramaic translations that circulated in Syria and Iraq in late antiquity, but very little of that literature survives today.

Moreover, the document is pseudepigraphic, meaning that it refers its own composition to a mythical figure, Hermes Trismegistus. This Hermes was the creation of Egyptian intellectuals—mainly priests—who wrote philosophical dialogues in Greek during the latter Roman period (ca. 150–400). He

Explanation and Analysis of the Document

Although its historical relevance is clear, the meaning of the text inscribed on the Emerald Tablet is more elusive. Even scholars frequently state that its alchemical symbolism cannot be understood, but, in fact, a great deal of meaning can be extracted from it. The tablet refers to some work performed by the alchemist, but this is never described in specific detail so that the reader might understand what it is. A hallmark of ancient magical texts is the omission of some vital part of instruction passed verbally from master to disciple. Of course, the author may simply have been playing with that tradition and not really have had any secret process in mind. Arabic writers may have taken this unnamed object or process as referring to the heavenly journey of Hermes/Enoch, since line 8 states, "It ascends from the earth to the heaven and again it descends to the earth." One obvious interpretation is that the text is an allegorical description of an alchemical process, possibly the creation of the philosopher's stone.

Tomb painting of the god Thoth
(The god Thoth, from the Tomb of Prince Khaemwaset II, son of Ramesses III [c.1187-1156 BC] New Kingdom [painted limestone], Egyptian 20th Dynasty [1200-1085 BC]) / Valley of the Queens, Thebes, Egypt / The Bridgeman Art Library International)

The Renaissance-era German magician Heinrich Cornelius Agrippa certainly read the text this way. For him, the "one thing" of lines 2 and 3 was nothing less than the principle of life, which alchemists of his era believed existed in all living things—including the *sal nitrum* (nitric acid) of the alchemists, which went into making fertilizer and gunpowder and which, when boiled, gave off the "vital spirit" (oxygen). If this principle of life could be obtained in what alchemists conceived of as an abstract or potential state from its particular manifestation in air or from something that naturally fertilizes the growth of life (like dung), it ought to be the philosopher's stone, which held the secrets of creation: transmutation and salvation.

For Isaac Newton, the "one thing" is also the reaction that gives the human being the same power to create that God exercised at the beginning of the universe—"that which is above is like that which is below to do the miracles of one only thing." The reaction is between the sun and moon, that is, mercury and sulfur in Newton's understanding, which can "marry," so to speak, because the one is constantly changing into the other already in the natural world. By the late seventeenth century, the scientific side of alchemy had advanced far enough that Newton thought that "mercury" was a coded name for acids and "sulfur" for bases. Newton believed that Jesus, as distinct from God the Father, was the active spirit that sparked this reaction to accomplish creation, as suggested in line 11.

It is unlikely that the author of the Emerald Tablet had any such chemical reactions as those of Agrippa and Newton in mind, since the chemistry used by ancient alchemists was far simpler than that of later eras. But the chemical side of alchemy was constantly changing, and what alchemists did in the laboratory in antiquity—and what they could have described in the allegorical language of the document—is not nearly as well understood as what transpired during the Renaissance because of the relative lack of ancient texts. In any case, it would seem that two substances, sun and moon, are combined and blackened (as nourished by the earth) in a heated retort exposed to the wind, or air, to produce a new substance. The alchemist was free to read into the metaphor any chemical reaction he could contrive.

On another level of meaning, the document may be read as an abstract description of the occult operation of the world. It gives all the laws by which magic, astrology, and alchemy operate, in the same way that a physics textbook describes the operation of the world in scientific terms. These same principles informed the worldview of Greek philosophy, especially Neoplatonism, a combination of the teachings of Plato and Aristotle. So the Emerald Tablet can give a source for these laws in divine revelation, as in the Islamic tradition, or can justify the investigation of the occult sciences, as in the Renaissance.

The greatest of these laws is known by the Stoic technical term *sympathy*, but it is an idea that has existed throughout human civilization and may be part of human evolution. Sympathy is the idea that all things and beings are interconnected in the vast fabric of reality in such a way that things and beings sometimes behave in ways that reflect action elsewhere in the universe—that is, they behave sympathetically. This irrationally conceived idea has little value as a way of explaining the universe and is broadly contradicted by the discoveries of modern science. But the notion is nevertheless intuitive and was widely accepted as valid in antiquity, since the human mind has evolved to seek logical connections between events in order to understand the potential consequences of natural occurrences as well as their own and others' actions. In antiquity and the Middle Ages, in the absence of scientific understanding, the sympathetic connections among nature and living organisms seemed to be confirmed by all sorts of observations, such as the way plants grow in response to sunlight or the way the tides are governed by the moon. More to the point, once the world is understood in this way, there arises the notion that action may be taken to influence or control it. Many people have come to believe that in special cases, when a human being imparts an action on a certain thing, nature will impart an equivalent action on another. From this perspective, if a priest dons a sheepskin to make himself look like a cloud and dances during a drought, then clouds may appear, and it may rain. If a magician makes a doll and gives it the name of a specific person and then

Essential Quotes

> "That which is below is like that which is above and that which is above is like that which is below to do the miracles of one only thing."

> "And as all things have been arose from one by the mediation of one: so all things have their birth from this one thing by adaptation."

> "It ascends from the earth to the heaven and again it descends to the earth and receives the force of things superior and inferior."

> "Hence I am called Hermes Trismegist, having the three parts of the philosophy of the whole world."

hammers a nail through its heart, then that person may feel pain or desire. If someone has chronic pain in his stomach, he may see fit to find the constellation in the heavens that corresponds to the stomach, and then if he wears an amulet made from a gem that also corresponds to the same region of the sky, his pain may be cured.

After the Emerald Tablet reassures the reader that it is a true text (something done by most occult writings), it makes its classic statement of the sympathetic connections of the universe: "That which is below is like that which is above and that which is above is like that which is below." In other words, there is an inherent connection between the human and the divine worlds, and what is done in one will also be accomplished in the other; this notion can be compared to the biblical phrase "on earth as it is in heaven" (Matthew 6:10). In the *Asclepius*, part of the philosophical Hermetica, the universe is presented as entirely contained and penetrated by God, so that everything is a part of God and God suffuses everything. Energies (such as light) from the planets circulate and control the system of the world in the same way that blood and the other humors do the human body.

Whatever process the Emerald Tablet literally describes, it must be a chemical reaction that takes place in the natural world; but it is not described in mechanistic terms. Rather, from line 4, "The Sun is its father, the moon its mother," and, from line 5, "the wind hath carried it in its belly, the earth its nourse." These names probably stand for the four elements of Greek philosophy—with the sun equivalent to fire, moon to water, wind to air, and earth to itself—but the reactive process they undergo is described as an act of human procreation. This illustrates another basic principle subscribed to in magic: that the natural world is alive and behaves as a living organism. When it creates something, it will do so in the manner of other living creatures. This kind of anthropomorphism allows the different parts of the natural world to be personified as gods or spirits, with whom one may talk and interact, through prayer and ritual, as with anyone else. At the same time, it logically allows sympathetic reactions between its parts.

The human is a microcosm, a scale model of the universe that is in sympathetic harmony with the larger world outside. The soul is part of heaven, while the body is part of the earth, and they are connected by sympathy just as the parts of the world are, or rather because they are different parts of the same macrocosmic body. Precisely because the human is a little god, he can use magic for creation, as with the ever-elusive alchemical philosopher's stone. But the idea of the stone is only an outward symbol. The return of the soul is what makes it a divine creator: "It ascends from the earth to the heaven and again it descends to the earth and receives the force of things superior and inferior." This completes the Emerald Tablet's theoretical description of the occult. The universe is bound by sympathy into a single body of which the human is a microcosm and a mediator. Because he and he alone can move between the upper and the lower, the divine and the physical, he can become godlike instead of merely physical and so can create and control through the power of magic, as expressed in alchemy, astrology, herbalism, or any other occult science: as in line 9, "By this means ye shall have the glory of the whole world thereby all obscurity shall fly from you." This also relates to the Emerald Tablet's own explanation in line 13 of the mysterious epithet Trismegistus as, "having the three parts of the philosophy of the whole world." Hermes is great in three respects: relating to the divine, relating to the world, and relating to the human link between them.

Audience

Greco-Roman Egypt in many respects resembled a colonized country of the modern world. Its educated priestly class resisted the influence of Greco-Roman culture but also could not help absorbing it, to the degree that its members wrote their own literature in Greek rather than any form of Egyptian. One goal of the Hermetica was to present Greek learning and science as having originally been Egyptian. This was successful insofar as the Hermetica began to circulate outside Egypt in late antiquity, and claims that Egypt was the original source of philosophy were taken seriously. The technical Hermetica, like the Emerald Tablet, were originally written for a small group of educated Egyptian priests working as alchemists (or herbalists or astrologers and so on, according to the various subject matters of the treatises) but later became of interest to intellectuals throughout the Roman and Iranian empires and eventually in the Arab world, after the Islamic conquests of the eighth century.

Alchemists, unlike philosophers but like every other class of specialized worker in antiquity, from glassblowers to physicians, were anxious that their writings remain secrets shared only with other experts in the field. The Emerald Tablet, in particular, was important not only to Arab alchemists and occultists but also to the whole intellectual community of the Muslim world, as it helped establish the genealogy of knowledge it embraced. In medieval and Renaissance Europe, the Emerald Tablet again spread from being a concern only of alchemists to reach the wider intellectual community in the wake of the resurgence of Neoplatonism at the end of the fifteenth century.

Impact

In the Islamic world, the myth of Hermes Trismegistus as an ancient prophet, of which the Emerald Tablet was offered as important evidence, helped legitimize not only alchemy but indeed the whole of Greek philosophy, which could have been attacked and rejected by Muslim scholars as "pagan" and therefore unworthy of concern. By treating Hermes Trismegistus as one of Muhammad's forerunners as a holy prophet, medicine, alchemy, philosophy, astrology, and all the arts he supposedly revealed to humankind could be harmonized with Islam.

Although the Emerald Tablet had been translated into Latin in the middle of the twelfth century, alchemy in western Europe was primarily a practical art. Alchemy again became a philosophical system once the ancient philosophy of Neoplatonism was revived in the late fifteenth century by the Florentine humanist Marsilio Ficino and his circle. In this environment, the Emerald Tablet was used to give alchemy a central place in Renaissance thought, a degree of priority it had lacked during the Middle Ages. Since the metaphysical assumptions of the document were the same as those of Neoplatonism, it permitted alchemy to become a practical tool of philosophical investigation. Humanists interested in the occult sciences, such as Agrippa and the abbot Trithemius, Johannes Heidenberg, could even use the philosophical doctrines presented in the Emerald Tablet to justify the connections they made between philosophy and magic.

Although he began with alchemy, Robert Boyle created the modern scientific practice of chemistry in the seventeenth century by applying the scientific method, as outlined by

---

Questions for Further Study

1. In the modern world, alchemy is regarded as at best a pseudo-science. In the Middle Ages, though, it was regarded as science. Why? What was the appeal of alchemy?

2. In what ways, if any, did alchemy contribute to the development of modern science?

3. The Emerald Tablet is about alchemy. Why is it included here, in a collection of texts having to do with religion? What connection did alchemy have with religious belief?

4. Much ancient writing, especially that having to do with alchemy, mystical beliefs, astrology, and so forth, was secret writing, shared only by initiates, priests, and other members of an "in group." Why do you think this was so? How does this differ from modern writing and publication, particularly in the sciences?

5. Read the entry on Paracelsus and be prepared to discuss how his work was similar to and different from the concepts contained in the Emerald Tablet.

Francis Bacon in his *Novum organum* (New Instrument), to the laboratory work of traditional alchemy. Around the same time, Isaac Newton, perhaps the most important physicist in history, made a quite different use of the Emerald Tablet. Newton was convinced that alchemy, if properly understood, could reveal the most profound spiritual as well as physical truths about the universe, and he spent most of his professional career engaged in alchemical experiments and research. Although he never made the discoveries he sought, his alchemical learning proved important in another way. Following René Descartes, scientists of Newton's age thought that the motion of an object could be influenced only by direct physical contact with another object. They specifically rejected the idea of occult sympathies acting on bodies as a superstitious relic of antiquity. Newton, however, because of his alchemical work—which included making the English translation of the Emerald Tablet used here—believed that such indirect forces could have effects on physical objects. This allowed him to make the imaginative leap to treat gravity as a force that acted between bodies with no physical connection, which he was then able to prove mathematically, resolving virtually all of the main problems facing the physicists of his day.

Precisely because of alchemy's associations with theology and magic, the art fell into disfavor during the Enlightenment, as the eighteenth-century philosophes dismissed all but the most practical aspects of it as superstition. The history of the Emerald Tablet was not quite concluded with the coming of modern science. In the late nineteenth and early twentieth centuries, an occult revival reacted against the Enlightenment and the scientific revolution, seeking to find meaning in the exploration of interior psychological conditions. Expressing its ideas in terms of magical traditions such as alchemy, this reaction gave rise to a host of New Age movements and belief systems. One of the most significant figures in this movement was the Swiss analytical psychologist Carl Jung, who struggled to find expression for his own unconscious mental actions in ancient mythology. The Emerald Tablet became a recurrent image in his dreams that eventually led him to compose his *Septem Sermones ad Mortuos* (*The Seven Sermons to the Dead*), a brief book in which he presents Gnostic and Hermetic doctrines as profound psychological truths, imitating the Emerald Tablet's reconciliation of seemingly paradoxical pairs of opposites.

Further Reading

■ Books

Copenhaver, Brian P., trans. *Hermetica: The Greek Corpus Hermeticum and the Latin Asclepius*. Cambridge, U.K.: Cambridge University Press, 1992.

Dobbs, Betty Jo Teeter. *The Foundations of Newton's Alchemy; or, "The Hunting of the Greene Lyon."* Cambridge, U.K.: Cambridge University Press, 1975.

Dobbs, Betty Jo Teeter. "Newton's Commentary on the Emerald Tablet of Hermes Trismegistus: Its Scientific and Theological Significance." In *Hermeticism and the Renaissance: Intellectual History and the Occult in Early Modern Europe*, ed. Ingrid Merkel and Allen G. Debus. Washington, D.C.: Folger Shakespeare Library, 1988.

Dobbs, Betty Jo Teeter. *The Janus Faces of Genius: The Role of Alchemy in Newton's Thought*. Cambridge, U.K.: Cambridge University Press, 1991.

Forbes, R. J. *Studies in Ancient Technology*. 2nd ed. Leiden, Germany: E. J. Brill, 1964.

Fowden, Garth. *The Egyptian Hermes: A Historical Approach to the Late Pagan Mind*. Cambridge, U.K.: Cambridge University Press, 1986.

Holmyard, E. J. *Alchemy*. Harmondsworth, U.K.: Penguin, 1957.

Jung, Carl Gustav. "Septem Sermones ad Mortuos." In *Memories, Dreams, Reflections*, ed. Aniela Jaffé and trans. Richard Winston and Clara Winston. New York: Pantheon Books, 1973.

Newman, William R. "From Alchemy to 'Chymistry.'" *The Cambridge History of Science*, Vol. 3: *Early Modern Science*, ed. Katharine Park and Lorraine Daston. Cambridge, U.K.: Cambridge University Press, 2006.

Newton, Isaac. "The Commentary on the Emerald Tablet." In *The Alchemy Reader: From Hermes Trismegistus to Isaac Newton*, ed. Stanton J. Linden. Cambridge, U.K.: Cambridge University Press, 2003.

Smith, Jonathan Z. *Map Is Not Territory: Studies in the History of Religions*. Leiden, Netherlands: E. J. Brill, 1978.

Van Bladel, Kevin. *The Arabic Hermes: From Pagan Sage to Prophet of Science*. Oxford, U.K.: Oxford University Press, 2009.

Zosimos of Panopolis. *On the Letter Omega*, ed. and trans. Howard M. Jackson. Missoula, Mont.: Scholars Press, 1978.

■ Journals

Obrist, Barbara. "Views on History in Medieval Alchemical Writings." *Ambix* 56, no. 3 (November 2009): 226–238.

■ Web Sites

"Corpus Hermeticum." Alchemist Web site.
http://www.levity.com/alchemy/corpherm.html

—Bradley A. Skeen

Emerald Tablet

1. 'Tis true without lying, certain most true.
2. That which is below is like that which is above and that which is above is like that which is below to do the miracles of one only thing.
3. And as all things have been arose from one by the mediation of one: so all things have their birth from this one thing by adaptation.
4. The Sun is its father, the moon its mother,
5. the wind hath carried it in its belly, the earth its nourse.
6. The father of all perfection in the whole world is here.
7. Its force or power is entire if it be converted into earth. Separate thou the earth from the fire, the subtle from the gross sweetly with great indoustry.
8. It ascends from the earth to the heaven and again it descends to the earth and receives the force of things superior and inferior.
9. By this means ye shall have the glory of the whole world thereby all obscurity shall fly from you.
10. Its force is above all force. [F]or it vanquishes every subtle thing and penetrates every solid thing.
11. So was the world created.
12. From this are and do come admirable adaptations whereof the means (Or process) is here in this.
13. Hence I am called Hermes Trismegist, having the three parts of the philosophy of the whole world.
14. That which I have said of the operation of the Sun is accomplished and ended.

Glossary

Hermes Trismegist or Hermes Trismegistus, a mythical philosopher and teacher of the magical system known as Hermiticism

Parchment page of a ninth-century Qur'an
(Kufic calligraphy from a Koran manuscript (parchment), Islamic School, [9th century] / Private Collection / The Bridgeman Art Library International)

Qur'an

ca. 610 –632

"Praise be unto him, who transported his servant by night, from the sacred temple of Mecca to the farther temple of Jerusalem."

Overview

The birth of Islam, the youngest of the three Abrahamic religions, began in 610 with the revelation of the Qur'an to Muhammad in a cave outside the Arabian city of Mecca. Driven by dissatisfaction with the religious life of his family and fellow citizens, the merchant Muhammad had retreated into the wilderness to build up his spiritual inner life through mystical contemplation. After years of this discipline, observed periodically for days or weeks at a time, something he had never expected happened: The archangel Gabriel began to dictate to him a scripture written by God, the new revelation of the Qur'an. The example of Muhammad's faith in his new revelation inspired his family and friends, who persuaded him, against his own reluctance, to begin to preach on the street corners of Mecca. His opposition to the traditional polytheist religion practiced in common by the whole city caused him and his followers to be exiled from Mecca, an event called the Hijra. But through skillful diplomacy and conquest, Muhammad became the ruler of the entire Arabian Peninsula by the time of his death in 632, and almost the whole population of his realm converted to Islam, the new faith in the Qur'an—the book that was gradually revealed to Muhammad throughout this lifetime.

The Qur'an is at the center of a large scriptural literature, including the Hadith, which governs interpretation of the Qur'an; Sharia law, which puts the principles of the Qur'an into formal jurisprudence; and the Sita (part of the Sunna), traditions handed down about the life of Muhammad, including his biography, the Sira. The Qur'an is not organized like the scriptures of Judaism or Christianity, the other Abrahamic faiths, but is grouped into books, or suras, by more or less loosely related subjects. Taken together, the Qur'anic literature calls for the worship of the same god as the older Abrahamic faiths (*Allah* being simply the Arabic cognate of the Hebrew name for god, El) and presents itself as a third revelation that corrects and completes the Hebrew Bible and New Testament. Muhammad, as the author of the Qur'an and founder of Islam, is one of history's religious virtuosi, or founders of successful new religious movements, like Zoroaster, the prophet of the first monotheistic region in the mid-second millennium BCE; Paul, whose missionary work spread his version of Christianity throughout the Roman Empire; and Mani, a Gnostic prophet of the mid-third century CE who claimed to be the Holy Spirit and the fulfillment of the prophecies of Zoroaster, Jesus, and the Buddha.

Context

Late antiquity, the time from the general crisis that almost saw the collapse of the Roman Empire in the middle of the third century until the completion of the Arab conquests in the century after Muhammad's death, saw a profusion of new literatures based upon the Jewish and Christian scriptures. The Mishnah and Talmudic literature, the system of commentaries on the Hebrew Bible that formed the main project of early rabbinic Judaism, created a new spiritual center for the Jewish world after Jewish national identity was lost in the failure of the Jewish revolt against Rome in 70 CE. At the same time, Christians produced a vast number of new gospels, quite different from the four Gospels of the New Testament, and other spiritual writings in conversation with the canonical texts; those gospels and writings are today called Gnostic scriptures. The point in both literatures was to find new meaning in traditional religious texts, so as to make them more useful in a world progressed several centuries from the original compositions; both movements were experiments with tradition. Rabbinic Judaism became a new form of Judaism that has endured into the modern world, while the Gnostics were brutally suppressed in favor of older forms of orthodoxy within the Christian tradition.

The Qur'an was an experiment of the same kind. Muhammad, who was almost certainly illiterate, was yet familiar with Jewish and Christian scripture, most likely from the personal contact with Jews and Christians that he is known to have had throughout his life. Both groups made a point of memorizing and reciting their scriptures. Even when scriptures were read in antiquity, they were almost always read aloud, such that the ancient experience of scripture, including the Qur'an, was primarily aural. Coming from a tradi-

Time Line

ca. 570
- Muhammad is born in Mecca.

ca. 605
- Muhammad marries the wealthy merchant Khadijah, who will become the first convert to Islam.

ca. 610
- Muhammad begins to receive the revelation of the Qur'an.

620
- Muhammad experiences the spiritual journeys called the Isra and Mi'raj.

622
- **July 22** The Hijra calendar is traditionally held to begin on this date.

622
- **September 24** Muhammad and his followers, expelled from Mecca, undertake the Hijra.

632
- **June 8** Muhammad dies.

644–656
- Caliph 'Uthman, under whom the Qur'an is traditionally codified, reigns.

ca. 800
- As suggested by modern scholars, by this time the Qur'an has assumed its final formation.

---

tional polytheist background, Muhammad was profoundly affected by the monotheist scriptures and embraced the idea of a single god enthusiastically. He proceeded to develop the Qur'an through his own contemplative spiritual practice as a mystical revelation. He then transmitted the text in oral form to his followers in bits and pieces throughout his life. In the Qur'an, Muhammad retells many of the same myths as the Jewish and Christian scriptures, of Creation, of the Flood, of divine judgment. He acknowledges the divine inspiration of the Jewish prophets in the Hebrew Bible as well as of Jesus. But Muhammad believed that Jews and Christians had failed in implementing monotheism correctly. He was well aware of the frequent urban rioting and political revolts occasioned by disagreements among Christian sects over the nature of the Trinity that plagued the cities of Roman Syria in the early seventh century. To his way of thinking, monotheism ought to bring unity, not discord. In the Qur'an, Muhammad purposefully set out to perfect and complete the Jewish and Christian revelations, which he considered partial, or at least preliminary, and defective.

One Christian attitude toward Judaism, reflected in Lactantius's *Divine Institutes* (ca. 310) and elsewhere, is that Christianity is the true religion of humanity given by God in the Garden of Eden, which was practiced by the Old Testament patriarchs but which, over time and through sin, was gradually corrupted into Judaism. In this view, Jesus came to restore what had been lost. The Qur'an adopts the same interpretation of history but sees Christianity as a second failed experiment. The Qur'an is a self-conscious reaction to the Hebrew Bible and New Testament and an attempt to rewrite them in a simpler, universalist manner. Muhammad succeeded to the extent that his new religion of Islam, as based on the Qur'an, became dominant nearly throughout the Roman and Sassanian empires. Between 632 and 715, Islam expanded by military conquest from its center on the Arabian Peninsula to absorb half the territories of the Roman Empire from Syria to Spain and the whole of Sassanian Iran, from Iraq into Inner Asia. Proselytization, especially within the expanding Mongol Empire, and further conquests extended Islam to much of the populations of Africa and India and throughout Indonesia. Today, a quarter of the world's population is Muslim.

After his death, Muhammad's companions began to make a serious effort to write down the Qur'an, which they had learned from him by memory. Muhammad's successor 'Uthman ibn 'Affan, who reigned as the third caliph, or supreme ruler of the Islamic world, from 644 to 656, ordered one of Muhammad's original scribes to make an official recension of the Qur'an based on the recollections and memoirs of the Prophet's other companions, and he then destroyed all other evidence outside of that recension. While Islamic tradition holds that the modern Qur'an is the same as 'Uthman's text, Western scholars suspect that the text must have continued evolving, especially in dialogue with other faiths, for as long as two centuries more, the period from which the earliest manuscripts of the Qur'an survive.

About the Author

Tradition ascribes the Qur'an to the Prophet, Muhammad. There is certainly no reason to question that Muhammad was the driving force behind the Qur'an and Islam, but the problem lies with the traditional nature of the sources. The Sira, or tradition about the life of Muhammad, was composed over a long period and at least partly as a commentary on the Qur'an, so agreement between the two texts is at best circular evidence for their historicity. Another problem is that the only surviving texts come from the end of the tradition in the ninth century, with no texts from earlier stages of development. Nor is there even a single source that lies outside this tradition. Modern scholars remain deeply divided on the reliability of the Sira tradition.

The received tradition of the Sira reports that Muhammad was born in the Arabian city of Mecca, where the Kaaba was already an important pilgrimage site in the polytheist religion of Arabia, about the year 570. After ris-

Muhammad receives the first revelation from Gabriel.
(Ms Or 20 f.45v Muhammad receives his first revelation through the angel Gabriel / Edinburgh University Library, Scotland / With kind permission of the University of Edinburgh / The Bridgeman Art Library International)

ing up from the disadvantageous position of an orphan to become a successful merchant through family connections and his own initiative, Muhammad began, when he was about forty years old, to pursue a contemplative practice in a cave in the desert. Soon the archangel Gabriel began dictating God's word directly to Muhammad. The prophet could not write—*Qur'an* means "recitation," as opposed to *scripture*, which means "writing"—but told these revelations to a small circle of companions as he continued to receive the text in bits and pieces up until his death in 632. Muhammad records having a mystical experience of a different character in 620, which Islamic tradition venerates as his night journey, in which he supposedly flew to Jerusalem and to heaven. Muhammad himself remembered the entire revelation and frequently repeated it, even dictating portions of it to scribes later in life.

The religion of the Qur'an was monotheist and claimed the shrine of the Kaaba for itself. Resistance to this idea by the non-Muslim Meccans forced Muhammad and his followers to flee in 622, an event called the Hijra, used as the beginning of the Islamic calendar. As an outsider, Muhammad was chosen by the people of Medina, an oasis near Mecca, to settle disputes between the contentious communities that lived there, including polytheist Arabs and Jews. Soon, most of the Arab population of Medina converted to Islam. After years of warfare with Mecca, Muhammad finally gained control of that city, too, and by 632, through a combination of conquest and skillful diplomacy, Muhammad had consolidated control of the entire Arabian Peninsula. He died on June 8, 632.

Explanation and Analysis of the Document

The Qur'an is divided into 114 chapters called *suras*. They are arranged, like the Mishnah (the rabbinic commen-

Essential Quotes

"They are infidels, who say, Verily God is Christ the son of Mary."

"O true believers, take not the Jews or Christians for your friends; they are friends the one to the other; but whoso among you taketh them for his friends, he is surely one of them."

"They are certainly infidels, who say, God is the third of three: for there is no God besides one God; and if they refrain not from what they say, a painful torment shall surely be inflicted on such of them as are unbelievers."

"God shall say, O Jesus son of Mary, remember my favour towards thee, and towards thy mother; . . . when I taught thee the scripture, and wisdom, and the law and the gospel; and when thou didst create of clay as it were the figure of a bird, by my permission, and didst breathe thereon, and it became a bird by my permission."

"Praise be unto him, who transported his servant by night, from the sacred temple of Mecca to the farther temple of Jerusalem, the circuit of which we have blessed, that we might show him some of our signs; for God is he who heareth, and seeth."

"And they say, We will by no means believe on thee, until thou . . . ascend by a ladder to heaven: neither will we believe thy ascending thither alone, until thou cause a book to descend unto us, bearing witness of thee, which we may read."

---

tary on the Hebrew Bible), in order from the longest to the shortest rather than by topic, or chronologically, or some other scheme. Each sura is further divided into verses. The two selections reprinted here deal with important points: sura V with the relationship of Islam to the other "religions of the book," Christianity and Judaism, and sura XVII with Muhammad's night journey and the mystical nature and authority of the Qur'an itself.

♦ Sura V

The fifth sura is titled "The Table" because it begins with a discussion of dietary restrictions. Besides limiting the diet of Muslims on pilgrimage to Mecca, Muhammad reinforces the prohibition of pork from the Hebrew Bible and plainly forbids Muslims from eating meat that comes from animals sacrificed to polytheist gods, giving a clear verdict on an issue that is the occasion of the apostle Paul's most famously indecisive comments in the Bible (I Corinthians 10:14–32). The text continues with a number of purity regulations, none of which, characteristically of Islam, are absolute but are to be practiced as circumstances allow.

Muhammad soon turns to the most important topic of this sura, Jews and Christians and their relationship to Islam. The Qur'an states that the original covenant of god with the twelve tribes of Israel was a true and efficacious religion, but the Jews allowed their tradition to become corrupt: "They dislocate the words of the Pentateuch"—that is, the first five books of the Hebrew Bible—"from their places and have forgotten part of what they were admonished" (5:13). The Qur'an repeats many of the anti-Semitic commonplaces that circulated among the Christian communities of the Roman Empire, such as that the Jews are cursed by God and that they are deceptive in their business practices. Nevertheless, Muhammad commands Muslims to be merciful to Jews.

Muhammad also considers the Christian scriptures to be corrupt. It is to the errors in the scriptures that he attributes the terrible strife that was raging in the Roman Empire about the nature of the Trinity. Muhammad tells the Christians that he will renew God's original message to them: "Now is our apostle come unto you, to make manifest unto you many things which ye concealed in the scriptures; and to pass over many things" (5:15). The Qur'an's judgment is that Jesus is in no way divine, that he is not the son of God but was only a human prophet like Moses or Muhammad himself. The text proceeds in the form of a debate, in which possible objections that might be made by Jews or Christians are answered directly by God. Briefly, the Jews are instructed to follow Islam. God revealed the Torah, which in its uncorrupted original form was identical to the Gospels, while both of them, again in their original form, were identical to the Qur'an, which is now being revealed a third time to make up for the corruption of the earlier texts (5:46).

There follows a long exposition in which Muslims are forbidden to associate with Jews and Christians. This could serve two functions, depending upon the time when the text was written. If the text indeed goes as far back as the time of Muhammad's residence in Medina, then it is an injunction to new Muslim converts from the Jewish community there to cut themselves off from family and a social network that might influence them to return to their traditional religion. Since, in his view, Muhammad offered Jews a perfected version of their own religion, he expected that they would be anxious to convert. But the Jews of Medina did not agree and proved highly resistant to Islam. Muhammad and his companions eventually defeated the three Jewish tribes of Medina in battle, exiling two of them and exterminating the third, killing all the adult males and enslaving the women and children. These seem like barbarous acts of cruelty today but were not exceptional in the ancient world. Indeed, the source for this tradition is the Sira itself, showing that Muslims did not find this action troubling. Alternatively, if the text of the Qur'an here reflects a later period of Islamic history, as some Western scholars suspect, the injunction against Muslims fraternizing with Jews could have been a means of discouraging insincere conversions that might have been made, for example, to avoid paying the special tax levied on non-Muslims (*dhimmis*) and other legal inequalities in the Islamic empire. Jews and Christians would have been less likely to make such a show of conversion if it meant cutting oneself off from family and community.

Muhammad turns his attention to Christianity and makes clear that any kind of Trinitarian formulation is to be considered blasphemous because God is a single, unique being. Jesus, therefore, cannot have been God. Muhammad attributes Trinitarian belief as well to scriptural corruption. The Qur'an asserts that Christians will be more easily converted than Jews. This, again, could reflect either Muhammad's own expectations, since he did not try to convert large numbers of Christians during his own lifetime and so did not meet as much resistance from them, or the actual experience of the first few centuries of Islamic rule, since it seems that some Christians, at least, in the newly conquered territories accepted Islam as a way out of sectarian strife.

After a brief return to the dietary rules for those on pilgrimage and a consideration of how Muslims ought to make wills, the text returns to Christianity. The document again emphasizes that Jesus was a human agent of God and that his miracles were performed by God on his behalf, not by his own power. The list of miracles includes Jesus's precocious speaking in the temple as a child (Luke 2:42–52), the healing of the man born blind (John 9:1–7), and raising the dead (John 11:41–44; Matthew 27:51–53). The miracle of Jesus's bringing a clay figurine of a bird to life, which comes from the folklore that circulated about Jesus in late antique Syria, is less familiar. It is recorded in the apocryphal Infancy Gospel of Thomas (2:1–5) as something Jesus did in Nazareth when he was a few years old. In fact, it is reported there that the young Jesus made a dozen such bird statues on the Sabbath. When someone complained that he was breaking the Sabbath prohibition against work, Jesus simply brought the figurines to life and ordered them to fly away. The story was common enough that it is also cited in the *Toldoth Jesu*, an anti-Christian Jewish "Life of Jesus" written not much later than the Qur'an.

The talk of a meal descending from heaven merely means that the celebration of the Eucharist is to be considered a divinely inspired ritual. Muhammad emphasizes again that neither Jesus nor his mother, Mary, are to be considered divine beings. The intercessory status given to Mary in early Christian theology—making her a mediator between the faithful and God—is often viewed by outsiders (including Protestants as well as Muslims) as equating Mary, too, with God. Jesus's own testimony before God at the last judgment is quoted against these propositions.

This sura mentions Sabians (5:69), who along with Jews, Christians, and Zoroastrians were considered people of the book, monotheists who were to be tolerated, albeit as second-class citizens, within Islamic society. What group Muhammad originally meant by the Sabians is far from clear. Perhaps it was the Mandaeans, a Gnostic group who venerate John the Baptist as their prophet and who lived until recently in Iraq (though, in the face of persecution through the modern-era Iraqi wars, almost the whole Mandaean population has been expelled, mostly to refugee camps in Syria but also to a growing émigré community in Sweden). However, the term *Sabian* was famously taken up by the polytheists of the city of Harran in Syria, who claimed to be Sabians to spare themselves forced conversion during the Arab conquests of the seventh century. As polytheists, they were subject to be exterminated if they did not convert. But once they were accepted as Sabians, several Harranian families moved to the newly founded city of Baghdad and became instrumental in translating Greek literature into

Arabic, laying the foundation for the Islamic philosophical achievements of the Middle Ages.

♦ Sura XVII

Sura XVII begins with the Qur'an's only description of one of the most important events from Muhammad's life, his so-called night journey. The tradition about the composition of the Qur'an already suggests that Muhammad had been practicing some form of mystical exercise, going alone periodically to a cave in the desert. Muhammad began to perceive the Qur'an itself as a result of this mysticism, as God revealed it to him through the angel Gabriel. Mysticism is a religious phenomenon, but it is also a psychological phenomenon and in that sense is quite well understood. The mystic—and as many great mystics have been women as men—turns one's senses away from the world, cutting oneself off from all the usual stimulation of sight and sound. A mystic may, like Muhammad, go away from other human beings, reduce the intake of food (which eventually quiets not only the desires associated with consumption and elimination but even sexual desires), and seek out a quiet, unchanging environment.

The mystic's attention can be focused away from the world through concentrating on activities that become automatic, like chanting or praying memorized prayers. Once the channels of perception are cleared, the mind begins to look inward, to perceive interiorities that are completely outside the realm of everyday experience and which cannot be easily committed to language. The new experiences can range from new perspectives on life as the mystic has experienced it to startling visions that make it seem as if an entirely new universe is being perceived. The same kind of experiences have been had by mystics from every part of the world and from every religion, whether polytheist, Jewish, Christian, or Buddhist. The same experience is also available to atheists. Increasingly, the changes in brain function that are associated with mystical experience can be directly observed with new imaging techniques such as PET scans. The role of religious tradition in mysticism is to give a framework for the mystic's understanding of his experience.

There can be little question that Muhammad gained the insight necessary to produce the Qur'an through a mystical practice. The first verse of sura XVII describes a mystical voyage that Muhammad experienced, a perception that he was traveling over a large part of the earth and to heaven and back in a single night. A later section (17:90–93) refers back to this experience and suggests that merely having the experience was not enough: Muhammad realized that he also needed to produce a book of scriptures so as to put Islam on the same footing as Judaism and Christianity.

The initial description of Muhammad's night journey is somewhat vague. God moves him from the Kaaba in Mecca to the furthest temple, which to Muhammad's audience could have suggested at least two places: either the Temple Mount in Jerusalem, where the Jewish temple built by Herod the Great (73–4 BCE) had once stood, or heaven. (The English Orientalist scholar George Sale's 1734 translation, used here, follows Islamic tradition and plainly calls this the Jerusalem temple, but there is no specific place name given in the Arabic text of the Qur'an.) Muhammad's later doubts about the experience make clear that he then went to heaven by ascending a ladder. It is not surprising that Muhammad expressed his experience in traditional religious terms. In ancient Semitic culture, heaven was considered a solid dome over a flat earth, so ascending to heaven merely involved a physical change in location. A ladder stretching from earth to heaven is perhaps the most typical Semitic expression of the connection between earth and heaven. The cult of stylites, Syrian holy men, both Christian and polytheist, who lived either for a few weeks each year or, in some cases, for their entire lives on top of pillars (in the manner of modern flagpole sitters), expressed the Semitic belief that merely gaining height is moving closer to God. The same idea is found in the Hebrew Bible, such as in Jacob's ladder, by which the angels go between heaven and earth (Genesis 28:12, 31:13, 45).

Islamic tradition did not hesitate to expand on the brief and obscure references to Muhammad's night journey in the Qur'an. According to the Sira, Muhammad first flew to Jerusalem and the Temple Mount, a journey called the Isra, on the magical steed Buraq. Once on the sacred mountain, Muhammad prayed with Abraham, Moses, and Jesus (stressing the continuity of the monotheistic faiths) and finally ascended to heaven (the Mi'raj) where he was given a tour by the angel Gabriel. The tour of heaven is a common motif of Semitic religious literature and can be found in many texts, including the apocryphal book of Enoch, the New Testament book of Revelation, and the Talmudic story of the four who entered Paradise. The religious interpretation of Muhammad's night journey tied it to monotheist tradition but also demanded a new revelation of scripture that became the Qur'an. As Islam grew, the new religious framework tied the mystical experience and the scripture ever more firmly back to their source in tradition.

Audience

According to the tradition that makes the Qur'an the revelation of God through the archangel Gabriel, Muhammad himself would count as the original audience, albeit, according to the same tradition, a reluctant one. Within the historical realm, Muhammad began to recite the Qur'an first to his wife, Khadijah. She had recognized the talent of the orphaned Muhammad early and had used her capital to set him up as a merchant before marrying him. She received the first recitation of the Qur'an seriously and encouraged Muhammad to go ahead with public preaching of his revelation. This brought Muhammad a small following in Mecca. But most of the city's population rejected him as a blasphemer against traditional religion, and he was eventually forced to leave the city with only a small band of the first Muslims.

As Muhammad became a more important figure politically and militarily, the number of those receptive to the Qur'an grew, until by the time of his death, when he had become ruler of the whole Arabian Peninsula, he had also extended the *ummah*, or community of Muslims, over the same area. Almost incredibly, given the meagerness of Muhammad's beginnings in life and as a preacher, he intended from very early on for the new religion of Islam to spread across the entire world and become the sole religion of the human race. In particular, he meant to encounter and convert the entire communities of followers of the three monotheistic religions that then flourished to the north of Arabia: not only Judaism and Christianity but the Zoroastrianism of the Iranian Empire as well. The Qur'an's claim to universalism for Islam descends from the same claims made for other late-antique religions, such as Manichaeanism and the Christianity that became the state religion of the Roman Empire. Within fifty years of Muhammad's death, Muslims had already conquered half of the Byzantine Empire and virtually all of Iran, bringing the Qur'an with them. The modern-day audience for the Qur'an is the entire *ummah* of one and a half billion Muslims throughout the world, stretching from Morocco to Indonesia and from Mali to Inner Asia, and including large Islamic immigrant communities in Europe and North America.

Impact

In the century after Muhammad's death, the Islamic caliphate established the only true world empire of antiquity, linking the whole of the Mediterranean with the Plateau of Iran to a center in the Middle East that was, for the first time since the original Persian Empire of Cyrus the Great (ca. 585–529 BCE), master of all its surrounding hinterlands and not constantly subject to threat of invasion from one direction or another. Islam and the Qur'an were central to this achievement, since the new monotheistic faith provided the empire with unity in a way that Christianity never did in the Roman Empire. Christianity was continuously a source of conflict in the Roman world, first in its contest with the traditional Roman religion and then in the subsequent states of near civil war between rival sects. One explanation the Muslims found for their own success was that God was punishing the Romans for wasting their strength in sectarian rivalry. The Qur'an is undoubtedly the foundation of the imperial Arab achievement. Accordingly, the Qur'an is also indirectly responsible for the exceptional achievements in science, philosophy, and poetry that characterized the medieval Arab world.

After the European Renaissance—which contact with the culturally superior Islamic civilization did much to spark—the Muslim world, its center then held by the Ottoman Empire, began to fall behind the West in the creation of new wealth, cultural initiative, and science and technology, and the empire was eventually colonized by the West, beginning in the sixteenth century. Though it is not entirely clear why Islamic civilization fell behind the West through this epoch, the influential scholar Ignác Goldziher has suggested that part of the answer lies in the Qur'an itself. In the face of geopolitical setbacks, beginning with the Mongol sack of Baghdad in 1258 and continuing through the loss of competitiveness with the West throughout the Renaissance and Enlightenment eras, the Islamic response was often to reinforce traditional identity as defined by the Qur'an rather than to adapt to change. In particular, the status of the Qur'an as the final authority in every area of life is at odds with acceptance of Western paradigms, such as of science and capitalism, that might have led to more practical geopolitical success. As the Islamic world was put under more and more stress, the reliance on religious authority made progress ever more difficult.

Today, many forces in Islam, such as the widespread Wahhabite movement based in Saudi Arabia, which is driving the radicalization of political discourse in Islamic states throughout the world, and the Islamic Republic of Iran, wish to use the Qur'an as a shield against what they view as Western intrusion into Islamic culture and even into traditional village culture, which forces like the Taliban, in Afghanistan, cannot separate from Islam. Muhammad's views expressed in the Qur'an envision Islam as an imperial power reigning over the whole world and followers of the "religions of the book" as subject peoples. Any liberal spirit in Islam calling for pluralism and religious liberty cannot rest easily with the Qur'anic view, any more than liberalism can rest easily on supports derived from Judeo-Christian scripture. The virtues of pluralism and freedom originated in the eighteenth-century Enlightenment and have had to make their way in the Western and Islamic worlds without much impulse from any deep spring of tolerance welling up from scripture. An insoluble difficulty in the conflict between Israel and the Arab world concerns the Temple Mount in Jerusalem, which Israel claims as in insuperable part of its national heritage but which many Muslims consider as part of their own heritage because of their belief that the al-Aqsa Mosque (the second-holiest site in Islam, after Mecca) marks the spot from which Muhammad ascended to heaven on his night journey.

Further Reading

■ Books

Asad, Muhammad. *The Road to Mecca*. New York: Simon and Schuster, 1954.

Berg, Herbert, ed. *Method and Theory in the Study of Islamic Origins*. Leiden, Netherlands: Brill, 2003.

Brockopp, Jonathan E., ed. *The Cambridge Companion to Muhammad*. Cambridge, U.K.: Cambridge University Press, 2010.

Donner, Fred M. *The Early Islamic Conquests*. Princeton, N.J.: Princeton University Press, 1981.

Fowden, Garth. *Empire to Commonwealth: Consequences of Monotheism in Late Antiquity*. Princeton, N.J.: Princeton University Press, 1993.

Goldziher, Ignác. *Mohammed and Islam,* trans. Kate Chambers Seelye. New Haven, Conn.: Yale University Press, 1917.

Ibn Hisham, 'Abd al-Malik. *The Life of Muhammad: A Translation of Ishaq's Sirat Rasul Allah.* Karachi, Pakistan: Oxford University Press, 1997.

Kennedy, Hugh. "Islam." In *Late Antiquity: A Guide to the Postclassical World,* ed. G. W. Bowersock, et al. Cambridge, Mass.: Belknap Press, 1999.

"Koran." In *Encyclopaedia Judaica,* vol. 10. Jerusalem, Israel: Keter, 1971.

Kroll, Jerome, and Bernard Bachrach. *The Mystic Mind: The Psychology of Medieval Mystics and Ascetics.* New York: Routledge, 2005.

Lactantius. *The Divine Institutes,* trans. William Fletcher. In *The Ante-Nicene Fathers,* vol. 7, ed. Alexander Roberts and James Donaldson. Buffalo, N.Y.: Christian Literature Company, 1886.

McAuliffe, Jane Dammen, ed. *Encyclopaedia of the Qur'an.* 6 vols. Leiden, Netherlands: Brill, 2001–2006.

McAuliffe, Jane Dammen, ed. *The Cambridge Companion to the Qur'an.* Cambridge, U.K.: Cambridge University Press, 2006.

Parrinder, Geoffrey. *Jesus in the Qur'an.* New York: Barnes & Noble, 1965.

Peter, F. E. *Muhammad and the Origins of Islam.* Albany: State University of New York Press, 1994.

Sale, George, trans. *The Koran: Commonly Called the Alkoran of Mohammed.* New York: American Book Exchange, 1880.

Wansbrough, John. *The Sectarian Milieu: Content and Composition of Islamic Salvation History.* Oxford, U.K.: Oxford University Press, 1978.

■ **Web Sites**

"Islam and Islamic Studies Resources." University of Georgia Web site.
    http://www.uga.edu/islam/

Shakir, M. H., trans. "The Koran." University of Michigan Digital Library Production Service Web site.
    http://quod.lib.umich.edu/k/koran/

—Bradley A. Skeen

Questions for Further Study

1. Describe the political circumstances in and around Mecca and Medina in which Muhammad created the Qur'an. How might these circumstances have influenced the shape of the Qur'an?

2. Over the course of history, many religions have risen and fallen. Why do you think Islam, as defined by the Qur'an, took root in the region and survived until today to claim well over a billion adherents? What fundamental appeal did Islam and the Qur'an have at the time?

3. Explain why an English-language translation of the Qur'an is likely to have a title such as *The Holy Qur'an* rather than just *Qur'an.*

4. Islam is described as an "Abrahamic" religion. What does this term mean? Who was Abraham? What relationship does Islam and the Qur'an bear to Judaism and Christianity as reflected in the Judeo-Christian Bible? What is meant by "religions of the book"?

5. Throughout religious history there has been a notable strain of mysticism and mystical revelations—not surprising, since religion by its very nature deals with matters unseen and largely unprovable. How would you compare the mystical revelations of Muhammad, as reflected in sura XVII, with the mystical revelations in the Gospel of Thomas or in the Persian Bayan?

Qur'an

Sura V

♦ **Entitled, The Table; Revealed at Medina. In the Name of the Most Merciful God.**

1. O True believers, perform your contracts. Ye are allowed to eat the brute cattle, other than what ye are commanded to abstain from; except the game which ye are allowed at other times, but not while ye are on pilgrimage to Mecca; God ordaineth that which he pleaseth. 2. O true believers, violate not the holy rites of God, nor the sacred month, nor the offering, nor the ornaments hung thereon, nor those who are travelling to the holy house, seeking favour from their Lord, and to please him. But when ye shall have finished your pilgrimage, then hunt. And let not the malice of some, in that they hindered you from entering the sacred temple, provoke you to transgress, by taking revenge on them in the sacred months. Assist one another according to justice and piety, but assist not one another in injustice and malice: therefore fear God; for God is severe in punishing. Ye are forbidden to eat that which dieth of itself, and blood, and swine's flesh, and that on which the name of any besides God hath been invocated; and that which hath been strangled, or killed by a blow, or by a fall, or by the horns of another beast, and that which hath been eaten by a wild beast, except what ye shall kill yourselves; and that which hath been sacrificed unto idols. It is likewise unlawful for you to make division by casting lots with arrows. This is an impiety. On this day, woe be unto those who have apostatized from their religion; therefore fear not them, but fear me. This day have I perfected your religion for you, and have completed my mercy upon you; and I have chosen for you Islam, to be your religion. But whosoever shall be driven by necessity through hunger to eat of what we have forbidden, not designing to sin, surely God will be indulgent and merciful unto him. They will ask thee what is allowed them as lawful to eat? Answer, Such things as are good are allowed you; and what ye shall teach animals of prey to catch, training them up for hunting after the manner of dogs, and teaching them according to the skill which God hath taught you. Eat therefore of that which they shall catch for you; and commemorate the name of God thereon; and fear God, for God is swift in taking an account. This day are ye allowed to eat such things as are good, and the food of those to whom the scriptures were given is also allowed as lawful unto you; and your food is allowed as lawful unto them. And ye are also allowed to marry free women that are believers, and also free women of those who have received the scriptures before you, when ye shall have assigned them their dower; living chastely with them, neither committing fornication, nor taking them for concubines. Whoever shall renounce the faith, his work shall be vain, and in the next life he shall be of those who perish. O true believers, when ye prepare yourselves to pray, wash your faces, and your hands unto the elbows; and rub your heads, and your feet unto the ankles; and if ye be polluted by having lain with a woman, wash yourselves all over. But if ye be sick, or on a journey, or any of you cometh from the privy, or if ye have touched women, and ye find no water, take fine clean sand, and rub your faces and your hands therewith; God would not put a difficulty upon you; but he desireth to purify you, and to complete his favour upon you, that ye may give thanks. Remember the favour of God towards you, and his covenant which he hath made with you, when ye said, We have heard, and will obey. Therefore fear God, for God knoweth the innermost parts of the breasts of men. O true believers, observe justice when ye appear as witnesses before God, and let not hatred towards any induce you to do wrong; but act justly; this will approach nearer unto piety; and fear God, for God is fully acquainted with what ye do. God hath promised unto those who believe, and do that which is right, that they shall receive pardon and a great reward. But they who believe not, and accuse our signs of falsehood, they shall be the companions of hell. O true believers, remember God's favour towards you, when certain men designed to stretch forth their hands against you, but he restrained their hands from hurting you; therefore fear God, and in God let the faithful trust. God formerly accepted the covenant of the children of Israel, and we appointed out of them twelve leaders: and God said, Verily, I am with you: if ye observe prayer, and give alms, and believe in my apostles, and assist them, and lend unto God on good usury, I will surely expiate your evil deeds from you, and I will lead you into gardens, wherein rivers flow: but he among you

who disbelieveth after this, erreth from the straight path. Wherefore because they have broken their covenant, we have cursed them, and hardened their hearts; they dislocate the words of the Pentateuch from their places, and have forgotten part of what they were admonished; and thou wilt not cease to discover deceitful practices among them, except a few of them. But forgive them, and pardon them, for God loveth the beneficent. And from those who say, We are Christians, we have received their covenant; but they have forgotten part of what they were admonished; wherefore we have raised up enmity and hatred among them, till the day of resurrection; and God will then surely declare unto them what they have been doing. O ye who have received the scriptures, now is our apostle come unto you, to make manifest unto you many things which ye concealed in the scriptures; and to pass over many things. Now is light and a perspicuous book of revelations come unto you from God. Thereby will God direct him who shall follow his good pleasure, into the paths of peace; and shall lead them out of darkness into light, by his will, and shall direct them in the right way. They are infidels, who say, Verily God is Christ the son of Mary. Say unto them, And who could obtain anything from God to the contrary, if he pleased to destroy Christ the son of Mary, and his mother, and all those who are on the earth? For unto God belongeth the kingdom of heaven and earth, and whatsoever is contained between them; he createth what he pleaseth, and God is almighty. The Jews and the Christians say. We are the children of God, and his beloved. Answer, Why therefore doth he punish you for your sins? Nay, but ye are men, of those whom he hath created. He forgiveth whom he pleaseth, and punisheth whom he pleaseth; and unto God belongeth the kingdom of heaven and earth, and of what is contained between them both; and unto him shall all things return. O ye who have received the scriptures, now is our apostle come unto you, declaring unto you the true religion, during the cessation of apostles, lest ye should say, There came unto us no bearer of good tidings, nor any warner: but now is a bearer of good tidings and a warner come unto you; and God is almighty. Call to mind when Moses said unto his people, O my people, remember the favour of God towards you, since he hath appointed prophets among you, and constituted you kings, and bestowed on you what he hath given to no other nation in the world. O my people, enter the holy land, which God hath decreed you, and turn not your backs, lest ye be subverted and perish. They answered, O Moses, verily there are a gigantic people in the land; and we will by no means enter it, until they depart thence; but if they depart thence, then will we enter therein. And two men of those who feared God, unto whom God had been gracious, said, Enter ye upon them suddenly by the gate of the city; and when ye shall have entered the same, ye shall surely be victorious: therefore trust in God, if ye are true believers. They replied, O Moses, we will never enter the land, while they remain therein: go therefore thou, and thy Lord, and fight; for we will sit here. Moses said. 'O Lord, surely I am not master of any except myself, and my brother; therefore make a distinction between us and the ungodly people.' God answered, Verily the land shall be forbidden them forty years; during which time they shall wander like men astonished in the earth; therefore be not thou solicitous for the ungodly people. Relate also unto them the history of the two sons of Adam, with truth. When they offered their offering, and it was accepted from one of them, and was not accepted from the other, Cain said to his brother, I will certainly kill thee. Abel answered, God only accepteth the offering of the pious; if thou stretchest forth thy hand against me, to slay me, I will not stretch forth my hand against thee, to slay thee; for I fear God the Lord of all creatures. I choose that thou shouldest bear my iniquity and thine own iniquity; and that thou become a companion of hell fire; for that is the reward of the unjust. But his soul suffered him to slay his brother, and he slew him; wherefore he became of the number of those who perish. And God sent a raven, which scratched the earth, to show him how he should hide the shame of his brother, and he said. Woe is me! am I unable to be like this raven, that I may hide my brother's shame? and he became one of those who repent. Wherefore we commanded the children of Israel, that he who slayeth a soul, without having slain a soul, or committed wickedness in the earth, shall be as if he had slain all mankind: but he who saveth a soul alive, shall be as if he had saved the lives of all mankind. Our apostles formerly came unto them with evident miracles; then were many of them, after this, transgressors on the earth. But the recompense of those who fight against God and his apostles, and study to act corruptly in the earth, shall be that they shall be slain, or crucified, or have their hands and their feet cut off on the opposite sides, or be banished the land. This shall be their disgrace in this world, and in the next world they shall suffer a grievous punishment; except those who shall repent, before ye prevail against them; for know that God is inclined to forgive, and merciful. O

Document Text

true believers, fear God, and earnestly desire a near conjunction with him, and fight for his religion, that ye may be happy. Moreover they who believe not, although they had whatever is in the earth, and. as much more withal, that they might therewith redeem themselves from punishment on the day of resurrection; it shall not be accepted from them, but they shall suffer a painful punishment.

They shall desire to go forth from the fire, but they shall not go forth from it, and their punishment shall be permanent. If a man or a woman steal, cut off their hands, in retribution for that which they have committed; this is an exemplary punishment appointed by God; and God is mighty and wise. But whoever shall repent after his iniquity, and amend, verily God will be turned unto him, for God is inclined to forgive and merciful. Dost thou not know that the kingdom of heaven and earth is God's? He punisheth whom he pleaseth, and he pardoneth whom he pleaseth; for God is almighty. O apostle, let not them grieve thee, who hasten to infidelity, either of those who say, We believe, with their mouths, but whose hearts believe not; or of the Jews, who hearken to a lie, and hearken to other people; who come not unto thee: they pervert the words of the law from their true places, and say, If this be brought unto you, receive it; but if it be not brought unto you, beware of receiving aught else; and in behalf of him whom God shall resolve to reduce, thou shalt not prevail with God at all. They whose hearts God shall not please to cleanse, shall suffer shame in this world, and a grievous punishment in the next: who hearken to a lie, and eat that which is forbidden. But if they come unto thee for judgment, either judge between them, or leave them; and if thou leave them, they shall not hurt thee at all. But if thou undertake to judge, judge between them with equity: for God loveth those who observe justice. And how will they submit to thy decision, since they have the law, containing the judgment of God? Then will they turn their backs, after this; but those are not true believers. We have surely sent down the law, containing direction, and light: thereby did the prophets, who professed true religion, judge these who Judaized; and the doctors and priests also judged by the book of God, which had been committed to their custody; and they were witnesses thereof. Therefore fear not men, but fear me: neither sell my signs for a small price. And whoso judgeth not according to what God hath revealed, they are infidels. We have therein commanded them, that they should give life for life, and eye for eye, and nose for nose, and ear for ear, and tooth for tooth; and that wounds should also be punished by retaliation: but whoever should remit it as alms, it should be accepted as an atonement for him. And whoso judgeth not according to what God hath revealed, they are unjust. We also caused Jesus the son of Mary to follow the footsteps of the prophets, confirming the law which was sent down before him: and we gave him the gospel, containing direction and light; confirming also the law which was given before it, and a direction and admonition unto those who fear God: that they who have received the gospel might judge according to what God hath revealed therein: and whoso judgeth not according to what God hath revealed, they are transgressors. We have also sent down unto thee the book of the Koran with truth, confirming that scripture which was revealed before it; and preserving the same safe from corruption. Judge therefore between them according to that which God hath revealed; and follow not their desires, by swerving from the truth which hath come unto thee. Unto every of you have we given a law, and an open path; and if God had pleased, he had surely made you one people; but he hath thought fit to give you different laws, that he might try you in that which he hath given you respectively. Therefore strive to excel each other in good works: unto God shall ye all return, and then will he declare unto you that concerning which ye have disagreed. Wherefore do thou. O prophet, judge between them according to that which God hath revealed, and follow not their desires; but beware of them, lest they cause thee to err from part of those precepts which God hath sent down unto thee; and if they turn back, know that God is pleased to punish them for some of their crimes; for a great number of men are transgressors. Do they therefore desire the judgment of the time of ignorance? but who is better than God, to judge between people who reason aright? O true believers, take not the Jews or Christians for your friends; they are friends the one to the other; but whoso among you taketh them for his friends, he is surely one of them: verily God directeth not unjust people. Thou shalt see those in whose hearts there is an infirmity, to hasten unto them, saying, We fear lest some adversity befall us; but it is easy for God to give victory, or a command from him, that they may repent of that which they concealed in their minds. And they who believe will say, Are these the men who have sworn by God, with a most firm oath, that they surely held with you? their works are become vain, and they are of those who perish. O true believers, whoever of you apostatizeth from his religion, God will certainly bring other people to supply his place, whom he will love, and who will love him; who shall be humble towards the believers, but severe to the unbelievers; they shall fight for the religion of God, and shall not fear the obloquy of the detractor. This is the bounty of God, he bestoweth it on whom he pleaseth: God is extensive and wise. Verily your protector is God, and his apostle, and those who believe, who observe the stated times of prayer, and give alms, and who bow down to worship. And whose taketh God, and his apostle, and the believers for his friends, they are the party of God, and they shall be victorious. O true believers, take not such of those to whom the scriptures were delivered before you, or of the infidels, for your friends, who make a laughing-stock and a jest of your religion; but fear God, if ye be true believers; nor those who, when ye call to prayer, make a laughing-stock and a jest of it; this they do because they are people who do not understand. Say, O ye who have received the scriptures, do ye reject us for any other reason than because we believe in God, and that revelation which hath been sent down unto us, and that which was formerly sent down, and for that the greater part of you are transgressors? Say, Shall I denounce unto you a worse thing than this, as to the reward which ye are to expect with God? He whom God hath cursed, and with whom he hath been angry, having changed some of them into apes and swine, and who worship Taghut, they are in the worse condition, and err more widely from the straightness of the path. When they came unto you, they said, We believe: yet they entered into your company with infidelity, and went forth from you with the same; but God well knew what they concealed. Thou shalt see many of them hastening unto inquity and malice, and to eat things forbidden; and woe unto them for what they have done. Unless their doctors and priests forbid them uttering wickedness, and eating things forbidden; woe unto them for what they shall have committed. The Jews say, the hand of God is tied up. Their hands shall be tied up, and they shall be cursed for that which they have said. Nay, his hands are both stretched forth; he bestoweth as he pleaseth: that which hath been sent down unto thee from thy Lord, shall increase the transgression and infidelity of many of them; and we have put enmity and hatred between them, until the day of resurrection. So often as they shall kindle a fire for war, God shall extinguish it; and they shall set their minds to act corruptly in the earth, but God loveth not the corrupt doers. Moreover, if they who have received the scriptures believe, and fear God, we will surely expiate their sins from them, and we will lead them into gardens of pleasure; and if they observe the law, and the gospel, and the other scriptures which have been sent down unto them from their Lord, they shall surely eat of good things both from above them and from under their feet. Among them there are people who act uprightly; but how evil is that which many of them do work! O apostle, publish the whole of that which hath been sent down unto thee from thy Lord: for if thou do not, thou dost not in effect publish any part thereof; and God will defend thee against wicked men; for God directeth not the unbelieving people. Say, O ye who have received the scriptures, ye are not grounded on anything, until ye observe the law and the gospel, and that which hath been sent down unto you from your Lord. That which hath been sent down unto thee from thy Lord shall surely increase the transgression and infidelity of many of them: but be not thou solicitous for the unbelieving people. Verily they who believe, and those who Judaize, and the Sabians, and the Christians, whoever of them believeth in God and the last day, and doth that which is right, there shall come no fear on them, neither shall they be grieved. We formerly accepted the covenant of the children of Israel, and sent apostles unto them. So often as an apostle came unto them with that which their souls desired not, they accused some of them of imposture, and some of them they killed: and they imagined that there should be no punishment for those crimes, and they became blind and deaf. Then was God turned unto them; afterwards many of them again became blind and deaf; but God saw what they did. They are surely infidels, who say, Verily God is Christ the son of Mary; since Christ said, O children of Israel, serve God, my Lord and your Lord; whoever shall give a companion unto God, God shall exclude him from paradise, and his habitation shall be hell fire; and the ungodly shall have none to help them. They are certainly infidels, who say, God is the third of three: for there is no God besides one God; and if they refrain not from what they say, a painful torment shall surely be inflicted on such of them as are unbelievers. Will they not therefore be turned unto God, and ask pardon of him? since God is gracious and merciful. Christ the son of Mary is no more than an apostle; other apostles have preceded him; and his mother was a woman of veracity: they both ate food. Behold, how we declare unto them the signs of God's unity; and then behold, how they turn aside from the truth. Say unto them, Will ye worship, besides God, that which can cause you neither harm nor profit? God is he who heareth and seeth. Say, O ye who have received the scriptures, exceed not the just bounds in your religion, by speaking beside the truth: neither follow the desires of people who have heretofore erred, and who have seduced many, and have gone astray from the strait path. Those among the children of Israel who believed not, were cursed by the tongue of David, and of Jesus the son of Mary. This befell them because they were rebellious and transgressed: they forbade not one another the wickedness which they committed; and woe unto them for what they committed. Thou shalt see many of them take for their friends those who believe not. Woe unto them for what their souls have sent before them, for that God is incensed against them, and they shall remain in torment for ever. But, if they had believed in God and the prophet, and that which hath been revealed unto him, they had not taken them for their friends: but many of them are evil-doers: Thou shalt surely find the most violent of all men in enmity against the true believers, to be the Jews and the idolaters: and thou shalt surely find those among them to be the most inclinable to entertain friendship for the true believers, who say, We are Christians. This cometh to pass, because there are priests and monks among them; and because they are not elated with pride. And when they hear that which hath been sent down to the apostle read unto them, thou shalt see their eyes overflow with tears, because of the truth which they perceive therein, saying, O Lord, we believe: write us down therefore with those who bear witness to the truth: and what should hinder us from believing in God, and the truth which hath come unto us, and from earnestly desiring that our Lord would introduce us into paradise with the righteous people. Therefore hath God rewarded them, for what they have said, with gardens through which rivers flow; they shall continue therein for ever; and this is the reward of the righteous. But they who believe not, and accuse our signs of falsehood, they shall be the companions of hell. O true believers, forbid not the good things which God hath allowed you; but transgress not, for God loveth not the transgressors. And eat of what God hath given you for food that which is lawful and good: and fear God, in whom ye believe. God will not punish you for an inconsiderate word in your oaths; but he will punish you for what ye solemnly swear with deliberation. And the expiation of such an oath shall be the feeding of ten poor men with such moderate food as ye feed your own families withal; or to clothe them; or to free the neck of a true believer from captivity; but he who shall not find wherewith to perform one of these three things, shall fast three days. This is the expiation of your oaths, when ye swear inadvertently. Therefore keep your oaths. Thus God declareth unto you his signs, that ye may give thanks. O true believers, surely wine, and lots, and images, and divining arrows, are an abomination of the work of Satan; therefore avoid them, that ye may prosper. Satan seeketh to sow dissension and hatred among you, by means of wine and lots, and to divert you from remembering God, and from prayer; will ye not therefore abstain from them? Obey God, and obey the apostle, and take heed to yourselves; but if ye turn back, know that the duty of our apostle is only to preach publicly. In those who believe and do good works, it is no sin that they have tasted wine or gaming before they were forbidden; if they fear God, and believe, and do good works, and shall for the future fear God, and believe, and shall persevere to fear him, and to do good; for God loveth those who do good. O true believers, God will surely prove you in offering you plenty of game, which ye may take with your hands or your lances, that God may know who feareth him in secret, but whoever transgresseth after this, shall suffer a grievous punishment. O true believers, kill no game while ye are on pilgrimage; whosoever among you shall kill any designedly, shall restore the like of what ye shall have killed, in domestic animals, according to the determination of two just persons among you, to be brought as an offering to the Caaba; or in atonement thereof shall feed the poor; or instead thereof shall fast, that he may taste the heinousness of his deed. God hath forgiven what is past, but whoever returneth to transgress, God will take vengeance on him; for God is mighty and able to avenge. It is lawful for you to fish in the sea, and to eat what ye shall catch, as a provision for you and for those who travel; but it is unlawful for you to hunt by laud, while ye are performing the rites of pilgrimage; therefore fear God, before whom ye shall be assembled at the last day. God hath appointed the Caaba, the holy house, an establishment for mankind; and hath ordained the sacred month, and the offering, and the ornaments hung thereon. This hath he done that ye might know that God knoweth whatsoever is in heaven and on earth, and that God is omniscient. Know that God is severe in punishing, and that God is also ready to forgive and merciful. The duty of our apostle is to preach only; and God knoweth that which ye discover, and that which ye conceal. Say, evil and good shall not be equally esteemed of, though the abundance of evil pleaseth thee; therefore fear God, O ye of understanding, that ye may be happy. O true believers, inquire not concerning things which, if they be de-

Document Text

clared unto you, may give you pain; but if ye ask concerning them when the Koran is sent down, they will be declared unto you: God pardoneth you as to these matters; for God is ready to forgive and gracious. People who have been before you formerly inquired concerning them; and afterwards disbelieved therein. God hath not ordained anything concerning Bahira, nor Saiba, nor Wasila, nor Hami; but the unbelievers have invented a lie against God: and the greater part of them do not understand. And when it was said unto them, Come unto that which God hath revealed, and to the apostle; they answered, That religion which we found our fathers to follow is sufficient for us. What though their fathers knew nothing, and were not rightly directed? O true believers, take care of your souls. He who erreth shall not hurt you, while ye are rightly directed: unto God shall ye all return, and be will tell you that which ye have done. O true believers, let witnesses be taken between you, when death approaches any of you, at the time of making the testament; let there be two witnesses, just men, from among you; or two others of a different tribe or faith from yourselves, if ye be journeying in the earth, and the accident of death befall you. Ye shall shut them both up, after the afternoon prayer, and they shall swear by God, if ye doubt them, and they shall say, We will not sell our evidence for a bribe, although the person concerned be one who is related to us, neither will we conceal the testimony of God, for then should we certainly be of the number of the wicked. But if it appear that both have been guilty of iniquity, two others shall stand up in their place, of those who have convicted them of falsehood, the two nearest in blood, and they shall swear by God, saying, Verily our testimony is more true than the testimony of these two, neither have we prevaricated; for then should we become of the number of the unjust. This will be easier, that men may give testimony according to the plain intention thereof, or fear lest a different oath be given, after their oath. Therefore fear God, and hearken; for God directeth not the unjust people. On a certain day shall God assemble the apostles, and shall say unto them, What answer was returned you, when ye preached unto the people to whom ye were sent? They shall answer, We have no knowledge but thou art the knower of secrets. When God shall say, O Jesus son of Mary, remember my favour towards thee, and towards thy mother; when I strengthened thee with the holy spirit, that thou shouldest speak unto men in the cradle, and when thou wast grown up; and when I taught thee the scripture, and wisdom, and the law and the gospel; and when thou didst create of clay as it were the figure of a bird, by my permission, and didst breathe thereon, and it became a bird by my permission; and thou didst heal one blind from his birth and the leper, by my permission; and when thou didst bring forth the dead from their graves, by my permission; and when I withheld the children of Israel from killing thee, when thou hadst come unto them with evident miracles, and such of them as believed not, said, This is nothing but manifest sorcery. And when I commanded the apostles of Jesus, saying, Believe in me and in my messenger; they answered, We do believe; and do thou bear witness that we are resigned unto thee. Remember when the apostles said, O Jesus, son of Mary, is thy Lord able to cause a table to descend unto us from heaven? He answered, Fear God, if ye be true believers. They said, We desire to eat thereof, and that our hearts may rest at ease, and that we may know that thou hast told us the truth, and that we may be witnesses thereof. Jesus, the son of Mary, said, O God our Lord, cause a table to descend unto us from heaven, that the day of its descent may become a festival day unto us, unto the first of us, and unto the last of us, and a sign from

Glossary

apostatizeth	that is, apostatizes, or abandons one's belief
Bahira, Saiba, Wasila, Hami	animals associated with idol worship
Caaba	also Ka'aba or Kaaba; a black, stone, cube-shaped building in Mecca that is the most sacred Muslim pilgrim shrine, believed to have been given by Gabriel to Abraham
Cain . . . Abel	two of the sons of Adam and Eve, noteworthy because Cain murdered Abel
David	the second king of the Israelites and the founder of the royal line from which Christ descended
Koran	a common (and slightly old-fashioned) variant of Qur'an

Document Text

thee; and do thou provide food for us, for thou art the best provider. God said, Verily I will cause it to descend unto you; but whoever among you shall disbelieve hereafter, I will surely punish him with a punishment wherewith I will not punish any other creature. And when God shall say unto Jesus, at the last day, O Jesus, son of Mary, hast thou said unto men, Take me and my mother for two gods beside God? He shall answer, Praise be unto thee! it is not for me to say that which I ought not; if I had said so, thou wouldst surely have known it: thou knowest what is in me, but I know not what is in thee; for thou art the knower of secrets. I have not spoken to them any other than what thou didst command me; namely, Worship God, my Lord and your Lord: and I was a witness of their actions while I stayed among them; but since thou hast taken me to thyself, thou hast been the watcher over them; for thou art witness of all things. If thou punish them, they are surely thy servants; and if thou forgive them, thou art mighty and wise. God will say, This day shall their veracity be of advantage unto those who speak truth; they shall have gardens wherein rivers flow, they shall remain therein for ever: God hath been well pleased in them, and they have been well pleased in him. This shall be great felicity. Unto God belongeth the kingdom of heaven and of earth, and of whatever therein is; and he is almighty. . . .

Sura XVII

♦ **Entitled, The Night-Journey; Revealed at Mecca. In The Name of the Most Merciful God**

Praise be unto him, who transported his servant by night, from the sacred temple of Mecca to the farther temple of Jerusalem, the circuit of which we have blessed, that we might show him some of our signs; for God is he who heareth, and seeth. And we gave unto Moses the book of the law, and appointed the same to be a direction unto the children of Israel, commanding them, saying, Beware that ye take not any other patron besides me. . . . When we bestow favours on man, he retireth and withdraweth himself ungratefully from us: but when evil toucheth him, he despaireth of our mercy. Say, Every one acteth after his own manner: but your Lord best knoweth who is most truly directed in his way. They will ask thee concerning the spirit: answer, The spirit was created at the command of my Lord: but ye have no knowledge given unto you, except a little. If we pleased, we should certainly take away that which we have revealed unto thee; in such case thou couldest not find any to assist thee therein against us, unless through mercy from thy Lord; for his favour towards thee hath been great. Say, Verily if men and genii were purposely assembled, that they might produce a book like this Koran, they could not produce one like unto it, although the one of them assisted the other. And we have variously propounded unto men in this Koran, every kind of figurative argument; but the greater part of men refuse to receive it, merely out of infidelity. And they say, We will by no means believe on thee, until thou cause a spring of water to gush forth for us out of the earth; or thou have a garden of palm-trees and vines, and thou cause rivers to spring forth from the midst thereof in abundance; or thou cause the heaven to fall down upon us, as thou hast given out, in pieces: or thou bring down God and the angels to vouch for thee; or thou have a house of gold; or thou ascend by a ladder to heaven: neither will we believe thy ascending thither alone, until thou cause a book to descend unto us, bearing witness of thee, which we may read. Answer, My Lord be

Glossary

Mecca	the city in modern-day Saudi Arabia where Muhammad was born; Islam's holiest city
Medina	the city in modern-day Saudi Arabia to which Muhammad moved in 622 after he and his followers were expelled from Mecca
Moses	the biblical patriarch who led the Israelites out of bondage in Egypt and delivered to them God's law in the form of the Ten Commandments
Pentateuch	the first five books of the Hebrew Bible, which Jews refer to as the Torah
Sabians	a Middle Eastern religious group entitled to religious toleration by Muslims
sacred month	possibly Muharram, the first month of the Islamic calendar
Taghut	an idol that is worshipped (rather than Allah)

Document Text

praised! Am I other than a man, sent as an apostle? And nothing hindereth men from believing, when a direction is come unto them, except that they say, Hath God sent a man for his apostle? Answer, If the angels had walked on earth as familiar inhabitants thereof, we had surely sent down unto them from heaven an angel for our apostle. Say, God is a sufficient witness between me and you for he knoweth and regardeth his servants. Whom God shall direct he shall be the rightly directed, and whom he shall cause to err thou shalt find none to assist, besides him. And we will gather there together on the day of resurrection, creeping on their faces, blind, and dumb, and deaf: their abode shall be hell, so often as the fire thereof shall be extinguished, we will rekindle a burning flame to torment them. This shall be their reward, because they disbelieve in our signs, and say, When we shall have been reduced to bones and dust, shall we surely be raised new creatures? Do they not perceive that God, who created the heavens and the earth, is able to create other bodies, like their present? And he hath appointed them a limited term, there is no doubt thereof: but the ungodly reject the truth, merely out of unbelief.

Tenzin Gyatso, the fourteenth Dalai Lama (The Dalai Lama [photo], / Dinodia / The Bridgeman Art Library International)

Shantideva: *Bodhicaryavatara*

ca. 700 –763

"Where is there hide to cover the whole world? The wide world can be covered with hide enough for a pair of shoes."

Overview

The *Bodhicaryavatara*, or "Introduction to the Path of the Bodhisattva," was composed by the Indian monk and poet Shantideva sometime in the eighth century. It is both a practical guide outlining meditation practice and proper monastic conduct and a philosophic treatise arguing for the importance and validity of the Mahayana Buddhist perspective. Two particularly important themes associated with Mahayana Buddhism are emptiness and the path of the bodhisattva. Mahayana Buddhist philosophy explicates a particularly detailed understanding of the concept of emptiness and promotes the path of the bodhisattva as key to the attainment of perfect wisdom.

The way in which Mahayana Buddhist philosophy explains emptiness and promotes the path of the bodhisattva marks a shift in Buddhist philosophy from the early Indian tradition associated with the Pali canon. The Pali canon is a set of Buddhist scriptures that were established as authentic by an early Indian school of Buddhism called Theravada around 25 BCE. Buddhists who follow the Theravadin tradition consider the texts of the Pali canon to be the oldest and most authentic. This position is challenged by Mahayanists.

The *Bodhicaryavatara* quickly became established as a basic text for teaching monastic conduct in Mahayana settings first in India and later across Asia. In the tenth century, Tibetan Buddhism was experiencing a revival, while Buddhism was declining in India. Many renowned teachers thus fled northern India for Tibet, bringing Mahayana texts and ideas with them. The *Bodhicaryavatara* became particularly revered as a teaching manual in the growing Tibetan monastic communities that were founded beginning in the tenth century and later.

Context

Early Indian Buddhism traces its origins to the Buddha's first teaching of the Four Noble Truths: that there is suffering, that the cause of suffering is attachment, that suffering can be overcome, and that there is a path to ending suffering that can be taught and learned. The Buddha, whose given name was Siddhartha Gautama and who lived around the turn of the fifth century BCE, explained that clinging to a sense of self is fundamental to the problem of attachment. Letting go of one's sense of self is not easy. Most people find some concept of individual personhood reassuring and dismiss the Buddhist concept of "no-self" as nihilistic without really understanding it. The challenge is to realize that adhering to the concept of no-self does not entail a lack of responsibility or concern for people at an individual level. Rather, no-self means that everyone and everything are interdependent.

Ideas related to the emerging Mahayana movement began to appear around 100 BCE. Mahayana Buddhism promotes selfless dedication to others, as associated with the ideal of the bodhisattva, as a way to put into action the realization that "no-self" entails connectedness to others. The Madhyamaka, or "Middle Way" philosophical system, was founded around the turn of the third century CE by Nagarjuna. Madhyamaka, with which Shantideva is associated, is one of several important philosophical schools of the Mahayana Buddhist tradition.

According to some legends, Shantideva composed the *Bodhicaryavatara* while he was a student at the ancient Buddhist university Nalanda early in the eighth century. According to this account, his teachers were not impressed with his diligence and were looking for a way to embarrass him into either working harder or leaving the university altogether. Their plan was to have him present a talk for the monastic community, with the expectation that he would make a complete fool of himself. Instead, he presented the ten very eloquent chapters of the *Bodhicaryavatara*, presenting the path of the bodhisattva.

All ten of the chapters are written in a poetic style that reflects considerable education. Shantideva's scholarly knowledge is revealed in his many references to Buddhist texts and ideas. In light of these two attributes alone, the story that he was a bumbling student seems unlikely. Be that as it may, the story itself supports an important motif that runs through the *Bodhicaryavatara*. The work of a bodhisattva is difficult and must be done for selfless reasons independent of worldly recognition. Aspiring bodhisattvas must work diligently and remain unconcerned about the judgment of others.

Time Line

CA. 563 –483 BCE	■ Siddhartha Gautama, the Buddha, is thought to have lived.
CA. 150 –250 CE	■ Nagarjuna lives and develops his Madhyamaka philosophy.
CA. 685	■ Shantideva is thought to have been born.
CA. 700 –763	■ Shantideva composes the *Bodhicaryavatara*.
CA. 763	■ Shantideva is believed to have died.
CA. 1000	■ The Indian logician Prajnakaramati composes an important commentary on Shantideva's *Bodhicaryavatara*.
1042	■ The Indian monk Atisha Dipankara Shrijnana arrives in the Tibetan kingdom of Guge.
CA. 1200 –1300	■ Buddhist texts originally written in the ancient Indian scholarly language of Sanskrit are lost in a series of invasions originating from Persia (now Iran).
1350 –1364	■ The Tibetan scholar Butön Rinchen Drup includes ten commentaries on the *Bodhicaryavatara* in his compilation of texts to be included in the Tenjur division of the Tibetan canon.
1907	■ Relying on Prajnakaramati's eleventh-century commentary, the renowned Buddhist scholar Louis de La Vallée Poussin publishes a French translation of the *Bodhicaryavatara*.
1994	■ Tenzin Gyatso, the fourteenth Dalai Lama, publishes *A Flash of Lightning in the Dark of Night: A Guide to the Bodhisattva's Way of Life*.

About the Author

Shantideva is regarded by modern scholars as one of the most influential intellectuals of his day. Despite this admiration, very little is known about his life—though many intriguing stories are told about him. These stories were composed several centuries after he lived and are filled with colorful but common Buddhist tropes, such as renunciation of royal birth and delayed recognition of hidden brilliance.

Scholars believe that Shantideva lived sometime between 685 and 763. While concrete biographical details are few, it is evident that Shantideva was a well-educated monk associated with the ancient Buddhist monastery of Nalanda and that he was particularly devoted to Manjushri, bodhisattva of wisdom. Shantideva wrote two influential books. In addition to the *Bodhicaryavatara*, he also composed the *Siksasamuccaya*, or "Compendium of Training," an anthology of choice selections drawn from more than one hundred Buddhist scriptures. He compiled these selections as scriptural support for his outline of proper conduct laid out in the ten chapters of his *Bodhicaryavatara*.

Explanation and Analysis of the Document

The *Bodhicaryavatara* is a manual for individuals who strive to live their lives in accordance with the Mahayana ideal of the bodhisattva. According to the Mahayana Buddhist perspective, the only way to attain the complete enlightenment of a buddha is by committing oneself to the dedicated service that defines the career of a perfect bodhisattva. The bodhisattva path is modeled after the life of Siddhartha Gautama and his transformation from birth as prince into Shakyamuni Buddha (where *Shakyamuni* means "Sage of the Shakyas," the people of his kingdom). In particular, it reflects the Buddha's dedicated service to others, as exemplified by his willingness to teach others how to reach the same level of enlightenment that he himself attained. The *Bodhicaryavatara* spells out in detail how to conduct one's life by modeling the bodhisattva ideal and describes how this conduct goes hand in hand with a complete understanding of the Buddhist concepts of emptiness and no-self.

The ideal of the bodhisattva appears in earlier Indian Buddhism, but the Mahayana Buddhist philosophical system developed this concept considerably. A bodhisattva is an enlightened being who is on his or her way to becoming a fully enlightened buddha but willingly puts off this moment in order to help others. Bodhisattvas are contrasted with the ideal of the arhat, which is associated with earlier Indian Buddhism. Arhats are followers of the Buddha who have realized a high level of understanding but are not yet enlightened Buddhas. From the Mahayana perspective, an exemplary arhat is primarily concerned with achieving personal liberation. By contrast, the example of the bodhisattva promoted by Mahayanists requires service to others as the only way to achieve the perspective of a fully enlightened Buddha. In the Mahayana view, the potential level of enlightenment that a bodhisattva can attain is much higher than the level of enlightenment available to an arhat.

Bodhisattvas gradually attain higher and higher levels as they become adept at the Six Perfections, or *paramitas*. These six virtuous qualities are generosity, proper conduct, patience, effort, mediation, and wisdom. The process of realizing each of the six perfections determines the structure of the *Bodhicaryavatara*. In the fifth chapter, "The Guarding of Awareness," which is presented here, Shantideva discusses the first two perfections: generosity and proper conduct. Chapters 6–9 focus on each of the remaining four perfections. The subtitles are not present in the original text but have been added for the sake of discussion.

♦ **Verses 1–8: The Importance of a Well-Trained Mind**

Before someone can start down the path to becoming a bodhisattva, the thought of wanting to become a bodhisattva must first occur to such a person. Put another way, becoming a bodhisattva begins in the mind. It is only after strengthening inner resolve to become a bodhisattva that a person can proceed with the training and discipline of the six perfections associated with becoming a full bodhisattva. Appropriately, before discussing the perfections of generosity and proper conduct that are the focus of this chapter, Shantideva begins by emphasizing the importance of learning to control one's own mind. As individuals become adept at each of the six perfections, they learn to take increasing control over their minds.

By describing the untrained mind as like a powerful elephant, Shantideva draws on a trope that is used frequently in Buddhist materials that describe the process of learning to meditate as similar to training a powerful, wild elephant. By alluding to the particularly destructive character of rutting elephants, Shantideva calls attention to the dangerous influence of sexual desire. There are two other gendered references in this set of verses. Verse 4 refers to "ogresses," and verse 8 mentions seductive "sirens." The point here is that particularly evil female beings populate the realms of hell—yet another reason to do everything possible to avoid rebirth in such a horrible place. Examples such as these that focus on the dangerous nature of women reflect both the social conditions of eighth-century India and Shantideva's intended audience: a monastic community of celibate males. Because this sort of reference is problematic to modern readers, some translators use less gender-specific terms in their English renditions of these verses as a way to promote the understanding of Shantideva's message among Western audiences.

According to Buddhist cosmology, there are three worlds: heaven, hell, and the world we live in on the earth. The precise number of hells varies according to different descriptions, but the most common system details eight cold and eight hot hells. Avici, or "no way out," is the lowest of the hot hells. Tortures in the hot hells include unrelenting punishments such as walking on a pavement of scalding iron.

These introductory verses refer to the Buddha with two epithets: the "Teacher of Reality" and the "Sage." While Buddhist cosmology describes three worlds, these verses

Wheel of Life (Dharmachakra) being turned by the Lord of Death

('Dharmachakra' Wheel of Life being turned by 'Yama' the Lord of Death, Tibetan, 1780-1850, Tibetan School / © National Museums of Scotland / The Bridgeman Art Library International)

explain that according to the Buddha, all three of these are projections of the mind. Attaining liberation entails completely understanding this fundamental aspect of the world.

♦ **Verses 9–13: The Perfections of Generosity and Conduct**

Shantideva introduces the perfection of generosity in response to a challenging question: If the perfection of generosity makes the universe free of poverty, how is it possible that "Protectors"—buddhas and bodhisattvas—became adept in the perfection of generosity and yet the world appears to be so impoverished? The answer to this question is something of a conundrum in itself. For buddhas and bodhisattvas, the universe is free of poverty, yet at the same time the vast majority of beings in the world experience suffering. Bodhisattvas perfect the expression of generosity by willingly and tirelessly helping others transform themselves and gradually realize the perfection of the universe.

In verse 11 Santideva defines the perfection of ethical conduct. The problem here concerns the inevitable harm that results from carrying out actions in the world. In other words, it is not possible to do good work without at times making mistakes. The Buddhist solution to this problem is to carry out activities with clear and positive intentions. This does not excuse any accidental or incidental harm,

Essential Quotes

> "Where is there hide to cover the whole world? The wide world can be covered with hide enough for a pair of shoes."

> "For there is nothing from which the sons of the Conqueror cannot learn. There is nothing which is not an act of merit for the good person who conducts himself in this way."

but the resulting bad karma, as well as the ability to recover from mistakes, is eased when one acts with positive intentions and mental attitude. Verse 12 alludes to slaying enemies. The point here is that by cultivating mental discipline and the ability to control one's anger, one is able to conduct oneself most appropriately. In the end, this is the most powerful weapon for overcoming enemies.

Verse 13 sums up the enormous challenge associated with the perfection of generosity and ties the performance of generosity to mental discipline. The generosity required of a bodhisattva is seemingly endless. It begins with each individual who takes a vow to proceed despite the daunting nature of the task. This is the meaning of one of the most quoted verses from this chapter of the *Bodhicaryavatara*, verse 13: "Where is there hide to cover the whole world? The wide world can be covered with hide enough for a pair of shoes alone." In other words, the entire world can be covered by the leather of the individual soles of the shoes of devoted persons as they walk across the earth, one step at a time, spreading enlightenment wherever they go.

♦ Verses 14–33: The Importance of Mental Discipline

The next fifteen verses reiterate the fundamental necessity of individual responsibility and mental outlook. The point is that while it is impossible to control external events, as individuals, if we have properly trained our minds, we can control how we react to external events. Verse 15 describes the potential rewards in store for those who train their minds and follow proper conduct. According to traditional Buddhist understanding, adepts with advanced meditation skills have the capacity to access supernormal dimensions. This is what it means to reach "the state of the Brahma gods." Brahma gods inhabit the highest heavens in the Buddhist cosmological system. The state of nirvana attained with complete enlightenment is beyond even this greatness.

Verse 17 describes the mind as containing the whole sum of dharmas. According to the Pali canon, elements called *dharmas* are the most fundamental principles of existence. Reference to the dharmas here may also refer to the teaching of the Buddha. The point is that understanding and disciplining the mind is of fundamental importance.

No matter how attentively one carries out other noble pursuits such as recitations and austerities, as mentioned in verse 16, practitioners will not succeed without first learning to train their minds. The next several verses elaborate on the negative consequences that will transpire if one does not have a sufficiently disciplined mind. These range from the inability to resist the dangers posed by bad company, such as wanton women, to rebirth in hell.

Verse 23 is a prayer offered by Shantideva to all who are willing to undertake the difficult but worthy practice of learning mind-training skills. After offering this prayer, verses 24 to 28 describe why training the mind is vital to maintaining a healthy body and enjoying a good life. The point is that anyone who is unwilling to train his or her mind is vulnerable to attacks by negative emotions such as anger and greed. When one's mind is controlled by such negative emotions, it is impossible to live a happy life.

With verses 29–33, Shantideva describes specific ways to cultivate mental prowess. He begins by reminding practitioners that mind control is something that must be practiced at all times and not just during formal meditation sessions. Fundamental to proper mental training is developing the habit of noticing when one's introspection is slipping and attending to this lapse immediately. If this is not done, one's mental state will only worsen.

♦ Verses 34–56: The Perfection of Proper Conduct

With verse 34, Shantideva describes proper conduct more directly. Proper conduct is absolutely linked to mental discipline. Verses 35–56 describe situations that are likely to arise as one is learning to meditate and what to do to address these problems. Verse 40 reiterates the analogy found at the beginning of this chapter that relates training the mind to reflect on the teachings of the Buddha, that is, "the Dharma," as requiring strength and concern similar to that needed to contain wild elephants.

Verse 46 refers to the Buddha as the Tathagata. In the scriptures collected in the Pali canon, the Buddha refers to himself using the term *Tathagata*, which can mean either "one who has gone thus" or "one who has come thus." This ambiguity was not lost on Mahayana philosophers. Buddhism explains the attainment of enlightenment in terms of reaching nirvana. Nirvana is explained as a place removed from the cycle of birth and death, called samsara. Whereas earlier Buddhist philosophy pictures the location of nirvana as far removed from the mundane world, Mahayana Buddhist philosophy understands nirvana and samsara as essentially one and the same; the difference between the two is a matter of mental attitude. From this perspective, a buddha is both one who has come and one who has gone. In this verse, practitioners are told that they should act in a manner that becomes a follower of the Buddha. Specifically, this means that whenever such a person notices that he or she is doing something destructive, it is important to recognize the behavior, reject it, and return to proper discipline.

Verses 48–53 list some twenty-seven specific precautions that bodhisattvas in training must bear in mind in order to maintain proper conduct. These must be committed to memory and understood with certainty, such that when each of these afflictions and meaningless distractions arise, practitioners are able to adamantly restrain their minds and remain resolutely "like a block of wood."

In verse 55 Shantideva lists characteristics of practitioners who consistently cultivate their minds with introspection. In verse 56 Shantideva offers advice to those who want to follow the path of the bodhisattva but are confronted with difficult situations. He gives two pieces of advice. Practitioners should not allow what others think to penetrate their personal sense of propriety, and they should keep a distance from others who are acting in immature ways. While keeping a distance, practitioners should nevertheless maintain a compassionate attitude; they should recognize that persons who are acting badly are inherently good but that struggling with afflictions has compromised their behavior.

♦ **Verses 57–67: Emptiness and No-Self**

With verse 57, Shantideva begins to tie together the important Mahayana concepts of the path of the bodhisattva and emptiness. Mahayana Buddhist philosophy explicates a more nuanced understanding of the concept of emptiness than earlier Buddhism. According to Mahayana Buddhist philosophy, even dharmas—which according to the Pali canon are the most fundamental factors of existence—can be broken up and are changing from moment to moment, because they, too, are subject to "the chain of dependent origination"—a system expounded by the Buddha that spells out precisely how everyone and everything is interrelated.

To thoroughly understand emptiness, one must be free of any delusions that there is a self. The Buddhist concept of no-self is not easy for most people to accept. The challenge is to realize that giving up self-attachment must be done out of concern for the well-being of others. Letting go of a sense of self entails relinquishing attachment to one's body. Verse 58 reminds practitioners of the value of birth as a human, a notion implied by the phrase "the best of opportunities." According to Buddhism, birth as a human is even better than birth as a god, because as a human one has the best chance at carrying out good deeds and eventually reaching enlightenment.

Mount Sumeru, also called Mount Meru, is the sacred mountain at the center of Buddhist cosmology that joins heaven and earth.

Beginning with verse 59, Shantideva encourages practitioners to reflect on the concept of no-self graphically. Verses 62–65 describe a mental practice involving wielding the knife of wisdom to meticulously dissect the nature of the body. This imaginatively gruesome task is presented as a way to dislodge any attachment to physicality. It is important to bear in mind that Shantideva is speaking to a monastic audience. Young monks, in particular, might find the challenges of physical desires particularly daunting. Thus, Shantideva is spelling out as graphically as possible the Buddhist concept of no-self.

One way to think about how the concept of no-self works is to focus on a machine that has many parts. Using the example of a car, one may consider what makes a car a car. Is it located in the wheels or the seats or the frame or the engine? The point is that all of these elements together make up the car; taking any of them away diminishes the whole such that it is no longer a car. This same exercise can be applied to a close examination of the human body, and this is what is described in verses 60–65.

The imaginative knife used to take apart the body is none other than the sword of wisdom, which has the capacity to cut through delusions. At the point where it seems Shantideva is encouraging the worst sort of ascetic masochism, the direction of the practice shifts. In verse 66 Shantideva allows that it is normal not to want to harm one's body. The point of deconstructing the body is not to throw the body out but to recognize that having a body is something positive. Having a body—especially a human body—allows one to serve others. This statement connects the Mahayana concepts of emptiness and the path of the bodhisattva. After mentally cutting the body to bits, the idea is to stop and recognize that the exercise is not about giving up. Emptiness is not nihilism. The point is to understand that the fullness of emptiness is the thorough integration of everything in the world. Bodhisattvas serve others because they recognize that in a deep sense they are connected to all others.

♦ **Verses 68–77: Mind over Body**

In Verses 68–69, Shantideva reminds practitioners that an important goal of training the mind is to develop sufficient resolve for the body to be subservient to the mind and not the other way around. In Buddhism, having a body, especially a human body, is precious. The body is anything but something to be disposed of lightly, and it is very important to take advantage of the opportunity to serve others in life. The ultimate goal of following the path of the bodhisattva is transformation into an enlightened buddha and the reward of freedom from the cycle of birth and death. Verses 71–77 describe practical and specific ways to carry out daily activities with a proper mind-set. By conducting themselves with care even as they perform mundane tasks, dedicated practitioners are told that they will grow closer and closer to the ideal of the perfect bodhisattva.

♦ **Verses 78–82: Karma and Proper Conduct**

Verse 78 introduces the Buddhist notion of karma, which means "action as based on the Sanskrit verb "to do or act." According to the principle of karma, the way in which individuals behave with respect to body, speech, and mind has consequences not only in this life but in all later rebirths as well. Thus, proper discipline concerns how practitioners conduct themselves physically in the world (verses 81 and 82) and how and what they speak (verse 79). Verse 80 provides an example of how a properly disciplined person should think. This verse explains that when interacting with another, one should give that person one's complete attention and also one should think to oneself that the generous act of looking at this person with an open heart provides an opportunity to reach enlightenment for oneself.

♦ **Verses 83–90: The Bodhisattva Path and Becoming Adept at the Six Perfections**

Verse 83 restates the goal of the path of the bodhisattva. As outlined earlier, a bodhisattva is an enlightened being who is on his or her way to becoming a fully enlightened buddha but willingly puts off this moment in order to help others. The bodhisattva reaches enlightenment by becoming adept in the six perfections. This process, which takes several lifetimes to accomplish, begins with the perfection of generosity. Verse 84 explains that one may even do "what is proscribed," or actions not ordinarily condoned, if such actions will be beneficial to others.

Verses 85 to 90 provide guidelines for difficult situations that a monk might confront when practicing the perfection of generosity, including what to do when faced with a person who has no interest in the teachings of the Buddha, such as a person who "when healthy, wears a turban on his head" or "whose head is veiled." Given the tensions that arose at times between Buddhists and Muslims, this may be an injunction not to proselytize to Muslim groups. More important, the point is that monks should not try to teach the dharma to anyone who does not first express an interest. Monks are also advised of precautions one should take when teaching women.

♦ **Verses 91–102: Proper Conduct for Monastic Living**

Verses 91–98 list specific rules of conduct that are particularly applicable to monastic living. Verse 98 mentions the Triskandha, or "Sutra of the Three Heaps," which is a list of daily confessions. "The Conqueror" is a term of

Questions for Further Study

1. In Mahayana Buddhist philosophy, what is the concept of "emptiness"? How does this concept differ from the understanding of the word in the West, where "emptiness" applied to a person implies lack of substance or superficiality? What might account for the differing understandings of the word?

2. This document invites comparison with the Noble Eightfold Path, part of the Pali canon and thus part of orthodox Theravada canon. What fundamental differences in religious vision do you see between the two documents? Why was this difference important?

3. The entry notes that the *Bodhicaryavatara* became popular with Tibetan monks in about the tenth century. But at roughly the same time and in the centuries that followed, the Bon faith was gaining a foothold in Tibet, as reflected in the entry gZi-brjid, and Buddhism and Bon historically competed in Tibet, even though Bon can be regarded as a form of Buddhism. Compare this document with gZi-brjid and be prepared to explain how Bon differed from Buddhism in Tibet.

4. Most people are familiar with "the Buddha," and even if they know next to nothing about Buddhism, they will picture in their minds a statue or picture of a seated, slightly rotund figure. But what is *a* buddha, at least according to the *Bodhicaryavatara*? How can a person achieve buddhahood in modern life, outside a monastery?

5. Compare this document with a document such as the Canons and Decrees of the Council of Trent. The canons and decrees were written to enforce religious orthodoxy in Renaissance Europe. The *Bodhicaryavatara* was written to promote a certain kind of religious practice in the Asian monastic community. The content of the two documents is obviously different, but examine them more fundamentally: How do the two documents reflect not just different religious traditions but different intellectual and cultural traditions as well?

respect for the Buddha, and the sons of the Conqueror are bodhisattvas. Mahayana acknowledges more than one buddha; thus, here the reference is to not just one Conqueror but to all the buddhas, or Conquerors.

Verses 99 and 100 provide a generous summation of the embracing wisdom of the *Bodhicaryavatara*. Practitioners striving to model themselves after the ideal of the bodhisattva should recognize that opportunities for practicing good conduct and acting generously are everywhere. Dedicated practitioners can profit from how they comport themselves as they carry out even the most mundane of tasks. Verses 101 and 102 summarize the commitment of bodhisattvas to selfless service to others.

♦ **Verses 103–106: References to Supporting Texts**

At the end of the text, Shantideva refers to several other texts in support of the ideas he has set out regarding the proper conduct of the bodhisattva and the relationship of proper conduct to the realization of enlightenment. By citing these texts, Shantideva displays the depth of his learning while underscoring the importance and validity of his presentation.

Verse 103 mentions the Srisambhava-vimoksa, or the "Biography of Srisambhava," which provides a vivid account of the importance of friendship. It is found in a Mahayana scripture called the Gandavyuha Sutra, or "Array of Flowers Sutra." The Gandavyuha Sutra is part of a still-larger collection of sutras called the Avatamsaka Sutra, which outlines the path of the bodhisattva in the form of a series of stories about a pilgrim by the name of Sudhana and his quest for teachings that will lead him to enlightenment.

Verse 104 mentions the Akasagarbha Sutra, another Mahayana text that spells out eight fundamental errors that must be avoided by anyone desiring to follow the path of the bodhisattva. Verse 105 refers to Shantideva's Siksasamuccaya, or "Compendium of Training," an anthology of choice selections that he drew from over one hundred Buddhist scriptures to support the discussions laid out in his *Bodhicaryavatara*.

Verse 106 cites Nagarjuna's Sutra Samuccaya, or "Compendium of All Sutras," a text that now exists only as a translation into Tibetan. Many Buddhist texts originally written in the ancient Indian scholarly language of Sanskrit were lost between the eleventh and thirteenth centuries. Before this happened, copies of some of these texts were brought to China and Tibet, where they were translated into the local language. When a Buddhist text is found to exist only in non-Indian languages such as Chinese and Tibetan, this may indicate the existence of an older text written in India that was lost. The fact that Shantideva mentions the Sutra Samuccaya suggests that he had access to an original copy of this text written in Sanskrit, which lends further credence to the authenticity of the surviving Tibetan translation. The Sutra Samuccaya is especially important because it quotes from other ancient Buddhist texts, some of which did not survive even in translation. Scholars use this sort of evidence to support arguments for the possibility of a version of the Buddhist canon that may predate the Pali canon. Shantideva's Siksasamuccaya is another rich source for this kind of scholarly sleuthing.

♦ **Verses 107–109: Summary**

In the final verses Shantideva summarizes the main point of the chapter: Monks who wish to follow in the steps of the ideal bodhisattva must begin by training themselves in the first two perfections, generosity and proper conduct. He also underscores that these two perfections are very much related: physical transformation effects moral transformation.

Audience

Shantideva composed the *Bodhicaryavatara* for a male monastic audience. While it argues persuasively for the validity of the Mahayana Buddhist perspective, initially it was read by dedicated Buddhist practitioners who were already convinced of the rightness of the Mahayana perspective. As a source of philosophical reflection and inspiration, the *Bodhicaryavatara* continues to play an important role in Buddhist monastic curricula throughout the world. While the original wording of Shantideva's composition reflects the needs of a celibate, male community, more recently translators have rendered his verses in gender-neutral language, making it more accessible to a wider audience. Thanks to this modernization, today more Buddhists and non-Buddhists outside of monastic environments read Shantideva's text for inspiration.

Impact

Shantideva's *Bodhicaryavatara* was enormously influential in its day. It quickly became established as a fundamental text for the teaching of monastic conduct. Two centuries after Shantideva composed his text, the Indian logician Prajnakaramati wrote an important commentary on it. During the reign of King Chanaka (953–983), Prajnakaramati was one of the most respected teachers at the ancient Indian Buddhist university of Vikramasila.

The *Bodhicaryavatara* played a significant role in the formation of Tibetan Buddhism. In 1042, less than a century after Prajnakaramati wrote his commentary at Vikramasila, Atisha Dipankara Shrijnana (982–1054), a monk from the same university, arrived in the Tibetan kingdom of Guge and established the Kadam school. Atisha brought a copy of the *Bodhicaryavatara* with him to use as a manual for instilling proper monastic conduct in the newly established Tibetan Buddhist monasteries. The Kadam school no longer exists, but the founders of the modern Gelug school trace their lineage back to the earlier school. The lineage of dalai lamas is associated with the Gelugpas.

Today there are four main schools associated with Tibetan Buddhism: the Nyingma, Gelug, Sakya, and Kagyu. The fact that important scholars from each of these four schools have written commentaries on the *Bodhicaryavatara* speaks to the high degree of respect associated with it. In the fourteenth century, the Kagyu scholar Butön Rinchen Drup included the *Bodhicaryavatara*, together with ten commentaries, in the collection of texts he placed in the Tenjur division of the Tibetan canon; he also wrote an extensive commentary on Shantideva's work. The Tenjur and Kanjur are the two divisions of the Tibetan Buddhist canon. The Kanjur comprises texts of various types, all of which are understood as the words of the Buddha. The Tenjur comprises commentaries by Indian Buddhist masters. Addressing a broad range of subjects, the Tenjur includes discussions of treatises on Madhyamaka and other philosophical schools, sutra commentary, stories about the Buddha's previous life as a bodhisattva, and studies concerning language, medicine, crafts, and other topics. Many Tibetan theological ideas as well as liturgies for rituals are drawn on material found in Shantideva's *Bodhicaryavatara* and his *Siksasamuccaya*.

Relying on a copy of Prajnakaramati's eleventh-century commentary on the *Bodhicaryavatara*, the renowned Buddhist scholar Louis de La Vallée Poussin published his *Introduction à la pratique des futurs Bouddhas* (Introduction to the Practice of Future Buddhas) in 1907. This French rendering of the *Bodhicaryavatara* was the first translation to appear in a Western language. More recently, the fourteenth Dalai Lama, Tenzin Gyatso, has written several commentaries on the *Bodhicaryavatara* and frequently quotes verse 55 from the tenth and final chapter: "For as long as space exists, and living beings endure, may I too remain, to dispel the misery of the world."

Further Reading

■ Books

Gyatso, Tenzin. *A Flash of Lightning in the Dark of Night: A Guide to the Bodhisattva's Way of Life*. Boston: Shambhala Publications, 1994.

Leighton, Taigen Dan. *Faces of Compassion: Classic Bodhisattva Archetypes and Their Modern Expression*. Boston: Wisdom Publications, 2003.

Rinpoche, Patrul. *The Words of My Perfect Teacher*, trans. Padmakara Translation Group. 2nd ed. Boston: Shambhala Publications, 1998.

—Cynthia Col

Shantideva: *Bodhicaryavatara*

Chapter 5: The Guarding of Awareness

1 One who wishes to guard his training must scrupulously guard his mind. It is impossible to guard one's training without guarding the wandering mind.

2 Rutting elephants roaming wild do not cause as much devastation in this world as the roaming elephant, the mind, let free, creates in Avici and other hells.

3 But if the roaming elephant, the mind, is tethered on every side by the cord of mindfulness, every danger subsides, complete prosperity ensues.

4 So too tigers, lions, elephants, bears, serpents, and all malign beings, and all the guards of hell, ogresses, demons.

5 All These are bound through the binding of a single mind, and through the taming of a single mind, all are tamed,

6 Since all fears and incomparable sufferings arise from the mind alone. So it was taught by the Teacher of Reality.

7 Who fashioned the weapons in hell so industriously? Who the pavement of scalding iron? And who sired those sirens?

8 Every single thing arises from the evil mind, sang the Sage. So there is nothing dangerous in the three worlds other than the mind.

9 If the perfection of generosity consists in making the universe free from poverty, how can previous Protectors have acquired it, when the world is still poor, even today?

10 The perfection of generosity is said to result from the mental attitude of relinquishing all that one has to all people, together with the fruit of that act. Therefore the perfection is the mental attitude itself.

11 Where can fish and other creatures be taken where I might not kill them? Yet when the mental attitude to cease from worldly acts is achieved, that is agreed to be the perfection of morality.

12 How many wicked people, as unending as the sky, can I kill? But when the mental attitude of anger is slain, slain is every enemy.

13 Where is there hide to cover the whole world? The wide world can be covered with hide enough for a pair of shoes alone.

14 In the same way, since I cannot control external events, I will control my own mind. What concern is it of mine whether other things are controlled?

15 Even with the help of body and speech, no fruit comes from a dull mind that bears comparison with that from a sharp mind on its own, such as reaching the state of the Brahma gods.

16 The Omniscient One declared that all recitation and austerity, even though performed over a long time, is completely useless if the mind is on something else or is dull.

17 Those who have not developed this mind, which is recondite and contains the whole sum of dharmas, wander the compass in vain trying to attain happiness and destroy suffering.

18 Therefore I should manage and guard my mind well. If I let go of the vow to guard my mind, what will become of my many other vows?

19 In the same way that someone in the midst of a rough crowd guards a wound with great care, so in the midst of bad company should one always guard the wound that is the mind.

20 Fearing slight pain from a wound, I guard the wound with great care. Why not the wound that is the mind, in fear of the blows from the crushing mountains of hell?

21 The resolute aspirant who maintains this attitude, even when moving in bad company, even amongst young and wanton women, is not broken.

22 Let my possessions freely perish, my honour, my body and life, and let other good things perish, but never the mind.

23 I make this salutation with my hands to those who wish to guard their mind. With all your effort, guard both mindfulness and awareness.

24 Just as a man weak with illness is not fit for any work, so a mind distracted from these two is not fit for any work.

25 What is heard, reflected upon, or cultivated in meditation, like water in a leaky jar, does not stay in the memory of a mind which lacks awareness.

26 Many, though learned, possessing faith, and though absorbed in effort, are befouled by offences due to the fault of lacking awareness.

27 Though they have amassed meritorious deeds, they end up in an evil realm, plundered by the

27 ...thief, lack of awareness, who comes after the theft of mindfulness.

28 This band of robbers, the defilements, seeks out a point of access. When it has found one, it plunders and destroys life in a good realm.

29 Therefore mindfulness should never be taken from the door to the mind, and, if it does go, it should be reinstated, remembering the torment of hell.

30 Mindfulness comes easily to those fortunate people who practise wholeheartedly, through the instruction of their preceptor, because they live with their teacher, and out of fear.

31 The Buddhas and Bodhisattvas have unobstructed vision in all directions. Every single thing is before them. Before them I stand.

32 Meditating thus, one should remain possessed of shame, respect, and fear. One should recollect the Buddhas in this way at every moment.

33 Awareness comes and, once come, does not go again, if mindfulness remains at the door to the mind in order to act as guard.

34 At first then, I should continually generate such a state of mind as this: I should act at all times as if lacking senses, like a block of wood.

35 One should never cast the eyes to and fro for no purpose. The gaze should be bent low as if continually absorbed in meditation.

36 However, one might occasionally look to the horizon in order to rest the eyes, and if one notices someone within one's field of vision, one should look up to greet them.

37 In order to spot danger on the road and so forth, one may look to the four quarters for a moment. Standing at ease, one may look to the distance, looking behind only after turning right round.

38 One should go ahead or turn back only after looking forward or behind. Likewise, in all situations one should proceed only after ascertaining what is to be done.

39 Having once initiated an action with the intention of keeping one's body in a particular position, thereafter one should from time to time observe how the body is positioned.

40 In this way the rutting elephant, the mind, should be watched with all one's effort, so that, bound to the great post of reflection on the Dharma, it does not break loose.

41 One should so observe the mind, thinking "Where is mine wandering to?," as never to abandon the responsibility of concentration, even for a moment.

42 If one is not able to do so, in connection with some danger or elation, then one should act at will. For it is taught that the code of moral conduct may be overlooked at a time of giving.

43 One should think of nothing else other than that which one has decided to undertake, with heart fully involved there, until it is completed.

44 For in this way everything is done well. Otherwise neither this thing nor the other would be. Moreover, in that case, the defilement, lack of awareness, would certainly increase as well.

45 One should quell the eagerness that arises for the various kinds of idle chat that often take place, and for all objects of curiosity.

46 Mindful of the teaching of the Tathagata, fearful, one should abandon immediately any such actions as breaking up clods of earth, ripping grass, and drawing lines in the earth without any purpose.

47 When one wishes to move or to speak, first one should examine one's own mind, and then act appropriately and with self-possession.

48 When one notices that one's own mind is attracted or repelled, one should neither act nor speak, but remain like a block of wood.

49 When the mind is inflated or derisive, full of arrogance and vanity, exceedingly jocose, evasive, or deceiving,

50 When, seeming to advance oneself, it is only deprecating others, contemptuous and scornful, one should remain like a block of wood.

51 My mind seeks acquisitions, reverence, or renown, or again wants an audience and attention. Therefore I remain like a block of wood.

52 My mind longs to hold forth, averse to the good of others, seeking my own advantage, longing only for a congregation. Therefore I remain like a block of wood.

53 It is intolerant, idle, cowardly, impudent, also foul-mouthed, and biased in my own favour. Therefore I remain like a block of wood.

54 Noticing in this way that his mind is defiled or engaged in a fruitless activity, the hero should always firmly curb it with the antidote to that condition.

55 Determined, full of serene confidence, steady, full of application and respect, with humility and timidity, calm, eager to help others,

56 Unwearied by the mutually conflicting desires of the puerile, full of pity, knowing that they are like this as a result of the arising of defilement,

57 See, always in blameless matters I shall keep my mind at the will of myself and other beings, free from delusions, like an illusion!

58 At every moment continuously mindful that it has taken so long to gain the best of opportunities,

this is how I shall keep my mind, as unshakeable as Mount Sumeru.

59 Why else does the body offer no resistance when dragged this way and that by vultures greedy for flesh?

60 Why, mind, do you protect this carcass, identifying with it? If it is really separate from you, then what loss is its decay to you?

61 O Fool! You do not identify with a wooden doll even when it is pure. So why do you guard this festering contraption made of filth?

62 First, just in your mind, pull apart this bag of skin. With the knife of wisdom loosen the flesh from the cage of bones.

63 Cracking open the bones, too, look at the marrow within. Work out for yourself what essence is there.

64 Searching hard like this, you have found no essence here. Now explain why it is that you still continue to guard the body.

65 You will not eat it, unclean as it is, nor drink the blood, nor suck out the entrails. What will you do with your body?

66 Of course it is right to protect this wretched body, but as food for vultures and jackals, or as the implement of action for the benefit of humankind.

67 Even as you protect it so, ruthless death will snatch away your body and give it to the vultures. Then what will you do?

68 You do not give clothes and such to a servant if you think he is not going to stay. The body will eat and then go. Why do you make the outlay?

69 On that account, having given the body its wages, Mind, now look to your own needs, for a labourer does not receive all of the wealth he creates.

70 Apply to the body the notion of a ship, on account of the way it comes and goes. At your own command, set the body on course to fulfil the needs of beings.

71 One's own nature mastered in this way, one should always have a smiling face. One should give up frowning and grimacing, be the first to speak, a friend to the universe.

72 One should not throw down stools and other furniture violently with a crash, nor should one pound on doors. One should always delight in silence.

73 The crane, the cat, or the thief achieves his intended goal by moving quietly and gently. The aspirant should move in such a way at all times.

74 One should accept respectfully the advice of those who are able to direct others, who offer unsolicited aid. One should be the pupil of everyone all the time.

75 One should express one's appreciation of all that is well said. When one sees someone doing something meritorious, one should encourage them with praises.

76 One should speak of others' virtues in their absence, and repeat them with pleasure, and when one's own praise is spoken, one should reflect on that person's recognition of virtue.

77 Surely everything is undertaken for the sake of satisfaction, and yet even with money that is hard to find. Therefore I shall enjoy the pleasure of finding satisfaction in the virtues acquired by others through their hard work.

78 I lose nothing in this world and gain great bliss in the next, whereas animosities lead to the misery of enmity and in the next world great suffering.

79 One should speak confident, measured words, clear in meaning, delighting the mind, pleasing to the ear, soft and slow, and stemming from compassion.

80 One should always look at people directly, as if drinking them in with the eye: depending upon them alone, Buddhahood will be mine.

81 Great good arises from continuous devotion towards the fertile fields that are the Virtuous and our benefactors, and from the application of an antidote in the case of one who suffers.

82 One should be able and energetic, at all times acting upon one's own initiative. In all actions one should not leave any work to another.

83 Each of the perfections, beginning with generosity, is more excellent than its predecessor. One should not neglect a higher one for the sake of a lower, unless because of a fixed rule of conduct.

84 Realizing this, one should always be striving for others' well-being. Even what is proscribed is permitted for a compassionate person who sees it will be of benefit.

85 One should consume in moderation and share with those in difficulty, the helpless, and those observing the vows, and, apart from one's three robes, give away everything.

86 The body serves the True Dharma. One should not harm it for some inferior reason. For it is the only way that one can quickly fulfill the hopes of living beings.

87 Therefore one should not relinquish one's life for someone whose disposition to compassion is not as pure. But for someone whose disposition is comparable, one should relinquish it. That way, there is no overall loss.

88–9 One should not speak about the Dharma, which is profound and magnificent, to someone

Document Text

who is disrespectful, who, when healthy, wears a turban on his head, or who holds an umbrella, stick or knife, or whose head is veiled; nor to those who are inadequate, or to women without a man present. To the lesser and higher teachings one should show equal respect.

90 One should not restrict someone who is worthy of the higher teaching to the lesser teaching, nor, disregarding the matter of good conduct, beguile them with the Scriptures and spells.

91 It is not desirable to spit out tooth-cleaning sticks and phlegm in public, and it is also forbidden to urinate and so forth on land or into water that is usable.

92 One should not eat with a mouth overfull, noisily, nor with mouth wide open. One should not sit with a leg hanging down, likewise one should not rub both arms at the same time.

93 One should not travel with another's wife if unaccompanied, nor lie down with her, nor sit with her. One should notice and ask about what displeases people and avoid it all.

94 One should not indicate with a finger something that is to be done, but respectfully with the whole of the right hand. One should also point out the road in this way.

95 One should not throw up one's arms and shout at anyone when worked up over some trifle, but instead snap the fingers or the like. Otherwise one would be showing lack of restraint.

96 One should lie down to rest in the preferred direction, in the position in which the Protector passed away. Full of awareness, one should get up promptly, before one is told to do so without fail.

97 The conduct of the Bodhisattvas has been described as immeasurable. In the first place it is essential to engage in conduct that purifies the mind.

98 Three times, day and night, one should recite the Triskandha, so that, through recourse to the Conquerors and the Bodhisattvas, one's remaining transgressions cease.

99 One should apply oneself industriously to the trainings appropriate to the various situations in which one finds oneself, whether there at will, or subject to another.

100 For there is nothing from which the sons of the Conqueror cannot learn. There is nothing which is not an act of merit for the good person who conducts himself in this way.

101 One should do nothing other than what is either directly or indirectly of benefit to living beings, and for the benefit of living beings alone one should dedicate everything to Awakening.

102 Never, even at the cost of one's life, should one forsake a spiritual friend who upholds the Bodhisattva vow and is skilled in the meaning of the Mahayana.

103 One should also practise towards teachers the correct conduct according to the Srisambhavavimoksa. Both this and other things taught by the Buddha should be understood from the recitation of the Scriptures.

104 The principles of the training are found in the Scriptures. Therefore one should recite the Scriptures, and one should study the fundamental transgressions in the Akasagarbha Sutra.

Glossary

Akasagarbha Sutra	a Mahayana text that spells out eight fundamental errors that must be avoided by anyone who wants to follow the path of a bodhisattva
Avici	a realm similar to hell
bodhisattva	an enlightened being who is on his or her way to becoming a fully enlightened buddha but willingly puts it off to help others
Brahma	in contrast to Hinduism, one of several deities in Buddhism, all conceived as an all-encompassing divine force
Conqueror	a term of respect for the Buddha (Siddhartha Gautama)
dharma	the fundamental principle of existence
Mahayana	the Buddhist tradition (as opposed to Theravada Buddhism) that Shantideva practiced
Mount Sumeru	the sacred mountain that joins heaven and earth at the center of Buddhist cosmology

Document Text

105 The Compendium of the Training, the Siksa Samuccaya, should definitely be looked at repeatedly, since correct conduct is explained there in some detail.

106 Alternatively, one should just look at it briefly, and then with great care at the companion Compendium of Scriptures, the Sutra Samuccaya, compiled by the noble Nagarjuna.

107 One should look in those works at the training, that from which one is prohibited and that which is enjoined, and one should practise it thoroughly in order to guard the mind in the world.

108 In brief, this alone is the definition of awareness: the observation at every moment of the state of one's body and one's mind.

109 I shall express this by means of my body, for what use would there be in the expression of words? For someone who is sick what use could there be in the mere expression of medical knowledge?

Glossary

Protectors	buddhas and bodhisattvas
Sage	the Buddha (Siddhartha Gautama)
Siksasamuccaya	Shantideva's own "Compendium of Training," an anthology of selections drawn from over a hundred Buddhist scriptures
Srisambhava-vimoksa	or the "Biography of Srisambhava," which provides an account of the importance of friendship and is found in a Mahayana scripture called the Gandavyuha Sutra, or "Array of Flowers Sutra"
Sutra Samuccaya	a "Compendium of All Sutras" by Nagarjuna
Tathagata	the name the historical Buddha used to refer to himself
Teacher of Reality	the Buddha (Siddhartha Gautama)
Triskandha	"Sutra of the Three Heaps," a list of daily confessions

An illustration of the voyage of Saint Brendan
(St. Brendan in his ship, from the German translation of 'Navigatio Sancti Brendani Abbatis', c.1476 [vellum], German School, [15th century] / Universitatsbibliothek, Heidelberg, Germany / The Bridgeman Art Library International)

THE VOYAGE OF BRAN

ca. 700–800

"A wood with blossom and fruit / On which is the vine's veritable fragrance / A wood without decay, without defect / On which are leaves of golden hue."

Overview

The Voyage of Bran, Son of Febal, and His Adventure (*Immram Brain maic Febail ocus a Echtra*) is one of the most evocative of early Irish tales. Written around the eighth century CE, it tells of Bran's ocean voyage to an "otherworld" island sometime before the coming of Christianity to Ireland. Early Irish (Gaelic) tales of sea voyages to exotic islands were an established literary type known as *immrama* ("voyages" or, literally, "rowings about"). Typically in tales of this genre the heroes make an ocean voyage in a boat made of animal hide. They take with them a number of companions, some of whom are abandoned before the destination is reached. They encounter a number of exotic people and creatures on land and sea. These encounters often have a moral and sometimes an ironic character. Occasionally the travelers touch upon wider mythological or theological themes: the sovereignty of Ireland, the fall of Adam and Eve, the coming of Christ, and the events of the book of Revelation. At the end of the tale, the heroes return to Ireland to recount their adventures.

The Voyage of Bran, the earliest *immram* in date, shows all these features of the genre, but it is unusual in some other respects. Unlike the other *immrama*, whose personnel are explicitly Christian, its story commences in pre-Christian times but finishes many centuries in the future—implicitly after the coming of Christianity. The voyage is rather a brief element in the narrative, and the tale has some features more in common with tales of another established tale type, the *echtrae* ("excursions" or "outings"), in which there is more of a focus on description of the otherworld than on the journey. The otherworld (a modern term for a place with many names in Irish literature) of *The Voyage of Bran*, as in these other early Irish tales, is a fertile and abundant place. The denizens of the otherworld have apparently escaped the fall of Adam and Eve and continue to live without sin. Their otherworld appears to be both a place of supernatural adventure and a paradise similar in nature to the biblical Eden. The story of Bran's voyage is thus in part a narrative—at times challenging in its interpretation—of the journey from paganism to Christianity. It is also a conversation between the Christian Irish and characters from their earlier mythology.

Context

The exact context of *The Voyage of Bran* is open to interpretation. Ireland was converted to Christianity in the course of the fourth through seventh centuries CE. Saint Patrick, in the fifth century, wrote briefly in Latin about the Ireland of his era; narrative literature in Irish (Gaelic) was not recorded in writing until monastic culture flourished from the mid-sixth century onward. The date of *The Voyage of Bran*, one of the earliest narrative tales, is not easy to resolve with certainty. The death of the Ulster king Mongán mac Fiachnai is mentioned in the tale, which we know from other sources occurred in 627 CE. Therefore *The Voyage of Bran* was written at least after the first quarter of the seventh century. The consensus of scholarship, such as it is, would put the writing of the tale around the eighth century.

Old Irish is a language that can be dated by reference to sound changes that occur in a known sequence (philological dating). This relative sequence of forms is then anchored to some texts that have absolute historical dates. Precision is difficult in these matters, however, and the forms of language in *The Voyage of Bran* have been taken to suggest dates as far apart as 650 and 900 CE. Another approach to dating the tale involves attempting to reconstruct the process of copying and recopying the text (text transmission). Short comments by scribes in the manuscripts show that the tale derived from a copy in a now-lost collection, "The Book of Drumsnat," which was written in the north of Ireland in the later first millennium CE. The periods between phases of copying might, however, have been long or short; various scholars have placed the writing of "The Book of Drumsnat" as early as the seventh and as late as the tenth century CE.

As a very early narrative tale in Irish, *The Voyage of Bran* especially raises the question of whether it should be treated as a product of an already completely Christian context—the tale at the very least was written a couple of centuries after the time of Saint Patrick (who flourished around the mid-fifth century)—or whether we see its immediate sources as

Time Line	
CA. 400–500	■ Saints Palladius and Patrick promote the expansion of Christianity throughout Ireland. Patrick's *Confessio* is the first known work written in Ireland.
CA. 520–600	■ Monasticism is extended throughout Ireland.
627	■ Mongán mac Fiachnai is killed in Islay.
CA. 730	■ The Irish discover the Faeroe Islands.
CA. 700–800	■ *The Voyage of Bran* is thought to have been written.
CA. 795	■ The Irish visit Iceland (Thule).
795–796	■ Vikings raid Iona and Ireland; the Irish monasteries in the Faeroes are abandoned.
CA. 800–830	■ *The Voyage of Saint Brendan* is thought to have been written.
825	■ Dicuil writes *Book of the Measurement of the Earth*.

connected to the "pagan" past. What is known in Irish textual criticism as the anti-nativist position holds that all literary records, even poems with some evidence of having been oral texts, can be taken only to represent the mind-set of the Christian monks who wrote out the texts. Characters in the tale prophesy the birth of Christ. Attempts have been made to identify these Christian elements of *The Voyage of Bran* as intrusions into an older narrative, but there is little to justify such a reconstruction of the tale. The tale is part of a wider tradition of conversations between mortals and otherworld figures, some of whom appear to be pagan gods. This must be understood as a Christian literary tradition in early Ireland, though it might arise from a pre-Christian type.

By the central Middle Ages (1000–1500 CE), the Irish tradition had developed an elaborate schema for accommodating pre-Christian deities and mythological figures into a framework of prehistory. In this general vision, heroes and gods who lived in distinct past ages continue to inhabit places (*síd*) accessible under hills and lakes. These are "immanent" or "inherent" otherworlds, which seem, in effect, to be other dimensions of the places where we encounter them. In *The Voyage of Bran*, the sea god Manannán is encountered driving a chariot across a dry land that is in the same space as the ocean in which Bran sails. In another early text concerning Bran, a visitor from the otherworld comes from a land that is now drowned under Lough Foyle.

The background to the tale is therefore a Christian tradition that could accommodate the gods and heroes of Irish mythology into a parallel world. The epithet of Manannán, Mac Lir ("son of Sea"), whom Bran encounters in his voyage, is explained in the glossary of Cormac of Cashel (d. 908) as "whence the Irish and British called him the god of the sea." The unnamed otherworld woman whose verse opens the tale is a denizen of a sinless paradise. Bran himself may be a mythological figure. A figure with supernatural qualities named Bran or Brân occurs in Irish folklore and in medieval Welsh literature. It is not certain that a common figure underlies all the mythological persons of this name; nonetheless, it is suggestive that the figure of "Brân the Blessed" (Bendigeidfran) in Welsh literature is the brother of Manawydan fab Llyr, clearly a Welsh counterpart to the Irish Manannán Mac Lir. Whether these relationships between Irish and Welsh tradition are pre-Christian myths of shared origin or borrowings of post-Christian traditions between the two countries remains the subject of debate.

The conversations between mortals and immortals convey prophetic stories to the early Irish. Some early poetic dialogue (*immacaldam*) texts survive separately concerning Bran and Lough Foyle, the place at which Bran returns to Ireland from the otherworld. These shorter works, which describe a rather less overtly Christian otherworld than does *The Voyage of Bran* itself, may have been earlier sources used by the author of this text. Two long verses that exist within *The Voyage of Bran* are also in a sense almost conversations, though they are one-sided: They are monologues spoken to Bran by the visitors from the otherworld. That the speech of people from the otherworld is consistently framed in poetic monologues and dialogues is probably a literary device to signal its special, often prophetic, qualities.

An innovation of Bran's voyage tale is that Bran can reach part of the same immanent otherworld as is found in the dialogues by voyaging *over* the sea rather than into it. Real monastic voyages, recorded by the geographer Dicuil in 825, also took Irish monks to islands: as far as the Faeroe Islands around 730 and to Iceland as well as possibly Greenland around 795. These voyages, cut short by the advent of the Vikings in the region around 795, appear to have had specific theological interests in measuring the extent of the remaining unconverted nations (see Matthew 24:14) and the ways in which earth possibly related to the heavens at its edges. One lengthy Latin tale of around 830, *The Voyage of Saint Brendan*, probably based on an older *Life of Saint Brendan*, describes such voyages of monks into the waters north and west of Ireland. The Brendan story is fictional, but it incorporates details of the contemporary discoveries in the ocean.

The Voyage of Bran and *The Voyage of Saint Brendan* appear to have shared origins. Brendan's story takes Brendan and fourteen companions across many islands in the ocean before visiting a paradise island that can be identified as near to the north of Ireland. (Some particular parallels to Brendan's voyage will be discussed later in the detailed explanation and analysis of *The Voyage of Bran*.) Sacred islands were not, however, unknown in pre-Christian Celtic religion. Greek and Roman writers including Plutarch, Pomponius Mela, Strabo, and Pliny all describe religious men and women living on islands off the coasts of France, Wales, and Scotland. In some of these classical accounts of the Celts, some uninhabited islands were identified as the abodes of gods or of the dead—the latter belief also features in Irish folklore of the medieval and modern period. It is reasonable to believe that pre-Christian religious beliefs existed concerning sacred islands and that the idea of an otherworld island need not be purely from a context of monastic voyages.

About the Author

The Voyage of Bran is anonymously written, as indeed are most early Irish tales. The author was evidently an Irishman and almost certainly a monk. He probably wrote at Drumsnat in County Monaghan. If we accept that this monk was inspired in part by contemporary ocean voyaging, he may have written it during or after the time, in about 730–795, when discoveries in the Faeroe Islands, Iceland, and probably the Greenland Sea were reported back by Irish voyagers.

Whether the other materials the author used to create the tale included oral or written traditions remains undetermined. The tale has a tight structure that involves repetition of similar motifs. These repeated features show an author who has done more than put together separate elements to form a tale and may suggest that the poetry and prose are by a single author or at least a skilled literary artist, perhaps educated in native poetic tradition before entering the monastic life.

Explanation and Analysis of the Document

The Voyage of Bran is made up of both poetry and prose: Three relatively short sections of prose alternate with two long (and one short) poems that make up about 65 percent of the tale. The poems in *The Voyage of Bran* are recited to Bran and his followers by "otherworld" figures, who appear briefly as characters in the prose tale. These long poems comprise information conveyed from the otherworld to humanity; their distinct poetic form may be intended to signify that they are sacred or special in character. That the number of verses provided is less than the number specified in the text might be evidence of losses of text in its transmission, but it might also be a deliberate conceit to hint that something was withheld by Bran from the reader—perhaps because not everything revealed by the otherworld figures is fit to be known by humankind. This idea is suggested in the dialogues.

Aerial view of Faeroe Islands
(AP/Wide World Images)

♦ **Paragraphs 1 and 2**

In paragraphs 1 and 2 the author introduces the otherworld woman and a token of the otherworld. The woman is said to be from "unknown lands." These lands include the Land of Women, which Bran will soon visit. She is said to sing fifty verses (quatrains), of which twenty-eight are given here. These verses describe the land of "Emain," from which has also been carried an apple branch. The unnamed woman appears to be the same woman who is encountered at the end of the tale as the chief of the Land of Women, though this is never specified.

The branch of the tree is a token of the otherworld. Such tokens appear in other Irish tales. In the Latin Life of Saint Ailbe, the saint is drawn away to a paradise island that appears off the coast of Clare and returns carrying a fruiting branch. In an Irish (Gaelic) text, "Twelve Apostles of Ireland," a gathering of saints receives a flower from the "promised land," and a similar motif is in the tale "The Siege of the Men of Fálgae." In these cases the tokens are symbols of the fruitful nature of the otherworld. The fruit in Bran's case is explicitly an apple, which evokes particularly the fruit of Eden (Genesis 3:6). Whether an older idea of a fruitful pagan otherworld is incorporated into this vision is not certain, though it is likely.

Essential Quotes

> "A great birth will come after ages / That will not be in a lofty place / The son of a woman whose mate will not be known / He will seize the rule of the many thousands."

> "'Tis He that made the heavens / Happy he that has a white heart / He will purify hosts under pure water / 'Tis He that will heal your sicknesses."

> "Along the top of a wood has swum / Thy coracle across ridges / There is a wood of beautiful fruit / Under the prow of thy little skiff."

> "A wood with blossom and fruit / On which is the vine's veritable fragrance / A wood without decay, without defect / On which are leaves of golden hue."

> "We are from the beginning of creation / Without old age, without consummation of earth / Hence we expect not that there should be frailty / Sin has not come to us."

> "A noble salvation will come / From the King who has created us / A white law will come over seas / Besides being God, He will be man."

> "This shape, he on whom thou lookest / Will come to thy parts / 'Tis mine to journey to her house / To the woman in Linemag (Moylinny)."

♦ **Paragraphs 3–30**

The poem recited by the otherworld woman describes the nature of the otherworld (3–25), noting in passing its unfallen nature (10). She then describes the coming of a figure we may presume to be Christ (26–28), described as the creator of the world and the heavens. This figure will be of humble birth, not born in a "lofty place." He will be the son of a woman whose mate is not known. In the final verse the otherworld woman exhorts Bran to visit the otherworld.

The otherworld land of Emain is portrayed in this section as part of an island or set of islands in the ocean. The land is supported (paragraphs 4 and 6) by four feet. This could be a Christian image, echoing the pillars of the Tabernacle of Moses (Exodus 26:32). Later in the first poem (paragraph 19) there is a reference to "Emne," in which the otherworld women live (see also paragraph 60). The fact that Emne is free from treachery or death (paragraphs 9, 10, and 18) implies that it is an unfallen paradise. It is apparent here that a number of different names describe the same places. "Emain" and "Emne" are forms of the same word. The same land is also identified in the prose passages by the descriptive name Tír inna mBan ("Land of Women"). An Emain Ablach ("Emain of the Apples") appears in later Irish, Scottish, and Manx traditions as the home of Manannán. This is undoubtedly the same as the Emain here—but it may also be directly inspired by *The Voyage of Bran*. Emain is also the name of the historic capital of Ulster, which cannot have escaped a northern author.

In *The Voyage of Bran*, Emne/Emain contains a tree (7), which may be the apple tree from whence comes the branch, in which "birds call to the Hours." This has a parallel in *The Voyage of Saint Brendan*, in which Saint Brendan meets birds that are incarnations of the souls of angels who were driven out of heaven at the time of the fall. Brendan's birds chant the monastic Hours. In the Latin Life of Saint Malo (from Brittany), Saint Brendan and Saint Malo seek an ocean island named Imma, in which dwell the souls of angels. Bran's Emne may be just one version of a legendary island of unfallen souls that circulated in Irish literature and saints' lives.

A number of plains are referred to in *The Voyage of Bran* as places in which chariots race: Mag Findargat, Mag Argatnél, Mag Réin, and Mag Mon. Again, as with Emain/Emne, the names Findargat ("White Silver") and Argatnél ("Silver Cloud") share a name element—*argat* ("silver")—and both are said to be "southern" in location. In paragraph 13 a land of music is named Ciúin (which means "quiet"). At 20–21, Imchiúin (meaning "very quiet"), a slight variant on *ciúin*, is described as a land, close to Emne (or perhaps in it), in which little birds sing—so this might also be the same place as that in which the birds call on the Hours (paragraph 7). It seems likely that the plains—taking the point that these are places in which chariots travel, as in the case of Manannán—are to be understood as having later become stretches of sea. We are left with uncertainty as to how all these locations fit together, which is possibly deliberate. One other possible explanation is that the references indicate places that are understood as having changed their qualities and identities across time, but which in the minds of the inhabitants of the otherworld continue to exist in both older and newer forms—just as Lough Foyle is both the sea and the land drowned beneath it.

One other noteworthy point in this section concerns two possible hints of contemporary discoveries. The chanting birds of Saint Brendan are associated by the author of *The Voyage of Saint Brendan* with islands that have been taken by some critics to be based on descriptions of the Faeroe Islands, discovered in about 730. In *The Voyage of Saint Brendan* reference is also made to a column of crystal in the ocean, in the shade of which the heat of the sun can still be felt. Although this is not a literal description of an iceberg, there is a strong case to be made that it was inspired by an encounter with an iceberg by monks when voyaging beyond Iceland around 795. The reference here to a "pure-white cliff on the range of the sea / Which from the sun receives its heat" (paragraph 22) might conceivably be understood as referring to the same episode.

♦ **Paragraphs 31 and 32**

A brief prose interlude occurs before the next set of verses in which the woman and the branch are drawn back to the otherworld and Bran and his company go on the sea. Bran meets Manannán on the sea, who is said to sing thirty verses (the text has twenty-eight). The implication of the last sentence of the prose is that the verses that follow will tell Bran of the coming of Mongán mac Fiachnai. Here the author seems to be commenting on the verse from within the prose, which causes some to believe that the prose might be written to explain a preexisting verse from a different author. This section also says that Manannán is to go into Ireland "after long ages." This indicates that Bran's voyage is a long time before the seventh century, the time of Mongán.

♦ **Paragraphs 33–54**

Like the otherworld woman, Manannán opens his poem by describing the nature of otherworld (33–47), including in passing its unfallen nature (44–47) and then the coming of Christ, a leader who will be God and man at the same time (48). The last paragraph (60) exhorts Bran to visit the otherworld. This repeated order of topics in the two poems is one of a number of repetitions in the tale. Manannán describes to Bran the plains and forests of a world that exists under the ocean on which he sails. Three verses (45–47) explicitly refer to Satan and original sin; they indicate that the unfallen world is in some way a continuation of the biblical Eden.

In paragraphs 49–54, Manannán then tells a story of a son *he* will father: "A son would be born to him," Mongán son of Fiachnae (as we have been told in paragraph 32). The tale *The Conception of Mongán*, along with *The Voyage of Bran*, describes how Mongán was fathered in disguise by Manannán, who impregnates Caintigern, the wife of Fiachnae mac Baetáin. This longer account fills out the bare narrative provided in *The Voyage of Bran*. This is a motif very similar to the later medieval story of the conception of King Arthur, who is fathered by Uther, who impregnates the wife of the ruler of Cornwall while disguised as her husband.

Here, Manannán's account of his own earthly offspring Mongán, the son of a deity who would be accepted by an earthly man as his own son, is, in the context, clearly intended as echoing the story of Christ. This is one of the most provocative elements of the tale. That a hero might be fathered by a god is not uncommon in mythology; likewise his being raised in disguise by an earthly father. Coming immediately after the prophecy of the coming of Christ, however, the tale is surely suggesting a specific parallel.

♦ **Paragraphs 53–60**

These paragraphs describe Mongán mac Fiachnai, who was a historical king but also in legend was said to be fathered by Manannán. The Irish Annals, a brief early-medieval chronicle of Irish history, record that Mongán was killed by a stone in the Scottish island of Islay in 627. Islay is mentioned by Manannán in verse 56. The references to Mongán taking the form of various beasts—dragon, wolf, stag, salmon, seal, swan—indicate that he is a shape-shifter, a theme that appears in accounts of Mongán in later texts.

♦ **Paragraphs 60 and 61**

After the lengthy poems, the main voyage tale is relatively short. Bran and his companions come first to an island, the Island of Joy, in which the occupants are engaged in ceaseless, maniacal mirthfulness. One of the companions swims ashore and immediately becomes like the occupants and oblivious to his shipmates.

♦ **Paragraphs 62–66**

The last five paragraphs tell of Bran's stay in the otherworld and his brief return to Ireland before he sets off again into the ocean. After the visit to the Island of Joy, the companions travel a short distance to the Land of Women (Emne). Here they find limitless food and (implicitly) sexual activity without sin. Time passes almost without it being noticed, until they wish to return home. When they state their intent to return, the chief of the women warns them not to go ashore. The woman tells them to visit the companion they have left on the Island of Joy, though no explanation is given as to why this is significant. It may be that it is to draw their attention to the general danger of leaving their ship. The warning not to touch the land is a formula also found in early tale traditions from other countries in which people have traveled outside their regular time pattern.

On their return to Ireland, Bran and his followers arrive at the northern tip of Ireland, Srúb Broin (Bran's Point—or, literally, "Bran's nose") to find that time has passed to the extent that they have become figures from the distant past. They are told that *The Voyage of Bran* is a legend known to the Irish. Nechtan mac Collbrain goes ashore, but upon touching land he immediately turns to ashes. Bran recites a poem that makes clear that they have come back hundreds of years into the future. Passing through the sea itself can be a metaphor for baptism, as Paul says of the Israelites (1 Corinthians 10:1), but Bran's poem implies that though Nechtan crosses onto the land, he is not baptized by this act (compare paragraph 28: "He will purify hosts under pure water"). Bran and his followers are thus fated to belong now only to the otherworld—perhaps even only to the sea. Bran tells his story again, it is recorded in archaic writing (ogham), and he returns to sea.

Audience

The original audience of *The Voyage of Bran* is not really known, but the writing of the tale in the vernacular language (Gaelic) implies an intended audience larger than simply monks; *The Voyage of Saint Brendan*, by contrast, is in Latin and clearly intended for a monastic audience. Ireland is remarkable for the quantity and variety of its early literature in the vernacular. *The Voyage of Bran* is arguably one of the earliest of these vernacular tales. Vernacular tales, as opposed to their Latin counterparts, could have been read aloud to laypeople, though historians do not know whether this one was.

The Voyage of Bran, in contrast to the other *immrama*, was edited and translated into an accessible edition, in book form. This 1895 edition was often reprinted, and the translation has circulated widely on the Internet. The simple motif of a short voyage to an exotic otherworld has made it an appealing tale to general readers, and the tale's explicit claim to depict the "pagan" past has made this the most critically studied of the *immrama* in the modern era. Although it was somewhat neglected in the 1990s, the tale was central to "anti-nativist" critique in the 1970s and early 1980s. In contrast to *The Voyage of Saint Brendan*, *The Voyage of Bran* is more often read as a complete story rather than reconstructed to present a supposedly "real" ocean voyage, which has tended to be the treatment of the Latin voyage tales.

Questions for Further Study

1. Respond to the following statement: *The Voyage of Bran* is a literary text, not a religious one. What arguments would you make for either side of the issue?

2. Sometimes, geography is destiny (at least in part). What impact did Ireland's geography have on *immrama* in general and *The Voyage of Bran* in particular?

3. A considerable amount of the world's literature involves traveling to an island; think of *Treasure Island*, *Robinson Crusoe*, *The Swiss Family Robinson*, or *Lord of the Flies*, as well as many science fiction novels that involve traveling to a planet that is essentially an "island." What is the appeal of the island for writers such as the author of *The Voyage of Bran*? What symbolic significance can islands have?

4. What do you think explains the continuing appeal of *The Voyage of Bran*? In what ways does it speak to a readership other than one composed of medieval monks?

5. It is often noted that certain elements of Christianity are derived from "pagan" rituals and beliefs, which were taken over by the Christian Church and adapted for Christian use; examples include certain Christmas traditions and rituals, such as the Christmas tree. What can modern readers learn about the blend of earlier pagan beliefs and Christianity by reading *The Voyage of Bran*?

Impact

The Voyage of Bran undoubtedly inspired a wider set of tales concerning Mongán and the otherworld. It also shares in a literary vision of the ocean that had influence throughout Europe via versions of the Saint Brendan story, though which story inspired the other remains the subject of debate. Other vernacular *immrama*, most notably *The Voyage of Máel Dúin*, show the influence of *The Voyage of Bran*. The correspondences between the Bran/Manannán/Mongán stories and some Welsh tales, even if occasionally exaggerated, also point to knowledge of a version of this material in early Wales, probably through borrowing from Irish sources, which we know did occur around the ninth century.

John Carey in *Ireland and the Grail* has argued that the same or a similar collection of texts to those in "The Book of Drumsnat" was transmitted to Wales. In his view this collection ultimately gave rise to the idea of the Holy Grail that is at the center of the medieval Arthurian cycle of legend. He sees the suite of texts concerning Lough Foyle and Mongán as containing several episodes common to the Grail story: a journey through water to gain an object that enshrines sovereignty and prosperity.

The Voyage of Bran remains a widely read tale. When it was edited by Kuno Meyer in 1895, it was perceived as a tale describing the "Celtic legend of the beyond" or "blessed realm." The novelist J. R. R. Tolkien read the tale, and his vision of immortal elves who can live simultaneously in Middle Earth and in the blessed realm over the sea is likely to have been directly influenced by this evocative text.

Further Reading

■ **Books**

Carey, John. *A Single Ray of the Sun: Religious Speculation in Early Ireland*. Andover, Mass.: Celtic Studies Publications, 1999.

Carey, John. *Ireland and the Grail*. Andover, Mass.: Celtic Studies Publications, 2009.

Koch, John, and John Carey, eds. *The Celtic Heroic Age*. Andover, Mass.: Celtic Studies Publications, 1995.

Mac Mathúna, Séamus, *Immram Brain: Bran's Journey to the Land of the Women*. Tübingen, Germany: Niemeyer, 1985.

MacQuarrie, Charles. *The Biography of the Irish God of the Sea from "The Voyage of Bran" (700 A.D.) to "Finnegans Wake" (1939): The Waves of Manannán*. Lewiston, N.Y.: Edwin Mellen, 2004.

McCone, Kim. *Echtrae Chonnlai and the Beginnings of Vernacular Narrative Writing in Ireland*. Maynooth, Ireland: National University of Ireland, 2000.

Meyer, Kuno, and Alfred Nutt, eds. *The Voyage of Bran Son of Febal to the Land of the Living*. 2 vols. London: Nutt, 1895–1897.

Nagy, Joseph F. "Close Encounters of the Traditional Kind in Medieval Irish Literature." In *Celtic Folklore and Christianity: Studies in Memory of William W. Heist*, ed. Patrick Ford. Santa Barbara, Calif.: McNally and Loftin, 1983.

Ní Bhrolcháin, Muireann. *Early Irish Literature*. Dublin: Four Courts Press, 2009.

Wooding, Jonathan M. *The Otherworld Voyage in Early Irish Literature: An Anthology of Criticism*. Dublin: Four Courts Press, 2000.

—Jonathan Wooding

Document Text

THE VOYAGE OF BRAN

1. 'TWAS fifty quatrains the woman from unknown lands sang on the floor of the house to Bran son of Febal, when the royal house was full of kings, who knew not whence the woman had come, since the ramparts were closed.

2. This is the beginning of the story. One day, in the neighbourhood of his stronghold, Bran went about alone, when he heard music behind him. As often as he looked back, 'twas still behind him the music was. At last he fell asleep at the music, such was its sweetness. When he awoke from his sleep, he saw close by him a branch of silver with white blossoms, nor was it easy to distinguish its bloom from that branch. Then Bran took the branch in his hand to his royal house. When the hosts were in the royal house, they saw a woman in strange raiment on the floor of the house. 'Twas then she sang the fifty quatrains to Bran, while the host heard her, and all beheld the woman.

And she said:

3. "A branch of the apple-tree from Emain
   I bring, like those one knows;
   Twigs of white silver are on it,
   Crystal brows with blossoms.

4. "There is a distant isle,
   Around which sea-horses glisten:
   A fair course against the white-swelling surge,—
   Four feet uphold it.

5. "A delight of the eyes, a glorious range,
   Is the plain on which the hosts hold games:
   Coracle contends against chariot
   In southern Mag Findargat.

6. "Feet of white bronze under it
   Glittering through beautiful ages.
   Lovely land throughout the world's age,
   On which the many blossoms drop.

7. "An ancient tree there is with blossoms,
   On which birds call to the Hours.
   'Tis in harmony it is their wont
   To call together every Hour.

8. "Splendours of every colour glisten
   Throughout the gentle-voiced plains.
   Joy is known, ranked around music,
   In southern Mag Argatnél.

9. "Unknown is wailing or treachery
   In the familiar cultivated land,
   There is nothing rough or harsh,
   But sweet music striking on the ear.

10. "Without grief, without sorrow, without death,
    Without any sickness, without debility,
    That is the sign of Emain—
    Uncommon is an equal marvel.

11. "A beauty of a wondrous land,
    Whose aspects are lovely,
    Whose view is a fair country,
    Incomparable is its haze.

12. "Then if Aircthech is seen,
    On which dragonstones and crystals drop
    The sea washes the wave against the land,
    Hair of crystal drops from its mane.

13. "Wealth, treasures of every hue,
    Are in Ciuin, a beauty of freshness,
    Listening to sweet music,
    Drinking the best of wine.

14. "Golden chariots in Mag Réin,
    Rising with the tide to the sun,
    Chariots of silver in Mag Mon,
    And of bronze without blemish.

15. "Yellow golden steeds are on the sward there,
    Other steeds with crimson hue,
    Others with wool upon their backs
    Of the hue of heaven all-blue.

16. "At sunrise there will come
    A fair man illumining level lands;
    He rides upon the fair sea-washed plain,
    He stirs the ocean till it is blood.

17. "A host will come across the clear sea,
    To the land they show their rowing;
    Then they row to the conspicuous stone,
    From which arise a hundred strains.

18. "It sings a strain unto the host
    Through long ages, it is not sad,
    Its music swells with choruses of hundreds—
    They look for neither decay nor death.

19. "Many-shaped Emne by the sea,
    Whether it be near, whether it be far,
    In which are many thousands of motley women,
    Which the clear sea encircles.

20. "If he has heard the voice of the music,
    The chorus of the little birds from Imchiuin,
    A small band of women will come from a height
    To the plain of sport in which he is.

21. "There will come happiness with health
    To the land against which laughter peals,
    Into Imchiuin at every season
    Will come everlasting joy.

22. "It is a day of lasting weather
    That showers silver on the lands,
    A pure-white cliff on the range of the sea,
    Which from the sun receives its heat

23. "The host race along Mag Mon,
    A beautiful game, not feeble,
    In the variegated land over a mass of beauty
    They look for neither decay nor death.

24. "Listening to music at night,
    And going into Ildathach,
    A variegated land, splendour on a diadem of beauty,
    Whence the white cloud glistens.

25. "There are thrice fifty distant isles
    In the ocean to the west of us;
    Larger than Erin twice
    Is each of them, or thrice.

26. "A great birth will come after ages,
    That will not be in a lofty place,
    The son of a woman whose mate will not be known,
    He will seize the rule of the many thousands.

27. "A rule without beginning, without end,
    He has created the world so that it is perfect,
    Whose are earth and sea,
    Woe to him that shall be under His unwill!

28. "'Tis He that made the heavens,
    Happy he that has a white heart,
    He will purify hosts under pure water,
    'Tis He that will heal your sicknesses.

29. "Not to all of you is my speech,
    Though its great marvel has been made known:
    Let Bran hear from the crowd of the world
    What of wisdom has been told to him.

30. "Do not fall on a bed of sloth,
    Let not thy intoxication overcome thee,
    Begin a voyage across the clear sea,
    If perchance thou mayst reach the land of women."

31. Thereupon the woman went from them, while they knew not whither she went. And she took her branch with her. The branch sprang from Bran's hand into the hand of the woman, nor was there strength in Bran's hand to hold the branch.

32. Then on the morrow Bran went upon the sea. The number of his men was three companies of nine. One of his foster-brothers and mates was set over each of the three companies of nine. When he had been at sea two days and two nights, he saw a man in a chariot coming towards him over the sea. That man also sang thirty other quatrains to him, and made himself known to him, and said that he was Manannan the son of Ler, and said that it was upon him to go to Ireland after long ages, and that a son would be born to him, even Mongan son of Fiachna—that was the name which would be upon him.

So he sang these thirty quatrains to him:

33. "Bran deems it a marvellous beauty
    In his coracle across the clear sea:
    While to me in my chariot from afar
    It is a flowery plain on which he rides about.

34. "What is a clear sea
    For the prowed skiff in which Bran is,
    That is a happy plain with profusion of flowers
    To me from the chariot of two wheels.

35. "Bran sees
    The number of waves beating across the clear sea:

I myself see in Mag Mon
Red-headed flowers without fault.

36. "Sea-horses glisten in summer
As far as Bran has stretched his glance:
Rivers pour forth a stream of honey
In the land of Manannan son of Ler.

37. "The sheen of the main, on which thou art,
The white hue of the sea on which thou rowest about,
Yellow and azure are spread out,
It is land, and is not rough.

38. "Speckled salmon leap from the womb
Of the white sea, on which thou lookest:
They are calves, they are coloured lambs
With friendliness, without mutual slaughter.

39. "Though (but) one chariot-rider is seen
In Mag Mell of many flowers,
There are many steeds on its surface,
Though them thou seest not.

40. "The size of the plain, the number of the host,
Colours glisten with pure glory,
A fair stream of silver, cloths of gold,
Afford a welcome with all abundance.

41. "A beautiful game, most delightful,
They play (sitting) at the luxurious wine,
Men and gentle women under a bush,
Without sin, without crime.

42. "Along the top of a wood has swum
Thy coracle across ridges,
There is a wood of beautiful fruit
Under the prow of thy little skiff.

43. "A wood with blossom and fruit,
On which is the vine's veritable fragrance,
A wood without decay, without defect,
On which are leaves of golden hue.

44. "We are from the beginning of creation
Without old age, without consummation of earth,
Hence we expect not that there should be frailty,
The sin has not come to us.

45. "An evil day when the Serpent went
To the father to his city!
She has perverted the times in this world,
So that there came decay which was not original.

46. "By greed and lust he has slain us,
Through which he has ruined his noble race:
The withered body has gone to the fold of torment,
And everlasting abode of torture.

47. "It is a law of pride in this world
To believe in the creatures, to forget God,
Overthrow by diseases, and old age,
Destruction of the soul through deception.

48. "A noble salvation will come
From the King who has created us,
A white law will come over seas,
Besides being God, He will be man.

49. "This shape, he on whom thou lookest,
Will come to thy parts;
'Tis mine to journey to her house,
To the woman in Line-mag.

50. "For it is Moninnan, the son of Ler,
From the chariot in the shape of a man,
Of his progeny will be a very short while
A fair man in a body of white clay.

51. "Monann, the descendant of Ler, will be
A vigorous bed-fellow to Caintigern:
He shall be called to his son in the beautiful world,
Fiachna will acknowledge him as his son.

52. "He will delight the company of every fairy-knoll,
He will be the darling of every goodly land,
He will make known secrets—a course of wisdom—
In the world, without being feared.

53. "He will be in the shape of every beast,
Both on the azure sea and on land,
He will be a dragon before hosts at the onset,
He will be a wolf of every great forest.

54. "He will be a stag with horns of silver
In the land where chariots are driven,
He will be a speckled salmon in a full pool,
He will be a seal, he will be a fair-white swan.

55. "He will be throughout long ages
An hundred years in fair kingship,
He will cut down battalions,—a lasting grave—
He will redden fields, a wheel around the track.

Document Text

56. "It will be about kings with a champion
That he will be known as a valiant hero,
Into the strongholds of a land on a height
I shall send an appointed end from Islay.

57. "High shall I place him with princes,
He will be overcome by a son of error;
Moninnan, the son of Ler,
Will be his father, his tutor.

58. "He will be—his time will be short—
Fifty years in this world:
A dragonstone from the sea will kill him
In the fight at Senlabor.

59. "He will ask a drink from Loch Ló,
While he looks at the stream of blood,
The white host will take him under a wheel of clouds
To the gathering where there is no sorrow.

60. "Steadily then let Bran row,
Not far to the Land of Women,
Emne with many hues of hospitality
Thou wilt reach before the setting of the sun."

61. Thereupon Bran went from him. And he saw an island. He rows round about it, and a large host was gaping and laughing. They were all looking at Bran and his people, but would not stay to converse with them. They continued to give forth gusts of laughter at them. Bran sent one of his people on the island. He ranged himself with the others, and was gaping at them like the other men of the island. He kept rowing round about the island. Whenever his man came past Bran, his comrades would address him. But he would not converse with them, but would only look at them and gape at them. The name of this island is the Island of Joy. Thereupon they left him there.

62. It was not long thereafter when they reached the Land of Women. They saw the leader of the women at the port. Said the chief of the women: "Come hither on land; O Bran son of Febal! Welcome is thy advent!" Bran did not venture to go on shore. The woman throws a ball of thread to Bran straight over his face. Bran put his hand on the ball, which clave to his palm. The thread of the ball was in the woman's hand, and she pulled the coracle towards the port. Thereupon they went into a large house, in which was a bed for every couple, even thrice nine beds. The food that was put on every dish vanished not from them. It seemed a year to them that they were there,—it chanced to be many years. No saviour was wanting to them.

63. Home-sickness seized one of them, even Nechtan the son of Collbran. His kindred kept praying Bran that he should go to Ireland with him. The woman said to them their going would make them rue. However, they went, and the woman said that none of them should touch the land, and that they should visit and take with them the man whom they had left in the Island of Joy.

64. Then they went until they arrived at a gathering at Srub Brain. The men asked of them who it was came over the sea. Said Bran: "I am Bran the son of Febal," saith he. However, the other saith: "We do not know such a one, though the Voyage of Bran is in our ancient stories."

65. The man leaps from them out of the coracle. As soon as he touched the earth of Ireland, forthwith he was a heap of ashes, as though he had been in the earth for many hundred years. 'Twas then that Bran sang this quatrain:

"For Collbran's son great was the folly
To lift his hand against age,
Without any one casting a wave of pure water
Over Nechtan, Collbran's son."

Glossary

Ciuin	literally, "quiet"
Coracle	a small boat
Erin	Ireland
quatrains	verses

Document Text

66. Thereupon, to the people of the gathering Bran told all his wanderings from the beginning until that time. And he wrote these quatrains in Ogam, and then bade them farewell. And from that hour his wanderings are not known.

Japanese wind god
(Sliding doors depicting a wind god, Late Edo Period [detail], Kiitsu, Suzuki [1796-1858] / © Tokyo Fuji Art Museum, Tokyo, Japan / The Bridgeman Art Library International)

Nihongi

"We have now produced the Great-eight-island country, with the mountains, rivers, herbs, and trees. Why should we not produce someone who shall be lord of the universe?"

Overview

Originally compiled in the eighth century in response to an official call for a history of Japan, the *Nihongi* (Chronicles of Japan) was for over one thousand years perhaps the most authoritative work on the origins of Japan and its deities. It was not originally intended as a religious text, except insofar as the worship of the deities by their descendants was considered part of government at the time; as the centuries passed, however, the interpretive traditions centered on the *Nihongi* developed into major Shinto lineages. Even after it was downgraded in the nineteenth century in favor of the slightly older *Kojiki* (Records of Ancient Matters), the tales of the age of the gods found in the first two scrolls of the *Nihongi* remained part of the mythology of divine lineage that was officially supported until the end of World War II, and they are still studied for insight into early Japanese religion and politics.

Context

The *Nihongi*, also known as the *Nihon shoki*, was presented to the Japanese court in 720. It was the culmination of a long project of history and myth compilation that began with an edict of 681. Emperor Tenmu (r. 673–686) declared that the histories of the various clans were accumulating errors and ordered the commencement of an official project to consolidate and correct the true history of Japan. In fact, this was a project not to correct errors but to rewrite history. Tenmu had come to power in 673 after a bloody civil war, against a faction that supported his nephew and in which this nephew was killed. The newly produced histories would be designed to strengthen the legitimacy of Tenmu's rule. While religious matters were likely included from the beginning—they were unavoidable, since every major clan traced its lineage back to a deity—this was a very political project.

The *Nihongi* was not the first work to emerge from this royal order. The preface to the *Kojiki* states that it was presented to the court in 712—yet no mention of the *Kojiki* was included in later chronicles. A renewed order for an official history went out in 714, indicating that the *Kojiki* might have been thought incomplete or somehow unsatisfactory for the purpose; the new history was to be compiled by Ki Kiyondo and Miyake Fujimaro. Compared with the *Kojiki*, the *Nihongi* more closely resembles Chinese models of historical writing, and it was written in a style more similar to standard literary Chinese. The *Kojiki* ends in the early seventh century, whereas the *Nihongi* continues up until the end of the seventh century.

About the Author

Not much is known for certain about the compilers of the *Nihongi*, though there were certainly more than one. The record of the *Nihongi*'s presentation in 720 credits Prince Toneri (676–735), one of Tenmu's sons, with the project. However, a previously recorded royal order of 714 had commanded Ki Kiyondo and Miyake Fujimaro to compile a national history, and this order is usually associated with the *Nihongi*. Quite possibly Toneri subsequently joined the project as a sponsor; since he had been made an adviser to the crown prince in 719 and would later be prime minister, he would have made a powerful patron. Kiyondo was well known as a scholar of the Confucian classics, and his influence, or that of men like him, helps explain some of the detailed references to yin and yang and their properties. While the text of the *Nihongi* seems to show the work of at least two groups of compilers, further speculation is difficult.

Explanation and Analysis of the Document

The selection published here is from the very beginning of the *Nihongi*, from the first of two scrolls describing, as book I is titled, "The Age of the Gods." It addresses the origin of the very first deities (*kami*) and the creation of the Japanese islands. In beginning with the creation of the world, the *Nihongi* differs from Chinese models such as the *Shiji* (Records of the Grand Historian). Notably, the ruling family of Japan derived its authority, at least in part,

Time Line

672–673	The Jinshin War, a civil war, results in victory for Tenmu's faction.
673	Emperor Tenmu takes the throne of Japan.
681	Tenmu orders the correction of all works of history.
712	The *Kojiki* is presented to the court.
714	Ki Kiyondo and Miyake Fujimaro are ordered to compile a national history of Japan.
720	The *Nihongi* is presented to the court.
720–936	Court lecture series are held on the *Nihongi*, on average every thirty years.
ca. 950–1000	The Urabe family compiles *Nihon shoki shiki*, based on private notes taken at the official lectures.
1271–1301	Urabe Kanetomo composes *Shaku Nihongi*, an explanation and interpretation of the *Nihongi*.
ca. 1419	The Tendai Buddhist monk Ryohen produces his own interpretation of the text.
ca. 1450–1500	Yoshida Kanetomo establishes Yoshida Shinto, drawing on the Urabe family tradition of *Nihongi* scholarship.
ca. 1670	The philosopher Yamazaki Ansai combines Neo-Confucianism with a personal interpretation of the *Nihongi* to create Suika Shinto.
1790–1822	Motoori Norinaga publishes *Kojiki-den*, his interpretation of the *Kojiki* and an attack on the *Nihongi*.

from its divine ancestry—which also connected it with the other powerful clans in Japan. This helps explain why such a work of "history" should have so much mythology in it, and that mythology is what led to its use as a text of religious cosmology.

What is odd and interesting about the *Nihongi* is how it incorporates alternate versions of events into the text. These alternate versions are introduced with "In one writing it is said:— . . . ." These alternate versions are one of the main reasons that the text of the *Nihongi* is so hard to read, as they interrupt the main flow of the story. The chronology is further complicated in that the end of each alternate version is not clearly indicated in the text. It is also unclear exactly how many variant histories there were, as any source texts were chopped up to put each relevant variation after the corresponding main myth. Up to eleven variants have been calculated for one section of a myth.

This initial portion of the *Nihongi* can be divided into two sections: the first, consisting of the first twenty-four paragraphs, covers the earliest genealogies of the gods; the second section covers Izanagi and Izanami's creation of the Japanese islands and the major deities of the Japanese pantheon.

♦ A Chaotic Mass Like an Egg

The main narrative of the *Nihongi* starts by describing the chaos before creation. In and Yo are the Japanese readings for yin (dark, damp, female) and yang (bright, dry, male), the opposing essences from Chinese cosmology. Yin and yang initially exist in a chaotic egg-shaped mix—a description that comes from the *Huainanzi*, a Chinese text from the second century BCE. There is no creator deity that makes creation from this chaos—instead, the natural opposition of yin and yang cause them to separate. The lighter material forms heaven, and the heavier material forms the earth. Even so, the earth is still chaotic and not completely formed at this time. The text gives an image of how the unformed earth looked: There is a roiling ocean, and the land floats freely upon this ocean, like a fish.

At the border between heaven and earth, deities spontaneously arise and appear. The first is Kunitokotachi ("no Mikoto" being an honorific for deity names), who appears out of something that looks like a reed shoot. Kunitokotachi is followed by Kuni-no-satsuchi and Toyokumunu. All are described as "pure males," indicating that they exemplify yang. The reference to "the operation of the principle of Heaven" as the origin indicates that their generation was completely natural, spontaneous, and unforced.

♦ In One Writing It Is Said

The first variant version of the creation myth is introduced with the characteristic phrase. In this version, the creation of the first three deities is still spontaneous, and Kunitokotachi is still the first deity to appear—however, what generated Kunitokotachi is now described as something beyond description. Kunitokotachi is also given an alternate name of Kunisokotachi, showing that the alternate myths have been modified to be closer to the main text

White-robed Shinto priests performing a fire ritual at a shrine dedicated to Amaterasu in Ise, Japan
(AP/Wide World Photos)

version. Kuni-no-satsuchi is still the second deity, but the third deity is listed as Toyokuninushi, who is given seven alternate names (Toyokumunu being one of them).

These alternate names, when they appear in the text, might indicate that another clan genealogy is being incorporated into the official history. While at the time of the composition of the *Nihongi* the ruling clan claimed descent from Amaterasu, the sun goddess, other clans also claimed descent from important and powerful deities. Both the *Nihongi* and *Kojiki* incorporate these other deities into family trees and alliances, reflecting the royal lineage's relations with other clans. While these clans might have been able to trace their lineage back to one of these early gods, Amaterasu was depicted as having an unsurpassed quality befitting the ancestress of the ruling house, although that is more evident in the *Kojiki* than in the *Nihongi*.

The second alternate creation myth does not describe the creation of heaven, starting instead with when the earth was young and unformed. The very first deity to emerge from the reed shoot is named Umashiashikabihikoji. In this version Kunitokotachi (Kuni-no-tokotachi here) is the second deity to appear, followed by Kuni-no-satsuchi. Toyokumunu does not appear. The third variant is like the second, except the name Kunisokotachi is given for Kunitokotachi, and this account does not extend to the third generation of deities.

In the fourth variant, the first two deities appear not singly, one per generation, but as a pair. Kunitokotachi (again and often as Kuni-no-tokotachi) is paired with Kuni-no-satsuchi, implying that in this version they were considered not two male deities but one male and one female. The next deities to appear are Ama-no-minakanushi, Takamimusubi, and Kamimimusubi.

The fifth variant gives more detail for the generation of Kunitokotachi's and describes his appearance as predating the creation of heaven and earth. Here he might have functioned as more of a creator deity. In this version, the reed shoot is described as being inside something that resembled "a cloud floating over the sea." When the reed shoot took human shape, it turned into Kunitokotachi.

Essential Quotes

"Of old, Heaven and Earth were not yet separated, and the In and Yo not yet divided. They formed a chaotic mass like an egg which was of obscurely defined limits."

"Now the male deity turning by the left, and the female deity by the right, they went round the pillar of the land separately. When they met together on one side, the female deity spoke first and said:—'How delightful! I have met with a lovely youth.' The male deity was displeased and said:—'I am a man, and by right should have spoken first.'"

"After this Izanagi no Mikoto and Izanami no Mikoto consulted together, saying:—'We have now produced the Great-eight-island country, with the mountains, rivers, herbs, and trees. Why should we not produce someone who shall be lord of the universe?' They then together produced the Sun-Goddess."

"Izanagi no Mikoto had already reached the Even Pass of Yomi. So he took a thousand-men-pull-rock, and having blocked up the path with it, stood face to face with Izanami no Mikoto, and at last pronounced the formula of divorce. Upon this, Izanami no Mikoto said: 'My dear Lord and husband, if thou sayest so, I will strangle to death the people of the country which thou dost govern, a thousand in one day.'"

In the sixth variant, the first deity, usually named Kunitokotachi, is named Ama-no-tokotachi. His appearance is followed by Umashiashikabihikoji. There is another tradition embedded in this sixth alternate version, which gives the first deity's name as Kunitokotachi again, while describing the material he appeared from as being like floating oil.

♦ **The Next Deities Who Came into Being**

These passages return to the main version of the myth. After the third generation, deities are produced in pairs. First are Uhijini and Suhijini, who are also known as Uhijine and Suhijine, possibly reflecting different dialects of Old Japanese. Ohoto-nochi and Ohoto-mahe are next, and like Uhijini and Suhijini, they have similar alternate names. Another version of the myths (introduced as "one authority") lists the pair as Ohoto-no-he, divided into Ohotomahiko and Ohotomahime. "Hiko" and "hime" indicate that this was a male-female pair, which are not hard to find among deities of shrines in Japan. Yet another version gives their names as Ohotomuchi and Ohotomuhe. In the sixth generation are Omotaru and Kashikone, the latter of which has many names. Most of Kashikone's names have elements indicating unpleasantness, meaning that these two gods might have formed a benevolent-malevolent deity pair. Like male-female pairs, benevolent-malevolent pairs are not at all uncommon among shrine deities in Japan. The final generation is Izanagi and Izanami, who would produce the Japanese islands and are the most famous deities of Japan. One version lists them as the children of Kashikone (identified through the alternate name Awokashikine).

A new alternate version gives a different, patrilineal account of descent for the first deities: Kunitokotachi fathers Amekagami, and Amekagami fathers Ame-yorodzu, who fathers Ahanagi, who finally fathers Izanagi. The female deities are left out of this lineage, so their names are unclear.

The fourth through seventh generations contain eight deities in all, as each of these four generations consists of a pair. In the main version of the myth in the *Nihongi*, sexual reproduction has yet to be invented, so each male-female pair is described as appearing spontaneously; they are male and female, since the material of the universe has male and female essences, the yin and yang. (The alternate versions mentioned contradict this statement of nonsexual origins.) The last paragraph of this section introduces the final alternate genealogy, replacing Ohotonochi and Ohotomahe with Tsunoguhi and Ikuguhi.

♦ Izanagi no Mikoto and Izanami no Mikoto

This passage begins with Izanagi and Izanami in heaven, contemplating the unformed earth below. They stir the chaotic ocean with a jeweled spear and create an island, Onogorojima, to which they descend. Izanagi and Izanami then perform a courtship ritual, where they pretend not to know each other—possibly to avoid an incest taboo. Izanami, the female, greets the male first, and is chided for it. They perform the ritual of meeting again, with Izanagi speaking first. Having thus established the "proper" gender hierarchy, they then confirm the difference between male and female sexual organs. The two thus become a married pair.

Having established sexual relations with Izanagi, Izanami starts to give birth to the islands of Japan. Ahaji (in modern Japanese, Awaji, an island in the Inland Sea) is the first, but it is not counted as a full child but instead as the placenta. Ohoyamato-no-Toyoakitsu-shima (the Island of Great Yamato—actually an inland region on the island of Honshu near the city of Nara) and the islands of Iyo-no-futana and Tsukushi are born next. Oki and Sado islands, in the Sea of Japan, are twins in this myth, although in reality they are rather distant from each other. The "islands" (again, like Yamato, regions of Honshu and not separate islands) of Koshi, Ohoshima, and Kibi-no-Ko round out the set of eight (as Ahaji is excluded), leading to the name for Japan soon given: "the Great-eight-island country." It should be noted, however, that in Old Japanese, "eight" merely stood for "many" or "uncountable."

The creation of Tsushima and Iki, as well as many other small islands of Japan, is described as not being through Izanagi and Izanami but merely through the hardening of foam from the water. Tsushima and Iki are in the Sea of Japan, very close to the Korean Peninsula, and served as the gateway to the continent. This part of the myth indicates how the royal court might have viewed this border area. Izanami and Izanagi go on to produce the ocean, rivers, mountains, and plants. The last two are through two deities, Kukunochi, the ancestor of treelike plants, and Kayanohime, the ancestress of grasslike plants.

♦ They Then Together Produced the Sun-Goddess

The birth of the sun goddess is next described, as Izanami and Izanagi decide to create a deity to rule the universe. Oddly, the name of this goddess in the main text is Ohohirume-no-muchi, appearing as variants of Amaterasu only in the alternate texts. This suggests that the royal family did not always count Amaterasu as their main ancestress and also that Amaterasu was combined with other sun deities early in her history. The sun goddess is too radiant to stay on earth and so is sent to heaven to rule from there.

The next child produced is Tsukiyumi or, as he is more commonly known, Tsukiyomi, the moon god. He is sent to heaven to be consort to the sun goddess. Following Tsukiyomi, the leech child is born. The leech child is considered a failure and is sent adrift in a boat.

The third child of this trio is then produced, Sosanowo (more commonly known as Susanoo), a storm god. His behavior, violent and upset, is so destructive that Izanami and Izanagi send him to rule the netherworld. This ends the main version of the creation myth as related in the *Nihongi*. Izanami and Izanagi have created Japan and deities to rule heaven and the netherworld, and subsequently, as related later, Izanagi retires from the world. This version of the myth is not well known in Japan today—far more famous are the following variants, which describe Izanami's death and Izanagi's pursuit of her to the netherworld. It is possible that the main version of the tale in the *Nihongi* is only as old as the *Nihongi* itself: The main text of the myth ultimately concludes (beyond the scope of this excerpt) with Izanagi retiring by himself, with no mention of Izanami's fate.

A variant of the birth of the sun/moon/storms trio is described, where Izanagi alone is responsible for their creation, through the use of mirrors—thought of as magical in early Japan. In this version, Sosanowo is still sent to rule the netherworld as a result of his misbehavior.

♦ Now Izanami no Mikoto Was Burnt by Kagu Tsuchi

Finally, another variant myth is introduced (beginning "After the sun and moon, the next child . . .") that describes the death of Izanami once she gives birth to the god of fire. Izanami and Izanagi still produce the sun and moon, the leech child, and then Sosanowo. Sosanowo is sent to the netherworld, but their next child is a boat, in which they abandon the leech child. Here, the birth of Kagutsuchi, the fire god, is mentioned. All the following alternate versions are variants of this story line. In her death spasms, Izanami produces the earth goddess Haniyamahime and the water goddess Midzuhanome. Kagutsuchi weds Haniyamahime, and their child, Wakamusubi, is the source of agriculture and sericulture (silk making, which requires silkworms and mulberry leaves).

Three more variants are introduced. In the first, Izanami gives birth to, along with the earth goddess and water goddess, "the gourd of Heaven." These three create a set that can control the fire god: The gourd holds the water that can put the fire out, and earth (dirt) can smother a fire. In the next variant, the earth and water goddesses are formed from Izanami's bodily waste as she dies. Her vomit is also turned into a god, Kanayamahiko, who appears to be a metal deity. The next short variant does not mention any children born to Izanami (or from her body) as she dies. Instead her location of burial is stated, and this story is given as the origin of a local festival.

This section starts the longest set of variants and subvariants concerning the birth of the fire god and the death of

Izanami, and it contains some of the best-known episodes of the myth. Izanami and Izanagi, having produced the islands of Japan, move on to producing the other deities. The god of the wind, the gods of the sea, mountains, rivers, and trees, and the earth goddess are produced. At last, Kagutsuchi's birth comes to pass; he burns his mother, Izanami, and she dies ("suffered change and departed"). Izanagi, upset at the loss of Izanami, mourns her and produces a deity from his tears. He then takes his sword and cuts Kagutsuchi into three parts. Each part becomes a deity, as does Kagutsuchi's blood as it drips from the sword. These deities produce named offspring. Two subvariants of the tale differ in the names of the deities formed from Kagutsuchi's body and blood.

♦ **The Land of Yomi**

The variant continues with Izanagi following Izanami to the land of Yomi, otherwise known as the netherworld or the land of the dead. Izanami says that she has eaten the food of Yomi and tells Izanagi not to look at her. Izanagi disobeys her and, by the light of a torch made from his comb, sees Izanami's decaying body. He is frightened and flees. This episode is described as the source of some taboos about torches and combs. Izanami is outraged and sends the hags of the dead to chase after him. To delay them, he turns his headdress into grapes and his comb into bamboo shoots, which the hags eat. Izanami joins the pursuit and catches up to Izanagi at the gateway to the netherworld.

A subvariant is described where Izanagi turns his urine into a river to delay his pursuers. The formatting suggests that the following conclusion belongs to the subvariant. Izanagi blocks the road from the netherworld with a rock and divorces Izanami. Izanami threatens to kill a thousand people a day if he persists in divorcing her, but Izanagi replies that he will, in turn, cause fifteen hundred people to be born each day. Izanagi sheds himself of his polluted garments, all of which become deities. The next two paragraphs are somewhat contradictory: The first suggests that the entrance to the netherworld is not a physical location but the cessation of breathing as one dies; the second, however, gives names for the rock used to block the entrance to the netherworld, suggesting that it does have a physical location.

Izanagi then cleanses himself of the pollution he acquired in visiting the land of the dead, and he creates the major deities of Japan. Washing his body in the various waters, Izanagi produces further deities. Finally, washing his eyes, he produces the sun and moon deities, and washing his nose he produces Sosanowo. This version of the birth of the sun/moon/storms triad is closer to what is found in the *Kojiki* than the previous versions related above. As before, Sosanowo cries and rages and is banished, although in this tale the reason for Sosanowo's behavior is that he is mourning Izanami. This ends the first variant about the death of Izanami and the birth of the sun, moon, and storm deities. (A version of the story of Izanagi's purification is found in the Nakatomi clan's liturgy for the Grand Purification.)

The succeeding paragraphs introduce two variants about the death of Kagutsuchi, where again different deities are born from the body of the dead fire god. In the second variant, the element of fire is said to be found in rocks and vegetation because of Kagutsuchi's blood having splashed on them.

Another version of Izanagi's descent to underworld and his escape is next relayed. In this version, the "thunders" that are feasting on Izanami's corpse become Izanagi's pursuers; they are repelled with flung peaches. A final variant of Izanagi's visit to the underworld is very vague and may have been corrupted. In this version, Izanagi is not chased out after seeing Izanami's corpse but instead gets into an argument with her about propriety. They divorce, and Izanagi spits at her; the spittle is turned into a deity. Furthermore, Izanagi's purification also forms a deity. At the entrance to Yomi, Izanami relays her intention to remain in the land of the dead, citing exhaustion with the act of creation. A deity called Kukurihime then has an exchange with Izanagi that is not explained. At this point, Izanagi performs his ablutions. He enters the water three times, creating three deities. Finally, he produces the remaining deities of the world. This ends the variants about Izanagi's visit to the underworld. Following this, the *Nihongi* describes how Izanagi turns over the rule of the world to others and retires to a concealed place on the island of Awaji.

Audience

It is difficult to be certain about the audience of a work written some thirteen hundred years ago. As the *Nihongi* was presented only eight years after the *Kojiki*, one prominent theory is that they were intended for different audiences: The *Kojiki* was to be read at the Japanese court, while the *Nihongi* was to be shown to a continental audience. However, there is no evidence that the *Nihongi* was used in diplomatic relations, so it seems that it was intended for a domestic audience.

The appearance of the *Nihongi* shortly after the *Kojiki* may instead indicate some domestic unhappiness with the latter work—an argument that can be supported by the prominence of variant tales in the *Nihongi*. Where the *Kojiki* insists on one version of royal origins, the *Nihongi* allows for some (slightly) different tales. On the other hand, the *Kojiki* includes more clan names and histories than the *Nihongi* does and is more expansive geographically, indicating that the audience that prompted the *Nihongi* was centered on the court itself or very close to it. As most of the variant texts are found in the two scrolls dedicated to the age of the gods, the *Nihongi* may have been an attempt at appeasing ritual and scholarly lineages at court. In the modern era, scholars have been interested in the *Nihongi* for the light it can shed on the emergence of the Japanese state, particularly as its authority was reinforced by State Shinto, which established a patriarchal, imperial, and race-based origin for the modern Japanese state.

Impact

If the *Nihongi* was intended to bring consensus among various religious lineages of the court, it did not fully succeed. Members of two religious lineages, the Inbe and the Mononobe, would later bring two private histories involving the age of the gods to the court: An Inbe member submitted *Kogo shui* (Gleanings from Stories of Antiquity) in 807, and a Mononobe descendant referred to *Sendai kuji hongi* (also known as the *Kujiki—Records of Ancient Matters from Previous Ages*) in 936. In both cases, the members of these clans were arguing for their own traditions against the ritual dominance of others at court.

In all other respects, the *Nihongi* proved highly successful. From 721 to 936, court lecture series were held on the *Nihongi*, on average every thirty years. It was canonized as the first of six official national histories, the Rikkokushi, and thus was referred to when questions of Japan's past came up. The *Nihongi* was cited as a near-absolute authority when it came to authenticating myths (concerning, for example, local shrines and deities or the divine origins of poetry) in the medieval period. Many such references to the *Nihongi* are in fact spurious, referring to myths and deities that do not appear in the text at all. These myths incorrectly attributed to the *Nihongi* are often referred to as the "medieval *Nihongi*."

The reason why this strategy of misattribution was so successful was threefold. First, the population that had access to the text was very limited until the first printed edition appeared in 1599. Second, the text had become hard to read not long after its completion. This leads to the third point, that there was a well-developed tradition of esoteric interpretations of the text. These three circumstances helped spur several interpretive lineages based on the *Nihongi*. The earliest surviving exegesis, *Nihon shoki shiki*, dates to around the second half of the tenth century; the next, the *Shaku Nihongi*, was written between 1271 and 1301. By the fourteenth and fifteenth centuries, many religious interpretations of the text by courtiers, ritualists, and Buddhist scholars had appeared; among them was one by the Tendai Buddhist monk Ryohen, who produced his own interpretation of the text in 1419. The Urabe family's tradition of *Nihongi* interpretation gave its descendant Yoshida Kanetomo the authority to develop Yoshida Shinto in the late fifteenth century, and the *Nihongi* became a major text of Suika Shinto, which was developed by Yamazaki Ansai in the seventeenth century. Buddhist interpretations of the *Nihongi* were also important to Ryobu (Buddhist) Shinto.

The *Nihongi*'s status as Japan's ultimate mythological authority lasted only until the early nineteenth century. From 1790 through 1822, the Kokugaku (National Learning) philosopher Motoori Norinaga published a study of the *Kojiki* that simultaneously attacked the *Nihongi* as being inadequately Japanese. Norinaga's rejection of the "Chinese-tainted" *Nihongi* has had a lasting impact on the study of Shinto since that time. The *Nihongi* has remained an important text for Japanese mythology, though it was placed second to the more "authentic" *Kojiki*.

Questions for Further Study

1. What does this document, in conjunction with the Yengishiki, tell you about the emergence of Shinto in medieval Japan? How did the medieval Japanese regard their mythological history, and how did that history affect their lives?

2. What vested interest did the emperor and his descendants have in the mythology recorded in the *Nihongi*?

3. The creation myth recorded in the *Nihongi* bears obvious comparison with creation myths in the Western tradition, notably that recorded in Genesis. What fundamental differences in the creation accounts can you specify? What historical, cultural, or geographical factors might have accounted for these differences?

4. The concept of a sun goddess was common in early cultures; Amaterasu plays a prominent role in the Shinto pantheon, as did Re for the ancient Egyptians. Less is said about a moon god or goddess. Why do you think early cultures might have revered a moon god such as Tsukiyumi in Japan?

5. The *Nihongi* is referred to in the entry as Japan's "mythological authority." Do you think anything—documents, institutions, organizations, and so forth—functions as a "mythological authority" for the United States? Explain.

Further Reading

■ Books

Breen, John, and Mark Teeuwen, eds. *Shinto in History: Ways of the Kami.* London: Routledge, 2000.

Breen, John, and Mark Teeuwen. *A New History of Shinto.* Chichester, U.K.: Wiley-Blackwell, 2010.

Matsumae Takeshi. "Early Kami Worship," trans. Janet Goodwin. In *The Cambridge History of Japan*, Vol. 1: *Ancient Japan*, ed. Delmar Brown. Cambridge, U.K.: Cambridge University Press, 1993.

Ooms, Herman. *Imperial Politics and Symbolics in Ancient Japan: The Tenmu Dynasty, 650–800.* Honolulu: University of Hawaii Press, 2009.

Scheid, Bernhard. "Two Modes of Secrecy in the *Nihon shoki* Transmission." In *The Culture of Secrecy in Japanese Religion*, ed. Bernhard Scheid and Mark Teeuwen. New York: Routledge, 2006.

Taro, Sakamoto. *The Six National Histories of Japan*, trans. John S. Brownlee. Vancouver, Canada: UBC Press, 1991.

■ Journals

Borgen, Robert, and Marian Ury. "Readable Japanese Mythology: Selections from *Nihon shoki* and *Kojiki*." *Journal of the Association of Teachers of Japanese* 24, no. 1 (April 1990): 61–97.

Jun'ichi, Isomae. "Reappropriating the Japanese Myths: Motoori Norinaga and the Creation Myths of the *Kojiki* and *Nihon shoki*," trans. Sarah E. Thal. *Japanese Journal of Religious Studies* 27, nos. 1/2 (Spring 2000): 15–39.

Kirkland, Russell. "The Sun and the Throne: The Origins of the Royal Descent Myth in Ancient Japan." *Numen* 44, no. 2 (May 1997): 109–152.

■ Web Sites

"Kojiki and Nihon shoki (Nihongi)." Encyclopedia of Shinto Web site.
http://eos.kokugakuin.ac.jp/modules/xwords/entry.php?entryID=1243

—Kristina Burhmann

NIHONGI

Book I. The Age of the Gods.

♦ **Part I.**

Of old, Heaven and Earth were not yet separated, and the In and Yo not yet divided. They formed a chaotic mass like an egg which was of obscurely defined limits and contained germs.

The purer and clearer part was thinly drawn out, and formed Heaven, while the heavier and grosser element settled down and became Earth.

The finer element easily became a united body, but the consolidation of the heavy and gross element was accomplished with difficulty.

Heaven was therefore formed first, and Earth was established subsequently.

Thereafter Divine Beings were produced between them.

Hence it is said that when the world began to be created, the soil of which lands were composed floated about in a manner which might be compared to the floating of a fish sporting on the surface of the water.

At this time a certain thing was produced between Heaven and Earth. It was in form like a reed-shoot. Now this became transformed into a God, and was called Kuni-toko-tachi no Mikoto. . . .

Next there was Kuni no sa-tsuchi no Mikoto, and next Toyo-kumu-nu no Mikoto, in all three deities.

These were pure males spontaneously developed by the operation of the principle of Heaven.

In one writing it is said:—"When Heaven and Earth began, a thing existed in the midst of the Void. Its shape may not be described. Within it a Deity was spontaneously produced, whose name was Kuni-toko-tachi no Mikoto, also called Kuni-soko-tachi no Mikoto. Next there was Kuni no sa-tsuchi no Mikoto, also called Kuni no sa tachi no Mikoto. Next there was Toyo-kuninushi no Mikoto, also called Toyo-kumu-nu no Mikoto, Toyo-ka-fushi-no no Mikoto, Uki-fu-no-toyo-kahi no Mikoto, Toyo-kuni-no no Mikoto, Toyo-kuhi-no no Mikoto, Ha-ko-kuni-no no Mikoto, or Mi-no no Mikoto."

In one writing it is said:—"Of old, when the land was young and the earth young, it floated about, as it were floating oil. At this time a thing was produced within the land, in shape like a reed-shoot when it sprouts forth. From this there was a Deity developed, whose name was Umashi-ashi-kabi-hiko-ji no Mikoto. Next there was Kuni no toko-tachi no Mikoto, and next Kuni no sa-tsuchi no Mikoto."

In one writing it is said:—"When Heaven and Earth were in a state of chaos, there was first of all a deity, whose name was Umashi-ashi-kabi-hiko-ji no Mikoto. Next there was Kuni-soko-tachi no Mikoto."

In one writing it is said:—"When Heaven and Earth began, there were Deities produced together, whose names were, first, Kuni-no-toko-tachi no Mikoto, and next Kuni no sa-tsuchi no Mikoto." It is further stated:—"The names of the Gods which were produced in the Plain of High Heaven were Ama no mi-naka-nushi no Mikoto, next Taka-mi-musubi no Mikoto, next Kami-mi-musubi no Mikoto."

In one writing it is said:—"Before Heaven and Earth were produced, there was something which might be compared to a cloud floating over the sea. It had no place of attachment for its root. In the midst of this a thing was generated which resembled a reed-shoot when it is first produced in the mud. This became straightway transformed into human shape and was called Kuni no toko-tachi no Mikoto."

In one writing it is said:—"When Heaven and Earth began, a thing was produced in the midst of the Void, which resembled a reed-shoot. This became changed into a God, who was called Ama no toko-tachi no Mikoto. There was next Umashi-ashi-kabi-hiko-ji no Mikoto." It is further stated:—"There was a thing produced in the midst of the Void like floating oil, from which a God was developed, called Kuni toko-tachi no Mikoto."

The next Deities who came into being were Uhiji-ni no Mikoto and Suhiji-ni no Mikoto, also called Uhiji-ne no Mikoto and Suhiji-ne no Mikoto.

The next Deities which came into being were Oho-to nochi no Mikoto and Oho-to mahe no Mikoto.

One authority says Oho-to no he no Mikoto, otherwise called Oho-to-ma-hiko no Mikoto and Oho-to-ma-hime no Mikoto. Another says Oho-tomu-chi no Mikoto and Oho-tomu-he no Mikoto.

The next Gods which came into being were Omotaru no Mikoto and Kashiko-ne no Mikoto, also called Aya-kashiko-ne no Mikoto, Imi kashiki no Mikoto, or Awo-kashiki-ne no Mikoto, or Aya-kashiki no Mikoto.

Document Text

The next Deities which came into being were Izanagi no Mikoto and Izanami no Mikoto.

One writing says:—"These two Deities were the children of Awo-kashiki-ne no Mikoto."

One writing says:—"Kuni no toko-tachi no Mikoto produced Ame kagami no Mikoto, Ame kagami no Mikoto produced Ame yorodzu no Mikoto, Ame yorodzu no Mikoto produced Aha-nagi no Mikoto, and Aha-nagi no Mikoto produced Izanagi no Mikoto."

These make eight Deities in all. Being formed by the mutual action of the Heavenly and Earthly principles, they were made male and female. From Kuni no toko-tachi no Mikoto to Izanagi no Mikoto and Izanami no Mikoto are called the seven generations of the age of the Gods. . . .

In one writing it is said:—"The gods that were produced in pairs, male and female, were first of all Uhiji ni no Mikoto and Suhiji ni no Mikoto. Next there were Tsuno-guhi no Mikoto and Iku-guhi no Mikoto, next Omo-taru no Mikoto and Kashiko-ne no Mikoto, and next Izanagi no Mikoto and Izanami no Mikoto."

Izanagi no Mikoto and Izanami no Mikoto stood on the floating bridge of Heaven, and held counsel together, saying: "Is there not a country beneath ?" . . .

Thereupon they thrust down the jewel-spear of Heaven, and groping about therewith found the ocean. The brine which dripped from the point of the spear coagulated and became an island which received the name of Ono-goro-jima.

The two Deities thereupon descended and dwelt in this island. Accordingly they wished to become husband and wife together, and to produce countries.

So they made Ono-goro-jima the pillar of the centre of the land.

Now the male deity turning by the left, and the female deity by the right, they went round the pillar of the land separately. When they met together on one side, the female deity spoke first and said:—"How delightful! I have met with a lovely youth." The male deity was displeased, and said:—"I am a man, and by right should have spoken first. How is it that on the contrary thou, a woman, shouldst have been the first to speak? This was unlucky. Let us go round again." Upon this the two deities went back, and having met anew, this time the male deity spoke first, and said:— "How delightful! I have met a lovely maiden."

Then he inquired of the female deity, saying:—"In thy body is there aught formed?" She answered, and said:—"In my body there is a place which is the source of femininity." The male deity said:—"In my body again there is a place which is the source of masculinity. I wish to unite this source-place of my body to the source-place of thy body." Hereupon the male and female first became united as husband and wife.

Now when the time of birth arrived, first of all the island of Ahaji was reckoned as the placenta, and their minds took no pleasure in it. Therefore it received the name of Ahaji no Shima.

Next there was produced the island of Oho-yamato no Toyo-aki-tsu shima. . . .

Next they produced the island of Iyo no futa-na, and next the island of Tsukushi. Next the islands of Oki and Sado were born as twins. This is the prototype of the twin-births which sometimes take place among mankind.

Next was born the island of Koshi, then the island of Oho-shima, then the island of Kibi no Ko.

Hence first arose the designation of the Oho-yashima country.

Then the islands of Tsushima and Iki, with the small islands in various parts, were produced by the coagulation of the foam of the salt-water.

It is also stated that they were produced by the coagulation of the foam of fresh water. . . .

They next produced the sea, then the rivers, and then the mountains. Then they produced Ku-ku-no-chi, the ancestor of the trees, and next the ancestor of herbs, Kaya-no-hime. . . .

After this Izanagi no Mikoto and Izanami no Mikoto consulted together, saying:—"We have now produced the Great-eight-island country, with the mountains, rivers, herbs, and trees. Why should we not produce someone who shall be lord of the universe? They then together produced the Sun-Goddess, who was called Oho-hiru-me no muchi.

Called in one writing Ama-terasu no Oho kami.

In one writing she is called Ama-terasu-oho-hiru-me no Mikoto.

The resplendent lustre of this child shone throughout all the six quarters. Therefore the two Deities rejoiced, saying:—"We have had many children, but none of them have been equal to this wondrous infant. She ought not to be kept long in this land, but we ought of our own accord to send her at once to Heaven, and entrust to her the affairs of Heaven."

At this time Heaven and Earth were still not far separated, and therefore they sent her up to Heaven by the ladder of Heaven.

They next produced the Moon-god.

Called in one writing Tsuki-yumi no Mikoto, or Tsuki-yomi no Mikoto.

His radiance was next to that of the Sun in splendour. This God was to be the consort of the Sun-

Goddess, and to share in her government. They therefore sent him also to Heaven.

Next they produced the leech-child, which even at the age of three years could not stand upright. They therefore placed it in the rock-camphor-wood boat of Heaven, and abandoned it to the winds.

Their next child was Sosa no wo no Mikoto.

Called in one writing Kami Sosa no wo no Mikoto or Haya Sosa no wo no Mikoto.

This God had a fierce temper and was given to cruel acts. Moreover he made a practice of continually weeping and wailing. So he brought many of the people of the land to an untimely end. Again he caused green mountains to become withered. Therefore the two Gods, his parents, addressed Sosa no wo no Mikoto, saying:—"Thou art exceedingly wicked, and it is not meet that thou shouldst reign over the world. Certainly thou must depart far away to the Nether-Land." So they at length expelled him.

In one writing it is said:—"Izanagi no Mikoto said 'I wish to procreate the precious child who is to rule the world.' He therefore took in his left hand a white-copper mirror, upon which a Deity was produced from it called Oho-hiru-me no Mikoto. In his right hand he took a white-copper mirror, and forthwith there was produced from it a God who was named Tsuki-yumi no Mikoto. Again, while turning his head and looking askance, a God was produced who was named Sosa no wo no Mikoto. Now Oho-hirume no Mikoto and Tsuki-yumi no Mikoto were both of a bright and beautiful nature, and were therefore made to shine down upon Heaven and Earth, But Sosa no wo's character was to love destruction, and he was accordingly sent down to rule the Nether Land."

In one writing it is said:—"After the sun and moon, the next child which was born was the leech-child. When this child had completed his third year, he was nevertheless still unable to stand upright. The reason why the, leech-child was born was that in the beginning, when Izanagi no Mikoto and Izanami no Mikoto went round the pillar, the female Deity was the first to utter an exclamation of pleasure, and the law of male and female was therefore broken. They next procreated Sosa no wo no Mikoto. This God was of a wicked nature, and was. always fond of wailing and wrath. Many of the people of the land died, and the green mountains withered. Therefore his parents addressed him, saying: 'Supposing that thou wert to rule this country, much destruction of life would surely ensue. Thou must govern the far-distant Nether Land.' Their next child was the bird-rock-camphor-wood boat of Heaven. They forthwith took this boat and, placing the leech-child in it, abandoned it to the current. Their next child was Kagu tsuchi."

Now Izanami no Mikoto was burnt by Kagu tsuchi, so that she died. When she was lying down to die, she gave birth to the Earth-Goddess, Hani-yama-hime, and the Water-Goddess, Midzu-ha-no-me. Upon this Kagu tsuchi took to wife Hani-yama-hime, and they had a child named Waka-musubi. On the crown of this Deity's head were produced the silkworm and the mulberry tree, and in her navel the five kinds of grain.

In one writing it is said:—"When Izanami no Mikoto gave birth to Ho-no-musubi, she was burnt by the child, and died. When she was about to die, she brought forth the Water-Goddess, Midzu-ha-no-me, and the Earth-Goddess, Hani-yama-hime. She also brought forth the gourd of Heaven."

In one writing it is said:—"When about to give birth to the Fire-God, Kagu tsuchi, Izanami no Mikoto became feverish and ill. In consequence she vomited, and the vomit became changed into a God, who was called Kana-yama-hiko. Next her urine became changed into a Goddess, who was called Midzu-ha-no-me. Next her excrement was changed into a Goddess, who was called Hani-yama-hime.

In one writing it is said:—"When Izanami no Mikoto gave birth to the Fire-God, she was burnt, and died. She was, therefore, buried at the village of Arima in Kumano, in the province of Kiï. In the time of flowers, the inhabitants worship the spirit of this Goddess by offerings of flowers. They also worship her with drums, flutes, flags, singing and dancing."

In one writing it is said:—"Izanagi no Mikoto and Izanami no Mikoto, having together procreated the Great-eight-island Land, Izanagi no Mikoto said: 'Over the country which we have produced there is naught but morning mists which shed a perfume everywhere!' So he puffed them away with a breath, which became changed into a God, named Shina tohe no Mikoto. He is also called Shina tsu hiko no Mikoto. This is the God of the Wind. Moreover, the child which they procreated when they were hungry was called Uka no mi-tama no Mikoto. Again they produced the Sea-Gods, who were called Wata tsu mi no Mikoto, and the Mountain-Gods, who were called Yama tsu mi, the Gods of the River-mouths, who were called Haya-aki-tsubi no Mikoto, the Tree-Gods, who were called Ku-ku no chi, and the Earth-Goddess, who was called Hani-yasu no Kami. Thereafter they produced all manner of things whatsoever. When the time came for the Fire-God Kagu tsuchi to be born, his mother Izanami no Mikoto was burnt, and suf-

Document Text

fered change and departed. Then Izanagi no Mikoto was wroth, and said: 'Oh, that I should have given my beloved younger sister in exchange for a single child!' So while he crawled at her, head, and crawled at her feet, weeping and lamenting, the tears which he shed fell down and became a Deity. It is this Deity who dwells at Unewo no Konomoto, and who is called Naki-saha-me no Mikoto. At length he drew the ten-span sword with which he was girt, and cut Kagu tsu-chi into three pieces, each of which became changed into a God. Moreover, the blood which dripped from the edge of the sword became the multitudinous rocks which are in the bed of the Easy-River of Heaven. This God was the father of Futsu-nushi no Kami. Moreover, the blood which dripped from the hilt-ring of the sword spurted out and became deities, whose names were Mika no Haya-hi no Kami and next Hi no Haya-hi no Kami. This Mika no Haya-hi no Kami was the parent of Take-mika-suchi no Kami."

Another version is:—"Mika no haya-hi no Mikoto, next Hi no haya-hi no Mikoto, and next Take-mika-tsuchi no Kami."

"Moreover, the blood which dripped from the point of the sword spurted out and became deities, who were called Iha-saku no Kami, after him Ne-saku no Kami, and next Iha-tsutsu-wo no Mikoto. This Iha-saku no Kami was the father of Futsu-nushi no Kami."

One account says:—"Iha-tsutsu-wo no Mikoto, and next Iha-tsutsu-me no Mikoto."

"Moreover, the blood which dripped from the head of the sword spurted out and became deities, who were called Kura o Kami no Kami, next Kura-yamatsumi no Kami, and next Kura-midzu-ha no Kami.

Thereafter, Izanagi no Mikoto went after Izanami no Mikoto, and entered the land of Yomi. When he reached her they conversed together, and Izanami no Mikoto said: 'My lord and husband, why is thy coming so late? I have already eaten of the cooking-furnace of Yomi. Nevertheless, I am about to lie down to rest. I pray thee, do not thou look on me.' Izanagi no Mikoto did not give ear to her, but secretly took his many-toothed comb and, breaking off its end tooth, made of it a torch, and looked at her. Putrefying matter had gushed up, and maggots swarmed. This is why people at the present day avoid using a single light at night, and also avoid throwing away a comb at night. Izanagi no Mikoto was greatly shocked, and said: 'Nay! I have come unawares to a hideous and polluted land.' So he speedily ran away back again. Then Izanami no Mikoto was angry, and said: 'Why didst thou not observe that which I charged thee? Now am I put to shame.' So she sent the eight Ugly Females of Yomi (*Shikome, called by some Hisame*) to pursue and stay him. Izanagi no Mikoto therefore drew his sword, and, flourishing it behind him, ran away. Then he took his black head-dress and flung it down. It became changed into grapes, which the Ugly Females seeing, took and ate. When they had finished eating them, they again pursued Izanagi no Mikoto. Then he flung down his many-toothed comb, which forthwith became changed into bamboo-shoots. The Ugly Females pulled them up and ate them, and when they had done eating them, again gave chase. Afterwards, Izanami no Mikoto came herself and pursued him By this time Izanami no Mikoto had reached the Even Pass of Yomi."

According to one account, Izanagi no Mikoto made water against a large tree, which water at once turned into a great river. While the Ugly Females of Yomi were preparing to cross this river, Izanagi no Mikoto had already reached the Even Pass of Yomi. So he took a thousand-men-pull-rock, and having blocked up the path with it, stood face to face with Izanami no Mikoto, and at last pronounced the formula of divorce. Upon this, Izanami no Mikoto said: "My dear Lord and husband, if thou sayest so, I will strangle to death the people of the country which thou dost govern, a thousand in one day." Then Izanagi no Mikoto replied, saying, "My beloved younger sister, if thou sayest so, I will in one day cause to be born fifteen hundred." Then he said, "Come no further," and threw down his staff, which was called Funado no Kami. Moreover, he threw down his girdle, which was called Naga-chi-ha no Kami. Moreover, he threw down his upper garment, which was called Wadzura-hi no Kami. Moreover, he threw down his trowsers, which were called Aki-gui no Kami. Moreover, he threw down his shoes, which were called Chishik no Kami.

Some say that the Even Pass of Yomi is not any place in particular, but means only the space of time when the breath fails on the approach of death.

Now the rock with which the Even Pass of Yomi was blocked is called Yomi-do ni fusagaru Oho-kami. Another name for it is Chi-gayeshi no Oho-kami.

When Izanagi no Mikoto had returned, he was seized with regret, and said, "Having gone to Nay! a hideous and filthy place, it is meet that I should cleanse my body from its pollutions." He accordingly went to the plain of Ahagi at Tachibana in Wodo in Hiuga of Tsukushi, and purified himself. When at length he was about to wash away the impurities of his body, he lifted up his voice and said, "The upper stream is too rapid and the lower stream is too sluggish, I will wash in the middle stream." The God which was thereby produced was called Ya-so-maga-tsu-bi no Kami, and then to remedy these evils there were produced Deities named Kami-nawo-bi no Kami, and after him Oho-nawo-bi no Kami.

Moreover, the Deities which were produced by his plunging down and washing in the bottom of the sea were called Soko-tsu-wata-tsu-mi no Mikoto and Soko-tsutsu-wo no Mikoto. Moreover, when he plunged and washed in the mid-tide, there were Gods produced who were called Naka tsu wata-dzu-mi no Mikoto, and next Naka-tsutsu-wo no Mikoto. Moreover, when he washed floating on the surface of the water, Gods were produced, who were called Uha-tsu-wata-dzu-mi no Mikoto and next Uha-tsutsu-wo no Mikoto. There were in all nine Gods. The Gods Soko-tsutsu-wo no Mikoto, Naka-tsutsu-wo no Mikoto, and Soko-tsutsu-wo no Mikoto are the three great Gods of Suminoye. The Gods Soko-tsu-wata-dzu-mi no Mikoto, Naka-tsu-wata-dzu-mi no Mikoto, and Uha-tsu-wata-dzu-mi no Mikoto are the Gods worshipped by the Muraji of Adzumi.

Thereafter, a Deity was produced by his washing his left eye, which was called Ama-terasu-no-oho-Kami. Then he washed his right eye, producing thereby a Deity who was called Tsuki-yomi no Mikoto. Then he washed his nose, producing thereby a God who was called Sosa no wo no Mikoto. In all there were three Deities. Then Izanagi no Mikoto gave charge to his three children, saying, "Do thou, Ama-terasu no Oho-kami, rule the plain of High Heaven: do thou, Tsuki-yomi no Mikoto, rule the eight-hundred-fold tides of the ocean plain: do thou, Sosa no wo no Mikoto, rule the world." At this time, Sosa no wo no Mikoto was already of full age. He had, moreover, grown a beard eight spans long. Nevertheless, he neglected to rule the world, and was always weeping, wailing, and fuming with rage. Therefore Izanagi no Mikoto inquired of him, saying, "Why dost thou continually weep in this way ?" He answered and said, "I wish to follow my mother to the Nether Land, and it is simply for that reason that I weep." Then Izanagi no Mikoto was filled with detestation of him, and said, "Go, even as thy heart bids thee." So he forthwith drove him away.

In one writing it is said: "Izanagi no Mikoto drew his sword and cut Kagutsuchi into three pieces. One of these became Ikadzuchi no Kami, one became Oho-yama-tsu-mi no Kami, and one became Taka-wo-Kami." Moreover, it is said: "When he slew Kagutsuchi, the blood gushed out and stained the five hundred rocks which are in the midst of the eighty rivers of Heaven, forming thereby Gods who were called Iha-saku no Kami; next Ne-saku no Kami's child, Iha tsutsu-wo no Kami ; and next, Iha-tsutsu-me no Kami's child, Futsu-nushi no Kami."

In one writing it is said: "Izanagi no Mikoto cut Kagutsuchi no Mikoto into five pieces, which were each changed, and became the five Mountain-Gods. The first piece, viz., the head, became Oho-yama-tsu-mi; the second, viz. the trunk, became Naka-yama-tsu-mi; the third, viz. the hands, became Ha-yama-tsu mi; the fourth, viz. the loins, became Masa-katsu-yama-tsu-mi; and the fifth, viz. the feet, became Shiki-yama-tsu-mi.

At this time the blood from the wounds spurted out and stained the rocks, trees and herbage. This is the reason that herbs, trees, and pebbles naturally contain the element of fire."

In one writing it is said: "Izanagi no Mikoto, wishing to see his younger sister, went to the temporary burial-place. At this time, Izanami no Mikoto being still as she was when alive came forth to meet him, and they talked together. She spoke to Izanagi no Mikoto and said, 'My august Lord and husband, I beseech thee not to look at me.' When she had done speaking, she suddenly became invisible. It was then dark, so Izanagi no Mikoto lit a single light, and looked at her. Izanami no Mikoto was then swollen and. festering, and eight kinds of Thunder-Gods rested on her. Izanagi no Mikoto was shocked, and ran away. Then the thunders all arose and pursued him. Now by the roadside there grew a large peach tree, at the foot of which Izanagi no Mikoto concealed himself. He accordingly took its fruit and flung it to the thunders, upon which the thunders all ran away. This was the origin of the practice of keeping off evil spirits by means of peaches, Then Izanagi flung down his staff, saying: 'The thunders may not come beyond this.' It (the staff) was called Funado no Kami, and was originally called Kunado no Ohoji.

Of the so-called Eight Thunders, that which was on her head was called the Great Thunder; that which was on her breast was called the Fire-Thunder; that which was on her belly was called the Earth-Thunder; that which was on her back was called the Young-Thunder; that which was on her posteriors was called the Black-Thunder; that which was on her hand was called the Mountain-Thunder; that which was on her foot was called the Moor-Thunder; and that which was on her genitals was called the Cleaving-Thunder."

Document Text

In one writing it is said: "Izanagi no Mikoto followed after Izanami no Mikoto, and, arriving at the place where she was, spoke to her and said: 'I have come because I sorrowed for thee.' She answered and said, 'We are relations. Do not thou look upon me.' Izanagi no Mikoto would not obey, but continued to look on her. Wherefore Izanami no Mikoto was ashamed and angry, and said, 'Thou hast seen my nakedness. Now I will in turn see thine.' Then Izanagi no Mikoto was ashamed, and prepared to depart. He did not, however, merely go away in silence, but said solemnly, 'Our relationship is severed.' Again he said, 'I will not submit to be beaten by a relation.' And the God of the Spittle which he thereupon spat out was called Haya-tama no wo. Next the God of his purification was called Yomo-tsu-koto-saka no wo; two gods in all. And when he came to contend with his younger sister at the Even Pass of Yomi, Izanagi no Mikoto said, 'It was weak of me at first to sorrow and mourn on account of a relation.'

"Then said the Road-wardens of Yomi, 'We have a message for thee, as follows: "I and thou have produced countries. Why should we seek to produce more? I shall stay in this land, and will not depart along with thee."' At this time Kukuri-hime no Kami said something which Izanagi no Mikoto heard and approved, and she then vanished away.

"But, having visited in person the Land of Yomi, he had brought on himself ill-luck. In order, therefore, to wash away the defilement, he visited the Aha gate and the Haya-sufu-na gate. But the tide in these two gates was exceeding strong. So he returned and took his way towards Wodo in Tachibana. There he did his ablutions. At this time, entering the water, he blew out and produced Iha-tsu-tsu no Mikoto; coming out of the water, he blew forth and produced Oho-nawo-bi no Kami. Entering a second time, he blew out and produced Soko-tsutsu no Mikoto; coming out he blew forth and produced Oho-aya-tsu-bi no Kami. Entering again, he blew forth and produced Aka-tsutsu no Mikoto, and coming out he blew out and produced the various deities of Heaven and Earth, and of the Sea-plain."

Glossary

In	that is, "yin," representing dark, damp, and female
Izanagi no Mikoto and Izanami no Mikoto	Japan's most famous deities; producers of the nation's islands
leech-child	a failure in the production of Japanese islands that is sent adrift in a boat
viz.	an abbreviation of the Latin word *videlicet*, meaning "namely" or "as follows"
Yo	that is, "yang," representing bright, dry, and male
Yomi	the netherworld or land of the dead

Padmasambhava
(Thangka of Padmasambhava with other figures depicting Padmasambhava's emanation / © Oriental Museum, Durham University, UK / The Bridgeman Art Library International)

Tibetan Book of the Dead

ca. 750

"Fear that not. Know them to be the thought-forms of thine own intellectual faculties."

Overview

Bardo Thodol ("Liberation through Hearing,"), often known in the West as the Tibetan Book of the Dead, is a funerary text, a guide for the dead and dying, and a source of inspiration and support to many interested people around the world. It is perhaps among the best-known texts in world religious literature on the afterlife and the process of reincarnation. Its first publication in the West, in 1927, was edited by W. Y. Evans-Wentz, who rendered the title in English as the Tibetan Book of the Dead because of its similarities to the Egyptian Book of the Dead. The legendary Indian guru Padmasambhava, credited with bringing Buddhism to Tibet in the eighth century, is thought to have written the Bardo.

Ostensibly, the Tibetan Book of the Dead describes the experiences at the moment of one's death, the premortem-death-rebirth experience. In other words, it describes the experiences that the consciousness undergoes during the interval between death and the next rebirth. In this sense, a person's life includes the life he or she is now living, the next life, and the life in between (known as the bardo). In Tibetan religious traditions, death is something that need not be feared; rather, it is capable of providing a unique opportunity for a person to grow spiritually. In fact, Tibetan religions aim to transfigure death into an immortal state of spiritual enhancement and rejuvenation. The Bardo text was traditionally chanted or read aloud to the dying to guide them in achieving liberation. It teaches that after a person's awareness, or soul, leaves the bondage of the body, it begins to have a dreamlike experience that assumes various phases (*bardos*) both cheerful and terrifying, represented by peaceful and wrathful deities, respectively.

The book deals with preparation for a favorable rebirth during the intermediate stage between passing and rebirth. This is an experience wherein the dead person is aware that he or she is no longer in a body but rather in the process of total death and rebirth. It guides the dying person on the successful journey through the three *bardo* states, leading them, step by step, toward the most desirable rebirth. According to the Tibetan Book of the Dead, people can indeed be exempted from the Six Worlds (the Buddhist concept of the six cycles of rebirth) as long as they follow the instructions described in the book.

Altogether there are three *bardos* to go through: first, the *chikhai bardo* or "*bardo* of the moment of death," including instructions on the signs and symptoms of death; second, the *chonyid bardo* or "*bardo* of the experiencing of reality," concerning the karmic apparitions of the peaceful deities and the wrathful deities; and third, the *sidpa bardo* or "*bardo* of rebirth," featuring illusions that finally lead to rebirth. The *bardo* visions, or the different deities that appear to deceased persons, are simply their own psychological reflections or, rather, their own desires and cravings that keep them suffering in earthly life. If they see through all of them, they are able to live freely and discern all the complexities of their karma, that is, the endless causes and effects in their lives. They will be liberated from their endless rebirths. On the other hand, failure to do so will result in, a new round of repetition in the Six Worlds.

Context

Religion and spirituality are the hallmarks of Tibet and the Tibetans, each one exerting a ubiquitous influence over all aspects of Tibetan life and infused deeply into Tibetans' cultural veins. In the fourth century, Vajrayana Buddhism developed in India. Buddhism first entered Tibet in the seventh century, with the two wives of King Songsten Gampo: Princess Wencheng from China and Princess Bhrikuti Devi from Nepal. It was not until the end of the eighth century, however, that Buddhism came to have a noticeable influence in Tibet. The Tibetan king Trisong Detsen invited two Buddhist masters to translate important Buddhist texts into the Tibetan language; one of these masters was Padmasambhava. King Detsen made Buddhism the official religion of the Tibetan people in about 755. It should also be noted that before the seventh century, the Tibetan native religion Bon had a very strong hold in Tibetan society. Tibet, under Buddhism, became one of the most religious countries on earth, with most men leading a monastic life. The era saw the construction of countless magnificent monasteries, legions of monks, and the formation of typically Tibetan Buddhist doctrines and practices.

Time Line

300–400	■ Vajrayana Buddhism develops in India.
600–700	■ Buddhism enters Tibet with the two wives of King Songsten Gampo: Princess Wencheng from China and Princess Bhrikuti Devi from Nepal.
CA. 750	■ Padmasambhava composes the Tibetan Book of the Dead.
CA. 755	■ King Trisong Detsen of Tibet makes Buddhism the official religion of the Tibetan people.
755	■ King Detsen establishes a monastic community at Samyé based on Indian Mahayana Buddhism.
836–842	■ King Langdarma persecutes Buddhists and supports the native Bon religion. All monasteries are destroyed, and thousands of monks and laypeople are murdered.
1042	■ Atisa, an Indian monk, arrives in Tibet, starting a revival of Buddhism.
CA. 1365	■ According to tradition, Karma Lingpa discovers the Tibetan Book of the Dead on top of a mountain.

While the Indian spiritual teacher Padmasambhava is revered as a kind of deity, he was also a historical figure and a great religious teacher for the Tibetans. He was responsible not only for translating Buddhist texts into the Tibetan language but also for mixing Buddhism with the local Bon religion to formulate Tibetan Buddhism. In addition, he created the first Tibetan Buddhist School, Nyingma. Tibetan Buddhism was eventually able to replace the Bon religion, becoming firmly secured in Tibet by the eleventh century. Around the same time, Tibetan Buddhism occupied a dominant place in Central Asia, especially in Mongolia and Manchuria, where it was adopted as the state religion. By the thirteenth century, monks in the monasteries in Tibet began to have administrative power, running the bureaucracy and administering the country.

Tibetan Buddhism is characterized by a keen awareness of death; it serves as a reminder to people of the impermanence of life. Everything is dying, including presently living things, but Buddhists believe that people should not panic or despair over death. Instead, they should work toward a holistic understanding and acceptance of death as an inevitable part of their journey. The Tibetan Buddhist tradition recognizes two types of meditations regarding death. The first views death as inevitable and thus encourages people to make the most out of their lives. The second concerns the rehearsal or reenacting of the death process, helping people to die skillfully so they will no longer be subject to the ordinary uncontrolled death and rebirth—the Six Worlds mentioned earlier.

It is in this context—religious, sociological, and historical—that the Tibetan Book of the Dead came into being as a resource for guiding people through the stages between death and rebirth. The Tibetan Book of the Dead was written in the eighth century by Padmasambhava and subsequently discovered by Karma Lingpa, a fourteenth-century Tibetan *terton*, or "revealers of treasure." According to Tibetan tradition, the six-century interval between the composition and discovery of the book was essential to the very survival of Tibet, which was embroiled in a series of wars with its Asian neighbors. The ongoing military struggles called for fearless fighters who were unafraid of the prospect of dying in battle, so a book devoted to the skill of dying well had no place in society at that time.

About the Author

Padmasambhava, or Padmakara ("the Lotus Born"), was a sage-guru credited with transmitting Tantric Buddhism to Tibet and neighboring countries in the eighth century. He is a legendary figure in Tibetan Buddhist history, and much of his biographical information is mythic in nature. According to legend, the Buddha (Siddhartha Gautama) once said, "But . . . years from now, in the midst of an immaculately pure lake in the northwest land of Uddiyana, one will appear who is wiser and more powerful than myself. Born from the center of a lotus blossom, he will be known as Padmasambhava and will reveal the teachings of the Secret Mantras to deliver all beings from misery." The Tibetan king Trisong Detsen (740–798) invited Padmasambhava to defeat and pacify the local demons and evil deities who resisted the Buddhist teachings. Padmasambhava miraculously transformed them to the protectors and guardians of the Dharma, illustrating how Buddhism synthesized the native religions and became localized.

The story of Padmasambhava begins with his birth in the Milk Ocean Land in present-day Pakistan; he is said to have been born within the lotus flower upon the waters of the lake. In various portraits of him, his left hand holds a skull cup and his right hand holds a thunderbolt, connoting compassion. He is credited with building the Samyé, the first monastery of Tibet, and Nyingma, the first major school of Tibetan Buddhism, and is said to have hidden a number of religious treasures in caves, fields, and forests of the Himalayan areas to be found by future tertons, or spiritual treasure-finders. According to Tibetan tradition, the Bardo Thodol, or the Tibetan Book of the Dead, was one such hidden treasure. The life events of Padmasambhava's life are reenacted throughout the year by Tibetans. On the tenth of every lunar month, one of his twelve feats is narrated, and at the Nyingma monasteries, people perform rituals and dances in his honor.

Explanation and Analysis of the Document

W. Y. Evans-Wentz credited himself only as the compiler and editor of this text. The actual translation was done by Tibetan Buddhists, mainly Lama Kazi Dawa-Samdup (1868–1922), a teacher of English at the Maharaja's Boys' School in Gangtok, Sikkim. The passage excerpted here describes the *chonyid bardo*, or the "bardo of the experiencing of reality," which focuses on the karmic apparitions of the wrathful deities. To make the text more readily understandable to the modern readers of English, explanatory words and phrases have been added in brackets.

According to the Tibetan Buddhist tradition, a person's mind or soul is always free, be it at the time before conception in the mother's womb or at the time between death and rebirth. In order to pass through each of these intermediate stages successfully, an individual must know what happens in them and what kind of deities or apparitions will appear at specific times. With proper training (such as studying the Tibetan Book of the Dead), a person will know what death is like and will not be frightened by the unknown.

In the *bardo* state, a person will experience the manifestations of the one hundred peaceful (cheerful or gentle) and wrathful (fierce) deities as illusions in his or her unconsciousness: Fifty-eight of them are of a fierce countenance and forty-two of a gentle one. First, the peaceful deities of the heart center come to awareness as very bright and clear lights; then the wrathful deities manifest themselves. The wrathful deities, though, are not the embodiment of evil or sinister forces; instead, they are there to ward off evil spirits, fight threats to Buddhism, and protect humans by adding fear to the evil spirits. Thus, after the visitations of the cheerful deities from the first to the seventh day, the union of wrathful deities will appear from the eighth until the fourteenth day. From days eight through twelve, the Tathagatas ("Celestial Buddhas") appear in their horrifying and awe-inspiring demonic aspects as Herukas (that is, wrathful but enlightened beings that embody indivisible bliss) and their consorts.

◆ **Introduction**

The "Introduction" serves as an overview of the dawning of the seven wrathful deities. These deities, appearing in very frightening forms and often described in such horrifying terms as "blood-drinking," are actually embodiments of the various desires of human beings for the transient and materialistic mundane world. They are the opposite manifestations of the preceding joyful or happy deities or simply the negative forms of the same mental state. If sentient be-

Bardo Mandala, showing the period between birth and reincarnation
(Bardo Mandala, Thangka showing the period between death and reincarnation [gouache on cloth], Tibetan School [19th century] / Victoria & Albert Museum, London, UK / The Bridgeman Art Library International)

ings can realize and conquer these negative sentiments or cravings, there will be no obstacles on their way to eternal bliss and happiness. The passage also gives warning that whoever flees "through fear, terror, and awe" will "fall over the precipices into the unhappy worlds and suffer." For this reason, "to the abbots [or discipline-holders], to the doctors, and to those mystics who have failed in their vows, and to all the common people, this *Thodol* is indispensable." The Tibetan Book of the Dead was thought to have miraculous powers in guiding the hearers of it to achieve perfect buddhahood and enlightenment.

◆ **The Eighth Day**

From the eighth day onward, the wrathful deities appear. These wrathful deities are so dark and terrifying that, without proper meditation in advance, people would be horrified by their fierce appearance. On this day, the wrathful form of the Buddha Vairocana, called Buddha Heruka, appears to the dead person; with three faces, nine eyes, six arms, and four legs, he has eyebrows like the flames of lightning, and his red hair stands on end. Even his clothing and jewelry are frightening, and he has a cap on his head decorated with dried-up human skulls. Buddha Heruka is accompanied by his consort, called Krodeshvara, both of

Essential Quotes

"As for the common worldly folk, what need is there to mention them! By fleeing, through fear, terror, and awe, they fall over the precipices into the unhappy worlds and suffer."

"Therefore, this Thodol is the doctrine by which Buddhahood may be attained without meditation; the doctrine liberating by the hearing [of it] alone; the doctrine which leadeth brings of great evil karma on the Secret Path; the doctrine which produceth differentiation instantaneously [between those who are initiated into it and those who are not]."

"By so proclaiming [them], knowing them to be tutelary deities, merging [in them] in at-one-ment, Buddhahood will be obtained."

"[They] being thine own tutelary deity, be not terrified. In reality [they are] the Father-Mother Bhagavan Ratna-Sambhava. Believe in them. Recognition [of them] and the obtaining of liberation will be simultaneous."

"For instance, a person, upon recognizing a lion-skin [to be a lion-skin], is freed [from fear]; for though it be only a stuffed lion skin, if one do not know it to be so actually, fear ariseth, but, upon being told by some person that it is a lion-skin only, one is freed from fear."

"Fear that not. Know them to be the thought-forms of thine own intellectual faculties."

"If all existing phenomena shining forth as divine shapes and radiances be recognized to be the emanations of one's own intellect, Buddhahood will be obtained at that very instant of recognition."

"When suffering miseries of karmic propensities here, / May the blissfulness of the Clear Light dawn."

"However heavy the evil karma may be and however weak the remaining karma may be, it is not possible that liberation will not be obtained [if one but recognize]."

whom make terrifying roaring sounds. His body is embraced by the Mother, Buddha-Krotishaurima (called the Queen of Wrath), who holds up to his mouth a skull cup brimming with blood. At this point, the writer tells people not to be alarmed by the wrathful deities' fearful appearance, for they are only tutelary deities, the embodiment of a dead person's own intellect. As it is, the gruesome appearances are only the ugly aspects of people's nature, or rather, the deities deliberately assume a fearful countenance in order to reveal the darkness in people that needs to be eradicated.

♦ **The Ninth Day**

On the ninth day of the visions of the *chonyid bardo*, Vajra-Heruka appears. Vajra-Heruka is the wrathful manifestation of the Buddha Vajrasattva Aksobhya and his consort Vajra-Krodhesvari; together, they emerge from the dead person's brain. They preside over the eastern quarter of the wrathful deity mandala (a concentric diagram in the form of a circle). With a dark blue face, Vajra-Heruka has three heads, six arms, and four legs and is also crowned with skulls, wearing a fearsome necklace of many severed heads. In his right hand is a skull cup and a battle-ax; his left hand holds a bell, a *kapala* (a cup made with a human skull), and a plowshare. Vajra-Heruka embodies the crystal wisdom of the *dharmakaya* (the ultimate essence of the enlightened mind) and the impure *klesha* ("defilement," "affliction") of anger. This section of the book encourages people to believe in the wrathful deities, recognize them, and merge with them so that liberation and Buddha-hood will be obtained at once. The two qualities of wisdom and anger, as the book implies, are not readily compatible, for if people's intellect is blurred by anger, they can never think properly or apply their wisdom. Therefore, it is beneficial to keep a balanced view of gains and losses so that people will not become irritated by earthly deficiencies and failures.

♦ **The Tenth Day**

On the tenth day, one encounters Ratna-Heruka, who appears like Vajra-Heruka but is yellow rather than blue. He represents the south and the Buddha Ratnasambhava. He has three faces, six hands, and four feet; in the first of the six hands he holds a gem, in the middle a trident staff, and in the last a baton. In the first of the left hands, he holds a bell, in the middle a skull bowl, and in the last a trident staff. Ratna-Heruka manifests the wisdom of equality. He embodies people's overweening pride or vanity, which means that people tend to show off, regarding themselves as superior to others. Therefore, with this deity, people come to know that once they have unshackled themselves from their pride and vanity, they may reside immediately in the ideal realm of equality, attaining the state of the *sambhogakaya* (the "body of delight" or "bliss body"). In this sense, Ratna-Heruka's main significance is Buddha Ratnasambhava, who is characterized by enrichment, development, and progress. Thus, when we have abandoned the negative desires of vanity, pride, and arrogance, we can achieve equality and harmony, which are fundamental to a person's development, progress, and ultimate success.

♦ **The Eleventh Day**

On the eleventh day, the Bhagavan Padma-Heruka (Heruka of the Lotus) appears in a reddish-black color, with three faces, six hands, and four feet, with the right face white, the left blue, and the central darkish-red. He represents the West and the Buddha Amitabha. In the first of the right hands he holds a lotus, in the middle a trident staff, and in the last a club. In the first of the left hands, he holds a bell, in the middle a skull bowl filled with blood, and in the last a small drum. His body is embraced by the Mother Padma-Krotishaurima. His essence is the combination of two wisdoms: the wisdom that, like a mirror, can discern the true nature of things and the wisdom that, with a unique ability for multiplicity, addresses the diverse phenomena of the world. Without the earthly desires that distract people's true insight into things, the discriminating wisdom can help people see things as they really are. When applied to daily life, such wisdoms can aid people and warn them not to be attracted by the mere appearance of things, but rather to delve deep into their essence or nature.

♦ **The Twelfth Day**

On the twelfth day, the blood-drinking deity of the Karmic Order, Karma Heruka, accompanied by the Kerima, Htamenma, and Wang-chugma, meets the dead person face to face. Karma Heruka is green and represents the north and the Buddha Amoghasiddhi. He has three faces, six hands, and four feet, with the right face white, the left red, and the middle dark green. In the first of three hands on the right, he holds a sword, in the middle one a trident staff, and in the last a club. In the first of his left hands, he holds a bell, in the middle one a skull bowl, and in the last a plowshare. His body is embraced by the Mother Karma-Krotishaurima, her right hand clinging to his neck and the left one offering a red shell to his mouth.

Karma Heruka represents the negative human feeling of envy, which historically has been one of the most direct causes of the human being's unhappiness (one of the seven deadly sins, by Christian standards). According to the British philosopher and mathematician Bertrand Russell, envy is a universal and most unfortunate aspect of human nature; it not only renders the envious person unhappy but also may cause him or her to wish misfortune on others. Karma Heruka's essence is the fulfillment of actions; in other words, with this spiritual quality, a person is able to achieve success in everything that he or she does. When one gets rid of envy, one will be free and clear in judgment and evaluation, so accomplishment is very likely to be achieved.

♦ **The Thirteenth Day**

Eight *kerimas* (the *dakinis* that accompany the Herukas, one category of the wrathful deities) appear on the thirteenth day, surrounding the Krodeshvari-Heruka couples. There are two kinds of *kerimas*: Four Inner Dakinis of the cardinal directions (pure colors) and Four Outer Dakinis of the intermediate directions (mixed colors). They combine to represent the fierce, terrifying female counterparts of the eight male bodhisattvas, the compassionate and enlightened beings. Called the Eight Wrathful Ones and Htamenmas, they are terrifying zoomorphic deities—that is, deities given animal form.

Descriptions of the eight *kerimas* are listed in this section of the text: from the east, the Dark-Brown Lion-Headed One, with hands crossed on the breast and in the mouth holding a corpse and shaking the mane; from the south, the Red Tiger-Headed One, with the hands crossed downward and with protruding eyes; from the west, the Black Fox-Headed One, with the right hand holding a shaving knife and the left hand holding an intestine; from the north, the Dark-Blue Wolf-Headed One, with the two hands tearing open a corpse; from the southeast, the Yellowish-White Vulture-Headed One, carrying a gigantic corpse on the shoulder and holding a skeleton in the hand; from the southwest, the Dark-Red Cemetery-Bird-Headed One, carrying a gigantic corpse on the shoulder; from the northwest, the Black Crow-Headed One, the left hand holding a skull bowl, the right holding a sword, and her mouth eating heart and lungs; from the northeast, the Dark-Blue Owl-Headed One, holding a thunderbolt in the right hand and a skull bowl in the left.

◆ **The Fourteenth Day**

On the fourteenth day, the visions of the *chonyid bardo* end with a rich array of deities, among them Four Female Door-Keepers (the Four Yoginis of the Door) with animal heads and other powerful zoomorphic deities and Yoginis. The Four Female Door-Keepers also come from the dead person's own brain: From the east part of the brain comes the White Tiger-Headed Goad-Holding Goddess, bearing a blood-filled skull bowl in her left hand; from the south part, the Yellow Sow-Headed Noose-Holding Goddess; from the west part, the Red Lion-Headed Iron-Chain-Holding Goddess; and from the north part, the Green Serpent-Headed Bell-Holding Goddess. These Yoginis are the feminine forms of the masculine yogi. They are known to possess a steadfast mind, which they cultivate through the disciplined pursuit of transcendence, an idea that is at the core of yoga. Proper respect of Yoginis is a necessary part of the path to liberation, since a yogini is the sacred feminine force made incarnate.

Audience

According to the Tibetan Buddhist tradition, the Tibetan Book of the Dead is chanted to a dying or dead person for him or her to be liberated from the cycles of rebirth from the Six Realms, or the *samsara*. It is also intended for readers not necessarily facing death but seeking a way to a deeper realization of the meaning of their existence as

---

Questions for Further Study

1. If for no other reason than its title, the Tibetan Book of the Dead bears comparison with the Egyptian Book of the Dead. What differing visions of death do the two documents present? What cultural factors might have given rise to these differences?

2. How consistent is the vision of death, the afterlife, karma, reincarnation, and spirituality in the Tibetan Book of the Dead with the vision in the text gZi-brjid of Tibetan Buddhism?

3. With regard to Tibetan Buddhism, the entry states: "Everything is dying, including presently living things, but Buddhists believe that people should not panic or despair over death." Do you see any similarities between this view and the view expressed by Lucretius in *On the Nature of Things*? Explain.

4. In 2010, thirty-three miners were trapped a half mile below ground in Chile. They remained in this dark, underground "tomb" for sixty-nine days until they were rescued by being pulled up one by one in a metal cage or pod through a narrow shaft. Their plight and successful rescue, a kind of death and rebirth, attracted worldwide attention. Do you see any similarities between the story of the Chilean miners and the vision of death and reincarnation presented in the Tibetan Book of the Dead? Do you think miners in these circumstances would be more hopeful and optimistic about their circumstances if they had copies of the Book of the Dead with them, particularly the passage that reads, "When suffering miseries of karmic propensities here, / May the blissfulness of the Clear Light dawn"?

5. How do you think the Tibetan Book of the Dead would be explicated by a modern psychologist or psychiatrist?

humans. It guides the person through his or her encounter with the various apparitions or deities, both cheerful and wrathful, which in scientific terms are the positive and negative projections of human instincts and consciousness. For the modern reader, the *bardo* experience reflects one's psychological makeup, as in the form of heavy psychological pressure, nervous breakdowns, and insecurities in life. Once people have realized the process and features of dying and death, they will be more assured of their reason for living. The Tibetan Book of the Dead continues to be read—sometimes read aloud to a dying person—as a source of awareness of a high state of consciousness.

Impact

The Tibetan Book of the Dead is a spiritual guide that is both meaningful and essential to everyday life. It influences the way people view life and death: If people have a holistic view of their existence, they will no longer be oppressed by the fear of the inevitable dying and death. Unlike the West, which is a global trailblazer in science and technology, the East—especially Asian countries like China—has been very advanced in the spiritual and psychological spheres. The people of Eastern nations are seemingly more attuned to grasping the meaning of life through meditation and yoga. The Tibetan Book of the Dead tells us it is possible to recognize that all phenomena are actually none other than reflections of our true nature of mind. This text highlights the Eastern exploration of the psychic and spiritual world. It tells people that death is not the termination of life; rather, it is the beginning of another existence or another form of being; in other words, it is an extension of people's existence.

The history of Tibetan Buddhism during the first millennium of the Common Era was erratic at best. In the ninth century, King Langdarma launched persecutions of Buddhists and threw his support to the native Bon religion. Warfare flourished, monasteries were destroyed, and thousands of Buddhist monks and laypersons were murdered. Accordingly, the Tibetan Book of the Dead, along with other Buddhist texts, was hidden in caves and other secret places to be discovered in later centuries, when they were designated as *thermas*, a Tibetan word that means "treasures." The discoverers of the text were called *tertons*, and these spiritual leaders propagated Tibetan Buddhism in the centuries that followed. Buddhism revived in Tibet in the eleventh century with the arrival of Atisa, an Indian monk, and the establishment of the Sakya Order of Buddhism by Khon Kongchog Gyalpo, a member of a Tibetan noble family. In the twenty-first century, the Tibetan Book of the Dead continues to embody the Buddhist view of death as a journey upon which people should embark calmly and gracefully.

Further Reading

■ Books

Bechert, Heinz, and Richard Gombrich, eds. *The World of Buddhism*. London: Thames and Hudson, 1984.

Becker, Carl B. *Breaking the Circle: Death and the Afterlife in Buddhism*. Carbondale: Southern Illinois University Press, 1993.

Freemantle, Francesca. *Luminous Emptiness: Understanding the Tibetan Book of the Dead*. Boston: Shambhala Publications, 2001.

Kapleau, Philip. *The Zen of Living and Dying: A Practical and Spiritual Guide*. Boston: Shambhala Publications, 1997.

Langer, Rita. *Buddhist Rituals of Death and Rebirth: Contemporary Sri Lankan Practice and Origins*. New York: Routledge, 2007.

Mullin, Glenn H. *Death and Dying: The Tibetan Tradition*. Boston: Arkana, 1986.

Thondup, Tulku. *Peaceful Death, Joyful Rebirth: A Tibetan Buddhist Guidebook*. Boston: Shambhala Publications, 2006.

Wilson, Liz, ed. *The Living and the Dead: Social Dimensions of Death in South Asian Religions*. Albany: State University of New York Press, 2003.

Wilson, Martin. *Rebirth and the Western Buddhist*. 2nd ed. London: Wisdom Publications, 1987.

—Dong Zhao

Tibetan Book of the Dead

The Dawning of the Wrathful Deities, from the Eighth to the Fourteenth Day

♦ **Introduction**

Now the manner of the dawning of the Wrathful Deities is to be shown.

In the above *Bardo* of the Peaceful [Deities] there were seven stages of ambuscade. The setting-face-to-face at each stage should have [caused the deceased] to recognize either at one or another [stage] and to have been liberated.

Multitudes will be liberated by that recognition; [and] although multitudes obtain liberation in that manner, the number of sentient beings being great, evil *karma* powerful, obscurations dense, propensities of too long standing, the Wheel of Ignorance and Illusion becometh neither exhausted nor accelerated. Although [all be] set face-to-face in such detail, there is a vast preponderance of those who wander downwards unliberated.

Therefore, after the cessation [of the dawning] of the Peaceful and the Knowledge-Holding Deities, who come to welcome one, the fifty-eight flame-enhaloed, wrathful, blood-drinking deities come to dawn, who are only the former Peaceful Deities in changed aspect—according to the place [or psychic-centre of the *Bardo*-body of the deceased whence they proceed]; nevertheless, they will not resemble them.

This is the *Bardo* of the Wrathful Deities; and, they being influenced by fear, terror, and awe, recognition becometh more difficult. The intellect, gaining not in independence, passeth from one fainting state to a round of fainting states. [Yet], if one but recognize a little, it is easier to be liberated [at this stage]. If it be asked why? [the answer is]: Because of the dawning of the radiances—[which produce] fear, terror, and awe—the intellect is undistractedly alert in one-pointedness; that is why.

If at this stage one do not meet with this kind of teaching, one's hearing [of religious lore]—although it be like an ocean [in its vastness]—is of no avail. There are even discipline-holding abbots [or *bhikkhus*] and doctors in metaphysical discourses who err at this stage, and, not recognizing, wander into the *Sangsara*.

As for the common worldly folk, what need is there to mention them! By fleeing, through fear, terror, and awe, they fall over the precipices into the unhappy worlds and suffer. But the least of the least of the devotees of the mystic *mantrayana* doctrines, as soon as he sees these blood-drinking deities, will recognize them to be his tutelary deities, and the meeting will be like that of human acquaintances. He will trust them; and becoming merged into them, in at-one-ment, will obtain Buddhahood.

By having meditated on the description of these blood-drinking deities, while in the human world, and by having performed some worship or praise of them; or, at least, by having seen their painted likenesses and their images, upon witnessing the dawning of the deities at this stage, recognition of them will result, and liberation. In this lieth the art.

Again, at the death of those discipline-holding abbots and doctors in metaphysical discourses [who remain uninstructed in these *Bardo* teachings], however assiduously they may have devoted themselves to religious practices, and however in the human world, there will not come any phenomenal signs such as rainbow-halo [at the funeral-pyre] nor bone-reliques [from the ashes]. This is because when they lived the mystic [or esoteric] doctrines were never held within their heart, and because they had spoken contemptuously of them, and because they were never acquainted [through initiation] with the deities of the mystic [or esoteric] doctrines; thus, when these dawn on the *Bardo*, they do not recognize them. Suddenly [seeing] what they had never seen before, engendered, they pass into the miserable states because of that. Therefore, if the observers of the disciplines, and the metaphysicians, have not in them the practices of the mystic [or esoteric] doctrines, such signs as the rainbow-halo come not, nor are bone-reliques and seed-like bones ever produced [from the bones of their funeral-pyre]: these are the reasons for it.

The least of the least of *mantrayanic* [devotees]—who may seem to be of very unrefined manners, un-industrious, untactful, and who may not live in accordance with his vows, and who in every way may be inelegant in his habits, and even unable, perhaps, to carry the practices of his teachings to a successful issue—let no one feel disrespect for nor doubt him, but pay reverence to the esoteric [or mystic] doctrines [which he holdeth]. By that, alone, one obtaineth liberation at this stage.

Even though the deeds [of one paying such reverence] may not have been very elegant while in the human world, at his death there will come at least one kind of sign, such a rainbow-radiance, bone-images, and bone-reliques. This is because the esoteric [or mystic] doctrines possess great gift-waves.

[Those of, and] above, the mystic *mantrayanic* devotees of ordinary [psychic development], who have meditated upon the visualization and perfection processes and practiced the essences [or essence *mantras*], need not wander down this far on the *Chonyid Bardo*. As soon as they cease to breathe, they will be led into the pure paradise realms by the Heroes and Heroines and the Knowledge-Holders. As a sign of this, the sky will be cloudless; they will merge into rainbow radiance; there will be sun-showers, sweet scent of incense [in the air], music in the skies, radiances; bone-reliques and images [from their funeral-pyre].

Therefore, to the abbots [or discipline-holders], to the doctors, and to those mystics who have failed in their vows, and to all the common people, this *Thodol* is indispensable. But those who have meditated upon the Great Perfection and the Great Symbol will recognize the Clear Light at the moment of death; and, obtaining the *Dharma-Kaya*, all of them will be such as not to need the reading of this *Thodol*. By recognizing the Clear Light at the moment of death, they also will recognize the visions of the Peaceful and the Wrathful during the *Chonyid Bardo*, and obtain the *Sambhoga-Kaya*; or, recognizing during the *Sidpa Bardo*, obtain the *Nirmana-Kaya*; and, taking birth on the higher planes, will, in the next rebirth, meet with this Doctrine, and then enjoy the continuity of *karma*.

Therefore, this *Thodol* is the doctrine by which Buddhahood may be attained without meditation; the doctrine liberating by the hearing [of it] alone; the doctrine which leadeth brings of great evil *karma* on the Secret Path; the doctrine which produceth differentiation instantaneously [between those who are initiated into it and those who are not]: being the profound doctrine which Conferreth Perfect Enlightenment instantaneously. Those sentient beings who have been reached by it cannot go to the unhappy states.

This [doctrine] and the *Tahdol* [doctrine], when joined together being like unto a *mandala* of gold inset with turquoise, combine them.

Thus, the indispensable nature of the *Thodol* being shown, there now cometh the setting-face-to-face with the dawning of the Wrathful [Deities] in the *Bardo*.

♦ **The Eighth Day**

Again, calling the deceased by name, [address him] thus:

O nobly-born, listen undistractedly. Not having been able to recognize when the Peaceful [Deities] shone upon thee in the *Bardo* above, thou hast come wandering thus far. Now, on the Eighth Day, the blood-drinking Wrathful Deities will come to shine. Act so as to recognize them without being distracted.

O nobly-born, the Great Glorious Buddha-Heruka, dark-brown of colour; with three heads, six hands, and four feet firmly postured; the right [face] being white, the left, red, the central, dark-brown; the body emitting flames of radiance; the nine eyes widely opened, in terrifying gaze; the eyebrows quivering like lightning; the protruding teeth glistening and set over one another; giving vent to sonorous utterances of "a-la-la" and "ha-ha," and piercing whistling sounds; the hair of a reddish-yellow colour, standing on end, and emitting radiance; the heads adorned with dried [human] skulls, and the [symbols of the] sun and moon; black serpents and raw [human] heads forming a garland for the body; the first of the right hands holding a wheel, the middle one, a sword, the last one, a battle-axe; the first of the left hands, a bell, the middle one, a skull-bowl, the last one, a ploughshare; his body embraced by the Mother, Buddha-Krotishaurima, her right hand clinging to his neck and her left putting to his mouth a red shell [filled with blood], [making] a palatal sound like a crackling [and] a clashing sound, and a rumbling sound as loud as thunder; [emanating from the two deities] radiant flames of wisdom, blazing from every hair-pore [of the body] and each containing a flaming *dorje*; [the two deities together thus], standing with [one] leg bent and [the other] straight and tense, on a dais supported by horned eagles, will come forth from within thine own brain and shine vividly upon thee. Fear that not. Be not awed. Know it to be the embodiment of thine own intellect. As it is thine own tutelary deity, be not terrified. Be not afraid, for in reality is it the Bhagavan Vairochana, the Father-Mother. Simultaneously with the recognition, liberation will be obtained: if they be recognized, merging [thyself], in at-one-ment, into the tutelary deity, Buddhahood in the *Sambhoga-Kaya* will be won.

♦ The Ninth Day

But if one flee from them, through awe and terror being begotten, then, on the Ninth Day, the blood-drinking [deities] of the Vajra Order will come to receive one. Thereupon, the setting-face-to-face is, calling the deceased by name, thus:

O nobly-born, listen undistractedly. He of the blood-drinking Vajra Order named the Bhagavan Vajra-Heruka, dark-blue in colour; with three faces, six hands, and four feet firmly postured; in the first right hand [holding] a *dorje*, in the middle [one], a skull-bowl, in the last [one], a battle axe; in the first of the left, a bell, in the middle [one] a skull-bowl, in the last [one], a ploughshare: his body embraced by the Mother Vajra-Krotishaurima, her right [hand] clinging to his neck, her left offering to his mouth a red shell [filled with blood], will issue from the eastern quarter of thy brain and come to shine upon thee. Fear it not. Be not terrified. Be not awed. Know it to be the embodiment of thine own intellect. As it is thine own tutelary deity, be not terrified. In reality [they are] the Bhagavan Vajra-Sattva, the Father and Mother. Believe in them. Recognizing them, liberation will be obtained at once. By so proclaiming [them], knowing them to be tutelary deities, merging [in them] in at-one-ment, Buddhahood will be obtained.

♦ The Tenth Day

Yet, if one do not recognize them, the obscurations of evil deeds being too great, and flee from them through terror and awe, then, on the Tenth Day, the blood-drinking [deities] of the [Precious]-Gem Order will come to receive one. Thereupon the setting-face-to-face is, calling the deceased by name, thus:

O nobly-born, listen. On the Tenth Day, the blood-drinking [deity] of the [Precious]-Gem Order named Ratna-Heruka, yellow of colour; [having] three faces, six hands, four feet firmly postured; the right [face] white, the left, red, the central darkish yellow; enhaloed in flames; in the first of the six hands holding a gem, in the middle [one], a trident-staff, in the last [one], a baton; in the first of the left [hands], a bell, in the middle [one], a skull-bowl, in the last [one], a trident-staff; his body embraced by the Mother Ratna-Krotishaurima, her right [hand] clinging to his neck, her left offering to his mouth a red shell [filled with blood], will issue from the southern quarter of thy brain and come to shine upon thee. Fear not. Be not terrified. Be not awed. Know them to be the embodiment of thine own intellect. [They] being thine own tutelary deity, be not terrified. In reality [they are] the Father-Mother Bhagavan Ratna-Sambhava. Believe in them. Recognition [of them] and the obtaining of liberation will be simultaneous.

By so proclaiming [them], knowing them to be tutelary deities, merging in them at-one-ment, Buddhahood will be obtained.

♦ The Eleventh Day

Yet, though set face-to-face thus, if, through power of evil propensities, terror and awe being produced, not recognizing them to be tutelary deities, one flee from them, then, on the Eleventh Day, the blood-drinking Lotus Order will come to receive one. Thereupon the setting-face-to-face is, calling the deceased by name, thus:

O nobly-born, on the Eleventh Day, the blood-drinking [deity] of the Lotus Order, called the Bhagavan Padma-Heruka, of reddish-black colour; [having] three faces, six hands, and four feet firmly postured, the right [face] white, the left, blue, the central, darkish red; in the first of the right of the six hands holding a lotus, in the middle [one], a trident-staff, in the last, a club; in the first of the left [hands], a bell, in the middle [one], a skull-bowl filled with blood, in the last, a small drum; his body embraced by the Mother Padma-Krotishaurima, her right hand clinging to his neck, her left offering to his mouth a red shell [filled with blood]; the Father and Mother in union; will issue from the western quarter of thy brain and come to shine upon thee. Fear that not. Be not terrified. Be not awed. Rejoice. Recognize [them] to be the product of thine own intellect; as [they are] thine own tutelary deity, be not afraid. In reality they are the Father-Mother Bhagavan Amitabha. Believe in them. Concomitantly with recognition, liberation will come. Through such acknowledging, recognizing them to be tutelary deities, in at-one-ment thou wilt merge [into them], and obtain Buddhahood.

♦ The Twelfth Day

Despite such setting-face-to-face, being still led backwards by evil propensities, terror and awe arising, it may be that one recognize not and flee. Thereupon, on the Twelfth Day, the blood-drinking deities of the Karmic Order, accompanies by the Kerima, Htamenma, and Wang-chugma, will come to receive one. Not recognizing, terror may be produced. Whereupon, the setting-face-to-face is, calling the deceased by name, thus:

O nobly-born, on the Twelfth Day, the blood-drinking deity of the Karmic Order, named Karma-Herua, dark green of colour; [having] three faces, six hands, [and] four feet firmly postured; the right

Document Text

[face] white, the left, red, the middle, dark green; majestic [of appearance]; in the first of the right of six hands, holding a sword, in the middle [one], a trident-staff, in the last, a club; in the first of the left [hands], a bell, in the middle [one], a skull-bowl, in the last, a plough-share; his body embraced by the Mother Karma-Krotishaurima, her right [hand] clinging to his neck, the left offering to his mouth a red shell; the Father and Mother in union, issuing from the northern quarter of thy brain, will come to shine upon thee. Fear that not. Be not terrified. Be not awed. Recognize them to be the embodiment of thine own intellect. [They] being thine own tutelary deity, be not afraid. In reality they are the Father-Mother Bhagavan Amogha-Siddhi. Believe; and be humble; and be fond [of them]. Concomitantly with recognition, liberation will come. Through such acknowledging, recognizing them to be tutelary deities, in at-one-ment thou wilt merge [into them], and obtain Buddhahood. Through the *guru's* select teaching, one cometh to recognize them to be the thought-forms issuing from one's own intellectual faculties. For instance, a person, upon recognizing a lion-skin [to be a lion-skin], is freed [from fear]; for though it be only a stuffed lion skin, if one do not know it to be so actually, fear ariseth, but, upon being told by some person that it is a lion-skin only, one is freed from fear. Similarly here, too, when the bands of blood-drinking deities, huge of proportions, with very thick-set limbs, dawn as big as the skies, awes and terror are naturally produced in one. [But] as soon as the setting-face-to-face is heard [one] recognizeth them to be one's own tutelary deities and one's own thought-forms. Then, when upon the Mother Clear-Light—which one had been accustomed to formerly—a secondary Clear-Light, the Offspring Clear-Light, coming together like two intimate acquaintances, blend inseparably, and [therefrom] a self-emancipating radiance dawneth upon one, through self-enlightenment and self-knowledge one is liberated.

♦ The Thirteenth Day

If this setting-face-to-face be not obtained, good persons on the Path, too, fall back from here and wander into the *Sangsara*. Then the Eight Wrathful Ones, the Kerimas, and the Htamenmas, having various [animal] heads, issue from within one's own brain and come to shine upon one's self. There-upon the setting-face-to-face is, calling the deceased by name, thus:

O nobly-born, listen undistractedly. On the Thirteenth Day, from the eastern quarter of thy brain, the Eight Kerimas will emanate and come to shine upon thee. Fear that not.

From the east of thy brain, the White Kerima, holding a human corpse, as a club, in the right [hand]; in the left, holding a skull-bowl filled with blood, will come to shine upon thee. Fear not.

From the south, the Yellow Tseurima, holding a bow and arrow, ready to shoot; from the west, the Red Pramoha, holding a *makara*-banner; from the north, the Black Petali, holding a *dorje* and a blood-filled skull-bowl; from the south-east, the Red Pukkase, holding intestines in the right [hand] and [with] the left putting them to her mouth; from the south-west, the Dark-Green Ghasmari, the left [hand] holding a blood-filled skull-bowl, [with] the right stirring it with a *dorje*, and [she then] drinking it with majestic relish; from the north-west, the Yellowish-White Tsandhali, tearing asunder a head from a corpse, the right [hand] holding a heart, the left putting the corpse to the mouth and [she then] eating [thereof]; from the north-east, the Dark-Blue Smasha, tearing asunder a head from a corpse and eating [thereof]: these, the Eight Kerimas of the Abodes [or Eight Directions], also come to shine upon thee, surrounding the Five Blood-drinking Fathers. Yet be not afraid.

O nobly-born, from the Circle outside of them, the Eight Htamenmas of the [eight] regions [of the brain] will come to shine upon thee: from the east, the Dark-Brown Lion-Headed One, the hands crossed on the breast, and in the mouth holding a corpse, and shaking the mane; from the south, the Red Tiger-Headed One, the hands crossed downwards, grinning and showing the fangs and looking on with protruding eyes; from the west, the Black Fox-Headed One, the right [hand] holding a shaving-knife, the left holding an intestine, and [she] eating and licking the blood [therefrom]; from the north, the Dark-Blue Wolf-Headed One, the two hands tearing open a corpse and looking on with protruding eyes; from the south-east, the Yellowish-White Vulture-Headed One, bearing a gigantic [human-shaped] corpse on the shoulder and holding a skeleton in the hand; from the south-west, the Dark-Red Cemetery-Bird-Headed One, carrying a gigantic corpse on the shoulder; from the north-west, the Black Crow-Headed One, the left [hand] holding a skull-bowl, the right holding a sword, and [she] eating heart and lungs; from the north-east, the Dark-Blue Owl-Headed One, holding a *dorje* in the right [hand], and holding a skull-bowl in the left, and eating.

Document Text

These Eight Htamenmas of the [eight] regions, likewise surrounding the Blood-Drinking Fathers, and issuing from within thy brain, come to shine upon thee. Fear that not. Know them to be the thought-forms of thine own intellectual faculties.

◆ **The Fourteenth Day**

O nobly-born on the Fourteenth Day, the Four Female Door-Keepers, also issuing from within thine own brain, will come to shine upon thee. Again recognize. From the east [quarter] of thy brain will come to shine the White Tiger-Headed Goad-Holding Goddess, bearing a blood-filled skull-bowl in her left [hand]; from the south, the Yellow Sow-Headed Noose-Holding Goddess; from the west, the Red Lion-Headed Iron-Chain-Holding Goddess; and from the north, the Green Serpent-Headed Bell-Holding Goddess. Thus, issue the Four Female Door-Keepers also from within thine own brain and come to shine upon thee; as tutelary deities, recognize them.

O nobly-born, on the outer Circle of these thirty wrathful deities, Herukas, the twenty-eight various-headed mighty goddesses, bearing various weapons, issuing from within thine own brain, will come to shine upon thee. Fear that not. Recognize whatever shineth to be the thought-forms of thine own intellectual faculties. At this vitally important time, recollect the select teachings of the *guru*.

O nobly-born, [there will dawn] from the east the Dark-Brown Yak-Headed Rakshasa-Goddess, holding a *dorje* and a skull; and the Reddish-Yellow Serpent-Headed Brahma-Goddess, holding a lotus in her hand; and the Greenish-Black Leopard-Headed Great-Goddess, holding a trident in her hand; and the Blue Monkey-Headed Goddess of Inquisitiveness, holding a wheel; and the Red Snow-Bear-Headed Virgin-Goddess, bearing a short spear in the hand; and the White Bear-Headed Indra-Goddess, holding an intestine-noose in the hand: [these], the Six Yoginis of the East, issuing from within the [eastern quarter of thine own] brain, will come to shine upon thee; fear that not.

O nobly-born, from the south [will dawn] the Yellow Bat-Headed Delight-Goddess, holding a shaving-knife in the hand; and the Red Makara-Headed Peaceful-[Goddess], holding an urn in the hand; and the Red Scorpion-Headed Amrita-Goddess, holding a lotus in the hand; and the White Kite-Headed Moon-Goddess, holding a *dorje* in the hand; and the Dark-Green Fox-Headed Baton-Goddess, flourishing a club in the hand; and the Yellowish-Black Tiger-Headed Rakshasi, holding a blood-filled skull-bowl in the hand: [these] the Six Yoginis of the South, issuing from within the [southern quarter of thine own] brain, will come to shine upon thee; fear that not.

O nobly-born, from the west [will dawn] the Greenish-Black Vulture-Headed Eater-Goddess, holding a baton in the hand; and the Red Horse-Headed Delight-Goddess, holding a huge trunk of a corpse; and the White Eagle-Headed Mighty-Goddess, holding a club in the hand; and the Yellow Dog-Headed Rakshasi, holding a *dorje* in the hand and a shaving-knife and cutting [with this]; and the Red Hoopoo-Headed Desire-Goddess, holding a bow and arrow in the hand aimed; and the Green Stag-Headed Wealth-Guardian Goddess, holding an urn in the hand: [these], the Six Yoginis of the West, issuing from within the [western quarter of thine own] brain, will come to shine upon thee; fear that not.

O nobly-born, from the north [will dawn] the Blue Wolf-Headed Wind-Goddess, waving a pennant in the hand; and the Red Ibex-Headed Woman-Goddess, holding a pointed stake in the hand; and the Black Sow-Headed Sow-Goddess, holding a noose of fangs in the hand; and the Red Crow-Headed Thunderbolt-Goddess, holding an infant corpse in the hand; and the Greenish-Black Elephant-Headed Big-Nosed Goddess, holding in the hand a big corpse and drinking blood from a skull; and the Blue Serpent-Headed Water-Goddess, holding in the hand a serpent noose: [these], the Six Yoginis of the North, issuing from within [the northern quarter of] thine own brain, will come to shine upon thee; fear that not.

O nobly-born, the Four Yoginis of the Door, issuing from within the brain, will come to shine upon thee: from the east, the Black Cuckoo-Headed Mystic Goddess, holding an iron hook in the hand; from the south, the Yellow Goat-Headed Mystic Goddess, holding a noose in the hand; from the west, the Red Lion-Headed Mystic Goddess, holding an iron chain in the hand; and from the north, the Greenish-Black Serpent-Headed Mystic Goddess: [these], the Four Door-Keeping Yoginis, issuing from within the brain, will come to shine upon thee.

Since these Twenty-eight Mighty Goddesses emanate from the bodily powers of Ratna-Sambhava, [He] of the Six Heruka Deities, recognize them.

O nobly-born, the Peaceful Deities emanate from the Voidness of the *Dharma-Kaya*; recognize them. From the Radiance of the *Dharma-Kaya* emanate the Wrathful Deities; recognize them.

At this time when the Fifty-eight Blood-Drinking Deities emanating from thine own brain come to shine upon thee, if thou knowest them to be the radiances of thine own intellect, thou wilt merge, in the state of at-one-ment, into the body of the Blood-Drinking Ones there and then, and obtain Buddhahood.

O nobly-born, by not recognizing now, and by fleeing from the deities out of fear, again sufferings will come to overpower thee. If this be not known, fear being begotten of the Blood-Drinking Deities, [one is] awed and terrified and fainteth away: one's own thought-forms turn into illusory appearances, and one wandereth into the *Sangsara*; if one be not awed and terrified, one will not wander into the *Sangsara*.

Furthermore, the bodies of the largest of the Peaceful and Wrathful Deities are equal [in vastness] to the limits of the heaves; the intermediate, as big as Mt. Meru; the smallest, equal to eighteen bodies such as thine own body, set one upon another. Be not terrified at that; be not awed. If all existing phenomena shining forth as divine shapes and radiances be recognized to be the emanations of one's own intellect, Buddhahood will be obtained at that very instant of recognition. The saying, "Buddhahood will be obtained in a moment [of time]" is that which applieth now. Bearing this in mind, one will obtain Buddhahood by merging, in at-one-ment, into the Radiances and the *Kayas*.

O nobly-born, whatever fearful and terrifying visions thou mayst see, recognize them to be thine own thought-forms.

O nobly-born, if thou recognize not, and be frightened, then all the Peaceful Deities will shine forth in the shape of Maha-Kala; and all the Wrathful Deities will shine [forth] in the form of Dharma-Raja, the Lord of Death; and thine own thought-forms becoming Illusions [or *Maras*], thou wilt wander into the *Sangsara*.

O nobly-born, if one recognize not one's own thought-forms, however learned one may be in the Scriptures—both *Sutras* and *Tantras*—although practicing religion for a *kalpa*, one obtaineth not Buddhahood. If one recognize one's own thought-forms, by one important art and by one word, Buddhahood is obtained.

If one's thought-forms be not recognized as soon as one dieth, the shapes of Dharma-Raja, the Lord of Death, will shine forth on the *Chonyid Bardo*. The largest of the bodies of Dharma-Raja, the Lord of Death, equaling the heavens [in vastness]; the intermediate, Mt. Meru; the smallest, eighteen times one's own body, will come filling the world-systems. They will come having their upper teeth biting the nether lip; their eyes glassy; their hairs tied up on the top of the head; big-bellied, narrow-wasted; holding a [*karmic*] record-board in the hand; giving utterance from their mouth to sounds of "Strike! Slay!," licking [human] brain, drinking blood, tearing heads from corpses, tearing out [the] hearts: thus will [they] come, filling the worlds.

O nobly-born, when such thought-forms emanate, be thou not afraid, nor terrified; the body which now thou possessest being a mental-body of [*karmic*] propensities, though slain and chopped [to bits], cannot die. Because thy body is, in reality, one of voidness, thou needest not fear. The [bodies of the] Lord of Death, too, are emanations from the radiances of thine own intellect; they are not constituted of matter; voidness cannot injure voidness. Beyond the emanations of thine own intellectual faculties, externally, the Peaceful and the Wrathful Ones, the Blood-Drinking Ones, the Various-Headed Ones, the rainbow lights, the terrifying forms of the lord of Death, exist not in reality: of this, there is no doubt. Thus, knowing this, all the fear and terror is self-dissipated; and, merging in the state of at-one-ment, Buddhahood is obtained.

If thou recognizest in that manner, exerting thy faith and affection towards the tutelary deities and believing that they have come to receive thee amidst the ambuscades of the *Bardo*, think, "[I] take refuge [in them]"; and remember the Precious Trinity, exerting towards them [the Trinity] fondness and faith. Whosoever thine own tutelary deity may be, recollect now; [and] calling him by name, pray thus:
"[Alas!], wandering am I in the *Bardo*; run to my rescue;
Uphold me by thy grace, O Precious Tutelary!"
Calling upon the name of thine own *guru*, pray thus:
"[Alas!] wandering am I in the *Bardo*; rescue me!
[O] let not thy grace forsake me!"
Have faith in the Blood-Drinking Deities, too, and offer up this prayer:
"Alas! when [I am] wandering in the *Sangsara*, through force of overpowering illusions,
On the light-path of the abandonment of fright, fear, and awe,
May the bands of the Bhagavans, the Peaceful and Wrathful Ones, lead [me],
May the bands of the Wrathful Goddess Rich in Space be [my] rear-guard,
And save me from the fearful ambuscades of the *Bardo*,
And place me in the state of the Perfectly-Enlightened Buddhas.
When wandering alone, separated from dear friends,
When the void forms of one's own thoughts are shining here,
May the Buddhas, exerting the force of their grace,

Document Text

Cause not to come the fear, awe, and terror in the *Bardo*.
When the five bright Wisdom-Lights are shining here,
May recognition come without dread and without awe;
When the divine bodies of the Peaceful and the Wrathful are shining here;
May the assurance of fearlessness be obtained and the *Bardo* be recognized.
When, by the power of evil *karma*, misery is being tasted,
May the tutelary deities dissipate the misery;
When the natural sound of Reality is reverberating [like] a thousand thunders,
May they be transmuted into the sounds of the Six Syllables.
When unprotected, *karma* having to be followed here,
I beseech the Gracious Compassionate [One] to protect me;
When suffering miseries of *karmic* propensities here,
May the blissfulness of the Clear Light dawn;
May the Five Elements not rise up as enemies;
But may I behold the realms of the Five Orders of the Enlightened Ones."

Thus, in earnest faith and humility, offer up the prayer; whereby all fears will vanish and Buddhahood in the *Sambhoga-Kaya* will undoubtedly be won: important is this. Being undistracted, repeat it in that manner, three of [even] seven times.

However heavy the evil *karma* may be and however weak the remaining *karma* may be, it is not possible that liberation will not be obtained [if one but recognize]. If, nevertheless, despite everything done in these [stages of the *Bardo*], recognition is still not brought about, then—there being danger of one's wandering further, into the third *Bardo*, called the *Sidpa Bardo*—the setting-face-to-face for that will be shown in detail hereinafter.

Glossary

Bardo	the state between life and death
Chonyid Bardo	literally, "the experiencing of reality"
Dharma-Kaya	the ultimate essence of the enlightened mind
dorje	thunderbolt or diamond
Herukas	wrathful but enlightened beings that embody indivisible bliss
kalpa	an enormous unit or cycle of time
karma	the concept that the effects of a person's actions determine one's destiny in one's next incarnation
Kerima	a being that accompanies a Wrathful Deity
Mantrayana	a type of Buddhism also known as Tantric Buddhism
Nirmana-Kaya	the form of the Buddha that appears in the world to teach people the path to liberation
Sangsara	a round of life-death-rebirth
Sidpa Bardo	the bardo of rebirth
Sutras	religious verses, aphorisms, or extracts
Tantras	scriptures pertaining to any of several Hindu and Buddhist traditions
Thodol	literally, "liberation"
Vajra	the thunderbolt of the goddess Indra; also, a central Buddhist principle representing indestructible substance that penetrates emotional instability or uncertainty
Wrathful Deities	fierce deities that ward off evil spirits, fight threats to Buddhism, and protect humans by adding fear to the evil spirits

Page of text with decorative border from the Sahih al-Bukhari

(Ms 212/1162 Fol.239r Page of text with decorative border, from `Bukhari Sahih' [w/c, gold and ink on paper], Islamic School / Musee Conde, Chantilly, France / Giraudon / The Bridgeman Art Library International)

Sahih al-Bukhari

"None of you will have faith till he wishes for his (Muslim) brother what he likes for himself."

Overview

The Arabic word *hadith* literally means "story." As used in Islam, the Hadith are stories about the prophet Muhammad (d. 632), the founder of Islam. The Hadith report the Sunna, or practices of Muhammad, including what he said, what he did, and what he tacitly approved of. Each Hadith has two parts: the text reporting Muhammad's words and actions, called *matn* in Arabic, and the chain of narrators, or *isnad*. The chain of narrators begins with the narrator from whom the compiler of a collection of Hadith received the report and is traced back through the generations, ending with the narrator who reported witnessing what Muhammad said or did. Each person in the chain of narrators reports the story on the authority of the person from whom he or she received it. The Arabic word *sahih* means "sound," and the book of Hadith known as the Sahih al-Bukhari was an attempt to collect only those stories that the compiler considered to be sound, or authentic—that is, stories that he viewed as reliable because they could be traced back to Muhammad through an unbroken chain of trustworthy narrators.

Muslims generally refer to the canonized collections of Hadith as the "Six Books." In reality, though, nine works are recognized by Sunni Muslims as sources of authoritative Hadith. The most important of the nine canonized collections is the Sahih of Muhammad ibn Abu Abdullah ibn Ismail al-Bukhari, which is considered the most influential book after the Qur'an in Sunni Islam (that is, the dominant, orthodox branch of Islam, so called because of its reliance on the Sunna). In some ways, it can be said to be even more influential than the Qur'an itself, for Hadith add details and concepts to Islamic belief and doctrine that may not be found, or that are only alluded to, in the Qur'an.

Like all Hadith collections, the Sahih al-Bukhari is not meant to be read from beginning to end like a novel. It is meant to be used as a reference by those who want to find quickly and easily what Muhammad said or did in relation to day-to-day issues of belief and practice. It is divided into more than ninety chapters arranged by topics, from the opening chapter on revelation to the final chapter on the oneness of God. The topical arrangement allows Muslims to quickly find the answers they seek. The chapter under discussion here, "Iman" (translated as "Belief/Faith"), contains forty-nine Hadith that provide details of faith and practice that have helped to define Sunni Islam.

Context

From the time Muhammad first received his call to preach in 610, until the lifetime of al-Bukhari two centuries later, people were telling stories about Muhammad. These stories were passed down from generation to generation, first orally and then in writing. These stories recount Muhammad's life in detail: his birth and childhood, his first encounter with the angel Gabriel in 610 at the age of forty, his escape (*hijra*) from Mecca to Medina in 622, his successful return to Mecca in 630, and finally his death in Medina in 632. For Muslims, the most important event in Islamic history is Muhammad's flight from Mecca to Medina. Muslims use this event to mark the beginning of the Islamic era.

No detail of Muhammad's life was too personal to be recounted in the Hadith. Stories about him are used for a variety of purposes—to entertain and enlighten as well as to support particular beliefs and practices, whether personal or political. Hundreds of thousands of stories about Muhammad were in circulation during al-Bukhari's lifetime, and a number of people had undertaken to collect them. Fabrication of Hadith was a widely recognized problem. People were known to have invented stories about Muhammad for both pious purposes and personal or political ends.

Al-Bukhari is said to have decided to compile the Sahih after one of his contemporaries expressed the wish that someone would produce a concise but comprehensive work containing only authenticated reports. He was the first to attempt to develop a system of authentication that could determine the relative reliability with which such stories might be traced back to Muhammad. He spent his entire adult life traveling in search of Hadith and is said to have examined more than six hundred thousand Hadith, of which fewer than seven thousand were included in his collection. Even after his death, however, al-Bukhari remained

Time Line

610 — Muhammad ibn Abdullah receives his call to prophethood.

622 — Muhammad flees from Mecca to Medina. Muslims date the Islamic era from this year.

630 — Muhammad successfully returns to Mecca.

810 — Muhammad ibn Abu Abdullah ibn Ismail al-Bukhari is born in Bukhara.

821 — Al-Bukhari completes his elementary education and begins studying with Hadith scholars in Bukhara.

827 — Al-Bukhari travels with his mother and brother on pilgrimage to Mecca.

828 — Al-Bukhari writes his first two books in Medina; he begins traveling throughout the Muslim empire studying and teaching Hadith in all of the major cities, a process that continues until 864.

864 — Al-Bukhari settles in the village of Khartank, near Bukhara, where he spends the remaining years of his life.

870 — Al-Bukhari dies in Khartank.

1072 — Nizam al-Mulk orders a public reading of *Sahih al-Bukhari* in the newly founded Nizamiyya College in Nisapur.

---

just one of many scholars who collected, studied, and taught Hadith throughout the Muslim world. It took two more centuries for his Sahih to become part of the emerging canon of Sunni Hadith literature.

In the late eleventh century, one of the most important events in the canonization process took place: The grand vizier of the Seljuk Empire, Nizam al-Mulk, ordered the public reading of al-Bukhari's Sahih at his newly founded religious college, known as the Nizamiyya, in the Iranian city of Nisapur in 1072. This reading was attended by the children of the city's elite. The strong support of the ruling elite and the usefulness of al-Bukhari's topically ar-ranged collection of Hadith helped to earn the Sahih its position as the most authoritative work in the Sunni Hadith canon. We do not know exactly when al-Bukhari completed the Sahih. Like other works from his era, the dating of the Sahih is established according to the year in which its compiler died—in al-Bukhari's case, in 870.

About the Author

Muhammad ibn Abu Abdullah ibn Ismail al-Bukhari, born in the Central Asian city of Bukhara (in modern-day Uzbekistan) in 810, was of Persian descent. His father, Ismail, was a well-respected scholar of Hadith in his own right. Ismail died when al-Bukhari was still an infant, leaving a sizable fortune to the boy, his mother, and his older brother, Abdullah. Like other children of his time and place, al-Bukhari's elementary education took place at home, under his mother's tutelage. At the age of eleven, he went on to study Hadith with the local masters of Bukhara. In his late teens, he undertook the pilgrimage to Mecca with his mother and older brother, in the year 827. This voyage began the odyssey of studying and teaching Hadith throughout the Muslim empire that would occupy the next four decades of al-Bukhari's life. He is said to have written his first two books at the age of eighteen, while living in Medina. While numerous books are attributed to al-Bukhari, the most important is his Sahih, to which he is believed to have dedicated a quarter of his life. After nearly four decades of travel studying and teaching, in 864 al-Bukhari settled in the village of Khartank, near his birthplace of Bukhara. He died in Khartank in 870.

Explanation and Analysis of the Document

The excerpt from Sahih al-Bukhari presented here is the second chapter, titled "Iman." It contains forty-nine Hadith. This part of the Sahih provides an overview of the most important components of belief. The remarks in brackets in this excerpt denote the interpolation of the translator and are not part of the original Arabic. This chapter of the Sahih provides Muslims with concise, yet detailed information about the attitudes and actions that demonstrate the depth and sincerity of one's belief in God. Repetition is a key feature of the entire Sahih, and this chapter is no exception. In some cases particular reports are repeated in more than one place in the text, and in other cases the same ideas are repeated in different Hadith.

♦ The Five Pillars of Islam

The first Hadith lists what are commonly referred to as "the five pillars" of Islam. The term "five pillars" is so popular that it is found in all introductory texts on Islam. This Hadith is the source of that term, which does not appear anywhere in the Qur'an. The "five pillars" on which this Hadith says Islam is built are the testimony of faith (*shahada*), ritual prayer (*salat*), almsgiving (*zakat*), fasting (*siyam*), and pilgrimage (*hajj*). Each of these religious duties is mentioned or alluded to in various places throughout the Qur'an, but the Qur'an does not include such a concisely delineated list. By placing this Hadith at the beginning of the chapter on belief, al-Bukhari highlights the importance of these duties as the foundation of Muslim life and practices. Additional details of these foundational practices are found elsewhere in the Sahih, in separate chapters dedicated to each.

Al-Bukhari repeats the same or similar Hadith in different places in this chapter and throughout the Sahih. Because Hadith treating the same topic are found in different parts of the chapter, they are discussed thematically here, rather than in order. This is the way Muslims generally approach the study of the Hadith. With regard to almsgiving, Hadith 20 indicates that the Prophet went out of his way not to show favoritism toward those he may have loved in the distribution of alms. One of the Prophet's companions questions him repeatedly about why he did not give alms to one whom the companion considered the most worthy. The Prophet's exclamation indicates both that he did not wish to let his personal opinion influence the distribution of alms and that he feared favoritism on his part might corrupt the one he favored and put him on the path to Hell. Hadith 21 repeats almost verbatim the theme of Hadith 5, telling Muslims to "feed (the poor) and greet those whom you know and those whom you don't know."

Hadith 44 returns to the topic of religious duties, with which al-Bukhari began this chapter of the Sahih. Hadith 1 is brief, giving only a concise listing of the religious duties that have come to be known as the "five pillars" of Islam. In contrast, Hadith 44 is a longer, narrative report. It is one of the longest Hadith in the chapter and embeds the list of duties in the context of a larger story that illustrates how the followers of Muhammad's companions heard and related the words of Muhammad.

This story recounts a situation in which the narrator, Abu Jamra, learned of what the Prophet had said. He did not hear the words of the Prophet personally. Instead, he heard them from the Prophet's companion, Ibn 'Abbas. Abu Jamra begins by describing something of his relationship with Ibn 'Abbas and then gives the context in which Ibn 'Abbas related the story to him. After establishing the context in which he heard the story, Abu Jamra then recounts the story as told by Ibn 'Abbas. There are some important differences from Hadith 1 in the Prophet's instructions in this report. First, there is no mention of the pilgrimage. Instead, this Hadith mentions the obligation to pay one fifth of the spoils of war ("Al-Khumus"). Second, it prohibits consumption of alcoholic beverages by inference, in listing the names of the containers in which such beverages were made and saying that they are forbidden. This is an instance where the Hadith contains details not found in the Qur'an. Another key detail of Muslim worship not found in the Qur'an is the number of daily prayers, enumerated as five in Hadith 38.

Slot for giving alms (zakat) at the tomb of a ninth-century ruler of Morocco
(Slot for giving zakat in the Zaouia Moulay Idriss II [photo], / Fes, Morocco / © World Religions Photo Library / The Bridgeman Art Library International)

♦ **The Qualities of a Faithful Muslim**

Hadith 2–10 emphasize the distinctive qualities and attitudes of people who have attained faith. Hadith 2 informs us that there are more than sixty aspects of belief and emphasizes the quality of *haya*, which encompasses traits such as modesty, humbleness, self-discipline, self-respect, and scruples. Hadith 17 also identifies *haya* as a part of faith about which one believer should not preach to another. *Haya* is an inherent personal quality that stems from an individual's faith rather than from the preaching of another. Belief and faith in God instill these traits in the faithful believer, who then manifests them in his or her behavior.

Specific examples of the types of behaviors that represent the manifestation of the traits associated with *haya* are mentioned in Hadith 3–6. These Hadith variously describe the faithful believer as one who does not harm other Muslims by word or deed and who wishes for his fellow Muslim what he wishes for himself. Moreover, according to Hadith 3, a believer is also an emigrant (*muhajir*), one who abandons those things that are forbidden by God. The word *muhajir* historically refers to Muhammad and his original followers, who were forced to emigrate from Mecca to Medina in 622 because of the persecution they suffered at the hands of the pagan tribes of Mecca.

Essential Quotes

> "Allah's Apostle said: Islam is based on (the following) five (principles): 1. To testify that none has the right to be worshipped but Allah and Muhammad is Allah's Apostle. 2. To offer the (compulsory congregational) prayers dutifully and perfectly. 3. To pay Zakat (i.e. obligatory charity). 4. To perform Hajj. 5. To observe fast during the month of Ramadan."

> "A man asked the Prophet, 'What sort of deeds or (what qualities of) Islam are good?' The Prophet replied, 'To feed (the poor) and greet those whom you know and those whom you do not Know.'"

> "The Prophet said, 'None of you will have faith till he wishes for his (Muslim) brother what he likes for himself.'"

> "The Prophet said 'None of you will have faith till he loves me more than his father, his children and all mankind.'"

> "The Prophet said, 'Religion is very easy and whoever overburdens himself in his religion will not be able to continue in that way. So you should not be extremists, but try to be near to perfection and receive the good tidings that you will be rewarded; and gain strength by worshipping in the mornings, the nights.'"

The Meccan Muslims' status as emigrants afforded them and their descendents a degree of prestige in the early Muslim community. Hadith 3 redefines *muhajir* as anyone who abandons that which has been forbidden by God. In this way, all faithful believers can attain the same status as Muhammad and the early Muslims.

Hadith 5 extends the good behavior required of a faithful believer beyond the Muslim community by defining very good Muslims as those who feed the poor and greet others, whether they know them or not. This requirement is repeated later in this chapter, in Hadith 21. The greeting referred to here is the greeting of peace. The Arabic text uses the term *as-salaam*, which refers to the common greeting *as-salaamu alaikum* ("peace be upon you"). Feeding the poor and offering greetings of peace to others, whether one knows them or not, are behaviors that help to foster a just and civil society, which according to Islam is a duty incumbent on humanity in general and on believers in particular.

Hadith 7–10 introduce love for the Prophet as a key element of belief. Love for the Prophet and the desire to follow his example is what motivates students of the Hadith, both in the early centuries and today. Loving the Prophet, and others, should not be for his sake or for one's own. It should be for the sake of God, because Islam is submission to God alone.

Hadith 9 is essentially identical to Hadith 14. In addition to loving the Prophet and others only for the sake of God, these two Hadith say that the faithful should loathe the idea of reverting to a state of unbelief, because this would demonstrate being ungrateful (*kufr*) to God.

Hadith 10 states that loving the Ansar (literally, "helpers"), the residents of Medina who took in the Muslim emigrants when they were forced to flee from Mecca, is also a trait of faithful believers, while hating them is a sign of hypocrisy. Once again, belief engenders feelings that foster a sense of community, but hypocrisy gives rise to feelings that damage a sense of community. Treatment of the Ansar is taken up again later, in Hadith 17, where Muslims are enjoined to regard the *haya* of the Ansars as part of the faith.

Hadith 23–25 emphasize the proper behavior and attitudes expected of believers. The first declares the brotherly equality of master and slave. The master is responsible for dressing and feeding the slave as he himself dresses and eats. Moreover, the master must not ask the slave to undertake difficult tasks unless the master assists the slave in them. The structure of the story, where the narrator asks Abu Dhar why he and his slave are wearing the same kind of cloak, shows that such equality was something surprising to the people of the time. The second of these three Hadith prohibits Muslims from taking up arms against each other or helping a Muslim who intends to harm another Muslim. This reinforces the idea expressed earlier in the chapter that Muslims are not to harm one another by word or deed. Hadith 25 demonstrates how the Prophet explained the meaning of Qur'anic verses to his followers. In this case, he is elaborating on verse 83 of chapter 6 of the Qur'an, which is quoted at the beginning of Hadith 25. When the Prophet's companions asked him who among them had not done wrong, the Prophet clarified the issue by citing another verse of the Qur'an (31:13), where the wrongdoing is defined as worshiping others along with God. According to still other verses of the Qur'an, worshiping others with God is the only wrong that God does not forgive.

Hadith 40 further illustrates the gravity of animosity between Muslims. The prophet was on his way to inform the people which night during Ramadan is the night of Qadr, but he found two Muslims quarreling, and God caused the Prophet to forget the date. The importance of the night of Qadr is also discussed in Hadith 28. The latter Hadith emphasizes the importance of praying on the night of Qadr, which falls within Ramadan and is the night Muhammad first received revelation of the Qur'an from the angel Gabriel. The Arabic word *Qadr* means "destiny" or "power." The night of Qadr and its importance is highlighted in the five verses of chapter 97 of the Qur'an; verse 3 declares that the night of Qadr is "better than a thousand months."

◆ **Prohibitions**

Hadith 11 continues the focus of Hadith 2–10 on behavior, but from a negative perspective. Where the first Hadith lists those things a believer is obliged to do, this Hadith lists those things that a believer is not to do. This list of prohibitions was given to listeners in the context of swearing allegiance to Muhammad. As in the case of the first Hadith, this one, too, brings together, in one concise list, items that are scattered throughout the Qur'an and adds others not found there. There are six specific prohibitions: worshiping anything else along with God, stealing, sexual intercourse outside of marriage, killing one's children, making false accusations, and disobeying an order to do a good deed. Items 1–5 are found in various parts of the Qur'an. Item 6, however, is not included either directly or indirectly in the Qur'an. The Prophet's additional comments about sin and punishment are also found only in the Hadith, but they nonetheless represent the common Sunni understanding. Hadith 12 predicts that there will be a time when the faithful believer will need to distance himself from a corrupt society and take refuge with his herds in a mountain or valley, where he can practice his religion freely, without interference.

The focus on attitudes and actions is balanced by the idea in Hadith 13 that the believer is required to do only what is easy, and this is emphasized again in Hadith 35. Hadith 16 offers a metaphor that indicates that among the companions of the Prophet there were varying levels of faith and practice. In Hadith 32, the Prophet takes up this theme again by emphasizing that the religion is easy, and he warns against extremism. Moderation is highlighted as an essential quality of believers. The theme continues in Hadith 34, which informs Muslims that the reward for good deeds far outweighs the potential punishment for bad deeds. Even those whose deeds land them in Hell are offered hope. Hadith 15 (along with Hadith 36) informs believers that even after the final judgment, whoever has even a minute amount of faith will be removed from Hell, cleansed, and sent to heaven.

Hadith 26 and 27 introduce the problem of hypocrisy, delineating the characteristics that make a believer a hypocrite: lying, breaking promises, betraying trusts, dishonesty, and insulting others in disputes. Such actions damage others by word and deed and damage the sense of community that faith is supposed to foster. This theme is taken up in the final selection, Hadith 43–49, which stress sincerity and the importance of intention; these Hadith caution believers to avoid those things that, while they may not be lawful or prohibited, are doubtful. All actions will be judged according to the intention behind them, and believers must strive to be sincere in all their words and actions.

◆ **Jihad**

Hadith 18 is the basis for the widespread misconception that Islam was spread by the sword. While the Muslim empire did spread by military conquest, the people of conquered territories were seldom forced to convert. In most areas, it took a century or more for the majority of the population in conquered areas to become Muslim. This particular Hadith is one that Hadith opponents see as contradicting the Qur'an, which specifically orders fighting (*qital* in Arabic) only against those who begin hostilities against Muslims (Qur'an 2:190, 9:13). Muslims who attempt to reconcile this Hadith with the text of the Qur'an understand it in relation to Islam's emphasis on proselytizing. Like Christianity, Islam claims to be the truth from God, sent to all humanity. It is the responsibility of the Prophet to spread the message. They see fighting, in this instance, as synonymous with exerting a great deal of effort (*jihad* in Arabic).

Throughout the Sahih various things are defined as "jihad," which is generally understood by Muslims to be any effort undertaken for the sake of God. This includes caring for one's family, as seen in Hadith 46 and 47. Hadith 29 reiterates the importance of jihad. Muslim jurists recognize four kinds of jihad: jihad of the heart, jihad of the tongue, jihad of the hand, and jihad of the sword. The first is the believer's struggle to overcome personal weaknesses and strengthen the soul. The second is to argue against falsehood and to spread the message of truth. The third is good works, which include fulfilling one's family responsibilities, as later indicated in Hadith 46 and 47.

♦ The Status of Women

Hadith 22 is one of two Hadith about women in this chapter of the Sahih. In this Hadith, the Prophet recounts seeing in a vision that the majority of the people in Hell will be women who are ungrateful to their husbands. This is one of many misogynistic Hadith, which are said to have been disputed by no less than the Prophet's wife Aisha, who criticized a number of Muhammad's companions for inaccuracy in reporting what the Prophet had said about women. The other Hadith about a woman in this chapter is one attributed to Aisha, in which the Prophet cautioned Aisha's female guest against overzealous religious practices (Hadith 35).

♦ Ritual Observances and Ramadan

Hadith 28, 30, and 31 discuss the rewards of the month of Ramadan, the ninth month of the Muslim lunar calendar, in which Muslims fast each day from dawn to dusk. The first emphasizes the importance of praying on the night of Qadr, which falls within Ramadan and is the night Muhammad first received revelation from the angel Gabriel. The exact day in Ramadan is not known, but it is said to be one of the last ten nights of the month. Muslims are encouraged to offer extra prayers during these nights, seeking the blessings of the night of Qadr and the forgiveness of their past sins. The next Hadith in this group extends the same blessings to those who perform extra night prayers throughout the month. Because of this, many Muslims will spend each night of Ramadan praying in the mosque. The third Hadith offers Muslims blessings and forgiveness for the fast itself. Fasting and prayer are activities that strengthen the soul of the believer and encourage humbleness and good works, those essential qualities that were addressed in the beginning of the chapter.

Hadith 33 tells the story of the *qibla*, the direction to which Muslims turn in prayer. When Muhammad first arrived in Medina, he and his followers turned toward Jerusalem. However, he desired to pray toward the Ka'ba in Mecca, which Muslims believe was built by Abraham as the first house of worship to the One True God. By Muhammad's time, the Ka'ba was said to be filled with some 360 idols worshipped by the Arab pagans. An important part of Muhammad's mission was to rededicate the Ka'ba to the worship of the One True God. Although the change of direction caused friction between the Muslims and the Jewish tribes, facing the Ka'ba in prayer from Medina is seen as an important step in this process.

Another report that touches on the relationship between the Muslims and the Jews is Hadith 37. Unlike most of the Hadith in the Sahih, this is not a report about the Prophet Muhammad. It is a report about his companion, 'Umar ibn al-Khattab, who was the second leader of the community after Muhammad's death. In response to a Jew who suggested that the day of the revelation of the Qur'an, described in chapter 5, verse 3, should be taken by Muslims as a day of celebration, 'Umar tells him that the verse was revealed during Muhammad's farewell pilgrimage and that the day of revelation is, in fact, already a day of celebration by the Muslims.

♦ Fundamental Beliefs

Hadith 25 serves as an explanation of Qur'anic verses 6:83 and 31:13, emphasizing the seriousness of worshipping anything or anyone along with God. There is no greater wrongdoing in Islam.

Hadith 41 is another lengthy narrative Hadith that defines a number of important terms: *Iman*, *Islam*, and *Ihsan*. In defining these terms, the Hadith summarizes the key beliefs and practices of the religion. An important aspect of the story is that it describes the coming of the angel Gabriel in the form of a man to ask Muhammad for religious instruction while Muhammad was sitting among his companions. Muhammad's companions are not aware that the man is Gabriel until Muhammad informs them, after Gabriel has left.

The first word of Muhammad's reply in this Hadith is translated here and in other reports as "faith," but it is also the word for "belief." Those things in which Muslims must believe are God, the angels, the prophets (who bring God's guidance), and the day of resurrection and judgment, when all human beings will meet God. Islam is defined by absolute monotheism and the obligatory religious duties of prayer, charity, and fasting. Perfection of faith and practice results from a constant awareness of God's presence. Those who have not attained such a level of awareness are advised to remember that God is watching. Although the hour of judgment is known only to God, this Hadith goes on to describe the signs of the last days and the approach of that hour.

Following the detailed discussion of beliefs and practices is a single Hadith (42) that describes the encounter between the Roman emperor Heraclius and the leader of Muhammad's Meccan opponents, Abu Sufyan. The emperor asks Abu Sufyan about the size of the nascent Muslim community. In particular, he asks whether anyone was unhappy with Islam after embracing it. When Abu Sufyan replies in the negative, the emperor declares that this is the sign of a true faith. Muslims cite this Hadith to demonstrate that even the mighty Roman emperor recognized the validity of Islam.

Audience

Al-Bukhari's target audience was the Muslim community as a whole, the faithful of his own and later generations. It is not meant for an audience of readers but for seekers in search of knowledge and guidance. The Sahih is meant to provide Muslims with what al-Bukhari believed to be the most reliable and authentic stories about Muhammad's life. The content and arrangement of the work is designed to give Muslims a concise but comprehensive collection of reliable stories that serve as a basis of religious belief, law, and practice. The vast majority of Muslims do not learn Hadith by reading from the Sahih or any of the canonized collections. They learn Hadith from other Muslims, parents, teachers, and imams, who relate them orally when giving advice, lectures, and sermons.

Impact

Although the canonization of the Hadith literature would come two centuries or more after his death, al-Bukhari's magnum opus became the centerpiece of that canon. Part of the reason that it took centuries for the canon to emerge is that early generations of Muslims disputed the proper role and authority of the Hadith. Opponents of the Hadith objected to the transmission and recording of these stories on the basis that they might come to rival the Qur'an, the "Book of God." They also argued that the objectionable or embarrassing content of some Hadith made the religion an object of ridicule. For opponents of the Hadith, the Qur'an's command to obey God's messenger meant following only the Qur'an, which the Prophet had delivered at God's command.

Supporters of the Hadith argued that the Qur'an's command to obey God's messenger required accepting the stories that were related about him and were passed on through sound chains of reliable narrators. Moreover, supporters argued that without these stories, there would be no uniformity in religious practices, because the Qur'an does not describe the details of such obligatory practices as prayer and almsgiving. The supporters of Hadith eventually prevailed, and by the late eleventh century, more than four hundred years after the time of Muhammad, arguments against the authority of the Hadith disappear from the literature. The debates over that authority then reemerged in the latter half of the nineteenth century and continue today. Contemporary opponents of the Hadith remain in the minority, and the Hadith continue to have a profound influence on the day-to-day thinking and practice of the vast majority of the world's Muslims.

Al-Bukhari scrutinized the chains of narrators in an attempt to include only sound, authentic Hadith in his collection. He was not as concerned with the textual content (*matn*) of the Hadith. For this reason, the collection contains Hadith that seem to contradict other Hadith and even the Qur'an. This has served as a basis for criticism on the part of some later Hadith scholars, who argue that such contradictory texts should not be considered sound and authentic. They also argue that not all of the chains of transmitters were sound enough to warrant the designation of *sahih*. Other scholars, in particular, the fifteenth-century scholar Ibn Hajar al-Asqalani, wrote commentaries analyzing, explaining, and defending al-Bukhari's compilation. Ibn Hajar began working on his extensive commentary, titled *Fath al-Bari* ("Grant of the Creator"), in 1414 and completed it in 1438. Today, *Fath al-Bari* continues to be the most widely used and accepted commentary on al-Bukhari's Sahih.

After centuries of study and criticism, the Sahih al-Bukhari continues to be the most influential and respected Hadith collection, more than eleven hundred years after the death of its compiler. For generations, it has served the majority of the world's Muslims as a source of law and guidance, second in authority only to the Qur'an. In many

Questions for Further Study

1. What are the five pillars of Islam, and why do you think Muslims regarded each as important?

2. The Hadith, as the entry states, "describe the faithful believer as one who does not harm other Muslims by word or deed." Yet in contemporary life, reports of terrorist acts perpetrated by Muslims in which Muslims die have become almost routine. How can these actions on the part of some Muslims be reconciled with the teachings of the Hadith?

3. The Arabic word *jihad* is commonly seen today in newspapers and on news reports. What is the meaning of this term? How do the Hadith interpret jihad?

4. Why would an American Muslim turn to the east while praying? What historical circumstances account for this practice?

5. In what ways might this document be similar to the Pirke Avot of Judaism? In what ways are the two documents different?

ways, it has been even more influential in Muslim belief and practice than the Qur'an. For example, the Qur'an orders believers to establish prayer, but the actual number of daily prayers is found only in the Hadith. Likewise, the Qur'an insists on the absolute oneness of God and declares that God, the angels, and those with knowledge testify to that oneness, but the Hadith make that testimony a pillar of Islam. The Qur'an also mentions charity, fasting, and pilgrimage, and here, again, the Hadith establish them as pillars of Islam. This is why Sunni Muslim scholars since the time of the imam Muhammad ibn Idrisal-Shafi'i have argued that the Hadith are absolutely necessary. The uniformity of Sunni Islam throughout the world comes not from the Qur'an but from the Hadith. Because his Sahih is the most respected and authoritative collection of Hadith, al-Bukhari's influence on Islam is comparable to the influence of Saint Paul on Christianity. Just as Paul's letters in the New Testament help to shape Christian doctrine and practice, al-Bukhari's Sahih helps to shape Muslim doctrine and practice.

Further Reading

■ Books

Abdul Rauf, Muhammad. "Hadith Literature: The Development of the Science of Hadith." In *Arabic Literature to the End of the Umayyad Period*, ed. A. F. L. Beeston et al. Cambridge, U.K.: Cambridge University Press, 1983.

Brown, Jonathan A. C. *Hadith: Muhammad's Legacy in the Medieval and Modern World*. Oxford, U.K.: Oneworld Press, 2009.

Juynbol, G. H. A. *Muslim Tradition: Studies in Chronology, Provenance, and Authorship of Early Hadith*. Cambridge, U.K.: Cambridge University Press, 2008.

Musa, Aisha Y. *Hadith as Scripture: Discussions on the Authority of Prophetic Traditions in Islam*. New York: Palgrave, 2008.

Siddique, Muhammad Z. *Hadith Literature: Its Origins, Development, and Special Features*. Cambridge, U.K.: Islamic Texts Society, 1993.

■ Web Sites

The Hadith Library Web site.
   http://ahadith.co.uk/

"Sunnah and Hadith." University of Southern California's Center for Jewish-Muslim Engagement Web site.
   http://www.usc.edu/schools/college/crcc/engagement/resources/texts/muslim/hadith/

—Aisha Y. Musa

Sahih al-Bukhari

Hadith 1
Narrated / Authority Of: Ibn Umar
Allah's Apostle said: Islam is based on five [principles]: 1. To testify that none has the right to be worshipped but Allah and Muhammad is Allah's Apostle. 2. To offer the [compulsory congregational] prayers dutifully and perfectly. 3. To pay Zakat. 4. To perform Hajj. 5. To observe fast during the month of Ramadan.

Hadith 2
Narrated / Authority Of: Abu Huraira
The Prophet said, "Faith consists of more than sixty branches. And Haya is a part of faith."

Hadith 3
Narrated / Authority Of: Abdullah bin Amr
The Prophet said, "A Muslim is the one who avoids harming Muslims with his tongue and hands. And a Muhajir is the one who gives up all what Allah has forbidden."

Hadith 4
Narrated / Authority Of: Abu Musa
Some people asked Allah's Apostle, "Whose Islam is the best?" He replied, "One who avoids harming the Muslims with his tongue and hands."

Hadith 5
Narrated / Authority Of: Abdullah bin Amr
A man asked the Prophet, "What sort of deeds of Islam are good?" The Prophet replied, "To feed [the poor] and greet those whom you know and those whom you do not Know."

Hadith 6
Narrated / Authority Of: Anas
The Prophet said, "None of you will have faith till he wishes for his [Muslim] brother what he likes for himself."

Hadith 7
Narrated / Authority Of: Abu Huraira
Allah's Apostle said, "By Him in Whose Hands my life is, none of you will have faith till he loves me more than his father and his children."

Hadith 8
Narrated / Authority Of: Anas
The Prophet said "None of you will have faith till he loves me more than his father, his children and all mankind."

Hadith 9
Narrated / Authority Of: Anas
The Prophet said, "Whoever possesses the following three qualities will have the sweetness of faith: 1. The one to whom Allah and His Apostle becomes dearer than anything else. 2. Who loves a person and he loves him only for Allah's sake. 3. Who hates to revert to Atheism as he hates to be thrown into the fire."

Hadith 10
Narrated / Authority Of: Anas
The Prophet said, "Love for the Ansar is a sign of faith and hatred for the Ansar is a sign of hypocrisy."

Hadith 11
Narrated / Authority Of: Ubada bin As-Samit
who took part in the battle of Badr and was a Naqib, on the night of Al-'Aqaba pledge: Allah's Apostle said while a group of his companions were around him, "Swear allegiance to me for: 1. Not to join anything in worship along with Allah. 2. Not to steal. 3. Not to commit illegal sexual intercourse. 4. Not to kill your children. 5. Not to accuse an innocent person. 6. Not to be disobedient [when ordered] to do good deed." The Prophet added: "Whoever among you fulfills his pledge will be rewarded by Allah. And whoever indulges in any one of them [except the ascription of partners to Allah] and gets the punishment in this world, that punishment will be an expiation for that sin. And if one indulges in any of them, and Allah conceals his sin, it is up to Him to forgive or punish him [in the Hereafter]." 'Ubada bin As-Samit added: "So we swore allegiance for these."

Hadith 12
Narrated / Authority Of: Abu Said Al-Khudri
Allah's Apostle said, "A time will come that the best property of a Muslim will be sheep which he will take on the top of mountains and

the places of rainfall so as to flee with his religion from afflictions."

Hadith 13
Narrated / Authority Of: Aisha

Whenever Allah's Apostle ordered the Muslims to do something, he used to order them deeds which were easy for them to do. They said, "O Allah's Apostle! We are not like you. Allah has forgiven your past and future sins." So Allah's Apostle became angry and it was apparent on his face. He said, "I am the most Allah fearing, and know Allah better than all of you do."

Hadith 14
Narrated / Authority Of: Anas

The Prophet said, "Whoever possesses the following three qualities will taste the sweetness of faith: 1. The one to whom Allah and His Apostle become dearer than anything else. 2. Who loves a person and he loves him only for Allah's sake. 3. Who hates to revert to disbelief after Allah has brought him out from it, as he hates to be thrown in fire."

Hadith 15
Narrated / Authority Of: Abu Said Al-Khudri

The Prophet said, "When the people of Paradise will enter Paradise and the people of Hell will go to Hell, Allah will order those who have had faith equal to the weight of a grain of mustard seed to be taken out from Hell. So they will be taken out but they will be blackened. Then they will be put in the river of Haya' or Hayat, and they will revive like a grain that grows near the bank of a flood channel. Don't you see that it comes out yellow and twisted."

Hadith 16
Narrated / Authority Of: Abu Said Al-Khudri

Allah's Apostle said, "While I was sleeping I saw [in a dream] some people wearing shirts of which some were reaching up to the breasts only while others were even shorter than that. Umar bin Al-Khattab was shown wearing a shirt that he was dragging." The people asked, "How did you interpret it? O Allah's Apostle?" He [the Prophet] replied, "It is the Religion."

Hadith 17
Narrated / Authority Of: Abdullah bin Umar

Once Allah's Apostle passed by an Ansari who was admonishing to his brother regarding Haya'. On that Allah's Apostle said, "Leave him as Haya' is a part of faith."

Hadith 18
Narrated / Authority Of: Ibn Umar

Allah's Apostle said: "I have been ordered [by Allah] to fight against the people until they testify that none has the right to be worshipped but Allah and that Muhammad is Allah's Apostle, and offer the prayers perfectly and give the obligatory charity, so if they perform that, then they save their lives and property from me except for Islamic laws and then their reckoning will be done by Allah."

Hadith 19
Narrated / Authority Of: Abu Huraira

Allah's Apostle was asked, "What is the best deed?" He replied, "To believe in Allah and His Apostle. The questioner then asked, "What is the next [in goodness]? He replied, "To participate in Jihad in Allah's Cause." The questioner again asked, "What is the next [in goodness]?" He replied, "To perform Hajj 'Mubrur."

Hadith 20
Narrated / Authority Of: Sad

Allah's Apostle distributed [Zakat] amongst [a group of] people while I was sitting there but Allah's Apostle left a man whom I thought the best of the lot. I asked, "O Allah's Apostle! Why have you left that person? By Allah I regard him as a faithful believer." The Prophet commented: "Or merely a Muslim." I remained quiet for a while, but could not help repeating my question because of what I knew about him. And then asked Allah's Apostle, "Why have you left so and so? By Allah! He is a faithful believer." The Prophet again said, "Or merely a Muslim." And I could not help repeating my question because of what I knew about him. Then the Prophet said, "O Sa'd! I give to a person while another is dearer to me, for fear that he might be thrown on his face in the Fire by Allah."

Hadith 21
Narrated / Authority Of: Abdullah bin Amr

A person asked Allah's Apostle . "What deeds in or [what qualities of] Islam are good?" He replied, "To feed [the poor] and greet those whom you know and those whom you don't know."

Hadith 22
Narrated / Authority Of: Ibn Abbas

The Prophet said: "I was shown the Hell-fire and that the majority of its dwellers were women who were ungrateful." It was asked, "Do they disbelieve

in Allah?" He replied, "They are ungrateful to their husbands and are ungrateful for the favors and the good done to them. If you have always been good to one of them and then she sees something in you [not of her liking], she will say, 'I have never received any good from you.'"

Hadith 23
Narrated / Authority Of: Al-Marur
At Ar-Rabadha I met Abu Dhar who was wearing a cloak, and his slave, too, was wearing a similar one. I asked about the reason for it. He replied, "I abused a person by calling his mother with bad names." The Prophet said to me, "O Abu Dhar! Did you abuse him by calling his mother with bad names? You still have some characteristics of ignorance. Your slaves are your brothers and Allah has put them under your command. So whoever has a brother under his command should feed him of what he eats and dress him of what he wears. Do not ask them to do things beyond their capacity and if you do so, then help them."

Hadith 24
Narrated / Authority Of: Al-Ahnaf bin Qais
While I was going to help this man ['Ali Ibn Abi Talib], Abu Bakra met me and asked, "Where are you going?" I replied, "I am going to help that person." He said, "Go back for I have heard Allah's Apostle saying, 'When two Muslims fight each other with their swords, both the murderer as well as the murdered will go to the Hell-fire.'" I said, "O Allah's Apostle! It is all right for the murderer but what about the murdered one?" Allah's Apostle replied, "He surely had the intention to kill his companion."

Hadith 25
Narrated / Authority Of: Abdullah
When the following Verse was revealed: "It is those who believe and confuse not their belief with wrong" (6:83), the companions of Allah's Apostle asked, "Who is amongst us who had not done injustice?" Allah revealed: "No doubt, joining others in worship with Allah is a great injustice indeed." (31.13)

Hadith 26
Narrated / Authority Of: Abu Huraira
The Prophet said, "The signs of a hypocrite are three: 1. Whenever he speaks, he tells a lie. 2. Whenever he promises, he always breaks it. 3. If you trust him, he proves to be dishonest.

Hadith 27
Narrated / Authority Of: Abdullah bin Amr
The Prophet said, "Whoever has the following four [characteristics] will be a pure hypocrite and whoever has one of the following four characteristics will have one characteristic of hypocrisy unless and until he gives it up. 1. Whenever he is entrusted, he betrays. 2. Whenever he speaks, he tells a lie. 3. Whenever he makes a covenant, he proves treacherous. 4. Whenever he quarrels, he behaves in a very imprudent, evil and insulting manner."

Hadith 28
Narrated / Authority Of: Abu Huraira
Allah's Apostle said, "Whoever establishes the prayers on the night of Qadr out of sincere faith and hoping to attain Allah's rewards then all his past sins will be forgiven."

Hadith 29
Narrated / Authority Of: Abu Huraira
The Prophet said, "The person who participates in [Holy battles] in Allah's cause and nothing compels him to do so except belief in Allah and His Apostles, will be recompensed by Allah either with a reward, or booty [if he survives] or will be admitted to Paradise [if he is killed in the battle as a martyr]. Had I not found it difficult for my followers, then I would not remain behind any sariya going for Jihad and I would have loved to be martyred in Allah's cause and then made alive, and then martyred and then made alive, and then again martyred in His cause."

Hadith 30
Narrated / Authority Of: Abu Huraira
Allah's Apostle said: "Whoever establishes prayers during the nights of Ramadan faithfully out of sincere faith and hoping to attain Allah's rewards, all his past sins will be forgiven."

Hadith 31
Narrated / Authority Of: Abu Huraira
Allah's Apostle said, "Whoever observes fasts during the month of Ramadan out of sincere faith, and hoping to attain Allah's rewards, then all his past sins will be forgiven."

Hadith 32
Narrated / Authority Of: Abu Huraira
The Prophet said, "Religion is very easy and whoever overburdens himself in his religion will not be able to continue in that way. So you should not be extremists, but try to be near to perfection and

receive the good tidings that you will be rewarded; and gain strength by worshipping in the mornings, the nights."

Hadith 33
Narrated / Authority Of: Al-Bara bin Azib

When the Prophet came to Medina, he stayed first with his grandfathers or maternal uncles from Ansar. He offered his prayers facing Baitul-Maqdis for sixteen or seventeen months, but he wished that he could pray facing the Ka'ba. The first prayer which he offered facing the Ka'ba was the 'Asr prayer in the company of some people. Then one of those who had offered that prayer with him came out and passed by some people in a mosque who were bowing during their prayers [facing Jerusalem]. He said addressing them, "By Allah, I testify that I have prayed with Allah's Apostle facing Mecca." Hearing that, those people changed their direction towards the Ka'ba immediately. Jews and the people of the scriptures used to be pleased to see the Prophet facing Jerusalem in prayers but when he changed his direction towards the Ka'ba, during the prayers, they disapproved of it. Al-Bara' added, "Before we changed our direction towards the Ka'ba in prayers, some Muslims had died or had been killed and we did not know what to say about them [regarding their prayers]. Allah then revealed: 'And Allah would never make your faith [prayers] to be lost.'" (2:143).

Hadith 34
Narrated / Authority Of: Abu Huraira

Allah's Apostle said, "If any one of you improve his Islamic religion then his good deeds will be rewarded ten times to seven hundred times for each good deed and a bad deed will be recorded as it is."

Hadith 35
Narrated / Authority Of: Aisha

Once the Prophet came while a woman was sitting with me. He said, "Who is she?" I replied, "She is so and so," and told him about her [excessive] praying. He said disapprovingly, "Do [good] deeds which are within your capacity as Allah does not get tired [of giving rewards] but you will get tired and the best deed [act of Worship] in the sight of Allah is that which is done regularly."

Hadith 36
Narrated / Authority Of: Anas

The Prophet said, "Whoever said 'None has the right to be worshipped but Allah and has in his heart good [faith] equal to the weight of a barley grain will be taken out of Hell.' And whoever said: 'None has the right to be worshipped but Allah and has in his heart good [faith] equal to the weight of a wheat grain will be taken out of Hell.' And whoever said, 'None has the right to be worshipped but Allah and has in his heart good [faith] equal to the weight of an atom will be taken out of Hell.'"

Hadith 37
Narrated / Authority Of: Umar bin Al-Khattab

Once a Jew said to me, "O the chief of believers! There is a verse in your Holy Book which is read by all of you [Muslims], and had it been revealed to us, we would have taken that day [on which it was revealed] as a day of celebration." 'Umar bin Al-Khattab asked, "Which is that verse?" The Jew replied, "This day I have perfected your religion for you, completed My favor upon you, And have chosen for you Islam as your religion." (5:3) 'Umar replied, "No doubt, we know when and where this verse was revealed to the Prophet. It was Friday and the Prophet was standing at 'Arafat."

Hadith 38
Narrated / Authority Of: Talha bin Ubaidullah

A man from Najd with unkempt hair came to Allah's Apostle and we heard his loud voice but could not understand what he was saying, till he came near and then we came to know that he was asking about Islam. Allah's Apostle said, "You have to offer prayers perfectly five times in a day and night." The man asked, "Is there any more [praying]?" Allah's Apostle replied, "No, but if you want to offer the Nawafil prayers [you can]." Allah's Apostle further said to him: "You have to observe fasts during the month of Ramadan." The man asked, "Is there any more fasting?" Allah's Apostle replied, "No, but if you want to observe the Nawafil fasts [you can]." Then Allah's Apostle further said to him, "You have to pay the Zakat." The man asked, "Is there any thing other than the Zakat for me to pay?" Allah's Apostle replied, "No, unless you want to give alms of your own." And then that man retreated saying, "By Allah! I will neither do less nor more than this." Allah's Apostle said, "If what he said is true, then he will be successful [that is, he will be granted Paradise]."

Hadith 39
Narrated / Authority Of: Abu Huraira

Allah's Apostle said, "[A believer] who accompanies the funeral procession of a Muslim out of sincere faith and hoping to attain Allah's reward and remains with it till the funeral prayer is offered and the burial ceremonies are over, he will return with a reward of two Qirats. Each Qirat is like the size of the Uhud. He who offers the funeral prayer only and returns before the burial, will return with the reward of one Qirat only."

Hadith 40
Narrated / Authority Of: Abdullah

The Prophet said, "Abusing a Muslim is Fusuq and killing him is Kufr." Narrated 'Ubada bin As-Samit: "Allah's Apostle went out to inform the people about the [date of the] night of decree [Al-Qadr] but there happened a quarrel between two Muslim men. The Prophet said, "I came out to inform you about the night of Al-Qadr, but as so and so and so and so quarreled, its knowledge was taken away and maybe it was better for you. Now look for it in the 7th, the 9th and the 5th [of the last 10 nights of the month of Ramadan]."

Hadith 41
Narrated / Authority Of: Abu Huraira

One day while the Prophet was sitting in the company of some people, [the angel] Gabriel came and asked, "What is faith?" Allah's Apostle replied, "Faith is to believe in Allah, His angels, meeting with Him, His Apostles, and to believe in Resurrection." Then he further asked, "What is Islam?" Allah's Apostle replied, "To worship Allah Alone and none else, to offer prayers perfectly to pay the compulsory charity and to observe fasts during the month of Ramadan." Then he further asked, "What is Ihsan?" Allah's Apostle replied, "To worship Allah as if you see Him, and if you cannot achieve this state of devotion then you must consider that He is looking at you." Then he further asked, "When will the Hour be established?" Allah's Apostle replied, "The answerer has no better knowledge than the questioner. But I will inform you about its portents. 1. When a slave gives birth to her master. 2. When the shepherds of black camels start boasting and competing with others in the construction of higher buildings. And the Hour is one of five things which nobody knows except Allah. The Prophet then recited: "Verily, with Allah [Alone] is the knowledge of the Hour." (31.34) Then that man [Gabriel] left and the Prophet asked his companions to call him back, but they could not see him. Then the Prophet said, "That was Gabriel who came to teach the people their religion." Abu 'Abdullah said: He [the Prophet] considered all that as a part of faith.

Hadith 42
Narrated / Authority Of: Abdullah bin Abbas

I was informed by Abu Sufyan that Heraclius said to him, "I asked you whether they [followers of Muhammad] were increasing or decreasing. You replied that they were increasing. And in fact, this is the way of true Faith till it is complete in all respects. I further asked you whether there was anybody, who, after embracing his religion [Islam] became displeased and discarded it. You replied in the negative, and in fact, this is [a sign of] true faith. When its delight enters the heart and mixes with them completely, nobody can be displeased with it."

Hadith 43
Narrated / Authority Of: An-Numan bin Bashir

I heard Allah's Apostle saying, "Both legal and illegal things are evident but in between them there are doubtful things and most of the people have no knowledge about them. So whoever saves himself from these suspicious things saves his religion and his honor. And whoever indulges in these suspicious things is like a shepherd who grazes [his animals] near the Hima of someone else and at any moment he is liable to get in it. [O people!] Beware! Every king has a Hima and the Hima of Allah on the earth is His illegal things. Beware! There is a piece of flesh in the body if it becomes good the whole body becomes good but if it gets spoilt the whole body gets spoilt and that is the heart."

Hadith 44
Narrated / Authority Of: Abu Jamra

I used to sit with Ibn 'Abbas and he made me sit on his sitting place. He requested me to stay with him in order that he might give me a share from his property. So I stayed with him for two months. Once he told [me] that when the delegation of the tribe of 'Abdul Qais came to the Prophet, the Prophet asked them, "Who are the people? [Or] who are the delegates?" They replied, "We are from the tribe of Rabi'a." Then the Prophet said to them, "Welcome! O people [or O delegation of 'Abdul Qais]! Neither will you have disgrace nor will you regret." They said, "O Allah's Apostle! We cannot come to you except in the sacred month and there is the infidel tribe of Mudar intervening between you and us. So please order us to do something good so that we may inform our people whom we have left behind, and that we may enter Paradise." Then they asked about drinks [what is legal and what is illegal]. The Prophet ordered them to do four things and forbade them from four things.

Document Text

He ordered them to believe in Allah Alone and asked them, "Do you know what is meant by believing in Allah Alone?" They replied, "Allah and His Apostle know better." Thereupon the Prophet said, "It means: 1. To testify that none has the right to be worshipped but Allah and Muhammad is Allah's Apostle. 2. To offer prayers perfectly. 3. To pay the Zakat. 4. To observe fast during the month of Ramadan. 5. And to pay Al-Khumus." Then he forbade them four things, namely, Hantam, Dubba, Naqir Ann Muzaffat or Muqaiyar. The Prophet further said: "Memorize them [these instructions] and convey them to the people whom you have left behind."

Hadith 45
Narrated / Authority Of: Umar bin Al-Khattab
Allah's Apostle said, "The reward of deeds depends upon the intention and every person will get the reward according to what he has intended. So whoever emigrated for Allah and His Apostle, then his emigration was for Allah and His Apostle. And whoever emigrated for worldly benefits or for a woman to marry, his emigration was for what he emigrated for."

Hadith 46
Narrated / Authority Of: Abu Masud
The Prophet said, "If a man spends on his family [with the intention of having a reward from Allah] sincerely for Allah's sake then it is a [kind of] almsgiving in reward for him."

Hadith 47
Narrated / Authority Of: Sad bin Abi Waqqas
Allah's Apostle said, "You will be rewarded for whatever you spend for Allah's sake even if it were a morsel which you put in your wife's mouth."

Hadith 48
Narrated / Authority Of: Jarir bin Abdullah
I gave the pledge of allegiance to Allah's Apostle for the following: 1. Offer prayers perfectly, 2. pay the Zakat, 3. and be sincere and true to every Muslim.

Hadith 49
Narrated / Authority Of: Ziyad bin Ilaqa
I heard Jarir bin 'Abdullah [Praising Allah]. On the day when Al-Mughira bin Shu'ba died, he [Jarir] got up [on the pulpit] and thanked and praised Allah and said, "Be afraid of Allah alone Who has none along with Him to be worshipped. [You should] be calm and quiet till the [new] chief

Glossary

Al-Khumus	spoils of war
Allah's Apostle	Muhammad
Ansar	literally, "helpers"—the residents of Medina who took in the Muslim emigrants, including Muhammad, when they were forced to flee from Mecca
Baitul-Maqdis	an Arabic name for Jerusalem
battle of Badr	a battle fought on March 17, 624
Fusuq	an evil action
Hajj	pilgrimage
Hantam, Dubba, Naqir Ann Muzaffat or Muqaiyar	types of drinking vessels forbidden for Muslims because they were used for wine
Haya	personal qualities encompassing modesty, humbleness, self-discipline, self-respect, and scruples
Hayat	literally, "life," often used to refer to worldly things that prevent attainment of eternal life

Document Text

comes to you and he will come to you soon. Ask Allah's forgiveness for your [late] chief because he himself loved to forgive others." Jarir added, "Amma badu, I went to the Prophet and said, 'I give my pledge of allegiance to you for Islam.'" The Prophet conditioned [my pledge] for me to be sincere and true to every Muslim so I gave my pledge to him for this. By the Lord of this mosque! I am sincere and true to you [Muslims]. Then Jarir asked for Allah's forgiveness and came down [from the pulpit].

Glossary

Heraclius	a Roman emperor
Hima	a portion of land reserved for a country's ruler as grazing ground
Jihad	any effort undertaken for the sake of God
Ka'ba	located in Mecca, Saudi Arabia, believed by Muslims to have been built by Abraham as the first house of worship to the one true God but by Muhammad's time said to be filled with idols worshipped by Arab pagans
Kufr	ungrateful to God
Muhajir	an emigrant
Naqib	a tribal chief or leader
Nawafil prayers	extra, recommended (but not required) prayers
night of Qadr	or al-Qadr; the night Muhammad first received revelation from the angel Gabriel
Qirat	a unit of measurement for gold
Ramadan	Islamic holy month of fasting and prayer
Uhud	the site of a battle
Zakat	almsgiving

The investiture of Ali as imam

(Or Ms 161 fol.162r The Investiture of 'Ali at Ghadir Khumm, from 'The Chronology of Ancient Nations' by Al-Biruni, / Edinburgh University Library, Scotland / With kind permission of the University of Edinburgh / The Bridgeman Art Library International)

USUL AL-KAFI

921–940

"I have commenced and inaugurated this book of mine with the chapter on reason, the greatness of knowledge."

Overview

The Usul al-kafi is part of the Kitab al-kafi, a multivolume collection of over sixteen thousand Hadith that were compiled between 921 and 940 by Abu Ja'far Muhammad ibn Ya'qub ibn Ishaq al-Kulayni al-Razi (known as al-Kulayni) in the city of Baghdad. Hadith are the sayings of the prophet Muhammad (the founder of Islam, born in 570) and, in some instances, the sayings of those Shia imams believed by the Shia to be direct successors to Muhammad.

The Sunni and Shia branches of Islam have separate collections of Hadith. The primary difference between the two is that whereas Sunni Hadith focus on the person of Muhammad, Shia Hadith—from a Shia sect known as the Twelvers—focus on the sayings of Muhammad and the twelve imams who followed him. The Twelvers, also known as the Ithna 'Ashariyya, are the largest Shia sect and are the dominant sect in modern-day Iran.

It is important to distinguish between the Hadith and the Qur'an. Most Muslims believe that the Qur'an is the literal word of God received by the prophet Muhammad in a series of revelations over a twenty-two-year period beginning in 610. Shia Hadith are not the word of God but rather are the utterances of both Muhammad and the imams. Although they apply a premise of absolute infallibility to the Qur'an, Islamic scholars often refer to taking a scientific approach to Hadith, which involves determining their reliability. A Hadith is considered reliable if its transmission from Muhammad or one of the imams can be documented and traced. Although the Hadith in the Kitab al-kafi are not the word of God, most Islamic scholars generally agree that most of them are particularly reliable.

Context

The Usul al-kafi was written during a time of political strife and religious factionalism; although this volume is not a political document, it is reflective of the manner in which government and religion often fuse in crucial ways in the Islamic world. The Usul al-kafi was written in response to people who needed clarification of their faith, as the government was becoming progressively unstable and religious disputes rocked the Islamic world.

By the time the Usul al-kafi was written, the rapid expansion of Islam that had followed the death of Muhammad in 632 had slowed down. Islam had spread across northern Africa and had reached as far west as Spain and as far east as the Indus River. The Islamic world was governed by the Abbasid Caliphate (so named because its initial leaders descended from 'Abbas ibn 'Abd al-Muttalib, an uncle of Muhammad). While the Abbasids briefly converted to Shia Islam during their struggle for political dominance, they quickly returned to their Sunni origins after securing power. At the height of their reign, the Abbasids governed all of the Islamic world. They made their capital in Baghdad; by the middle of the eighth century, Baghdad rivaled Constantinople in size. It was a center of learning graced by mosques, palaces, observatories, and libraries.

By the beginning of the tenth century, when the Usul al-kafi was written, the Abbasids were in a period of decline, both in terms of political and religious unity. Shia separatism became firmly established in the early tenth century, as the Fatimids—the descendants of Muhammad's daughter Fatimah and his son-in-law Ali—broke away from the Sunni Abbasids and traveled to North Africa, ultimately conquering the Syrian coast and Egypt and making their capital Cairo. Other separate Shia dynasties that came to power during this time were the Buyids in Iran and Iraq and the Hamdanids in Syria. Almost immediately after the Usul al-kafi was written, the Abbasid caliph was reduced to performing religious functions. Ultimately, the Islamic world became far more factionalized and was no longer governed from a single dynastic seat.

The Usul al-kafi was compiled in response to the emergence of Shia separatism and the deep-seated uncertainty that accompanied it. As Abbasid power declined and the Shia appeared to be ascendant, people needed a statement of the basis of their faith and the particulars of their religious practice. As the Shia shifted from being a small, struggling minority to being a self-governing authority, the Usul al-kafi filled a need by providing references to how previous Shia leadership approached problems.

Time Line

570	The prophet Muhammad is born.
610	Muhammad begins to receive the Qur'an.
600	'Ali ibn Abi Talib is born; according to the Shia, 'Ali was the first imam.
622	Muhammad flees to Mecca.
846	Hassan ibn 'Ali al-Askari, the eleventh imam, is born.
869	The twelfth imam, Muhammad al-Mahdi, is born.
874	Al-Mahdi enters into occultation.
921	Al-Kulayni moves to Baghdad and begins work on the Kitab al-kafi.
940	Al-Kulayni dies in Baghdad.

The Usul al-kafi is strictly a Shia text. Unlike the Sunnis, the Shia believe that the first imams were designated by Allah as the sole and infallible interpreters of the revelations of God (Allah). They believe that the imamate was passed down from imam to imam, with each imam naming his own successor. According to Twelver Shia, the imamate passed from Muhammad's son-in-law 'Ali ibn Abi Talib (ca. 600–661) through ten more imams, the eleventh being Hasan ibn 'Ali al-Askari, born in 846, who died unexpectedly in 874. Al-Askari's successor, Muhammad al-Mahdi, was born in 869. Al-Mahdi assumed the imamate at age five, at which point he is believed to have gone into occultation. *Occultation* is a mystical concept in which the imam is considered to be very much alive but outside the vision of mere mortals. Many Twelver Shia believe that since humankind cannot exist without an imam, the twelfth imam, known as the Mahdi, will someday emerge from occultation. The Mahdi was believed to be in communication with various deputies for the first few decades following the death of al-Askari. These decades are called the period of minor occultation. The Usul al-kafi is considered particularly reliable because it was compiled during this period of minor occultation. The Mahdi is said to remain inaccessible in occultation today, and Shia believe that he will emerge at an unknown point in time. The Twelvers can be compared to the less popular Seveners—who believe that infallibility was extended only to the first seven imams.

In compiling the Usul al-kafi, al-Kulayni justified his work by asserting that Allah divided all humans into two categories: healthy, thinking people and unhealthy persons of unsound mind. The Qur'an holds that healthy, thinking people have a duty to educate others so as to invite humankind toward the unity of Allah. Al-Kulayni pointed out that it is difficult for "interrogative" people to fulfill this duty because there are conflicting statements regarding the utterances of Muhammad and the imams. Al-Kulayni compiled this collection of Hadith in the hope of remedying the need for a compilation of traditions.

About the Author

Since the Hadith in a collection are previously written works that have been handed down through time, we speak of who compiled them rather than who wrote them. Thus, we speak of al-Kulayni as the compiler of the Kitab al-kafi. Few details are known about his early life other than that he came from a scholarly family from the town of Kulayn, near modern-day Tehran. He was a scholar, teacher, and writer who was reasonably well traveled. Like his father, he was recognized as a *muhaddithun*—a scholar who specializes in Hadith. While we know that his writings went far beyond the Kitab al-kafi, few of them have been preserved.

Al-Kulayni began the Kitab al-kafi when he moved to Baghdad in 921, and he continued work on the compilation for the last twenty years of his life. A gloss of reliability is extended to the work because it was compiled during the minor occultation; the Shia presume that the Mahdi would have spoken out through one of his deputies if the text was erroneous. Twelver Muslims believe that every century has one outstanding Islamist scholar, or *mujadid*. The Kitab al-kafi is such a far-reaching and reliable work that al-Kulayni is credited with being the *mujadid* of the third century (corresponding roughly to the ninth century of the Christian era, in that the Islamic calendar begins with Muhammad's flight to Mecca in 622). Al-Kulayni is also known by the title *thiqat al-Islam*, meaning "reliable narrator." Al-Kulayni died in Baghdad in 940. He is buried in Kufah, roughly 110 miles south of Baghdad.

Explanation and Analysis of the Document

As noted, the Usul al-kafi is part of the Kitab al-kafi. The Arabic word *kitab* means "book," and *al-kafi* means "the necessary and sufficient." Thus, the title Kitab al-kafi can be translated as "the book containing that which is necessary and sufficient." This has been used for various puns, including one by Ayatollah Khomeini, the late Iranian political and religious leader, to the effect that merely having the al-kafi was not sufficient, one has to follow the precepts therein as well.

The Usul is one of the three volumes of the Kitab al-kafi, the other two being the Furu and Rawda. *Usul* means "roots" or "fundamentals." Usul al-kafi can be translated "sufficing fundamentals," the implication being that it provides the believer with a sufficient background (outside of the Qur'an) in the Islamic fundamentals of faith. The Usul al-kafi includes eight books of traditions that speak to the heart of Shia belief and practice. These eight books include Hadith relating to reason, knowledge, divine unity, faith, prayer, the Qur'an, and social ethics. The text included in this volume is the introduction to the Usul al-kafi. The brief introduction to the Usul al-kafi contains the fundamental precepts that separate Sunni and Shia Islam and provides a justification for producing the work. Al-Kulayni quickly builds the structure of an argument that legitimizes Shia doctrine and raises it from a political dispute to a religious and philosophical position.

♦ **All Praise Be to Allah . . .**

The first paragraphs of the Usul al-kafi speak to the unknowability and omniscience of Allah. Allah's power is so great that humans cannot possibly understand him. Ultimately he transcends our ability to reason, to imagine, to calculate, and to physically perceive. According to the Usul, this unknowability does not relieve humankind from a duty to try to understand Allah and what Allah wants. Realizing that humans were incapable of understanding him, Allah sent messengers as intermediaries. Al-Kulayni writes, "He has sent His messengers with glad tidings and due warnings. So that, if, thereafter one comes to grief it will be on his own account and if he comes to success it will also be on his own account." Ultimately, the responsibility of heeding Allah's message lies with humankind.

Since Allah is unknowable, it is only through Muhammad and the Qur'an that humankind can understand him. Al-Kulayni notes that the prophet Muhammad lived during a time of enormous ignorance, when most people were lacking any consciousness of God. According to al-Kulayni, Muhammad's transcription of the Qur'an provided a path out of this ignorance. Through the Qur'an, Allah stated very specifically what he wanted from people. By following the prescriptions in the Qur'an, people could be assured of salvation.

In these first paragraphs, al-Kulayni's argument is consistent with most Sunni doctrine. However, the text then quickly moves from establishing Muhammad and the Qur'an as being sent by Allah for the enlightenment of humanity to establishing Muhammad's son-in-law 'Ali ibn Abi Talib as Muhammad's "nominated executor"— that is, asserting that Allah declared through Muhammad that 'Ali ibn Abi Talib was Muhammad's successor. Moreover, says al-Kulayni, 'Ali likewise had the authority to name a divinely approved successor.

This leap is important in establishing the Kitab al-kafi as a particularly Shia text, undergirding the legitimacy of the Shia imamate and the infallibility of the first twelve imams. Whereas the Sunni refer to the first four successors to Muhammad (Abu Bakr, 'Uthman, 'Umar, and 'Ali) as the "four rightly guided caliphs," the Shia believe that succession

Arabic calligraphy with the names of Allah, Muhammad, Ali, and Ali's two sons, Hassan and Hussein (the second and third imams, respectively)
(Arabic calligraphy with the names of Muhammad, his son in law, Ali and Ali's two sons, Hassan and Hussein (coloured ink on paper), Ottoman School, (18th century) / Private Collection / Archives Charmet / The Bridgeman Art Library International)

should have run directly to Muhammad's son-in-law 'Ali, bypassing Abu Bakr, 'Uthman, and 'Umar. This essentially political struggle was the genesis of the Sunni-Shia split. Al-Kulayni's reference to 'Ali as Muhammad's nominated executor rests upon a long series of Hadith that are unique

Essential Quotes

"He is veiled without any veil and is concealed without any covering. He is recognised without being seen and has been described as being formless."

"He [Muhammad] departed (from the world) and has left behind him the book of Allah and his deputy (nominated executor, 'Ali ibn Abi Talib) the chief of the believers and the guide (Imam) for those who guard themselves against evil."

"Whoever among the Imams died, he used to nominate after him his successor as a declared luminous, righteous guide (Imam). Who would guide people (towards the Truth) and would be constant in his guidance. These guides (Imams) called the people towards Allah as His demonstrators and are designated by God as the patrons for His creation."

"God wanted them to refer to Imam (to know the Truth), forbidding all other people to pass hasty verdicts."

"If it had been proper for the people of health and peace to remain ignorant, then God would have never ordered them to be interrogative, and the need for sending the prophets with the books and the codes would never have arisen."

"I have commenced and inaugurated this book of mine with the chapter on reason, the greatness of knowledge, the great status of those who possess it, their high worth, the defectiveness of ignorance, the baseness of its possessor, and their lowered rank. Since reason is the axis on which every thing revolves, it is on the reason that all the argument rests."

---

to the Shia. Al-Kulayni confirms the Shia position that Muhammad's successor should be the progeny of Muhammad himself, because only these progeny had the received word of Allah. Al-Kulayni reframes this problem of succession as a religious one, saying that "God the Almighty explained His religion" to his progeny and gave them "the deep springs of divine knowledge" of which others were ignorant.

♦ Whoever among the Imams Died . . .

Al-Kulayni uses the legitimacy of 'Ali ibn Abi Talib as a springboard to his next argument about the infallibility of the imams. He points to a pattern of imamic succession wherein each imam was divinely inspired to nominate his own successor. Although these imams were mortal, al-Kulayni asserts that God designated them as leaders and invested them with unique knowledge so that they could inspire their followers. This idea is similar to the concept of papal infallibility. Here, al-Kulayni is referring to 'Ali and each of the eleven imams who followed him. Once again, this is a uniquely Shia—and, more narrowly, a Twelver Shia—concept. Al-Kulayni's repeated exhortation, "peace be upon him and his progeny" (sometimes rendered only as "p.b.u.h.a.h.p."), after invoking the name of Muhammad reveals that the deference al-Kulayni shows to Muhammad is extended to Muhammad's lawful successors. By declaring that this pattern of succession came from Allah by way of his messenger Muhammad, al-Kulayni legitimizes the Shia position.

Having established the basis of Shia epistemology, al-Kulayni begins to explain why he has undertaken the project of compiling Hadith. He speaks about the ignorance of people and how they "assist and help each other" and get farther away "from learnings and from the men of learning." He suggests that blind adoption of religion without true understanding is a shallow act from which individuals can be spared. Al-Kulayni asserts that Allah has created two kinds of humans—those who are healthy and sound and those who are unhealthy and unsound. It is the religious duty of those who are in the first category to bring others toward Allah so that humankind may be unified in its faith. Al-Kulayni states that this elevated category of humans has been singled out by God. Unless this educated class honors its religious duty, "the entire structure of divine books, prophet and education falls to the ground." Al-Kulayni claims that this duty arises because Allah "deemed ignorance about Him and the denial of His religion highly improper." Unlike the text's earlier propositions, this assertion is so important that al-Kulayni bolsters it with Qur'anic support by quoting sura (verses) from four Qur'anic chapters: al-A'raf, Yunus, at-Tawbah, and ah-Nahl (translated as "the Heights," "Jonah," "the Repentance," and "the Bees," respectively).

In the passages that follow, al-Kulayni asserts that God ordered healthy people to be "interrogative," meaning that they should ask questions and think deeply. This ability to question, more than any other, is what separates humans from animals. Al-Kulayni uses this point to cycle back to his initial premise—that blind adoption of religion without true understanding is a shallow act. Like the Hebrew prophet who says that "wisdom is the principal thing; therefore get wisdom and with all the getting get understanding" (Proverbs 4:7), al-Kulayni reminds the reader that knowledge and understanding are the a priori values of religious worship and that it is incumbent on every thinking person to have a teacher or some other means by which to study and learn. Acquiring the knowledge of "religion and God consciousness" separates those who merely go through the motions of religious observance from those with true knowledge and insight.

At this point, al Kulayni diverts from the subject ever so slightly to introduce an idea that he will come back to regarding how to distinguish a reliable Hadith from an unreliable one. Al-Kulayni states that "evidence without the knowledge of what is witnessed is not at all acceptable." Thus, Kulayni rules out hearsay evidence in support of a Hadith. This is the foundation for what Shia scholars refer to as a scientific approach to the study of Hadith; a Hadith is considered reliable only if its transmission from Muhammad or one of the imams can be documented and traced. Al-Kulayni will return to the issue of reliability later in the introduction. However, in the meantime, he reverts to his discussion regarding distinguishing rote observation from true knowledge. He quotes the words of an imam who proposes that true knowledge and understanding have the effect of deepening faith and making the believer more steadfast. That is, says al-Kulayni, if knowledge is derived from authentic sources such as the Qur'an, or Muhammad, or (most pointedly) Muhammad's progeny (the successor imams), then faith will be as unmovable as mountains. However, those who do not recognize the legitimacy of the imams, he continues—here drawing the proverbial line in the sand between the Shia and Sunni—will not be able to distinguish religious truths from errors. In this way, al-Kulayni repudiates the entire canon of Sunni scholarship.

♦ **You (the Interrogator) Have Spoken . . .**

Al-Kulayni now returns to the idea he began to develop earlier: the importance of distinguishing reliable Hadith from unreliable Hadith. He recognizes that there are many conflicting versions of particular traditions (quotes from Muhammad and the imams are called traditions) that amount to hearsay. He recognizes that the lack of expertise about conflicting versions of a particular tradition has created enormous demand for a text so that people "could act thereon with genuine traditions from the truthful Imams." Al-Kulayni claims that there is no place for individual discrimination between these versions. Instead, the correct approach is to retain those Hadith that are consistent with the Qur'an and reject those that are not consistent with it. Hadith that were repeated with the intention of obeying the imam are more likely to be reliable that those that were circulated for other reasons.

Al-Kulayni brings his introduction to a close by thanking Allah for enabling him to compile these Hadith. He notes that the collection intentionally begins with a chapter on the human being's ability to reason because it is upon reason that all argument rests. This attribute is particularly important because whereas Sunni Sharia law relies upon analogy, Shia jurisprudence is based upon reason. Philosophically, this is important because in pre-Islamic times the opposite of ignorance was considered to be understanding and self-control. As Shia philosophy evolved, the opposite of ignorance was held to be reason. Thus, al-Kulayni returns once again to his earlier theme of rectifying ignorance and provides the justification of his book.

Audience

As stated in the introduction of the Kitab al-kafi, the intended audience for al-Kulayni's text was intelligent people who sought religious understanding and who could then teach and lead others. Since al-Kulayni was writing in a Shia stronghold, we may assume that he was writing for a Shia audience and, presumably, to those who were receptive to Shia authority.

One of the strengths in these volumes is that al-Kulayni refrained from editorializing about the Hadith, leaving further analysis to subsequent commentators. Because of this, the document retains its original freshness. Usul al-kafi has spawned commentary of its own, and there is a rich Shia tradition of examining and weighing the reliability of the Hadith presented therein. The commentary on the Usul began almost immediately after publication by such figures as the famous Shia scholar Al-Shaykh al-Saduq. Other collections of Shia Hadith exist. Together with three other collections by other authors, the Kitab al-kafi makes up the famous Al-Kutub al-Arba'ah, or "Four Books," that Shia scholars rely upon. However, these volumes merely add to al-Kulayni's work, rather than superseding it. In modern times, the Usul al-kafi remains a foundational work that retains a vital place in Shia discourse. It is consistently referred to by contemporary Shia legal scholars and political leaders to exhort people to the faith and also to serve as a source of legal authority. Among non-Islamists, the text occupies a significant space in medieval studies.

Impact

The impact of the Kitab al-kafi, and the Usul al-kafi contained therein, on the evolution of Shia Islam cannot be overestimated. The quality of its scholarship was immediately recognized by the tenth-century Persian theologian and historian Abu Ja'far Muhammad ibn Jarir al-Tabari, who wrote that "al-kafi among the four Shia books is like the sun among the stars." It rapidly became one of the four canonical Shia texts of Hadith, the other three being Man la yahduruhu al-Faqih, Tahdhib al-Ahkam, and Al-Istibsar. The Kitab al-kafi is the largest of these collections and one of the oldest.

Part of the reason for the quick acceptance of this text was that it provided a much-needed explanation of the faith to a growing body of faithful. The succession problems that gave rise to the Shia began immediately upon the death of Muhammad. These early years were marked by a series of unsuccessful insurrections against the Sunnis. The Usul al-kafi was written during a significant gap in that cycle of insurrection and persecution, during which Shia Islam gained footholds in India, Syria, Iran, Iraq, and Egypt. During this time, the focus of the Shia faithful was more intellectual than military. In providing a justification for their faith and an explanation of its practices, the Usul al-kafi met an enormous need.

Today, Shia continues to be the dominant strand of Islam in Iran, Iraq, Azerbaijan, and Bahrain. There is also a sizable Shia minority in Pakistan, Afghanistan, Syria, India, Kuwait, Saudi Arabia, and Yemen. It is not coincidental that some of these regions—such as Iran, Iraq, Syria, and India—correspond to the regions of Shia separatism established in the tenth century.

The Usul al-kafi continues to have contemporary legal application in countries such as Iran that practice Shia Sharia law. Sharia law involves applying religious doctrine to resolve civil and criminal disputes. Legal scholars look to both the Qur'an and the Hadith when searching for legal rules and precedents. Reliance on the Hadith constitutes part of the foundation for what is referred to as the dominant usuli-rationalist approach in legal theory and, by extension, contemporary jurisprudence. Today, the Usul al-

Questions for Further Study

1. This document invites comparison with the Hadith presented in Sahih al-Bukhari. In comparing the documents, do you detect any differences in underlying viewpoints, concerns, or beliefs? What might account for these differences?

2. Both Usul al-kafi and, in China, the Book of Rites were written partly in response to social and political upheaval. Explain how the two documents are similar—and how they differ—in responding to that upheaval and speculate on the factors that might have caused these similarities and differences.

3. Why, in the view of Shia (and Sunni) Islam are the Hadith even necessary? How would you respond to a statement to the effect that the Qur'an is the only text necessary for Muslims?

4. Considerable emphasis is placed on the authenticity of the Hadith. Yet the Hadith in Usul al-kafi were compiled some two centuries after Muhammad. How do you think Islamic scholars in the Middle Ages were able to document the authenticity of the Hadith? How did they know they could trust their sources?

5. If Usul al-kafi "provided a much-needed explanation of the faith," as the entry states, in what respect could it be regarded as bearing similarities to the Nicene Creed and the function that document fulfilled for Christianity? Explain.

kafi is referred to in the most seemingly unlikely matters of Islamic law and Islamic finances.

The Usul al-kafi also had a profound impact on Shia philosophy, when philosophy became integrated into the Shia intellectual world in the thirteenth century. This philosophy is particularly rooted in the sayings of the imams. Without the preservation of the sixteen thousand Hadith contained in al-Kulayni's work, this philosophy would be impoverished indeed.

Further Reading

■ Books

Lapidus, Ira. *History of Islamic Societies*. New York: Cambridge University Press, 1988.

Lewis, Bernard, ed. *The World of Islam: Faith, People, Culture*. London: Thames and Hudson. 1976.

Küng, Hans. *Islam: Past, Present, and Future*, trans. John Bowden. Oxford, U.K.: Oneworld Publications, 2007.

Newman, Andrew J. *The Formative Period of Twelver Shi'ism: Hadith as Discourse between Qum and Baghdad*. Richmond, U.K.: Curzon Press, 2000.

Rogerson, Barnaby. *The Heirs of the Prophet Muhammad*. London: Little, Brown, 2006.

■ Web Sites

Howard, I. K. A. "Great Shia Works: 'Al-Kafi' by Al-Kulayni," Al-Islam.org Web site.
   http://www.al-islam.org/al-serat/kulayni-howard.htm

Nasr, Seyyed Hossein. "The Qur'an and Hadith: As Source and Inspiration of Islamic Philosophy." I-epistemology.net Web site.
   http://i-epistemology.net/philosophy/14-the-quran-and-Hadith-as-source-and-inspiration-of-islamic-philosophy.html

—Cy Ashley Webb

Document Text

Usul al-kafi

In the Name of Allah, the Beneficent, the Merciful

All praise be to Allah Who is praised for His bounties, worshipped for His Might, obeyed in His reign, feared for His Majesty. He possesses all things that allure, His commands pervade all through His creation. He is elevated to the extent He liked. He is too near to find, too high for everyone to see, Whose beginning has no beginning and Whose eternity has no end, Who existed before the existence of all things and Who is an eternal supporter of all things. The Conqueror Whom the preservation of the things does not tire. The Almighty Who is in a class by Himself in His sublimity throughout His realm, the unique in His Might because of His power. Who, out of His Wisdom, manifested His signs (proofs) and mercy for His creation. Who out of His Might and Wisdom originated all things anew from the very beginning. Nothing existed (at that time) to falsify His being the originator (of all things), nor did any other cause (of creation) exist to nullify His being the (first) originator. All alone He created what He liked and as He liked to manifest His Wisdom and the truth of His being the Nourisher. Reason cannot grasp Him. Imagination cannot reach Him. Eyes cannot see Him. Measurement cannot encompass Him. Every explanation fails in His description. Eyes are blurred in seeing Him. Attributing different qualities to Him goes astray in His description.

He is veiled without any veil and is concealed without any covering. He is recognised without being seen and has been described as being formless. He is described as having no corporal form. There is no God save Him, the great the elevated. Imagination goes astray in trying to reach the reality about Him (Godhood). Thoughts get confounded in trying to reach His finality. No flight of fancy can touch Him. He is all knowing, all hearing. He (Allah) has offered proofs (of truth and reality) through His messengers (peace be upon them) and has explained things through reasons. He has sent His messengers with glad tidings and due warnings. So that, if, thereafter one comes to grief it will be on his own account and if he comes to success it will also be on his own account, so that people should understand what they do not know about their Lord and they should recognise God's Lordship after their having denied it. And, so that people should believe in His unity after believing in His plurality. To Him (Allah) do we accord such a praise as is the solace of the souls, as secures God's pleasure and as will acquit us of our gratitude for His perfect bounties, abundant favours and graceful tests.

I am a witness to there being no God save Him. Who has no partner, the one, the eternally Besought and Who has taken no wife nor a son. And I have been witness to Muhammad (peace be upon him and his progeny), His select slave, and to his being sent as a messenger when the coming of such messengers had been suspended. The period when the nations were in deep slumber, when ignorance prevailed, distress and affliction were rampant, firm pledges were being violated, people were blinded against all truth, when oppression was in great vogue and honesty was being obliterated.

So (under the circumstances such as these) did Allah send His book to him (Muhammad, the prophet) containing description and explanation (of all good), a book readable (Qur'an) in Arabic language totally free from all slant, so that mankind may guard itself against every evil. This book (Qur'an) describes clearly before the people the distinct path (of truth) with reason and knowledge. It also elucidates the (divine) religion, describing the imperatives imposed on them by Allah, the things which God has revealed and announced for the people. This book contains guidance for salvation, and is a milestone leading towards the right path.

The Prophet delivered what he received (from God) and acknowledged whatever was ordained. He bore the weight of the responsibilities of prophethood on him. He exercised patience to please His Lord. He strove in the way of God and consulted his people and called them towards their salvation. He roused them to the remembrance of God and guided them towards the right path. Afterwards he built the highways and erected the light house for the guidance of mankind and raised minarets, the flags of which fluttered high for the people to watch. All this He did so that people should not go astray, since he (the Prophet) was very kind and merciful to them.

When his (Prophet's) period of life ended and his days were done, God took out his soul and brought it to Himself. Now he is with God in a state where

God is pleased with each of his actions. He is venerable and his share of divine rewards is the greatest. He departed (from the world) and has left behind him the book of Allah and his deputy (nominated executor, 'Ali ibn Abi talib) the chief of the believers and the guide (Imam) for those who guard themselves against evil. May peace of Allah be upon him. Both of them (the Prophet and 'Ali, his executor) were comrades and close associates. Each one of whom bore witness to the integrity of the other. ('Ali) the Imam spoke for God about (the import) of His book (Qur'an) in respect of the imperatives, God has imposed upon the people for His obedience and the obedience of the Imam (the divinely appointed guide). He also spoke (towards God), about the rule and rights of the Imam, through whom God intended perfecting His religion, expressing His commands, offering His reasons and arguments and (finally) His effulgence (guidance).

He did all this through those who were the fountain spring of all divinely chosen, the unique, the righteous, belonging to the house (progeny) of our Prophet Muhammad, may peace of Allah be upon him and upon his progeny. God the Almighty explained His religion through them and lighted through them the path that leads to Him and through them He unearthed the deep springs of divine knowledge. God appointed them as the milestones on the highways of God consciousness, sign posts for His religion and ushers between Himself and His creation. He made them the doorways which lead to divine rights, secrets' and the realisation of obligations of God consciousness. Further, God informed them His secrets and mysteries.

Whoever among the Imams died, he used to nominate after him his successor as a declared luminous, righteous guide (Imam). Who would guide people (towards the Truth) and would be constant in his guidance. These guides (Imams) called the people towards Allah as His demonstrators and are designated by God as the patrons for His creation. Because of their guidance the people adopt religion and Godliness and due to them the cities get illuminated (with Truth and guidance). God the Almighty designated them as the life and soul of the people, beacon lights in darkness, keys to the fort of knowledge and as the bedrock of His religion (Islam). God determined obedience and submission to the Imams as obedience and acme of submission to Himself and His religion, in respect of the commands known to them. Regarding God's commands unknown to them, God wanted them to refer to Imam (to know the Truth), forbidding all other people to pass hasty verdicts. God also forbade them from rejecting them and not accepting the verdicts passed by the Imams in respect of those divine commands they do not know, God did all this at the time He intended redeeming the people, He liked, from the curse of darkness (of misguidance), from the rampant ambiguity (in faith). May peace of Allah be upon Muhammad and upon the folk of his house, the righteous, from whom Allah wish as to wipe out uncleanliness away from them (the folk of the house) and cleanse them with thorough cleansing.

To come to the point, I have fully comprehended your complaint about the people of our time how proverbially they are accustomed to ignorance and how they assist and help each other in rehabilitating its ways and means and in getting farther away from learnings and from the men of learning. Until the plant of learning not only gets dried up but is also completely uprooted from their life. It is because they have all helped in elevating the state of ignorance in wiping off learning and the men of learning.

And you have asked me whether it is proper for the people to take up a stand in ignorance and to adopt religion without knowing religion, believing all its theories and concepts in all excellence, and also following it in every way. But they are doing it all blindly in following their fore-fathers, ancestors and their chiefs, completely relying upon their thoughts and reasons in matters (of religion) small or big.

Know thou, my brother, may God be merciful to you, verily, God the Almighty has brought human beings into existence as distinct from the animals, in respect of intelligence and understanding of which they are compounded, and has imposed upon them the load of imperatives and preventives. Afterwards Allah of the highest praised, has divided them into two categories—the healthy, the sound and the second the unhealthy and disabled. God has singled out the former category for the enforcement of His imperatives and preventives after perfecting in them the (intelligence and understanding) the instrument of His (arduous) responsibility, and has relieved the disabled and the unhealthy of this heavy task of responsibility, as they have been created as beings quite unfit for the task of discipline and education. God has made the people of sound health the instrument of safety and preservation of the later category. And has made discipline and education as the instrument of safety and preservation of the former. Should ignorance have been made permissive for the former, the very responsibility (of imperatives and preventives) would have been taken away from them. Once this is made permissible, the entire structure of divine books, prophet and education falls to the ground.

In this case, the divine books, the prophets and their education would have been nullified and the whole set up would have come to naught. In that case we would have had to turn to the beliefs and concepts of atheism. Hence, Providence in its justice and wisdom requires from men (of sagacity) that they should, in view of their nature and the very purpose of their creation, single themselves out to shoulder the burden of certain imperatives and prohibitions, lest their existence may not be regarded as in vain and purposeless. And so that they should glorify God, regard Him as one, and acknowledge His Lordship. And so that they should know God to be the creator and their All-giver, since the evidence of His Lordship is manifest, His arguments are self-evident and His symbols are unmistakable. They (people of health, peace and sagacity) should invite mankind towards Unity of Allah, the Almighty. They themselves bear witness, on the basis of their own existence that they have their creator, Who is their Lord, Who is worshipped. It is because there are wonderful signs of His Providence within themselves. Allah Himself accorded to them God consciousness since, for Him it was not proper for such people to remain without His awareness and in ignorance of (His) religion and His commandments. It is because Allah in His Wisdom deems ignorance about Him and the denial of His religion highly improper, as He Himself has said:

"Has not the compact of the Book been taken touching them, that they should say concerning God nothing but the truth?" (*al-A'raf*, 7:169).

Allah has (also) said:

"No; but they have cried lies to that whereof they comprehended not the knowledge" (*Yunus*, 10:39).

So mankind has been earmarked for (divine) imperatives and prohibitions and it has been ordained to speak the truth. Men have not been allowed to remain in ignorance (regarding the ultimate truth and the divine imperatives and prohibitions). Hence Allah has ordained mankind to be interrogative (in this connection) and to acquire understanding in the religion (of Allah) saying:

"But why should not a party of every section of them go forth, to become learned in religion, and to warn their people when they return to them" (*at-Tawbah*, 9:122).

Allah has further said: "Question the people of the remembrance, if it should be that you do not know" (*ah-Nahl*, 16:43).

If it had been proper for the people of health and peace to remain ignorant, then God would have never ordered them to be interrogative, and the need for sending the prophets with the books and the codes would never have arisen. In that case all mankind would have been maimed and disabled and would have remained on the animal plane. Had all this been so, then all mankind would have been set at naught within the twinkling of an eye. When there is no justification for its (mankind) existence without a code and education, then it is incumbent on each and every perfectly sound individual to have a teacher, a guide, a director, a preventer, a code, an education and interrogation to discharge his responsibilities. The privilege of a sage and a lucky rightful and a brilliant statesman is to endeavour in the acquisition of the knowledge of religion and God consciousness on account of which God is worshipped by His creation, which (in essence) is God's unity, divine code, divine commandments, divine imperatives and preventives, His admonitions and His etiquette. If it is established that the divine proofs are there, that our responsibilities are evident, that our life span is very short, that evasion and procrastination are unacceptable, then the divine condition, on account of which God is worshipped by His creatures, is to discharge all divine obligations consciously, in true belief and with due insight, so that (the divine obligations) performer be deemed praiseworthy in the eye of God and be entitled to divine rewards in high compensation. Since the one who performs divine obligations without knowledge and insight, does not really know what he has performed and in whose obedience he has done so; and because the ignorant can neither have any confidence in what have they done in the performance of divine obligations, nor can he truly believe in his deeds, for the simple reason that the believer can never believe unless he is the knower of the things he believes in, without the least doubt; and because of this reason, neither can the sceptic be like those who in all submission long for and fear God, nor can they have that nearness to God which a sage with true belief has. Thus has God observed:

"Save such as have testified to the truth and that knowingly" (*az-Zukhruf*, 43:86).

Evidence is acceptable on the basis of the knowledge of what is witnessed. Evidence without the knowledge of what is witnessed is not at all acceptable. In the case of a person performing divine duties in a state of doubt and uncertainty without the knowledge of insight (into them) is left to Allah's Will either to accept it in His grace, or to reject it totally since the indispensable condition laid by God on the person for whom they (divine duties) are made imperative, is to act upon them with knowledge, insight and conviction, so that such people may not be included among those whom God has described with the following words:

"And among men there is such a one as worships God upon the very edge—if good befalls him he is at rest in it, but if a trial befalls him he turns completely over; he loses this world and the world to come; that is indeed the manifest loss" (al-hajj 22:11).

For this reason, the entrance of such a type of man in religion without knowledge and belief in it and his exist also therefrom, is without knowledge and belief. The 'Alim (the Imam) has observed:

"The faith of a man accepted knowingly remains steadfast, and is of profit for him. Whoever enters the house of faith without knowledge, makes his exit from that house in the same way in which he entered it." The Imam (peace be upon him) has said, "Whoever derives his faith from the knowledge of the Book of Allah and the precepts of the Prophet of God (peace be upon him and his progeny) is more difficult to be dislodged from his faith than the mountains are, from their places. And the faith of a person derived from the words of the mouth of the people is repudiated by the people themselves."

The Imam added, "He, who does not recognize our (Imams from the progeny of Prophet Muhammad—p.b.u.h.a.h.p.) case in the light of Qur'an, will not be able to turn the errors aside."

For this reason false and detestable faiths fulfilling all the conditions of infidelity and polytheism hold their sway over the people of our time. All this, (the recognition and non-recognition of our position) depends upon the favour and disfavour of God. Whomsoever God grants His favour of keeping his faith steady, He also creates such conditions for him as will lead to derive his faith from the Book of Allah and the precepts of Prophet (Muhammad) with knowledge, belief and insight. It is such people that are firmer in their faith than the high mountains in their places. Should God intend alienating Himself from a person, then, the faith He lends him is rendered superficial and temporary—may God protect us all from this situation. God provides such a person with ways and means on account of which he begins perceiving only the superficial beauty of every thing. He takes to following every thing blindly, and he starts interpreting (the scriptures) without knowledge and insight. The case of such a person entirely rests on the Will of God the Almighty whether to rectify his faith or to forfeit it from him altogether. Such a person cannot remain in peace when he is a believer in the morning and infidel in the evening or vice versa. All this is because he falls in for everything that appears great to him and accepts everything with a glittering appearance. The 'Alim (the Imam)—peace be upon him—has observed: "God, the Almighty has so created His prophets as to infuse prophethood into their blood and so they cannot remain except as prophets (peace be upon them all). He has also created their vicegerents in the same mode; so they cannot remain except as the vicegerents (of the prophets). He lent faith temporarily to another group of people, so that should He so like, He may perfect it into them or forfeit it from them altogether. These words of Allah hold true in the case of such people: "And then a lodging-place, and then a repository" (al-An'am, 6:98).

You (the interrogator) have spoken of matters that are difficult for you. Your main difficulty is that you do not know the truth because of the conflicting versions of traditions coming from different narrators. And you know that conflicting versions of traditions have their own causes and effects. Further, your problem is that you do not find whether any expert knowledge (of the authenticity of narrators) can be relied upon and whom you can approach, talk to and have your problem solved. And for all this you earnestly want to have a book with you, inclusive of all branches of the science of religion, which could wholly satisfy all the students of religion and which seekers of guidance could turn to, and from which they could derive the specific knowledge of religion they intend to, and they could act thereon with genuine traditions from the truthful Imams (the divinely appointed guides), which (Book) ensures the practice on the codified divine law. And finally by means of which (Book) the divine obligations and the precepts of the prophet could be implemented. And you have said, "In case such a book is compiled then I can hope by God that with His grace and help it will lead our brethren in faith their and our (Muslim) community to their truthful guides—the Imams."

O' brother! may God guide you. It is up to no person to discriminate between different versions of the traditions of the Imams according to his own light and except on the basis of the verdicts (criterion) laid down by the Imam himself. The verdict of the Imam is:

Document Text

"Check it up with the text of the Book of God (Qur'an), accept it if it agrees with the text and reject it if it does not."

The verdict further lays down, "Let alone the agreeing with what is on the lips of general people since the truth is just the opposite." The third verdict lays down: "Accept what is held in common by all the narrators quoting us. Since there can be no doubt about what is unanimously held by all." (The narrators of our traditions—a hadith.) But, to our knowledge, very few such contradicting traditions can be solved on the basis of the above described criterion. In the case of such (contradicting) traditions the best, the simpler and the more comprehensive solution is to leave all knowledge (regarding contradicting traditions) to the Imam himself. Imam has given us the easiest solution to choose and follow any of the versions among such contradicting traditions. The Imam has said, "Whatever you have accepted and followed with the intention of obeying (the Imam) is valid for you."

Thus has Allah made (the task of selecting and collecting the traditions) easy. All praise is due to Allah, that He has enabled me to compile the book you have requested for. I hope this book will be after your liking. There may be some deficiency (in this work of mine) but there is none in the sincerity of intention to counsel my people, which is essential (especially) in the case of our brethren and coreligionists. Simultaneously we ourselves earnestly desire to be among the participants deriving benefits (from this book) and among those who act upon it in this age and in the ages hereafter coming, till the Day of Judgment. God the Almighty is one, His Prophet Muhammad (peace be upon him and his progeny) the last of the prophets, is one and the divine code is also one. What Muhammad, the Prophet (p.b.u.h.a.h.p.) declared to be unlawful is unlawful till the Day of Judgment. The chapter on divine proofs has slightly been expanded although the expansion is not in the measure the chapter deserves, since it was distasteful for us to reducing any portion thereof.

We hope that Allah, the great and the Almighty, will make it easy for us and will grant us further span of life for the fulfillment of our objective of making this chapter widest and fullest, in the manner it deserves, provided Allah wills since all power and might is His. With Him are all our longings for increased help and favour. May Allah's peace and blessings be upon our chief, Muhammad the Prophet and upon his progeny—the purified, the excellent.

I have commenced and inaugurated this book of mine with the chapter on reason, the greatness of knowledge, the great status of those who possess it, their high worth, the defectiveness of ignorance, the baseness of its possessor, and their lowered rank. Since reason is the axis on which every thing revolves, it is on the reason that all the argument rests. All divine rewards and punishments are in accordance with it. (It is Allah that grants the favour of reason.)

Glossary

al-A'raf, al-An'am, al-hajj, ah-Nahl, at-Tawbah, az-Zukhruf, Yunus	the names of suras, or books, of the Qur'an
'Ali ibn Abi talib	Muhammad's cousin and son-in-law; the fourth caliph, or leader, of Islam according to Sunni Muslims but the first legitimate successor to Muhammad according to Shia Islam
Muhammad	the founder of Islam
Prophet	that is, Muhammad
Qur'an	the Islamic sacred scripture
p.b.u.h.a.h.p.	"peace be upon him and his progeny"

Izanami and Izanagi creating the Japanese islands
(Kobayashi Eitaku, Izanami and Izanagi Creating the Japanese Islands, William Sturgis Bigelow Collection, 11.7972, © 2010 Museum of Fine Arts, Boston. All rights reserved.)

Yengishiki

"Let the sovereign gods tranquilly take with clear hearts, as peaceful offerings and sufficient offerings the great offerings which I set up."

Overview

Yengishiki (often spelled *Engishiki* or *Engishiki*), a document whose title is generally translated as some variation of "The Ordinances of Engi" or "The Procedures of the Engi Era," is in part a Shinto text compiled during the reign of the Japanese emperor Daigo, who ruled from 897 to 930. One of the emperor's ministers, Fujiwara no Tokihira, began compiling the text in 905. After the minister's death in 909, the text was completed by his brother, Fujiwara no Tadahira, in 927. The ordinances were not implemented until 967.

The Yengishiki includes some fifty volumes of ordinances specifying how earlier Japanese legal codes, specifically the Konin-shiki of 820 and the Jogan-shiki of 871, were to be applied. Many of these codes dealt, for example, with succession to the throne as well as matters of criminal law (*ritsu*) and civil law (*ryo*). But about ten of the volumes deal with Shinto rituals, prayers (*norito*), and ceremonies connected with ascension to the throne. The excerpts reproduced here include several of the Shinto rituals mandated by the Yengishiki: "The Harvest Ritual," "The Ritual for the Wind-Gods," "The Fire Ritual," "The Ritual for Evil Spirits," "The Road-Gods' Ritual," "Rituals to the Sun-Goddess," and "The Purification Ritual."

Context

Shinto, sometimes called Shintoism, is a religion that resists description and categorization. The word *Shinto* derives from two Chinese characters: *shin*, which means "god," and *to*, which means "the way," much as "the Way" is used in Daoism, a philosophy of life developed in sixth-century China. Accordingly, *Shinto* can be translated as "the way of the gods." In many respects, Shinto is less a formal religion than an embodiment of Japanese history and culture, with an overlay of many elements of folk belief. The religion has no particular founder, no dogmas, no formalized theology, no seat of authority, no saints or holy figures, no places that are considered holy, and few formal prayers. It also has no sacred scripture, although a document called the *Kojiki* ("Records of Ancient Matters"), written in the eighth century, comes close to being scriptural and forms the basis for some of the mythology that appears in the Shinto prayers and rituals of the Yengishiki. Shinto is best described as a life philosophy, a set of rituals and practices that allow people to forge and maintain a relationship with the gods of Shinto, the *kami*. Even the *kami* are hard to describe. The word is often translated as "gods" or "divinities," but a better translation would be "spirits of nature," "life forces," or "the sacredness in things." The spirits of departed ancestors can also be considered *kami*.

The origins of Japanese civilization, and therefore of Shinto, are shrouded in history and legend. Archaeological evidence suggests that sometime around 35,000 to 30,000 BCE, humans first migrated to the Japanese islands, probably from Mongolia or Siberia through Korea or alternatively from Polynesia westward across the Pacific Ocean. A more stable civilization evolved sometime around 10,000 BCE, the start of the Jomon Period. This period extended to about 400 BCE, and it is believed that Shinto beliefs had emerged in Japan by late in the Jomon Period. During this time in Japan's history, the concept of the *kami* originated. Japanese society was organized around separate clans that were not connected by a central government or sense of a national identity. A chieftain headed each of the various clans, and every clan worshipped a divinity, a *kami*. The chieftain's job, in part, was to oversee the ceremonies devoted to the *kami*.

The clans were often in conflict with one another. When one clan defeated another, the *kami* of the defeated clan became subject to that (or those) of the victorious clan. In this way, the hierarchy of the *kami* constantly shifted. Later, when a more centralized Japanese government with a supreme emperor at its head evolved, the belief in *kami* was used to give legitimacy to the emperor's authority. Because the emperor claimed direct descent from the sun goddess Amaterasu, the emperor's clan was more powerful than any other clan and thus held the right to rule Japan.

Two historical events had major importance for the development of Shinto. The first was the introduction of writing in the fifth century; the second was the arrival of Buddhism in the sixth. By the seventh century, Japan had become dominated by its much-larger neighbor, China, so

Time Line

673	■ Emperor Tenmu seizes the throne of Japan and orders that a history of Japan be compiled.
712	■ The *Kojiki* ("Record of Ancient Matters"), the oldest surviving Japanese text, is written down.
794	■ The Heian Period of Japanese history begins.
897	■ Emperor Daigo assumes the throne of Japan.
901	■ The Engi era of Emperor Daigo's reign begins, lasting until 923.
905	■ Emperor Daigo orders Fujiwara no Tokihira to begin compiling the Yengishiki.
909	■ Fujiwara no Tokihira dies.
912	■ Fujiwara no Tokihira's brother, Fujiwara no Tadahira, resumes the task of compiling the Yengishiki.
927	■ The Yengishiki is completed.
967	■ The ordinances contained in the Yengishiki are implemented.

many elements of Japanese culture came to reflect Chinese influences, including Buddhist beliefs. The more advanced Chinese had thoroughly documented their history, and under their influence Japanese writers began to do the same, though none of their earliest works survive. Their goal was in part to incorporate themes from Chinese religion and culture into their texts as a way of impressing the Chinese and to establish the divine right of Japanese emperors to rule.

In 673 CE, Emperor Tenmu seized power in Japan, but his hold over the throne was tenuous, owing to continued opposition from rival ethnic groups and clans, including the aboriginal people of Japan, the Ainu. To legitimize his rule by showing that he descended from the gods, Tenmu ordered that a history of Japan be compiled. This history was transmitted orally until 712, when it was written down as the *Kojiki*, a text that cemented the court's legitimacy. The *Kojiki* is the earliest surviving text written by the Japanese.

Shinto, however, was widely regarded as a folk religion, filled with superstitions and myths. "Real" religion, for many Japanese, was Chinese Buddhism. In the centuries that followed, Shinto and Buddhism coexisted and amalgamated in a process referred to as *Shinbutsu shugo,* a phrase formed from the Japanese characters for "Shinto," "Buddhism," "learn," and "join together." This state of affairs would last until the end of the Edo Period (1600–1867).

The Yengishiki was compiled during the reign of Emperor Daigo in the Heian Period, which began in 794 after the capital of Japan was moved to Heian-kyo (present-day Kyoto). His reign was divided into "eras," a common practice in the Japanese calendar, with each era defined by some important event or set of events. The first of the eras, called the Kanpyo era, extended from 889 to 898; the second, the Shotai era, extended from 898 to 901. The third was named the Engi era and lasted from 901 to 923; although it is unclear what event or events marked the beginning of the Engi era, because records were destroyed, it is possible that an eclipse of the sun played a role. Accordingly, the Yengishiki is called "The Ordinances of Engi." (The fourth and final era of Daigo's reign was called the Encho era.)

The Heian Period is regarded as a high point in Japanese culture, a period of artistic and cultural flowering at the imperial court, particularly among the aristocracy. Power nominally lay with the emperor but, in fact, was wielded by a clan whose family name was Fujiwara. Although the period was marked by stability, imperial control over the provinces was shaky, and many of the great clans ignored the efforts of the imperial court to impose Chinese-style systems of law and taxation. During this period, the Fujiwara clan intermarried with the imperial family, and some of its members were appointed to high office. Daigo's predecessors had tried to check the power of the Fujiwara clan, but with limited success. Daigo was the first Heian emperor who was able to do so, at least in part. Nevertheless, the clan continued to acquire estates and wealth, as did other prominent families. They were able to obtain title to lands in perpetuity, evade taxes, and avoid government inspection of their lands. Accordingly, central control in Japan was weakening, and in the decades after Daigo's death, the Fujiwara clan was able to assert near absolute control over the imperial court. In effect, by the year 1000, the Fujiwara had become perpetual dictators. Meanwhile, the government was becoming increasingly decentralized, and Japan lacked any sense of being a single nation under the direct control of the imperial family.

It was in this context, then, that Emperor Daigo ordered the compilation of the Yengishiki as part of an ongoing effort to legitimize the rule of the emperor and impose some unity on Japan. Again, some 80 percent of "The Ordinances of Engi" deal with administrative matters and law, updating earlier legal and administrative texts. The remaining 20 percent, however, focus on Shinto rituals and practices and include twenty-seven *norito,* or prayers. As far as is known, this was the first time these prayers were reduced to writing, but they were undoubtedly used for hundreds of years before the Yengishiki was compiled.

About the Author

In one sense, no one "authored" the Yengishiki, which was a compilation and updating of content that had already been written. The text was compiled under the orders of Emperor Daigo beginning in 905. To carry out the task, he appointed members of the powerful Fujiwara clan. The compilation was begun by Fujiwara no Tokihira, who was born in Kyoto in 871. His father, Fujiwara Mototsune, had created and occupied the post of *kampaku*, or chancellor, allowing him to issue edicts in the name of the emperor and thus increase the influence of the family. On his death, Tokihira became head of the family at the age of twenty-one. In the court of Emperor Daigo, he held a post as minister, but he did not find great favor at the court, as the emperor tried to check the power and influence of the Fujiwara clan. When he died in 909, the project of compiling the Yengishiki was taken over by his brother, Fujiwara no Tadahira, who was born in 880. Throughout the remainder of Emperor Daigo's reign, Tadahira enjoyed even less power and influence than his older brother had, although he was appointed to a ministry post in 924. When Emperor Daigo abdicated the throne in favor of three-year-old Emperor Suzaku, Tadahira was appointed regent. Then in 936 he was named prime minister and, later, chancellor. He died in 949.

Explanation and Analysis of the Document

The excerpts reproduced here include several examples of the rituals prescribed by the Yengishiki. These rituals reflect Shinto culture and beliefs, and many of them draw on the mythology of Shinto as reflected in the earlier *Kojiki*. In most cases the rituals take the form of prayers, but in some instances the text describes ritual practices as well.

♦ The Harvest Ritual

It comes as no surprise that a religious ritual in an early culture had to do with the harvest, a time when people thanked the gods for their bounty. The Harvest Ritual was celebrated on the fourth day of the second month of each year at the Office for the Worship of the Shinto gods. Additionally, it was practiced in the provinces by the chiefs of the local administration. It is unknown who specifically the harvest gods were, though several are specified in the *Kojiki*. In ritual sacrifices, it was common to offer the "first fruits" of the harvest to the gods. Thus, this prayer says that "I will fulfil their praises by presenting the first-fruits in a thousand ears, and in many hundred ears"—"ear" here meaning the grain-bearing tip of the stem of a cereal plant, typically corn or wheat, but in Japan, the rice plant. The reference to "dripping of foam" and "drawing the mud" refers to the process of preparing the soupy soil of rice fields for young plants. The prayer goes on to say that the person will offer clothing, beer, and the fruits of the plain; "bitter herbs" might have included chamomile, peppermint, dandelion, milk thistle, and yarrow, herbs often used in rituals and for medicinal purposes. Further, the reader of the prayer offers a horse for the god to ride

A Shinto temple
(A view of the Temple of Two Lions, Tokyo, Japan, 1923 [autochrome], Courtellemont, Gervais [1863-1931] / National Geographic Image Collection / The Bridgeman Art Library International)

on, a cock to tell the time, and a domesticated boar for the god's food. The "grandchild" is the grandchild of Amaterasu, the sun goddess; in time, this word was used to refer to any successor to the throne of Japan.

♦ The Ritual for the Wind-Gods

"The Ritual for the Wind-Gods" is a prayer that addresses crop failure, specifically failure brought about by high winds. "At Tatsuta" is likely a reference to a shrine devoted to Tatsuta-hime, the Shinto goddess of autumn and the harvest. The ritual transmits a legend that purports to account for its origin and for the establishment of the shrine. Centuries earlier, a series of violent storms had devastated the crops. Diviners and others had tried to learn the cause of this disaster, but their efforts were in vain until the Wind-Gods revealed themselves to the emperor in a dream. They made a bargain with him: In the future, they would bless and ripen the crops if he built for them a shrine and made offerings to them.

♦ The Fire Ritual

"The Fire Ritual" draws heavily on the Shinto creation myth contained in the *Kojiki*. The myth runs as follows:

Essential Quotes

"I declare in the presence of the sovereign gods of the Harvest, if the sovereign gods will bestow . . . the late-ripening harvest which they will bestow . . . then I will fulfil their praises by presenting the first fruits in a thousand ears, and in many hundred ears."

"When the two pillars, the divine Izanagi and Izanami's augustness, younger sister and elder brother, had intercourse, and she had deigned to bear the many tens of countries of the countries, and the many tens of islands of the islands, and had deigned to bear the many hundred myriads of gods, she also deigned to bear her dear youngest child of all, the Fire-producer god."

"Let the sovereign gods tranquilly take with clear hearts, as peaceful offerings and sufficient offerings the great offerings which I set up, piling them upon the tables like a range of hills providing bright cloth, glittering cloth, soft cloth, and coarse cloth."

"I declare in the presence of the From-Heaven-shining great-deity . . . he will pile up the first fruits like a range of hills in the great presence of the Sovereign great goddess, and will peacefully enjoy the remainder."

"The Maiden-of-Descent-into-the-Current, who dwells in the current of the swift stream which boils down the ravines from the tops of high mountains, and the tops of the low hills, shall carry out to the great sea plain the offenses which are cleared away and purified."

Before creation, chaos existed as a formless oiliness. The first gods and goddesses emerged from this chaos onto the Plain of High Heaven. They were born as eight pairs of men and women who were both mates and siblings. The eighth of these pairs—Izanagi and Izanami—would be the first to have children. Standing on the Floating Bridge of Heaven, they dipped a jeweled spear into the chaos, and when they pulled the spear out, drops fell from it, forming the Japanese island of Onogoro. Izanagi and Izanami descended to Onogoro, where they built a palace and a ceremonial pillar and devised a wedding ritual around the pillar. After they completed the wedding ritual, they produced "children"—a reference to the other islands of Japan and the spirits that ruled them, the *kami*.

During the wedding ceremony, Izanami, the woman, spoke first, causing the other deities to believe that her union with Izanagi was corrupted, so they ordered that the ceremony be repeated, with Izanagi speaking first. After this second marriage, the couple produced additional gods, including Kagutsuchi, the fire-god. In giving birth to the fire-god, Izanami was severely burned and died. She was sent to Yomi, the underworld or the Nether Regions, where Izanagi located her in a castle she had built for herself. He could not see her, but he could talk to her, and he persuaded her to return with him to the world they had created. Izanami pleaded with Izanagi not to look at her until they returned home, but Izanagi so longed to see her that he succumbed to the temptation to look at her—only to discover that she was a rotting corpse because she had eaten the food of the underworld. She was humiliated, so she dispatched a legion of demons to chase Izanagi.

Izanagi, pursued by the demons and by Izanami herself, fled. When they finally confronted each other at the entrance to the underworld, they agreed to divorce; Izanagi would rule the realm of the living, and Izanami would rule that of the dead. Izanagi returned to earth, where he bathed in a stream and purified himself. Out of his eyes and nose, three major deities emerged: Amaterasu, the sun goddess and ruler of heaven; Tsukiyomi, the moon-god and ruler of night; and Susano-o, the god of violence and ruler of the ocean. Afterward, Izanagi returned to heaven and remained there.

The purpose of many Shinto rituals is to appease or avoid evil spirits. The Fire Ritual fulfills a similar purpose, with offerings that are similar to those made in the Harvest Ritual.

♦ **The Ritual for Evil Spirits**

Shinto begins with the belief that people are naturally good but that evil spirits cause them to do bad things. Once again, the purpose of many Shinto rituals is to ward off evil spirits and to achieve a state of purification. The Ritual for Evil Spirits is consistent with this view. The ritual again references the creation of the world, as outlined in the discussion of "The Fire Ritual." It then notes that the gods wanted to subdue the evil spirits of the plain; consequently, they dispatched a succession of heroic gods for that purpose, including Amenohohi, one of the sons of the sun goddess Amaterasu; then Takemikuma; and then Ameno-waka-hiko. Finally, two gods—Futsunushi and Takemadzuchi—achieved success. Futsunushi was the *kami* of swords and lightning and one of Amaterasu's generals. He has also been characterized as the divine personification of the sacred sword called Futsu-no-Mitama and the ancestral deity of the Fujiwara clan. Futsunushi was accompanied by Takema-dzuchi, and together these two "pillars" descended from the heavens and subdued the evil spirits of the plain. They were able to "soften the gods who were turbulent" and to cause the "Sovereign Grandchild's augustness to descend from heaven"—again, a reference to any emperor. The ritual then concludes with a sacrificial offering. Again, reference is made to the creation of the world. Reference is also made to "Yamato," which is simply another term used for Japan at the time. Japan is perceived as a peaceful country, and implicit throughout the description of the country is the Shinto belief in Japan's superiority to all other lands on earth because it was divinely created. At the ritual's end, a series of offerings is made, including cloth, a mirror, beads, a bow and arrows, a sword, a horse, liquor, grain, herbs, fish, and others. The purpose of the ritual is conveyed in the final word, "tranquil." By exorcising evil spirits, the nation can find peace and tranquility.

♦ **The Road-Gods' Ritual**

In Shinto, *kami* can represent virtually anything, including all manner of natural phenomena—among them, mountains, forests, the seas, rivers—as well as human-made objects such as roads, bridges, and gates. In this ritual prayer, the priest appeals to the *kami* that protect the roads. This type of prayer might have been used, for example, when envoys ("servants of the monarch") were dispatched and had to travel over the roads. The prayer calls on the gods ("You and Maiden of the Many Road-forkings and Come-no-further Gate") to ward off evil spirits, here conceived as "roughly acting and hating." These two gods originated from the rock that Izanagi used to block the road when demons were pursuing him. The priest appeals to the road gods to take sacrificial offerings and pile them up as a way of protecting people on the roads.

♦ **Rituals to the Sun-Goddess**

Historically, the cult of the sun has been dominant in Japanese culture. The name for Japan, "Nippon," means "source of the sun," and the Japanese flag consists simply of a white field with a red disk representing the sun. Accordingly, the central deity in Shinto is Amaterasu, called here the "From-Heaven-shining-great deity." According to Shinto mythology, she was the ruler of the Plain of Heaven and the eldest daughter of Izanagi (although the legends are not always consistent about genealogy). She was so radiant that her parents sent her up a celestial ladder to heaven, where she rules. The mythology also says that her brother, the storm god, ravaged the earth. She retreated to a cave to escape the noise, closing it with a large boulder and thus depriving the world of light. In her absence, evil spirits ruled the earth. The other gods tried to persuade her to come out, but to no avail—that is, until Uzume, the Shinto goddess of joy and happiness, succeeded. The dawn is conceived as a streak of light that escaped when she emerged from the cave. Later, she created rice fields and taught the art of weaving. The Japanese imperial family claimed descent from her.

"Oho-Nakitomi" refers to one of the hereditary families that in ancient times oversaw Shinto ceremonies at court. Again, "Mikado" is a generic term for the emperor. The ritual is a sacrificial one in which offerings are made to the sun goddess, who in turn will provide blessings to the entire extent of the country. "Ise" is the name of a city in Japan that is the site of the Ise Great Shrine to Amaterasu.

♦ **The Purification Ritual**

The concept of purification is central to Shinto. Shinto is essentially an optimistic religion. It requires no savior or messiah, nor does it require redemption. It does, however, ask people to lead simple, pure lives in accordance with nature—which perhaps explains why modern housing codes in Japan call for the presence of a garden and a window out of which the garden can be seen. Purification rituals are a way to achieve this purity and simplicity by casting out evil.

"The Purification Ritual" lists heavenly offenses and earthly offenses. The heavenly offenses have to do primarily with agriculture and interference with community functions. Among them are breaking down ridges, covering up ditches, releasing irrigation sluices, and flaying animals that are alive. Earthly offenses include such things as leprosy, blights, and disasters caused by thunderstorms; these are termed "earthly" offenses because they could result from a curse and wreak havoc on the entire community. The ritual, then, consists of sweeping away these offenses with a broom made of grass.

Audience

The audience for the Yengishiki was many layered. Its primary audience consisted of court officials, administrators, civil functionaries, and other members of Japan's governmental apparatus, from the imperial court down to local communities. To the extent that the Yengishiki deals with matters involving succession to the throne, it functioned as a kind of constitution. Additionally, a target audience for those portions of the Yengishiki having to do with Shinto rituals and prayers included any persons who conducted or led rituals and prayers, especially priests. By standardizing prayers and rituals, the Yengishiki imposed a kind of unity on Japanese culture at a time in the nation's history when it tended toward fragmentation.

Impact

The Yengishiki was completed and presented to the emperor in 927. However, its immediate impact was nil, for revisions continued to be made in the decades that followed, and the provisions of the text were not implemented until 967. At the time, there was no hurry, for many of the provisions of the Yengishiki were already contained in earlier books, notably the Konin-shiki of 820 and the Jogan-shiki of 871. Further, in the decades that followed, Japan continued to experience a degree of political turmoil. Suzaku became the titular emperor in 930, with Fujiwara Tadahira serving as regent (one who rules for a monarch who is a minor) until 949, after Murakami became the hereditary emperor in 946. In the meantime, the power of landed and wealthy clans in the provinces continued to grow. The central government continued to lose power and influence outside the capital, giving rise to rebellions. One example was the rebellion led by Taira Masakado, who created a kingdom in the Kanto area and proclaimed himself emperor. Thus, the release of the Yengishiki did not occur until 967, with the ascension of Emperor Reizai to the throne.

One concrete impact of the Yengishiki has to do with its list of official Shinto shrines—2,861 of them. The Yengishiki also enshrines 3,132 "heavenly and earthly deities," allocating them to provinces and districts. Throughout the country, people took pride in the fact that their shrine was a *shikinaisha,* or "shrine listed in the *shiki.*" In the centuries that followed, a class of national scholars called *kokugaku* devoted considerable study to the portions of the Yengishiki having to do with the *norito* (prayers) as well as to the list of deities. They wrote commentaries, including *Norito ko* ("On Norito") by Kamo no Mabuchi, *Engishiki norito kogi* ("Lectures on Engishiki Norito") by Suzuki Shigetane, and *Jinmyocho kosho* ("Studies of Jinmyocho") by Ban Nobutomo. At the same time, aristocrats venerated the Yengishiki and transmitted it to their descendants, for they regarded it as a primary source for annual rites and court protocols.

Questions for Further Study

1. Compare the impact of Chinese Buddhism on Japanese society with its impact on Tibetan society as reflected in the entries gZi-brjid and *Tibetan Book of the Dead*. What does this comparison tell you about the influence of Buddhism in Asia during the Middle Ages?

2. To what extent did the clan structure of Japanese society and the accompanying instability of the central government contribute to the creation of the Yengeshiki?

3. A central feature of many religions has been the offering of sacrifices to the gods. What were the purposes for which medieval Japanese offered such sacrifices? How did the nature of these sacrifices reflect something unique about Japanese culture and history?

4. The entry notes that Shinto has become a kind of folk religion and the number of people who identify themselves as Shinto has declined. Why do you think Japanese people continue to practice Shinto rituals? Do you think that non-Japanese people living in the United States practice rituals that are in any way analogous to Shinto rituals?

5. Compare and contrast the role of the sun goddess, Amaterasu, in Shinto with the sun god Re in ancient Egypt, as explicated in "Great Hymn to the Aten."

Together with the *Kojiki,* the Yengishiki continues to define Shinto. In the nineteenth century, Shinto became a way of marshalling the support of the people and fostering a sense of intense patriotism in the face of Western expansionism. Into the twentieth century, Shinto and emperor worship—of the kind fostered in the early texts—justified the aggressive expansion of the Japanese empire throughout the Pacific in the 1930s and after the outbreak of World War II. This period of "State Shinto" ended abruptly in 1945 with the Japanese surrender at the end of World War II, and the Japanese emperor then abandoned his claim that he ruled by divine authority or that he was a living god. Because Shinto had been used to justify the excesses of Japanese nationalism and the desire for territory before and during the war, many Japanese people became disillusioned with Shinto, and the number of people who identified themselves as followers of Shinto fell sharply. Still, many Japanese continued to practice Shinto rituals. After World War II, Shinto reverted to a kind of folk religion. People visit Shinto shrines, for example, to improve their lot in life by remaining on good terms with their ancestors and the *kami.* New religions have emerged in Japan, many of them incorporating Shinto beliefs. Shinto has become not a state-sponsored religion but a set of cultural values that in large part define Japanese culture, a culture that, in turn, was defined in part by the Yengishiki.

Further Reading

■ Books

Evans, Ann Llewellyn. *Shinto Norito: A Book of Prayers.* Victoria, B.C., Canada: Trafford Publishing, 2002.

Hurst, G. Cameron, III. "The Heian Period." In *A Companion to Japanese History,* ed. William M. Tsutsui. Oxford, U.K.: Blackwell Publishing, 2007.

Kitagawa, Joseph. *Religion in Japanese History.* New York: Columbia University Press, 1966.

Morris, Ivan. *The World of the Shining Prince: Court Life in Ancient Japan.* London: Oxford University Press, 1964.

Picken, Stuart D. G. *Sourcebook in Shinto: Selected Documents.* Westport, Conn.: Praeger, 2004.

Picken, Stuart D. G. *The A to Z of Shinto.* Lanham, Md.: Scarecrow Press, 2006.

■ Web Sites

"Encyclopedia of Shinto." National Learning Institute for the Dissemination of Research on Shinto and Japanese Culture Web site.
   http://eos.kokugakuin.ac.jp/modules/xwords

"Shinto in Japan." iSchool's "Shinto and Its Impact on the World" Web site.
   http://school.phippy.com/shinto/index.html

—Michael J. O'Neal

Yengishiki

The Harvest Ritual

I declare in the presence of the sovereign gods of the Harvest, If the sovereign gods will bestow, in many-bundled spikes and in luxuriant spikes, the late-ripening harvest which they will bestow, the late-ripening harvest which will be produced by the dripping of foam from the arms, and by drawing the mud together between the opposing thighs, then I will fulfil their praises by presenting the first-fruits in a thousand ears, and in many hundred ears; raising high the beer-jars, filling and ranging in rows the bellies of the beer-jars, I will present them in juice and in grain. As to things which grow in the great field plain—sweet herbs and bitter herbs; as to things which dwell in the blue sea plain things wide of fin, and things narrow of fin, down to the weeds of the offing, and weeds of the shore; and as to Clothes, with bright cloth, glittering cloth, soft cloth, and coarse cloth will I fulfil their praises. And having furnished a white horse, a white boar, and a white cock, and the various kinds of things in the presence of the sovereign gods of the Harvest, I fulfil their praises by presenting the great Offerings of the sovereign Grand-child's augustness.

The Ritual for the Wind-Gods

I declare in the presence of the sovereign gods, whose praises are fulfilled at Tatsuta.

Because they had not allowed, firstly the five sorts of grain which the Sovereign Grand-child's augustness, who ruled the great country of many islands at Shikishima, took with ruddy countenance as his long and lasting food, and the things produced by the people, down to the least leaf of the herbs, to ripen, and had spoilt them not for one year, or for two years, but for continuous years, he deigned to command: "As to the Heart of the god which shall come forth in the divinings of all the men who are learned in things, declare what god it is."

Whereupon the men learned in things divined with their divinings, but they declared that no Heart of a god appears.

When he had heard this, the Sovereign Grand-child's augustness deigned to conjure them, saying: "I sought to fulfil their praises as heavenly temples and country temples, without forgetting or omitting, and have so acted, but let the god, whatever god he be, that has prevented the things produced by the people of the region under Heaven from ripening, and has spoilt them, make known his Heart."

Hereupon they made the Sovereign Grand-child's augustness to know in a great dream, and made him to know their names, saying:

"Our names, who have prevented the things made by the people of the region under Heaven from ripening and have spoilt them, by visiting them with bad winds and rough waters, are Heaven's Pillars augustness and Country's Pillars augustness." And they made him to know, saying: "If for the Offerings which shall be set up in our presence there be furnished various sorts of Offerings, as to Clothes, bright cloth, glittering cloth, soft cloth, and coarse cloth, and the five kinds of things, a shield, a spear, and a horse furnished with a saddle; if our house be fixed at Wonu, in Tachinu, at Tatsuta, in a place where the morning sun is opposite, and the evening sun is hidden, and praises be fulfilled in our presence, we will bless and ripen the things produced by the people of the region under Heaven, firstly the five sorts of grain, down to the least leaf of the herbs."

Therefore hear, all ye wardens and vergers, by declaring in the presence of the sovereign gods that, having fixed the House-pillars in the place which the sovereign gods had taught by words and made known, in order to fulfil praises in the presence of the sovereign gods, the Sovereign Grandchild's augustness has caused his great Offerings to be lifted up and brought, and has fulfilled their praises, sending the princes and counselors as his messengers.

The Fire Ritual

I declare with the great ritual, the Heavenly ritual, which was bestowed on him at the time when, by the Word of the Sovereign's dear progenitor and progenitrix, who divinely remain in the plain of high Heaven, they bestowed on him the region under Heaven, saying: "Let the Sovereign Grandchild's augustness tranquilly rule over the country of fresh spikes which flourishes in the midst of the reed-moor, as a peaceful region."

When the two pillars, the divine Izanagi and Izanami's augustnesses, younger sister and elder brother, had intercourse, and she had deigned to bear the many tens of countries of the countries, and the many tens of islands of the islands, and had deigned to bear the many hundred myriads of gods, she also deigned to bear her dear youngest child of all, the Fire-producer god, and her hidden parts being burnt, she bid in the rocks, and said: "My dear elder brother's augustness, deign not to look upon me for seven nights of nights and seven days of sunshine"; but when, before the seven days were fulfilled, he looked, thinking her remaining hidden to be strange, she deigned to say: "My hidden parts were burnt when I bore fire." At such a time I said, "My dear elder brother's augustness, deign not to look upon me, but you violently looked upon me"; and after saying, "My dear elder brother's augustness shall rule the upper country; I will rule the lower country," she deigned to hide in the rocks, and having come to the flat hill of darkness, she thought and said: "I have come hither, having born and left a bad-hearted child in the upper country, ruled over by my illustrious elder brother's augustness," and going back she bore other children. Having born the Water-goddess, the gourd, the river-weed, and the clay-hill maiden, four sorts of things, she taught them with words, and made them to know, saying: "If the heart of this bad-hearted child becomes violent, let the Water-goddess take the gourd, and the clay-hill maiden take the river-weed, and pacify him."

In consequence of this I fulfil his praises, and say that for the things set up, so that he may deign not to be awfully quick of heart in their great place of the Sovereign Grandchild's augustness, there are provided bright cloth, glittering cloth, soft cloth, and coarse cloth, and the five kinds of things; as to things which dwell in the blue sea plain, there are things wide of fin and things narrow of fin, down to the weeds of the offing and weeds of the shore; as to liquor, raising high the beer-jars, filling and ranging in rows the bellies of the beer-jars, piling the offerings up, even to rice in grain and rice in ear, like a range of hills, I fulfil his praises with the great ritual, the heavenly ritual.

The Ritual for Evil Spirits

I (the diviner), declare: When by the word of the progenitor and progenitrix, who divinely remaining in the plain of high Heaven, deigned to make the beginning of things, they divinely deigned to assemble the many hundred myriads of gods in the high city of Heaven, and deigned divinely to take counsel in council, saying: "When we cause our Sovereign Grandchild's augustness, to leave Heaven's eternal seat, to cleave a path with might through Heaven's manifold clouds, and to descend from Heaven, with orders tranquilly to rule the country of fresh spikes, which flourishes in the midst of the reed-moor as a peaceful country, what god shall we send first to divinely sweep away, sweep away and subdue the gods who are turbulent in the country of fresh spikes"; all the gods pondered and declared: "You shall send Amenohohi's augustness, and subdue them," declared they. Wherefore they sent him down from Heaven, but he did not declare an answer; and having next sent Takemikuma's augustness, he also, obeying his father's words, did not declare an answer. Ameno-waka-hiko also, whom they sent, did not declare an answer, but immediately perished by the calamity of a bird on high. Wherefore they pondered afresh by the word of the Heavenly gods, and having deigned to send down from Heaven the two pillars of gods, Futsunushi and Takemika-dzuchi's augustness, who having deigned divinely to sweep away, and sweep away, and deigned divinely to soften, and soften the gods who were turbulent, and silenced the rocks, trees, and the least leaf of herbs likewise that had spoken, they caused the Sovereign Grandchild's augustness to descend from Heaven.

I fulfil your praises, saying: As to the Offerings set up, so that the sovereign gods who come into the heavenly house of the Sovereign Grandchild's augustness, which, after he had fixed upon as a peaceful country—the country of great Yamato where the sun is high, as the center of the countries of the four quarters bestowed upon him when he was thus sent down from Heaven—stoutly planting the house-pillars on the bottom-most rocks, and exalting the cross-beams to the plain of high Heaven, the builders had made for his shade from the Heavens and shade from the sun, and wherein he will tranquilly rule the country as a peaceful country may, without deigning to be turbulent, deigning to be fierce, and deigning to hurt, knowing, by virtue of their divinity, the things which were begun in the plain of high Heaven, deigning to correct with Divine-correcting and Great-correcting, remove hence out to the clean places of the mountain streams which look far away over the four quarters, and rule them as their own place. Let the sovereign gods tranquilly take with clear hearts, as peaceful offerings and sufficient offerings the great offerings which I set up, piling them upon the tables like a range of hills, providing bright cloth, glittering cloth, soft cloth, and coarse cloth, as a thing to see plain in—a mirror: as things to play with—beads: as things to shoot off with—a bow and arrows: as things to strike and cut with—a sword: as a thing which gallops out—a horse; as to liquor—raising high the beer-jars, filling and ranging in rows the bellies of the beer-jars, with grains of rice and ears; as to the things which dwell in the hills things soft of hair, and things rough of hair; as to the things which grow in the great field plain—sweet herbs and bitter herbs; as to the things which dwell in the blue sea plain things broad of fin and things narrow of fin, down to weeds of the offing and weeds of the short, and without deigning to be turbulent, deigning to be fierce, and deigning to hurt, remove out to the wide and clean places of the mountain streams, and by virtue of their divinity be tranquil.

The Road-Gods' Ritual

HE (the priest) says: "I declare in the presence of the sovereign gods, who like innumerable piles of rocks, sit closing up the way in the multitudinous road-forkings . . . fulfil your praises by declaring your names, Youth and Maiden of the Many Road-forkings and Come-no-further Gate, and say: for the offerings set up so that you may prevent the servants of the monarch from being poisoned by and agreeing with the things which shall come roughly acting and hating from the Root-country, the Bottom-country, that you may guard the bottom of the gate when they come from the bottom, guard the top when they come from the top, guarding with nightly guard and with daily guard, and, may praise them peacefully take the great offerings which are set up by piling them up like a range of hills—that is to say, providing bright cloth, etc., and sitting closing-up the way like innumerable piles of rock in the multitudinous road-forkings, deign to praise the Sovereign Grandchild's augustness eternally and unchangingly, and to bless his age as a luxuriant age."

Rituals to the Sun-Goddess

HE (the priest envoy) says: "Hear all of you, ministers of the gods and sanctifiers of offerings, the great ritual, the Heavenly ritual, declared in the great presence of the From-Heaven-shining-great deity, whose praises are fulfilled by setting up the stout pillars of the great house, and exalting the cross-beam to the plain of high Heaven at the sources of the Isuzu river at Udji in Watarahi."

He says: "It is the Sovereign's great Word. Hear all of you, ministers of the gods and sanctifiers of offerings, the fulfilling of praises on this seventeenth day of the sixth moon of this year, as the morning sun goes up in glory, of the Oho-Nakatomi, who—having abundantly piled up like a range of hills the tribute thread and sanctified liquor and food presented as of usage by the people of the deity's houses attributed to her in the three departments and in various countries and places, so that she deign to bless his (the Mikado's) life as a long life and his age as a luxuriant age eternally and unchangingly as multitudinous piles of rock; may deign to bless the children who are born to him, and deigning to cause to flourish the five kinds of grain which the men of a hundred functions and the peasants of the countries in the four quarters of the region under Heaven long and peacefully cultivate and eat, and guarding and benefiting them deign to bless them—is hidden by the great offering-wands."

I declare in the great presence of the From-Heaven-shining-great deity who sits in Ise. Because the Sovereign great goddess bestows on him the countries of the four quarters over which her glance extends, as far as the limit where Heaven stands up like a wall, as far as the bounds where the country stands up distant, as far as the limit where the blue clouds spread flat, as far as the bounds where the white clouds lie away fallen—the blue sea plain as far as the limit whither come the prows of the ships without drying poles or paddles, the ships which continuously crowd on the great sea plain, and the roads which men travel by land, as far as the limit whither come the horses' hoofs, with the baggage-cords tied tightly, treading the uneven rocks and tree-roots and standing up continuously in a long path without a break—making the narrow countries wide and the hilly countries plain, and as it were drawing together the distant countries by throwing many tens of ropes over them—he will pile up the first-fruits like a range of hills in the great presence of the Sovereign great goddess, and will peacefully enjoy the remainder.

The Purification Ritual

Amongst the various sorts of offenses which may be committed in ignorance or out of negligence by Heaven's increasing people, who shall come into being in the country, which the Sovereign Grand-

Document Text

child's augustness, hiding in the fresh residence, built by stoutly planting the house-pillars on the bottom-most rocks, and exalting the cross-beams to the plain of high Heaven, as his shade from the Heavens and shade from the sun, shall tranquilly rule as a peaceful country, namely, the country of great Yamato, where the sun is seen on high, which be fixed upon as a peaceful country, as the center of the countries of the four quarters thus bestowed upon him—breaking the ridges, filling up watercourses, opening sluices, doubly sowing, planting stakes, flaying alive, flaying backward, and dunging; many of such offenses are distinguished as Heavenly offenses, and as earthly offenses; cutting living flesh, cutting dead flesh, leprosy, proud flesh, the offense committed with one's own mother, the offense committed with one's own child, the offense committed with mother and child, the offense committed with child and mother, the offense committed with beasts, calamities of crawling worms, calamities of a god on high, calamities of birds on high, the offenses of killing beasts and using incantations; many of such offenses may be disclosed.

When he has thus repeated it, the Heavenly gods will push open Heaven's eternal gates, and clearing a path with might through the manifold clouds of Heaven, will hear; and the country gods, ascending to the tops of the high mountains, and to the tops of the low hills, and tearing asunder the mists of the high mountains, and the mists of the low hills, will bear.

And when they have thus heard, the Maiden-of-Descent-into-the-Current, who dwells in the current of the swift stream which boils down the ravines from the tops of the high mountains, and the tops of the low hills, shall carry out to the great sea plain the offenses which are cleared away and purified, so that there be no remaining offense; like as Sbinato's wind blows apart the manifold clouds of Heaven, as the morning wind and the evening wind blow away the morning mist and the evening mist, as the great ships which lie on the shore of the great port loosen their prows,

Glossary

Amaterasu	the sun goddess and ruler of heaven
Amenohohi, Takemikuma, Ame-no-waka-hiko, Futsunushi, Takema-dzuchi	heroic gods sent to subdue evil spirits
dripping of foam . . . drawing the mud	reference to the process of preparing the soupy soil of rice fields for young plants
grandchild	grandchild of Amaterasu, the sun goddess; used to refer to any successor to the throne of Japan
Ise	the name of a city in Japan that is the site of the Ise Great Shrine to Amaterasu
Izanagi and Izanami	in the Shinto creation myth, one of the eight pairs of gods and goddesses to emerge from chaos onto the Plain of High Heaven and the first to have children
Mikado	a generic term for the emperor
Oho-Nakitomi	one of the hereditary families that in ancient times oversaw Shinto ceremonies at court
Shikishima	a town in Japan
Sovereign Grandchild's augustness	a reference to any Japanese emperor, as being descended from the sun goddess
Tatsuta	probably a reference to a shrine devoted to Tatsuta-hime, the Shinto goddess of autumn and the harvest
Yamato	another name for Japan at the time

and loosen their sterns to push out into the great sea plain; as the trunks of the forest trees, far and near, are cleared away by the sharp sickle, the sickle forged with fire; so that there cease to be any offense called an offense in the court of the Sovereign Grandchild's augustness to begin with, and in the countries of the four quarters of the region under Heaven.

And when she thus carries them out and away, the deity called the Maiden-of-the-Swift-cleansing, who dwells in the multitudinous meetings of the sea-waters, the multitudinous currents of rough sea-waters shall gulp them down.

And when she has thus gulped them down, the lord of the Breath-blowing-place, who dwells in the Breath-blowing-place, shall utterly blow them away with his breath to the Root-country, the Bottom-country.

And when he has thus blown them away, the deity called the Maiden-of-Swift-Banishment, who dwells in the Root-country, the Bottom-country, shall completely banish them, and get rid of them.

And when they have thus been got rid of, there shall from this day onward be no offense which is called offense, with regard to the men of the offices who serve in the court of the Sovereign, nor in the four quarters of the region under Heaven.

[Then the high priest says:]

Hear all of you how he leads forth the horse as a thing that erects its ears toward the plain of high Heaven, and deigns to sweep away and purify with the general purification, as the evening sun goes down on the last day of the watery moon of this year.

O diviners of the four countries, take the sacrifices away out of the river highway, and sweep them away.

Vishnu and his avatars

(Vishnu and His Avatars, c.10th century [sandstone], Indian School, [10th century] / Museum of Fine Arts, Houston, Texas, USA / Agnes Cullen Arnold Endowment Fund / The Bridgeman Art Library International)

Vishnu Purana

ca. 1045

"Contemplative devotion is the union with Brahma, effected by that condition of mind which has attained perfection through those exercises which complete the control of self."

Overview

The Vishnu Purana is one of the earliest of the eighteen major Puranas ("ancient stories") revered by the Hindus. It is considered to be one of the most important Puranas and for this reason is referred to by the name Puranaratna, which means "Gem of Puranas." Like some of the other Puranas, the Vishnu Purana is presented in the form of a dialogue, in this instance with the sage Parashara (or Parasara) teaching his disciple Maitreya how Vishnu, as the Supreme Being, takes care of his devotees and how one should evolve spiritually for the attainment of liberation. Major topics discussed in the Puranas include creation myths, narratives of battles fought between the Asuras (sinful, materialistic, power-seeking deities) and Devas (benevolent supernatural beings), the avatars (appearances, manifestations, or incarnations) of Vishnu, and stories and genealogies surrounding legendary kings. The Vishnu Purana glorifies Vishnu as the supreme lord of the universe, in whom the whole universe abides. The text may have been composed to unify disparate philosophic worldviews and people of all castes and to elevate Vaishnavism—one of the divisions of Hinduism, which sees Vishnu as the central god—as the only sure means for spiritual success.

The authorship of the entire Vishnu Purana is attributed to the legendary Vyasa (literally, "Arranger"), who is believed to be the author of all the Puranas as well as the editor of the ancient Vedas, the earliest Hindu sacred texts. Included in the class of *smriti*—"that which has to be remembered"—by India's Vedic sages and handed down orally from very ancient times, this Purana incorporates very old stories that might have undergone several revisions before their final redaction sometime around 1045. It is unknown where this text was finally composed, a common problem with the ancient Hindu texts, which do not directly or indirectly allude to their original place and time of composition to suggest their ancientness and divine authorship. Scholars seem resigned to the belief that the absence of texts glorifying particular places and people or providing similar information makes it nearly impossible to determine the origin of the Puranas.

Context

Because Hinduism dates back thousands of years, when written records were not kept, it is difficult to date its founding and development. Among nineteenth-century scholars, the "classical theory" of the origins of Hinduism prevailed. According to this view, the roots of Hinduism lay in the Indus Valley civilization and date back to 4000 BCE. In about 1500 BCE the area was invaded by Aryans, or Indo-European tribes from Central Asia, and the Indus Valley civilization disappeared. The invading tribes brought with them a religion called Vedism, and, according to the theory, Hinduism developed out of a mingling of Vedism and the Indus Valley culture.

More-recent scholars have rejected the classical theory, arguing that there was no Aryan invasion and that Hinduism developed directly out of the beliefs of the Indus Valley culture. Astronomers even point to a specific date for the "founding" of Hinduism. One of Hinduism's sacred texts describes the positions of the stars when Krishna, a Hindu god, was born; the stars were in this position in 3102 BCE. Another significant date is the year 600 BCE, when the Rig Veda, one of Hinduism's most sacred texts, was officially codified.

In the early centuries of the Common Era, various Hindu sects emerged, each dedicated to a specific god or goddess. Today, most Hindus are followers of one of three major divisions within Hinduism. One is called Vaishnavism, which sees Vishnu, "the Preserver," as the central god; the followers of Shivaism see Shiva, "the Destroyer," as the central god; the Shaktis worship Devi, or the mother aspect of the divine. In rural areas, many Hindus worship a village god or goddess who influences such matters as fertility and disease.

Scholars recognize six major epochs in Hindu history. The pre-Vedic epoch gave way to the Vedic epoch in roughly 1700 BCE. It was during the Vedic period, which lasted until 500 BCE, that most of the Hindu scriptures, including the Vedas, were written down and most of the basic beliefs of Hinduism were formulated. The epoch of ascetic reformism, marked by the growth of Buddhism and Jainism, extended roughly from 500 BCE to 200 BCE. It was during the ensuing fourth epoch, that of classical Hinduism, when Hinduism's two great epic poems, the Mahabharata and the Ramayana, were composed. The Mahabharata contains the

Time Line

CA. 1700 –1200 BCE	■ During the early Vedic epoch, the Rig Veda is composed.
CA. 1000 –500 BCE	■ The later Vedic period sees the first appearance of the word *Purana*, meaning "old story" or "mythological narrative."
CA. 557 BCE	■ Mahavira, originally Vardhamana, attains a state of highest knowledge and begins to establish precepts of Jainism.
CA. 528 BCE	■ Siddhartha Gautama, the founder of Buddhism, achieves enlightenment and begins teaching his doctrine.
CA. 500 BCE	■ As the Vedic civilization ends, its religion evolves into early Hinduism.
CA. 300 BCE	■ The great Indian epic poem Mahabharata, traditionally attributed to Vyasa, who is also the author of Puranas, is composed in Sanskrit; it includes the Bhagavad Gita.
CA. 600 BCE	■ The revised accreted texts of most of the Puranas assume their final form as they exist today.
CA. 1045	■ According to one scholarly opinion, the Vishnu Purana undergoes its last revisions.

Bhagavad Gita, the first literature on the Bhakti devotional movement in Hinduism, centered on unmitigated loving devotion. Lasting until 1100 CE, the classical epoch saw a great outpouring of philosophical works and the development of numerous schools of thought, leading into the fifth epoch, which was marked by the growth of Hindu sects. The modern epoch began around 1850; since then Hinduism has seen increasing contact with Western cultures and ways of thinking, primarily because India was a British colony during much of this time.

It is very difficult to assign any definite date to the Vishnu Purana, and the tentative dates given by scholars are speculative and vary broadly. The mythological conception is that this Purana records descriptions of activities beginning in the Varaha Age—the mythical age when Vishnu incarnated as a boar (Varaha) in order to save the earth from demons. Such stories were first handed down through oral tradition, while various revisions or additional stories may have been introduced over time. Regarding the composition of the Vishnu Purana in the present form, dates ranging from 700 BCE to 1045 CE have been proposed by different scholars. Book III, chapter XVIII (the first excerpt here) gives some hint of the era of the text's composition, as it refers to the time when the historical Buddha was not yet regarded or appropriated in the Vaishnava tradition as an incarnation of Vishnu—an idea that finds expression in other Puranas, such as the Bhagavata Purana and Matsya Purana. By comparing different Puranas, some scholars argue that this story of Vishnu's delusive form was an interpolation in a very late period or, at the earliest, typifies the time when Brahmanical religion was gaining popularity before about 320 CE.

About the Author

Vyasa is often considered the original scribe of all the Puranas, including the one under discussion. The third chapter of book III of this Purana narrates that Vishnu, in the person of Vyasa (also called Veda Vyasa), divides the original single Veda into four Vedas—Rig, Yajus, Saman, and Atharvan—in every Dvapara Age (the third age in the eternal cycle of time, according to Hindu mythology). This legendary Vyasa is believed to have been born as a son of Parashara and a non-Aryan princess called Satyavati, and he is said to have had perfect knowledge of all time. It is difficult to talk about the real authorship of this text in its historical setting, for such texts survived and were transformed through a long oral tradition and even the name Vyasa is often regarded as a title given to many ancient compilers of a large body of Hindu sacred texts, including the Puranas. The Vishnu Purana itself mentions that it was transmitted orally for a long time, beginning with Brahma, the creator of the Hindu universe, through Parashara, before being compiled by Vyasa.

Explanation and Analysis of the Document

Chapter XVIII of book III raises various issues, such as the mythic battle between the opposing divine and demonic forces, the supremacy of Vishnu as the Ultimate God, the significance of Vedic religion, and the relationship between the orthodox and heterodox religions of the time. The text gives a picture of an ancient Indian society in which Vedic and non-Vedic religions are locked in an intense ideological rivalry. It also shows how religious narratives must have been potent tools for maintaining and consolidating social unity. Chapter VII of book VI, in contrast, concentrates on the theme of yoga ("contemplative devotion") and instructs devotees how to sever oneself from the bonds of material existence and be liberated from the cycle of rebirths. The text also teaches how one can progress along a spiritual path that leads to attainment of Vishnu, or final liberation in which the devotee reaches the abode of the Supreme God Vishnu.

◆ **Book III: Chapter XVIII**

In this chapter, Parashara narrates to Maitreya how the ultimate god Vishnu sent "the great delusion" in the form of an ascetic in order to induce the *daityas* ("demons," or "foes of gods") to denounce their Vedic religion by teaching them heretical doctrines. The narrator argues that the religion of the Vedas was the true religion that had originally protected the demons and provided them with their powers. However, they misused their divine power by seizing upon the three worlds and appropriating the offerings made to the gods. It was then that the almighty Vishnu, upon the gods' request, emitted an illusory form from his own body and sent him to defeat and destroy the demons.

Paragraphs 1 and 2: The opening paragraphs suggest the role of Vishnu in the conversion of the demons from the Vedic to unorthodox religions such Jainism and Buddhism. In this text, the illusory form sent by Vishnu is not regarded as his incarnation appearing on earth for the well-being of earthly creatures, although the mythical battle between the gods and the demons ultimately restores order. Nonetheless, the person sent by Vishnu is regarded as a form of Vishnu himself.

Parashara narrates how the "delusive being" sent by Vishnu approached the ascetics, the "lords of the Daitya race," who were practicing acts of penance by the side of the Narmada River. This "arch deceiver" falsely taught the demons various doctrines that would, as he claimed, either lead the demons to heaven or liberate them from future existence (rebirths). He thus converted the entire race to different heterodox religious worldviews—such as Jainism, Buddhism, and that of the Varhospatyas (materialists)—and misled them from the religion of the Vedas. Sometimes, this being appeared as a Jain mendicant, with his head shaved and carrying peacock feathers. As scholars have noted, he taught doctrines such as *syadvada*, a theory of postulations in seven different categories (a thing is; a thing is not; it is and is not; it is not definable; it is, but it is not definable; it is not, and neither is it definable; it is, and it is not, and it is not definable). At other times, the master deluder posed as a compassionate ascetic—referring to the Buddha (spelled "Bauddha" here)—who falsely taught that the *daityas* should refrain from killing animals for ritual sacrifice, as practiced by the followers of Vedic religion, and that the world subsists without any ultimate support. According to Parashara, the sole purpose of this person (a form of Vishnu) was to persuade the demons to abandon their own faith—that is, the practices enjoined by the Vedas and the laws—in order to defeat and destroy them. He postulates that Jainism and Buddhism were originally propounded by this person and that they were nothing more than "heresies."

Paragraphs 3 and 4: These paragraphs show how the same master deluder taught other "erroneous tenets," such as those of the Lokayatas (meaning "materialistic" or "atheistic"; also called Varhospatyas), and helped the gods to win their battle against the demons. The chapter thus far gives the reader a picture of both the literal demonizing of other religious sects by the Vedic orthodoxy and the intense ri-

Yogis

(Yogis, Indian School / Private Collection / Photo © Luca Tettoni / The Bridgeman Art Library International)

valry and ideological battle between the opposing groups. The text specifies some of the objections unorthodox people had toward the Vedic religion, which was remarkable for its belief that the gods, ancestors, spirits, and sages needed sacrifices, especially grains; its strong belief in sacrificial rituals, involving offerings of butter and other substances and, at times, animal sacrifices; its emphasis on the supremacy of the Brahmins and the three Vedas originally considered authoritative (the Rig Veda, Yajur Veda, and Sama Veda); and its faith in the *sraddha*, or *shraddha*, ritual of feeding and offering things to the priests, which means offering them directly to deceased ancestors. In contrast, the unorthodox religions were based on rationality and did not believe in anything unseen and speculative, one of the reasons they often laughed at general Vedic practices: "If an animal slaughtered in religious worship is thereby raised to heaven, would it not be expedient for a man who institutes a sacrifice to kill his own father for a victim?" However, from the perspective of the narrator, the "armour of religion" sustains one and gives one the necessary strength to fight outside forces.

Paragraph 5: In this paragraph, a further difference between the Vedic and non-Vedic religions is highlighted. Here, Parashara suggests that a heretic is anyone who does not follow the traditional religious order and discards "the garment of the Vedas," becoming naked. The Vedic religion is defined as based on the traditional hierarchy of castes and four or-

Essential Quotes

"'The precepts,' they cried, 'that lead to the injury of animal life (as in sacrifices) are highly reprehensible. . . . If an animal slaughtered in religious worship is thereby raised to heaven, would it not be expedient for a man who institutes a sacrifice to kill his own father for a victim?'"

"Remaining in a place where there is too great an intermixture of the four castes is detrimental to the character of the righteous. Men fall into hell who converse with one who takes his food without offering a portion to the gods, the sages, the manes, spirits, and guests."

"This soul is (of its own nature) pure, and composed of happiness and wisdom. The properties of pain, ignorance, and impurity, are those of nature (Prakriti), not of soul."

"Contemplative devotion is the union with Brahma, effected by that condition of mind which has attained perfection through those exercises which complete the control of self: and he whose contemplative devotion is characterized by the property of such absolute perfection, is in truth a sage, expectant of final liberation from the world."

"The mind of man is the cause both of his bondage and his liberation: its addiction to the objects of sense is the means of his bondage; its separation from objects of sense is the means of his freedom."

"When endowed with the apprehension of the nature of the object of inquiry, then, there is no difference between it (individual and) supreme spirit: difference is the consequence of the absence of (true) knowledge."

ders of life ("the religious student, the householder, the hermit, and the mendicant") and is regulated by the practice of food offerings to "the gods, the sages, the manes, spirits, and guests." The narrator speaks from a strictly orthodox standpoint; for example, "there is no fifth state"—that is, there are only the four conditions listed—there is no chance for the unorthodox who are outside the Vedic system, and there is no forgiveness for those who desert their religion. Deserters of this type are "impure" and are led directly to hell, along with those who converse with such people.

Paragraphs 6 and 7: Parashara then illustrates what could happen if one is associated with the heretic in one or the other form. He recounts a story of a king and a queen, their chance encounter with a heretic, and the bad karmic results endured by the king as a consequence of his conversation. The narrative thus justifies what was postulated earlier—that even a mere conversation with heretics is bound to result in bad rebirths and can only be rectified by very arduous expiations.

Besides the law of karma, this passage places emphasis on perceived wifely virtues, such as devotion to husband, benevolence, sincerity, humility, and discretion. It also gives insight into the contemporary suttee, or sati, practice, the custom of a wife's suicidal ascension onto the funeral pyre of her husband upon his death. In this story, the queen sacrifices herself on the king's cremation pile twice in her different births (with the husband's many beastly reincarnations occuring in between) in order to follow her husband. After her first suttee, the queen, reborn as a princess, is endowed with "knowledge of the events of her preexistence" as a result of her good karma. There also surfaces here the belief that heroic death on the battlefield leads one to heaven. The king, having been reborn as a Kshatriya ("warrior," or "protector of gentle people"), fights and dies in battle and is appropriately sent to heaven. The text gives some idea about the princess's right to choose her future husband, a practice that seems to have operated at least in royal households of the Indian Subcontinent.

Paragraphs 8 and 9: Parashara ends this narrative with the moral that a follower of the Vedas should "carefully avoid the discourse or contact of an unbeliever," especially while in devotional worship or practicing religious rites, because any association with the heretic demands expiation. He asserts, "Let not a person treat with even the civility of speech, heretics, those who do forbidden acts. . . . Intercourse with such iniquitous wretches, even at a distance, all association with schismatics, defiles."

♦ **Book VI: Chapter VII**

In this chapter, Parashara is narrating a story to Maitreya and discusses the nature of ignorance and the benefits of yoga, translated here as "contemplative devotion." The story concerns Kesidhwaja and Khandikya, former rivals who share their religious ideas in friendly terms and benefit from each other's knowledge. They talk about many important points, such as the "nature of ignorance," the human soul, the constituents of the universe in relation to the Supreme God, the relationship between the human soul and the godhead (Brahma, Vishnu), and finally yoga as a sure method of training the mind for liberation. The chapter theologizes yoga from the Vaishnava point of view and discusses how one spiritually evolves by strictly following the eightfold noble path of Yoga and attains liberation through perfection in yoga practice.

Paragraphs 1 and 2: These paragraphs contain a dialogue between Kesidhwaja and Khandikya about the worldly ambitions and the duties of the warrior class, Kshatriyas, as narrated by Parashara to Maitreya. The context of the dialogue is that Khandikya's kingdom was seized by Kesidhwaja. Having been driven from his palace, Khandikya then became a mendicant, beyond desire and selfishness of any kind. Here, Khandikya realizes that he was unable to do the duties of the warrior class and protect his kingdom; therefore, the takeover of the kingdom by a more capable one was justified. In the previous chapter (not included here), Khandikya taught Kesidhwaja about the ways of doing penance for the death of a cow, and, as a gift for his teaching, Kesidhwaja now instructs Khandikya in the doctrine of the soul.

Kesidhwaja distinguishes between the soul and the body. He argues that the soul by its inherent nature is pure, but when it is associated with Prakriti (the world of becoming), it assumes the qualities of gross nature. He explains that the human body is composed of five elements—ether, air, fire, water, and earth—and that human beings are confined to bodily existence because of their attachment to worldly things. He further states that by imputing selfhood to what is not self (namely, the body and worldly existence), and by regarding something that is not actually one's own as one's property, the human being is bound to the realm of ignorance. As a consequence, he accrues bodily karma and revolves in the world of birth and rebirth. Kesidhwaja instructs that it is through the practice of contemplative devotion (yoga), that one can be free from "worldly sorrows" and attain liberation from the world of birth and rebirth.

Paragraphs 3 and 4: In these paragraphs, Kesidhwaja talks about how one can train one's mind through yoga and be liberated from the cycle of birth, death, and rebirth. He argues that the mind is the root cause of both bondage and liberation, and therefore one has to first restrain the mind from the objects of the senses and continue meditating on the Supreme Being. He stresses that both the soul and the Supreme Being have a similar "nature," and therefore one can be united with Brahma, the ultimate Self, through perfection in yoga. Here, the perfection of yoga means following the noble eightfold path of Yoga and cultivating one's virtues and practice. Through the ensuing paragraphs, he elaborates the eight limbs of Yoga: *yana* (abstentions, moral restraints), *niyama* (ethical observances), *asana* (posture), *pranayama* (breath control), *pratyahara* (withdrawal of the senses), *dharana* (concentration), *dhyana* (meditation), and *samadhi* (full meditative absorption).

Paragraphs 5 and 6: Kesidhwaja expounds how through perfection in yoga and the cultivation of supreme virtues, one abides one's mind in Brahma (the ultimate Self), which is defined as both "with or without form" and as both "supreme and secondary." He regards Brahma as another name of Vishnu and stresses that the one who knows him "recognises no distinctions" and has the knowledge that all those who are seen and unseen are pervaded by the single "imperishable form of Vishnu," the supreme lord of the universe. However, Kesidhwaja cautions that this ultimate form cannot be contemplated by the sages in their early devotions; only through devoted yoga practice and constant meditation, progressing one's focus from the gross to the more subtle forms of Hari (another name for Vishnu), can one contemplate the ultimate form. He also postulates that the spiritual faculties of the beings in this world manifest in different ways and have different gradations.

Paragraphs 7–9: After his extensive elaboration of the eight limbs of Yoga, Kesidhwaja concludes that the yogi, or yogic sage, acquires discriminative knowledge and attains the supreme Brahma through perfection in yoga. This attainment is defined as the identification of the individual soul with the supreme Brahma (again, Vishnu). Kesidhwaja also states that the absence of knowledge earlier led to the distinction between the individual soul and the supreme Self, but with the dawn of the knowledge of Yoga, ignorance is removed, and one finds oneself in complete oneness with the supreme Self. The narration ends with Kesidhwaja returning to his city, installing his son on the throne, and retiring into the woods to accomplish his devotions.

Audience

As it is written, Parashara narrates the entire Vishnu Purana to Maitreya, who is thus the first audience. In historical terms, it appears that the text was composed with the express aim of showing the superiority of the Vedic religion over heterodox religions of the time. Written from the perspective of the orthodox Brahmins, this Purana represents an attempt to consolidate the Vedic order of life and ways of thinking. The text seems to have been composed for the first three traditional Hindu classes of people—Brahmins, Kshatriyas, and Vaishyas—directing them to preserve the traditional social order and traditional religious practices. The modern reader thus gains insight into the prevailing ideological rivalry between the Vedic and other religious systems of the time. The Vishnu Purana specifically targets the Jain, Buddhist, and Lokayata doctrines by demonizing them through the mythology that their religions are false and were enunciated by the "delusive" form of Vishnu himself.

Impact

The way the Buddha story is cast in the narrative, it appears that the text was purposefully composed to consolidate the traditional Vedic religious practice and dissuade people from opting for other religions. Although it legitimizes other heterodox faiths by stating that they were the creations of Vishnu himself, it disparages and demonizes them and sanctifies the Vedic religious order as the only true and original one. Similarly, the second excerpt on yoga is completely theologized, and Yoga is defined from the Vaishnava perspective. As Vishnu is now the ultimate God in whom and from whom everything emanates, yoga becomes the definite means for one's unity with God and therefore for ultimate liberation.

While yoga philosophy was originally not theistic, the nonsectarian theological conception slowly entered the practice through the time of its refinement by Patanjali (ca. 200 BCE). Later, depending on the sectarian affiliation, yoga was related to a particular deity, such as Shiva or Vishnu or other forms of divine power. The theologization of yoga in the sectarian fashion (that is, as a means to reach a particular deity) must have served the needs of

---

Questions for Further Study

1. What factors do you think might have accounted for the division of Hinduism into sects—primarily Vaishnavism, Shivaism, and the Shaktis—in the early centuries of the Common Era?

2. Most religions at one time or another have had to deal with heterodox or heretical views. How does the Vishnu Purana address the issue of "false" religions such as Buddhism and Jainism? How does Hinduism's response to supposedly false religious beliefs differ from that of Christianity, as reflected in a document such as the Canons and Decrees of the Council of Trent?

3. The Vishnu Purana states: "This soul is (of its own nature) pure, and composed of happiness and wisdom. The properties of pain, ignorance, and impurity, are those of nature (Prakriti), not of soul." How, then, do you think that Hindus who adhere to the teachings of the Vishnu Purana explain the existence of evil people: Adolf Hitler, serial killers, child molesters, and the like?

4. The word *Vedic* is often used in discussions of the history of Hinduism. To what does this word refer? What meaning would it have for a Hindu?

5. If the Puranas are "ancient stories" that take up such issues as creation, the genealogies and stories surrounding ancient kings, and battles between good and evil, to what extent do they in general, and the Vishnu Purana in particular, resemble the Judeo-Christian Bible, specifically Genesis and Exodus? In what sense do they resemble a work such as the *Epic of Gilgamesh*?

diverse peoples wishing to incorporate the philosophy in their religious doctrine. Nonetheless, because of the lack of information regarding the immediate historical setting of the Vishnu Purana, it is difficult to assess the impact of the text on contemporary people.

In the modern era, puranic works are often recited in Sanskrit—the language in which the texts were originally transmitted and codified—in a public setting. The recitation of a particular puranic text is then followed by storytelling in the vernacular language suitable to the public gathered to celebrate the occasion and listen to the divine narratives. Among orthodox Hindus, belief in puranic stories is very strong, and most such followers regard the stories as real happenings of the past. However, more liberal-minded Hindus tend to take the puranic stories just as a means to inspire devotion to a particular form of god or goddess.

Further Reading

■ Books

Dayal, Thakur Harendra. *The Vishnu Purana: Social, Economic and Religious Aspects*. Delhi: Sundeep Prakashan, 1983.

Kane, Pandurang Vaman. *History of Dharmashastra: Ancient and Medieval Religious and Civil Law*. Vol. 5. Poona, India: Bhandarkar Oriental Research Institute, 1962.

Michaels, Axel. *Hinduism: Past and Present*, trans. Barbara Harshav. Princeton, N.J.: Princeton University Press, 2004.

Rocher, Ludo. *A History of Indian Literature*, Vol. 2: *The Puranas*. Wiesbaden, Germany: Otto Harrassowitz, 1986.

Wilson, H. H. *The Vishnu Purana: A System of Hindu Mythology and Tradition*. Calcutta: Punthi Pustak, 1972.

■ Journals

Datta, K. S. R. "The Vishnu-Purana and Advaita." *Purana* 20 (1978): 193–196.

Dikshitar, V. R. Ramachandra. "The Age of the Vishnu Purana." *Indian Historical Quarterly* 7, no. 2 (1931): 370–372.

Hazra, Rajendra Chandra. "The Date of the Vishnu Purana." *Annals of the Bhandarkar Oriental Research Institute* 18 (1936–1937): 265–275.

Kennedy, J. "The Gospels of the Infancy, the Lalita Vistara, and the Vishnu Purana: Or the Transmission of Religious Legends between India and the West." *Journal of the Royal Asiatic Society* (1917): 209–243, 469–540.

O'Flaherty, Wendy Doniger. "The Origin of Heresy in Hindu Mythology." *History of Religions* 10, no. 4 (May 1971): 271–333.

Roy, S. N. "Date of Vishnu Purana's Chapters on Maya-Moha." *Purana* 7 (1965): 276–287.

Sharma, Arvind. "A Note on H. H. Wilson's Interpretation of the Role of Rajas in Cosmic Creation in the Vishnu Purana." *Purana* 19 (1977): 347–350.

Varadachari, V. "Similes in the Vishnu Purana," *Purana* 3 (1961): 228–234.

—Nawaraj Chaulagain

Vishnu Purana

Book III: Chapter XVIII

PARASHARA.—After this, the great delusion, having proceeded to earth, beheld the Daityas engaged in ascetic penances upon the banks of the Narmada river; and approaching them in the semblance of a naked mendicant, with his head shaven, and carrying a bunch of peacock's feathers, he thus addressed them in gentle accents: "Ho, lords of the Daitya race! wherefore is it that you practise these acts of penance? is it with a view to recompense in this world, or in another?" "Sage," replied the Daityas, "we pursue these devotions to obtain a reward hereafter; why should you make such an inquiry?" "If you are desirous of final emancipation," answered the seeming ascetic, "attend to my words, for you are worthy of a revelation which is the door to ultimate felicity. The duties that I will teach you are the secret path to liberation; there are none beyond or superior to them: by following them you shall obtain either heaven or exemption from future existence. You, mighty beings, are deserving of such lofty doctrine." By such persuasions, and by many specious arguments, did this delusive being mislead the Daityas from the tenets of the Vedas; teaching that the same thing might be for the sake of virtue and of vice; might be, and might not be; might or might not contribute to liberation; might be the supreme object, and not the supreme object; might be effect, and not be effect; might be manifest, or not be manifest; might be the duty of those who go naked, or who go clothed in much raiment: and so the Daityas were seduced from their proper duties by the repeated lessons of their illusory preceptor, maintaining the equal truth of contradictory tenets; and they were called Arhatas, from the phrase he had employed of "Ye are worthy (Arhatha) of this great doctrine;" that is, of the false doctrines which he persuaded them to embrace.

The foes of the gods being thus induced to apostatize from the religion of the Vedas, by the delusive person sent by Vishnnu, became in their turn teachers of the same heresies, and perverted others; and these, again, communicating their principles to others, by whom they were still further disseminated, the Vedas were in a short time deserted by most of the Daitya race. Then the same deluder, putting on garments of a red colour, assuming a benevolent aspect, and speaking in soft and agreeable tones, addressed others of the same family, and said to them, "If, mighty demons, you cherish a desire either for heaven or for final repose, desist from the iniquitous massacre of animals (for sacrifice), and hear from me what you should do. Know that all that exists is composed of discriminative knowledge. Understand my words, for they have been uttered by the wise. This world subsists without support, and engaged in the pursuit of error, which it mistakes for knowledge, as well as vitiated by passion and the rest, revolves in the straits of existence." In this manner, exclaiming to them, "Know!" (Budhyadwam), and they replying, "It is known" (Budhyate), these Daityas were induced by the arch deceiver to deviate from their religious duties (and become Bauddhas), by his repeated arguments and variously urged persuasions, When they had abandoned their own faith, they persuaded others to do the same, and the heresy spread, and many deserted the practices enjoined by the Vedas and the laws.

The delusions of the false teacher paused not with the conversion of the Daityas to the Jaina and Bauddha heresies, but with various erroneous tenets he prevailed upon others to apostatize, until the whole were led astray, and deserted the doctrines and observances inculcated by the three Vedas. Some then spake evil of the sacred books; some blasphemed the gods; some treated sacrifices and other devotional ceremonies with scorn; and others calumniated the Brahmans. "The precepts," they cried, "that lead to the injury of animal life (as in sacrifices) are highly reprehensible. To say that casting butter into flame is productive of reward, is mere childishness. If Indra, after having obtained godhead by multiplied rites, is fed upon the wood used as fuel in holy fire, he is lower than a brute, which feeds at least upon leaves. If an animal slaughtered in religious worship is thereby raised to heaven, would it not be expedient for a man who institutes a sacrifice to kill his own father for a victim? If that which is eaten by one at a Sraddha gives satisfaction to another, it must be unnecessary for one who resides at a distance to bring food for presentation in person." "First, then, let it be determined what may be (rationally) believed by mankind, and then," said their preceptor, "you will find that felicity may be

Document Text

expected from my instructions. The words of authority do not, mighty Asuras, fall from heaven: the text that has reason is alone to be acknowledged by me, and by such as you are." By such and similar lessons the Daityas were perverted, so that not one of them admitted the authority of the Vedas.

When the Daityas had thus declined from the path of the holy writings, the deities took courage, and gathered together for battle. Hostilities accordingly were renewed, but the demons were now defeated and slain by the gods, who had adhered to the righteous path. The armour of religion, which had formerly protected the Daityas, had been discarded by them, and upon its abandonment followed their destruction.

Thus, Maitreya, you are to understand that those who have seceded from their original belief are said to be naked, because they have thrown off the garment of the Vedas. According to the law there are four conditions or orders of men (of the three first castes), the religious student, the householder, the hermit, and the mendicant. There is no fifth state; and the unrighteous man who relinquishes the order of the householder, and does not become either an anchoret or a mendicant, is also a naked (seceder). The man who neglects his permanent observances for one day and night, being able to perform them, incurs thereby sin for one day; and should he omit them, not being in trouble, for a fortnight, he can be purified only by arduous expiation. The virtuous must stop to gaze upon the sun after looking upon a person who has allowed a year to elapse without the observance of the perpetual ceremonies; and they must bathe with their clothes on should they have touched him: but for the individual himself no expiation has been declared. There is no sinner upon earth more culpable than one in whose dwelling the gods, progenitors, and spirits, are left to sigh unworshipped. Let not a man associate, in residence, sitting, or society, with him whose person or whose house has been blasted by the sighs of the gods, progenitors, and spirits. Conversation, interchange of civilities, or association with a man who for a twelvemonth has not discharged his religious duties, is productive of equality of guilt; and the person who eats in the house of such a man, or sits down with him, or sleeps on the same couch with him, becomes like him instantaneously. Again; he who takes his food without shewing reverence to the gods, progenitors, spirits, and guests, commits sin. How great is his sin! The Brahmans, and men of the other castes, who turn their faces away from their proper duties, become heretics, and are classed with those who relinquish pious works. Remaining in a place where there is too great an intermixture of the four castes is detrimental to the character of the righteous. Men fall into hell who converse with one who takes his food without offering a portion to the gods, the sages, the manes, spirits, and guests. Let therefore a prudent person carefully avoid the conversation, or the contact, and the like, of those heretics who are rendered impure by their desertion of the three Vedas. The ancestral rite, although performed with zeal and faith, pleases neither gods nor progenitors if it be looked upon by apostates.

It is related that there was formerly a king named Satadhanu, whose wife Saivya was a woman of great virtue. She was devoted to her husband, benevolent, sincere, pure, adorned with every female excellence, with humility, and discretion. The Raja and his wife daily worshipped the god of gods, Janarddana, with pious meditations, oblations to fire, prayers, gifts, fasting, and every other mark of entire faith, and exclusive devotion. On one occasion, when they had fasted on the full moon of Kartika, and had bathed in the Bhagirathi, they beheld, as they came up from the water, a heretic approach them, who was the friend of the Raja's military preceptor. The Raja, out of respect to the latter, entered into conversation with the heretic; but not so did the princess; reflecting that she was observing a fast, she turned from him, and cast her eyes up to the sun. On their arrival at home, the husband and wife, as usual, performed the worship of Vishnu, agreeably to the ritual. After a time the Raja, triumphant over his enemies, died; and the princess ascended the funeral pile of her husband.

In consequence of the fault committed by Satadhanu, by speaking to an infidel when he was engaged in a solemn fast, he was born again as a dog. His wife was born as the daughter of the Raja of Kasi, with a knowledge of the events of her preexistence, accomplished in every science, and endowed with every virtue. Her father was anxious to give her in marriage to some suitable husband, but she constantly opposed his design, and the king was prevented by her from accomplishing her nuptials. With the eye of divine intelligence she knew that her own husband had been regenerate as a dog, and going once to the city of Vaidisa she saw the dog, and recognised her former lord in him. Knowing that the animal was her husband, she placed upon his neck the bridal garland, accompanying it with the marriage rites and prayers: but he, eating the delicate food presented to him, expressed his delight after the fashion of his species; at which she was much ashamed, and, bowing reverently to him, thus spake to her degraded spouse: "Recall to memory, illustrious prince, the ill-timed politeness on account of which you have been born as a dog, and are now fawning upon me. In consequence of speaking to a heretic, after bathing in a sacred river, you have been condemned to this abject birth. Do you not remember it?" Thus reminded, the Raja recollected his former condition, and was lost in thought, and felt deep humiliation. With a broken spirit he went forth from the city, and falling dead in the desert, was born anew as a jackal. In the course of the following year the princess knew what had happened, and went to the mountain Kolahala to seek for her husband. Finding him there, the lovely daughter of the king of the earth said to her lord, thus disguised as a jackal, "Dost thou not remember, oh king, the circumstance of conversing with a heretic, which I called to thy recollection when thou wast a dog?" The Raja, thus addressed, knew that what the princess had spoken was true, and thereupon desisted from food, and died. He then became a wolf; but his blameless wife knew it, and came to him in the lonely forest, and awakened his remembrance of his original state. "No wolf art thou," she said, "but the illustrious sovereign Satadhanu. Thou wast then a dog, then a jackal, and art now a wolf." Upon this, recollecting himself, the prince abandoned his life, and became a vulture; in which form his lovely queen still found him, and aroused him to a knowledge of the past. "Prince," she exclaimed, "recollect yourself: away with this uncouth form, to which the sin of conversing with a heretic has condemned you!" The Raja was next born as a crow; when the princess, who through her mystical powers was aware of it, said to him, "Thou art now thyself the eater of tributary grain, to whom, in a prior existence, all the kings of the earth paid tribute." Having abandoned his body, in consequence of the recollections excited by these words, the king next became a peacock, which the princess took to herself, and petted, and fed constantly with such food as is agreeable to birds of its class. The king of Kasi instituted at that time the solemn sacrifice of a horse. In the ablutions with which it terminated the princess caused her peacock to be bathed, bathing also herself; and she then reminded Satadhanu how he had been successively born as various animals. On recollecting this, he resigned his life. He was then born as the son of a person of distinction; and the princess now assenting to the wishes of her father to see her wedded, the king of Kasi caused it to be made known that she would elect a bridegroom from those who should present themselves as suitors for her hand. When the election took place, the princess made choice of her former lord, who appeared amongst the candidates, and again invested him with the character of her husband. They lived happily together, and upon her father's decease Satadhanu ruled over the country of Videha. He offered many sacrifices, and gave away many gifts, and begot sons, and subdued his enemies in war; and having duly exercised the sovereign power, and cherished benignantly the earth, he died, as became his warrior birth, in battle. His queen again followed him in death, and, conformably to sacred precepts, once more mounted cheerfully his funeral pile. The king then, along with his princess, ascended beyond the sphere of Indra to the regions where all desires are for ever gratified, obtaining ever-during and unequalled happiness in heaven, the perfect felicity that is the rarely realised reward of conjugal fidelity.

Such, Maitreya, is the sin of conversing with a heretic, and such are the expiatory effects of bathing after the solemn sacrifice of a horse, as I have narrated them to you. Let therefore a man carefully avoid the discourse or contact of an unbeliever, especially at seasons of devotion, and when engaged in the performance of religious rites preparatory to a sacrifice. If it be necessary that a wise man should look at the sun, after beholding one who has neglected his domestic ceremonies for a month, how much greater need must there be of expiation after encountering one who has wholly abandoned the Vedas? one who is supported by infidels, or who disputes the doctrines of holy writ? Let not a person treat with even the civility of speech, heretics, those who do forbidden acts, pretended saints, scoundrels, sceptics, and hypocrites. Intercourse with such iniquitous wretches, even at a distance, all association with schismatics, defiles; let a man therefore carefully avoid them.

These, Maitreya, are the persons called naked, the meaning of which term you desired to have explained. Their very looks vitiate the performance of an ancestral oblation; speaking to them destroys religious merit for a whole day. These are the unrighteous heretics to whom a man must not give shelter, and speaking to whom effaces whatever merit he may that day have obtained. Men, indeed, fall into hell as the consequence of only conversing with those who unprofitably assume the twisted hair, and shaven crown; with those who feed without offering food to gods, spirits, and guests; and those who are excluded from the presentation of cakes, and libations of water, to the manes. . . .

Book VI: Chapter VII

"BUT," said Kesidhwaja, "why have you not asked of me my kingdom, now free from all annoyance? what else except dominion is acceptable to the warrior race?" "I will tell you," replied Khandikya, "why I did not make such a demand, nor require that territory which is an object of ignorant ambition. It is the duty of the warrior to protect his subjects in peace, and to kill in fight the enemies of his sway. It is no fault that you should have taken my kingdom from one who was unable to defend it, to whom it was a bondage, and who was thus freed from the incumbrance of ignorance. My desire of dominion originated in my being born to possess it: the ambition of others, which proceeds from human frailties, is not compatible with virtue. To solicit gifts is not the duty of a prince and warrior: and for these reasons I have not asked for your kingdom, nor made a demand which ignorance alone would have suggested. Those only who are destitute of knowledge, whose minds are engrossed by selfishness, who are intoxicated with the inebriating beverage of self-sufficiency, desire kingdoms; not such as I am."

When king Kesidhwaja heard these words, he was much pleased, and exclaimed, "It is well spoken!" Then addressing Khandikya affectionately, he said, "Listen to my words. Through desire of escaping death by the ignorance of works I exercise the regal power, celebrate various sacrifices, and enjoy pleasures subversive of purity. Fortunate is it for you that your mind has attached itself to the dominion of discrimination. Pride of your race! now listen to the real nature of ignorance. The (erroneous) notion that self consists in what is not self, and the opinion that property consists in what is not one's own, constitute the double seed of the tree of ignorance. The ill judging embodied being, bewildered by the darkness of fascination, situated in a body composed of the five elements, loudly asserts, 'This is I:' but who would ascribe spiritual individuality to a body in which soul is distinct from the ether, air, fire, water, and earth (of which that body is composed)? What man of understanding assigns to disembodied spirit corporeal fruition, or lands, houses, and the like, that it should say, 'These are mine?' What wise man entertains the idea of property in sons or grandsons begotten of the body after the spirit has abandoned it? Man performs all acts for the purpose of bodily fruition, and the consequence of such acts is another body; so that their result is nothing but confinement to bodily existence. In the same manner as a mansion of clay is plastered with clay and water, so the body, which is of earth, is perpetuated by earth and water (or by eating and drinking). The body, consisting of the five elements, is nourished by substances equally composed of those elements: but since this is the case, what is there in this life that man should be proud of? Travelling the path of the world for many thousands of births, man attains only the weariness of bewilderment, and is smothered by the dust of imagination. When that dust is washed away by the bland water of real knowledge, then the weariness of bewilderment sustained by the wayfarer through repeated births is removed. When that weariness is relieved, the internal man is at peace, and he obtains that supreme felicity which is unequalled and undisturbed. This soul is (of its own nature) pure, and composed of happiness and wisdom. The properties of pain, ignorance, and impurity, are those of nature (Prakriti), not of soul. There is no affinity between fire and water, but when the latter is placed over the former in a caldron it bubbles and boils, and exhibits the properties of fire. In like manner, when soul is associated with Prakriti it is vitiated by egotism and the rest, and assumes the qualities of grosser nature, although essentially distinct from them, and incorruptible. Such is the seed of ignorance, as I have explained it to you. There is but one cure of worldly sorrows, the practice of devotion; no other is known."

"Then," said Khandikya, "do you, who are the chief of those versed in contemplative devotion, explain to me what that is; for in the race of the descendants of Nimi you are best acquainted with the sacred writings in which it is taught." "Hear," replied Kesidhwaja, "the account of, the nature of contemplative devotion, which I impart to you, and by perfection in which the sage attains resolution into Brahma, and never suffers birth again. The mind of man is the cause both of his bondage and his liberation: its addiction to the objects of sense is the means of his bondage; its separation from objects of sense is the means of his freedom. The sage who is capable of discriminative knowledge must therefore restrain his mind from all the objects of sense, and therewith meditate upon the Supreme Being, who is one with spirit, in order to attain liberation; for that supreme spirit attracts to itself him who meditates upon it, and who is of the same nature, as the loadstone attracts the iron by the virtue which is common to itself and to its products. Contemplative devotion is the union with Brahma, effected by that condition of mind which has attained perfection through those exercises which complete the control of self: and he whose contemplative devotion is characterized by the property of such absolute perfection, is in truth a sage, expectant of final liberation from the world.

"The sage, or Yogi, when first applying himself to contemplative devotion is called the novice or practitioner (Yoga yuj); when he has attained spiritual union he is termed the adept, or he whose meditations are accomplished. Should the thoughts of the former be unvitiated by any obstructing imperfection, he will obtain freedom, after practising devotion through several lives. The latter speedily obtains liberation in that existence (in which he reaches perfection), all his acts being consumed by the fire of contemplative devotion. The sage who would bring his mind into a fit state for the performance of devout contemplation be devoid of desire, and observe invariably continence, compassion, truth, honesty, and disinterestedness: he must fix his mind intently on the supreme Brahma, practising holy study, purification, contentment, penance, and self-control. These virtues, respectively termed the five acts of restraint (Yana), and five of obligation (Niyama), bestow excellent rewards when practised for the sake of reward, and eternal liberation when they are not prompted by desire (of transient benefits). Endowed with these merits, the sage self restrained should sit in one of the modes termed Bhadrasana, &c., and engage in contemplation. Bringing his vital airs, called Prana, under subjection, by frequent repetition, is thence called Pranayama, which is as it were a seed with a seed. In this the breath of expiration and that of inspiration are alternately obstructed, constituting the act twofold; and the suppression of both modes of breathing produces a third. The exercise of the Yogi, whilst endeavouring to bring before his thoughts the gross form of the eternal, is denominated Alambana. He is then to perform the Pratyahara, which consists in restraining his organs of sense from susceptibility to outward impressions, and directing them entirely to mental perceptions. By these means the entire subjugation of the unsteady senses is effected; and if they are not controlled, the sage will not accomplish his devotions. When by the Pranayama the vital airs are restrained, and the senses are subjugated by the Pratyahara, then the sage will he able to keep his mind steady in its perfect asylum."

Khanddikya then said to Kesidhwaja, "Illustrious sage, inform me what is that perfect asylum of the mind, resting on which it destroys all the products of (human) infirmity." To this, Kesidhwaja replied, "The asylum of mind is spirit (Brahma), which of its own nature is twofold, as being with or without form; and each of these is supreme and secondary. Apprehension of spirit, again, is threefold. I will explain the different kinds to you: they are, that which is called Brahma, that which is named from works, and that which comprehends both. That mental apprehension which consists of Brahma is one; that which is formed of works is another; and that which comprehends both is the third: so that mental apprehension (of the object or asylum of the thoughts) is threefold. Sanandana and other (perfect sages) were endowed with apprehension of the nature of Brahma. The gods and others, whether animate or inanimate, are possessed of that which regards acts. The apprehension that comprehends both works and spirit exists in Hiranyagarbha and others, who are possessed of contemplative knowledge of their own nature, and who also exercise certain active functions, as creation and the rest. Until all acts, which are the causes of notions of individuality, are discontinued, spirit is one thing, and the universe is another, to those who contemplate objects as distinct and various; but that is called true knowledge, or knowledge of Brahma, which recognises no distinctions, which contemplates only simple existence, which is undefinable by words, and is to be discovered solely in one's own spirit. That is the supreme, unborn, imperishable form of Vishnu, who is without (sensible) form, and is characterised as a condition of the supreme soul, which is variously modified from the condition of universal form. But this condition cannot be contemplated by sages in their (early) devotions, and they must therefore direct their minds to the gross form of Hari, which is of universal perceptibility. They must meditate upon him as Hiranyagarbha, as the glorious Vasava, as Prajapati, as the winds, the Vasus, the Rudras, the suns, stars, planets, Gandharbas, Yakshas, Daityas, all the gods and their progenitors, men, animals, mountains, oceans, rivers, trees, all beings, and all sources of beings, all modifications whatever of nature and its products, whether sentient or unconscious, one-footed, two-footed, or many-footed; all these are the sensible form of Hari, to be apprehended by the three kinds of apprehension. All this universal world, this world of moving and stationary beings, is pervaded by the energy of Vishnu, who is of the nature of the supreme Brahma. This energy is either supreme, or, when it is that of conscious embodied spirit, it is secondary. Ignorance, or that which is denominated from works, is a third energy; by which the omnipresent energy of embodied spirit is ever excited, and whence it suffers all the pains of repeated worldly existence. Obscured by that energy

Document Text

(of ignorance or illusion), the energy that is denominated from embodied spirit is characterised by different degrees of perfection in all created beings. In things without life it exists in a very small degree: it is more in things that have life, but are (without motion): in insects it is still more abundant, and still more in birds; it is more in wild animals, and in domestic animals the faculty is still greater: men have more of this (spiritual) faculty than animals, and thence arises their authority over them: the faculty exists in an ascending degree in Nagas, Gandharbas, Yakshas, gods, Sakra, Prajapati, and Hiranyagarbha: and is above all predominant in that male (Vishnu) of whom all these various creatures are but the diversified forms, penetrated universally by his energy, as all-pervading as the ether.

"The second state of him who is called Vishnu, and which is to be meditated upon by the (advanced) sage, is that imperceptible, shapeless form of Brahma, which is called by the wise, 'That which is,' and in which all the before described energies reside. Thence proceeds the form of the universal form, the other great form of Hari, which is the origin of those manifested forms (or incarnations) that are endowed with every kind of energy, and which, whether the forms of gods, animals, or men, are assumed by him (Hari) in his sport. This active interposition of the undefinable god, all-comprehending and irresistible, is for the purpose of benefiting the world, and is not the necessary consequence of works. This form of the universal form is to be meditated upon by the sage for the object of purification, as it destroys all sin. In the same manner as fire, blazing in the wind, burns dry grass, so Vishnu, seated in the heart, consumes the sins of the sage; and therefore let him resolutely effect the fixation of his mind upon that receptacle of all the three energies (Vishnu), for that is the operation of the mind which is called perfect Dharana: and thus the perfect asylum of individual as well as universal spirit, that which is beyond the three modes of apprehension, is attained, for the eternal emancipation of the sage. The minds of other beings, which are not fixed upon that asylum, are altogether impure, and are all the gods and the rest, who spring from acts. The retention or apprehension by the mind of that visible form of Vishnu, without regard to subsidiary forms, is thence called Dharana; and I will describe to you the perceptible form of Hari, which no mental retention will manifest, except in a mind that is fit to become the receptacle of the idea. The meditating sage must think (he beholds internally the figure) of Vishnu, as having a pleased and lovely countenance, with eyes like the leaf of the lotus, smooth cheeks, and a broad and brilliant forehead; ears of equal size, the lobes of which are decorated with splendid pendants; a painted neck, and a broad breast, on which shines the Srivatsa mark; a belly falling in graceful folds, with a deep-seated navel; eight long arms, or else four; and firm and well-knit thighs and legs, with well-formed feet and toes. Let him, with well-governed thoughts, contemplate, as long as he can persevere in unremitting attention, Hari as clad in a yellow robe, wearing a rich diadem on his head, and brilliant armlets and bracelets on his arms, and bearing in his hands the bow, the shell, the mace, the sword, the discus, the rosary, the lotus, and the arrow. When this image never departs from his mind, whether he be going or standing, or be engaged in any other voluntary act, then he may believe his retention to be perfect. The sage may then meditate upon the form of Vishnu without his arms, as the shell, mace, discus, and bow; and as placid, and bearing only his rosary. When the idea of this image is firmly retained, then he may meditate on Vishnu without his diadem, bracelets, or other ornaments. He may next contemplate him as having but one single limb, and may then fix his whole thoughts upon the body to which the limbs belong. This process of forming a lively image in the mind, exclusive of all other objects, constitutes Dhyana, or meditation, which is perfected by six stages; and when an accurate knowledge of self, free from all distinction, is attained by this mental meditation, that is termed Samadhi.

"(When the Yogi has accomplished this stage, he acquires) discriminative knowledge, which is the means of enabling living soul, when all the three kinds of apprehension are destroyed, to attain the attainable supreme Brahma. Embodied spirit is the user of the instrument, which instrument is true knowledge; and by it that (identification) of the former (with Brahma) is attained. Liberation, which is the object to be effected, being accomplished, discriminative knowledge ceases. When endowed with the apprehension of the nature of the object of inquiry, then, there is no difference between it (individual and) supreme spirit: difference is the consequence of the absence of (true) knowledge. When that ignorance which is the cause of the difference between individual and universal spirit is destroyed finally and for ever, who shall ever make that distinction between them which does not exist? Thus have I, Khandikya, in reply to your question, explained to you what is meant by contemplative devotion, both fully and summarily. What else do you wish to hear?"

Document Text

Khandikya replied to Kesidhwaja, and said, "The explanation which you have given me of the real nature of contemplative devotion has fulfilled all my wishes, and removed all impurity from my mind. The expression 'mine,' which I have been accustomed to use, is untruth, and cannot be otherwise declared by those who know what is to be known. The words 'I' and 'mine' constitute ignorance; but practice is influenced by ignorance. Supreme truth cannot be defined, for it is not to be explained by words. Depart therefore, Kesidhwaja; you have done all that is necessary for my real happiness, in teaching me contemplative devotion, the inexhaustible bestower of liberation from existence."

Accordingly king Kesidhwaja, after receiving suitable homage from Khandikya, returned to his city. Khandikya, having nominated his son Raja, retired to the woods to accomplish his devotions, his whole mind being intent upon Govinda: there his entire thoughts being engrossed upon one only object, and being purified by practices of restraint, self-control, and the rest, he obtained absorption into the pure and perfect spirit which is termed Vishnu. Kesidhwaja also, in order to attain liberation, became averse from his own perishable works, and lived amidst objects of sense (without regarding them), and instituted religious rites without expecting therefrom any advantages to himself. Thus by pure and auspicious fruition, being cleansed from all sin, he also obtained that perfection which assuages all affliction for ever.

Glossary

anchoret	a hermit
Bauddhas	or Buddhas, that is, followers of Buddhism
Bhagirathi	a river in India and the source stream of the Ganges River
Brahma	the ultimate Self
Brahmins	members of the highest of the four Hindu castes; priests
Daityas	demons, foes of god
Govinda	one of the names of Krishna
Hari	another name for Vishnu
Hiranyagarbha	literally, the "golden fetus" or "golden womb," the source of the creation of the Universe in Indian philosophy
Indra	the king of the gods and the god of the storm
Kartika	a month of the Hindu calendar, named after the Hindu god Karttikeya
Kesidhwaja	a king who shares religious ideas with Khandikya
Maitreya	the person to whom the Vishnu Purana is addressed
Parashara	the narrator of the Vishnu Purana
Srivatsa mark	the "Endless Knot," a mark on the breast of Vishnu
Vedas	the most ancient sacred writings of Hinduism
Vishnu	the preserver god in Hinduism

Page from the Mishneh Torah

(Page from the Mishneh Torah, c.1351 (vellum), Jewish School, (14th century) / National Library, Jerusalem, Israel / Giraudon / The Bridgeman Art Library International)

Mishneh Torah

1170–1180

"Every Israelite has a duty to study whether he is poor or rich, whether healthy or suffering, whether young or very old."

Overview

The Spanish-born Jewish philosopher Moses ben Maimon, usually called Maimonides, is best known for composing two texts: *The Guide for the Perplexed*, a philosophical work, and the *Mishneh Torah*, also known as the Maimonidean Code. The fourteen-volume *Mishneh Torah* established Maimonides as the leading rabbinic authority of his generation and, many believe, of all time. Maimonides aimed to compose a work from which the entire Oral Law governing Jewish life might be studied systematically. He hoped that his *Mishneh Torah* would provide Jews with a text that could reinvigorate religious study in a time of cultural decline and religious apathy. Maimonides composed this work between 1170 and 1180. The title *Mishneh Torah*, which means "repetition and summary of the Torah," indicates its intent. The subtitle *Sefer Yad ha-Chazaka* ("Book of the Strong Hand") is a play on the numerical equivalent of the Hebrew word "hand," which comes out to 14—the number of volumes in the *Mishneh Torah*.

Maimonides wrote that he intended the *Mishneh Torah* to be a comprehensive explanation of the Jewish oral tradition. A person who had mastered the written Torah and then his *Mishneh Torah* would have no need for any other religious reference work. Maimonides' intent to create a single guidebook has some similarities to the motivation of Rabbi Judah the Prince, who compiled the Mishnah around the year 200 CE, almost a thousand years earlier. As Maimonides saw it, Judah made the controversial decision to reduce the oral tradition to writing because the increasing difficulties of the times made it necessary. In Judah's time, the Roman Empire was strengthening, and increasing numbers of Jews were leaving the land of Israel, propelled by social instability and economic crisis; likewise, Maimonides saw his code as providing a comparable pedagogical tool that would serve a similar function.

Context

Muslims won a decisive military victory in 711 CE, bringing Visigoth rule to an end on the Iberian Peninsula. The Catholic Visigoths had persecuted the Jews, and so the Jews of Spain welcomed the Muslim conquerors. Non-Muslims of monotheistic faiths were regarded as *diman*, the plural of *dhimmi*—an Islamic term meaning the "people of the pact of protection" and used in reference to People of the Book, namely, Jews and Christians. *Diman* had fewer legal rights than Muslims but were allowed to live in Muslim-ruled areas. Even though Jews were subjected to discriminatory legislation, their status improved dramatically over the next few centuries of Islamic rule in Spain. The period of stability in the region helped usher in what was seen as the golden age of Spain, a time of cultural diversity and intellectual openness; however, the tolerance that characterized the golden age came to an end with the arrival of the Almohads in the middle of the twelfth century, which coincided with the Christian reconquest of northern Spain. Maimonides was born in the late 1130s, about ten years before the beginning of Almohad rule. Such unfortunate timing had a tremendous impact on his entire life.

In his introduction to the *Mishneh Torah*, Maimonides explains that severe vicissitudes prevailed in his time, causing Jews to lose the ability to comprehend Talmudic literature properly. He bemoans the disappearance of the wisdom of wise men, quoting from the book of Isaiah, "And the wisdom of its wise shall fail /And the prudence of its prudent shall vanish" (29:14). Maimonides explains that because the current generation had low scholarly attainments, they were unable to understand the commentaries of the Geonim, the rabbinic scholars of the earlier generations who had written commentaries on various facets of the Talmud. Their writings, which they had taken care to present in a clear format, were now so difficult to understand that only a few could properly comprehend them.

If the current generation was unable to understand the commentaries, they were even less able to understand the Talmud itself. The Talmud is the written form of the Oral Law, which tradition explains was given to Moses by God at Mount Sinai, along with the Written Law. The Talmud consists of the Mishnah, brief statements compiling legal opinions, and the Gemara, transcripts of discussion on the Mishnah. The Mishnah organizes its material on the basis of subject matter rather than biblical context. It puts these subjects into six orders, each of which is divided into a number of subcategories. The Mishnah was redacted

Time Line

1137 or 1138
- **March 30** Moses ben Maimon, or Maimonides, is born in Córdoba, Spain.

1148
- The Almohads conquer Córdoba, resulting in the exodus of most of the Jewish community, including Maimonides' family.
- Maimonides begins his wanderings around southern Spain and North Africa, having difficulty finding a secure Jewish community in which to settle.

1160
- Maimonides settles in Fez, Morocco, where he remains for about five years.

1165
- **April 18** Maimonides and his family sail to the port of Acco (Acre) in the land of Israel before traveling on to Egypt.

1166
- Maimonides and his family finally settle in Fustat (now part of Old Cairo), Egypt, where they remain.

1169 or 1170
- Maimonides' younger brother David dies in a shipwreck on the way to India, forcing Maimonides to begin working as a physician in order to support David's family, as well as his own.

1170
- Maimonides starts the fourteen-volume *Mishneh Torah*.

1171
- Maimonides is appointed *nagid*, the prince or leader of the Egyptian Jewish community.

1180
- Maimonides completes the *Mishneh Torah*.

1204
- **December** Maimonides dies in Fustat, Egypt.

---

around the year 200 CE by Rabbi Judah the Prince, a controversial decision due to the fact that the Oral Law was intended to be transmitted verbally. In the three or four centuries following the redaction of the Oral Law into the Mishnah, sages working in both Babylonia and the land of Israel continued to discuss the issues presented in the Mishnah. The Jerusalem and Babylonian Talmuds had the same Mishnah but different Gemara.

About the Author

Moses ben Maimon, known as Maimonides, was the most distinguished of all medieval Jewish philosophers and is considered one of the greatest Torah scholars in history. Maimonides is his Greek name, the suffix "-ides" meaning "son of." His Hebrew name was Rabbi Moses ben Maimon; therefore, in rabbinic literature, he was known by the acronym Rambam. Maimonides' unmatched rabbinic learning earned him the title "the Great Eagle." He was also called the Mordecai of his generation because of his selfless involvement in the local Jewish community. Many praised him by citing the popular adage "from Moses to Moses, there arose no one like Moses."

Maimonides was born in Córdoba, Spain, in 1137 or 1138. Córdoba at the time was under enlightened Muslim rule, a cultural Mecca for Jews and Christians as well as Muslims. But the Almohads, an intolerant Muslim group that gave non-Muslims the choice of conversion or expulsion, conquered the area in 1148. Jews were attacked by rioters, and synagogues were destroyed. It is possible that Maimonides' family had to pretend to convert in order to avoid death. They fled from Córdoba, traveling around through southern Spain and North Africa for about ten years, settling for a time in Fez, Morocco.

Maimonides and his family continued their travels in search of a permanent home. In 1165 the Maimon family left Morocco for Acco in the land of Israel and the following year traveled overland to Fustat (now part of Old Cairo), Egypt. Trained as a medical doctor, Maimonides worked as physician to the sultan of Egypt and also tended to patients in his home. He wrote ten treatises on medicine, some of which were used as textbooks in medieval medical schools.

The Guide for the Perplexed, completed in 1190, was ostensibly a letter written to a student who was torn between his love of philosophy and the teachings of Judaism. In this Arabic work, Maimonides vigorously rejects a literal understanding of phrases that ascribe corporeality to God. Rather, he insists that the Torah spoke in the language of human beings and that the Torah did not intend to suggest that God has fingers, toes, or any other body parts. To argue otherwise, Maimonides stresses, is a material conception of God, which is idolatrous.

Maimonides became the most important rabbinic sage in the world after penning the *Mishneh Torah*. When he died in 1204, Egyptian Jews observed three full days of mourning, a sign of great respect. They ascribed the verse in the first book of Samuel to his life: "The ark of God has been taken" (I Samuel 4:11). Maimonides was buried in Tiberias, in the land of Israel.

Explanation and Analysis of the Document

The text from the *Mishneh Torah* is taken from *The Book of Knowledge*, the opening volume of Maimonides' fourteen-volume legal masterpiece. The initial chapters of each of the five treatises in the volume are reproduced here. Whereas much of the *Mishneh Torah* covers rather technical legal material, *The Book of Knowledge* explains the basic principles of the Jewish faith, proper behavior, the obligation to study Torah, the prohibition against idolatry, and the religious obligation to repent. These five treatises provide a window into the worldview of medieval Judaism.

Maimonides titled his book of religious law the *Mishneh Torah*, which means "repetition and summary of the Torah," because he intended to list all of the commandments in the Hebrew Bible. The commandments, called the *mitzvot* in Hebrew, are believed to have been given by God to Moses at Mount Sinai. The religious Jew is obligated to observe all 613 of them in their entirety. According to Talmudic tradition, 365 are negatives, and 248 are positives. A negative commandment is something one should not do, and a positive commandment is something one is obligated to do.

The *Mishneh Torah* includes an entire list of the commandments in the Torah, regardless of whether they could be observed at the time of the writing of the work. Because of the destruction of the Temple in Jerusalem by the Romans in the year 70 CE, many of the commandments relating to the functioning of the priests and the offering of sacrifices could no longer be observed. Maimonides nevertheless includes these commandments because his interest is not only in the practical observance of Jewish law in his day but also in a full understanding of Judaism in its entirety.

Maimonides
(Statue of Moses Maimonides (bronze), Spanish School / Plaza de Tiberiades, Cordoba, Spain / Ken Welsh / The Bridgeman Art Library International)

♦ **Treatise 1: The Foundation of the Torah**

Maimonides begins by listing the Ten Commandments, which are relevant to the category that he calls "The Foundation of the Torah." These are laws related to the belief in God and the proper relationship with Him. God is not a male figure, but Hebrew words are either masculine or feminine, and many of the references to God utilize the masculine form. Maimonides emphasized that God is incorporeal, meaning that God has no body.

Drawing heavily from Aristotle, Maimonides stresses that the foundation of wisdom is to understand that there is a primary reality that caused everything to be. That primary reality is God. If God did not exist, nothing else would have come into this world. On the other hand, God could exist even if nothing else did because God's existence is independent of the reality of any animate or inanimate objects. Maimonides then cites proof texts from various biblical sources, including "the Lord is the true God," from Jeremiah, and "there is no one like unto Him," from the book of Deuteronomy.

There are positive as well as negative commandments associated with the broad category of "The Foundation of the Torah." It is a positive to affirm that God exists, as it is written in the book of Exodus "I am the Lord thy God." It is a negative commandment to reject the belief that there are any other gods, as it is written in the book of Exodus "Thou shalt have no other gods before me." God is an absolute single unity, unlike other unities in the universe that may be divided into parts.

Maimonides emphasizes that God has no bodily form. He points out, however, that certain biblical references can be misunderstood quite easily, leading readers to believe that God has bodily parts. For example, in the book of Exodus, the Torah speaks of "under His feet," "written with the finger of God," and "the hand of the Lord." Maimonides explains in great depth that the Torah uses these images because it speaks to people in language they can understand; that is, these expressions are intended to be metaphorical rather than literal. Maimonides expands on the metaphorical nature of such statements in his philosophic work, *A Guide for the Perplexed*.

♦ **Treatise 2: Discernment**

In the second treatise, Maimonides discusses eleven commandments that relate to the religious obligation to imitate the ways of God. Maimonides begins this treatise with a discussion of the different personality types. Writing in the medieval period and using a language that has masculine and feminine forms, he phrases everything in the male form; nevertheless, the text can apply to women as well

Essential Quotes

> "The very foundation and firm support of all wisdom is to know that there is a primary reality which caused all to be; and that all that exists in heaven and earth and all between heaven and earth could not exist without the truth of this reality."

> "The right way is the middle path. It is found in all dispositions of man and is equally removed from both extremes and is not near to either. For this reason the ancient sages commanded that man should examine his inclinations continually, weigh them and direct them intentionally to the middle path in order to have a sound body."

> "Every Israelite has a duty to study whether he is poor or rich, whether healthy or suffering, whether young or very old and in failing strength, even if he is poor and supported by charity or begs from door to door. Even if he is a married man with a wife and children, it is a duty to set aside time to study, day and night, as the verse says: 'Thou shalt meditate therin day and night'."

> "[Abraham] broke the images and began to tell the people that it was proper to worship only the Lord of the Universe, to bow down to Him and to offer sacrifice and drink offerings so that all future creatures might recognise Him. It was proper to destroy and smash the idols so that the people should not err by them like those who think there is no god save images."

> "In these times when there is no Temple standing and we have no altar for atonement, there is nothing left but repentance. Repentance atones for all transgressions. Even one who has done evil all his days, if he repents, will have nothing of his wickedness held against him in the end."

as men. Among the examples he gives is that of the hotheaded man, who is always agitated, while the calm man remains serene in even the most unpleasant circumstances. One type of person displays arrogance, while another shows humility; one type of person is obsessed by ever-increasing desires, while another is satisfied with his lot in life.

Following Aristotle's view, Maimonides urges his readers to avoid the extremes in terms of disposition. Instead of allowing oneself to move too far in any one direction, one should try to remain on the path of the good, which is the middle path. As it is written in the book of Deuteronomy, "walk in His ways." By this, Maimonides suggests that we should try to imitate God. Just as God is called gracious, we should try to be gracious. Just as God is called merciful, we should try to be merciful. As the prophets explained, God is "slow to anger," "righteous," "upright," "perfect," "mighty," and "strong." The pedagogical purpose in listing these divine attributes is to make it known to people that these are the good paths, which it is the duty of all religious people to follow in order to be like God. All people can integrate these traits into their personalities by practicing them repeatedly until they become habitual and rooted in the soul. This is how Abraham had instructed his children to follow in the ways of God.

♦ **Treatise 3: The Study of the Torah**

There are only two commandments relating to the study of the Torah, both of them positive. Torah study was considered one of the most important religious acts that could be undertaken. Maimonides begins by stating that women, servants, and small children are excused from studying the Torah. This is a reference to the fact that these groups were exempt from performing positive, time-bound commandments because, owing to their domestic responsibilities, they might not be able to complete a specific religious act during a limited and specific time period. Anyone who might not be able to perform a given ritual act during the allotted interval would not be obliged to perform it. Furthermore, notes Maimonides, people are obligated to teach others only that which they are obligated to learn themselves; for this reason, women are not expected to teach the Torah to their children.

In contrast, a man is obligated to teach not only his child but also his grandchild, as it is written in the book of Deuteronomy "Teach them thy sons, and thy sons' sons." It is also a commandment for every scholar in Israel to teach anyone who seeks to learn. Maimonides explains that when the book of Deuteronomy states "and thou shalt teach them diligently unto thy children," the word *children* is understood to mean all students. Teachers are allowed to charge for their services. If a person has not been taught by his father and his father has not hired a tutor for him, then that person has the obligation to study the Torah on his own when he becomes an adult. Maimonides explains that learning is important not only for its own sake but also because study brings forth action. Nevertheless, the reverse is not the case—action does not lead to learning.

Maimonides states that one's own study takes precedence over one's child's study, unless the child is smarter than the parent. Even so, the adult is not allowed to give up studying entirely, because there is a commandment that remains valid.

A man should first study Torah extensively and only then marry. If he marries first, he is likely to become so preoccupied with earning a living and other duties related to his wife and children that he is unlikely to be able to concentrate. However, if he is so obsessed with sex that he cannot concentrate on his studies, then he should marry before trying to study the Torah.

When a child begins to speak, he should be taught two verses from the book of Deuteronomy, "Moses commanded us a law" and "Hear, O Israel." Subsequently, children should be taught additional verses according to their ability until they are six or seven years old, when they should be given over to a teacher.

Every Jew has the duty to study, whether they are rich or poor, healthy or sick. Every person has the duty to set aside time to study Torah, as it is written in the book of Joshua "Thou shalt meditate therein day and night." Maimonides reminds his readers that the ancient sages needed to work in order to support themselves and their families but even so studied day and night in order to pass on the oral tradition from Moses, the original teacher of the Jews.

Study time should be divided into three parts: one part for the written Torah, one part for the oral Torah, and a third part "to understand things completely." This third part of Torah study is the study of the Talmud, the transcripts of debates between the sages in which "the Torah is expounded until one grasps the principle of the rules." Maimonides gives an example of an artisan who works three hours each day and spends nine hours studying. Of these nine hours, he should study the written Torah for three and the oral Torah for three and "investigate his knowledge and understanding of matters one from another" for three.

A woman who studies the Torah receives a smaller reward than a man, because she is not under the obligation to study Torah. The sages did not require females to study Torah regularly because they understood that a woman might have to take care of her children or perform other vital household tasks that could not wait. Since women are not required to study Torah, they can do so on an optional basis rather than as a means of fulfilling a divine commandment.

A father should not teach his daughter the Torah because, according to Maimonides, most women do not have the capacity to apply themselves to learning. This statement must be understood in the context of Maimonides' time—the Middle Ages. Men and women had clearly definable roles in society in the twelfth century, and any deviation from those norms could result in scandal and crisis. However, while Maimonides urges fathers not to teach their daughters the written Torah, if they do, "there is no impropriety in that."

♦ **Treatise 4: Idolatry**

Maimonides lists no fewer than fifty-one commandments relating to idolatry, forty-nine of them negative. Judaism prohibits any form of idolatry, which is not limited to the worship of an idol itself but also could involve the worship of any artistic representation of God. The commandments listed in this treatise relate to the religious obligation to avoid following the ways of the worshippers of the stars who rejected the belief in one God. In *The Guide for the Perplexed*, Maimonides argues that the earliest idolaters did not believe that their idols were gods. Rather, they understood that their idols were only representations of God and that the idols were worshipped as an intermediary between God and humankind. Eventually, the existence of the one true God was forgotten, and people began to worship the idols as if they were actually gods.

Maimonides goes on to recount the history of idolatry. In the days of Enosh, Adam's grandson, people began to believe that because God made the stars and the planets to rule the universe, these stars and planets should be worshipped. They did not say that there was no God, so they were not atheists; nevertheless, the belief in the stars and planets as entities worthy of praise, glory, and honor in order to reach the will of the Creator is the basis of idolatry. Maimonides condemns this belief in the strongest possible terms.

Maimonides also explains that later, false prophets arose, who said that God had commanded them to serve a certain star or alternatively all of the stars. They brought offerings and built temples, making images to which people should bow down and worship. One prophet said that an image that he had invented was the form of a particular star that had been revealed to him by God. The idolaters made images in their temples coming together to worship these idols. The priests of the idolaters told people that by respecting and worshipping the idols they would prosper. Eventually, God was forgotten and people recognized only the idols that slowly took the place of the one God. Only a handful of individuals, such as Enosh, Methuselah, Noah, Shem, and Eber, continued to recognize the one true God. The vast majority of humankind went astray until the time of Abraham, who rediscovered the true God.

When Abraham was young, he pondered how it was possible for the universe to revolve without a driver to control it. He had no teacher who could help him understand monotheism because he was "sunk in Ur of the Chaldees among foolish idolaters." Even his father and mother worshipped the stars along with everyone else. And so Abraham followed in their ways at first. But he struggled to realize the divine truth and came to the realization that there must be one God and that God had to have created everything. There could be no other God except the one true God. This realization hit Abraham when he was forty years old. As soon as he understood this basic religious truth, he began to tell people that it was important to worship the one God of the universe. Idols were false gods and should be destroyed. Because of this advocacy, the local king tried to have him executed, and he escaped from Ur to Haran. There he began to proselytize, going from city to city until he reached Canaan. In Israel, the book of Genesis recounts, "Abraham called there on the name of the Lord, the everlasting God." His sons Isaac and Jacob continued his mission.

After the children of Israel went to Egypt, they relapsed into idolatry because of local influences. Only the tribe of Levi remained faithful to the commandments of their fathers, never engaging in idolatry. In order to reinforce the true religion, God chose Moses to convey the message of monotheism to the people of Israel. As Maimonides explained, when Moses prophesied, God chose the people of Israel for His inheritance and crowned them with the Commandments.

♦ **Treatise 5: Repentance**

This treatise explains one commandment, which is the positive injunction to repent. Repentance is the only way to atone for sin in the absence of the Jerusalem Temple.

If a person transgresses, breaking any of the positive or negative commandments of the Torah, he or she must repent. It does not matter whether this transgression was unintentional or intentional, the book of Numbers states that when a man or woman commits a sin of any type they shall confess what they have done. In the times of the Temple in Jerusalem, the transgressor would bring a sacrifice as part of this process. It is not enough to make restitution in money matters unless one has also confessed to one's wrongdoing and promised not to repeat such actions. In the case of a capital crime or a crime in which the person has been sentenced to receive lashings, the punishment itself does not absolve the person in the absence of confession and repentance.

A scapegoat is sent away to atone for all of Israel. As the book of Leviticus explains, Aaron shall designate all of the inequities of the children of Israel onto the scapegoat. This scapegoat therefore atones for all of the transgressions committed by the children of Israel whether minor or major, deliberate or accidental. Nevertheless, the actual sinner must repent as well in the case of major offenses.

In Maimonides' time, when there was no Temple left standing and "we have no altar for atonement," the only vehicle for being forgiven for transgressions was repentance. Repentance can atone for transgression if done in completely sincerity. Even a person who has been evil for many years will not have his wickedness held against him if he sincerely repents. As is written in the book of Ezekiel, "As for the wickedness of the wicked, he shall not fall thereby in the day that he turneth from his wickedness."

The Day of Atonement atones for those who repent, as the book of Leviticus makes clear: "For on that day shall the priest make an atonement for you." There are some transgressions that are atoned for immediately and others that are not forgiven until later. Maimonides concludes by listing specific circumstances that might have an impact on how and when the atonement process would be complete.

Audience

Maimonides was writing for rabbinic scholars as well as the average Jew. Since his *Mishneh Torah* was an explanation of the entire Torah, he envisioned it as an educational tool for all Jews throughout the world. Indeed, he hoped that any Jew who had mastered the written Torah and then the *Mishneh Torah* would never need to consult another work on religious law. While he aimed to explain the basic principles of Judaism, he wrote on a highly theoretical level that intended to transmit an esoteric doctrine not comprehensible to the common folk. He developed his philosophic approach to Judaism further in *The Guide for the Perplexed*.

Impact

The *Mishneh Torah* was a controversial work for a number of reasons. Some believed that Maimonides intended his work to supersede the Talmud, the authoritative collection of debates among the sages that recorded the Oral Law given by God to Moses at the same time as the Written Law. Since the *Mishneh Torah* included every decision rendered by the Talmud, it would therefore be theoretically unnecessary to continue to refer back to Talmudic literature. Critics felt this would undermine the entire culture of rabbinic study that had become the cornerstone of Jewish scholarship.

Maimonides was also attacked because he did not cite any of his sources. This made it impossible for other rabbis to check the validity of his decisions. Maimonides seemed to be telling other scholars they should accept his positions as authoritative simply because of his obvious brilliance. But those who opposed his positions on various issues wanted to be able to study his sources in order to potentially refute his arguments. Without sources, they were left in the dark. Rabbi Abraham ben David of Posquières wrote a gloss on the entire *Mishneh Torah*, harshly criticizing many of the Maimonidean positions.

Despite substantial opposition, the *Mishneh Torah* was regarded as the masterly summary of the Talmud and rabbinic thought up until Maimonides' times. While it did not become a definitive code or supplant the classic works of ancient Judaism, it did transform the nature of Jewish legal study. Some Jewish legal authorities argued that no legal decision could be made that opposed a Maimonidean position, even in cases where Maimonides seemed to go against the most obvious understanding of a Talmudic discussion. Even eight hundred years after its compilation, the *Mishneh Torah* continues to be one of the basic sources for the study of the Jewish tradition.

Further Reading

■ Books

Angel, Marc. *Maimonides, Spinoza and Us: Toward an Intellectually Vibrant Judaism*. Woodstock, N.Y.: Jewish Lights Publishing, 2009.

Davidson, Herbert A. *Moses Maimonides: The Man and His Works*. New York: Oxford University Press, 2004.

Davidson, Herbert A. *Maimonides the Rationalist*. Oxford, U.K.: Littman Library of Jewish Civilization, 2011.

Kellner, Menachem. *Maimonides' Confrontation with Mysticism*. Oxford, U.K.: Littman Library of Jewish Civilization, 2006.

Kraemer, Joel. *Maimonides: The Life and World of One of Civilization's Greatest Minds*. New York: Doubleday Religion, 2010.

Nuland, Sherwin. *Maimonides*. New York: Schocken, 2008.

Rudavsky, Tamar M. *Maimonides*. New York: Wiley-Blackwell, 2010.

Shapiro, Marc. *The Limits of Orthodox Theology: Maimonides' Thirteen Principles Reappraised*. Oxford, U.K.: Littman Library of Jewish Civilization, 2003.

Shapiro, Marc. *Studies in Maimonides and His Interpreters*. Scranton, Pa.: University of Scranton Press, 2008.

Stroumsa, Sarah. *Maimonides in His World: Portrait of a Mediterranean Thinker*. Princeton, N.J.: Princeton University Press, 2009.

■ Web Sites

Jacobs, Joseph, et al. "Moses Ben Maimon." JewishEncyclopedia.com.
http://www.jewishencyclopedia.com/

Seeskin, Kenneth. "Maimonides." Stanford Encyclopedia of Philosophy Web site.
http://plato.stanford.edu/archives/spr2010/entries/maimonides

—Dana Evan Kaplan

Questions for Further Study

1. What is the distinction between "written law" and "oral law" in Judaism? What is the source of each of these sets of laws? Why is the distinction important?

2. What historical and political events prompted Maimonides, in part, to write the *Mishneh Torah*?

3. What is the conception of God contained in the *Mishneh Torah*? Provide details. How does this conception of God differ from that contained in a document such as Thomas Aquinas's *Summa theologiae*.

4. Roughly a millennium earlier, the Sefer Yetzirah was an attempt to arrive at an understanding of the nature of God and creation. How does the conception of God and creation in that document contrast with that of the *Mishneh Torah*?

5. The entry states that the *Mishneh Torah* provides readers with a window into medieval Judaism. Explain what you "see through the window." How would you describe medieval Judaism based on your reading of the document?

Mishneh Torah

Treatise 1

THE FOUNDATION OF THE TORAH

The Laws concerning the foundations of the Torah are six positive and four negative, namely:

1. To know that there is a God.

2. Not to support that there is another.

3. To believe in His unity.

4. To love Him.

5. To fear Him.

6. To hallow His name.

7. Not to profane His name.

8. Not to destroy anything which bears His name.

9. To listen to a prophet who speaks in His name.

10. Not to test (tempt) Him.

♦ Chapter 1

1. The very foundation and firm support of all wisdom is to know that there is a primary reality which caused all to be; and that all that exists in heaven and earth and all between heaven and earth could not exist without the truth of this reality.

2. If He were not, nothing could have been called into existence.

3. On the other hand, if all other beings did not exist, He would remain; for His existence does not depend on theirs. He would not cease if they ceased—blessed be He! He is not dependent upon one of them. So the reality of His being is not comparable to the reality of any other existing thing.

4. This is what the prophet said, "the Lord is the true God" (Jeremiah 10:10), and the Torah states: "there is no one like unto Him," implying that He alone is the Truth and there is no other Truth like His Truth (Deuteronomy 4:39).

5. This reality is God of the universe and Lord of all the earth. He guides the celestial spheres with a might which is complete and unceasing, for the sphere turns continually which it could not do without a cause. The Blessed One turns it although He has no body or hand.

6. To understand this is the positive commandment which states: "I am the Lord thy God" (Exodus 20:2). Anyone who believes that there is another god violates the negative commandment which says: "Thou shalt have no other gods before me" (Exodus 20:3) for he denies the very principle upon which all depends.

7. God is one, neither two nor more, but a unity, unlike other unities in the universe which may have many parts or like a body which is divided into parts. So the unity of God is quite different from anything else in the world. If there were many deities it would mean that they had body and form because individuals only differ from one another in bodily form. If the Creator had a body and form He would have an end, a ceasing. It is impossible to imagine a body that does not end and whose strength does not wane. Our God—blessed be He!—has strength to which there is no end and does not falter because the sphere continues to revolve for ever by His force which is not a bodily force. Because He is incorporeal, none of the happenings which occur to parts of a body can be attributed to Him, so it is impossible that He should be but one. The understanding of monotheism is a positive commandment (Deuteronomy 6:4).

8. The Torah and the prophesies proclaim that the Holy One has no bodily form, for it is said: "He is Lord in heaven above and in earth beneath" (Deuteronomy 4:39) and a body cannot be in two places at once. Further on Sinai no bodily form was seen (Deuteronomy 4:15) and Isaiah said: "To whom then will ye liken me, or shall I be equal?" (Isaiah 40: 25).

Document Text

9. This being so, why were there allusions in the writings of the Torah to "under His feet" (Exodus 24:10); "written with the finger of God" (Exodus 31:18); "the hand of the Lord" (Exodus 9:3); "the eyes of the Lord" (Deuteronomy 11:12); "the ears of the Lord" (Numbers 11:18); and such like? All these expressions are related to the capacity of men who only understand material things, and the Torah spoke the language that men could understand. These sayings are all metaphorical. When it is said: "If I whet my glittering sword" (Deuteronomy 32:41), has He a sword and does He kill? All is allegorical. Elsewhere a prophet said that he saw the Holy One and that His "garment was white as snow" (Daniel 7:9); and another saw Him with dyed garments of Bozrah, (Isaiah 63:1). At the Red Sea, Moses our teacher saw the Lord as a "man of war" engaged in battle (Exodus 15:3); and upon Sinai clothed as a reader of the congregation (Exodus 19:19), meaning that He has no likeness or form. All these expressions are images and visions of the prophets. The truth is that the mind of man is not able to understand nor is he able to penetrate here, as the verse states: "Canst thou by searching find out the Almighty unto perfection?" (Job 11:7).

10. What did Moses our teacher want to understand when he asked: "I beseech thee, shew me thy glory" (Exodus 33: 18)? He sought to know in his heart the reality of the existence of the Holy One—blessed be He!—in the same way as he recognised individual persons whose appearance was engraved on his heart and distinguished from all others. So Moses our teacher wished to see in his mind the Holy One separated from all other creatures until he understood His reality as it is. The Blessed One answered that it is not in the power of living man, compounded of body and soul, to grasp that reality in its perfection. But the Holy One did make known to Moses what no one has known before or since; and he grasped the truth of a reality which was different from all other things, in the same way as one can recognise by body and clothes someone whom one sees from behind and can recognise as different from other men. The verse which suggests this states: "and thou shalt see my back parts: but my face shall not be seen" (Exodus 33:23).

11. Since it is clear that the Holy One has neither body nor form, it is also clear that nothing that happens to bodies can happen to Him, no joining or dividing, no position or measure, no ascent or descent, no right or left, no front or back, no sitting or standing. As He is not influenced by time, He has no beginning or end or any measure in years, nor does He change for there is nothing changeable in Him. There is no death or life in Him as in living bodies; no folly or wisdom such as are found in man. He neither sleeps nor wakens, is neither angry nor laughs, does not rejoice or grieve, has no silence or speech like the speech of man. The sages said also that in Heaven there was no sitting, no standing, no competition or weariness.

12. Because of this all the descriptions of the Holy One in the Torah, and those uttered by the prophets, are merely metaphorical and figurative. For example, it states: "He that sitteth in the heavens shall laugh" (Psalm 2:4), "they have provoked me to anger" (Deuteronomy 32:21), "the Lord rejoiced" (Deuteronomy 28:63), and the like. The sages said that the Torah is written in the speech of ordinary men. It is also written, "do they provoke me to anger?" (Jeremiah 7:19), and "I am the Lord, I change not" (Malachi 3:6). If the Holy One was sometimes angry and sometimes mirthful, he would be subject to change for such attributes are only found in dark and lowly bodies dwelling in houses of clay, made of dust. But the Holy One—blessed be He!—is exalted above all that.

Treatise 2

DISCERNMENT

In this treatise, eleven commandments (five positive and six negative) are listed and explained.

1. To imitate the ways of the Lord.

2. To keep close to those who have knowledge of Him.

3. To love neighbours.

4. To love strangers.

5. Not to hate neighbours.

6. To rebuke a wrongdoer.

7. Not to put anyone to shame.

8. Not to humiliate the unfortunate.

9. Not to be a tale bearer.

10. Not to take revenge.

11. Not to bear a grudge.

♦ **Chapter 1**

1. There are many widely different temperaments among the children of men. There is the hot tempered man who is always angry and the calm man, serene in disposition who is never angry, or if he shows anger, it is only a little anger in many years. One man is arrogant, another quite humble; one is obsessed by desire and never satisfied, another so pure in heart that he does not even long for the few needs of the body. There is the greedy man who would never be satisfied with all the wealth in the world, as the saying goes "He that loveth silver shall not be satisfied with silver" (Ecclesiastes 5:10). Another shortens his life because he is satisfied with the little which is insufficient for his needs and will not look for or try to get what he needs. One will mortify himself to starvation, hoard everything and will not eat a pennyworth without pain to himself, while another scatters his goods as he fancies. So it is with all the temperaments, for example, cheerfulness and gloom, miserliness and generosity, cruelty and kindness, timidity and courage, and so on.

2. Between all these extremes there are intermediate degrees which differ from each other. There are some dispositions which are inborn in man and depend upon the nature of his body and these predispose him to certain temperaments. Others are not inherited but are learned from other men or selected because of some ideas in the heart, or because a man has heard that this trend would be good for him, and he thinks it proper, and he conducts himself accordingly until it is fixed in his heart.

3. The two opposite extremes in all dispositions are not the good way, and it is not fitting for a man to follow them or to be instructed in them. If a man finds his nature tending towards one of them, or ready for one of them, or has already learned it, and conducts himself accordingly he turns himself towards goodness and goes along the path of the good which is the straight path.

4. The right way is the middle path. It is found in all dispositions of man and is equally removed from both extremes and is not near to either. For this reason the ancient sages commanded that man should examine his inclinations continually, weigh them and direct them intentionally to the middle path in order to have a sound body. For example, one ought not to be a hot tempered man and given to anger, nor without feeling like the dead, but between the two, not becoming enraged except in a great matter when anger is needed to prevent something happening again. So also he should only crave for what the body requires and cannot live without, as was said: "The righteous eateth to the satisfying of his soul" (Proverbs 13:25). Likewise he ought not to toil at his business but acquire what is necessary for life from day to day, as the saying goes: "A little that a righteous man hath is better than the riches of many wicked" (Psalm 37:16). He ought not to be too tight-fisted nor squander his money but give charity within his means and lend to one in need. He should not be always cheerful and laughing nor distressed and mournful, but should be glad all his days in moderation, and receive all men with a friendly countenance. So should it be with all the different dispositions for that is the path of wise men. Men of equanimity are called wise.

5. The man who is excessively critical of himself and leaves the middle path, tending towards one extreme or another, is called pious. For example, one who abandons arrogance and goes to the other extreme of humility is called pious, for that is the character of piety. If one keeps in the middle path and is also humble, one is called wise for that is the characteristic of wisdom. This applies in all dispositions. The ancient pious men turned from the mean towards the two extremes, some leaning towards piety others towards wisdom more than is demanded by the Law. We however are required to go in the middle paths for they are good and straight, as was said: "walk in His ways" (Deuteronomy 28:9).

6. Concerning this command the teaching was thus; even as God is called gracious, be thou gracious; even as He is called merciful, be thou merciful; even as He is called holy, be thou holy. In this way the prophets gave attributes to God such as "slow to anger," "of great mercy," "righteous," "upright," "perfect," "mighty," and "strong" and so on, in order to make known that these are

Document Text

the good and straight paths which it is the duty of a man to follow and so to be like the Lord, as far as he is able.

7. How does a man accustom himself to these dispositions until they are fixed in him? He should do once, twice and thrice the things that belong to the middle path and repeat them until they become easy for him and need no effort. Then they become rooted in his soul. Because these attributes are applied to the Creator and are the middle way which we must follow, they are called the Lord's way. This was how Abraham had instructed his children when the Lord said: "I know him, that he will command his children and his household after him, and they shall keep the way of the Lord" (Genesis 18:19). He who follows this way brings well being and blessing to himself, so "that the Lord may bring upon Abraham that which he hath spoken of him" (Genesis 18:19).

Treatise 3

THE STUDY OF THE TORAH

Two positive commandments are contained in this Treatise and they are:

(a) To study the Torah.

(b) To honour those who study and understand it.

◆ **Chapter 1**

1. Women, servants and small children are excused from studying but the father of a little boy is obliged to teach him the Torah, as the verse says: "And ye shall teach them your children, speaking of them" (Deuteronomy 11:19). A woman is not obliged to teach her child, for only those whose duty it is to study have a duty to teach.

2. Just as a man has a duty to teach his child, he has a duty to teach his grandchild, as the verse says: Teach them thy sons, and thy sons' sons" (Deuteronomy 4:9), and not only his children and grandchildren. For it is a command that every scholar in Israel should teach those who seek learning, even although they are not his children. The verse says: "And thou shalt teach them diligently unto thy children" (Deuteronomy 6:7). By tradition pupils are also called children. The verse in 2 Kings 2:3 says: "And the sons of the prophets … came forth" (meaning pupils). Why then is one commanded to teach children and grandchildren? In order to attend to one's children before grandchildren, and grandchildren before the children of one's friends.

3. It is a duty to hire a teacher to teach one's child but it is not a duty to teach a friend's child for nothing. Anyone not taught by his father must educate himself when he becomes mature. The verse in Deuteronomy 5:1 says: "That ye may learn them, and keep, and do them." Generally speaking, one finds that learning leads to action, for study brings forth action, but action does not lead to learning.

4. If one is anxious to study Torah and has a son studying, one's own study comes before the son's. If the son is the cleverer and the more able to understand what he learns, the son comes first. However, although the son comes first, one may not give up study because the same command to teach the son applies to teaching oneself.

5. A man should study first and then marry. If he marries first, his mind is not free to study, but if he finds his desire overcomes him and his mind is not free, he should marry and study Torah afterwards.

6. At what age is it a father's duty to teach the Torah? When the child begins to speak, he should be taught two verses: "Moses commanded us a law" (Deuteronomy 33:4) and "Hear, O Israel" (Deuteronomy 6:4). After that the child should be taught little by little, verse by verse, according to his development, until he is six or seven years old, and then he should be put under a children's teacher.

7. If it is the custom in the region to hire a children's teacher, this must be done, and it is a duty to pay until the child can read the whole written law. In a place where it is customary to teach the written Torah for reward, it is permitted to take pay, but it is forbidden to teach the oral tradition for pay. The verse says: "Behold, I have taught you statutes and judgments, even as the Lord my God commanded me" (Deuteronomy 4:5), meaning, "what I learned for nothing so you must teach for nothing what came from me," likewise, "when you teach the next generations, teach them for nothing as you were taught by me." If no man can be found to teach without payment, teaching must be paid for, as the verse says: "Buy the truth" (Proverbs

23:23). Can he therefore teach for nothing? The same verse says: "sell it not." Learn from this that it is forbidden to teach the oral law for hire although your teacher did so.

8. Every Israelite has a duty to study whether he is poor or rich, whether healthy or suffering, whether young or very old and in failing strength, even if he is poor and supported by charity or begs from door to door. Even if he is a married man with a wife and children, it is a duty to set aside time to study, day and night, as the verse says: "Thou shalt meditate therein day and night" (Joshua 1:8).

9. Among the great scholars of Israel some were hewers of wood and drawers of water, and some were blind, but in spite of that they studied by day and night. They were of those who passed on the verbal tradition from mouth to mouth from Moses our teacher.

10. For how long is it a duty to study the Law? To the day of death. The verse says: "Lest they depart from thy heart all the days of thy life" (Deuteronomy 4:9). When one does not study one forgets.

11. It is a duty to divide the time for study into three parts, one third for the written word, one third for the oral tradition and one third to understand things completely, and deduce one from another, and to compare one thing with another, and to know the rules by which the Torah is expounded until one grasps the principle of the rules and knows which things are forbidden, which are permitted and which are learned by tradition. This study is known as Gemara.

12. To give an example, an artisan busies himself with his work for three hours each day and spends nine hours in study. Of the nine hours, for three he ought to study the written law, for three the oral law and for three investigate his knowledge and understanding of matters one from another. Traditional matters are included in the Holy Writ and their explanations are in the oral law. The subjects relating to the *Pardes* are in the *Gemara* generally. When do these rules apply? When a man begins to study. When he has acquired knowledge he has no need to study the Holy Writ or to busy himself with the oral tradition, and he should then read the written law and oral law at fixed times (so that he may not forget any of the laws of the Torah) and turn every day to the *Gemara* according to the capacity of his heart and the equanimity of his mind.

13. A woman who studies the Torah has a reward but not the reward of a man because she is not commanded to do it. One who does something which is not mandatory has not the reward of one who obeys a command, but a smaller reward. Although she has a reward, the sages commanded that a man should not teach his daughter the Torah because most women have not the capacity to apply themselves to learning; they change the matters of the Torah into nonsense because of their poor understanding. The sages said of anyone who taught his daughter the Torah that it was as if he taught indecency and, according to tradition, this applies to teaching of the oral law. As regards the written Torah, he should not start to teach her at all, but, if he does, there is no impropriety in that.

Treatise 4

IDOLATRY

Fifty-one commandments, two positive and forty-nine negative, are enumerated here. They are:

1. Not to follow idolaters (worshippers of the stars).

2. Not to follow evil thoughts and sights of the eyes.

3. Not to blaspheme.

4. Not to worship idols in the customary way.

5. Not to bow down to them.

6. Not to make a graven image for oneself.

7. Not to make a graven image for another.

8. Not to make any image even for its beauty.

9. Not to entice others to serve it.

10. To burn an idolatrous city.

11. Not to rebuild it.

12. Not to benefit from any of its wealth.
13. Not to entice anyone to serve an idol.
14. Not to love an enticer.
15. Not to stop hating an idolater.
16. Not to save him.
17. Not to plead for him.
18. Not to refrain from testifying against him.
19. Not to prophesy in the name of idolatry.
20. Not to listen to such prophesy.
21. Not to prophesy falsely even in the name of the Lord.
22. Not to fear to destroy a false prophet.
23. Not to swear in the name of idolatry.
24. Not to practise necromancy.
25. Not to practise sorcery.
26. Not to sacrifice to Moloch (burning first born in sacrifice).
27. Not to set up a pillar.
28. Not to bow down to a figure made of stone.
29. Not to plant a grove.
30. To destroy idols and their belongings.
31. Not to benefit from idol worship and its belongings.
32. Not to enjoy their plated ornaments.
33. Not to make a covenant with idolaters.
34. Not to show them favours.
35. Not to let them dwell in our land.
36. Not to follow their customs or dress.
37. Not to practise witchcraft.
38. Not to practise divination.
39. Not to practise augury.
40. Not to practise enchantment.
41. Not to seek the spirits of the dead.
42. Not to consult those who practice spiritualism.
43. Not to consult augurers.
44. Not to practise magic.
45. Not to round off the side curls of the head.
46. Not to destroy the corners of the beard.
47. Man shall not adorn himself in women's clothes.
48. A woman shall not adorn herself in armour or the clothes of a man.
49. Not to practise tattooing.
50. Not to lacerate oneself.
51. Not to tear one's hair for the dead.

An elucidation of all these commandments is given in the following chapters.

♦ **Chapter 1**

1. In the days of Enosh the children of mankind erred grievously and rejected the advice of the wise men of that generation, and Enosh himself suffered from that. Their mistake was to say that "because God made the stars and planets to rule the universe and placed them on high to share honour with them, for they are ministers who render service in His presence, they are worthy of praise, glory and honour." They also said that, "It is the will of God—blessed be He—to exalt and honour what He exalted and honoured, just as a king desires to honour those who stand before him: such is the prerogative of a king." When this idea arose in their hearts, they began to build temples, to offer sacrifices, and to praise and glorify them in words. Because of a wrong belief they bowed down before the stars in order to reach the will of the Creator. This is the basis of idolatry and was the verbal tradition of the worshippers who

knew its origin. They did not say that there was no god except one special star. Jeremiah said: "Who would not fear Thee, O King of nations? for to Thee doth it appertain … there is none like unto Thee. But they are altogether brutish and foolish; the stock is a doctrine of vanities" (Jeremiah 10:7–8), meaning "All know that Thou art alone, but by mistakes and folly they think that vanity is Thy will."

2. After a long time there arose among the children of men false prophets who said that God had commanded them to serve such and such a star, or all the stars. They brought offerings and libations to drink in certain quantities, built a temple and made an image for all the people, men, women and children to bow down before it. A prophet made it known that an image, which he had invented in his heart, was the form of a particular star, revealed to him in prophecy. In this way, they began to make images in the temples and under groves, and on the hill tops and high places where they congregated and bowed down. The people were told that "this image did good or evil and was worthy of worship and awe." The priests said to them that by "such service you will prosper and have good fortune, so do so and so, or don't do so and so." Then other deceivers arose who said that the star itself, or the planet or messenger had spoken with them and told them to serve the idol and to worship it by doing one thing and not another. The service of images by different ceremonies with sacrifice and bowing down before them spread throughout the world. After a long time the great and awful Name was forgotten and the people, men, women and children, only recognised an image of wood or stone and the temple of stone which they had been brought up from infancy to serve by bowing down, and by swearing by its name. The wise men among them, the priests and such like, thought that there was no god except the stars and planets whose images were made in their likenesses. So the Rock of the universe had no one to recognise Him except solitary persons like Enosh, Methuselah, Noah, Shem and Eber. Thus the world continued to revolve until a pillar of the world was born—Abraham, our father.

3. When this mighty one grew up, he began to think hard. Even when young, he thought by day and night and wondered how it was possible for the universe to revolve without a driver to turn it, for it was impossible for it to do that by itself. He had no teacher or instruction in the matter, for he was sunk in Ur of the Chaldees among foolish idolaters. His father and mother and all the people worshipped the stars, and he worshipped with them. His heart struggled to reach the way of Truth and to understand the correct line of thought. He realised that there was one God who led the planets and that He had created all and that there was no other god except Him. He knew that all were mistaken and that what caused them to err was worship of the images which drove the Truth out of their minds. Abraham was forty years old when he recognised his Creator and, as soon as he recognised and understood, he began to think of changing the sons of Ur of the Chaldees to spread judgment among them and to teach that theirs was not the way of truth. He broke the images and began to tell the people that it was proper to worship only the Lord of the Universe, to bow down to Him and to offer sacrifice and drink offerings so that all future creatures might recognise Him. It was proper to destroy and smash the idols so that the people should not err by them like those who think there is no god save images. When he had won them by his evidence, the king sought to kill him and by a miracle he escaped to Haran. There he stood up and made known to all that there was one God in the Universe who should be served and whom he proclaimed. He went forward from city to city and from country to country until he reached the land of Canaan and proclaimed the Name of the Lord, as the verse states: "Abraham called there on the name of the Lord, the everlasting God" (Genesis 21:33). When the people collected round him and questioned him about his words, he explained to each according to his intelligence until he turned them to the way of Truth. Thousands and tens of thousands gathered and became Abraham's household and he planted in their hearts this great principle. He wrote books and taught Isaac his son, and Isaac taught and advised and instructed his son, Jacob, and made him a teacher. Jacob our father taught all his children and appointed Levi head of the school of learning—to teach the way of the Lord and to fulfil Abraham's commands. Jacob commanded his children not to cease continual support for the Levites so that learning might not be forgotten. So the movement advanced in strength among the sons of Jacob and their associates so that a people arose who knew the Lord. When the children of

Israel had spent a long time in Egypt they relapsed into idolatry from local customs. But the tribe of Levi remained faithful to the commandments of their fathers and were never idolaters. Soon the root which Abraham had planted would have been uprooted and the children of Jacob would have returned to the errors of the world but for the love of the Lord for us. To maintain the oath with Abraham He appointed Moses, our master, as lord of all the prophets and made him His messenger. When Moses our teacher prophesied, the Lord chose the people of Israel for His inheritance and crowned them with the commandments. He made known to them the way of His service and what would be the judgment against idolatry and all its erring followers.

Treatise 5

REPENTANCE

This deals with one positive commandment that the sinner shall repent of his guilt and confess it before the Lord. The explanation of this command and the principles related to it are given in this treatise.

♦ Chapter 1

1. If a man transgresses one of the positive or negative commands of the Torah, whether intentionally or by mistake, when he repents and turns back from the sin it is a duty to confess before the Lord—blessed be He! The verse states: "When a man or woman shall commit any sin … they shall confess their sin which they have done" (Numbers 5: 6,7) and this is a confession in words and the confession is a positive command. How is it done? The sinner says: "I beseech Thee Great Name, I have sinned. I have been perverse and transgressed before thee, I have done so and so. Now behold. I repent and am ashamed of my deed and I shall not repeat it again." This is the fundamental form of confession. Whoever elaborates his confession and prolongs it is praiseworthy. But the transgressor or guilty one when bringing sacrifices for mistakes or deliberate misdeeds will not be pardoned by a sacrifice until he repents and confesses in words, as the verse says: "he shall confess that he hath sinned" (Leviticus 5:5). Also all under sentence of death from the *Beth Din* and those sentenced to lashings do not atone by death or the lashing unless they repent and confess. Anyone who injures his fellow man or damages him in money matters, even if he makes recompence for what is due, does not have atonement until he has confessed and turned from such doings for ever. As the verse states: Any sin that men commit … they shall confess their sin which they have done" (Numbers 5:6,7).

2. The scapegoat because it is sent away atones for the sins of all Israel. The High Priest confesses over it for the whole of Israel. As the verse says: Aaron shall … confess him all the iniquities of the children of Israel" (Leviticus 16:21). The scapegoat atones for all the transgressions mentioned in the Torah, the minor and major, the deliberate or accidental and whether done knowingly or in ignorance. The goat atones for all who repent, but if the sinner does not repent, the goat only atones for minor offences. What are minor and major transgressions? The major sins are those which carry the death penalty of the *Beth Din* or *karet*. False swearing, although it does not imply *karet*, is a major sin. All other negative and positive commands which do not involve *karet* are minor.

3. In these times when there is no Temple standing and we have no altar for atonement, there is nothing left but repentance. Repentance atones for all transgressions. Even one who has done evil all his days, if he repents, will have nothing of his wickedness held against him in the end. The verse says: "As for the wickedness of the wicked, he shall not fall thereby in the day that he turneth from his wickedness" (Ezekiel 33:12). The Day of Atonement (Yom Kippur) itself atones for those who repent, even as the verse states: "For on that day shall the priest make an atonement for you" (Leviticus 16:30).

4. Although repentance atones for everything and the Day of Atonement itself atones, there are some transgressions which are atoned for at once and there are others which are not forgiven for some time. For example, if a man sins against a positive commandment which does not carry *karet* and he repents, he is forgiven straight away; of such the verse says: "Return ye backsliding children, and I will heal your backslidings" (Jeremiah 3:22). If he transgresses a negative command which does not deserve *karet* or the death penalty of the *Beth Din* and he repents, it is suspended till the Day of Atonement pardons; of such the verse says: "For on that

Document Text

day shall the priest make an atonement for you" (Leviticus 16:30). If he sinned and deserved *karet* or execution from the *Beth Din*, repentance and the Day of Atonement suspends them and the sufferings which follow for him complete the atonement. Forgiveness and atonement are not complete until suffering comes to him; of such it is said: "Then will I visit their transgressions with the rod, and their iniquity with stripes" (Psalm 89:32). When does this apply? To one who does not profane the Holy Name when he has sinned. But he who blasphemed the Holy Name, even if he repented and was still penitent on the Day of Atonement and suffering came to him, is not completely forgiven until his death. Repentance and the Day of Atonement and suffering may suspend judgment but only death atones, as the verse says: "Surely this iniquity shall not be purged from you till ye die" (Isaiah 22:14).

Glossary

Beth Din	a rabbinical court
Bozrah	an ancient city in Edom, or modern-day Jordan
Canaan	the ancient name for the region that encompasses modern-day Israel, Lebanon, and the Palestinian territories
Enosh	often spelled Enos, the first son of Seth, mentioned in the book of Genesis as one of Adam's descendants
Gemara	one of the early records of the oral tradition of the Torah
Haran	an ancient Assyrian city where Abraham lived part of his life
Isaac	Abraham's son and the father of Jacob
Jacob	Isaac's son and the father of the Twelve Tribes of Israel
karet	literally "excision," or the cutting of the soul, which causes premature earthly death and a severing of the soul's connection with God
Levi	one of Jacob's twelve sons and the progenitor of the tribe of Israel, which gave Israel its priests
Methuselah, Noah, Shem and Eber	figures in the biblical listing of generations descended from Adam
Moses	the biblical patriarch who led the Jewish people out of slavery in Egypt to Mount Sinai, where he received the Written Law (the Ten Commandments) and the Oral Law
Pardes	exposition of the Torah in rabbinical Judaism
Torah	the first five books of the Hebrew Bible, commonly referred to as the Old Testament in Christianity: Genesis, Exodus, Leviticus, Numbers, and Deuteronomy
Ur of the Chaldees	an ancient biblical city whose location remains the subject of dispute

The creation of Adam through the breath of God
(The Creation of Adam (mosaic), Italian School, (12th century) / Palatine Chapel, Palermo, Sicily, Italy / Alinari / The Bridgeman Art Library International)

Book of the Bee

ca. 1200 –1300

"No one who does not obtain remission (of sins) in this world can be free from the penalty of examination in that day."

Overview

The Book of the Bee was written in the thirteenth century CE by the Nestorian Christian bishop Solomon (Shelemon), a metropolitan bishop of Basra (al-Basrah), in what is now Iraq. Bishop Solomon wrote the Book of the Bee during the Pax Mongolica, the era when the Mongols' four great khanates stretched from China to Persia and into eastern Europe, controlling the Silk Road and ruling vast lands that were home to many of the world's religions. During this time, the learned Nestorians occupied many administrative positions within the Mongol Empire, enjoying a time of relative peace for their church. As a general history spanning the time before Creation to Judgment Day, the Book of the Bee represents Bishop Solomon's commentary on elements of the Old and New Testaments as well as theological speculations on such matters as good and evil and the afterlife.

The Book of the Bee actually raises more theological and philosophical questions than it answers, as readers can find a multitude of seemingly contradictory statements. However, the bishop's purpose was to recount earlier discussions held with his friend and peer, not necessarily to provide definitive answers to these questions. The book evokes the highly symbolic nature of Catholicism and serves as a record of the historical circumstances from which the Nestorian Church evolved in the Near East.

Context

The Nestorian Church, also called the Church of the East, has its origins in the first century after the Crucifixion of Jesus. After the visitation of the Holy Spirit upon Jesus's apostles on Pentecost, several of the apostles, including Thomas, Bartholomew, and Andrew—along with perhaps many of the Persian Jews converted at the event—are believed to have spread the gospel not just to the Roman Empire but as far as the Persian Empire to the east and beyond to India and Central Asia.

Nestorius, a monk from Antioch, was elected patriarch of Constantinople in 428. Nestorius's beliefs were influenced by previous fathers of Antiochene theology, who believed that Christ had two natures, human and divine, and that human nature was the subject of Jesus's suffering on earth, thus keeping the divine nature (Logos) from being diminished. Thus, Jesus, perfect and complete as human, is consubstantial with God, perfect and complete in divinity; the two are united as one person. Accordingly, the Nestorian formula for the nature of Christ held that there are two real natures united in a single person without confusion or change. In the ensuing theological and political rivalries of the time, Nestorius's beliefs were deemed heretical, and he was exiled to Egypt. The Church of the East, however, eventually adopted his theology, setting it at odds with the Catholic Church in Rome.

The Nestorian Church, with its home originally in Syria, used the Syriac language—the Christian name for Aramaic—throughout its history. Unlike the Catholic Church in Rome, it was never to become the state religion of any particular empire. Under a variety of rulers to include Persians (who favored Zoroastrianism) and Muslims, the Nestorian Church, while usually occupying a respected position because of its learning and tax revenues, was often viewed with suspicion, particularly after Rome adopted Christianity as its state religion. This resulted in periods of persecution, sometimes entailing hundreds of thousands of deaths. In India, where the apostle Thomas established churches in both the northern and southern parts of the subcontinent, Christianity became a permanent, though minority, feature of the overwhelmingly Hindu urban areas. In the millennium after the fall of Rome in the West, the Nestorian missionary effort would take the church south to the Arabian Peninsula and east to China, where thriving Nestorian communities remained well into the thirteenth century.

For much of its history, the Nestorian Church was more highly organized and had a much greater membership than either the Roman or Greek Orthodox churches of the West. The Nestorian Church was noted for its theological and medicinal studies. Nestorians worked with Muslim scholars to translate Greek and Roman learning into Arabic and were often found in positions of power, including as court officials and physicians to the caliphs. The church spread farther eastward through the efforts of monks, traders, and artisans, and monasteries

Time Line

150	The earliest Christians are living in Edessa, a region that is now part of Turkey.
196	Christian communities are established in the Persian Empire.
252	The Sassanid Dynasty assumes power in the Persian Empire.
313	Constantine issues the Edict of Toleration, which legalizes Christianity in the Roman Empire.
340	The Sassanids begin persecution of the Persian Church, which lasts until early in the next century.
428	Nestorius is ordained patriarch of Constantinople.
431	Nestorius is condemned as a heretic by the Third Ecumenical Council of Ephesus.
636	The armies of Islam begin to conquer the Middle East and North Africa.
850	The Abbasid Dynasty removes the Nestorian patriarch and begins to persecute Christians.
CA. 1200–1300	The Book of the Bee is written by Mar Shelemon, or Bishop Solomon, of Basra.
1258–1401	The Mongols effectively rule over Persia (Il-Khanate).

were established in episcopal sees along with schools, libraries, and hospitals.

With the Mongol conquest of the Islamic Persian Empire in the thirteenth century, the Church of the East found itself in a favorable situation. The Nestorians flourished among the religiously tolerant Mongols, whose empire reached from China to Persia. During the Mongols' reign, as with the caliphs, Nestorians found themselves installed in positions of administration and as physicians to the various khans. At perhaps its height in the late thirteenth century, the Church of the East boasted metropolitan sees throughout Asia, including the Middle East, India, Turkestan, and China, and had churches as far away as Siberia and possibly Korea, Japan, and Southeast Asia. It was around this time that Bishop Solomon wrote the Book of the Bee.

About the Author

Not much is known about the author, Mar Shelemon, or Bishop Solomon. He was a native of Akhlât, in Armenia, and was the Nestorian metropolitan bishop of Basra in the thirteenth century CE. He was present at the consecration of the Nestorian patriarch Sabrisho' IV bar Qayyoma, who as patriarch bore the title of "Catholicos," in 1222. In catalogs of ecclesiastical works he is stated to have written, besides the Book of the Bee, a treatise on the heavens and the earth, various short discourses, prayers, and poems.

Explanation and Analysis of the Document

The Book of the Bee contains an introduction with an apology and sixty chapters, most of which are twenty-five lines or fewer in length. The purpose of the book, as noted by the author, is to provide information gleaned from the Old and New Testaments "concerning God's dispensation in the two worlds." The chapters generally follow the chronology of the Christian Bible with some diversions as well as theological discussions concerning the nature of the afterlife and Judgment Day. As a trained scholar, Bishop Solomon uses many sources outside the Christian Bible in constructing his arguments. The excerpted chapters provide a sense of the Nestorian viewpoint at a time when Christian theological discussion was mature with centuries of discourse, not only within the Church of the East but also with the Roman and Greek churches, Judaism, Islam, and to a lesser extent Asian religions. Wording in parentheses are the editor's clarifications of the text.

♦ **Introduction and Apology**

The apology to the Book of the Bee contains information regarding the author and the book's purpose and a discussion of why and how religious texts are studied. The author, Bishop Solomon, indicates that he is writing to a lifelong friend as a means of summarizing their theological discussions. Solomon uses both the Christian Bible and the teachings of "the Fathers and the Doctors" to formulate his discourses. In a fascinating metaphor, he describes the process of building religious arguments as equivalent to the life of a bee. Just as the bee goes from source to source to gather pollen and then turns it into honey and wax, so, too, has Bishop Solomon drawn on various sources to form a worldly foundation and a spiritual roof for his arguments. He then shifts the metaphor to relate theological research to the work of a gardener who plants and tends his garden. The author warns that if the fruits of his garden are too few,

Nestorian basilica in Basra
(The Basilica at Bosra [photo], / Bosra, Syria / © Julian Chichester / The Bridgeman Art Library International)

then the visitor should seek out the roots to be further satisfied, thus enjoining the reader to go to the source material to inquire further if his explanations seem inadequate. As a final warning, Solomon notes that just as eating too much honey can cause one to vomit, delving too far into the meaning of sacred texts robs them of their sweetness, implying that one can also "vomit" up one's beliefs.

♦ Creation

Bishop Solomon's initial commentaries expound upon elements of the creation story found in Genesis. In chapter 1, he notes that there was no single time when God thought of creating the universe, that it was always in his mind, an image reinforcing the eternal nature of God. Humans have seniority over the other species of the world because the idea of the human being was thought of first in the mind of God, even though the other creatures were created first. And while the other creatures were created by God in the silence of the universe with a spoken word, Adam was formed directly by God's hands, and it was the actual breath of God that infused life into him, making Adam a living soul with knowledge of good and evil. This makes the human body a temple for God to dwell in, a position very close to other religious views that the soul or spark of the human being's nature is part of the divine. When Adam perceived that he was a created being and that there was a creator, the idea of God formed in his mind—an awareness very similar to what the angels experienced (as noted in chapter 7).

In chapters 2 and 3, the bishop comments on the nature of the divine power to create the universe. The original substances from which the universe is formed were created strictly through the will of God; heaven, the elements, the angels, and darkness came into being from nothingness. Each of these substances was separate, with unformed earth under the waters, air above the waters, and fire above the atmosphere, and with each described using the fundamental concepts of hot, cold, moist, and dry. The bishop refutes the notion that the "Spirit" mentioned in Genesis 1:2 refers to the Holy Spirit, insisting it refers only to the air.

Where Genesis does not mention angelic beings in its opening chapters, chapters 5 and 7 of the Book of the Bee, discussing angels, are based on tradition and learning carried down through the centuries since even before the birth of Jesus. Bishop Solomon's discourse mirrors the angelic hierarchies of the Catholic Church and can be compared to discussions of angels found in Judaism, Islam, and Zoroastrianism, of which the author would have been well aware. The angels are in the presence of God and perform services for God based on their class. The lower order, the Principalities, Archangels, and Angels, are "ministers who wait upon

Essential Quotes

> "'When thou findest honey, eat (only) so much as is sufficient for thee, lest, when thou art sated, thou vomit it;' that is to say, do not enquire (too closely) into the divine words."

> "As the natural child in the womb of his mother knows not her who bears him, nor is conscious of his father, who, after God, is the cause of his formation; so also Adam, being in the mind of the Creator, knew Him not. And when he was created, and recognised himself as being created, he remained with this knowledge six hours only, and there came over him a change, from knowledge to ignorance and from good to evil."

> "The foundation of all good and precious things, of all the greatness of God's gifts, of His true love, and of our arriving in His presence, is Death."

> "No one who does not obtain remission (of sins) in this world can be free from the penalty of examination in that day. Not that there is torture or pleasure or recompense before the resurrection; but the soul knows everything it has done whether of good or evil."

> "The penalty of Gehenna is a man's mind; for the punishment there is of two kinds, that of the body and that of the mind. That of the body is perhaps in proportion to the degree of sin, and He lessens and diminishes its duration; but that of the mind is for ever, and the judgment is for ever."

created things," essentially supernatural guides for humanity, including the guardian angels, who are assigned to a person from birth through to the final resurrection. Angels are above humankind in that they have a greater intellect, allowing them to understand more of the nature and design of the universe. Human beings, however, have stronger desires; this inclination is both negative and positive, in that desires, which tie people to the material world, lead them to sin but also to want to be more godlike. The demons, on the other hand, have greater anger than that of other rational beings, which by the nature of emotion—selfish and introspective—leaves them constantly in a sinful state.

Because the angels were not spoken into being but were created directly from the will of God, they believed that they were self-sufficient, that is, godlike. When God created light by not only willing it but also commanding it vocally, the angels became aware of the presence of God, and through their knowledge of his power they began eternal praise and worship of him. The bishop notes that light has no warmth, light being disassociated from fire and established as a separate element. Like philosophers from the Greeks on, Solomon speculates on the nature of light and its association with the divine; unlike the Platonists or Neoplatonists, he sees light as a created thing separate from God and not as emanations of God.

♦ **Concerning the Afterlife**

The last five chapters of the Book of the Bee deal with the afterlife. Chapters 56, 59, and 60 are of interest because of the manner in which the bishop discusses various beliefs concerning the soul, God's mercy, the afterlife, and resurrection. To begin, the bishop states one of the core beliefs of the Church of the East even today: that death is God's gift to humankind. While on the surface this would seem a contradiction, the majority religions today—Hinduism, Buddhism, Judaism, Christianity, and Islam—view the physical time the human being spends on earth as only a temporary state, one that contains conditions for distraction from the divine will (sin, karma, and so on). Thus the end of life, if one has lived in accordance with God's will, leads one not to dismay but instead to a state in which one is in the divine presence. In discussing this end state, the bishop is compiling both church thought and traditional speculations, so the text sometimes seems contradictory.

In the opening paragraph of chapter 56, the bishop notes that humans die in five ways: naturally, voluntarily, accidentally, through violence, and through divine punishment (such as the Flood). Of these, only the first is "natural." The others involve some act of will—even accidents, which are caused by an agency connected with the person's actions. However, all of these reasons for dying are interwoven into God's will, which cannot be understood by either humans or angels until resurrection, when all rational beings will understand it. When a person dies, the soul goes out of the body, and angels escort it. The angels do not defend the soul as devils examine it; the deeds a person performed in life become the determinant for whether the devils seize the soul and take it to Gehenna (Hell) or whether the soul proceeds on its way to the divine presence. In God's presence, the soul forgets its earthly existence—although in the very next sentence the bishop notes that "the soul knows everything that it has done whether of good or evil."

In the next paragraph, five different viewpoints on where the soul goes are listed, including to heaven or Paradise if good or to the "abyss of Eden outside Paradise" (Gehenna) if bad, while various traditions indicate that the soul somehow remains with or near the body. Souls, and hence humankind, may have knowledge of the truth, but it is a baby's knowledge; true knowledge will come only with resurrection. As with other Catholic faiths, the Nestorians believe in the power of prayer and the intercession of saints. The prayers of the righteous, both living and deceased, are heard by God and can affect the living. Moreover, the souls of those who lived good lives "hold spiritual conversation with each other," implying an afterlife that is engaging and active.

Chapter 59 concerns the consequences in the afterlife for both sinners and the righteous. In the first paragraph, Bishop Solomon uses a short logical discussion to argue that there must be punishment for sinners in order for there to be happiness for the godly. However, unlike the usual vision of hell as fire, molten rock, and physically agonizing torments, the bishop explains that the real torment of sinners is mental. The punishment of the sinner is tied to human intelligence, which is refined and made more acute at resurrection. Thus, the joy of the righteous and the anguish of the sinner are beyond anything the living can comprehend. The importance of intelligence is a consistent theme in the Book of the Bee. From the angels to the human soul, the bishop believes that rationality is the foundation of what the world is all about. Intelligence allows humankind to make decisions in earthly life, and intelligence continues into the afterlife to one's great joy or torment depending upon what kind of decisions were made in life.

The second paragraph of chapter 59 describes the afterlife for the godly. The "light" of the righteous is not the elemental light but is instead some of the "light" of God, continuing the argument that as temples of God, humans share God's light. There follows a note about the proportionality of that light for the righteous and of torment for the sinners, each according to how they lived. For the righteous, the more holy they were in life, the brighter the light. Yet in the next part of the chapter, the bishop makes the argument that all will be resurrected equally in the sight of God. There will be no names and no social distinctions, whether gender, class, nationality, ethnicity, age, or any other condition. All will arise as did Jesus, as a perfectly formed human, thirty-three years of age. Presumably, the proportional light distinguishing the most righteous ceases to be so after the final resurrection.

Chapter 60 provides a further interesting, though somewhat contradictory, look at the afterlife. In this chapter, Bishop Solomon argues for the mercy of God, but the arguments are not complete; he never truly answers the questions of whether torment for sinners is eternal or whether God's mercy is complete. The bishop draws on the lost Book of Memorials and on the writings of three early Christian scholars in this chapter: Isaac, bishop of Nineveh, Assyria (in modern-day Iraq), in the late seventh century, a prolific ascetic author whose works were a foundation of Nestorian piety for several centuries; Theodore the Expositor, bishop of Mopsuestia (now Yakapinar, Turkey) from about 392 to 428 and author of the Book of Pearls (also since lost); and Diodorus, or Diodore (ca. 330–390), bishop of Tarsus (in modern-day Turkey) and teacher of Theodore of Mopsuestia.

Solomon begins the chapter with an observation about religious teaching, noting that those teachers who preach warnings of fire and brimstone terrify and cause despair—which is good for those who cannot think for themselves or control their lives—while other teachers encourage by expounding on God's mercy. As quoted, the Book of Memorials indicates that humans should repent of sins in this world or suffer retribution in the next, which will be exacted "to the uttermost farthing." To exact punishment to such a degree indicates there will be nothing left to exact, which means that there will be an end to punishment. Thus, once that retribution is carried out, the soul will be purified, and God will be satisfied.

The quotations cited by the bishop illustrate the universalist position that God's intent is to dispense grace, not justice, which is a human motive. Divine punishment makes no sense without eventual divine mercy because, as the bishop indicates, what would be the point of eternal torment if the purpose behind the agony is to elicit understanding of one's mistakes and sins and regret for them? If immortality is humankind's eventual reward, it makes more sense for punishment to conclude, so that the immortal life of the soul is one of unending joy in the presence of God. In closing, Bishop Solomon quotes Diodorus's Book of the Dispensation at length, affirming that God allots punishments and rewards according to what each soul deserves. The cited text reiterates that the punishment for sinners is really the mental anguish of having failed in life. Punishment for the body is "perhaps in proportion to the degree of sin," and God shows mercy by lessening it according to his will, but punishment of the mind is forever, and "the judgment is for ever." In keeping with the sense of recording the flavor of his philosophical and theological conversations with his friend from long before, the bishop leaves several thoughts open-ended. For example, punishment of the mind is said to be forever, but since intelligence is what defines humanity in this life and the afterlife and God intends to show mercy to humankind, then does God's mercy extend even to mental punishment or not? Or will perhaps the greater truth to be revealed at resurrection allow the soul to fully understand and forgive itself?

Audience

According to the author, Bishop Solomon, the Book of the Bee was written by him as a form of personal correspondence with a longtime friend and peer, Bishop Narses. As the text roughly notes, Bishop Narses was located in Khoni-Shabor, also called Beth-Wazik, a town on the Little Zab River near its junction with the Tigris River, in present-day Iraq. Almost nothing else is known about Bishop Narses or what he actually did with the text. Copies were ultimately made, a number of which survived to the present day.

The modern audience for the text includes the contemporary congregation of the modern equivalent of the Nestorian Church. Although it is not a large sect, the Church of the East signed an agreement with the Roman Catholic Church in 1994 and is now considered part of that church order. Syriac (or Aramaic), the language that Jesus would have spoken, is still the official language of the Church of the East, and many of their beliefs are still practiced.

The history of Christianity has typically focused on its spread to the West, through Greece and the Roman Empire and then into the nations of Europe and the British Isles and onward to the New World. Less emphasis tends to be placed on the spread of the Christian Church to the East, largely because the Eastern versions of Christianity are less "orthodox" (from the perspective of the West) and because the cultures and the historical records are complex and incomplete. The Book of the Bee, however, provides the modern reader with insight into a different version of Christianity as it was practiced in a region of the world with a complex, diverse religious history that too often remains unfamiliar to Westerners.

Impact

The Book of the Bee has had little impact outside the Nestorian Church, except perhaps among seminarians, bib-

---

Questions for Further Study

1. The Nestorian Church flourished in the Middle Ages but then largely (but not entirely) disappeared. Why? What historical factors might have accounted for the rise and decline of Nestorianism?

2. Few people would probably regard death as "God's gift to humankind," as the entry states. Why did the Church of the East hold this belief? How did the Nestorian view of death differ from that of another culture, such as that reflected in, for example, the Tibetan Book of the Dead, the Egyptian "Great Hymn to the Aten," or Lucretius's *On the Nature of Things*?

3. The Book of the Bee reflects a wide range of cultural and religious influences, including those from Jews, Muslims, Zoroastrians, Hindus, and Buddhists, among others. What cultural and geographical factors contributed to this? In what ways is the Book of the Bee different from more insulated medieval European documents on religion, for example Francis of Assisi's "Canticle of the Creatures"?

4. A fundamental Nestorian belief—that Christ had "two real natures united in a single person without confusion or change"—was regarded as heretical by the Christian Church in Rome? Why? What did the Church in the West find so outrageous about this view?

5. Does it surprise you to learn that "the Nestorian Church was more highly organized and had a much greater membership than either the Roman or Greek Orthodox churches of the West"? Why or why not? What factors might have accounted for this organization and membership?

lical scholars, and historians of religion. The most complete translation of the book from its original Syriac was made by Ernest A. Wallis Budge in 1886. For his translation, Budge used elements from four editions of the manuscript, each of which dates to three or more centuries after the original was written. While the historical presence of the Book of the Bee is mentioned in many sources, there are no readily available analytical references. Thus, while it is accessible to the public, the document is mostly of interest to audiences with immediate concerns as to the content. But with additional historical research in the process of being published about the Nestorian Church and its importance to history, the fascinating Book of the Bee may in the future receive richer attention and analytical focus.

Although the Nestorian Church no longer exists as such today, an understanding of the Book of the Bee is helpful to the modern student of religion in several ways. First, the Book of the Bee provides insight into the argumentation of religious doctrine as practiced in the early and middle ages of Christianity. The Nestorians had direct relationships with scholars of many faiths that most Europeans at the time would not have bothered with or did not even know about—primarily Jews and Muslims but also Zoroastrians, Hindus, Buddhists, and others—and had access to a far greater body of knowledge than did western Europeans. The influence of these faiths is evident in the Book of the Bee. Second, the book gives insight into a church that, while at its peak influence politically, was struggling to survive and would, after the downfall of the Mongol khanates, undergo persecution and internal corruption that would essentially seal its fate. Finally, the author's intriguing commentary on Christian doctrine certainly remains relevant. Modern science has not uncovered the "physical" truths behind much of what is discussed in the Book of the Bee, but from a metaphysical perspective the discourse presented by Bishop Solomon can still be considered pertinent almost eight hundred years later.

Further Reading

■ **Books**

Baum, Wilhelm, and Dietmar W. Winkler. *The Church of the East: A Concise History*. New York: RoutledgeCurzon, 2003.

Foltz, Richard C. *Religions of the Silk Road: Overland Trade and Cultural Exchange from Antiquity to the Fifteenth Century*. New York: St. Martin's Press, 1999.

Jenkins, Philip. *The Lost History of Christianity: The Thousand-Year Golden Age of the Church in the Middle East, Africa, and Asia—and How It Died*. New York: HarperOne, 2008.

Kim, Sebastian, and Kirsteen Kim. *Christianity as a World Religion*. London: Continuum, 2008.

Moynahan, Brian. *The Faith: A History of Christianity*. New York: Doubleday, 2002.

■ **Web Sites**

Dickens, Mark. "The Tarsakan Pages: Syriac Christianity in Central Asia." Oxus Communications Web site.
    http://www.oxuscom.com/nestpage.htm

"History of the Nestorian Church." Nestorian.org Web site.
    http://www.nestorian.org/history_of_the_nestorian_churc.html
"Nestorius and Nestorianism." Catholic Encyclopedia, New Advent Web site.
    http://www.newadvent.org/cathen/10755a.htm

—Dale A. Hueber

Book of the Bee

TRUSTING in the power of our Lord Jesus Christ, we begin to write this book of gleanings called "The Bee," which was composed by the saint of God, Mar Solomon, metropolitan of Perath-Maishan, that is Bassorah (al-Basrah), one of His companions. O Lord, in Thy mercy help me. Amen.

♦ FIRST, THE APOLOGY.

"The children ought not to lay up treasures for the parents, but the parents for the spiritual children," saith the blessed Paul; therefore we are bound to repay thee the debt of love, O beloved brother and staff of our old age, saint of God, Mar Narses, bishop of Khoni-Shabor Beth-Wazik. We remember thy solicitude for us, and thy zeal for our service, which thou didst fulfil with fervent love and Christ-like humility. And when we had loving meetings with each other from time to time, thou wert wont to ask questions and to make enquiries about the various things which God hath wrought in His dispensation in this material world, and also as to the things that He is about to do in the world of light. But since we were afflicted with the Mosaic defect of hesitancy of speech, we were unable to inform thee fully concerning the profitable matters about which, as was right, thou didst enquire; and for this reason we were prevented from profitable discourse upon the holy Books. Since, then, God has willed and ruled our separation from each other, and the sign of old age, which is the messenger of death, hath appeared in us, and we have grown old and come into years, it has seemed good to us, with the reed for a tongue and with ink for lips, to inform thee briefly concerning God's dispensation in the two worlds. And, behold, we have gleaned and collected and gathered together chapters and sections relating to this whole universe from the garden of the divine Books and from the crumbs of the Fathers and the Doctors, having laid down as the foundation of our building the beginning of the creation of this world, and concluding with the consummation of the world to come. We have called this book the "Book of the Bee," because we have gathered of the blossoms of the two Testaments and of the flowers of the holy Books, and have placed them therein for thy benefit. As the common bee with gauzy wings flies about, and flutters over and lights upon flowers of various colours, and upon blossoms of divers odours, selecting and gathering from all of them the materials which are useful for the construction of her handiwork; and having first of all collected the materials from the flowers, carries them upon her thighs, and bringing them to her dwelling, lays a foundation for her building with a base of wax; then gathering in her mouth some of the heavenly dew which is upon the blossoms of spring, brings it and blows it into these cells; and weaves the comb and honey for the use of men and her own nourishment: in like manner have we, the infirm, hewn the stones of corporeal words from the rocks of the Scriptures which are in the Old Testament, and have laid them down as a foundation for the edifice of the spiritual law. And as the bee carries the waxen substance upon her thighs because of its insipidity and tastelessness, and brings the honey in her mouth because of its sweetness and value; so also have we laid down the corporeal law by way of substratum and foundation, and the spiritual law for a roof and ceiling to the edifice of the spiritual tower. And as the expert gardener and orchard-keeper goes round among the gardens, and seeking out the finest sorts of fruits takes from them slips and shoots, and plants them in his own field; so also have we gone into the garden of the divine Books, and have culled therefrom branches and shoots, and have planted them in the ground of this book for thy consolation and benefit. When thou, O brother, art recreating thyself among these plants, those which appear and which thou dost consider to be insipid and tasteless, leave for thy companions, for they may be more suitable to others (than to thee); but, upon those which are sweet, and which sweeten the palate of thy understanding, do thou feed and satisfy thy hunger. If, however, owing to their fewness, they do not fill thee, seek in succession for their roots, and from thence shall thy want be satisfied. Know also, O brother, that where there is true love, there is no fear; and where there is freedom of speech, there is no dread; and we should not dare to be so rash as to enter upon these subjects, which are beyond the capacity of our simple understanding, unless we relied upon thy immaculate love; because, in the words of one of the inspired,

"When thou findest honey, eat (only) so much as is sufficient for thee, lest, when thou art sated, thou vomit it;" that is to say, do not enquire (too closely) into the divine words.

♦ CHAPTER I. OF GOD'S ETERNAL INTENTION IN RESPECT OF THE CREATION OF THE UNIVERSE.

IT is well for us to take the materials for our discourse from the divine Scriptures, that we may not stray from the straight paths of the way of truth. The blessed David saith, "Lord, thou hast been our dwelling-place in all generations, before the mountains were conceived." David, the harpist of the Spirit, makes known thereby, that although there was a beginning of the framing of Adam and the other creatures when they were made, yet in the mind of God it had no beginning; that it might not be thought that God has a new thought in respect of anything that is renewed day by day, or that the construction of Creation was newly planned in the mind of God: but everything that He has created and is about to create, even the marvellous construction of the world to come, has been planned from everlasting in the immutable mind of God. As the natural child in the womb of his mother knows not her who bears him, nor is conscious of his father, who, after God, is the cause of his formation; so also Adam, being in the mind of the Creator, knew Him not. And when he was created, and recognised himself as being created, he remained with this knowledge six hours only, and there came over him a change, from knowledge to ignorance and from good to evil. Hence, when Divine Providence wished to create the world, the framing of Adam was first designed and conceived in the mind of God, and then that of the (other) creatures; as David saith, "Before the mountains were conceived." Consequently, Adam is older than the (other) creatures in respect of his conception, and the (other) creatures are older than Adam in respect of their birth and their being made. And whereas God created all creatures in silence and by a word, He brought forth Adam out of His thoughts, and formed him with His holy hands, and breathed the breath of life into him from His Spirit, and Adam became a living soul, and God gave him the knowledge of the difference between good and evil. When he perceived his Creator, then was God formed and conceived within the mind of man; and man became a temple to God his maker, as it is written, "Know ye not that ye are the temple of God, and that the Spirit of God dwelleth in you?" And again, "I will dwell in them, and walk in them."

♦ CHAPTER II. OF THE CREATION OF THE SEVEN NATURES (SUBSTANCES) IN SILENCE.

WHEN God in His mercy wished to make known all His power and His wisdom, in the beginning, on the evening of the first day, which is Sunday, He created seven natures (substances) in silence, without voice. And because there was as yet none to hear a sound, He did well to create them in silence, that He might not make anything uselessly; but He willed, and heaven, earth, water, air, fire, and the angels and darkness, came into being from nothing.

♦ CHAPTER III. OF EARTH, WATER, AIR, AND FIRE.

THE earth was toh we-boh, that is to say, was unarranged and unadorned, but plunged in the midst of the waters. The waters were above it, and above the waters was air, and above the air was fire. The earth is by nature cold and dry. Dry land appeared on the third day, when the trees and plants were created; and the waters were separated therefrom on the second day, when the firmament was made from them. Water is by nature cold and moist. As touching the "Spirit which was brooding upon the face of the waters," some men have ignorantly imagined it to have been the Holy Spirit, while others have more correctly thought it to have been this air (of ours). Air is by nature hot and moist. Fire was operating in the upper ether, above the atmosphere; it possessed heat only, and was without luminosity until the fourth day, when the luminaries were created: we shall mention it in the chapter on the luminaries. Fire is by nature hot and dry. . . .

♦ CHAPTER V. OF THE ANGELS.

THE Angels consist of nine classes and three orders, upper, middle and lower. The upper order is composed of Cherubim, Seraphim, and Thrones: these are called "priests" (kumre), and "chief priests," and "bearers of God's throne." The middle order is composed of Lords, Powers and Rulers: these are called "priests" (kahne), because they receive revelations from those above them. The lower order consists of Principalities, Archangels and Angels: and these are the ministers who wait upon created things. . . . The Angels are a motion which has spiritual knowledge of everything that is on earth and in heaven. With each and every one of us is an angel of this group—called the guardian angel—who directs man from his conception until the general resurrection. . . . The fathers, when they have been deemed worthy at any time to see our Lord in a revelation, have seen Him in heaven, surrounded by the Cherubim and Seraphim. Hence some say that there are angels above the heavens. All these celestial hosts have revelations both of

Document Text

sight and of hearing; but the Cherubim have revelations by sight only, because there is no mediator between them and God. The angels have an intellect superior to that of the rest of rational beings; man has stronger desire, and the demons a greater degree of anger. . . .

♦ CHAPTER VII. OF EFFUSED (CIRCUMAMBIENT) LIGHT.

WHEN the holy angels were created on the evening of the first day, without voice, they understood not their creation, but thought within themselves that they were self-existent beings and not made. On the morning of the first day God said in an audible and commanding voice, "Let there be light," and immediately the effused light was created. When the angels saw the creation of light, they knew of a certainty that He who had made light had created them. And they shouted with a loud voice, and praised Him, and marvelled at His creation of light, as the blessed teacher saith, "When the Creator made that light, the angels marvelled thereat," etc.; and as it is said in Job, "When I created the morning star, all my angels praised me." Now by nature light has no warmth. . . .

♦ CHAPTER LVI. OF DEATH AND THE DEPARTURE OF THE SOUL FROM THE BODY.

THE foundation of all good and precious things, of all the greatness of God's gifts, of His true love, and of our arriving in His presence, is Death. Men die in five ways. Naturally; as David said, "Unless his day come and he die," alluding to Saul. Voluntarily; as when Saul killed himself in the battle with the Philistines. By accident; such as a fall from a roof, and other fatal accidents. By violence, from devils and men and wild beasts and venomous reptiles. By (divine) chastisement; as the flood in the days of Noah, and the fire which fell upon the Sodomites, and other such like things. But (side by side) with all these kinds of fatalities runs the providence of God's government, which cannot be comprehended by the creatures, restraining (them) where it is meet (to restrain), and letting (them) loose where it is fitting (to let loose). This government is not comprehended in this world, neither by angels nor by men; but in the world which is to come all rational beings will know it. When the soul goes forth from the body, as Abba Isaiah says, the angels go with it: then the hosts of darkness go forth to meet it, seeking to seize it and examine it, if there be anything of theirs in it. Then the angels do not fight with them, but those deeds which the soul has wrought protect it and guard it, that they come not near it. If its deeds be victorious, then the angels sing praises before it until it meets God with joy. In that hour the soul forgets every deed of this world. Consequently, no one who does not obtain remission (of sins) in this world can be free from

Glossary

Before the mountains were conceived	quotation from the Old Testament book of Psalm, chapter 90, verse 2
Book of Memorials	a lost work by Isaac, bishop of Nineveh
The children ought not to lay up treasures for the parents . . .	quotation from the New Testament book of 2 Corinthians, chapter 12, verse 14
David	the second king of the Israelites and founder of the royal line from which Christ descended
Diodorus	bishop of Tarsus and teacher of Theodore the Expositor
Gehenna	the place where children were sacrificed to the god Moloch
I will dwell in them, and walk in them	quotation from the New Testament book of 2 Corinthians, chapter 6, verse 16
Isaac	bishop of Nineveh in the latter half of the seventh century
Know ye not that ye are the temple of God . . .	quotation from the New Testament book of 1 Corinthians, chapter 3, verse 16

the penalty of examination in that day. Not that there is torture or pleasure or recompense before the resurrection; but the soul knows everything that it has done whether of good or evil.

As to where the souls abide from the time they leave their bodies until the resurrection, some say that they are taken up to heaven, that is, to the region of spirit, where the celestial hosts dwell. Others say that they go to Paradise, that is, to the place which is abundantly supplied with the good things of the mystery of the revelations of God; and that the souls of sinners lie in darkness in the abyss of Eden outside Paradise. Others say that they are buried with their bodies; that is to say, as the two were buried in God at baptism, so also will they now dwell in Him until the day of the resurrection. Others say that they stand at the mouth of the graves and await their Redeemer; that is to say, they possess the knowledge of the resurrection of their bodies. Others say that they are as it were in a slumber, because of the shortness of the time; for they point out in regard to them that what seems to us a very long time is to them as a momentary nod (or wink) in its shortness. . . . Those who say that they are like an infant which has no knowledge, shew that they call even the knowledge of the truth ignorance in comparison with that knowledge of the truth which shall be bestowed upon them after the resurrection.

That the souls of the righteous pray, and that their prayers assist those who take refuge with them, may be learned from many . . . Therefore it is right for those who have a holy man for a friend, to rejoice when he goes to our Lord in Paradise, because their friend has the power to help them by his prayers. Like the blind disciple of one of the saints mentioned in the Book of the Paradise, who, when his master was dying, wept bitterly and said, "To whose care dost thou leave the poor blind man?" And his master encouraged him, and said to him, "I believe in God that, if I find mercy in His sight, at the end of a week thou wilt see;" and after some days he did see. The souls of the righteous also hold spiritual conversation with each other, according to the Divine permission and command which moves them to this by necessary causes. Neither those who have departed this life in the flesh are hindered from this (intercourse), nor those who are still clad in their fleshly garments, if they live their life in them holily. . . .

♦ **CHAPTER LIX. OF THE HAPPINESS OF THE RIGHTEOUS AND THE TORMENT OF SINNERS, AND IN WHAT STATE THEY ARE THERE.**

IT is right for us to know and explain how those suffer, who suffer in Gehenna. If they do suffer, how can we say that they are impassible? And if they do not suffer, then there is no torture for sinners; and if there be no torture for sinners in proportion to their sins, neither can there be happiness for the righ-

Glossary

Lord, thou hast been our dwelling-place . . .	quotation from the Old Testament book of Psalms, chapter 90, verse 1
Mar	in Syriac, "my lord," a title of respect given to bishops
Mosaic	pertaining to the Old Testament patriarch Moses
Saul	the first king of the Israelites
Spirit which was brooding upon the face of the waters	quotation from the Old Testament book of Genesis, chapter 1, verse 2
Theodore the Expositor	Bishop of Mopsuestia from 392 to 428 and author of *The Book of Pearls,* now lost
Unless his day come and he die	quotation from the Old Testament book of 1 Samuel, chapter 26, verse 10
When I created the morning star, all my angels praised me	quotation from the Old Testament book of Job, chapter 38, verse 4

teous as a reward for their labours. The suffering wherewith the Fathers say that sinners will suffer in Gehenna is not one that will pain the limbs, such as the blows of sticks, the mutilation of the flesh, and the breaking of the bones, but one that will afflict the soul, such as grief for the transgression of what is right, repentance for shameful deeds, and banishment from one to whom he is bound in love and for whom his affection is strong. For in the resurrection we shall not be without perception, like the sun which perceives not his splendour, nor the moon her brilliancy, nor the pearl its beauty; but by the power of reason we shall feel perfectly the delight of our happiness or the keen pain of our torture. So then by that which enables the righteous to perceive the pleasure of their happiness, by that selfsame thing will the wicked also perceive the suffering of their torment; (that is) by the power capable of receiving pleasure, which is the intelligence. Hence it is right for us to be certain that intelligence will not be taken away from us, but it will receive the utmost purification and refinement. . . . The pleasure of that world is something beyond all comparison more glorious and excellent and exalted than those of this world; and the torment of yonder is likewise something beyond all comparison more severe and more bitter than any that is here.

. . . The light of the righteous is not of a natural origin like this elemental light (of ours), but some of the light of our Lord—whose splendour surpasses ten thousand suns—is diffused and shed upon them. Each saint shines in proportion to his purity, and holiness and refinement and sincerity. . . . So also with the sinners in Gehenna; their sentence will not be alike, for in proportion to the sin of each will be his torment. . . . In the new world there will be no distinctive names for ranks and conditions of human beings; and as every name and surname attributed to God and the angels had its origin from this world, and names for human beings were assigned and distributed by the government of this world, in the world of spiritual and intellectual natures there will be neither names nor surnames among them, nor male nor female, nor slave nor free, nor child nor old man, nor Ethiopian nor Roman (Greek); but they will all rise in the one perfect form of a man thirty-three years of age, as our Lord rose from the dead. In the world to come there will be no companies or bands but two; the one of the angels and the righteous, who will mingle and form one Church, and the other of the devils and sinners in Gehenna.

♦ **CHAPTER LX. WHETHER MERCY WILL BE SHEWN TO SINNERS AND THE DEVILS IN GEHENNA, AFTER THEY HAVE BEEN TORMENTED AND SUFFERED AND BEEN PUNISHED, OR NOT? AND IF MERCY IS TO BE SHEWN TO THEM, WHEN WILL IT BE?**

SOME of the Fathers terrify us beyond our strength and throw us into despair; and their opinion is well adapted to the simple-minded and trangressors of the law. Others of them encourage us and bid us rely upon Divine mercy; and their opinions are suitable and adapted to the perfect and those of settled minds and the pious. In the "Book of Memorials" it is thus written: "This world is the world of repentance, but the world which is to come is the world of retribution. As in this world repentance saves until the last breath, so in the world to come justice exacts to the uttermost farthing. And as it is impossible to see here strict justice unmingled with mercy, so it is impossible to find there strict justice mingled with mercy." Mar Isaac says thus: "Those who are to be scourged in Gehenna will be tortured with stripes of love; they who feel that they have sinned against love will suffer harder and more severe pangs from love than the pain that springs from fear." Again he says: "The recompense of sinners will be this: the resurrection itself will be their recompense instead of the recompense of justice; and at the last He will clothe those bodies which have trodden down His laws with the glory of perfection. This act of grace to us after we have sinned is greater than that which, when we were not, brought our nature into being." Again he says: "In the world which is to come grace will be the judge and not justice." Mar Theodore the Expositor . . . would never have said, "Until thou payest the uttermost farthing," unless it had been possible for us to be freed from our sins through having atoned for them by paying the penalty; neither would He have said, "he shall be beaten with many stripes," or "he shall be beaten with few stripes," unless it were that the penalties, being meted out according to the sins, should finally come to an end. . . .

So also the blessed Diodorus, who says in the "Book of the Dispensation": "A lasting reward, which is worthy of the justice of the Giver, is laid up for the good, in return for their labours; and torment for sinners, but not everlasting, that the immortality which is prepared for them may not be worthless. They must however be tormented for a short time, as they deserve, in proportion to the measure of their iniquity and wickedness, according to the amount of the wickedness of their deeds. This they will have to bear, that they suffer for a short time; but immortal and unending happiness is prepared for them. . . ."

Again he says: "God pours out the wages of reward beyond the measure of the labours (wrought), and in the abundance of His goodness He lessens and diminishes the penalty of those who are to be tormented, and in His mercy He shortens and reduces the length of the time. But even thus He does not punish the whole time according to (the length of) the time of folly, seeing that He requites them far less than they deserve, just as He does the good beyond the measure and period (of their deserts); for the reward is everlasting. It has not been revealed whether the goodness of God wishes to punish without ceasing the blameworthy who have been found guilty of evil deeds (or not), as we have already said before. But if punishment is to be weighed out according to sin, not even so would punishment be endless. . . . The penalty of Gehenna is a man's mind; for the punishment there is of two kinds, that of the body and that of the mind. That of the body is perhaps in proportion to the degree of sin, and He lessens and diminishes its duration; but that of the mind is for ever, and the judgment is for ever." . . . To Him be glory and dominion and praise and exaltation and honour for ever and ever. Amen and Amen.

Arabs defending the Spanish city of Mallorca from Christian forces
(Arabs defending the city of Mallorca from attack by King James I, fragment of 'The Conquest of Mallorca', 1285-90 [fresco] / Museo de Arte de Catalunya, Barcelona, Spain / Mithra-Index / The Bridgeman Art Library International)

Ibn al-'Arabi: The Meccan Illuminations

1203–1224

"The Truly Real manifests Himself to (the Heart), which (alone) encompasses Him, in 'seventy thousand veils of light and darkness.'"

Overview

The Meccan Illuminations (or Openings or Revelations) is the English title of *Al-Futuhat al-Makiyya*, a Sufi mystical text written in Arabic by the Spanish-born Muhyiddin Muhammad ibn al-'Arabi over a twenty-one year period, from 1203 to 1224. Its 560 chapters span all branches of Islamic learning and revolve around the concept of *tawhid*, or the unity and oneness of God. In this massive encyclopedic work, Ibn al-'Arabi thoroughly covers many topics from the Qur'an (Islam's sacred scripture) as well as prayer and fasting, theology, ontology (the study of the nature of being and existence), and metaphysics (the study of ultimate and fundamental reality).

In *The Meccan Illuminations*, Ibn al-'Arabi tells of various dreams and visions in which he saw and spoke with God, Muhammad, Jesus, the other prophets, and some angels. He also describes visions in which he sees and speaks with his dead teachers. It is because of these visions and dreams that he calls himself the Seal of the Muhammadan Saints, and it is because of them that he writes *The Meccan Illuminations*. The book also includes accounts of miracles performed by Ibn al-'Arabi and his teachers.

Chapter 367, reproduced here, narrates the *mi'raj* of Ibn al-'Arabi, signifying an ascent akin to that of Muhammad in 621. According to Islamic belief, upon being visited by the angel Gabriel, Muhammad literally traveled from Mecca to Jerusalem in one night, a journey that would have taken many days, on the back of a steed that had wings and could fly. The journey continued onward to a place in the heavens where Muhammad encountered earlier prophets such as Moses. Finally, he descended again physically to earth. Ibn al-'Arabi's related narrative is significant in two ways: It provides a nonliteral interpretation of the *mi'raj* of Muhammad. And because in the *mi'raj* of Ibn al-'Arabi, a man who is not a prophet claims to have gone on the same journey as Muhammad, the miracle of the *mi'raj* is represented as possible for others.

Ibn al-'Arabi's writing style has posed many challenges to readers and translators, as he combines specialized mystical and philosophical language with frequent jumps from one topic to another. Whether intentionally, in order to create a state of bewilderment in the reader as preparation for mystical experience, or to imitate the style of the Qur'an, his explanations of certain topics are dispersed among many chapters, if not many books. As a result, despite his great place in the history of Islam, knowledge of Ibn al-'Arabi has been limited in the West. His work was not widely translated or studied until the late 1950s, and much remains to be done.

Context

Sufism, an ascetic and mystical strand of Islam dating from an early period of the religion, was widely established by the ninth century, and many Sufi orders had been formed. Great Sufi thinkers prior to Ibn al-'Arabi included Hasan al-Basri (d. 728?), Sahl al-Tustari (d. 896), Abu Bakr al-Wasiti (d. 932), and al-Kushayri (or Qushayri, d. 1074).

The Meccan Illuminations dates from the time of the Crusades, a series of intermittent wars between Muslims and Christian Europeans over the Holy Land. Islamic Spain (Andalusia or Al-Andalus), which Muslims had conquered in the eighth century, was also under siege in what Christians called the Reconquista—the "reconquest" of Spain by Christian forces. While the Spanish city of Toledo was reclaimed by the Christians in 1085, Jerusalem, captured by the Crusaders in 1099, was taken back by the Muslims in 1187. Meanwhile, an Andalusian culture of science, medicine, art, and philosophy flourished in Spain. Many Islamic structures, such as the Alhambra of Granada, survive as a legacy of Islamic Spain.

Despite wars and instability across the Muslim world, Qur'anic scholarship, compiling of Hadith (reports of the sayings and activities of Muhammad and his companions), and Sufi teachers and their disciples were all flourishing, producing works that traveled as far and wide as their authors. However, not all scholarship was celebrated at the time, and some authors were prosecuted as heretical. In Ibn al-'Arabi's time a great Persian Sufi philosopher, Suhrawardi, was executed for heresy in Syria.

Ibn al-'Arabi deals with questions raised by many philosophers and theologians before him. For example, the ques-

Time Line

621	The *mi'raj*, or ascent, of Muhammad to heaven is said to have taken place.
632	Muhammad dies in Mecca.
711	Muslims begin their conquest of Spain.
874	Abu Yazid al-Bistami (or Bayazid Bistami), the Persian Sufi author of an earlier *mi'raj* narrative, dies.
1165	Ibn al-'Arabi is born in Murcia, Spain.
1191	Suhrawardi, a mystical philosopher and contemporary of Ibn al-'Arabi, is executed in Syria.
1198	Ibn al-'Arabi experiences a vision that inspires his pilgrimage to Mecca and subsequent account in *The Meccan Illuminations*.
1224	Ibn al-'Arabi completes *The Meccan Illuminations*.
1240	Ibn al-'Arabi dies in Syria.
1251	The centuries-long Reconquista completes the return of all Iberian cities except Granada to Christian hands.
1328	Ibn Taymiyya, one of Ibn al-'Arabi's chief critics, dies in Syria.
1958	Henry Corbin publishes *L'imagination créatrice dans le soufisme d'ibn 'Arabi* (later translated as *Creative Imagination in the Sufism of Ibn 'Arabi* and as *Alone with the Alone*), introducing the Sufi master's thought to the West.

tion of the multiplicity or unity of God had been a topic of great debate throughout the medieval period. Philosophers and theologians debated how God could be one and at the same time have many attributes. Some philosophers argued that if God is one, then God cannot have any attributes. Ibn al-'Arabi's solution to this problem involved the idea of *Wahdat al-Wujud*, or the unity of existence. Although he did not use this term himself, it is often used to describe his philosophy, especially with regard to his concept of *tawhid*, or the unity of God. Despite the world's multiplicity, the world is one in all its components, and it is one with God.

Knowledge of the world, Ibn al-'Arabi argued, is not acquired through the rational methods of the philosophers but rather through *dhawq* (literally "taste"), a word that here signifies immediate mystical experience. Knowledge obtained in this way is different from discursive knowledge. A *wali*, or saint, is like a prophet in being able to acquire true knowledge of God in this way and to see reality clearly. Unlike a prophet, however, the *wali* has no obligation to spread this knowledge to others.

Ibn al-'Arabi's esoteric style of writing was common in the medieval period. The Isma'ilis, an offshoot of the minority Shia sect of Islam, believed that the Qur'an had an inner and an outer meaning; they themselves wrote in two levels of meaning. Moses Maimonides (d. 1204), the great Jewish philosopher of Spanish origin, displayed the same style of writing in his *Guide for the Perplexed* (originally composed in Judeo-Arabic), scattering his discussion of certain topics throughout many chapters of a book, covering a great number of subjects, and assuming that the reader had vast knowledge. Some modern scholars argue that this method was specifically designed to hide his true message from those unable to understand it.

About the Author

Ibn al-'Arabi's full name was Abu 'Abdallah Muhammad ibn 'Ali ibn al-'Arabi al-Ta'i al-Hatimi. Known as al-Shaykh al-Akbar, the Greatest Master or Teacher, Ibn al-'Arabi is one of the supreme Sufi masters. He wrote hundreds of books of philosophy and Qur'anic commentary, many of which are extant in manuscript form.

Ibn al-'Arabi was born in 1165 in Murcia, Spain, and educated in Seville. In Córdoba he met the renowned Aristotelian philosopher Ibn Rushd (known in the West as Averroes). Ibn al-'Arabi was a youth at the time, but Ibn Rushd is said to have admired his intellect. A frequent traveler, Ibn al-'Arabi lived in Andalusia (Spain), Fès (Morocco), Tunis (Algeria), Baghdad (Iraq), Anatolia (or what is today Turkey), and Aleppo (Syria), and he was accompanied on many of his journeys by his friend and disciple 'Abd Allah al-Habashi. He finally settled in Damascus, Syria, where he married and had at least two sons. He spent the last seventeen years of his life in Damascus, dying there in 1240.

In Damascus Ibn al-'Arabi wrote and taught. One of his most important students was Muzaffar al-Din Musa, who (as al-Ashraf) ruled Damascus for nearly a decade beginning in 1229. To this student, Ibn al-'Arabi gave permission to teach 290 of his works. Even though he was a Sufi, Ibn al-'Arabi did not follow a traditional Sufi path, as he neither had a *shaykh* (Sufi master) whom he followed nor did he establish a Sufi order for his students. Yet his visions inspired works that became standard textbooks in later Sufi orders throughout Iran and Turkey.

In 1198 Ibn al-'Arabi had a vision of Moses, Isa (the Qur'anic name for Jesus), and Muhammad that led him to travel to Mecca (Islam's holiest city) in 1201. He describes this vision, and the many others he had throughout his life, in *The Meccan Illuminations*. It was at Mecca that he received another vision allowing him to write *The Meccan Illuminations*. In *The Meccan Illuminations*, he describes his early years, before receiving his visions, as *al-Jahiliyya*, or the age of ignorance, similar to that before the advent of Islam. These visions were Ibn al-'Arabi's most important source of knowledge. He emphasized this when he described three ways of acquiring knowledge: through the intellect, through experience, and through revelation.

Ibn al-'Arabi was a poet as well as a philosopher. His works include a *diwan* (collection) of poetry, and verse is interspersed in his philosophical and theological works as well. In *Turjuman al-ashwaq* (The Interpreter of Desire), his love poems, Ibn al-'Arabi describes a woman whose beauty inspired him. Some scholars think that these poems were a result of erotic love for a woman, but others believe that he was moved by his love for the divine.

Explanation and Analysis of the Document

As a Sufi text, the *mi'raj* account in chapter 367 of *The Meccan Illuminations* is mystical in nature, combining material from the Qur'an with philosophy, and prose with poetry. It resembles the Neoplatonic concept of the soul's ascent to God through knowledge, an idea based on the belief that the unknowable first principle and source of reality transcends being and thought. In Ibn al-'Arabi's thought, though, knowledge itself, not God, is the end point.

The introduction cites various verses from the Qur'an to make metaphysical arguments about God and the world—namely, that God is everywhere and always close to every human being but that the humans need signs to be made aware of this presence. Thus, miracles play a great role in the worldview of Ibn al-'Arabi, and his *mi'raj* begins by emphasizing that the purpose of miracles is to allow one to see God's signs. As Ibn al-'Arabi does not read the Qur'an literally, so also the miracles he describes are not to be construed literally. He emphasizes that one ought to read the Qur'anic verses about God's throne together with the verses that describe God as closer to a person than his jugular vein. Even though God is great, and God has a throne, God is not far off in heaven.

In the same way, the journey of the *mi'raj* is at once a journey through a person's inner states as well as God's manifestations, rather than through physical space. Ibn al-'Arabi's description of his own *mi'raj* is shocking and disorienting because it either elevates the status of Ibn al-'Arabi so that he is almost Muhammad-like (and, in fact, he calls himself the seal of saints), or calls into question whether Muhammad's miraculous experience is as singular and significant as it is seen. As a result, the reading of both

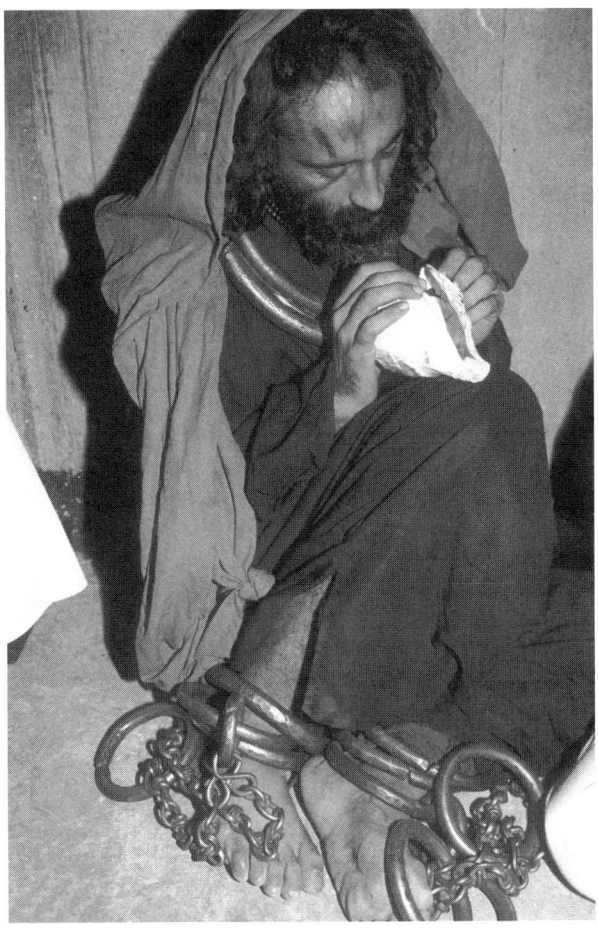

A modern-day Sufi mystic
(Sufi mystic wearing chains and anklets at the Mausoleum of Hazrat Shahbaz Qalander [photo], / Sehwan Sharif, Sindh Province, Pakistan / © World Religions Photo Library / The Bridgeman Art Library International)

descriptions invites a reexamination of whether literal readings of religious texts are sufficient. Thus, a reader who might have always taken accounts of the Prophet's *mi'raj* as historical might consider seeing the event as a metaphor, and this then gives the text/event new meanings. One figurative reading that results is that the *mi'raj* can be seen as a metaphor for one's journey to knowledge of God and the world, with the ascent signifying different levels of learning and different layers of meaning.

♦ I. Introduction: The Context and Purpose of the Spiritual Journey

The Qur'anic verse quoted in the first paragraph, about God's being "closer to man than his jugular vein" (50:16) is fundamental for Muslim mystics, having inspired Sufism from the beginning. According to Ibn al-'Arabi, the purpose of a *mi'raj*, or ascent to the heavens, is not so that the person can see God—after all, God is in the world below as well—but to bring into stronger relief God's signs, so that once the person descends, he can see and better understand the signs available to everyone on earth. Referring to

Essential Quotes

"As for the saints, they have spiritual journeys in the intermediate world during which they directly witness spiritual realities (ma'ani) embodied in forms that have become sensible for the imagination; these (sensible images) convey knowledge of the spiritual realities contained within those forms."

"So when the servant has become aware of what we have just explained, so that he knows that he is not (created) according to the form of the world, but only according to the form of God (al-Haqq), then God makes him journey through His Names, in order to cause him to see His Signs (Kor. 17:1) within him."

"Now when (the spiritual traveler) has completed his share of the journey through the Names and has come to know the Signs which the Names of God gave him during that journey, then he returns and 'reintegrates' his self with a composition different from that initial composite nature, because of the knowledge he has gained which he did not have when he was 'dissolved' (in the ascending phase of that journey)."

"Then they were lacking in the knowledge of the way things are, to the extent of what they missed, since the world was non-existent for them. So they were lacking the True Reality (al-Haqq) to the extent of that (aspect) of the world which was veiled from them. Because the whole world is precisely the Self-manifestation (tajalli) of the Truly Real, for whoever really knows the Truly Real."

"The Truly Real manifests Himself to (the Heart), which (alone) encompasses Him, in 'seventy thousand veils of light and darkness.' Thus He manifests Himself to the Heart of His servant through those (veils)— for 'if He were' to manifest Himself without them, 'the radiant splendors of His Face would burn up' the creaturely part of that servant."

Muhammad and his ascent to heaven from Jerusalem, he quotes the Qur'an (here abbreviated "Kor."): "I only made him journey by night in order that he see the Signs, not (to bring him) to Me: because no place can hold Me and the relation of all places to Me is the same." (Parentheses are used by the translator of the Qur'anic text to clarify the meaning that is not necessarily spelled out in the Arabic but which is obvious to someone reading the original.)

♦ III. The Spiritual Journey of the Saints

Ibn al-'Arabi states that all *walis* (saints, or friends of God) undertake spiritual journeys in which they perceive forms otherwise inaccessible to the senses. It is on these journeys that a saint uses the imagination in order to truly apprehend the world. Ibn al-'Arabi's ascent is slightly different from other spiritual journeys, however, in that what he saw was different from what others had seen before him.

He distinguishes between his journey and Muhammad's, which he describes as "sensible," or sensory. In other words, whereas the Prophet's journey took place in body and spirit, Ibn al-'Arabi's was solely spiritual.

More specifically, the *mi'raj* is spiritual in the sense that the saint, or *wali*, gradually leaves behind his body and his connection to the physical world while ascending from one level to another. The ultimate goal is to let go of everything material and be in the presence of God. The body, like everything else in the physical world, is thus like a veil. It prevents the believer from understanding the nature of God and stands as a barrier between humanity and God.

The ultimate destination of ascent is the realization of oneness with God, so that the spiritual voyager finally sees the unity of existence and is no longer able to distinguish between self and God. It is through this union that the human is able to know that we are created in the image of God. Ibn al-'Arabi describes the journey as a passage through God's names, because being created in the form of God means that the human being has all the characteristics described by the ninety-nine names of God, which represent states of the human's inner being.

This new knowledge profoundly changes the saint, who returns a different person even if the physical self is regained in the descent. The changes are not immediately visible to others, but they become apparent when the saint speaks, as they did when Muhammad described his journey to his companions. The response that would be expected if a saint were to describe such a journey is that he would be accused of heresy or taken to be insane. However, a small group of learned people would believe the account, thus causing a dispute. For this reason Ibn al-'Arabi tells the reader undertaking such a journey to share only what has been learned but not the manner of learning. In other words, do not do what Ibn al-'Arabi is doing; instead, communicate only the teachings.

Note the image of a mirror. By sharpening one's intellect or practicing in preparation for such a journey, "polishing the mirror of his soul," one can transform oneself from a mere physical object to a reflection of God. Through this cleaning, the mirror itself becomes less and less visible, and the viewer more so. This metaphor recalls the act of unveiling that takes place on the journey toward heaven—as one sheds one's physicality, one layer after another, the truth, and God, lose veil after veil in a process known to Sufis as *kashf*. Ibn al-'Arabi finally compares the saint's knowledge of God with that of the ordinary human. Ordinary human beings who see God through many veils construct "likenesses" of God (in violation of the Qu'ran), whereas the saint possesses actual knowledge of God.

◆ **IV. Ibn 'Arabi's Personal *Mi'raj***

The first part of chapter IV, "The Departure from the Elemental World," begins the description of the *mi'raj*. Ibn al-'Arabi is borne on Buraq, the winged steed that had transported Muhammad to heaven. In the first heaven, the traveler meets Adam, a perfect man (*insan kamil*), without sin, like Muhammad. Then, in "Adam and the First Heaven," Ibn al-'Arabi asks Adam about hell and whether he or his community would suffer in it. Adam's response is shocking: He says that there will be no suffering in hell, as God's anger has ended.

In sections C, D, and E (omitted here), Ibn al-'Arabi ascends through three further levels of heaven, where he meets, successively, Jesus, Joseph, and Enoch (or Idris). In the fifth level (part F), he meets Aaron, the brother of Moses, and engages in philosophical discourse with him and Yahya (John the Baptist). Yahya emphasizes that each person follows a unique path to heaven: "Each person has a path, that no one else but he travels." What matters is the journey itself: "They come to be through the traveling itself." A discussion with Aaron follows on the nature of reality and what is real. The traveler asks whether, in the quest for God, physical reality actually disappears. Aaron replies, enigmatically, that "the whole world is precisely the Self-manifestation (*tajalli*) of the Truly Real, for whoever really knows the Truly Real."

In part G, Moses is questioned about seeing God and about the meaning of the Qur'anic verse 7:143, which says that no one sees God while alive. Moses answers that he had, in fact, died, seen God, and then awakened. Moses then goes on to say that upon seeing God, he learned that he always had seen God but never knew it. As William Chittick has noted, according to Ibn al-'Arabi, "God Himself is the spirit of the cosmos, while the cosmos is His body."

Finally, in the seventh level of heaven (part H), we meet Abraham. The "Inhabited House" is a place of prayer created by Abraham and, in effect, Islam's first "mosque." Here, Ibn al-'Arabi encounters the "Truly Real," which encompasses God in "seventy thousand veils of light and darkness." This is an allusion to the fundamental Islamic belief that God has no shape or color. In order to reach God, a person must pass through veils of darkness—that is, the material world—then through veils of light. Thus, God "manifests Himself to the Heart of His servant through those (veils)—for 'if He were' to manifest Himself without them, 'the radiant splendors of His Face would burn up' the creaturely part of that servant."

Audience

Ibn al-'Arabi's intended readership was probably first and foremost a Sufi audience, but it did not exclude the learned scholars of the Qur'an and other Islamic disciplines. Perhaps the original readers were expected to approach the text only with a Sufi master, who would guide the student through the text stage by stage, in a journey similar to that of Ibn al-'Arabi's *mi'raj*, or ascent to God.

In the medieval period, Ibn al-'Arabi's work was also read in India, where it influenced the works of many Muslim authors. *The Meccan Illuminations* continues to be read today by Sufis all over the world, and Ibn al-'Arabi continues to be seen as one of the greatest Sufi saints and thinkers of all time. Today he is revered not only in Iran, Turkey, and other centers of Sufi learning but even in the West, where Orientalists and scholars of Middle Eastern and Islamic studies have studied and translated his work.

Non-Sufi readers celebrate Ibn al-'Arabi's work because it appears to provide a pluralistic understanding of the world and religion's role in it. Ibn al-'Arabi stands with Rumi and Hafez, the great Persian poet-mystics of the thirteenth and fourteenth centuries, as essential reading for interfaith groups seeking to find similarities between religions and possibilities for coexistence.

Impact

Even during his lifetime Ibn al-'Arabi's writings were copied and disseminated widely. After his death, Sufi writers continued their investigations where he left off—focusing on his metaphysics rather than on moral or practical aspects of worship. Also after his death, many hagiographies were composed, and his biography was written by numerous medieval historians. His tomb in Damascus is still visited by Muslims, and above the entrance are inscribed two lines of his poetry: "In every age there is one after whom it is named; / for the remaining ages I am the one."

Hundreds of commentaries on *The Meccan Illuminations* were written in the six centuries after Ibn al-'Arabi's death, the earliest by Sadr al-Din al-Qunawi (d. 1274), his stepson, and Mu'ayyid al-Din al-Jandi. Al-Qunawi describes Ibn al-'Arabi's work as *mashrab al-tahqiq*, "the school of realization," which is neither philosophy nor theology (*kalam*). Ibn al-'Arabi also had his enemies. He was accused of heresy after his death by Ibn Taymiyya and others, and his work was considered atheistic and rejected by many scholars of the strict Hanbali school of Islamic law. His books were burned in Egypt. Such rejection had been the fate of other ecstatic Muslim mystics such as the Persian al-Hallaj, executed for his teachings in 922, and al-Bistami, a ninth-century Persian Sufi who was shunned because of his controversial sayings (for example, "I am I; there is no God but I; so worship me!") and his claim that he had traveled through the seven heavens in a dream. Ibn al-'Arabi's influence nonetheless spread across the Muslim world and beyond. His philosophy may have influenced such great Western thinkers as the Catalan mystic Ramon Llull (d. 1315), the Italian poet Dante (d. 1321), and the Dutch philosopher Baruch Spinoza (d. 1677). The works of Ibn al-'Arabi were introduced to the West in modern times by the French scholar Henry Corbin, beginning in 1958 with *L'imagination créatrice dans le soufisme d'ibn 'Arabi*, or *Creative Imagination in the Sufism of Ibn 'Arabi*.

Further Reading

■ Books

Addas, Claude. *Quest for the Red Sulphur: The Life of Ibn 'Arabi*, trans. Peter Kingsley. Cambridge, U.K.: Islamic Texts Society, 1993.

Ates, A. "Ibn al-Arabi, Muhyi'l-Din Abu Abd Allah Muhummad b. Ali b. Muhammad b. al-Arabi al-Hatimi al-Tai known as al-

---

Questions for Further Study

1. Describe the relationship between Sufism and Islam. For reference, consult other entries on Islamic documents such as the one on the Qur'an or the one titled Usul al-kafi.

2. Sufism is a mystical sect of Islam. In what sense, then, does it bear similarities with Jewish mysticism, as represented by the entry Sefer Yetzirah? How does the mysticism of *The Meccan Illuminations* differ from that contained in a document such as *Calling Humanity* by José Trigueirinho?

3. *The Meccan Illuminations* deals in part with the nature of God—specifically the question of the unity or oneness of God and whether God can have attributes. How does Ibn al-'Arabi answer this question? How would you answer the question?

4. Both Ibn al-'Arabi and Maimonides, the author of the *Mishneh Torah*, were born and lived in Spain at roughly the same time. Although the two writers represent different religious traditions, what do the two entries, taken together, tell you about the religious community of Spain during the Middle Ages?

5. Do you believe that the author intended for readers to take his account of his journey literally? Or do you think he regarded the account as symbolic? Explain your reasoning.

Shaykh al-'Akbar." In *Encyclopaedia of Islam*, ed. P. Bearman, et al., 2nd ed. Leiden, Netherlands: Brill, 2010.

Chittick, William. *The Sufi Path of Knowledge: Ibn al-'Arabi's Metaphysics of Imagination*. Albany: State University of New York Press, 1989.

Chittick, William. "Two Chapters from the Futuhat al-Makiyya." In *Muhyiddin ibn 'Arabi: A Commemorative Volume*, ed. S. Hirtenstein and M. Tiernan. Rockport, Mass.: Element Books, 1993.

Chittick, William. "Ibn 'Arabi and His School." In *Islamic Spirituality: Manifestations*, ed. S. H. Nasr. New York: Crossroad, 1997.

Corbin, Henry. *Alone with the Alone: Creative Imagination in the Sufism of Ibn 'Arabi*, trans. Ralph Manheim. Princeton, N.J.: Princeton University Press, 1998.

Hirtenstein, Stephen. *The Unlimited Mercifier: The Spiritual Life and Thought of Ibn 'Arabi*. Ashland, Ore.: White Cloud Press, 1999.

Knysh, Alexander. "Ibn Arab." *Medieval Islamic Civilization: An Encyclopedia*, ed. Josef W. Meri. New York: Routledge, 2005.

Sells, Michael. *Early Islamic Mysticism: Sufi, Qur'an, Mi'raj, Poetic and Theological Writings*. New York: Paulist Press, 1996.

■ **Journals**

Abdul Haq, Muhammad. "Significance of the Isra'-Mi'raj in Sufism." *Islamic Quarterly* 34, no. 1 (1990): 32–58.

Elmore, Gerald. "New Evidence on the Early Life of Ibn al-'Arabi." *Journal of the American Oriental Society* 117, no. 2 (1997): 347–349.

Halligan, Fredrica. "The Creative Imagination of the Sufi Mystic Ibn Arabi." *Journal of Religion and Health* 40, no. 2 (Summer 2001): 275–287.

Morris, James. "The Spiritual Ascension: Ibn Arabi and the Mi'raj." *Journal of the American Oriental Society* 107, no. 4 (October–December 1987): 629–652, and 108, no. 1 (January–March 1988): 63–77.

Sells, Michael. "Ibn 'Arabi's Polished Mirror: Perspective Shift and Meaning Event." *Studia Islamica* 67 (1988): 121–149.

■ **Web Sites**

Clark, Jane. "Ibn Arabi and Religions." Oxford Centre for Mission Studies Web site.
http://www.ocms.ac.uk/docs/20050208_JClark.pdf

"Ibn Arabi." Stanford Encyclopedia of Philosophy Web site.
http://plato.stanford.edu/entries/ibn-arabi/

Muhyiddin Ibn 'Arabi Society Web site.
http://www.ibnarabisociety.org/index.html

—Shatha Almutawa

Document Text

IBN AL-'ARABI: *THE MECCAN ILLUMINATIONS*

I. Introduction: The Context and Purpose of the Spiritual Journey

... God said *"There is nothing like His likeness [and He is the All-Hearing, the All-Seeing]"* (Kor. 42:11), so He described Himself with a description that necessarily belongs only to Him, which is His saying: *"And He is with you wherever you are"* (Kor. 57:4). Thus He is with us wherever we are, in the state of His "descending to the heaven of this world during the last third of the night," in the state of His being *mounted upon the Throne* (Kor. 5:20; etc.), in the state of His being in the "Cloud," in the state of His being *upon the earth and in heaven* (Kor. 43:84; etc.), in the state of His being *closer to man than his jugular vein* (Kor. 50:16)—and all of these are qualifications with which only He can be described.

Hence God does not move a servant from place to place in order that (the servant) might see Him, but rather "so that He might cause him to see of His Signs" (Kor. 41:53; etc.) those that were unseen by him. He said: *"Glory to Him Who made His servant journey one night from the Sacred Place of Worship to the Furthest Place of Worship, whose surroundings We have blessed, so that We might cause him to see of Our Signs!"* (Kor. 17:1) And similarly, when God moves (any) servant through his (inner spiritual) states in order also to cause him to see His Signs, He moves him through *His* states.... (*I.e.*, God) says: "I only made him journey by night in order that he see the Signs, not (to bring him) to Me: because no place can hold Me and the relation of all places to Me is the same. For I am such that (only) 'the heart of My servant, the man of true faith, encompasses Me.' so how could he be 'made to journey to Me' while I am '*with him wherever he is*' (Kor. 57:4)?!" ...

III. The Spiritual Journeys of the Saints

As for the saints, they have spiritual journeys in the intermediate world during which they directly witness spiritual realities (*ma'ani*) embodied in forms that have become sensible for the imagination; these (sensible images) convey knowledge of the spiritual realities contained within those forms. And so they have a (spiritual) journey on the earth and in the air, without their ever having set a sensible foot in the heavens. For what distinguished God's Messenger from all the others (among the saints) was that his *body* was made to journey, so that he passed through the heavens and spheres in a way perceptible by the senses and traversed real, sensible distances. But all of that from the heavens (also belongs) to this heirs, (only) in its spiritual reality (*ma'na*), not its sensible form.

So as for what is above the heavens, let us mention what God made me directly witness in particular of the journey of the People of God. For their journeys are different (in form) because they are embodied spiritual realities, unlike the sensible journey (of the Prophet). Thus the ascensions (*ma'arij*) of the saints are the ascensions of (their) spirits and the vision of (their) hearts, (the vision) of forms in the intermediate world and of embodied spiritual realities. And we have already mentioned what we directly witnessed of that in our book called "*The Nocturnal Journey*," along with the order of (the stages of) the voyage....

Therefore whenever God wishes to journey with the spirits of whomever He wishes among the heirs of His messengers and His saints, *so that He might cause* them *to see His Signs* (Kor. 17:1)—for this is a journey to increase (their) knowledge and open the eye of (their) understanding—the modalities of their journey are different (for different individuals): and among them are those whom He causes to journey *in* Him.

Now this journey (in God) involves the "dissolving" of their composite nature. Through this journey God (first of all) acquaints them with what corresponds to them in each world (of being), by passing with them through the different sorts of worlds, both composite and simple. Then (the spiritual traveler) leaves behind in each world that part of himself which corresponds to it: the form of his leaving it behind is that God sends a barrier between that person and that part of himself he left behind in that sort of world, so that he is not aware of it. But he still has the awareness of what remains with him, until eventually he remains (alone) with the divine Mystery which is the "specific aspect" extending from God to Him. So when he alone remains (without any of those other attachments to the world), then God removes from him the barrier of the veil and he remains with God, just as everything else in him remained with (the world) corresponding to it.

Hence throughout this journey the servant remains God and not-God. And since he remains God and not-God, He makes (the servant) travel—with respect to Him, not with respect to (what is) not-Him—*in Him*, in a subtle spiritual (*ma'nawi*) journey. . . .

So when the servant has become aware of what we have just explained, so that he knows that he is not (created) according to the form of the world, but only according to the form of God (*al-Haqq*), then God *makes him journey* through His Names, *in order to cause him to see His Signs* (Kor. 17:1) within him. Thus (the servant) comes to know that He is what is designated by every divine Name—whether or not that Name is one of those described as "beautiful." It is through those Names that God appears in His servants, and it is through Them that the servant takes on the different "colorings" of his states: for They are Names in God, but "colorings" (of the soul) in us. And they are precisely the "affairs" with which God is "occupied": so it is in us and through us that He acts just as we (only) appear in Him and through Him. . . .

Thus when God makes the saint (*al-wali*) travel through His most beautiful Names to the other Names and (ultimately) all the divine Names, he comes to know the transformations of his states and the states of the whole world. And (he knows) that that transformation is what brings those very Names to be in *us*, just as we know that the transformations of (our) states (manifest) the specific influences (*ahkam*) of those Names. . . . So there is no Name that God has applied to Himself that He has not also applied to us: through (His Names) we undergo the transformations in our states, and with them we are transformed (by God) . . . .

Now when (the spiritual traveler) has completed his share of the journey through the Names and has come to know the Signs which the Names of God gave him during that journey, then he returns and "reintegrates" his self with a composition different from that initial composite nature, because of the knowledge he has gained which he did not have when he was "dissolved" (in the ascending phase of that journey). Thus he continues to pass through the different sorts of worlds, taking from each world that (aspect of himself) which he had left there and reintegrating it in his self, and he continues to appear in each successive stage (of being) until he arrives back on earth.

So "he awakens among his people" (like the Prophet), and no one knows what happened to occur to him in his innermost being (*sirr*) until he speaks (of his journey). But then they hear him speaking a language different from the one they are used to recognizing as his; and if one of them says to him "What is this?," he replies that "God made me journey by night and then caused me to see whatever Signs of His He wanted (me to see)." So those who are listening say to him: "You were not gone from us, so you were lying in what you claimed about that."

And the jurist (*faqih*) among them says: "This fellow is laying claim to prophethood (*nubuwwa*), or his intellect has become deranged: so either he is a heretic—in which case he ought to be executed—or else he is insane, in which case we have no business talking with him." Thus *"a group of people make fun of him"* (Kor. 49:11), others *"draw a lesson from him"* (Kor. 59:2), while others have faith in what he says, and thus it becomes a subject of dispute in the world. But the *faqih* was unaware of (the true meaning of) His saying: *"We shall show them Our Signs on the horizons and in their souls . . ."* (Kor. 41:53), since (God) does not specify one group rather than (any) other.

Therefore whoever God may cause to see something of these Signs in the way we have just mentioned should mention (only) *what* he has seen, but he should not mention the way. For then people will have credence in him and will look into what he says, since they will only deny what he says if he makes a claim about the way (he acquired that knowledge).

Now you should know that (in reality) there is no difference with regard to this journey between ordinary people and the person (distinguished by) this way and this characteristic. That is because (this spiritual journey) is in order to see the (divine) Signs, and the transformations of the states of ordinary people are (likewise) all Signs: they are *in* those Signs, but *"they do not notice"* (Kor. 23:56; etc.). Hence this sort (of traveler) is only distinguished from the rest of (his fellow) creatures, *those who are veiled* (Kor. 83:15), by what God has inspired in his innermost being either through his thinking and inquiry with his intellect, or, through his preparation, by polishing the mirror of his soul, for the unveiling of these Signs to him by way of inner unveiling and immediate witnessing, direct experience and ecstatic "finding."

Thus ordinary people (when they object to those who speak of this spiritual voyage) are denying precisely That within Which they are and through Which they subsist. So if (the traveler) did not mention the *way* in which he obtained the inner knowledge of these things, no one would deny or dispute him. For all of the (ordinary) people—and I do not exclude a single one of them—are "making up likenesses for God"; they have always agreed and cooperated in that, so not one of them criticizes another for doing it. God says: "*Do not make up likenesses for God . . .*" (Kor. 16:74)—yet they remain blind to that Sign.

But as for *the friends of God* (Kor. 10:64–66), they do not make up likenesses for God. For *God is the One Who makes up likenesses for the people* (Kor. 14:25; 24:35), because of His knowledge of the underlying intentions (of those symbols), since *God knows, but* we *do not know* (see Kor. 16:74; 3:66; 2:216). Thus the saint (the one truly "close to God") observes the likenesses God has made, and in that immediate witnessing he actually *sees* precisely what connects the likeness and That Which it symbolizes: for the likeness is precisely what is symbolized, with respect to that which connects them, but it is different insofar as it is a likeness. So the saint "does not make up likenesses for God"; instead, he truly *knows* what God symbolized with those likenesses. . . .

IV. Ibn 'Arabi's Personal *Mi'raj*

♦ IV-A. *The Departure from the Elemental World*

So when God wished to "journey with me to cause me to see (some) of His Signs" in His Names among my names—and that was the portion of our inheritance from the (Prophet's) nocturnal journey—He removed me from my place and ascended with me on the Buraq of my contingency. Then He penetrated with me into my (natural) elements...

So I passed through into the first heaven: nothing remained with me of my bodily nature that I (needed to) depend on or to which I (had to) pay attention.

♦ IV-B. *Adam and the First Heaven*

. . . Therefore I and my children are (all) in the Right Hand of the Truly Real (*al-Haqq*), while everything in the world other than us is in the other divine Hand.

I said: "Then we shall not be made to suffer (in Hell)?"

And (Adam) replied: "If (God's) Anger were to continue (forever), then the suffering (of the damned) would continue. But it is happiness that continues forever, although the dwellings are different, because God places in each abode (of Paradise and Gehenna) that which comprises the enjoyment of the people of that abode, which is why both abodes must necessarily be 'filled up' (*see* Kor. 11:119; etc.). For the (divine) Anger has already come to an end with the 'Greater Reviewing': (God) ordered that (His) limits be established; so they were established, and when they were established (His) Anger disappeared. (This is) because the sending down of the (divine) Message (*tanzil al-risala*) actually *is* precisely the establishment (and application) of (God's) limits for *those with whom He is angry* (Kor. 1:7), and nothing remains (after that) but (His) Good Will and *Mercy which encompasses every thing* (Kor. 7:156). So when these 'limits' (and the punishments flowing from them) have come to an end, then the (divine) authority comes back to the universal Mercy with regard to everything."

Thus my father Adam granted me the benefit of this knowledge when I was unaware of it, and that was divine good tidings for me in the life of this world, in anticipation (of its full realization in the hereafter). Therefore the Resurrection comes to an end with time, as God said: "[*The angels and the Spirit ascend to Him in a Day whose extent is*] *of fifty thousand years*" (Kor. 70:4), and this is the period of the establishment (and application) of the (divine) limits.

. . . Hence the creatures are entirely submerged in (God's) Mercy, and the authority of the (other divine) Names (only) continues in their intrinsic opposition, but *not in us*. So you should know that, for it is a rare and subtle knowledge that (most people) do not realize. Instead, ordinary people are blind to it: there is no one among them who, if you were to ask him "Are you content to have applied to yourself (the influence) of those Names that give you pain?," would not reply "No!" and have the influence of that painful Name applied to someone else in his stead. But such a person is among the most ignorant of people concerning the creatures—and he is even more ignorant of the Truly Real!

So this (experience of) immediate witnessing informed (us) concerning the continuation of the authority (*hukm*) of the Names (*i.e.*, other than those of Mercy) with regard to those Names (in themselves), but not in us. For those Names are *relations* whose realities are intrinsically opposed, so that they (can) never become united (in a way that would erase their inherent relational distinctions). But God extends His Mercy to (all) His servants wherever they are, since Being in its entirety *is* Mercy. . . .

♦ IV-F. *Aaron and the Fifth Heaven*

Next I alighted to stay with Aaron, and (there) I found Yahya, who had already reached him before me. So I said to (Yahya): "I didn't see you on my path: is there some other path there?"

And he replied: "Each person has a path, that no one else but he travels."

I said: "Then where are they, these (different) paths?"

Then he answered: "They come to be through the traveling itself."

. . . I said: "O Aaron, some people among the true Knowers have claimed that the existence (of the external world) disappeared with regard to them, so that they see nothing but God, and so that nothing of the world remains with them that might distract them, in comparison with God. Nor is there any doubt that they (really) are in that (spiritual) rank, as opposed to those like you. Now God has informed us that you said to your brother (Moses) when he was angry (with you for having allowed the Israelites to worship the golden calf): '... *so do not cause (our) enemies to gloat over me!*' (Kor. 7:151). Thus you posited their having a certain power (over you in the external world), and this condition is different from the condition of those true Knowers (who experience the 'disappearance' of the external world)."

Then he replied: "They spoke sincerely (about their experience). However, they did not have any more than what was given them by their immediate experience *(dhawq)*. But look and see—did what disappeared from them (in that state actually) disappear from the world?"

"No," I answered.

He said: "Then they were lacking in the knowledge of the way things are, to the extent of what they missed, since the world was non-existent for them. So they were lacking the True Reality *(al-Haqq)* to the extent of that (aspect) of the world which was veiled from them. Because the whole world is precisely the Self-manifestation *(tajalli)* of the Truly Real, for whoever really knows the Truly Real. *So where are you going? It is only a reminder to the worlds* (Kor. 81:26-27) of the way things are!" . . .

♦ **IV-G. *Moses and the Sixth Heaven***

. . . After that I said to him: "Surely God has chosen you over the people with His Message and His Word.' But you requested the vision (of God), while the Messenger of God said that 'not one of you will see His Lord until he dies'?"

So he said: "And it was just like that: when I asked Him for the vision (of God), He answered me, so that '*I fell down stunned*' (Kor. 7:143). Then I saw Him in my '(state of) being stunned'."

I said: "While (you were) dead?"

He replied: "While (I was) dead."

. . . He said: ". . . So I did not see God until I had died. It was then that I '*awakened,*' so that I knew *Who* I saw. And it was because of that that I said '*I have returned to you*' (Kor. 7:143), since I did not return to anyone but Him."

Then I said to him: "You are among the group of 'those who know God,' so what did you consider the vision of God (to be) when you asked Him for it?"

And he said: "(I considered it to be) necessary because of rational necessity."

I said: "But then what was it that distinguished you from others?"

He said: "I was seeing Him (all along), and yet I didn't use to *know* that it was Him! But when my 'dwelling' was changed and I saw Him, then I knew *Who* I saw. Therefore when I 'awoke' I was no longer veiled, and my vision (of God) went on accompanying me throughout all eternity. So this is the difference between us and *those who are veiled* (Kor. 83:15) from their knowledge (of God) by what they see. Yet when they die they see the Truly Real, since the 'dwelling' (of divine Vision) distinguishes Him for them. Therefore if they were returned (to this world as I was), they would say the same thing as we did."

I said: "Then if death were the 'dwelling' of the vision of God, every dead person would see him—but God has described them (at Kor. 83:15) as being '*veiled*' from seeing Him!?"

He said: "Yes, those are '*the ones who are veiled*' from the knowledge that what (they see) *is* God. But what if you yourself had to meet a person with whom you were not personally acquainted, whom you were looking for (simply) by name and because you needed him? You could meet him and exchange greetings with him, along with the whole group of those you encountered, without discovering his identity: then you would have seen him and yet not have seen him, so you would continue looking for him while he was right where you could see him! Hence one cannot rely on anything but knowledge. That is why we (Knowers of God) have said that Knowledge is His very Essence, since if Knowledge were not His very Essence, what was relied on (i.e., our knowledge) would be other than God—for nothing can be relied on but knowledge."

I said: "Now God indicated the mountain to you (at Kor. 7:143) and mentioned about Himself that '*He manifested Himself to the Mountain*' (Kor. 7:143). [So how do these theophanies differ?]"

Then he replied: "Nothing resists His Self-manifestation; therefore the particular condition *(hal)* necessarily changes [according to the 'locus' of each

Document Text

theophany]. Hence for the mountain being '*crushed flat*' was like Moses' being '*stunned*': God says '*Moses*' (Kor. 7:144), and (He) Who crushed it stunned me."

I said to him: "God has taken charge of teaching me, so I (only) know about Him to the extent of what He bestows on me."

Then he replied: "That is just how He acts with the Knowers of God, so take (your spiritual knowledge) from Him, not from the world. And indeed you will never take (such knowledge) except to the extent of your predisposition (*isti'dad*). So do not let yourself be veiled from Him by the likes of us (prophets)! For you will never come to know about Him by means of us anything but what we know about Him through His Self-manifestation. Thus we too only give you (knowledge) about Him to the extent of your predisposition. Hence there is no difference [between learning from us and directly from God], so attach yourself to Him! For He only sent us to call you all to *Him*, not to call you to us. (His Message) is *a Word (that is) the same between us and you: that we should worship none but God, and that we should not associate anything with Him, and that some of us should not take others as lords instead of God* (Kor. 3:64)."

I said: "That is how it came in the *Qur'an*!"
He said: "And that is how He is."

I said: "With what did you hear 'God's Speech'?"
He said: "With my hearing."
I said: "And what is your 'hearing'?"
He said: "*He* (is)."
I said: "Then by what were you distinguished (from other men)?"
He said: "By an immediate personal experience (*dhawq*) in that regard, which can only be known by the person who actually experiences it."
I said: "So those who possess such immediate experiences are like that?"
"Yes," he said, "and (their) experiences are according to (their spiritual) ranks."

◆ **IV-H.** *The Seventh Heaven: Abraham and the Temple of the Heart*

. . . Then I saw the *Inhabited House* (Kor. 52:4), and suddenly there was my Heart—and there were the angels who "enter It every day"! The Truly Real manifests Himself to (the Heart), which (alone) encompasses Him, in "seventy thousand veils of light and darkness." Thus He manifests Himself to the Heart of His servant through those (veils)—for "if He were" to manifest Himself without them, "the radiant splendors of His Face would burn up" the creaturely part of that servant.

Glossary

Aaron	the brother of Moses and the first high priest of Israel
Gehenna	the underworld; hell
Kor.	an abbreviation of "Koran" and an alternate English rendering of Qur'an; the numbers refer first to the sura, or chapter, and then to the specific verse(s)
Moses	the Hebrew patriarch and lawgiver to the Israelites, best remembered for leading the Israelites out of bondage in Egypt and for receiving the Ten Commandments on Mount Sinai
theophanies	manifestations of God that are not visible
Yahya	John the Baptist, the forerunner of Jesus who prepared the way for Jesus's arrival

Thor catching a serpent, from the Snorra Edda
(Thor Catching the Midgard Serpent, from 'Melsted's Edda' [pen & ink and w/c on paper], Icelandic School, [18th century] / Arni Magnusson Institute, Reykjavik, Iceland / The Bridgeman Art Library International)

SNORRA EDDA

ca. 1220

"Odin . . . set off from Turkey and took with him a very great following, young people and old, men and women, and they took with them many precious things."

Overview

The name *Edda* is given to two interrelated bodies of mythology originating in Iceland in the thirteenth century. *Snorra Edda* (otherwise called the "younger" or "prose" Edda) is attributed to the Icelandic chieftain Snorri Sturluson and was probably composed around 1220. The *Poetic Edda* (or "elder" Edda) is a manuscript from about 1270 that collects a number of anonymous poems about the Norse gods and legendary heroes. Many of these poems are likely to be much older than the manuscript itself, and some may date back to the period before the conversion of Iceland to Christianity around 1000. *Snorra Edda* also quotes from several of the poems that are preserved in the *Poetic Edda*, proving that these texts were in circulation in Iceland before the *Poetic Edda* manuscript was produced.

Snorra Edda, excerpted here, comprises four distinct sections. The last two, entitled "Skáldskaparmál" (The Language of Poetry) and "Háttatal" (List of Poetic Meters), make up a technical treatise about the composition of Old Norse verse and are only tangentially related to pagan mythology, in that "Skáldskaparmál" contains several individual myths that relate to poetry or explain features in the poems that Snorri cites. The most important section of *Snorra Edda* viewed as a document of pre-Christian culture is "Gylfaginning" (The Tricking of Gylfi), which is excerpted here and provides an overview of all of Norse mythology. It takes the form of a dialogue between three of the Aesir—the Old Norse pagan gods—and King Gylfi, who elicits information from the Aesir with a series of naive-sounding questions about their beliefs. Additionally, a prologue precedes "Gylfaginning," providing a pseudohistorical context, expressed in learned and obviously Christian language, for the mythology that follows.

Context

Snorra Edda was written during a period of relatively rapid change in Iceland. The island had been discovered in 874 by the Vikings, who were Norse explorers and warriors, although a handful of Irish monks had actually preceded them. During the period ranging from 930 to 1262, Iceland was a commonwealth ruled by a body of chieftains, who formed a parliament that is often cited as the world's oldest. There was nothing in the way of a central government, so laws were enforced locally, sometimes through blood feuds (spurred by the obligation of a family to avenge a death or injury to one of its members at the hands of another family). During these years, Iceland's population grew steadily, and the exploits of its settlers provided considerable material for sagas about them. Most of these settlers were pagans who worshipped Norse gods, but by the 900s pressure was growing throughout Europe to convert to Christianity. In 995, King Olaf I Tryggvason ascended the throne of Norway and tried to convert the kingdom to Christianity. By about the year 1000, many Icelanders were converting, and Christianity became the nation's "official" religion, although pagans were allowed to continue to worship in their own way. The first Christian bishops were arriving in Iceland by the mid-eleventh century. Then, the eleventh and twelfth centuries saw the consolidation of more centralized authority, reducing the influence and independence of many of the local chieftains and placing power in the hands of a few families and their leaders. This period, from about 1200 to 1262, is called the "Age of the Sturlungs," a reference to one of the two major clans that fought for control of Iceland; Snorri Sturluson was himself a member of the Sturlung clan. To gain control, the family became vassals of the Norwegian monarch, enabling them to subdue the other clans. The clans eventually capitulated and accepted the sovereignty of Norway and the Norwegian monarch.

Together, the two Eddas make up one of the most important surviving sources for the study of the Scandinavian pagan religion that Iceland's earliest settlers brought with them. The traditional, polytheistic religions of northern Europe were gradually replaced by Christianity over a period ranging from the sixth and seventh centuries (in England) to the twelfth century (in Sweden and Finland). Very few authentic written sources survive from the pagan period, such that to reconstruct Scandinavian paganism, historians have had to combine archaeological evidence with much later textual material. There is thus a very substantial

Time Line

CA. 874	Iceland is discovered by the Vikings, Norse explorers, and warriors.
900–1000	Most of the mythological poems later preserved in the *Poetic Edda* are composed.
995	King Olaf I Tryggvason ascends the throne of Norway and attempts to convert the kingdom to Christianity.
999–1000	Iceland formally adopts Christianity as the national religion.
1056	The first Christian bishop arrives in Iceland.
1179	Snorri Sturluson is born in Hvammur, Iceland.
1200	The "Age of the Sturlungs" begins.
CA. 1200	Snorri writes the *Snorra Edda*.
1230s	Civil war erupts in Norway over the issue of succession to the throne.
1241	Snorri is killed by agents of the king of Norway, Haakon IV.
1270	A collection of Norse poems dubbed the Codex Regius manuscript is composed.
CA. 1300	The oldest surviving manuscript of *Snorra Edda* is written.
1643	The title *Poetic Edda* is first given to the Codex Regius manuscript.

chronological gap—of at least two hundred years—between the end of paganism as a dominant religion and the writing of *Snorra Edda*. Accordingly, its usefulness and reliability as a witness to pre-Christian religious culture have often been questioned.

There is no evidence that what is now known as the *Snorra Edda* was ever considered a sacred text: Norse paganism possessed no sacred book analogous to the scriptures of the Judeo-Christian-Islamic type. Moreover, *Snorra Edda* was written down by Christians in a Christian nation. It does draw on traditions that appear to originate in a much earlier period, but it also shows clear signs of having been reworked for a Christian audience, although the author tries to present his narrative as a straightforward account of what pagans believed. Neither of the Eddas tells very much about religious practice: They are almost entirely mythological texts, and one of the challenges facing historians of religion is to work out how these entertaining tales of the gods relate to what earlier pagans actually believed and how these beliefs manifested in people's daily lives.

The meaning of the title *Edda* is difficult to determine and probably has no bearing on the content of the texts. It is most likely derived from the Old Icelandic word for "great-grandmother"—implying that these stories might have been passed down from generation to generation—or from the Latin verb *edo,* which means "to compose poetry." There is no evidence that the term *Edda* was ever applied to a body of myths in the pagan period itself. Even in the thirteenth and fourteenth centuries, only *Snorra Edda* bore this title; the *Poetic Edda* manuscript is untitled and, after being known as the Codex Regius manuscript, was given its Eddic name in the seventeenth century.

It is important to distinguish between the contexts that produced the myths contained in the Eddas and the Eddas themselves. *Snorra Edda* and the *Poetic Edda* both preserve material that is likely to have existed in some form—in earlier manuscripts, perhaps, or prior to them in oral tradition—for generations before their creation in the thirteenth century. While it is impossible to identify with certainty the context that produced either the "original" myths or the orally transmitted poems that preserved them, the *Snorra Edda* itself is undoubtedly rooted in thirteenth-century Iceland. It stemmed from a relatively new antiquarian interest in the pagan past, which by this time could be viewed with scholarly detachment as a distinct historical epoch that had now passed. The initial focus of this new wave of Icelandic scholarship was on poetry: Scholars like Snorri Sturluson began to view traditional poetry as a subject worthy of academic study, and they wanted to both perpetuate traditional forms of literature and encourage their contemporaries to produce new verse in the old manner. (Snorri himself was a most accomplished poet who favored traditional forms in his own poems.) This focus was partly a question of national prestige: Icelanders were very conscious of the importance of their poetic heritage, which provided direct links back to their ancestors. Old poems were also regarded as supplying crucial evidence about the history of Iceland, and their preservation was an important corollary of the flourishing of Scandinavian historical writing in the twelfth century.

The oldest poems known to medieval Icelanders originated in the settlement period (ca. 870–1000) and thus were the products of a pagan culture. Traditionally, Old Norse poetry had been closely bound up with pagan religion: The chief of the gods, Odin, was also the god of poetry and the wellspring of artistic inspiration. Poetry from the

Red-figure cup depicting scenes from the Trojan War
(Attic red-figure cup depicting scenes from the Trojan War, c.490 BC [pottery] [detail], Brygos Painter [c.500-475 BC] / Louvre, Paris, France / Giraudon / The Bridgeman Art Library International)

pre-Christian era abounds in references to the gods and allusions to myths, and it seems that *Snorra Edda* was produced partly as a response to the thirteenth-century revival of interest in pagan verse. *Snorra Edda* is, in part, a technical manual about how to compose and appreciate traditional forms of poetry, but to do so fully, its audience needed to understand the place of myth within that poetry. Snorri therefore added a mythological handbook, "Gylfaginning," to his work in order to explain the mythological background of the poems that he discusses later in the Edda.

Snorra Edda displays quite clearly the new interest in pagan culture, poetry, and mythology that permeated thirteenth-century Icelandic writing, but it should be remembered that the work is the product of a learned, Christian milieu. Even if some pagan mythological traditions were then still alive in Scandinavia, in the sense that people remembered the stories or some of the poems, they could be appreciated only as historical phenomena—as products of a dead culture that had been superseded by Christianity, and not as part of a living belief system.

About the Author

The author of *Snorra Edda* is perhaps the most famous figure in the history of medieval Iceland. Snorri Sturluson, born in 1179 in Hvammur, Iceland, was an extremely influential and wealthy chieftain and a lawyer who served two terms as Iceland's law-speaker, the highest office in the country. Contemporary sources portray him as a wily and manipulative political operator. They are largely silent, however, about his role in the production of Old Norse literature; his biography—which forms part of a text called Íslendinga saga (The Story [or History] of the Icelanders), written by his nephew Sturla Thordarson—mentions only that Snorri "had some books of sagas put together," a reference that is ambiguous about both his authorship and the nature of the books in question. Alongside the *Snorra Edda*, Snorri is often credited with writing the great collection of historical sagas known as Heimskringla and—more dubiously—with Egils saga, a biography of medieval Iceland's greatest poet, from whom Snorri was descended on his mother's side.

Although his authorship of prose works is doubtful, Snorri had a well-founded contemporary reputation as a poet, and the last part of *Snorra Edda* is structured around a long poem in honor of the Norwegian rulers King Haakon IV Haakonsson and Earl Skúli Baardsson, whom Snorri is known to have visited during two trips abroad (in 1218–1220 and 1237–1239); there is thus circumstantial evidence to suggest that Snorri really did write "Háttatal." In the end, Snorri fell out with the Norwegian royal family,

Essential Quotes

"Almighty God created heaven and earth and all things in them, and lastly two humans from whom generations are descended, Adam and Eve, and their stock multiplied and spread over all the world. But as time passed mankind became diverse: some were good and orthodox in faith, but many more turned aside to follow the lusts of the world and neglected God's commandments."

"And so they believed that he ruled all things on earth and in the sky, of heaven and the heavenly bodies, of the sea and the weathers. But so as to be better able to give an account of this and fix it in memory, they then gave a name among themselves to everything, and this religion has changed in many ways as nations became distinct and languages branched."

"Odin . . . set off from Turkey and took with him a very great following, young people and old, men and women, and they took with them many precious things. And whatever countries they passed through, great glory was spoken of them, so that they seemed more like gods than men."

"King Gylfi was clever and skilled in magic. He was quite amazed that the Æsir-people had the ability to make everything go in accordance with their will. He wondered whether this could be as a result of their own nature, or whether the divine powers they worshipped could be responsible."

"Gangleri began his questioning thus: 'Who is the highest and most ancient of all gods?' High said: 'He is called All-father in our language. . . . He lives throughout all ages and rules all his kingdom . . . .' Then spoke Just-as-high: 'He made heaven and earth and the skies and everything in them.' Then spoke Third: 'But his greatest work is that he made man and gave him a soul that shall live and never perish.'"

who at that time had designs on gaining control of Iceland. After initially siding with the Norwegians, Snorri fell foul of the king as something approaching civil war engulfed Norway, and he was killed by one of King Haakon IV's new Icelandic allies in 1241.

The earliest surviving manuscript of *Snorra Edda* (also known as the *Uppsala Edda*), which was written around 1300, attributes the whole text to Snorri, in a heading that states: "This book is called Edda. Snorri Sturluson has put it together according to the manner in which it is arranged." There is then a brief list of contents, confirming that the scribe of the manuscript differentiated between "Háttatal," "Skáldskaparmál," and the "stories about the Aesir" now known as "Gylfaginning." The Uppsala manuscript does not mention the prologue in this list, but the prologue is indeed present, as it is in all four of the main manuscripts of *Snorra Edda*. Some scholars have suggested that Snorri did not write the prologue to the *Snorra Edda*, since it seems to be notably more Christian in tone than the rest of the work. However, it is pointless to speculate about the authorship of individual parts of *Snorra Edda*, with the likely exception of "Háttatal." Either the text is the work of Snorri alone, or else it has been put together by some later hand and then falsely attributed to Snorri; either way, all the evidence suggests that *Snorra Edda* has always been thought to comprise the four sections, just as the Uppsala manuscript states. The prologue is integral to the Edda as a whole, whether or not the text that survives matches what Snorri Sturluson originally composed.

Explanation and Analysis of the Document

This excerpt from *Snorra Edda* comprises the whole of the prologue and the first chapters of "Gylfaginning." These sections are key to understanding the Edda as a whole, and particularly to determining the author's attitude toward pagan religion. The prologue sets out the text's scholarly interpretative framework and acts as an introduction to, and apology for, the culture of Snorri's pagan Norse ancestors. The beginning of "Gylfaginning," meanwhile, uses a distinctive narrative device—the frame narrative—that places further distance between the audience and the phenomena of paganism that Snorri wishes to describe.

♦ Prologue

The prologue to *Snorra Edda* begins with the strikingly Christian statement that "Almighty God created heaven and earth," echoing the opening of Genesis. It is clear at once that Snorri's approach to paganism is that of an outsider looking in, and his main concern in beginning is to account for pagan religion as an outdated historical phenomenon in the context provided by universal Christian history. In this long introductory paragraph, Snorri places the origins of pagan belief within a chronology provided by the Old Testament: He mentions both Adam and Eve and the story of Noah's flood, in each case noting that early humankind tended to forget God's commandments as nations grew populous and divided from one another.

To explain how people went from forgetting the true God to worshipping false deities, Snorri suggests that paganism arose from a fundamental misunderstanding of the natural world. God granted all people a degree of innate rational wisdom, by which early pagans sought to understand their surroundings. By making observations about the world—and Snorri gives several convoluted examples of such thought processes—pagans eventually arrived at a sort of natural religion, believing that inanimate objects have some kind of life force. Extrapolating from these observations, pagans then began to imagine that some kind of higher power must control the natural world. It seems that the pagans were already groping toward the idea of a single, supreme God, but because they had earthly rather than spiritual understanding, they could not recover God's true identity. It is notable that Snorri never blames pagans for their beliefs or suggests that they had been deceived by Satan, as many medieval Christian authors claimed. Snorri represents the development of pagan religions as a rational, if misguided, process; he does not judge pagans in the way that most Christian theorists did.

The rest of the prologue provides a detailed, but spurious account of how paganism developed in Scandinavia. The dominant mode of interpretation in this part of the text is informed by euhemerism—a popular theory in the medieval world that explained away pagan gods by reducing them to human heroes who, over time, came to be worshipped on account of their superior qualities and achievements. Snorri purports to believe that the Norse gods were ultimately descended from the heroes of the Trojan War. Troy, which Snorri situates "near the middle of the world," in Turkey, is represented as the very best of places, and its inhabitants were the very best of people. This idea was quite common in medieval Europe, where, despite the disdainful Christian attitude toward pagan religion itself, a nation's descent from the noble pagan heroes of classical legend had considerable cachet. The Icelanders were certainly aware of the prestige of the Troy story, since a version called *Trójumanna saga* was composed in Old Norse; Snorri almost certainly got most of his version of these events from a version of that saga.

Ancient Troy is a long way in space and time from Scandinavia, however, and Snorri needs to use an ingenious (but disingenuous) device to connect the two regions. He has observed the superficial similarity between the god name *Thor* and the Old Norse name for Troy, *Trója*. Thus, he invents for King Priam a son named "Tror," whom the Norse people call "Thor." On the basis of this false etymology, Snorri is able to construct a full genealogy for the Norse gods that eventually links the Trojans to Odin. In all other sources—and, indeed, in "Gylfaginning"—Odin is Thor's father, but here Snorri manipulates the gods' family tree in order to place this "Tror/Thor" back in Troy. Many of the other names in the gods' genealogy are drawn from Germanic legend, rather than from pagan religion proper.

It is Odin who decides to relocate to Scandinavia, and on his journey there Snorri outlines the euhemeristic process by which people in the northern lands began to worship the human Aesir (or Æsir)—a name that Snorri falsely translates as "men of Asia"—as gods. The prologue concludes with Snorri's linking the gods with the royal families of the different Scandinavian nations; deriving the royal family line from the gods was also a common trope in medieval Norse historical writing. He also attributes the fact that a single language was spoken all across Scandinavia to the Aesir's travels across the region, during which time their "Asian" language, the language of Troy, was universally adopted.

♦ "Gylfaginning"

The story of "Gylfaginning" begins in the same pseudohistorical world outlined in the prologue. At this point in Snorri's version, the Aesir are still humans, although mythological features enter the narrative right from the start. The protagonist, Gylfi, is a legendary king of Sweden who is known from other sources, including the poem *Ragnarsdrápa*, by Bragi Boddason (known as Bragi the Old), which Snorri quotes to support his account of how Gylfi was tricked into giving up some of his lands by Gefiun, one of the Aesir. From the beginning of the text, the Aesir are shown to be deceitful, and this is an important theme throughout "Gylfaginning." Snorri uses this theme as a way of distancing his audience from the mythological information that he relates; since the Aesir are consistently deceitful and the information they give unreliable, the Christian audience is given hints that pagan myths contain no religious truth—a fact Snorri points out explicitly in an address to his readers at the start of "Skáldskaparmál."

The poems that Snorri cites in this section are examples of skaldic court poetry, attributed to named historical Scandinavian poets. In contrast to the poems of the *Poetic Edda*, this type of verse is not primarily mythological, though poets often allude to the pagan gods in obscure language and make reference to stories known from the Eddas. The stanzas quoted here are both attributed to Norwegian poets from the ninth and tenth centuries. This is the type of poetry with which Snorri is concerned in "Skáldskaparmál," but once Gylfi enters the Aesir's hall, he hears only anonymous Eddic (mythological) poems. It seems likely that this is a deliberate device that helps to separate the "real" world—which Gylfi inhabits—from the mythical world of the Aesir, since the Eddic poems are considered purer iterations of the myths.

When Gylfi decides to visit the Aesir in order to test whether they are human or divine, he is shown into a mysterious hall, called Asgard, where he meets three characters called High, Just-as-high, and Third. These figures are all aspects of Odin; High and Third are found elsewhere as names for the god. The decision to divide Odin into three distinct characters serves a narrative purpose, as much of "Gylfaginning" is based on a tripartite structure in which each god-character in turn reveals a piece of mythological information. It is also possible, however, that Snorri was influenced by the idea of the Holy Trinity in ascribing three separate identities to a single deity.

Once Gylfi, assuming the name of Gangleri, has entered Asgard, the opening frame-narrative concludes, and the main part of "Gylfaginning" begins with a challenge. Gylfi and the Aesir are to exchange knowledge with each other; whoever is proved wiser at the end will win—and the loser cannot expect to leave Asgard unharmed. This structure echoes traditional knowledge contests that are also found in the *Poetic Edda*. To underline this point, Snorri later quotes from "Vafthrudnismal," a poem that provides mythological information in the form of a contest between Odin and a giant named Vafthrudnir. (Although Vafthrudnir is the one quoted in this text, in the poem, Odin wins, just as he does in the majority of knowledge-exchange myths.)

From this point in the narrative, "Gylfaginning" assumes a question-and-answer format, which is an effective means of giving a lot of information in a short space. Gylfi asks the three Aesir a question, and either High alone responds or each of them responds in turn. High usually gives the essential or fullest answers, followed by Just-as-high and then Third, whose replies sometimes modify or even contradict those of his fellow respondents. Gylfi's questions seem straightforward and—to anybody who knows anything about Norse mythology—naive. But, in fact, they have been carefully chosen both to move the narrative along and perhaps to influence the audience's perception of the information that the Aesir give.

Gylfi begins by asking about the Aesir's supreme god. In response, they name "All-Father," which is a traditional cognomen, or distinguishing name, for Odin. They do not refer to themselves as gods, but it is clear at this point in the text that the Aesir, though powerful, are still subordinate to a higher power whom they worship. A list of alternative names for Odin follows, which is a reflection of a widespread phenomenon in Norse pagan culture: All the gods, and Odin in particular, had a very wide range of bynames that reflected different aspects of their character or abilities.

What is remarkable about this Odin, however, is that he sounds suspiciously like the omnipotent Christian Creator-God. He created the whole world and everything in it; he endowed humankind with a soul; and good people dwell with him in Valhalla, while the wicked go to Hel, a place of punishment much like the Christian hell. None of these features much resemble Odin as known from other sources. Indeed, Snorri goes on to tell a story of the creation of the universe in which Odin has a different role altogether. It seems that Snorri means to refer to the notion expressed in the prologue that pagans originally had some knowledge of God but forgot his name. So here, Odin performs the Christian God's functions but goes by the name of the chief of the Aesir.

A long section in "Gylfaginning" is devoted to an account of the creation of the universe. It is based upon an amalgam of different traditions, combining information from the Eddic poems "Völuspá," "Völuspá hin skamma" (or "Shorter Völuspá") "Vafthrudnismal," and "Grimnismal." But these poems provide different information about the creation, and in combining them Snorri produces a version of events that resembles none of the individual poems and which may not reflect genuine pagan beliefs very closely at all. "Völuspá" is Snorri's most important poetic source, since it is the only text in the *Poetic Edda* that tells the whole history of the pagan universe, from its creation to its eventual destruction at Ragnarök, the Norse apocalypse. Snorri follows the chronology of "Völuspá" throughout "Gylfaginning," although he adds much information that is not found in that poem.

Although High has already told Gylfi that Odin created the world and everything that belongs to it, this section contradicts that statement by making the creation an almost-spontaneous process based on natural forces. In this schema, Odin is not the first being in the world but rather is descended from frost-giants, who were the first "race" to appear in the universe. Overall, the Aesir's account of how the cosmos came into being is famously convoluted and hard to follow, perhaps because of Snorri's difficulty in reconciling the several different versions of the myth that the poems preserve.

To begin with, there was just Ginnungagap, the "Mighty Void." This name does not appear anywhere else, although "Völuspá" says that "the void was expansive" (*gap var ginnunga* in Old Norse). Snorri may have coined the name on the basis of that poem's statement. Ginnungagap was presumably completely empty, but according to the Aesir, two landmasses later arose that began to fill it. Niflheim, in the north, was cold; Muspell (or Muspellsheim) was its polar opposite, being a very hot and fiery land in the southern region. In this version of the creation, the elemental opposition of heat and cold provides the motor for the universe's development. As the ice from Niflheim encounters the warmth emanating from the south, it melts and then hardens again, like clinker (incombustible matter) in a furnace. Some scholars have seen in this account a particularly Icelandic viewpoint, since the creation of land here seems to resemble the process by which a volcanic landscape—successively liquid and solid—is created. It is notable that the division of the universe into three zones—hot in the south, cold in the north, and temperate in the middle—closely parallels Snorri's description of the earth's geography in the prologue.

In this account of the mythology, the universe itself is made out of the body of Ymir, the primeval giant. While the idea of the creation of the cosmos through the dismemberment of a single being is paralleled in other world mythologies—and this story is also found in the *Poetic Edda*—Gylfi seems to doubt the Aesir's testimony, which is admittedly rather confused. Gylfi's questions are pointed: If Ymir was the first being in the universe, what did he live on? High replies by saying that Ymir was suckled by the great cow, Audhumla (who does not appear in the poetic sources). Gylfi's follow-up question demands to know, therefore, what the cow could possibly have eaten; it seems that questions of this type may serve not solely to test the Aesir's knowledge but also to show up the logical inconsistencies in their story. If Ymir was the being out of which everything else was created, how did Audhumla come into being? Did she preexist Ymir, or was she somehow part of creation?

At the end of this section there is another crucial reference to the relationship between the Aesir's knowledge and the nature of their religion. Here, High reintroduces Odin, who he now refers to as one of the gods, the "rulers of heaven and earth." But it is clear that Gylfi does not share High's belief in Odin as the "greatest and most glorious" god, since High has to try to persuade Gylfi that "you would do well to agree to call him that too." This reminds the reader that Gylfi is not a representative of paganism but an external observer who remains detached from the religious content of the information he receives. In this respect, Gylfi might well be seen as representing the author's own position: He is interested in finding out about paganism, but he is never taken in by the false knowledge that the Aesir seek to promulgate. One should also note that in Snorri's version of these events, the god Odin logically cannot be identical with the All-Father who existed outside the universe, since this Odin has a biological origin, descending directly from Ymir—even though the Aesir explicitly deny that Ymir is a god.

The final part of the section on the universe's creation deals in more detail with the way in which the world achieved its final form and its inhabitants came to life. The majority of information here is taken from the Eddic poems "Vafthrudnismal" and "Grimnismal," and there are relatively few signs that Snorri has manipulated his sources for effect. A possible sign of Christian influence, however, is in High's description of the great flood of blood that followed Ymir's killing at the hands of Odin and his brothers. In the episode as it is presented here, a frost-giant named Bergelmir becomes a Noah figure, escaping the flood in his "ark" and thereby preserving the giant race. However, the poem that tells the same story, and from which Snorri has High recite lines, does not mention an "ark." Rather, it says that Bergelmir was laid on a "box," perhaps referring to a coffin. Snorri either has misunderstood his source or—more likely—has once again taken the opportunity to introduce a parallel between pagan and Christian mythology in order to support the points made in the prologue about the ways in which paganism grew out of a distorted impression of Christian truth.

Although the pagan gods do not create the universe in this version of the myth, they are responsible for shaping it, as the Aesir describe in some detail. Odin and his brothers also give life to humankind when they animate some tree trunks that they find on the shore. Some scholars have suggested that the names given to the first humans, Ask and Embla, resemble Adam and Eve rather suspiciously, although these names are also found in "Völuspá." Another important link to the prologue is provided when High tells Gylfi that the Aesir refer to the gods' chief city, Asgard, as Troy. Through this device, the audience is reminded that the people telling the story, for all their great knowledge and uncanny abilities, are not gods but people, and they exist within the historical framework that Snorri established in the prologue.

At this point in the structure of "Gylfaginning," the Aesir's speeches change slightly, as they start to tell Gylfi longer stories in response to his questions; eventually, they almost abandon the question-and-answer format in favor of simply relating whole myths. This section concludes with the first reference in the text to the end of the pagan world, known as Ragnarök, with which "Gylfaginning" concludes and which High foreshadows here, providing a signpost to the idea that the doom of the old gods is inevitable; there is, ultimately, no future in paganism.

Audience

While the original audience of the mythology related in *Snorra Edda* was undoubtedly a pagan one, no evidence survives to reveal in what contexts they were performed or passed around in the pre-Christian period. Some scholars have suggested that the myths had a direct connection to pagan religious practice; some may even have had a ritual function. These links, however, are highly controversial and remain unproved.

The Eddas themselves seem to have been created for a literary elite in thirteenth-century Iceland—probably a relatively small group of scholars and writers who were interested in traditional Icelandic culture. Judging by the contents of surviving manuscripts and a few references to the text in other works, *Snorra Edda* was viewed as being a work primarily about poetry rather than religion. Its main audience, therefore, was probably found among poets and poetry enthusiasts. By the time the latest medieval manuscript of *Snorra Edda* was written around 1350, however, traditional skaldic poetry had begun to go out of fashion once again, and no more is heard of the Eddas in the medieval period. It was only after the Reformation that a new generation of antiquarians turned to *Snorra Edda* and began to treat it as a source of information about pagan mythology and religion. At the same time, the manuscript of the *Poetic Edda* was rediscovered and given this title.

Impact

Neither of the Eddas is a sacred text; neither has any direct and unambiguous connection to pagan religion. They are both retrospective compilations of mythological lore that were produced by people who did not believe in the gods who populate the stories. *Snorra Edda* displays obvious signs of having been written with a Christian audience in mind, approaching paganism from a learned Christian viewpoint. As such, the reliability of the Eddas' testimony about pagan beliefs is open to question. At the same time, the two Eddas, taken together, provide the fullest account of Norse mythology that survives; they surely preserve a good amount of much older material that did, in fact, originate in the pagan culture of pre-Christian Scandinavia. *Snorra Edda*, in particular, is an essential reference tool that allows historians to make sense of older Norse poetry that would otherwise be extremely obscure. The Eddas' value to the study of Old Norse religion and culture therefore remains extremely important. Without them, the myths of the pagan North would survive merely as scattered fragments, and the process of reconstructing pre-Christian Norse religious culture would be even more difficult than it is today. When approached critically and combined with historical and archaeological evidence, the Eddas give an unparalleled glimpse into the pagan world, even though the versions of the myths that they present are at least partly viewed through the eyes of medieval Christians.

Questions for Further Study

1. *Snorra Edda* was written during an era when Iceland was converting from an older pagan Norse religion to Christianity. How does the document represent a blend of earlier pagan beliefs and the newer Christian beliefs?

2. The *Snorra Edda* originated in the pagan Norse mythology and legends of first-millennium Iceland. In what sense, then, can the document be said to resemble the *Nihongi* of Japan, which likewise was written during the medieval period? In particular, how did geography play a role in the shape of the legends?

3. Faiths such as Wicca tended to originate in northern Europe. Can you trace any similarities between the legendary material and worldview of Icelanders as reflected in the *Snorra Edda* and those of Wiccans as reflected in Gerald Gardner's *Book of Shadows*?

4. The medieval sagas of Scandinavia and Iceland continue to be studied by scholars for their literary qualities, in much the same way they study, for example, the epics by Homer or the ancient *Epic of Gilgamesh.* Later, in the nineteenth century, scholars became interested in northern European stories that today are commonly called fairy tales; the collections by the Grimm brothers are noteworthy examples. Do you see any similarities between the legends transmitted in the *Snorra Edda* and traditional Germanic fairy tales you may be familiar with (examples might include "Cinderella," "Little Red Riding Hood," "Hansel and Gretel," and "Rumpelstiltskin")?

5. The word *Paganism* often has negative connotations, implying ignorance and backwardness. Yet, as the entry states, the author of the *Snorra Edda* recognized that "pagans eventually arrived at a sort of natural religion, believing that inanimate objects have some kind of life force." Do you believe that there exists a "life force" in the objects of the natural world? Explain.

Further Reading

■ **Books**

Abram, Christopher. *Myths of the Pagan North: The Gods of the Norsemen*. London: Continuum Books, 2011.

Gunnell, Terry. "Eddic Poetry." In *A Companion to Old Norse–Icelandic Literature and Culture*, ed. Rory McTurk. Oxford, U.K.: Blackwell, 2004.

Larrington, Carolyne, trans. *The Poetic Edda*. Oxford, U.K.: Oxford University Press, 1996.

Lindow, John. "Mythology and Mythography." In *Old Norse–Icelandic Literature: A Critical Guide*, ed. Carol J. Clover and John Lindow. Ithaca, N.Y.: Cornell University Press, 1985.

Lindow, John. *Norse Mythology: A Guide to the Gods, Heroes, Rituals, and Beliefs*. New York: Oxford University Press, 2001.

Snorri Sturluson. *Edda*, trans. Anthony Faulkes. London: J. M. Dent & Sons, 1987.

Turville-Petre, E. O. G. *Myth and Religion of the North: The Religion of Ancient Scandinavia*. London: Weidenfeld and Nicholson, 1964.

Wanner, Kevin J. *Snorri Sturluson and the Edda: The Conversion of Cultural Capital in Medieval Scandinavia*. Toronto: University of Toronto Press, 2008.

■ **Web Sites**

Enoksen, Lars Magnar. "What Does a Mythological Text in Snorra Edda Tell Us about the Ritual Ceremonies That Surrounded Glíma Fights in Ancient Times?"
http://www.glima-deutschland.net/documents/Glima-History.pdf

—Christopher Abram

Snorra Edda

Prologues

Almighty God created heaven and earth and all things in them, and lastly two humans from whom generations are descended, Adam and Eve, and their stock multiplied and spread over all the world. But as time passed mankind became diverse: some were good and orthodox in faith, but many more turned aside to follow the lusts of the world and neglected God's commandments, and so God drowned the world in a flood together with all creatures in the world except those who were in the ark with Noah. After Noah's flood there lived eight people who inhabited the world and from them generations have descended, and it happened just as before that as the world came to be peopled and settled it turned out to be the vast majority of mankind that cultivated desire for wealth and glory and neglected obedience to God, and this reached such a pass that they refused to mention the name of God. But who was there then to tell their children of the mysteries of God? So it happened that they forgot the name of God and in most parts of the world there was no one to be found who knew anything about his creator. But even so God granted them earthly blessings, wealth and prosperity for them to enjoy in the world. He also gave them a portion of wisdom so that they could understand all earthly things and the details of everything they could see in the sky and on earth. They pondered and were amazed at what it could mean that the earth and animals and birds had common characteristics in some things, though there was a difference of quality. One of the earth's characteristics was that when it was dug into on high mountain tops, water sprang up there and there was no need to dig further for water there than in deep valleys. It is the same with animals and birds, that it is just as far to blood in the head as in the feet. It is a second property of the earth that every year there grows on the earth vegetation and flowers and the same year it all falls and fades. It is the same with animals and birds, that their hair and feathers grow and fall off every year. It is the third property of the earth, that when it is opened and dug, then vegetation grows on the soil which is uppermost on the earth. Rocks and stones they thought of as equivalent to teeth and bones of living creatures. From this they reasoned that the earth was alive and had life after a certain fashion, and they realized that it was enormously old in count of years and mighty in nature. It fed all creatures and took possession of everything that died. For this reason they gave it a name and traced their ancestry to it. Similarly they learned from their elderly relatives that after many hundreds of years had been reckoned there was the same earth, sun and heavenly bodies. But the courses of the heavenly bodies were various, some had a longer course and some a shorter. From such things they thought it likely that there must be some controller of the heavenly bodies who must be regulating their courses in accordance with his will, and he must be very powerful and mighty; and they assumed, if he ruled over the elements, that he must have existed before the heavenly bodies; and they realized that if he ruled the course of the heavenly bodies, he must rule the shining of the sun and the dew of the sky and the produce of the earth which is dependent on it, and similarly the wind of the sky and with it the storm of the sea. But they did not know where his kingdom was. And so they believed that he ruled all things on earth and in the sky, of heaven and the heavenly bodies, of the sea and the weathers. But so as to be better able to give an account of this and fix it in memory, they then gave a name among themselves to everything, and this religion has changed in many ways as nations became distinct and languages branched. But they understood everything with earthly understanding, for they were not granted spiritual wisdom. Thus they reasoned that everything was created out of some material.

The world was divided into three regions. From south to west and in up to the Mediterranean sea, this part was called Africa. The southern part of this section is hot and burned up by the sun. The second part from west and to the north and in up to the sea, this is called Europe or Enea. The northern part there is cold so that vegetation does not grow and habitation is impossible. From the north and over the eastern regions right to the south, that is called Asia. In that part of the world is all beauty and splendour and wealth of earthly produce, gold and jewels. The middle of the world is there too; and just as the earth there is more beautiful and better in all respects than in other places, so too mankind there was most honoured with all blessings, wisdom and strength, beauty and every kind of skill.

Near the middle of the world was constructed that building and dwelling which has been the most splendid ever, which was called Troy. We call the land there Turkey. This place was built much larger than others and with greater skill in many respects, using the wealth and resources available there. Twelve kingdoms were there and one high king, and many countries were subject to each kingdom. In the city there were twelve chief languages. The twelve rulers of the kingdoms were superior to other people who have lived in the world in all human qualities.

The name of one king there was Munon or Mennon. He was married to the daughter of the high king Priam; she was called Troan. They had a son, he was called Tror; we call him Thor. He was brought up in Thrace by a duke whose name was Loricus. When he was ten he inherited his father's weapons. He was as beautiful to look at when he came among other people as when ivory is inlaid in oak. His hair is more beautiful than gold. When he was twelve he had reached his full strength. Then he lifted from the ground ten bearskins all at once and then he killed his foster-father Loricus and his wife Lora or Glora and took possession of the realm of Thrace. We call this Thrudheim. Then he travelled through many countries and explored all quarters of the world and defeated unaided all berserks and giants and one of the greatest dragons and many wild animals. In the northern part of the world he came across a prophetess called Sibyl, whom we call Sif, and married her. No one is able to tell Sif's ancestry. She was the most beautiful of all women, her hair was like gold. Their son was Loridi, who took after his father; his son was Einridi, his son Vingethor, his son Vingenir, his son Moda, his son Magi, his son Sescef, his son Bedvig, his son Athra, whom we call Annar, his son Itrmann, his son Heremod, his son Scialdun, whom we call Skiold, his son Biaf, whom we call Biar, his son Iat, his son Gudolf, his son Finn, his son Friallaf, whom we call Fridleif. He had a son whose name was Woden, it is him that we call Odin. He was an outstanding person for wisdom and all kinds of accomplishments. His wife was called Frigida, whom we call Frigg. Odin had the gift of prophecy and so did his wife, and from this science he discovered that his name would be remembered in the northern part of the world and honoured above all kings. For this reason he became eager to set off from Turkey and took with him a very great following, young people and old, men and women, and they took with them many precious things. And whatever countries they passed through, great glory was spoken of them, so that they seemed more like gods than men. And they did not halt their journey until they came north to the country that is now called Saxony. Odin stayed there a long while and gained possession of large parts of that land.

There Odin put in charge of the country three of his sons; one's name was Veggdegg, he was a powerful king and ruled over East Saxony; his son was Vitrgils, his sons were Vitta, father of Hengest, and Sigar, father of Svebdegg, whom we call Svipdag. Odin's second son was called Beldegg, whom we call Baldr; he had the country that is now called Westphalia. His son was Brand, his son Friodigar, whom we call Frodi, his son was Freovin, his son Wigg, his son Gewis, whom we call Gavir. Odin's third son's name was Síggi, his son Rerir. This dynasty ruled over what is now called France, and from it is descended the family called the Volsungs. From all these people great family lines are descended. Then Odin set off north and came to a country that they called Reidgotaland and gained possession of all he wished in that land. He set over the area a son of his called Skiold; his son was called Fridleif. From them is descended the family called the Skioldungs; they are kings of Denmark, and what was then called Reidgotaland is now called Jutland.

After that Odin went north to what is now called Sweden. There was there a king whose name was Gylfi, and when he learned of the arrival of the men of Asia (who were called Æsir), he went to meet them and offered Odin as much power in his realm as he wished himself. And such was the success that attended their travels that in whatever country they stopped, there was then prosperity and good peace there, and everyone believed that they were responsible for it because the people who had power saw that they were unlike other people they had seen in beauty and wisdom. Odin found the conditions in the country attractive and selected as a site for his city the place which is now called Sigtunir. He also organized rulers there on the same pattern as had been in Troy, set up twelve chiefs in the place to administer the laws of the land, and he established all the legal system as it had previously been in Troy, and to which the Turks were accustomed.

After that he proceeded north to where he was faced by the sea, the one which they thought encircled all lands, and set a son of his over the realm which is now called Norway. He is called Sæming,

Document Text

and the kings of Norway trace their ancestry back to him, as do earls and other rulers, as it says in "Haleygiatal." And Odin took with him a son of his whose name was Yngvi, who became king in Sweden, and from him are descended the family lines known as the Ynglings. These Æsir found themselves marriages within the country there, and some of them for their sons too, and these families became extensive, so that throughout Saxony and from there all over the northern regions it spread so that their language, that of the men of Asia, became the mother tongue over all these lands. And people think they can deduce from the records of the names of their ancestors that those names belonged to this language, and that the Æsir brought the language north to this part of the world, to Norway and to Sweden, to Denmark and to Saxony; and in England there are ancient names for regions and places which one can tell come from a different language from this one.

Gylfaginning

King Gylfi was ruler in what is now called Sweden. Of him it is said that he gave a certain vagrant woman, as a reward for her entertainment, one plough-land in his kingdom, as much as four oxen could plough up in a day and a night. Now this woman was one of the race of the Æsir. Her name was Gefiun. She took four oxen from the north, from Giantland, the sons of her and a certain giant, and put them before the plough. But the plough cut so hard and deep that it uprooted the land, and the oxen drew the land out into the sea to the west and halted in a certain sound. There Gefiun put the land and gave it a name and called it Zealand. Where the land had been lifted from there remained a lake; this is now called Lake Mälar in Sweden. And the inlets in the lake correspond to the headlands in Zealand. Thus says the poet Bragi the Old: "Gefiun drew from Gylfi, glad, a deep-ring of land so that from the swift-pullers steam rose: Denmark's extension. The oxen wore eight brow-stars as they went hauling their plunder, the wide island of meadows, and four heads."

King Gylfi was clever and skilled in magic. He was quite amazed that the Æsir-people had the ability to make everything go in accordance with their will. He wondered whether this could be as a result of their own nature, or whether the divine powers they worshipped could be responsible. He set out to Asgard and travelled in secret and assumed the form of an old man and so disguised himself. But the Æsir were the wiser in that they had the gift of prophecy, and they saw his movements before he arrived, and prepared deceptive appearances for him. When he got into the city he saw there a high hall, so that he could scarcely see over it. Its roof was covered with gilded shields like tiles. Thiodolf of Hvinir refers thus to Val-hall being roofed with shields: "On their backs they let shine—they were bombarded with stones—Svafnir's hall-shingles, those sensible men."

In the doorway of the hall Gylfi saw a man juggling with knives, keeping seven in the air at a time. This man spoke first and asked him his name. He said it was Gangleri and that he had travelled trackless ways; he requested that he might have a night's lodging there and asked whose hall it was. The man replied that it belonged to their king. "And I can take you to see him. Then you can ask him his name yourself."

And the man turned ahead of him into the hall. Gylfi followed, and the door immediately shut on his heels. He saw there many apartments and many people, some engaged in games, some were drinking, some were armed and were fighting. He looked around and thought many of the things he saw were incredible. Then he said: "Every doorway, before you go through, should be peered round, for you cannot know for certain where enemies may be sitting waiting inside."

He saw three thrones one above the other, and there were three men, one sitting in each. Then he asked what the name of their ruler was. The man who had brought him in replied that the one that sat in the lowest throne was king and was called High, next to him the one called Just-as-high, and the one sitting at the top was called Third. Then High asked the newcomer whether he had any further business, though he was welcome to food and drink like everyone else there in the High one's hall. He said that he wished first to find out if there was any learned person in there. High said he would not get out unscathed unless he was more learned, and "Stand out in front while you ask: he who tells shall sit."

Gangleri began his questioning thus: "Who is the highest and most ancient of all gods?"

High said: "He is called All-father in our language, but in Old Asgard he had twelve names. One is All-father, the second Herran or Herian, the third Nikar or Hnikar, the fourth Nikuz or Hnikud, the fifth Fiolnir, the sixth Oski, the seventh Omi, the eighth Biflidi or Biflindi, the ninth Svidar, the tenth Svidrir, the eleventh Vidrir, the twelfth Ialg or Ialk."

Then Gangleri asked: "Where is this god, what power has he, and what great works has he performed?"

High said: "He lives throughout all ages and rules all his kingdom and governs all things great and small."

Then spoke Just-as-high: "He made heaven and earth and the skies and everything in them."

Then spoke Third: "But his greatest work is that he made man and gave him a soul that shall live and never perish though the body decay to dust or burn to ashes. And all men who are righteous shall live and dwell with him himself in the place called Gimle or Vingolf, but wicked men go to Hel and on to Niflhel; that is down in the ninth world."

Then spoke Gangleri: "What was he doing before heaven and earth were made?"

Then High replied: "Then he was among the frost-giants."

Gangleri spoke: "What was the beginning? And how did things start? And what was there before?"

High replied: "As it says in 'Voluspa': 'It was at the beginning of time, when nothing was; sand was not, nor sea, nor cool waves. Earth did not exist, nor heaven on high. The mighty gap was, but no growth.'"

Then spoke Just-as-high: "It was many ages before the earth was created that Niflheim was made, and in its midst lies a spring called Hvergelmir, and from it flow the rivers called Svol, Gunnthra, Fiorm, Fimbulthul, Slidr and Hrid, Sylg and Ylg, Vid, Leiptr; Gioll is next to Hel-gates."

Then spoke Third: "But first there was the world in the southern region called Muspell. It is bright and hot. That area is flaming and burning and it is impassable for those that are foreigners there and are not native to it. There is one called Surt that is stationed there at the frontier to defend the land. He has a flaming sword and at the end of the world he will go and wage war and defeat all the gods and burn the whole world with fire. Thus it says in 'Voluspa': 'Surt travels from the south with the stick-destroyer. Shines from his sword the sun of the gods of the slain. Rock cliffs crash and troll-wives are abroad, heroes tread the road of Hel and heaven splits.'"

Gangleri spoke: "What were things like before generations came to be and the human race was multiplied?"

Then spoke High: "These rivers, which are called Elivagar, when they had got so far from their source that the poisonous flow that accompanied them began to go hard like the clinker that comes from a furnace, it turned to ice; and when this ice came to a halt and stopped flowing, the vapour that was rising from the poison froze on the top in the same direction and turned to rime, and this rime increased layer upon layer right across Ginnungagap."

Then spoke Just-as-high: "Ginnungagap, the part that faces in a northerly direction, was filled with the weight and heaviness of ice and rime and there was vapour and a blowing inwards from it. But the southerly part of Ginnungagap cleared up in the face of the sparks and molten particles that came flying out of the world of Muspell."

Then spoke Third: "Just as from Niflheim there arose coldness and all things grim, so what was facing close to Muspell was hot and bright, but Ginnungagap was as mild as a windless sky. And when the rime and the blowing of the warmth met so that it thawed and dripped, there was a quickening from these flowing drops due to the power of the source of the heat, and it became the form of a man, and he was given the name Ymir. But the frost-giants call him Aurgelmir, and from him are descended the generations of frost-giants, as it says in the *Shorter Voluspa*: 'All sibyls are from Vidolf, all wizards from Vilmeid, all sorcerers from Svarthofdi, all giants from Ymir come.'"

And here it is told by the giant Vafthrudnir where Aurgelmir came from, together with the sons of giants, first, that wise giant: "When from Elivagar shot poison drops and grew until from them came a giant in whom our ancestries all converge: thus ever too terrible is all this."

Then spoke Gangleri: "How did generations grow from him, and how did it come about that other people came into being, or do you believe him to be a god whom you have just spoken of?"

Then High replied: "Not at all do we acknowledge him to be a god. He was evil and all his descendants. We call them frost-giants. And it is said that when he slept, he sweated. Then there grew under his left arm a male and a female, and one of his legs begot a son with the other, and descendants came from them. These are frost-giants. The ancient frost-giant, him we call Ymir."

Then spoke Gangleri: "Where did Ymir live, and what did he live on?"

"The next thing, when the rime dripped, was that there came into being from it a cow called Audhumla, and four rivers of milk flowed from its teats, and it fed Ymir."

Then spoke Gangleri: "What did the cow feed on?"

High said: "It licked the rime-stones, which were salty. And the first day as it licked stones there came from the stones in the evening a man's hair, the second day a man's head, the third day there was a com-

Document Text

plete man there. His name was Buri. He was beautiful in appearance, big and powerful. He begot a son called Bor. He married a wife called Bestla, daughter of the giant Bolthorn, and they had three sons. One was called Odin, the second Vili, the third Ve. And it is my belief that this Odin and his brothers must be the rulers of heaven and earth; it is our opinion that this must be what he is called. This is the name of the one who is the greatest and most glorious that we know, and you would do well to agree to call him that too."

Then spoke Gangleri: "How did they get on together, which group was the more powerful?"

Then High replied: "Bor's sons killed the giant Ymir. And when he fell, so much blood flowed from his wounds that with it they drowned all the race of frost-giants, except that one escaped with his household. Giants call him Bergelmir. He went up on to his ark with his wife and was preserved there, and from them are descended the families of frost-giants, as it says here: 'Countless winters before the earth was created, then was Bergelmir born. That is the first I remember, when that wise giant was laid on a box.'"

Then Gangleri replied: "What did Bor's sons do then, if you believe that they are gods?"

High said: "There is not just a little to be told about that. They took Ymir and transported him to the middle of Ginnungagap, and out of him made the earth, out of his blood the sea and the lakes. The earth was made of the flesh and the rocks of the bones, stone and scree they made out of the teeth and molars and of the bones that had been broken."

Then spoke Just-as-high: "Out of the blood that came from his wounds and was flowing unconfined, out of this they made the sea with which they encompassed and contained the earth, and they placed this sea in a circle round the outside of it, and it will seem an impossibility to most to get across it."

Then spoke Third: "They also took his skull and made out of it the sky and set it up over the earth with four points, and under each corner they set a dwarf. Their names are Austri, Vestri, Nordri, Sudri. Then they took molten particles and sparks that were flying uncontrolled and had shot out of the world of Muspell and set them in the middle of the firmament of the sky both above and below to illuminate heaven and earth. They fixed all the lights, some in the sky, some moved in a wandering course beneath the sky, but they appointed them positions and ordained their courses. Thus it is said in ancient sources that by means of them days were distinguished and also the count of years, as it says in 'Voluspa': 'The sun did not know where her dwelling was. The moon did not know what power he had. The stars did not know

Glossary

brow-stars	that is, eyes
deep-ring of land	the island of Zealand, the largest island of Denmark
Haleygiatal	a poem written by Eyvind (or Eyvindr) Skaldaspiller in about 985
hall-shingles	shields
lord	earth
Odin	a major god in Norse mythology and the ruler of Asgard, one of the nine worlds and the homeland of the Aesir, the race of warrior gods
scree	loose rock
Skinfaxi	literally, "shining mane"
Sol	the sun
stick-destroyer	that is, fire
Svafnir	that is, the god Odin
swift-pullers	oxen
Voluspa	that is, "Völuspá," the first poem of the *Poetic Edda*, telling the story of the creation of the world

where their places were.' That is what it was like above the earth before this took place."

Then spoke Gangleri: "This is important information that I have just heard. That is an amazingly large construction and skilfully made. How was the earth arranged?"

Then High replied: "It is circular round the edge, and around it lies the deep sea, and along the shore of this sea they gave lands to live in to the races of giants. But on the earth on the inner side they made a fortification round the world against the hostility of giants, and for this fortification they used the giant Ymir's eyelashes, and they called the fortification Midgard. They also took his brains and threw them into the sky and made out of them the clouds, as it says here: 'From Ymir's flesh was earth created, and from blood, sea; rocks of bones, trees of hair, and from his skull, the sky. And from his eyelashes the joyous gods made Midgard for men's sons, and from his brains were those cruel clouds all created.'"

Then spoke Gangleri: "A great deal it seems to me they had achieved when earth and heaven were made and sun and stars were put in position and days were separated—and where did the people come from who inhabit the world?"

Then High replied: "As Bor's sons walked along the sea shore, they came across two logs and created people out of them. The first gave breath and life, the second consciousness and movement, the third a face, speech and hearing and sight; they gave them clothes and names. The man was called Ask, the woman Embla, and from them were produced the mankind to whom the dwelling-place under Midgard was given. After that they made themselves a city in the middle of the world which is known as Asgard. We call it Troy. There the gods and their descendants lived and there took place as a result many events and developments both on earth and aloft. In the city there is a seat called Hlidskialf, and when Odin sat in that throne he saw over all worlds and every man's activity and understood everything he saw. His wife was called Frigg Fiorgvin's daughter, and from them is descended the family line that we call the Æsir race, who have resided in Old Asgard and the realms that belong to it, and that whole line of descent is of divine origin. And this is why he can be called Allfather, that he is father of all the gods and of men and of everything that has been brought into being by him and his power. The earth was his daughter and his wife. Out of her he begot the first of his sons, that is Asa-Thor. He was possessed of power and strength. As a result he overcomes all living things.

"Norfi or Narfi was the name of a giant who lived in Giantland. He had a daughter called Night. She was black and dark in accordance with her ancestry. She was married to a person called Naglfari. Their son was called Aud. Next she was married to someone called Annar. Their daughter was called Iord. Her last husband was Delling, he was of the race of the Æsir. Their son was Day. He was bright and beautiful in accordance with his father's nature. Then Allfather took Night and her son Day and gave them two horses and two chariots and set them up in the sky so that they have to ride around the earth every twenty-four hours. Night rides in front on the horse called Hrimfaxi, and every morning he bedews the earth with the drips from his bit. Day's horse is called Skinfaxi, and light is shed over all the sky and sea from his mane."

Then spoke Gangleri: "How does he control the course of the sun and moon?"

High said: "There was a person whose name was Mundilfæri who had two children. They were so fair and beautiful that he called the one Moon and his daughter Sol, and gave her in marriage to a person called Glen. But the gods got angry at this arrogance and took the brother and sister and set them up in the sky; they made Sol drive the horses that drew the chariot of the sun which the gods had created, to illuminate the worlds, out of the molten particle that had flown out of the world of Muspell. The names of these horses are Arvak and Alsvinn. Under the shoulders of the horses the gods put two bellows to cool them, and in some sources it is called ironblast. Moon guides the course of the moon and controls its waxing and waning. He took two children from the earth called Bil and Hiuki as they were leaving a well called Byrgir, carrying between them on their shoulders a tub called Sæg; their carrying-pole was called Simul. Their father's name is Vidfinn. These children go with Moon, as can be seen from earth."

Then spoke Gangleri: "The sun moves fast, almost as if she was afraid, and she would not be able to go any faster if she was in terror of her death."

Then High replied: "It is not surprising that she goes at great speed, he comes close who is after her. And she has no escape except to run away."

Then spoke Gangleri: "Who is it that inflicts this unpleasantness on her?"

High said: "It is two wolves, and the one that is going after her is called Skoll. She is afraid of him and he will catch her, and the one that is running ahead of her is called Hati Hrodvitnisson, and he is trying to catch the moon, and that will happen."

Document Text

Then spoke Gangleri: "What is the origin of the wolves?"

High said: "A certain giantess lives east of Midgard in a forest called Ironwood. In that forest live trollwives called Iarnvidiur. The ancient giantess breeds as sons many giants and all in wolf shapes, and it is from them that these wolves are descended. And they say that from this clan will come a most mighty one called Moongarm. He will fill himself with the lifeblood of everyone that dies, and he will swallow heavenly bodies and spatter heaven and all the skies with blood. As a result the sun will lose its shine and winds will then be violent and will rage to and fro. Thus it says in 'Voluspa': 'In the east lives the old one, in Ironwood, and breeds there Fenrir's kind. Out of them all comes one in particular, sun's snatcher in troll's guise. He gorges the life of doomed men, reddens gods' halls with red gore. Dark is sunshine for summers after, all weathers hostile. Know you yet, or what?'"

A fresco of Saint Francis in the Lower Church of the Papal Basilica in Assisi
(St. Francis [fresco], Martini, Simone [1284-1344] / San Francesco, Lower Church, Assisi, Italy / Giraudon / The Bridgeman Art Library International)

Francis of Assisi: "Canticle of the Creatures"

1224–1225

"Blessed are those who endure in peace, for by You, Most High, shall they be crowned."

Overview

Francis of Assisi's "Canticle of the Creatures" (in Italian "Cantico di frate Sole," sometimes translated as "Canticle of Brother Sun") is the earliest Italian vernacular text in the now-extinct Umbrian dialect. It was written toward the end of Francis's life (1224–1225) and expressed his religious experience and understanding of the world in a hymn of praise to the "Most High, good God." A canticle is a sacred song or chant based on biblical verse and written in the tradition of the medieval *lauda*; this particular canticle was composed by Francis after a night of extreme physical and emotional pain that brought new insight into the meaning of his own suffering as well as a better understanding of what it means to be human in a creation that signifies God. Francis wrote the "Canticle of the Creatures" to praise God and express his experience of harmony with creation.

The significance of the "Canticle" lies both in its poetic originality and in its vision of the world that gives access to God. It countered dualistic understandings of the Creation and provided a basis for the possibility of encountering the sacred in the created realm. It continues to be a point of reference for reflection on the relationship between humans, God, and the world, especially in the context of today's environmental crises.

Context

The broad context for the "Canticle of the Creatures" is cultural. Both the Catholic Church and society in thirteenth-century Europe were highly stratified, with well-defined roles and positions for everyone and everything. Through its teaching and the central role it played in Western European life in the Middle Ages, the Catholic Church had an impact on every dimension of human experience. The Gregorian Reform of the eleventh century, with its intention of freeing the church from lay control, achieved its purpose of a clear separation between clergy and laity, which translated on the practical level into the general perception of the clear separation of the secular from the sacred. The preached reform ideology connected the priesthood with direct access to God through their sacramental power and demanded of clerics a cultic holiness expressed in celibacy. One of the implications of this ideology was that the laity—immersed as they were in materiality (characterized especially by their freedom to marry)—had no direct access to the sacred and were dependent on priests and monks for their spiritual well-being. Control of the spiritual, sacred realm became the reserved prerogative of the clergy and monks, while the laity occupied that space described as secular with no possibility of crossing these boundaries. It was at this period, in fact, that rood screens were installed in churches in the West, clearly delineating the sacred from the secular with the separation of churchgoers from direct access to the altar, where only the clergy ministered. This had implications for how the laity understood themselves and their lives in the world in relation to God.

This perception of separation and distinction of the sacred from the secular began to give way during the twelfth century with the appearance of lay apostolic movements and the emergence of the order of penitents. As a result of crusade preaching and spirituality, lay men and women began to claim an active role in their own spiritual lives. Groups of men and women came together in their own homes to lead a more explicit and self-conscious Christian life. In their meetings, translations of passages of the synoptic Gospels were read, reflected on, and discussed, as they supported each other in their Christian lives and work. The laity began to claim for themselves the right to live the life of the apostles, which was understood to require a life of poverty in imitation of Christ and his twelve apostles. Some claimed that living like an apostle gave one the right to preach, a claim that brought them into conflict with the hierarchy of the church. Some of these lay apostolic groups, such as the Waldensians, were eventually accused of heresy over this issue, and while some members complied with the demand of the hierarchy to stop preaching, others refused and continued to be problematic for the church throughout the Middle Ages. As noted by André Vauchez, the French Dominican priest Dominic Chenu described these developments as an "evangelical renewal" of the church and suggested that this signaled a new equilibrium between nature and grace, as the laity claimed from their secular location the ability to encounter God.

Time Line

1182	Francis of Assisi is born.
1198	Innocent III is elected as pope.
1209	Innocent III gives oral approval to the proposed life plan of Francis and his eleven first followers.
1212	**March** Clare of Assisi joins the brotherhood, and the Poor Sisters have their origin at the Church of Our Lady in the valley below Assisi.
1215	**November** The Fourth Lateran Council is held in Rome.
1217	The brotherhood is divided into geographical provinces in Western Europe and beyond.
1219	Francis travels to the Middle East during the Fifth Crusade and meets with the Sultan al-Malek al-Kamel in late August.
1220	September 1220---Francis returns to Italy, recalled there because of problems within the brotherhood. He resigns as general minister of the brotherhood in a chapter held in Assisi.
1221–1223	Francis is directly involved in the revision of the Rule of the Friars Minor, which is approved by Pope Honorius III in November of 1223.
1224	**September** Francis is marked with the wounds of the crucified Christ while at prayer on Mount La Verna in Tuscany.
1224–1225	Extremely sick and almost totally blind, Francis spends the winter in a hut of the brothers near San Damiano, where he is cared for by Clare and where he composes the "Canticle of the Creatures."

In addition to these problematic issues of religious practice, there was another—that of the more insidious dualistic heresy rampant in Western Europe, whose adherents were known as Cathars. The Cathars posited two distinct principles at the origin of the created order, a positive good principle that created the spiritual realm as opposed to an evil principle that created the material realm. Cathars denied the goodness of the created material world and even of the human body and procreation. They saw it as their task to escape as much as possible from imprisonment in matter in order to live in a purely spiritual realm. The Cathar religion was an organized sect with its own hierarchy and religious rites. Given the role of asceticism and mortification in orthodox Christian practice, it was not always easy to tell the difference between an orthodox Christian who fasted and a heretical Cathar who abstained from food and sex. In addition, given the Cathar emphasis on poverty as the renunciation of evil materiality, Cathars appeared to be more worthy of imitation than some of the orthodox clergy and hierarchy who lived a worldly life. Both of these developments—the rise of lay apostolic groups and the problem of Cathar dualism—provide the general context against which the "Canticle of the Creatures" expressed an appreciation of creation as reflecting the goodness of God.

The more specific context for the "Canticle of the Creatures" is the religious experience of Francis of Assisi. Francis shared the new evangelical spirit of the laity in common with many of these new lay apostles. His conversion led him not to leave the world and enter a monastery but rather to enter directly into the world created by God, where he experienced the grace of God in his care for lepers, the action which marked the beginning of his new life. Francis did leave Assisi, a thriving merchant town organized for the purpose of accruing wealth and assisting other wealthy and powerful men to protect and amass even more. From this social organization the poor and the sick were excluded—only those who had capital or skills were welcomed within Assisi's walls. Lepers thus symbolized everything alien to Assisi's purposes and understanding of life, as they represented sickness, weakness, and poverty, a reality that Assisi excluded. It was with the lepers that Francis found God, and he came to experience with the lepers and the poor the reality of brotherhood and sisterhood in Christ, who in his incarnation came to be with humanity in poverty and weakness. Francis and his brothers experienced creation as God's good gift intended for all, and they developed an ethic of sharing and support, thus ensuring the circulation of God's good gifts to everyone. Creation spoke God's goodness and generosity and was to be respected as such and was to be available for everyone. It was this experience of life in the world that finds expression in the "Canticle of the Creatures."

About the Author

The son of a wealthy Italian merchant named Pietro Bernardone, Francis of Assisi (1182–1226) was given the name Giovanni at his baptism but was later known by the name Francesco Bernardone. Francis (the anglicized version of the Italian Francesco) experienced a conversion in 1206 that led him to follow in the footprints of Jesus Christ. Leaving behind his comfortable merchant life in Assisi, he began to associate with and care for the poor, the sick, and the marginalized who lived outside the walls of Assisi. By 1209 eleven men had come to share his life and vision, and together they traveled to Rome to seek approval from the church for their way of life. Pope Innocent III gave them oral permission to live the life of disciples, which they described in their *propositum vitae* (plan of life) with citations from the gospel. In brotherhood with all and without claiming anything as their own, they lived itinerant lives, supporting themselves and caring for the sick and poor through manual labor. The small brotherhood grew rapidly and even welcomed clerics into its midst. While there was no specific work or ministry that identified them as Friars Minor, they followed the example of Christ in the Gospels and witnessed to the Gospel through their Christian example of brotherhood, especially through their renunciation of power and ownership.

While Francis had no intention of founding a Catholic religious order, the rapid growth of the movement and its popularity led the hierarchy to insist that the brothers live by an approved rule. Coming together annually in chapter meetings, the brothers discussed their lived experience in the light of their initial proposal for living, and they clarified and expanded on this from year to year. This developed into the Rule of the Friars Minor, which was formally approved, but not without significant difficulties and problems in the process, by Pope Honorius III in 1223.

Conflicts within the brotherhood, different understandings of the purpose of Minorite life, and the interests of the hierarchy in shaping the Friars Minor into a pastoral ministerial force within the church led Francis to resign as minister of the brothers upon his return from the Middle East in September 1220, after his meeting there with the Muslim Sultan al-Malek al-Kamel, whom he approached as a brother during the Fifth Crusade. Francis continued to lead the process of the revision of the Rule of the Friars Minor until its confirmation in 1223, but his experience of the divisions and conflicts within the brotherhood led him to grow more and more frustrated with the direction the order was taking. In addition, he returned from the Middle East severely ill with ailments of the eyes and stomach, so that his last years were passed in great suffering, both spiritual and physical. While he was no longer juridical leader of the order, Francis continued to provide a living example of the commitment of the lesser brothers. He was marked with the wounds of the crucified Christ in September 1224, and his physical suffering increased even more. During the winter of 1224–1225, Francis spent some months near the monastery of San Damiano in Assisi, where Clare of Assisi and her sisters dwelled. Clare cared for Francis in his illness. There, after one very difficult night of temptation, Francis almost despaired, but he was assured in a dream that his suffering would ultimately lead him into God's kingdom. In response to this assurance, Francis composed the "Canticle of the Creatures," which he then had set to music. He intended that the brothers who preached should sing this song to give praise to the "Most High, good God." Francis died in Assisi on October 4, 1226. Two years later he was canonized a saint in the Catholic Church.

Time Line

1226
- **October 4** — Francis dies in Assisi and is buried the next day is his parish church of San Giorgio.

1228
- **July 16** — Francis is canonized Saint Francis of Assisi by Pope Gregory IX.

Explanation and Analysis of the Document

The oldest manuscript of the "Canticle of the Creatures" is the mid-thirteenth-century Codex 338 of the Communal Library in Assisi. The manuscript included space for musical notation, but this was not entered on the manuscript. While Francis's authorship has never been doubted, the hagiographical sources—scholarly studies of the saints—suggest that after he composed the "Canticle" he taught the poem to his brothers and asked brother Pacifico to set it to music, thus implying that it was written down sometime after its composition. This same mid-thirteenth-century hagiographical source suggests that the "Canticle" was composed in three stages: verses 1 through 9 written during Francis's winter stay at San Damiano after a night of great suffering and temptation, verses 10 and 11 added later that summer when a dispute between the bishop and the mayor of Assisi erupted, and verses 12 through 14 added shortly before Francis's own death in October 1226. Most recent scholarship disputes this three-stage theory based on the structural unity of the poem itself, the consistent use of rhyme and assonance throughout the poem, and the studied use of the *cursus* (a literary device that chooses specific words with accented syllables to indicate the end of a section).

The primary literary sources for Francis's "Canticle" were the Bible and the liturgy, both of which were familiar to him through his daily prayer of the Divine Office. The "Canticle of the Three Young Men," from the book of Daniel 3, was prayed for the liturgical hour of lauds on all Sundays and feast days. This text begins with praises of God; turns to invite the angels and heavenly beings to praise God; then moves down to the earth to enlist the creatures of the earth, including animals, in the praise of God, and closes with an exhortation to praise God at all times. Francis's "Canticle" differs in that he eliminates any reference to angels and animals while reducing everything under heaven to the four elements—earth, wind (or air), fire, and water—suggesting a distinct approach to creation. Psalm 148 was also present in the Divine Office and presents the elements of creation as the actors in giving praise to God, as opposed to the passive voice accorded them in Francis's "Canticle." Francis's experience and understanding were certainly informed by these texts, and his own composition "The Praises to Be Said at All the Hours" was made up of phrases taken from

Pope Innocent III approving the Order of Friars Minor
(Pope Innocent III Approving the Rule [fresco] [b/w photo], Gozzoli, Benozzo di Lese di Sandro [1420-97] / San Francesco, Montefalco, Italy / Alinari / The Bridgeman Art Library International)

the "Canticle of the Three Young Men" and from the book of Revelation 4 and 5; it was prayed eight times a day, one time before each daily hour of the Divine Office. Together with the Lord's Prayer, these texts, which were prayed day after day, shaped Francis's perception of the created world as a sacred reality.

Verses 1 and 2 of the "Canticle of the Creatures" introduce God as "Most High," powerful and good, to whom alone praise belongs, while describing humans as unworthy even to speak God's name. That creation belongs to God and not to humans is clearly stated here at the outset of the poem, a conviction that stands as the basis for Francis's practice of poverty and the complete rejection of ownership of any kind. Creation is a gift of the good God and is intended to provide for the needs of all through sharing. The centrality of the good God from which everything comes and to which everything returns is presented as the primary motive for praise.

Since humans are unable even to mention God's name, God should be praised through creation: "*Laudato sie, mi' Signore, cum tutte le Tue creature,*" which can be translated as "be praised by means of all your creatures" (verses 3 and 4). Here, the passage from the Lord's Prayer "hallowed be Thy name" is reflected in the grammatical construction of the phrase. The purpose of creation, that is, of each creature, is to praise God. The first named creature in the "Canticle," "Sir Brother Sun" (verse 3) speaks of or signifies the "Most High" through his very nature of being light, echoing the first verses of John's Gospel, which state that God is light and in God there is no darkness. The designation of the sun as "Sir" and "Brother" personifies the sun with relational names and properties that will continue to be employed throughout the "Canticle." This naming and defining of creation as brother and sister reflect Francis's experience of universal brotherhood and sisterhood, which was the fruit of his conversion and expresses the experi-

Essential Quotes

> *"Blessed are those who endure in peace for by You, Most High, shall they be crowned."*

> *"Praise and bless my Lord and give Him thanks and serve Him with great humility."*

ence of harmony in creation. The importance of relationship as the identifying characteristic of everything that exists in both the human and nonhuman world is written into the very foundation of creation; furthermore, the notion of interconnectedness demands that the commitments and practices of human beings reflect and respect that reality in the way they deal with each other and with every aspect of creation.

Verses 5 through 11 follow the same structure. Each sentence begins with the passive subjunctive construction of "Praised be you, my Lord," followed in the original text by the Italian preposition *per*. The translation of this preposition has been the subject of discussion for more than a century because it can be rendered in at least four different ways: *Per* can express causation ("for") or agency ("by") or instrumentality ("by means of") or, finally, mediation ("through"). Each of these meanings can be applied to the text and expresses the multifaceted relationship between God and creation described in the "Canticle." Following this phrase and preposition, the verses identify elements of creation from the heavens down to the earth in a balanced set of relationships: Brother Sun (verse 3), Sister Moon and the stars (verse 5), Brother Wind (verse 6), Sister Water (verse 7), Brother Fire (verse 8), and Sister Mother Earth (verse 9). Additionally, and also in contrast to the "Canticle of the Three Young Men" and Psalm 148, where the creatures are simply listed by name, in the "Canticle of the Creatures" they are described in terms of their beauty, power, usefulness, and goodness—parts of the very constitution they have received from their creator. Francis gives his uninterrupted attention to the concrete realities, expressing them differently from philosophical or symbolic medieval readings of creation. Every creature possesses a unique visage and voice that makes it valuable in itself. In other words, the creatures are living and conscious goods from God. The elements that are encountered in ordinary daily experience provide an image of and reflect their source. Thus, the moon and stars are "clear and precious and beautiful"; wind gives God's "sustenance" to creatures; water is "humble and precious and chaste;" fire is "beautiful and playful and robust and strong." Earth "sustains and governs" humans and stands in striking contrast to the Genesis story of Creation, wherein Adam is given dominion over all.

The elements listed in verses 3 through 9 represent the three spheres of heaven (sun, moon, and stars) and the four elements (wind, water, fire, and earth). These seven elements reflect the seven days of Creation and express the order and goodness symbolized by the number seven. Included in this description of the Creation is all space and time (the three heavenly spheres) and everything that exists on earth (the four elements). In other words, each created thing, beginning with Brother Sun down to Mother Earth herself, "bears a likeness" to the "Most High, good God"—creation reveals God's continuing care for what God created. Perhaps most important, God continues to communicate Godself through creation.

To this point in the "Canticle of the Creatures," the focus has been on nonhuman creation. Humans enter the song only in verses 10 through 14, precisely through qualities that describe the human being as both creature and dependent on God. In these verses, the qualities that are highlighted reflect the more fragile and painful experiences of being human: infirmity, tribulation, and death; clearly, the "Canticle of the Creatures" is infused with the feelings of temptation and suffering that Francis experienced toward the end of his life. Physical sickness, weakness, and emotional distress regarding the developments with the brotherhood became temptations for Francis, leading him to question the very meaning of his own life. Reassured in a dream that it was though this experience of brokenness and fragility that he would enter the kingdom of God, Francis was transformed through "pardon for [God's] love" and was able to "endure in peace" as he faced his own death. But what Francis expresses here goes deeper than an insight into his own difficulties. What God is to be praised for is the human ability to "give pardon" and "bear infirmity and tribulation" and sustain all this in "peace" (verses 10 and 11). In fact, Francis describes in these verses the real created nature of the human person—an identity that he tried to avoid prior to his conversion but that he later saw reflected in the brokenness and sickness of the lepers with whom he lived and worked. Through this work, Francis came to understand who Jesus Christ was: God's son who humbled himself and took on the ordinary human condition of frailty. Francis reflected on this in his "Letter to the Faithful," which he wrote after his return from the Middle East:

"The Most High Father made known from heaven through his holy angel Gabriel this Word of the Father—so worthy, so holy and glorious—in the womb of the holy and glorious virgin Mary, from whose womb he received the flesh of our humanity and frailty." And citing Saint Paul, Francis commented that although Christ was rich, he chose poverty in this world (2 Corinthians 8:9). It is thus Christ who reveals the true meaning of being brother and sister. The implications of Christ's choice of weakness and poverty in this world reveal the real nature of the human person. To reject or avoid this dimension of human experience, or to try to escape from it, is the sin that leads to eternal death (verse 13).

It is the human being who accepts his created weak and fragile identity as a brother of Christ who is finally invited to "praise and bless my Lord and give him thanks and serve him with great humility" in the final verse of the "Canticle." This invitation to praise, bless, and thank God is made in the active voice; only the reconciled human being is able to join in the song of creation, and this invitation is directed to all the hearers of the "Canticle." The "Canticle of the Creatures" summarizes and expresses the very meaning of Franciscan life, celebrating as it does creation as a good gift of the good God. It signifies God's intention for creation to be a fraternal space in which all can share in the goodness of God and through its respectful use to allow creation to achieve its purpose in praise of its creator. The "Canticle of the Creatures" expresses the Franciscan vision of reality.

Audience

The second volume of *Francis of Assisi, Early Documents*, titled *The Founder*, describes both the composition of the "Canticle of the Creatures" and its intended audience: "[Francis] said that he wanted one of them who knew how to preach, to preach to the people. After the sermon, they were to sing the *Praises of the Lord* as minstrels of the Lord." In other words, the "Canticle" was Francis's attempt to share and promote the early brotherhood's perception of life and creation with everyone the brothers met, from popes and kings at the highest levels of medieval church and society down to the poor, the lepers, and those who might be considered the most insignificant, lowly human beings.

Impact

The impact of the "Canticle of the Creatures" can be seen in the positive response to the ministry and preaching of the brothers. The growth of the movement known today as the Secular Franciscans was exponential. Secular Franciscans associated themselves with the vision and spirituality of the Franciscans while continuing their life in the world as married or single. The "Canticle" countered the dualistic vision of the Cathars and fostered a theological vision that celebrated the possibility of choosing both God and the world. The "Canticle" also affected the development of a more realistic artistic style connected with the Italian painter Giotto and his school as a prelude to the Italian Renaissance. In addition, it fostered the development of experimental science through the works of the Franciscans Roger Bacon and William of Ockham. The "Canticle" provided a basis for John Duns Scotus's Franciscan theology, with his focus on the concrete particular and the "thisness" of every created thing, which in turn inspired the poety of the nineteenth-century English-born priest Gerard Manley Hopkins. The "Canticle of the Creatures"

Questions for Further Study

1. Imagine that the writers of the Humanist Manifesto and Francis of Assisi were engaged in a debate. What conflicting positions would the two parties adopt? How would each respond to the other?

2. What relevance does "Canticle of the Creatures" have for contemporary concern with environmental issues? What do you think Francis's reaction would have been to the 2010 oil spill in the Gulf of Mexico or any other environmental disaster?

3. What issues was the Catholic Church confronting in the years up to and including Francis's life? How did those issues have an impact on Francis's thinking?

4. What is dualism? In what way is "Canticle of the Creatures" a response to dualist theology?

5. What were "lay apostolic groups," and why did the Church hierarchy oppose them? What does this opposition tell you about the nature of the Church in the thirteenth century?

continues to inspire theologians and Christian ecologists with a vision of creation that needs to be recovered in order to preserve nature; it suggests an experience of creation in terms of relationship rather than domination.

Further Reading

■ Books

Armstrong, Regis J., J. A. Wayne Hellmann, and William J. Short, eds. *Francis of Assisi, Early Documents.* Vol. 1: *The Saint.* New York: New City Press, 1999; Vol. 2: *The Founder.* New York: New City Press, 2000.

Brown, Raphael. "Appendix VIII: The Canticle of Brother Sun." In *Saint Francis of Assisi,* ed. Omar Englebert. Chicago: Franciscan Herald Press, 1965.

Cunningham, Lawrence. *Saint Francis of Assisi.* Boston: Twayne Publishers, 1976.

Doyle, Eric. *St. Francis and the Song of Brotherhood.* New York: Seabury Press, 1981.

Leclercq, Eloi. *The Canticle of Creatures: Symbols of Union.* Chicago: Franciscan Herald Press, 1978.

Lehmann, Leonhard. *Francis, Master of Prayer.* Delhi, India: Media House, 1999.

Manselli, Raoul. *Saint Francis of Assisi.* Chicago: Franciscan Herald Press, 1984.

Nairn, Thomas. "St. Francis of Assisi's *Canticle of Creatures* as an Exercise of the Moral Imagination." In *Finding Voice to Give God Praise,* ed. Kathleen Hughes. Collegeville, Minn.: Liturgical Press, 1998.

Sorrell, Roger. *St. Francis of Assisi and Nature.* New York: Oxford University Press, 1988.

Vauchez, André. *The Spirituality of the Medieval West.* Kalamazoo, Mich.: Cistercian Publications, 1993.

■ Journals

Coy, Susanna. "The Problem of 'Per' in the *Cantico di Frate Sole.*" *Modern Language Notes* 91 (1976): 1–11.

Fumagalli, Edoardo. "Saint Francis, The *Canticle,* The *Our Father.*" *Greyfriars Review* 19 (2005 Supplement).

Kopaczynski, Germain. "Saint Francis and the Divine Adjectives." *Miscellanea Francescana* 82 (1992): 462–470.

Pozzi, Giovanni. "The Canticle of Brother Sun: From Grammar to Prayer." *Greyfriars Review* 4 (1992): 1–21.

Schmucki, Octavian. "The Mysticism of St. Francis in the Light of His Writings." *Greyfriars Review* 3, no. 3 (1989): 259–263.

■ Web Sites

Muscat, Noel. Franciscan Studies Web site.
  http://i-tau.org/wp/?page_id=32

—Michael W. Blastic

Francis of Assisi: "Canticle of the Creatures"

Most High, all-powerful, good Lord,
Yours are the praises, the glory, and the honor, and all blessing,

To You alone, Most High, do they belong,
and no human is worthy to mention Your name.

Praised be You, my Lord, with all Your creatures,
especially Sir Brother Sun,
Who is the day and through whom You give us light.

And he is beautiful and radiant with great splendor;
and bears a likeness of You, Most High One.

Praised be You, my Lord, through Sister Moon and the stars.
in heaven You formed them clear and precious and beautiful.

Praised be You, my Lord, through Brother Wind,
and through the air, cloudy and serene, and every kind of weather,
through whom You give sustenance to Your creatures.

Praised be You, my Lord, through Sister Water,
who is very useful and humble and precious and chaste.

Praised be You, my Lord, through Brother Fire,
through whom You light the night,
and he is beautiful and playful and robust and strong.

Praised be You, my Lord, through our Sister Mother Earth,
who sustains and governs us,
and who produces various fruit with colored flowers and herbs.

Praised be You, my Lord, through those who give pardon for Your love,
and bear infirmity and tribulation.

Blessed are those who endure in peace
for by You, Most High, shall they be crowned.

Praised be You, my Lord, through our Sister Bodily Death,
from whom no one living can escape.

Woe to those who die in mortal sin.
Blessed are those whom death will find in Your most holy will,
for the second death shall do them no harm.

Praise and bless my Lord and give Him thanks
and serve Him with great humility.

Glossary

canticle	a song, usually one with a liturgical message and based on the Bible

Thirteenth-century French manuscript page from the Summa theologiae

(Ms de Vauclair 160 Fol.1 Page from the 'Somme de Theologie' by St. Thomas Aquinas [1225-74] [vellum], French School, [13th century] / Bibliotheque Municipale, Laon, France / Giraudon / The Bridgeman Art Library International)

Thomas Aquinas: *Summa theologiae*

1266–1273

"It is necessary to arrive at a first mover, put in motion by no other; and this everyone understands to be God."

Overview

The magnum opus of the medieval Christian philosopher and theologian Thomas Aquinas, the *Summa theologiae* (also known as *Summa theologica*, "Summary of Theology") is a massive work that aims to expound all of Christian theology as systematically as possible. It is written in Latin, the universal language of medieval European scholarship and law. At its broadest level, the *Summa* depicts in philosophical terms the relationship between God and humanity and delineates how human reconciliation with God is made possible through Christ. Spanning three volumes treating God, humanity, and Christ the Redeemer, the *Summa* is arranged as 518 questions divided into 2,652 articles. Each article states the negative and positive sides of the proposition under examination, the arguments pro and con, and then Aquinas's solution. The first and most famous volume (from which our excerpts are drawn) deals with the theological enterprise as well as the existence and nature of God. The second volume deals with humanity, examining the purpose of life, the cardinal and theological virtues, venial and mortal sins, and kinds of law. The third volume deals with Christ vis-à-vis his Incarnation, the sacraments he explicitly or implicitly instituted, and his Resurrection. The *Summa* is arguably the preeminent construction of Scholasticism, a theological method that was practiced among the three Abrahamic religions (Judaism, Christianity, and Islam) from the eleventh to the fourteenth centuries and that attempted to reconcile faith and reason. Accordingly, the *Summa* argues both for the rationality of the Christian faith and for the validity of employing philosophy in the service of theology. Philosophy can be used to show the error of unbelievers and to enrich and deepen the faith of believers. By harmonizing the life of the spirit with the life of the mind, Aquinas endeavored to furnish a genuinely rational and universal view of all existence.

Aquinas's great synthesis of theology and philosophy amounted to a grand medieval cathedral of ideas, with the Trinitarian God and divine redemptive grace at its inner sanctum. One can picture this cathedral as having two stories, the bottom accessible to all humanity through native intelligence (which Aquinas took to be the *imago Dei*, or image of God) and the top accessible to Christians through faith. The bottom story is nature, containing philosophy (especially that of Aristotle) and everything that Aquinas felt philosophy could logically prove, such as the existence of God. The top story is grace, containing supernatural revelation and everything Aquinas felt it could logically prove, like the Trinity and God's Incarnation as Jesus of Nazareth. In sum, reason possesses a realm distinct from yet lower than grace—namely, nature—and faith possesses a realm distinct from and higher than nature—namely, grace. Such a distinction between nature and grace was completely unknown to previous Christian theologians, who considered these two items inseparable. Despite their separateness, Aquinas emphasized that nature points upward toward grace, and grace completes and elevates nature—rendering each realm the necessary complement of the other.

Context

The *Summa theologiae* contributed prominently to the thirteenth-century academic debates raging at such universities as Paris, Bologna, Salerno, Oxford, Cambridge, Montpellier, Padua, Salamanca, and Toulouse and sparked by the recovery of the works of Plato and Aristotle. These Greek and Latin classics had been virtually lost to the Western world after the decline of the Roman Empire but, through their Arabic versions preserved by Muslim scholars, returned to Western circulation in the eleventh century, when Jewish scholars began to translate them from Arabic into Latin. This philosophical revival generated three competing schools of thought: realism, moderate realism or conceptualism, and nominalism. Realism, rooted in the philosophy of Plato, maintained that there are universals of goodness, justice, and beauty that exist apart from individual human acts of goodness, justice, and beauty. Summarized by the phrase *universalia ante rem* (universals exist before created things), realism claimed that a just act, for instance, is merely a shadow or imperfect copy of the reality of justice that exists independently apart from that act. Further, realism alleged that faith precedes knowledge as its foundation, namely, *credo ut intelligam* (I believe in order that I may

Time Line

1225 — Thomas Aquinas is born near Roccasecca, Italy.

1230 — Thomas begins his primary education at nearby Monte Cassino, the monastery founded by Benedict of Nursia.

1242 — Thomas matriculates at the University of Naples and enters the Dominican order.

1244 — Enroute to Rome, Thomas is kidnapped by his brothers and imprisoned in the family castle, during which time he studies the Bible, the *Sentences* of Peter Lombard, and the works of Aristotle.

1245 — After his father releases him from custody, Thomas enters the University of Paris.

1248 — Thomas accompanies his master, Albertus Magnus, to continue his studies at the Dominican school in Cologne.

1256 — Upon earning his doctorate of theology, Thomas embarks upon his teaching career at the University of Paris.

1266 — Thomas starts writing the *Summa theologiae*, which he later claims (despite appearances) to have never completed.

1273 — Thomas's mystical experiences lead him to retire from writing and to devote his time completely to the spiritual life.

1274 — *March 7* Thomas dies while traveling to the Council of Lyons at the request of Pope Gregory X.

1323 — Thomas is canonized as a saint and given the title "Angelic Doctor" by Pope John XXII.

---

know). Faith must be first because the existence of universals depends on the existence of an immaterial realm, which there is, by definition, no physical way to prove.

Conceptualism, rooted in the philosophy of Aristotle, maintained that universals indeed exist but do so in particular things as their common nature; thus humanity exists as the common nature of people. The reason why universals objectively exist is their correspondence to ideas in the mind of God. Summarized by the phrase *universalia in re* (universals exist in created things), conceptualism is the school that the *Summa* endorses and for which it offers the most powerful medieval defense. Conceptualism affirmed that knowledge precedes faith as its foundation, or, in the words of Aquinas, *intelligo ut credam* (I know in order that I may believe). Nominalism, the *via moderna* (modern way) challenging the Platonic and Aristotelian *via antiqua* (old way), maintained that universals do not exist in reality. Rather, they are nothing more than "names," or linguistic handles, that humans have invented to conveniently describe the world; hence *universalia post rem* (universals after created things). In addition, nominalism divorced the realm of faith from the realm of knowledge, making the two entirely separate and having nothing to do with each other.

As a result, many nominalists held to a "double-truth model" in which the truths of faith (or theology) exist independently of, and may well contradict, the truths of knowledge (or philosophy). It was this idea that Aquinas found most damaging to Christianity and in need of refutation in that it denied that the truths of faith counted as knowledge and rendered such "truths" meaningless, as they would no longer correspond to objective facts. Aquinas combated the double-truth model by reconstructing Christian theology according to the philosophy of Aristotle. For Aquinas, faith is based on knowledge and reason: "Faith presupposes reason as grace presupposes nature." By the time of Aquinas, Aristotle had already been subject to interpretation and study by leading Muslim thinkers like Ibn Rushd (known in the West as Averroës, 1126–1198) and leading Jewish thinkers like Moses ben Maimon (known as Maimonides, 1135–1204). In drawing on their scholarship, the *Summa* informs Christian thought with much of the best medieval Jewish and Islamic philosophy.

About the Author

Thomas Aquinas stands as the scholastic theologian par excellence: The theology of this "Angelic Doctor" has either unofficially or officially served as the norm for the Roman Catholic Church since his lifetime. Thomas was born in 1225 to wealthy parents of the landed gentry at the family castle near Roccasecca, located between Rome and Naples in the Kingdom of Sicily. He obtained his primary education at the famed monastery of Monte Cassino founded by Benedict of Nursia. He then matriculated at the University of Naples, where he encountered two forces that revolutionized his life. First, the Western rediscovery of Aristotelian philosophy captivated him, as he found it the standard of sound reason. Second, the Dominicans, a relatively new order of friars founded by Saint Dominic de Guzman (1170–1221), was a popular religious renewal movement that greatly appealed to Aquinas and many other young intellectuals. But the Dominicans were considered *dominicares*, or fanatical "hounds of the Lord," by the wealthy and powerful elite of society, including Thomas's father, Landulf de Aquino. So when Thomas joined the Dominican order as a novice friar and moved into their house, Landulf commissioned his other sons to kidnap and "deprogram" Thomas so that he would return to his senses and play his assigned social role. Nevertheless, after two years of confinement in the family castle, Thomas could not be dissuaded from becoming a scholar of Aristotle among the Dominican friars. Granting defeat, his father finally released him from custody.

Leaving Italy as soon as possible to avoid recapture by his family, Aquinas quickly rejoined the Dominican order at the University of Paris, where he studied under the great scholastic master Albertus Magnus (1193–1280), whom he followed to a new Dominican school in Cologne in 1248. Although Thomas's fellow students dubbed him "the dumb ox" because he was rather obese and shy, Albertus recognized his brilliance and prophetically declared before the entire student body, "We call this lad a dumb ox, but I tell you that the whole world is going to hear his bellowing." Upon his graduation in 1256, Aquinas pursued a teaching career at the University of Paris, a hotbed of the controversy over Aristotelian philosophy. There he composed many works of theology, foremost among which were the multivolume sets *Summa contra Gentiles* ("Contra Gentiles"), his apologetic defense of Christianity against Muslim scholars in Spain and North Africa, and *Summa theologiae*, his systematic theology. Writing on virtually every conceivable topic in the university curriculum, Aquinas quickly grew famous and received acclamation from leaders of both church and state. Less than a year before his death on March 7, 1274, he suddenly retired from writing for no apparent reason. When his colleagues encouraged him to return to his scholarship, Aquinas replied, "I cannot, because all that I have written seems like straw to me compared to the things being revealed to me." Some scholars view this as a kind of nervous breakdown. Thomas's own perspective was that he was having such profound mystical experiences of the "beatific vision," or the heavenly glory of God, which he had written about as the goal of human redemption, that he felt it more important to attend to his spiritual life than to his literary output.

Explanation and Analysis of the Document

We begin by calling attention to the scholastic genre in which Aquinas wrote. This logically meticulous genre first inquires into a disputed point; thus Question 1, Article 1 asks, "Whether, besides philosophy, any further doctrine is required?" It proceeds to discuss the known negative answers to the question, such as "Objection 1: It seems that, besides

Time Line

1567 — Thomas is made "Universal Doctor of the [Roman Catholic] Church" by Pope Pius V.

1879 — Pope Leo XIII's encyclical *Aeterni Patris* ("Of the Eternal Father") pronounces Thomas's theology as the standard for the Roman Catholic Church.

philosophical science, we have no need of any further knowledge." Afterward, the writer presents the affirmative view, introduced by "On the contrary" or "I answer that" and then refutes each negative answer in sequence, such as "Reply to Objection 1." Frequently Aquinas substantiates both the negative answers and his own positive positions with traditional authorities, including biblical passages, statements by church fathers, creeds, and quotations from councils, as well as "the Philosopher," namely, Aristotle.

♦ Treatise on Sacred Doctrine

Question 1, Articles 1–6: At the outset Thomas's purpose in the *Summa theologiae* becomes immediately apparent: to integrate theology and philosophy without subordinating theology to philosophy and without reducing either of these two sciences (*scientia*, or species of knowledge) to the other. While both theology and philosophy are necessary for understanding God, theology is the queen or "chief of the sciences," served by philosophy as its necessary handmaiden. Thomas's opening six articles make one of his most notable and controversial contributions to Christian theology: the distinction between a natural knowledge of God accessible to all humanity and a special knowledge of God accessible to the faithful. The former knowledge encompasses philosophy and the other nontheological sciences, while the latter knowledge equals "sacred doctrine," or theology. Both natural knowledge and sacred doctrine constitute "sciences," since each employs reason, logic, and evidence, but they are grounded upon two different sets of axioms. The axioms of natural knowledge constitute the information gained from the five senses, while the axioms of sacred doctrine constitute the information gained from the Bible. Because God is the creator of the physical world and the ultimate author of scripture, both sciences are the logical outcrops of different forms of divine revelation, which can be called "natural revelation" and "special revelation." Sacred doctrine is both "practical" and "speculative," insofar as the relevance of some theological matters pertains directly to daily life while the relevance of others pertains to eternal life and will become apparent only in the hereafter. Since wisdom orders things according to their highest governing principle and since the truths God has supernaturally revealed are said truths, sacred doctrine alone is properly called wisdom and amounts to one unified science. Though theology and philosophy amount to two radically different

Thomas Aquinas
(St Thomas Aquinas [1225-1274], Bartolommeo, Fra [Baccio della Porta]
[1472-1517] / Museo di San Marco dell'Angelico, Florence, Italy / The
Bridgeman Art Library International)

ways of knowing, they do not contradict each other but rather cohere with one another, for both are fountains of *scientia* from the same divine wellspring.

Aquinas admitted that a certain happiness in this life can be achieved by the exercise of our natural powers, such that the unbeliever can realize the highest goal proportionate to human powers (the *bonum ultimum*). The existence of this goal and the means for achieving it are discoverable by philosophy. However, this *bonum ultimum* is still incomplete and imperfect, as humans must move beyond the natural to the supernatural goal of their existence. This supernatural goal (the *summum bonum*) is the final good, which cannot be known by unaided reason but only through theology. Thus the natural end, insofar as it cannot satisfy humanity, points beyond itself to the supernatural and satisfactory end. In seeking the natural, insisted Thomas, humanity is heading in the right direction but not traveling far enough. In other words, the natural end is imperfect because it is incomplete, not because it is wrong. Complete and perfect happiness is found in God alone.

Question 1, Articles 7 and 8: Sacred doctrine, for Thomas, is "a matter of argument" that necessarily complements philosophy. This is because the human mind unaided by scripture can reach only the vestibule to faith, while sacred doctrine allows us to move from the vestibule into the house of God. Theology is a higher science than philosophy owing both to the certainty of its data, as human perception can err but scripture cannot, and to the superior excellence of its object of study, namely, God. Thomas noted that theology utilizes logic not to prove scripture—in terms of either its doctrinal validity or its historical reliability—which he regarded as a futile enterprise, since God is already known to be truthful, but to formulate coherent doctrines from scripture and to defend their rationality.

Question 1, Article 9: If God is incomprehensible, as Aquinas believed, then how can the Deity ever be described, much less studied, using human language? The answer, says Aquinas, is through metaphor, a notion that has since been styled the "principle of analogy." For God's creation of the world points to a basic analogy of being between God and the world—there exists continuity between God and the world as a result of the expression of the being of God in the being of the world. Thus it is valid to use "material," "corporeal things" as metaphors for God. In so doing, theology does not reduce God to the level of corporeal things; instead, it affirms that there are "similitudes" between God and corporeal things, which allow the latter to serve as pointers to God. Moreover, metaphor allows only persons who are spiritually receptive to receive the truth, since they are unlikely to abuse it, while truth's inherent ambiguity hides it from the "unworthy."

Question 1, Article 10: In Article 10 we find the classic articulation of Aquinas's hermeneutic (methodology for interpreting scripture), known as the *quadriga* on account of the four "senses" conveyed by every biblical "word" or passage. The term *quadriga* originally referred to a four-horse chariot. Just as the chariot needed all four horses to advance in a straight line, so scripture needs all four senses to lead people down the straight path to eternal life. First, the "historical or literal" sense denotes the plain, factual meaning of the text. Second, the "allegorical sense" refers to the abstract spiritual principle embodied by the text. This sense was often followed in place of the historical sense when interpreting commands regarding ceremony, diet, and dress in the "Old Law," or Mosaic Torah, which the New Testament declared no longer binding on Christians. It also trumped the historical sense when the literal reading affirmed something contrary to God's perfection, such as God's commanding the slaying of various Canaanite peoples. Third, the "moral" or "tropological" sense designates the text's lessons for the believer's ethical and devotional life. Fourth, the "anagogical sense" alludes to the elements of the text that foreshadow things that, though not yet having obtained, will obtain in the glorious new heaven and new earth.

♦ **Treatise on the One God**

Question 2, Article 3: Although God is properly the object of theological investigation, this does not imply that nothing about God can be known through natural revelation. In fact, Aquinas argues that the existence of God can be indisputably proved five times over via philosophy alone. Through these proofs, even a person who had never heard of Christianity could deduce that God exists. These *quinque*

Essential Quotes

> "This science . . . transcends all others. . . . Now one speculative science is said to be nobler than another, either by reason of its greater certitude, or by reason of the higher worth of its subject-matter. In both these respects this science surpasses other speculative sciences. . . . The purpose of this science . . . is eternal bliss; to which . . . the purposes of every practical science are directed. Hence . . . from every standpoint, it is nobler than other sciences."

> "Since therefore grace does not destroy nature but perfects it, natural reason should minister to faith as the natural bent of the will ministers to charity. . . . Hence sacred doctrine makes use also of the authority of philosophers in those questions in which they were able to know the truth by natural reason . . . but properly uses the authority of the canonical Scriptures as an incontrovertible proof, and the authority of the doctors of the Church . . . merely as probable."

> "Whatever is in motion must be put in motion by another. If that by which it is put in motion be itself put in motion, then this also must needs be put in motion by another, and that by another again. But this cannot go on to infinity. . . . Therefore it is necessary to arrive at a first mover, put in motion by no other; and this everyone understands to be God."

viae (five ways), or five proofs for God's existence, stand as perhaps Aquinas's most enduring legacy; their soundness has remained a matter of lively debate among professional philosophers and theologians to this day. All five ways appeal to human experiences of the natural world, surmising that these experiences could not happen apart from the existence of God. In short, God can be known naturally as the necessary cause of his effects in the natural order.

The first way is "the argument from motion," predicated upon the observation that many things in the world are constantly changing or "moving." For anything in the natural world that is moving, it must have been moved by something already moving. That is to say, natural things do not just move on their own; they are moved by something else. So for the motion of any natural entity, there is another moving entity that caused its motion; if that entity is natural, there is another moving entity that caused its motion. Accordingly, when we trace these causes backward, we find a whole chain of moving things lying behind the world as it is at present. But since an infinite regress is impossible, there must be a single moving thing at the beginning of the chain.

However, this original moving thing cannot be something in the natural world, or else it would need to have been moved by something else. Therefore this original moving thing at the beginning of the chain must be supernatural, which, Aquinas notes, "everyone understands to be God." Within this argument, Aquinas introduced a significant Aristotelian distinction between two modes of being: potentiality and actuality. In every movement, something potential is becoming actual. But no potency can actualize itself, and thus the actualization of any potency requires a previous actuality. For this reason, the ultimate "first mover, put in motion by no other," or Unmoved Mover who set the natural world in motion, must be *actus purus* (pure actuality).

The second way is "from the nature of the efficient cause," predicated upon the observation that everything that comes into being, regardless of whether or not it moves thereafter, has been brought into being by something else. But everything in the universe has come into being. Consequently, the first thing in the history of the universe requires an efficient, or productive, cause, but this cause cannot be anything in the universe, since at that point nothing else in the universe existed. Therefore, this "first efficient cause," "to which everyone gives the name of God," must transcend the space-time universe.

The third way is "taken from possibility and necessity," predicated upon the observation that some things exist contingently while other things exist necessarily. In other words, it is *logically possible* for some things to come into existence or to go out of existence, even if those things neither came into existence nor will go out of existence. Such things are called contingent. On the other hand, it is *logically impossible* for other things to come into existence or to go out of existence; they simply exist necessarily. But then the question arises: Why do contingent things exist at all? For unlike necessary things, which are self-sustaining by their very nature, contingent things could cease to exist and so do not sustain their own existence. Hence Aquinas contends that every contingent thing depends for its existence on a necessary thing. All this leads to the central issue: What about the set of "things in nature," namely, the universe itself? Is it contingent or necessary? Notice here that Aquinas is not asking whether or not the universe, in fact, came into existence, as he realized that apart from scripture (which is not part of natural revelation and thus is off-limits to this argument), no evidence was available in his day to establish whether the universe had a beginning. (In fact, Aristotle held that the universe never came into existence.) Rather, Aquinas is asking whether or not it is *logically possible* for the universe to either begin to exist or cease to exist. Since not one but both of these are logical possibilities, it follows that the universe cannot sustain its own existence. Hence there must be a necessary being outside the universe, namely, God, who sustains the universe in existence.

The fourth way is "taken from the gradation to be found in things," predicated upon the existence of such human values as goodness, truth, and nobility. However, we recognize that some human goods are better or worse than others, and even the greatest human goods are always capable of improvement. Such gradations or value judgments require an objective standard or yardstick against which they are measured. Since humans cannot, by definition, reach the greatest goods, as there are always potentially goods just a little bit better, human societies could not have devised this objective standard. Hence this objective standard must be the character, or nature, of God himself. (Even though male pronouns are used for God in English translation of the *Summa*, the original Latin does not specify gender, and Thomas regarded God as beyond gender distinctions.)

The fifth way is "taken from the governance of the world," predicated upon the clear purposes that unconscious natural processes (for example, planetary motion) and objects (for example, plants) seem to contain, such as maintaining the order of the cosmos, growth, reproduction, and the like. As unconscious entities, they could not have given themselves these purposes. For this reason, "some intelligent being" must have instilled various purposes within these entities. Because no animal or human intelligence could have instilled such purposes, the intelligent being under discussion can only be God.

Audience

Thomas's intended audience consisted of university students earning theology degrees, for whom the *Summa* was designed as a comprehensive textbook. Fulfilling and far surpassing this goal, the *Summa* immediately became essential reading not only for students but also for all of Thomas's academic contemporaries in the Scholastic movement, regardless of school (conceptualist, realist, or nominalist) or religion (Christian, Jewish, or Muslim). However, the *Summa* was neither intended for nor read by medieval laypeople, most of whom were illiterate. Until the Protestant Reformation, the *Summa* served as a staple in the theology curricula of all European universities, with professors and students emulating, modifying, or refuting it depending on the philosophical slant of each university.

In recent times, the Second Vatican Council (1962–1965) seemed to displace Thomas's thought with post-Enlightenment philosophical trends, limiting his modern audience. However, the fluidity of such trends coupled with the so-called failure of modernity led Pope John Paul II in 1998 to issue *Fides et ratio* ("Faith and Reason"), an encyclical that reasserted the primacy of Thomas for the Roman Catholic Church. While recognizing his importance in stimulating continued dialogue, secular philosophers are split on the validity of Thomas's claims, finding in them either points of support or foils for their own thinking.

Impact

Recognized as the authoritative expression of conceptualism, the *Summa*'s system of thought became appropriately known as Thomism. From the early fourteenth century onward, Thomism became one of several competing forms of Christian philosophy, alongside the realist Augustinianism (named after the early theological giant Augustine of Hippo [354–430]), the quasi-nominalism of John Duns Scotus (ca. 1266–1308), and the nominalism of William of Ockham (ca. 1280/88–1348/49). Accordingly, Pope John XXII canonized Aquinas as a saint and gave him the title "Angelic Doctor" in 1323. Because of its meticulous reason and logic, Thomism emerged as a valuable ally against sixteenth-century Protestantism and Anabaptism and secured its place as the leading school of Catholic thought. Thus Pope Pius V declared Aquinas the "Universal Doctor of the [Roman Catholic] Church" in 1567.

With the advent of the Enlightenment in the seventeenth century, many in the West came to embrace a secular worldview based on scientific rationalism with no room for religion, here regarded as superstition. This separation of science and religion, foreshadowed centuries earlier by the nominalist double-truth model, was widened by Charles Darwin's publication of *On the Origin of Species* (1859). Hence the nineteenth-century Roman Catholic Church needed a fully integrated Christian worldview that allowed for the truth of evolution and other scientific discoveries and demonstrated their consistency with theology, which, far from superstition, comprised a science and the highest branch thereof. Harmonizing natural reason with religious knowledge, the *Summa* provided precisely such an integrated worldview, leading Pope Leo XIII in his 1879 encyclical *Aeterni Patris* ("Of the Eternal Father") to pronounce it as the official theology of the Roman Catholic Church. In the 1960s the Second Vatican Council opened Roman Catholicism to a variety of philosophical perspectives, such that Thomas was no longer considered the Church's exclusive voice. But the modern revival of Thomas's thought, chartered in 1998 by *Fides et ratio*, has returned Thomas to the premier rank among the many available Catholic perspectives and thereby places him in fruitful dialogue with contemporary philosophy.

Further Reading

■ Books

Cairns, Earle E. *Christianity through the Centuries*. 3rd. rev. ed. Grand Rapids, Mich.: Zondervan, 1996.

Chesterton, Gilbert K. *St. Thomas Aquinas*. New York: Sheed and Ward, 1933.

Davies, Brian. *The Thought of Thomas Aquinas*. Oxford, U.K.: Clarendon, 1992.

Gilson, Étienne. *The Christian Philosophy of St. Thomas Aquinas*, trans. L. K. Shook. South Bend, Ind.: University of Notre Dame Press, 1956.

McCabe, Herbert. *On Aquinas*, ed. Brian Davies. London: Continuum, 2008.

McGrath, Alister E. *Historical Theology*. Malden, Mass.: Blackwell, 1998.

McGrath, Alister E. *Christian Theology*. 3rd. ed. Malden, Mass.: Blackwell, 2001.

Olson, Roger E. *The Story of Christian Theology*. Downers Grove, Ill.: InterVarsity Press, 1999.

Stump, Eleonore. *Aquinas*. New York: Routledge, 2003.

■ Web Sites

Browning, Mark. "St. Thomas Aquinas." Christian Classics Ethereal Library Web site.
   http://www.ccel.org/a/aquinas

Kennedy, Daniel. "St. Thomas Aquinas." Catholic Encyclopedia, New Advent Web site.
   http://www.newadvent.org/cathen/14663b.htm

McInerny, Ralph, and John O'Callaghan. "Saint Thomas Aquinas." Stanford Encyclopedia of Philosophy Web site.
   http://plato.stanford.edu/entries/aquinas/

—Kirk R. MacGregor

Questions for Further Study

1. The *Summa theologiae* is one of the great works of the medieval period. Why? What insights about the medieval mind-set does it hold for modern readers?

2. Over the centuries, numerous cultures throughout the world have produced at least one major work that outlines a theology and a philosophy that influenced people well into the future. Select a milestone work from another culture—the Analects of Confucius, for example, or the Bhagavad Gita—and, in comparing it with the *Summa theologiae*, explain why each work had such an impact on the culture that produced it.

3. What was "nominalism," and what part did the nominalist philosophy play in Aquinas's work?

4. What was the relationship between Thomism and the emerging field of evolutionary science in the nineteenth century? Why did the *Summa theologiae* attain new relevance in light of evolutionary theory?

5. Aquinas says that the purposes of every practical science are directed toward "eternal bliss." Do you think that most contemporary scientists would agree or disagree with this statement? Explain.

Thomas Aquinas: *Summa Theologiae*

First Part: Treatise on Sacred Doctrine

♦ **QUESTION 1—THE NATURE AND EXTENT OF SACRED DOCTRINE (TEN ARTICLES)**

To place our purpose within proper limits, we first endeavor to investigate the nature and extent of this sacred doctrine. Concerning this there are ten points of inquiry:

(1) Whether it is necessary?

(2) Whether it is a science?

(3) Whether it is one or many?

(4) Whether it is speculative or practical?

(5) How it is compared with other sciences?

(6) Whether it is the same as wisdom?

(7) Whether God is its subject-matter?

(8) Whether it is a matter of argument?

(9) Whether it rightly employs metaphors and similes?

(10) Whether the Sacred Scripture of this doctrine may be expounded in different senses?

Article 1—Whether, besides philosophy, any further doctrine is required?

Objection 1: It seems that, besides philosophical science, we have no need of any further knowledge. For man should not seek to know what is above reason: "Seek not the things that are too high for thee." But whatever is not above reason is fully treated of in philosophical science. Therefore any other knowledge besides philosophical science is superfluous.

Objection 2: Further, knowledge can be concerned only with being, for nothing can be known, save what is true; and all that is, is true. But everything that is, is treated of in philosophical science—even God Himself; so that there is a part of philosophy called theology, or the divine science, as Aristotle has proved (Metaph. vi). Therefore, besides philosophical science, there is no need of any further knowledge.

On the contrary, It is written: "All Scripture, inspired of God is profitable to teach, to reprove, to correct, to instruct in justice." Now Scripture, inspired of God, is no part of philosophical science, which has been built up by human reason. Therefore it is useful that besides philosophical science, there should be other knowledge, i.e. inspired of God.

I answer that, It was necessary for man's salvation that there should be a knowledge revealed by God besides philosophical science built up by human reason. Firstly, indeed, because man is directed to God, as to an end that surpasses the grasp of his reason: "The eye hath not seen, O God, besides Thee, what things Thou hast prepared for them that wait for Thee." But the end must first be known by men who are to direct their thoughts and actions to the end. Hence it was necessary for the salvation of man that certain truths which exceed human reason should be made known to him by divine revelation. Even as regards those truths about God which human reason could have discovered, it was necessary that man should be taught by a divine revelation; because the truth about God such as reason could discover, would only be known by a few, and that after a long time, and with the admixture of many errors. Whereas man's whole salvation, which is in God, depends upon the knowledge of this truth. Therefore, in order that the salvation of men might be brought about more fitly and more surely, it was necessary that they should be taught divine truths by divine revelation. It was therefore necessary that besides philosophical science built up by reason, there should be a sacred science learned through revelation.

Reply to Objection 1: Although those things which are beyond man's knowledge may not be sought for by man through his reason, nevertheless, once they are revealed by God, they must be accepted by faith. Hence the sacred text continues, "For many things are shown to thee above the understanding of man." And in this, the sacred science consists.

Reply to Objection 2: Sciences are differentiated according to the various means through which knowledge is obtained. For the astronomer and the physicist both may prove the same conclusion: that the earth, for instance, is round: the astronomer by means of mathematics (i.e. abstracting from matter), but the physicist by means of matter itself. Hence there is no reason why those things which may be learned from philosophical science, so far as they can be known by natural reason, may not also be taught us by another science so far as they fall within revelation. Hence theology included in sacred doctrine differs in kind from that theology which is part of philosophy.

Article 2—Whether sacred doctrine is a science?

Objection 1: It seems that sacred doctrine is not a science. For every science proceeds from self-evident principles. But sacred doctrine proceeds from articles of faith which are not self-evident, since their truth is not admitted by all: "For all men have not faith." Therefore sacred doctrine is not a science.

Objection 2: Further, no science deals with individual facts. But this sacred science treats of individual facts, such as the deeds of Abraham, Isaac and Jacob and such like. Therefore sacred doctrine is not a science.

On the contrary, Augustine says (De Trin. xiv, 1) "to this science alone belongs that whereby saving faith is begotten, nourished, protected and strengthened." But this can be said of no science except sacred doctrine. Therefore sacred doctrine is a science.

I answer that, Sacred doctrine is a science. We must bear in mind that there are two kinds of sciences. There are some which proceed from a principle known by the natural light of intelligence, such as arithmetic and geometry and the like. There are some which proceed from principles known by the light of a higher science: thus the science of perspective proceeds from principles established by geometry, and music from principles established by arithmetic. So it is that sacred doctrine is a science because it proceeds from principles established by the light of a higher science, namely, the science of God and the blessed. Hence, just as the musician accepts on authority the principles taught him by the mathematician, so sacred science is established on principles revealed by God.

Reply to Objection 1: The principles of any science are either in themselves self-evident, or reducible to the conclusions of a higher science; and such, as we have said, are the principles of sacred doctrine.

Reply to Objection 2: Individual facts are treated of in sacred doctrine, not because it is concerned with them principally, but they are introduced rather both as examples to be followed in our lives (as in moral sciences) and in order to establish the authority of those men through whom the divine revelation, on which this sacred scripture or doctrine is based, has come down to us.

Article 3—Whether sacred doctrine is one science?

Objection 1: It seems that sacred doctrine is not one science; for according to the Philosopher (Poster. i) "that science is one which treats only of one class of subjects." But the creator and the creature, both of whom are treated of in sacred doctrine, cannot be grouped together under one class of subjects. Therefore sacred doctrine is not one science.

Objection 2: Further, in sacred doctrine we treat of angels, corporeal creatures and human morality. But these belong to separate philosophical sciences. Therefore sacred doctrine cannot be one science.

On the contrary, Holy Scripture speaks of it as one science: "Wisdom gave him the knowledge [scientiam] of holy things."

I answer that, Sacred doctrine is one science. The unity of a faculty or habit is to be gauged by its object, not indeed, in its material aspect, but as regards the precise formality under which it is an object. For example, man, ass, stone agree in the one precise formality of being colored; and color is the formal object of sight. Therefore, because Sacred Scripture considers things precisely under the formality of being divinely revealed, whatever has been divinely revealed possesses the one precise formality of the object of this science; and therefore is included under sacred doctrine as under one science.

Reply to Objection 1: Sacred doctrine does not treat of God and creatures equally, but of God primarily, and of creatures only so far as they are referable to God as their beginning or end. Hence the unity of this science is not impaired.

Reply to Objection 2: Nothing prevents inferior faculties or habits from being differentiated by something which falls under a higher faculty or habit as well; because the higher faculty or habit regards the object in its more universal formality, as the object of the "common sense" is whatever affects the senses, including, therefore, whatever is visible or audible. Hence the "common sense," although one faculty, extends to all the objects of the five senses. Similarly, objects which are the subject-matter of different philosophical sciences can yet be treated of by this one single sacred science under one aspect precisely so far as they can be included in revelation. So that in this way, sacred doctrine bears, as it were, the stamp of the divine science which is one and simple, yet extends to everything.

Article 4—Whether sacred doctrine is a practical science?

Objection 1: It seems that sacred doctrine is a practical science; for a practical science is that which ends in action according to the Philosopher (Metaph. ii). But sacred doctrine is ordained to action: "Be ye doers of the word, and not hearers only." Therefore sacred doctrine is a practical science.

Objection 2: Further, sacred doctrine is divided into the Old and the New Law. But law implies a moral science which is a practical science. Therefore sacred doctrine is a practical science.

On the contrary, Every practical science is concerned with human operations; as moral science is concerned with human acts, and architecture with buildings. But sacred doctrine is chiefly concerned with God, whose handiwork is especially man. Therefore it is not a practical but a speculative science.

I answer that, Sacred doctrine, being one, extends to things which belong to different philosophical sciences because it considers in each the same formal aspect, namely, so far as they can be known through divine revelation. Hence, although among the philosophical sciences one is speculative and another practical, nevertheless sacred doctrine includes both; as God, by one and the same science, knows both Himself and His works. Still, it is speculative rather than practical because it is more concerned with divine things than with human acts; though it does treat even of these latter, inasmuch as man is ordained by them to the perfect knowledge of God in which consists eternal bliss. This is a sufficient answer to the Objections.

Article 5—Whether sacred doctrine is nobler than other sciences?

Objection 1: It seems that sacred doctrine is not nobler than other sciences; for the nobility of a science depends on the certitude it establishes. But other sciences, the principles of which cannot be doubted, seem to be more certain than sacred doctrine; for its principles—namely, articles of faith—can be doubted. Therefore other sciences seem to be nobler.

Objection 2: Further, it is the sign of a lower science to depend upon a higher; as music depends on arithmetic. But sacred doctrine does in a sense depend upon philosophical sciences; for Jerome observes, in his Epistle to Magnus, that "the ancient doctors so enriched their books with the ideas and phrases of the philosophers, that thou knowest not what more to admire in them, their profane erudition or their scriptural learning." Therefore sacred doctrine is inferior to other sciences.

On the contrary, other sciences are called the handmaidens of this one: "Wisdom sent her maids to invite to the tower."

I answer that, Since this science is partly speculative and partly practical, it transcends all others speculative and practical. Now one speculative science is said to be nobler than another, either by reason of its greater certitude, or by reason of the higher worth of its subject-matter. In both these respects this science surpasses other speculative sciences; in point of greater certitude, because other sciences derive their certitude from the natural light of human reason, which can err; whereas this derives its certitude from the light of divine knowledge, which cannot be misled: in point of the higher worth of its subject-matter because this science treats chiefly of those things which by their sublimity transcend human reason; while other sciences consider only those things which are within reason's grasp. Of the practical sciences, that one is nobler which is ordained to a further purpose, as political science is nobler than military science; for the good of the army is directed to the good of the State. But the purpose of this science, in so far as it is practical, is eternal bliss; to which as to an ultimate end the purposes of every practical science are directed. Hence it is clear that from every standpoint, it is nobler than other sciences.

Reply to Objection 1: It may well happen that what is in itself the more certain may seem to us the less certain on account of the weakness of our intelligence, "which is dazzled by the clearest objects of nature; as the owl is dazzled by the light of the sun" (Metaph. ii, lect. i). Hence the fact that some happen to doubt about articles of faith is not due to the uncertain nature of the truths, but to the weakness of human intelligence; yet the slenderest knowledge that may be obtained of the highest things is more desirable than the most certain knowledge obtained of lesser things, as is said in de Animalibus xi.

Reply to Objection 2: This science can in a sense depend upon the philosophical sciences, not as though it stood in need of them, but only in order to make its teaching clearer. For it accepts its principles not from other sciences, but immediately from God, by revelation. Therefore it does not depend upon other sciences as upon the higher, but makes use of them as of the lesser, and as handmaidens: even so the master sciences make use of the sciences that supply their materials, as political of military science. That it thus uses them is not due to its own defect or insufficiency, but to the defect of our intelligence, which is more easily led by what is known through natural reason (from which proceed the other sciences) to that which is above reason, such as are the teachings of this science.

Article 6—Whether this doctrine is the same as wisdom?

Objection 1: It seems that this doctrine is not the same as wisdom. For no doctrine which borrows its principles is worthy of the name of wisdom; seeing that the wise man directs, and is not directed (Metaph. i). But this doctrine borrows its principles. Therefore this science is not wisdom.

Objection 2: Further, it is a part of wisdom to prove the principles of other sciences. Hence it is called the chief of sciences, as is clear in Ethic. vi. But this doctrine does not prove the principles of other sciences. Therefore it is not the same as wisdom.

Objection 3: Further, this doctrine is acquired by study, whereas wisdom is acquired by God's inspiration; so that it is numbered among the gifts of the Holy Spirit. Therefore this doctrine is not the same as wisdom.

On the contrary, It is written: "This is your wisdom and understanding in the sight of nations."

I answer that, This doctrine is wisdom above all human wisdom; not merely in any one order, but absolutely. For since it is the part of a wise man to arrange and to judge, and since lesser matters should be judged in the light of some higher principle, he is said to be wise in any one order who considers the highest principle in that order: thus in the order of building, he who plans the form of the house is called wise and architect, in opposition to the inferior laborers who trim the wood and make ready the stones: "As a wise architect, I have laid the foundation." Again, in the order of all human life, the prudent man is called wise, inasmuch as he directs his acts to a fitting end: "Wisdom is prudence to a man." Therefore he who considers absolutely the highest cause of the whole universe, namely God, is most of all called wise. Hence wisdom is said to be the knowledge of divine things, as Augustine says (De Trin. xii, 14). But sacred doctrine essentially treats of God viewed as the highest cause—not only so far as He can be known through creatures just as philosophers knew Him—"That which is known of God is manifest in them"—but also as far as He is known to Himself alone and revealed to others. Hence sacred doctrine is especially called wisdom.

Reply to Objection 1: Sacred doctrine derives its principles not from any human knowledge, but from the divine knowledge, through which, as through the highest wisdom, all our knowledge is set in order.

Reply to Objection 2: The principles of other sciences either are evident and cannot be proved, or are proved by natural reason through some other science. But the knowledge proper to this science comes through revelation and not through natural reason. Therefore it has no concern to prove the principles of other sciences, but only to judge of them. Whatsoever is found in other sciences contrary to any truth of this science must be condemned as false: "Destroying counsels and every height that exalteth itself against the knowledge of God."

Reply to Objection 3: Since judgment appertains to wisdom, the twofold manner of judging produces a twofold wisdom. A man may judge in one way by inclination, as whoever has the habit of a virtue judges rightly of what concerns that virtue by his very inclination towards it. Hence it is the virtuous man, as we read, who is the measure and rule of human acts. In another way, by knowledge, just as a man learned in moral science might be able to judge rightly about virtuous acts, though he had not the virtue. The first manner of judging divine things belongs to that wisdom which is set down among the gifts of the Holy Ghost: "The spiritual man judgeth all things." And Dionysius says (Div. Nom. ii): "Hierotheus is taught not by mere learning, but by experience of divine things." The second manner of judging belongs to this doctrine which is acquired by study, though its principles are obtained by revelation.

Article 7—Whether God is the object of this science?

Objection 1: It seems that God is not the object of this science. For in every science, the nature of its object is presupposed. But this science cannot presuppose the essence of God, for Damascene says (De Fide Orth. i, iv): "It is impossible to define the essence of God." Therefore God is not the object of this science.

Objection 2: Further, whatever conclusions are reached in any science must be comprehended under the object of the science. But in Holy Writ we reach conclusions not only concerning God, but concerning many other things, such as creatures and human morality. Therefore God is not the object of this science.

On the contrary, The object of the science is that of which it principally treats. But in this science, the treatment is mainly about God; for it is called theology, as treating of God. Therefore God is the object of this science.

I answer that, God is the object of this science. The relation between a science and its object is the same as that between a habit or faculty and its object. Now properly speaking, the object of a faculty or habit is the thing under the aspect of which all things are referred to that faculty or habit, as man and stone are referred to the faculty of sight in that they are colored. Hence colored things are the proper objects of sight. But in sacred science, all things are treated of under the aspect of God: either because they are God Himself or because they refer to God as their beginning and end. Hence it follows that God is in very truth the object of this science. This is clear also from the principles of this science, namely, the articles of faith, for faith is about God. The object of the principles and of the whole science must be the same, since the whole science is contained virtually in its principles. Some, however, looking to what is treated of in this science, and not to the aspect under which it is treated, have asserted the object of this science to be something other than God—that is, either things and signs; or the works of salvation; or the whole Christ, as the head and members. Of all these things, in truth, we treat in this science, but so far as they have reference to God.

Reply to Objection 1: Although we cannot know in what consists the essence of God, nevertheless in this science we make use of His effects, either of nature or of grace, in place of a definition, in regard to whatever is treated of in this science concerning God; even as in some philosophical sciences we demonstrate something about a cause from its effect, by taking the effect in place of a definition of the cause.

Reply to Objection 2: Whatever other conclusions are reached in this sacred science are comprehended under God, not as parts or species or accidents but as in some way related to Him.

Article 8—Whether sacred doctrine is a matter of argument?

Objection 1: It seems this doctrine is not a matter of argument. For Ambrose says (De Fide 1): "Put arguments aside where faith is sought." But in this doctrine, faith especially is sought: "But these things are written that you may believe." Therefore sacred doctrine is not a matter of argument.

Objection 2: Further, if it is a matter of argument, the argument is either from authority or from reason. If it is from authority, it seems unbefitting its dignity, for the proof from authority is the weakest form of proof. But if it is from reason, this is unbefitting its end, because, according to Gregory (Hom. 26), "faith has no merit in those things of which human reason brings its own experience." Therefore sacred doctrine is not a matter of argument.

On the contrary, The Scripture says that a bishop should "embrace that faithful word which is according to doctrine, that he may be able to exhort in sound doctrine and to convince the gainsayers."

I answer that, As other sciences do not argue in proof of their principles, but argue from their principles to demonstrate other truths in these sciences: so this doctrine does not argue in proof of its principles, which are the articles of faith, but from them it goes on to prove something else; as the Apostle from the resurrection of Christ argues in proof of the general resurrection. However, it is to be borne in mind, in regard to the philosophical sciences, that the inferior sciences neither prove their principles nor dispute with those who deny them, but leave this to a higher science; whereas the highest of them, viz. metaphysics, can dispute with one who denies its principles, if only the opponent will make some concession; but if he concede nothing, it can have no dispute with him, though it can answer his objections. Hence Sacred Scripture, since it has no science above itself, can dispute with one who denies its principles only if the opponent admits some at least of the truths obtained through divine revelation; thus we can argue with heretics from texts in Holy Writ, and against those who deny one article of faith, we can argue from another. If our opponent believes nothing of divine revelation, there is no longer any means of proving the articles of faith by reasoning, but only of answering his objections—if he has any—against faith. Since faith rests upon infallible truth, and since the contrary of a truth can never be demonstrated, it is clear that the arguments brought against faith cannot be demonstrations, but are difficulties that can be answered.

Reply to Objection 1: Although arguments from human reason cannot avail to prove what must be received on faith, nevertheless, this doctrine argues from articles of faith to other truths.

Reply to Objection 2: This doctrine is especially based upon arguments from authority, inasmuch as its principles are obtained by revelation: thus we ought to believe on the authority of those to whom the revelation has been made. Nor does this take away from the dignity of this doctrine, for although the argument from authority based on human reason is the weakest, yet the argument from authority based on divine revelation is the strongest. But sacred doctrine makes use even of human reason, not, indeed, to prove faith (for thereby the merit of faith would come to an end), but to make clear other things that are put forward in this doctrine. Since therefore grace does not destroy nature but perfects it, natural reason should minister to faith as the natural bent of the will ministers to charity. Hence the Apostle says: "Bringing into captivity every understanding unto the obedience of Christ." Hence sacred doctrine makes use also of the authority of philosophers in those questions in which they were able to know the truth by natural reason, as Paul quotes a saying of Aratus: "As some also of your own poets said: For we are also His offspring." Nevertheless, sacred doctrine makes use of these authorities as extrinsic and probable arguments; but properly uses the authority of the canonical Scriptures as an incontrovertible proof, and the authority of the doctors of the Church as one that may properly be used, yet merely as probable. For our faith rests upon the revelation made to the apostles and prophets who wrote the canonical books, and not on the revelations (if any such there are) made to other doctors. Hence Augustine says (Epis. ad Hieron. xix, 1): "Only those books of Scripture which are called canonical have I learned to hold in such honor as to believe their authors have not erred in any way in writing them. But other authors I so read as not to deem everything in their works to be true, merely on account of their having so thought and written, whatever may have been their holiness and learning."

Article 9—Whether Holy Scripture should use metaphors?

Objection 1: It seems that Holy Scripture should not use metaphors. For that which is proper to the lowest science seems not to befit this science, which holds the highest place of all. But to proceed by the aid of various similitudes and figures is proper to poetry, the least of all the sciences. Therefore it is not fitting that this science should make use of such similitudes.

Objection 2: Further, this doctrine seems to be intended to make truth clear. Hence a reward is held out to those who manifest it: "They that explain me shall have life everlasting." But by such similitudes truth is obscured. Therefore, to put forward divine truths by likening them to corporeal things does not befit this science.

Objection 3: Further, the higher creatures are, the nearer they approach to the divine likeness. If therefore any creature be taken to represent God, this representation ought chiefly to be taken from the higher creatures, and not from the lower; yet this is often found in Scriptures.

On the contrary, It is written : "I have multiplied visions, and I have used similitudes by the ministry of the prophets." But to put forward anything by means of similitudes is to use metaphors. Therefore this sacred science may use metaphors.

I answer that, It is befitting Holy Writ to put forward divine and spiritual truths by means of comparisons with material things. For God provides for everything according to the capacity of its nature. Now it is natural to man to attain to intellectual truths through sensible objects, because all our knowledge originates from sense. Hence in Holy Writ, spiritual truths are fittingly taught under the likeness of material things. This is what Dionysius says (Coel. Hier. i): "We cannot be enlightened by the divine rays except they be hidden within the covering of many sacred veils." It is also befitting Holy Writ, which is proposed to all without distinction of persons—"To the wise and to the unwise I am a debtor"—that spiritual truths be expounded by means of figures taken from corporeal things, in order that thereby even the simple who are unable by themselves to grasp intellectual things may be able to understand it.

Reply to Objection 1: Poetry makes use of metaphors to produce a representation, for it is natural to man to be pleased with representations. But sacred doctrine makes use of metaphors as both necessary and useful.

Reply to Objection 2: The ray of divine revelation is not extinguished by the sensible imagery wherewith it is veiled, as Dionysius says (Coel. Hier. i); and its truth so far remains that it does not allow the minds of those to whom the revelation has been made, to rest in the metaphors, but raises them to the knowledge of truths; and through those to whom the revelation has been made others also may receive instruction in these matters. Hence those things that are taught metaphorically in one part of Scripture, in other parts are taught more openly. The very hiding of truth in figures is useful for the exercise of thoughtful minds and as a defense against the ridicule of the impious, according to the words "Give not that which is holy to dogs."

Reply to Objection 3: As Dionysius says, (Coel. Hier. i) it is more fitting that divine truths should be expounded under the figure of less noble than of nobler bodies, and this for three reasons. Firstly, because thereby men's minds are the better preserved from error. For then it is clear that these things are not literal descriptions of divine truths, which might have been open to doubt had they been expressed under the figure of nobler bodies, especially for those who could think of nothing nobler than bodies. Secondly, because this is more befitting the knowledge of God that we have in this life. For what He is not is clearer to us than what He is. Therefore similitudes drawn from things farthest away from God form within us a truer estimate that God is above whatsoever we may say or think of Him. Thirdly, because thereby divine truths are the better hidden from the unworthy.

Article 10—Whether in Holy Scripture a word may have several senses?

Objection 1: It seems that in Holy Writ a word cannot have several senses, historical or literal, allegorical, tropological or moral, and anagogical. For many different senses in one text produce confusion and deception and destroy all force of argument. Hence no argument, but only fallacies, can be deduced from a multiplicity of propositions. But Holy Writ ought to be able to state the truth without any fallacy. Therefore in it there cannot be several senses to a word.

Objection 2: Further, Augustine says (De util. cred. iii) that "the Old Testament has a fourfold division as to history, etiology, analogy and allegory." Now these four seem altogether different from the four divisions mentioned in the first objection. Therefore it does not seem fitting to explain the same word of Holy Writ according to the four different senses mentioned above.

Objection 3: Further, besides these senses, there is the parabolical, which is not one of these four.

On the contrary, Gregory says (Moral. xx, 1): "Holy Writ by the manner of its speech transcends every science, because in one and the same sentence, while it describes a fact, it reveals a mystery."

I answer that, The author of Holy Writ is God, in whose power it is to signify His meaning, not by words only (as man also can do), but also by things themselves. So, whereas in every other science things are signified by words, this science has the property, that the things signified by the words have themselves also a signification. Therefore that first signification whereby words signify things belongs to the first sense, the historical or literal. That signification whereby things signified by words have themselves also a signification is called the spiritual sense, which is based on the literal, and presupposes it. Now this spiritual sense has a threefold division. For as the Apostle says the Old Law is a figure of the New Law, and Dionysius says (Coel. Hier. i) "the New Law itself is a figure of future glory." Again, in the New Law, whatever our Head has done is a type of what we ought to do. Therefore, so far as the things of the Old Law signify the things of the New Law, there is the allegorical sense; so far as the things done in Christ, or so far as the things which signify Christ, are types of what we ought to do, there is the moral sense. But so far as they signify what relates to eternal glory, there is the anagogical sense. Since the literal sense is that which the author intends, and since the author of Holy Writ is God, Who by one act comprehends all things by His intellect, it is not unfitting, as Augustine says (Confess. xii), if, even according to the literal sense, one word in Holy Writ should have several senses.

Reply to Objection 1: The multiplicity of these senses does not produce equivocation or any other kind of multiplicity, seeing that these senses are not multiplied because one word signifies several things,

Glossary

Abraham, Isaac and Jacob	patriarchs of the Jewish people in the Old Testament
As a wise architect, I have laid the foundation	from the biblical book of 1 Corinthians, chapter 3, verse 10
As some also of your own poets said	from the biblical book of Acts, chapter 17, verse 28
Augustine	Saint Augustine of Hippo, author of *On the Trinity* (in Latin, abbreviated as De Trin.), *On the Usefulness of Believing* (in Latin, abbreviated as De util. cred.), the *Epistle to Hieronymus* (or Saint Jerome, abbreviated in Latin as Epis. ad Hieronymi), and *Enchiridion* (Greek for "handbook")
Be ye doers of the word, and not hearers only	from the biblical book of James, chapter 1, verse 22
Bringing into captivity every understanding . . .	from the biblical book of 2 Corinthians, chapter 10, verse 5

but because the things signified by the words can be themselves types of other things. Thus in Holy Writ no confusion results, for all the senses are founded on one—the literal—from which alone can any argument be drawn, and not from those intended in allegory, as Augustine says (Epis. 48). Nevertheless, nothing of Holy Scripture perishes on account of this, since nothing necessary to faith is contained under the spiritual sense which is not elsewhere put forward by the Scripture in its literal sense.

Reply to Objection 2: These three—history, etiology, analogy—are grouped under the literal sense. For it is called history, as Augustine expounds (Epis. 48), whenever anything is simply related; it is called etiology when its cause is assigned, as when Our Lord gave the reason why Moses allowed the putting away of wives—namely, on account of the hardness of men's hearts; it is called analogy whenever the truth of one text of Scripture is shown not to contradict the truth of another. Of these four, allegory alone stands for the three spiritual senses. Thus Hugh of St. Victor (Sacram. iv, 4 Prolog.) includes the anagogical under the allegorical sense, laying down three senses only—the historical, the allegorical, and the tropological.

Reply to Objection 3: The parabolical sense is contained in the literal, for by words things are signified properly and figuratively. Nor is the figure itself, but that which is figured, the literal sense. When Scripture speaks of God's arm, the literal sense is not that God has such a member, but only what is signified by this member, namely operative power. Hence it is plain that nothing false can ever underlie the literal sense of Holy Writ.

Treatise on the One God

♦ QUESTION 2—THE EXISTENCE OF GOD (THREE ARTICLES)

. . .

Article 3—Whether God exists?

Objection 1: It seems that God does not exist; because if one of two contraries be infinite, the other would be altogether destroyed. But the word "God" means that He is infinite goodness. If, therefore, God existed, there would be no evil discoverable; but there is evil in the world. Therefore God does not exist.

Objection 2: Further, it is superfluous to suppose that what can be accounted for by a few principles has been produced by many. But it seems that everything we see in the world can be accounted for by other principles, supposing God did not exist. For all natural things can be reduced to one principle which is nature; and all voluntary things can be reduced to one principle which is human reason, or will. Therefore there is no need to suppose God's existence.

On the contrary, It is said in the person of God: "I am Who am."

Glossary

But these things are written that you may believe	from the biblical book of John, chapter 20, verse 31
Damascene	Saint John of Damascus, author of *De fide orthodoxa* (abbreviated here as De Fide Orth.), or *Exposition of the Orthodox Faith*
de Animal	*Historia de animalibus* (*History of Animals*) by Aristotle
Destroying counsels and every height . . .	from the biblical book of 2 Corinthians, chapter 10, verses 4 and 5
Dionysius	Dionysius the Areopagite, converted to Christianity by Saint Paul; author of *Caelestis hierarchia* (Coel. Hier.), or *Celestial Hierarchy*
embrace that faithful word which is according to doctrine . . .	from the biblical book of Titus, chapter 1, verse 9
Ethic	Aristotle's *Ethics*

Document Text

I answer that, The existence of God can be proved in five ways.

The first and more manifest way is the argument from motion. It is certain, and evident to our senses, that in the world some things are in motion. Now whatever is in motion is put in motion by another, for nothing can be in motion except it is in potentiality to that towards which it is in motion; whereas a thing moves inasmuch as it is in act. For motion is nothing else than the reduction of something from potentiality to actuality. But nothing can be reduced from potentiality to actuality, except by something in a state of actuality. Thus that which is actually hot, as fire, makes wood, which is potentially hot, to be actually hot, and thereby moves and changes it. Now it is not possible that the same thing should be at once in actuality and potentiality in the same respect, but only in different respects. For what is actually hot cannot simultaneously be potentially hot; but it is simultaneously potentially cold. It is therefore impossible that in the same respect and in the same way a thing should be both mover and moved, i.e. that it should move itself. Therefore, whatever is in motion must be put in motion by another. If that by which it is put in motion be itself put in motion, then this also must needs be put in motion by another, and that by another again. But this cannot go on to infinity, because then there would be no first mover, and, consequently, no other mover; seeing that subsequent movers move only inasmuch as they are put in motion by the first mover; as the staff moves only because it is put in motion by the hand. Therefore it is necessary to arrive at a first mover, put in motion by no other; and this everyone understands to be God.

The second way is from the nature of the efficient cause. In the world of sense we find there is an order of efficient causes. There is no case known (neither is it, indeed, possible) in which a thing is found to be the efficient cause of itself; for so it would be prior to itself, which is impossible. Now in efficient causes it is not possible to go on to infinity, because in all efficient causes following in order, the first is the cause of the intermediate cause, and the intermediate is the cause of the ultimate cause, whether the intermediate cause be several, or only one. Now to take away the cause is to take away the effect. Therefore, if there be no first cause among efficient causes, there will be no ultimate, nor any intermediate cause. But if in efficient causes it is possible to go on to infinity, there will be no first efficient cause, neither will there be an ultimate effect, nor any intermediate efficient causes; all of which is plainly false. Therefore it is necessary to admit a first efficient cause, to which everyone gives the name of God.

The third way is taken from possibility and necessity, and runs thus. We find in nature things that are possible to be and not to be, since they are found to be generated, and to corrupt, and consequently, they are possible to be and not to be. But it is impossible for these always to exist, for that which is possible not to be at some time is not. Therefore, if everything is possible not to be, then at one time there could have

Glossary

For all men have not faith	from the biblical book of 2 Thessalonians, chapter 3, verse 2
For many things are shown to thee above the understanding of man	from the biblical book of Ecclesiastes, chapter 3, verse 25
Gregory	Saint Gregory the Great, author of *Morals*
Hugh of St. Victor	a French theologian and author of *De sacramentis ecclesiasticis* (here abbreviated Sacram.)
I am Who am	from the biblical book of Exodus, chapter 3, verse 14
Metaph	*Metaphysics,* a work by Aristotle
Osee	a minor Old Testament prophet and author of the book of Osee, or Hosea
that science is one which treats only of one class of subjects	from Augustine's *On the Trinity*

Document Text

been nothing in existence. Now if this were true, even now there would be nothing in existence, because that which does not exist only begins to exist by something already existing. Therefore, if at one time nothing was in existence, it would have been impossible for anything to have begun to exist; and thus even now nothing would be in existence—which is absurd. Therefore, not all beings are merely possible, but there must exist something the existence of which is necessary. But every necessary thing either has its necessity caused by another, or not. Now it is impossible to go on to infinity in necessary things which have their necessity caused by another, as has been already proved in regard to efficient causes. Therefore we cannot but postulate the existence of some being having of itself its own necessity, and not receiving it from another, but rather causing in others their necessity. This all men speak of as God.

The fourth way is taken from the gradation to be found in things. Among beings there are some more and some less good, true, noble and the like. But "more" and "less" are predicated of different things, according as they resemble in their different ways something which is the maximum, as a thing is said to be hotter according as it more nearly resembles that which is hottest; so that there is something which is truest, something best, something noblest and, consequently, something which is uttermost being; for those things that are greatest in truth are greatest in being, as it is written in Metaph. ii. Now the maximum in any genus is the cause of all in that genus; as fire, which is the maximum heat, is the cause of all hot things. Therefore there must also be something which is to all beings the cause of their being, goodness, and every other perfection; and this we call God.

The fifth way is taken from the governance of the world. We see that things which lack intelligence, such as natural bodies, act for an end, and this is evident from their acting always, or nearly always, in the same way, so as to obtain the best result. Hence it is plain that not fortuitously, but designedly, do they achieve their end. Now whatever lacks intelligence cannot move towards an end, unless it be directed by some being endowed with knowledge and intelligence; as the arrow is shot to its mark by the archer. Therefore some intelligent being exists by whom all natural things are directed to their end; and this being we call God.

Reply to Objection 1: As Augustine says (Enchiridion xi): "Since God is the highest good, He would not allow any evil to exist in His works, unless His omnipotence and goodness were such as to bring good even out of evil." This is part of the infinite goodness of God, that He should allow evil to exist, and out of it produce good.

Glossary

The eye hath not seen, O God, besides Thee . . .	from the biblical book of Isaiah, chapter 64, verse 4
The spiritual man judgeth all things	from the biblical book of 1 Corinthians, chapter 2, verse 15
They that explain me shall have life everlasting	from the biblical book of Ecclesiastes, chapter 24, verse 31
This is your wisdom and understanding . . .	from the biblical book of Deuteronomy, chapter 4, verse 6
Wisdom gave him the knowledge [scientiam] of holy things	from the biblical book of Wisdom, chapter 10, verse 10
Wisdom is prudence to a man	from the biblical book of Proverbs, chapter 10, verse 23
Wisdom sent her maids to invite to the tower	from the biblical book of Proverbs, chapter 9, verse 3

Reply to Objection 2: Since nature works for a determinate end under the direction of a higher agent, whatever is done by nature must needs be traced back to God, as to its first cause. So also whatever is done voluntarily must also be traced back to some higher cause other than human reason or will, since these can change or fail; for all things that are changeable and capable of defect must be traced back to an immovable and self-necessary first principle, as was shown in the body of the Article.

After fleeing Chinese rule and trekking through the Himalayas, the first group of Tibetan refugees enters India (May 1959).
(AP/Wide World Photos)

gZi-brjid

ca. 1400

"This sphere of bon, the unborn universal basis, / is unimpeded knowing and the very form of knowledge."

Overview

The gZi-brjid, or "The Glorious," is a fundamental text of the Tibetan Bon religion, said to have been spiritually transmitted to Londen Nyingpo, who recorded the revelation, in the fourteenth century. This twelve-volume text contains a biography and the teachings of Tonpa Shenrab Miwoche, the founder of Bon. Bon originally referred to practices associated with ancient Tibetan folk traditions. Over the centuries, Bon gradually developed a religious institutional structure, and in many respects it has merged with Tibet's official religion, Buddhism. Bon is considered the oldest extant religious tradition in Tibet. Bon adherents refer to themselves as Bonpos.

The gZi-brjid presents Tonpa Shenrab's life and teachings in sixty-one "episodes." In episode 16, found in the fourth volume, Shenrab teaches the meditation practices that represent Bon's highest teaching: Dzogchen, or the Great Perfection. There are three versions of the gZi-brjid, referred to as the Southern Treasure, the Northern Treasure, and the Central Treasure. The version of the Dzogchen teaching as it is reproduced here, "The Supreme Way," appears as the ninth chapter of the Southern Treasure.

Context

Historians interested in Bon have many obstacles to surmount: While sifting through clues scattered across various texts, ferreting out fact from fiction, historians must also recognize that fabulous legends play an important role in shaping cultures and contain truths beyond the confines of modern historical record building. The ancient history of Bon reaches back to prehistoric times, and many of the earliest records are written in an archaic script. Furthermore, both natural disasters and active persecutions of Bon have resulted in the destruction of many of its earliest written records.

According to Bonpos, Tonpa Shenrab was one of three brothers who learned the teachings of Bon in a primordial heaven far removed from this world. In order to relieve the suffering of all sentient beings, the three were advised by the Deity of Compassion to guide humanity in three successive ages. The oldest brother arrived in a former age. The youngest brother will arrive during a later age. The middle brother, Tonpa Shenrab, was born into this world in the land of Olmo Lungring some eighteen thousand years ago. According to Bon histories, Tonpa Shenrab lived for over eight thousand years, between 16016 BCE and 7816 BCE. During his lifetime, he visited Tibet only once, while in pursuit of stolen horses. He found the Tibetans uncivilized and not yet ready to accept his teachings.

Olmo Lungring, where Shenrab was said to be born, is described in Bon texts as lying to the west of Tibet in a place called Tazig. Scholars have proposed various geographical possibilities as the location of Olmo Lungring and Tazig and debated their relationship to the Bon kingdom of Zhang Zhung. Sources are inconsistent as to whether these three are distinct places or alternative and somewhat interchangeable designations for the same place. For the location of Tazig, some scholars have proposed a region that currently lies within the borders of Uzbekistan in Central Asia, while others have suggested a more distant region such as ancient Persia. Mount Kailash in Tibet is sometimes equated with a legendary mountain called Yungdrung Gutsek, which is described as rising up in the middle of Olmo Lungring to join heaven and earth. While Yungdrung Gutsek is not explicitly mentioned in episode 16 of the gZi-brjid (the selection analyzed here), the references to Mount Kailash in the text have cosmic associations that evoke Yungdrung Gutsek and its symbolic representation of the "Nine Ways of Bon."

Yungdrung Gutsek is a mountain that serves as the central pivot around which the universe revolves. Yungdrung Gutsek means "nine stacked *yungdrungs*," referring to the Bon symbol for eternal indestructible truth, for permanence and indestructible wisdom. The *yungdrung* looks like a left-turning swastika (although this ancient symbol has nothing to do with Nazi ideology). This four-sided mountain features nine levels, with each in the form of a *yungdrung*. The nine *yungdrungs* represent the system of the Nine Ways of Bon described in the gZi-brjid. Tibetan Buddhists use the symbol of the *vajra* to represent a similar concept.

Although the actual geographic location—and, more broadly, the historical existence—of Olmo Lungring may

Time Line	
CA. 16016–7816 BCE	■ According to legend, Tonpa Shenrab Miwoche, the founder of Bon, lives in the land of Olmo Lungring.
CA. 640	■ The Tibetan king Songtsen Gampo marries two Buddhist princesses, Bhrikuti from Nepal and Wen Cheng from China. These marriages mark the introduction of Buddhism to Tibet.
645	■ Songtsen Gampo annexes the western Tibetan kingdom of Zhang Zhung, creating the first unified Tibetan empire.
CA. 684	■ Drigum Tsenpo, the eighth Tibetan king, launches the first of two major persecutions of Bon. Drigum Tsenpo will be the first Tibetan king to have an actual tomb; previous kings are thought to have returned to heaven.
CA. 740–800	■ King Trisong Detson rules during this period and invites the Indian Tantric master Padmasambhava and other Buddhist teachers to Tibet; he ultimately establishes Buddhism as the official state religion, initiating a suppression of Bon in Tibet.
836	■ Lang Darma becomes king of Tibet and is a patron of Bon.
842	■ Lang Darma becomes king of Tibet and is a patron of Bon.
1017	■ Shenchen Luga discovers a number of important concealed Bon texts.
1290–1364	■ The Tibetan monk and scholar Buton Rinchen Drup lived at this time and collected and categorized sacred Tibetan texts to be included in the Kanjur (Words of the Buddha) and Tenjur (Commentaries on the Words of the Buddha) of the Tibetan Buddhist canon.
1360	■ Londen Nyingpo, the author of the gZi-brjid, is born.

be impossible to identify conclusively, scholarly reflection on possibilities is still productive. The evidence that scholars use to propose various locations for Olmo Lungring is drawn from linguistic clues and patterns of thinking that suggest that over the course of history some ancient Bon ideas may have come from Central Asian sources and ideas originating from the ancient civilizations of the Indus Valley. According to adherents, Bon is the origin of these ideas and predates all religions in the world.

While Olmo Lungring may exist only in another dimension, scholars are more confident that the Bon kingdom of Zhang Zhung existed as an independent state until 645. At this time the Tibetan king Songtsen Gampo (ca. 617–650) annexed Zhang Zhung—where the father of one of his wives was the king—and thereby created the first unified Tibetan empire. Both Bon and Buddhism were freely practiced in Songtsen Gampo's empire, as represented among his many wives: Although Songtsen Gampo's funeral rites were performed according to Bon tradition, Buddhist histories emphasize the religious outcome of his marriages to the princesses Bhrikuti (the daughter of King Amsuvarma of Nepal) and Wen Cheng (the daughter of Emperor Taizong of the Tang Dynasty of China). These two princesses are said each to have brought to Tibet a sacred statue of the Buddha Shakyamuni, representative of the Buddhism of their native countries, thereby introducing that religion to Tibet. The history of Bon and Buddhism in Tibet therafter was one of strongly mutual influence.

After Buddhism became established in Tibet, rivalry arose between these two spiritual traditions, leading to further persecutions and suppressions. According to Bon accounts, the first persecution of Bon took place during the rule of the seventh-century Tibetan king Drigum Tsenpo, who suppressed the religion by destroying many of its texts. Contentions between Bon and Buddhist adherents became particularly pronounced in the late eighth century, when King Trisong Detson invited the Indian Tantric master Padmasambhava to teach in Tibet. Trisong Detson went on to erect the country's first Buddhist monastery, and he ultimately decreed Buddhism to be the official religion of the Tibetan Empire. The subsequent suppression of their religion led many Bon priests and teachers to flee Tibet.

A few decades later, in 836, the Tibetan prince Lang Darma killed his brother and ascended the throne of Tibet. Lang Darma was a patron of the Bonpos, and Buddhism fell out of favor during his brief rule. But in 842 Lang Darma himself was murdered, by a Buddhist monk, and that event led both to the fall of the first Tibetan dynasty and to the end of the first dissemination of Buddhism in Tibet.

After the collapse of the Tibetan Empire in the ninth century, little is known about either Bon or Buddhism until the year 1017, when two boxes containing bilingual scriptures, written in the languages of both Zhang Zhung and Tibet, were unearthed by Shenchen Luga, considered one of Tonpa Shenrab's descendants. This discovery ushered in a revival of Bon in Tibet, where over the course of the next several centuries many Bon monasteries were established.

When the Tibetan monk and historian Buton Rinchen Drup (1290–1364) first compiled the scriptures that became the Tibetan Buddhist canon in the fourteenth century—dividing them into the Kanjur (Words of the Buddha) and Tenjur (Commentaries on the Words of the Buddha)—he rejected many texts from the Nyingma Buddhist lineage because he detected the influence of Bon ideas and was unable to trace them to Sanskrit originals. The Nyingma tradition is the oldest of the four major schools of Tibetan Buddhism, reflecting the Tantric teachings of Padmasambhava, and among many similarities between Bon teachings and those of the Nyingma school, a notable parallel occurs in the meditative practice that both traditions call Dzogchen.

In the late fourteenth century, a Bon adherent named Londen Nyingpo recorded a text that he said had been spiritually transmitted to him regarding the origins of Bon: His work, the gZi-brjid, was received with enthusiasm in the context of the Bon revival. Its twelve volumes were included among the texts of the Bon canon that were compiled, codified, edited, and finally carved into woodblocks and printed in the mid-eighteenth century in eastern Tibet.

The Bon canon of doctrinal texts and associated literature is divided (like the Tibetan Buddhist canon) into two parts, the Kanjur and Katen. The Kanjur fills 178 volumes divided into four parts and contains the words of Tonpa Shenrab. The Katen consists of more than three hundred volumes of commentaries on the texts of the Kanjur. Because the gZi-brjid is understood as having been originally spoken by Tonpa Shenrab, it is collected in the Kanjur section of the Bon canon.

Bon teachings and practices are applicable to all aspects of life, including ethical and moral behavior and the development of love, compassion, joy, and equanimity. Whereas Buddhism tends to emphasize otherworldly concerns, Bon tends to focus more on the affairs of this world.

About the Author

According to adherents, Londen Nyingpo wrote down the gZi-brjid verbatim in the latter half of the fourteenth century, after hearing the scripture from a supernatural sage. From an historical point of view, Londen was a poet who wrote this and many other Bon texts. He was born in 1360 in the Khyungpo region of Kham, a Tibetan region that has been broken up into areas now incorporated into several provinces of western China. While Londen Nyingpo is understood as the historical author of the text, Bonpos (followers of the Bon tradition) understand his gZi-brjid as a revelation of a teaching originally taught by Tonpa Shenrab.

Explanation and Analysis of the Document

The gZi-brjid is a twelve-volume text that presents the life and teachings of Tonpa Shenrab in sixty-one "episodes." The excerpt presented below is episode 16, found in the

Time Line

CA. 1750
- The Bon canon, organized into the Kanjur and Katen, is compiled, codified, and edited.

1961–1963
- The exiled Bon monk Lopon Tenzin Namdak collaborates with Professor David Snellgrove on *The Nine Ways of Bon*: Excerpts from "gZi-brjid."

1967
- Lopon Tenzin Namdak founds the new Menri Monastery in Dolanji, India, with abbot Lungtok Tenpa'i Nyima as leader of this worldwide spiritual center for the Bon religion.

fourth volume. In this episode, Shenrab teaches the meditation practices of Dzogchen, or the Great Perfection, to Tshad-med gTsug-phud. (Transliteration of Tibetan script often does not reflect how the language sounds; the phonetic spelling of this name is *tse me tsuk pu*.) Tshad-med gTsug-phud asks three questions. Shenrab's response to the first question is short. Each of Shenrab's responses to the second and third questions has four subtopics.

♦ **The First Question**
Shenrab responds to Tshad-med gTsug-phud's request for a basic overview of the system of the Nine Ways of Bon: "We beg you to tell us by explaining in detail." Shenrab first states that *bon* is something beyond the reach of normal intellectual understanding. He then continues with a general description of distinguishing features of *bon* in an effort to describe it in terms that can be understood, at least in part, by thoughtful humans. He explains that *bon* can be understood in a general way from three perspectives—as basis, way, and result—and also in a more specialized way from four perspectives—as insight, contemplation, practice, and result.

♦ **The Second Question**
In the second question, Tshad-med gTsug-phud presses Shenrab for more details: "What are the characteristics of the Basis? How should 'release' come from the Basis? How should one advance along the Way? How should one gain the Result?" Shenrab responds with an overview of each of these three perspectives. With regard to the nature of the basis, Shenrab describes the fundamental nature of the unconditioned truth of *bon*, which is at the root of everything. In this section he describes primordial, undifferentiated existence before the coming-to-be of the phenomenal universe as we now know it. The ultimate goal according to *bon* is to attain release from the ignorance associated with the cycle of birth and death. This state of release is associated with the enlightened understanding of Buddhas. In the second part of this response, Shenrab contrasts the

Ruins of a Tibetan monastery, abandoned during the 1959 uprising
(AP/Wide World Photos)

afflictions associated with ignorance with the state of happiness and complete knowledge that Buddhas enjoy.

"The Buddhas of past, present and future come forth from this basis," says Shenrab. Whereas Buddhists revere Siddhartha Gautama, or Shakyamuni, as the first historical Buddha, Bonpos consider Shakyamuni as a later Buddha, and they believe Tonpa Shenrab was the first Buddha to emerge from the primordial basis. When scholars analyze Bon biographies of Tonpa Shenrab, the structure and themes are similar to the life of Shakyamuni Buddha. Indeed, many scholars have viewed the Bon literature as being drawn from Buddhist sources, with some scholars dismissing Bon texts as blatant plagiarism and Bon beliefs as less-sophisticated intellectually. Bon adherents, however, assert that their belief system is far older than Buddhism and that it is the Buddhists who copied ideas from Bon scriptures.

In the third part of his response, Shenrab explains that the capacity to attain primordial knowledge is a "natural condition" found in the mind. Advancing in the direction of this attainment involves a process of learning to relax and allowing primordial knowledge to emerge spontaneously in the mind in its natural state. In the fourth part of his response, Shenrab describes the result of meditation, the fruit that is the reward for complete mastery of the Nine Ways of Bon. Shenrab describes in a series of analogies the limitless powers attained by a person who masters the way.

♦ **The Third Question**

With his third question, Tshad-med gTsug-phud presses Shenrab for the characteristics of the four more specialized ways of thinking about the Nine Ways of Bon. Shenrab addresses each of them: insight, contemplation, practice, and result. Shenrab first describes the characteristics of insight, which he presents in ways that obliquely demonstrate (for the knowledgeable listener) the differences between Bonpo philosophy and Tibetan Buddhist philosophy. This section not only offers the modern reader a fuller sense of the Bon ideas described but also demonstrates some of the tensions that still persist between Tibetan Bon and Tibetan Buddhist adherents. Over the course of history, Tibetan Bon scholars and Tibetan Buddhist scholars have had heated debates over fundamental differences in their philosophical positions.

For instance, Tibetan Buddhist philosophy traces many of its ideas to the Indian philosopher Nagarjuna. Nagarjuna is associated with promulgating the important Mahayana (or "Great Vehicle") Buddhist principle of the two truths: ultimate truth and conventional truth. Nagarjuna's principle of the two truths pervades Tibetan Buddhist phil-

Essential Quotes

> "This precious thing, the Thought of Enlightenment, / the state of primeval buddhahood, / the essence of knowledge in its natural state, / the absolute purity of the unconditioned, / void of any basis whatsoever in physical and metaphysical notions, / unaffected in any way, this Great Unmoved / has no first existing origin, / has no intermediate way and progressive stages, / and has no final attainable stage."

> "First as for the nature of the Basis, / in the prime state, timeless and unoriginated, / there is no effective cause for the buddhas of past, present and future, / there is no admixture of causal conditions (for the producing) of beings / of the threefold world."

> "The Way causes magical emanations to arise from the Basis, / and these (emanations) appear as the delusion of ignorance. / As for their cause, they spring from ignorance, / and the five lights in their own self-nature act as causal conditions."

> "This Thought of Enlightenment which is void and selfless, / the state of knowledge in its natural condition / is really one's own mind in the form of buddhahood. / It is the sphere of bon, the unborn universal basis / with unimpeded power of action and self-manifesting reflective power."

> "This sphere of bon, the unborn universal basis, / is unimpeded knowing and the very form of knowledge, / the single thing which possesses no duality, / the 'substance' of the great Supreme Vehicle. / It is free from the extreme notions of viewed and viewer. / It is the sphere of bon where nothing is seen by looking. / It is the unviewed state of mind in its own clarity."

osophical discussions. According to this philosophy, when a person attains enlightenment, that person no longer requires the crutch of conventional truth because at that point he is able to understand ultimate truth. By contrast, Bon promotes a central principle of "unbounded wholeness." According to this principle, the capacity to attain enlightenment is within the mind right now. From the Bon perspective there is only primordial perfect wisdom. Access to this "unbounded wholeness" is attained by individuals who are able to cut through the obscurations preventing their minds from accessing it.

A Khyun (or *khyung* bird) is a symbol used in Bon scriptures to evoke the idea of unbounded wholeness. As Shenrab speaks of the characteristics of insight, he describes it in terms of the actions of Khyun: When the "Khyun appears in the sky, he cuts smoothly through the three atmospheric levels and subdues all creatures who have claws." That is, the unbounded wholeness of wisdom subdues ignorance like a Khyun cuts through all levels of attainment in a focused pursuit of all creatures who have claws (an image that could refer to evil or simply resistance to truth). Tibetan Buddhism uses the Garuda bird as a similar symbol but describes the process in terms of cutting through the ignorance that is associated with conventional truth in order to attain ultimate truth.

In the next two sections of his response, Shenrab discusses contemplation and practice. In Bon meditation, practitioners first learn how to enter into and remain in a state of mind referred to as the "natural state," described as spontaneous, effortless, and unaffected by extremes. After adherents have mastered preliminary practices, they are ready to move on to more advanced practices, in which "all . . . is playfulness." Shenrab then presents the attainment of the "Perfection of Wisdom" as the ultimate reward for complete mastery of the meditative practices.

Most scholars consider the scriptures comprising the Perfection of Wisdom to be originally Buddhist texts, but Bonpos maintain that the texts have always been theirs. As stated earlier, the twelve volumes of the Bon Kanjur are divided into four parts. The texts collected in the second section contain Perfection of Wisdom scriptures that duplicate the Buddhist Perfection of Wisdom teachings, associated with the first spreading of Mahayana Buddhist ideas. Adherents of Mahayana Buddhism believe that the Buddha spoke the Perfection of Wisdom and other Mahayana scriptures at an event referred to as the "Second Turning of the Wheel." In their view, at that time there was no one on earth capable of hearing the wisdom contained in these teachings or even accessing the higher plane where the Buddha spoke these teachings. For this reason the Buddha hid these teachings in the land of the Nagas for a later time when humanity would have matured sufficiently to grasp their meaning. Buddhist legends claim that the Indian philosopher Nagarjuna retrieved many of these scriptures from the land of the Nagas. Available historical evidence favors Buddhist claims. Nevertheless, Bon adherents have a long spiritual connection with Perfection of Wisdom scriptures that cannot be dismissed. The fact that both spiritual traditions claim these same teachings is evidence of some of the common ground that they both share.

Audience

The initial audience for the teachings described in the gZi-brjid was most likely monastic practitioners of Tibetan Bon in the time of Londen Nyingpo and after. These practitioners must have been willing to commit to several years of hermetic retreat to master the techniques sketched out in these verses. The larger audience for the text over time, however, has been adherents of Bon and others in the modern world—thanks to translations of the text that have enabled scholarship and made possible numerous books about Bon generally and Dzogchen practice in particular. Newfound modern interest in indigenous religions and, in the West, interest in non-Western religions have combined to create a modern audience for a text that offers modes of contemplation and meditation, leading to a purer, more tranquil life.

Impact

The gZi-brjid played an important role in the resurgence of Bon in Tibet, which had begun in the eleventh century but gained momentum in the fourteenth century. In the modern world, as more texts such as the gZi-brjid have become available in the West, scholars have had to reconsider initial impressions of Bon as merely an unsystematic composite of magical rituals and unoriginal and unsophisticated ideas. Bon practices predate the introduction of Buddhism in Tibet, and Bon maintains a long oral tradition. Both Buddhists and Bon traditions draw on teachings that they claim predate available written texts. Like Buddhism and many other religious traditions, Bon teachings were communicated orally for centuries. Clearly Tibetan Bon and Tibetan Buddhist ideas are indebted to each other. Increased knowledge has provided both scholars and adherents of Bon and Buddhism the opportunity to rethink their ideas about the evolution of these two great religions. Scholars no longer dismiss Bon as a mere repository of unorthodox ideas. Scholars also recognize that Tibetan Buddhism is infused with Bon rituals and, like Bon, has a long tradition of revealed scriptures; they also acknowledge that not all Buddhist scriptures can be traced to Sanskrit originals.

Buddhist and Bon leaders alike were forced to flee Tibet—many finding refuge in India and others in the West—during the 1959 Tibetan uprising against the country's Chinese Communist occupiers. Bon and Buddhist monasteries and texts were destroyed by the Chinese army during the revolt, making it considerably more difficult for subsequent researchers to find concrete historical evidence about either of the Tibetan religions. The forced emigration of many Bon leaders nonetheless had the positive effect of bringing Bon texts and teachers to the West. The Bonpo senior teacher Lopon Tenzin Namdak, for example, was one of the refugees who fled Tibet, and in the following years, between 1961 and 1963, he lived in London and collaborated with the eminent Tibetologist David Snellgrove on the selection and translation of texts included in *The Nine Ways of Bon: Excerpts from "gZi-brjid"* (1967). Lopon Tenzin Namdak then returned to India to purchase land for the founding of a central home for the Tibetan Bonpo refugee community; in 1967 in Dolanji he founded the Menri Monastery, named after what had been the leading Bon monastery in Tibet, established in the early fifteenth century. The monastery's abbot, Lungtok Tenpai Nyima (born in 1926), is considered the worldwide spiritual leader of the Bon religion.

Working with Bonpo scholars on the English translation texts collected in *The Nine Ways of Bon*, Snellgrove changed his understanding and estimation of the Bonpos. Earlier he had dismissed Bon beliefs as dominated by ignorance and superstition. The publication of the English translation of selections of this text together with Snellgrove's renewed interest and respect for the Bonpos has had considerable effect on the acceptance of Bon in the West.

Until recently the Buddhist tradition recognized only four major schools: Nyingma, Kagyu, Sakya, and Geluk. This situation changed when the fourteenth Dalai Lama, Tenzin Gyatso, publically recognized Bon as a fifth Buddhist tradition. The Dalai Lama has been particularly active in supporting the efforts of Bonpo refugees in India and the establishment of Bonpo monastic communities outside China and Tibet. The Western audience for Bon has grown with the arrival of learned Bon teachers together with increasing numbers of Bon scriptures now available in English and other Western languages. Today, Bonpo practitioners throughout the world rely on truths conveyed in the gZi-brjid.

Further Reading

■ Books

Namkhai, Norbu. *The Cycle of Day and Night: Where One Proceeds along the Path of the Primordial Yoga: An Essential Tibetan Text on the Practice of Dzogchen*, trans. and ed. John Myrdin Reynolds. 2nd ed. Barrytown, N.Y.: Station Hill Press, 1987.

Powers, John. "Bon: A Heterodox System." In *Introduction to Tibetan Buddhism*. Ithaca, N.Y.: Snow Lion Publications, 1995.

Snellgrove, David L. *The Nine Ways of Bon: Excerpts from "gZi-brjid."* 2nd ed. Bangkok: Orchid Press, 2009.

Tashi Gyaltsen, Shardza. *Heart Drops of Dharmakaya: Dzogchen Practice of the Bon Tradition*, trans. and ed. Lopon Tenzin Namdak. Ithaca, N.Y.: Snow Lion Publications, 2002.

Wangyal, Tenzin. *Wonders of the Natural Mind: The Essence of Dzogchen in the Native Bon Tradition of Tibet*, ed. Andrew Lukianowicz. Ithaca, N.Y.: Snow Lion Publications, 2000.

■ Web Sites

Bon Foundation Web site.
   http://www.bonfoundation.org

Ligmincha Institute Web site.
   http://www.ligmincha.org

—Cynthia Col

Questions for Further Study

1. Describe the relationship between the Tibetan Bon religion and Buddhism. Why do you think the Bon faith emerged in Tibet as both an offshoot of Buddhism and, in some senses, an opposing religion?

2. The entry notes that "Tonpa Shenrab lived for over eight thousand years, between 16016 BCE and 7816 BCE." Many of the figures in the Hebrew scriptures are reported to have lived to great ages; indeed, Methuselah is a biblical figure whose name has become synonymous with advanced age. Why do you think early scriptures extended long life spans to historical-mythical figures?

3. A good many early scriptural texts, including the gZi-brjid, were transmitted orally until they were written down at a later date. What challenges does this present for historians in dating documents, determining their authorship, and judging their authenticity?

4. The document states that in the "sphere of *bon* . . . nothing is seen by looking. / It is the unviewed state of mind in its own clarity." How does this view, which seems broadly characteristic of Eastern religions, differ from the view of experience commonly adopted in the West?

5. "gZi-brjid" is an odd-looking title. What does it mean? Why is it written in such a seemingly strange way? In a larger sense, what issues do translators face when translating a document such as this one?

gZi-brjid

CHAPTER IX. THE SUPREME WAY

Then Tshad-med gTsug-phud said:
O all-knowing teacher, the splendour and protector of living beings,
You have said that the 84,000 ways of *bon* are compressed into Nine Ways.
The highest of them all,
the great Way, the *bon* which consists of nine "trunks,"
you have committed to my keeping.
As for the religious truths (*bon*) of this Supreme Way,
what are their characteristics
and how does one distinguish differences both of a general and special kind?
We beg you to tell us by explaining in detail.

So he spoke and the Teacher replied:
Listen *Tshad-med gTsug-phud*, listen!
This precious thing, the Thought of Enlightenment,
the state of primeval buddhahood,
the essence of knowledge in its natural state,
the absolute purity of the unconditioned,
void of any basis whatsoever in physical and metaphysical notions,
unaffected in any way, this Great Unmoved
has no first existing origin,
has no intermediate way and progressive stages,
and has no final attainable stage,
for it lacks characteristics of going and coming.
But although it is thus inexpressible in words,
in order to avoid the extreme notions of eternity and nihilism,
and to give guidance to ignorant beings,
it has to be explained and expressed in words.
In general this summit of all (nine) Ways is explained in three parts,
as Basis, as Way and as Result.
In a special way it is explained in four parts,
as Insight, as Contemplation, as Practice
and as the Result of supreme achievement.
Divided into its separate distinctions,
it spreads out into 84,000 parts,
but in its compressed form it becomes a single dot.

So he spoke, and again they asked:
O all-knowing Teacher,
You have said that in general there are three parts in the Supreme Vehicle,
the Basis, the Way, and the Result.
What are the characteristics of the Basis?
How should "release" come from the Basis?
How should one advance along the Way?
How should one gain the Result?

The Teacher replied:
Listen, Shen *Tshad-med gTsug-phud*!
First as for the nature of the Basis,
in the prime state, timeless and unoriginated,
there is no effective cause for the buddhas of past, present and future,
there is no admixture of causal conditions (for the producing) of beings
of the threefold world.
Before physical and metaphysical states originated,
at the beginning the "King of Knowledge" is first.
This is the natural state, the state of knowledge, the universal basis,
void and unpredicated.
It is neither existence nor non-existence.
No name, physical or metaphysical, applies to it.
It is unconditioned by either good or evil.
It is not emptiness and it is not manifestation.
It is not eternity and it is not nihilism.
It is neither blessedness nor misery.
It is neither buddha nor living being.
It lacks colour, form and shape.
It is the boundless infinite sphere of *bon*.
It cannot be regarded as interrupted, limited or ending.
No term, physical or metaphysical can be applied to it.
It is spoiled by no notion of fault or of virtue.
It possesses no cause for good or evil.
It has no colour, is neither black nor white, nor large nor small.
It cannot be investigated with regard to its extent or its narrowness, its
limits or its centre.
Its area cannot be measured in miles.
It remains without beginning or end, without change or decline.
It does not increase or decrease.
It cannot be exhausted and it does not lessen.
It cannot be lost or separated.

It does not come into existence and it is not destroyed.
It is not produced from a cause or destroyed by circumstances.
It is not spoiled by circumstances and no cause is present.
For example—like the sphere of the sky
it is clear, blank and solitary,
remaining in a state of nothingness.
To begin with then, this is the nature of the Basis.

Secondly as for the way "release" comes from this Basis,
this universal basis is the unborn sphere of *bon*
void in its prime state and unpredicated,
for in this emptiness where nothing exists
there is no erring into the extreme views of eternity and nihilism,
and in this infinite unmoving expanse
waves appear somehow and by their movement
knowledge arises from this essence of emptiness.
For example it is like the orb of the sun.
In this pure "spontaneity" of the knowledge of emptiness
there resounds the "self-sound" of the unimpeded void
and thence there arise the five lights in their own self-nature,
and their rays reach everywhere in their self-nature.
It appears as "being," but it is really not so,
It appears as "non-being," but does not fall into extreme views.
It is the unchanging "Primeval King,"
the unmoving form of the "Great Ancestor."
The buddhas of past, present and future come forth from this basis.
It is the spontaneous "All Good,"
of whom names and terms are mere indications.
In reality what is indicated is altogether transcendent.
It is the great primeval purity,
unaffected by anything, tranquil and self-existing.
From the beginning of time it is free from delusion and defilement.
It is the causeless "First Buddha,"
not produced from a cause and not destroyed by circumstances.
It is the Buddha without beginning or end.
Its sound is emptiness, the absolute body.
Its light is the great purity.
Its rays are manifold, the body of phenomenal manifestation.
The lights of the five colours are the Five Wisdoms.
They do not have counterparts in reflection elsewhere,
for they are (already) perfected in the self-characterized *mandala* sphere.

This is the unchanging essence, the sphere of *bon*,
the state and self-nature which are free from association and separation.
It is the body of primeval buddhahood,
but by the term "Buddha" it is no more than indicated.
In reality it is that unaffected state of absolute tranquillity,
The Single Dot. What wonder!
By knowing it, (one uses it as) a basis for being released in buddhahood.
The pure, the unchanging, the very essence!
The way of the perfect self-characterized *mandala*!
The sphere of self-existing self-nature!
Five gods, five bodies, five realms,
five families, five powers, five eyes,
perfect in everything, and known by the name of "Buddha."
The abiding Basis and the Way of "release"
are Basis or Way according to each particular view
and to them is attached the appellation of "buddhahood."

As for the manner of ignorant beings' delusion,
it was said above that in this great unmoving expanse
waves appear somehow and by their movement
knowledge arises from the essence of emptiness.
In the spontaneity of unimpeded knowledge
Sound, Light and Rays, all three, shine by reflective power.
The Way causes magical emanations to arise from the Basis,
and these (emanations) appear as the delusion of ignorance.
As for their cause, they spring from ignorance,
and the five lights in their own self-nature act as causal conditions.
Not knowing the self-characterized *mandala* (as sole origin),
the knower is deluded with regard to causal conditions
(thinking the appearances) arise elsewhere,
As a result of the knower's disquisitive knowing, it all appears
as the phenomenal world.
The delusion of conceiving non-being as being comes from the act of conceiving.
The delusion that there is nothing but the self comes from disquisitive thinking.
The delusion of mental suffering comes from the feelings.
The delusion of self-distrust with regard to Sound arises from fear.
The delusion of attachment to Light arises from perplexity.

Document Text

The delusion of thought-emanations with regard to the Rays arises from beguilement.
As a result of pursuing these delusions, it all appears as the (Six) Spheres
(of possible rebirth).
With regard to the light of white rays
there is first attachment and delusion of appearances.
Then the mind is perplexed and *Wrath* emerges,
and it all appears as the sphere of the hot and cold hells.
So a shadow is cast over the intention of great loving-kindness.
With regard to the light of red rays
There is first attachment and delusion of appearances.
Then the mind is perplexed and *Desire* arises,
and it all appears as the sphere of hungry and thirsty tormented spirits.
So a shadow is cast over the intention of great generosity.
With regard to the light of blue rays
there is first attachment and delusion of appearances.
Then the mind is perplexed and *Mental Torpor* arises,
and it all appears as the sphere of stupid beasts.
So a shadow is cast over the intention of great knowledge.
With regard to the light of yellow rays
there is first attachment and delusion of appearances.
Then the mind is perplexed and *Envy* arises,
and it all appears as the sphere of wretched men.
So a shadow is cast over the intention of magnanimity.
With regard to the light of green rays
there is first attachment and delusion of appearances.
Then the mind is perplexed and *Pride* arises,
and it all appears as the sphere of contentious titans.
So a shadow is cast over the intention of tranquillity.
With regard to the light with rays coloured in equal parts
there is first attachment and delusion of appearances.
Then the mind is perplexed and *Disquisitive Thought* arises,
and it all appears as the sphere of the falling gods.
So a shadow is cast over the intention of unity and sameness.
Form is produced with the formless as cause.
One is bound with the bonds of the Five *Maras*, the Five Evils, the Five
Molestations(*klesa*klesa*),
and sinks in the ocean of suffering and desire.
The river of birth, old age, sickness and death flows on
and (rebirth in) the Six Spheres goes on continuously like a circular
chain of water buckets.
In the power of others without gaining power over oneself
one wanders through wretched states of existence.
Such is the way ignorant beings are deluded.
As for the characteristics of Release and Delusion,
ignorance is produced with the Basis as its cause,
and although delusion is not recognized on the Way,
it exists in the first place as the Sound of the Basis.
The molestations and the Five Evils must be cleansed.
Advance must be made on the Way of Salvation.
The Result, namely buddhahood, must be achieved.
Knowing that perceives must become clear.
Such is the difference between Release and Delusion.

Thirdly, as for how one should advance along the path,
this Thought of Enlightenment which is void and selfless,
the state of knowledge in its natural condition
is really one's own mind in the form of buddhahood.
It is the sphere of *bon*, the unborn universal basis
with unimpeded power of action and self-manifesting reflective power.
Whatever the appearance it manifests, it is correspondingly void,
for both appearance and voidness are absolutely pure.
It is the absolute *bon* with reflective power self-produced from itself,
the absolute *bon* sphere of all
characterizable *bon* elements.
In this basic state which is perfect from all time
there is no advance and no coming and going.
It is the state of mind itself, unaffected and effortless,
the unmoving, all-pervading expanse of absolute *bon*.
There is nothing to be learned in its regard,
for what might be learned and the learner are both the self-knowing mind.
The teaching by signs and by methods
is merely an application referring to the absolute.
It is just a matter of knowing how it really is.
It is just an understanding of knowledge itself.
It is just a combination of understanding and release.
The knowledge of pure knowing shines translucent on the face of the
emptiness of the universal basis.
The intellect with its various characteristics which emerge and return
remains translucent with (such seeming) separateness in a state of absolute unity.
It remains at one in the pure ultimate.
The manner of application referring to this state
is really comprised within the sphere of the universal basis.
It is the inseparable combination of manifestation and voidness.

Document Text

It is the sphere of the play of bliss and voidness mutually inseparable,
It is the Thought of Enlightenment where knowing and voidness are inseparable.
Such is this state of unity! How wonderful!
The knower is produced in the universal basis
just as earth, air, fire and water are produced in sky.
Appearing and returning, the realms of existence come into being on a very vast scale.
They are translucent with (seeming) separateness in a state of absolute unity.
It remains at one in the pure ultimate.
The manner of application referring to this state
is really comprised in the sphere of the "universal womb" (*bhaga*),
It is the inseparable combination of manifestation and voidness.
It is the sphere of the play of bliss and voidness mutually inseparable.
It is the Thought of Enlightenment where knowing and voidness are inseparable.
Such is this state of unity! How wonderful!

Just relax spontaneously in mind itself in its abiding condition.
"Staying" and "darting," "emerging" and "sinking" are a single state.
Talk of manifestation and voidness is stopped.
The (supreme) form and knowledge are the reflective power of the "Two-in-One."
In that which is absolutely perfect from all time
the extreme ideas of advancement and of the one who advances just do not exist,
In the self-produced play of physical and metaphysical notions (acted)
by mind itself abiding in its own condition,
the term "manner of advancement" is a mere appellation.
This is the third subject, the manner of advancement.

Fourthly as for gaining the Result,
the sphere of *bon*, the unborn universal basis,
the non-dual single form,
of unimpeded power of action and self-manifesting reflective power,
the "single-flavoured" sphere, neither physical nor metaphysical,
is eternally unborn and deathless.
The phenomenal world, physical and metaphysical notions,
pertain from all time to the "beyond."
The essential nature of this spontaneously produced self-nature
is (absolute) form and knowledge as "Two-in-One."
Without striving for any qualities, it is spontaneously perfect,
so there can be no gaining or not gaining of any achievement.
But in knowing this natural state
there is a way of relaxing upon things as they are,
and having got them stable,
self-knowledge becomes manifest,
so that in the self-characterized mandala
manifestation and voidness are in unity,
and in the unified play of bliss and emptiness
knowledge and emptiness are spontaneously produced,
with superb qualities surpassing all thought.
Like the sky, like Mount *Kailasa*, like the ocean,
it cannot be measured, it cannot be appraised.
Although unmoved from its single form
a hundred million manifestations spread forth,
showing itself anyhow, wherever anyone is converted,
and in keeping with the characteristics of the four elements
acting absolutely in absolute space.
It is the deathless Swastika body, free of *Mara*,
As it is lifeless, disease, poisons and weapons cannot destroy it.
(He who has realized this is like) a bird in the sky and a fish in the ocean.
He splits rocks as by lightning and gathers in (magically) aromatic shrubs.
He raises Mount *Kailasa* in his hand and sucks up the ocean.
He pulls back the waters as with a noose and transfixes the planets.
He treads the whole universe under the sole of one foot.
He possesses the supreme unchanging form.
Although only one sound resounds, all living beings hear the sounds of
their own languages in their different styles of speech.
He knows effortlessly and in their self-nature the 84,000 elements of *bon*,
and he translates them into the 360 styles of speech.
Firm in word and sanctifying power towards all living beings,
he causes joy to arise at the word of truth.
He removes suffering by means of the melody of *Brahma*
and he subdues all things to the word of the Buddhas.
They listen, whoever they are, to their directed work.
He possesses the supreme unhindered Speech with the 60 divisions of
Brahma sound.

Document Text

Although unmoved from a single state of thought, whatever thought
might convert them is produced for the living beings of the Six
Spheres of existence.
With the purposeful knowledge of one who knows
he explains in detail the different characterized notions for converting
whatever kind of being it may be.
He knows the order of the places of rebirth for past, present and future,
He sends forth and regathers the rays of light of the 60 divisions of
contemplative thought in a process of contraction and expansion.
He possesses the Mind of Sameness free of all illusion.
Although unmoved from a single state of good quality,
in the sight of various living beings
leaves and fruits and flowers seem to be produced on the spread tree of paradise.
There are wonderful things for each case,
medicine for illness and potion for poison,
a wish-granting gem for those in want
and an escort for those who are frightened, (all) understood (as suits the case).
To the foolish crowds he is whatever protector they need.
He is adorned with the major and minor marks (of a buddha),
with all the eighty minor marks quite perfect.
He is a centre of worship for all and the object of their homage.
Like the crest gem of the king of birds,
he is the splendour of living beings, their splendid protector.
He possesses all those qualities which come out well.
Although he performs just a single act,
he converts living beings whoever they are and wherever they are,
leaning easily towards them wherever they are, like a post in the mud.
The Four Actions of pacifying, prospering, empowerment, destroying,
and the "Flow" (as fifth),
long life, wealth, good fortune, prosperity and so on,
quelling hindrances and demons, victory in battle, acting like a world-conqueror,
the fields for acts of conversion surpass all thought.
In the central country of our suffering world, in this universe of 1,000 times 3,000 worlds
he is born as a king with wife and son and entourage,
and performing the twelve great acts,
he is the glory of those who guide living beings.

So he possesses action which is effortlessly self-produced.
Such is the last item on how to gain the Result.

Thus in the case of the *bon* of the Supreme Vehicle,
first there is the nature of the Basis,
secondly how "release" comes from this Basis,
thirdly how one should advance along the Way,
and lastly how one should gain the Result.
Tshad-med gTsug-phud, Shen who manifest yourself in various ways,
act as the splendour of living beings!

So the Teacher spoke, and *Tshad-med gTsug-phud* said again:
O Light of Teachers, Splendour of living beings, whose mind knows all things!
Concerning this top vehicle, the Supreme One,
the nature of the Basis, the Way and the Result has been dealt with above,
but what are the characteristics of the (other) four,
Insight, Contemplation, Practice and Result?
Bring forth the essence (of their meaning) from the centre of your thought,
and tell us, we beg.

So he asked, and the Teacher replied:
Listen, O you who are gathered here,
Tshad-med gTsug-phud, listen with respect!
Concerning Insight, Contemplation, Practice and the Result of
supreme achievement
in this top vehicle, the Supreme One,
first I shall explain Insight.
This sphere of *bon*, the unborn universal basis,
is unimpeded knowing and the very form of knowledge,
the single thing which possesses no duality,
the "substance" of the great Supreme Vehicle.
It is free from the extreme notions of viewed and viewer.
It is the sphere of *bon* where nothing is seen by looking.
It is the unviewed state of mind in its own clarity.
It is the single thing which possesses no duality,
the "substance" of the great Supreme Vehicle.
There is no realization of it by grasping at what comes into existence.
It is the sphere of the primeval empty absolute
There is no denying it by grasping at what comes to an end.
It is the primeval self-produced "sky" of knowledge.
It is the state of mind where nothing is born and nothing impeded

Document Text

It is the sphere of the non-dual single one.
It is the "substance" of the great Supreme Vehicle.
There is no realization of it by grasping at existence.
It is the primeval unenvisaged form of *bon*.
There is no denying of it by grasping at non-existence.
It is the primeval realm of perfect enjoyment.
It is the state of mind where nothing exists and nothing does not exist.
It is the sphere of the non-dual single one.
It is the "substance" of the great Supreme Vehicle.
There is no realization of it by grasping at eternity.
It is the primeval non-abiding "passage from sorrow" (*nirvatia*).
There is no denial of it by grasping at nihilism.
Primevally a whole variety springs forth from it somehow.
It is the state of mind where there is neither eternity nor nihilism.
It is the sphere of the non-dual single one.
It is the "substance" of the great Supreme Vehicle.
There is no real substance by grasping at appearances.
It is the sphere of the primeval empty absolute.
There is no non-entity by grasping at emptiness.
It is the state of primeval unimpeded "play."
It is the state of mind where neither appearance nor emptiness exists.
It is the sphere of the non-dual single one.
It is the "substance" of the great Supreme Vehicle.
It is free of the extreme notions of existence and non-existence, of
eternity and nihilism, of appearances and emptiness, of being born
and being stopped, free of these four extreme pairs.
In this great insight free of all extremes phenomenal existence has passed beyond sorrow.
There is no origination, continuing, dissolution, and emptiness of ages and existences,
no happiness and unhappiness, no sense of the arising of good and evil,
no seizing upon hopes and fears.
For example in the wide expanse of the sky
the four elements, fire, water, earth and air
originate, continue, dissolve and become void,
but within the sky itself there is no sense of their emergence.
In the same way in the wide expanse of true mind
(there arise) the characterizable magical forms which emerge from mind,
but within the mind itself there is no sense of their emergence.
In phenomenal existence which is the tremulation of mind

there is no cause for avoiding or accepting anything.
In physical and metaphysical states which are the "play" of true *bon*
there is no measuring of good and bad, virtue and evil.
As regards gods and demons, which are the magical forms of mind,
the extremes of benefit and of harm do not exist.
For example when the Khyun appears in the sky,
he cuts smoothly through the three atmospheric levels
and subdues all creatures who have claws.
In the same way when the sun appears in the sky,
it subdues all other lights
and brightens places of dark ignorance.
Likewise if one seals the "substance" of this Great Vehicle with the seal
of non-discriminating insight,
one quells all the hosts of discriminations
and all the lower vehicles are cowed.
It is everything, and yet there is nothing.
It is free of the four extreme views, and yet it has no central position.
It is the all-pervading *bon* itself with no outward movement and no limits,
the state of primeval buddhahood, primeval unaffected pervasiveness.
Such is the insight of the "substance" of the Great Vehicle.

Secondly as for the explanation of Contemplation,
the "substance" of the great Supreme Vehicle
is the precious Thought of Enlightenment itself,
pure, spontaneously produced, uncompounded.
Primevally unaffected and effortless,
it is free from such extremes as an object of contemplation and a contemplating agent.
If there were an object of contemplation, it would be possible to affect the absolute.
If there were a contemplating agent, mind itself would be defiled.
Unmoved, uncontrived and unadulterated,
it is the "ever-fresh," the natural, the middle way.
It is the great bliss, the state of *bon* itself.
Unaffected in its state by any (other) state,
it abides as such a state in just such a state.
It is the king of contemplation itself.
But in order to explain it by words,
the precious Thought of Enlightenment
is taught as a set of three, example, substance and sign.
For example, (it is said to be) like the sky.
As substance, it pervades everywhere,
As sign, it abides free of all partiality.
It is contemplation free of the defect of extremes.

Document Text

Thirdly I shall explain the Practice.
The "substance" of the great Supreme Vehicle
is the precious Thought of Enlightenment,
that Sameness which does not distinguish physical and metaphysical states.
It is free of the extremes of avoidance and acceptance.
It is self-produced form in the state of the absolute,
the single dot, of which "practice" is playfulness.
What is practised and the practiser are both self-thought.
Although practised, it is the reflective power of self-produced mind.
Unpractised, it abides as the Single One,
There is no cause for anything practised.
The term "practice" is a word (referring to) characteristics.
In terms of such verbal reference, thought is like the sky,
where appearances are produced like fire, water, earth and air.
In the self-nature of the sky all practice is playfulness.
It is practice without avoidance or acceptance.

Fourthly I shall explain the Result.
The precious Thought of Enlightenment
is the "substance" of the great Supreme Vehicle,
the non-discriminating sphere of selfless insight,
the absolute state of non-directed contemplation,
self-produced reflective power acting in non-action,
the supreme achievement free of hopes and fears,
the primeval "state beyond wisdom" (viz. *Perfection of Wisdom*),
the absolute sphere where nothing is born and nothing stops.
Its characterizing quality is the action of Discriminating Wisdom.
In this primeval buddhahood there is absence of the extreme notions of
achievement and achiever.
If there were anything to be achieved, the absolute would be contrived.
If there were anyone to do the achieving, mind itself would be adulterated.
If there were much contriving and adulterating, causes and conditions would arise.
This precious Thought of Enlightenment,
the "substance" of the great Supreme Vehicle,
has not sprung from a cause and is not destroyed by conditions.
It is Knowledge without cause and conditions,
the Swastika body which is both lifeless and deathless (free of *Mara*),
and it holds the unchanging Result.
This precious Thought of Enlightenment,
the "substance" of the great Supreme Vehicle,
has nothing to be avoided under the name of physical states,
has nothing to be accepted under the name of metaphysical states.
It is that Sameness where the physical and the metaphysical are indistinguishable.
and it holds the Result which is free of hopes and fears.
The precious Thought of Enlightenment,

Glossary

bon	distinct from uppercase "Bon," the underlying philosophy of the Bon faith
Brahma	the god of creation
buddhas	those who have achieved enlightenment
Khyun	the khyung bird, a symbol used in Bon scriptures to evoke the idea of unbounded wholeness
Mandala	a usually circular geometric design symbolizing the universe and used as an aid to meditation
Mara	a personification of death in spiritual life
Mount *Kailasa*	a peak in the Himalayas in Tibet
Swastika	a reference to the *yungdrung*, the Bon symbol for eternal indestructible truth and wisdom and not to be confused with the infamous Nazi symbol
Tshad-med gTsug-phud	the name of the student who is listening to Shenrab

the "substance" of the great Supreme Vehicle,
has nothing to be avoided under the name of the Five Evils,
has nothing to be accepted under the name of the Five Wisdoms.
It is that Sameness where faults and virtues are indistinguishable,
and it holds the Result of the "single-flavoured much."
This precious Thought of Enlightenment,
the "substance" of the great Supreme Vehicle,
has no authenticity which can be conceived of as a self,
has no discriminating power which can conceive of others.
It is that Sameness where self and others are indistinguishable,
and it holds the Result in the Sameness of non-duality.
This precious Thought of Enlightenment,
the "substance" of the great Supreme Vehicle,
has no effective form which can be conceived of as a unity,
has no distinctions which can be conceived of as many.
It is that Sameness which is unaffected and effortless,
and it holds the Result which is a single dot.
This precious Thought of Enlightenment,
the "substance" of the great Supreme Vehicle,
is buddhahood without beginning and end,
the state of primeval buddhahood,
the changeless selfhood, the sphere of *bon*,
the changeless essence, the sky of knowing,
the changeless state, the sphere of thought,
state and nature with no joining and no separation,
indistinguishable as physical or metaphysical,
imperceptible as happiness or misery,
no acceptance and no rejection of virtues and faults,
inconceivable as self or other,
unhindered as Method and Wisdom,
changeless essence, body of knowledge,
whose manifestation is the land of gems and gold,
wondrous gem that grants all wishes,
tree of paradise (laden) with good things,
in action like a universal monarch,
whose twofold effect is a treasury of elixir.
It contains the unimpeded achievement.
It is the absolute truth of the Supreme Vehicle.
Tshad-med gTsug-phud, all-manifesting Shen,
bring to perfection for all beings
the "substance" of the great Supreme Vehicle,
the "substance" of Insight, Contemplation, Practice and Result.
Thus he spoke.

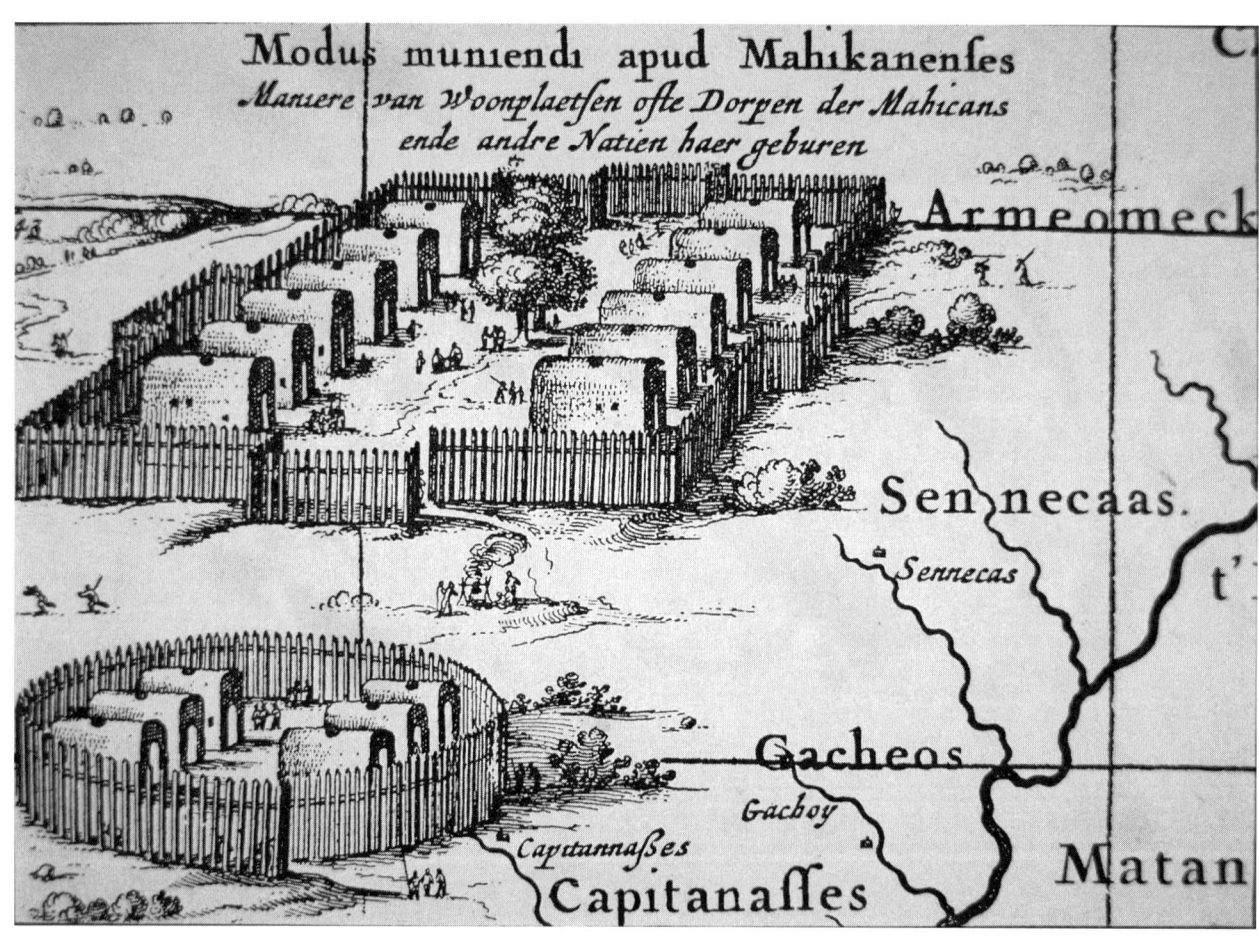

An Iroquois village
(Iroquois Village, 1651 [engraving], Visscher, Nicolaes [Claes] Jansz [1586-1652] / Private Collection / Peter Newark American Pictures / The Bridgeman Art Library International)

Mohawk Thanksgiving Address

ca. 1451

"We have been given the duty to live in balance and harmony with each other and all living things."

Overview

The Thanksgiving Address is an ancient Haudenosaunee (Iroquois) expression of gratitude that acknowledges connection to all beings. The address is known to have existed at the latest since the formation of the Haudenosaunee Confederacy—perhaps around 1451—when its ritual use was established by the Peacemaker, but it was likely passed down through oral tradition for untold centuries before. The word *Haudenosaunee* means "the People of the Longhouse" (or, technically, "They Are Building a Longhouse"), and it is the name of a confederated group of six (originally five) Native American nations, including the Mohawk. *Longhouse* refers to the characteristic structures in which they lived—immense rectangular structures made of logs that housed numerous families. The longhouse was more than just a shelter; it became a metaphor for the cultural and social values of the Haudenosaunee. The Haudenosaunee recite this address at the beginning and at the end of any important gathering of their people, whether the event is religious, political, or social. It can be recited in any one of the Haudenosaunee languages or even in English, when English is the primary shared language of those gathered together. Among Mohawk of the northeastern United States and southeastern Canada, the Thanksgiving Address, some form of which has been in use for at least a thousand years, is called "Ohén:ton Karihwatéhkwen," which means "Words before All Else" or "Words That Come before All Else." This refers to the practice of reciting the Thanksgiving Address at the beginning of a gathering, before events commence, and at the end of a gathering, before the people depart.

Context

The roots of the Thanksgiving Address could be said to extend back to about 10,000 BCE, when indigenous peoples migrated to the Northeastern Woodlands, a region that comprises modern-day New England, parts of the Upper Midwest, and parts of southeastern Canada. It is known that by about 4500 BCE these people were subsisting on deer, caribou, and sea mammals. A thousand years later their diet included fish, small land mammals, and fowl, and they were using tools such as canoes, fishnets and hooks, stone bowls, and woodworking tools. By 1000 BCE they were making pottery, living in rectangular houses made of bark and saplings, and using slash-and-burn agricultural techniques to cultivate corn, beans, squash, sunflowers, and tobacco. Semipermanent settlements were forming, and longhouse villages were coming into use. Additionally, warfare among tribes emerged as the tribes competed for usable land and as the Iroquoian-speaking nations expanded into present-day Upstate New York.

There are six Haudenosaunee nations, each of which has its own distinct language. The original Five Nations of the Haudenosaunee Confederacy were the Seneca, the Cayuga, the Onondaga, the Oneida, and the Mohawk. Haudenosaunee traditional lands originally stretched across present-day upstate New York, extending from the Genesee River (the western border of Seneca lands); continuing east through the Finger Lakes (Cayuga lands), Onondaga Lake (Onondaga lands), and Oneida Lake (Oneida lands); and ending at the Hudson River (the eastern border of Mohawk lands). The Tuscarora are the sixth nation. Their original territory was near that of the Five Nations, but well before European colonization they had migrated southward to land in present-day North Carolina. After a difficult period of warfare with newly arrived English colonists from 1711 to 1713, they moved northward and were welcomed into the traditional lands of the Oneida people as long-lost relatives. In 1722, the Tuscarora were formally admitted to the Haudenosaunee Confederacy. Sometimes this alliance of nations is referred to as the "Iroquois Confederacy," or the "League of Peace and Power."

It is not known exactly when the Thanksgiving Address was first composed, but it is clear that the address is part of an ancient oral tradition. It is at least as old as the Haudenosaunee Confederacy itself. In Haudenosaunee oral tradition, the Confederacy of the Five Nations was established by a revered man known as "the Peacemaker" and his friend Ayonhwathah (Hiawatha). The date of the confederation of the formerly separate nations is not known precisely, but scholarly consensus dates it sometime between 1450 and 1600. Some scholars have ventured to identify more spe-

Time Line	
CA. 10,000 BCE	■ Indigenous peoples migrate into the geographical area now known as the Northeastern Woodlands, the region comprising modern-day New England, parts of the Upper Midwest, and parts of southeastern Canada.
CA. 4500 BCE	■ Peoples in the Northeastern Woodlands consume deer, caribou, and sea mammals.
CA. 3500 BCE	■ Peoples in the Northeastern Woodlands consume fish, small land mammals, and fowl and employ the technologies of canoes, stone bowls, woodworking tools, fishnets, and fishhooks.
CA. 1000 BCE	■ Peoples in the Northeastern Woodlands make pottery, live in rectangular houses made of saplings and bark, and employ slash-and-burn agriculture to cultivate corn, beans, squash, sunflowers, and tobacco; village culture comes into being. Warfare between groups rises in frequency because of competition for arable land.
1142 CE	■ According to some accounts, the Haudenosaunee Confederacy is created by the Peacemaker, Ayonhwathah, and Jigonsaseh, as the Five Nations form an alliance under the Great Law of Peace and Power; the Peacemaker establishes the ritual recitation of the Thanksgiving Address within the Five Nations.
1451	■ Astronomical phenomena contained in Seneca traditions occur; these phenomena suggest this as a later date for the formation of the Five Nations and the ritual use of the Thanksgiving Address.
1536	■ Similar astronomical phenomena suggest to some historians that the Five Nations may have been formed at this date.
1600–1700	■ The Haudenosaunee Confederacy expands significantly.

cific dates on the basis of a particular detail of Seneca oral tradition. According to the Seneca, their nation—the last to join the original Haudenosaunee Confederacy—formally affiliated in a year during which a "black sun" (eclipse) took place at the time of the second hoeing season. The only years between 1450 and 1600 in which such an astronomical event was visible in Seneca territory during that agricultural season are 1451 and 1536. However, some recent scholarship proposes that the Haudenosaunee Confederacy may have been created as early as 1142. These scholars are using both astronomical data and Haudenosaunee oral histories to arrive at this date, but their conclusions are disputed by some prominent archaeologists.

According to the tradition of the Haudenosaunee, the Peacemaker created the Gayanashagowa, the Great Law of Peace that transformed the Five Nations from a state of enmity to one of unbreakable alliance. The Great Law was in effect a constitution; in fact, Benjamin Franklin consulted with the Haudenosaunee, and the U.S. Constitution reflects many of the ideals of the Great Law. While it is impossible to determine whether the Peacemaker was involved in the composition or further elaboration of the Thanksgiving Address or whether he was just reminding the people of its importance, it is known that the Peacemaker was instrumental in mandating its ritual use throughout the Five Nations on political occasions. In the Great Law, the Peacemaker required the recitation of the Thanksgiving Address in order to open council meetings of the appointed chiefs of the Five Nations.

The legend of the Peacemaker and his activities fleshes out the context for the Thanksgiving Address. In his mission to establish peace among the Five Nations, his first follower was the woman Yegowaneh (or Jigonsaseh), the "Mother of Nations." The Seneca claim her as their own, but the Mohawk say she was a member of the Neutral (Chonnonton or Attawandaron) nation. In any event, the Peacemaker renamed her Jigonsaseh ("She Whose Face Is Doubly New") in honor of her wisdom and sent her as an emissary to the Oneida and Mohawk nations, spreading his message of peace. The next person the Peacemaker encountered was Ayonhwathah (Hiawatha). In many versions of the story, Ayonhwathah was a man torn apart by inconsolable grief because his wife and (three or seven) daughters had died (or were killed). He cried incessantly as he wandered on his own, unable to bear living among others. As he mourned, Ayonhwathah eventually came upon a lakeside. There he found shells, which he strung together with rushes and carried as a symbol of his grief. He named these strung shells "wampum," and he vowed to give them to anyone he could find whose despair could match his own, as a symbol of empathy and consolation.

The Peacemaker heard of Ayonhwathah's great suffering, created his own fourteen strings of wampum, and approached Ayonhwathah with them in hand. Each of the wampum strings the Peacemaker gave to Ayonhwathah had a specific meaning and function: to dry tears, to unplug the ears, to unstop the throat, to restore the body to wholeness, to wipe the blood from the ground, to bring light into the darkness, to make the sky beautiful again, to bring the sun back into the sky, to smooth the earth over the grave of the deceased, to gently bind the deceased's bones together, to gather the scattered kindling and relight the longhouse fire, to raise up the minds of all the people, to dispel the insanity of grief, and to replace the torch that had been carried through the longhouse to announce a death. Later, when this ritual was used to ceremonially install a man into a chieftainship, a fifteenth string of wampum would symbolize the restoration of the deceased chief in the form of his successor.

Ayonhwathah was moved by the Peacemaker's action and embraced him. This exchange is known to the Haudenosaunee people as the creation of the ritual called the Condolence Ceremony, which was to establish the path to reconciliation of all of the warring nations. Ayonhwathah joined the Peacemaker in his efforts to reconcile the nations and taught them this healing ritual. Their cycle of vengeance was ended through mutual condolence—the ritualized drying of tears, opening of ears, clearing of throats, soothing of wounds, and restoration of beauty and light. At last, the combined efforts of the Peacemaker, Ayonhwathah, and Jigonsaseh brought about a cessation of warfare, and the Five Nations agreed to embark together on a new path of peace. They joined together to create a sacred confederation, guided and governed by the Peacemaker's Gayanashagowa, the Great Law of Peace.

The first nation the Peacemaker persuaded to accept his message and follow the path of peace was the Mohawk nation. According to legend, he built a campfire whose smoke would announce his presence to a nearby Mohawk village. Villagers came to his campsite to find out who he was and what he wanted. After the Peacemaker explained his mission, the Mohawk were skeptical and concluded that he had to pass a test to prove his power. He was to climb a tree growing next to the nearby falls, and the Mohawk would cut it down; if the Peacemaker survived the fall, that would be a demonstration of his power and they would listen to his message. The Peacemaker agreed to the test, but when the Mohawk cut down the tree, the Peacemaker disappeared into the falls and did not come to the surface. The Mohawk returned to their village, but the next morning a wisp of smoke appeared in the distance; the Mohawk investigated and discovered the Peacemaker alive and well. They invited him to their village and proceeded to accept the Great Law.

However, one man resisted accepting the Great Law, even though the rest of his nation had agreed to embrace it. This was Adodaroh (Tadadaho), the chief of the Onondaga Nation, who was a disturbed and bloodthirsty man feared by all. Adodaroh was terrifying in appearance, with snakes entwined in his hair and twisted about his body. Some versions of the story describe (or hint at) Adodaroh being so depraved as to consume human flesh. Together, the Peacemaker, Jigonsaseh, and Ayonhwathah sang a six-verse song of thanksgiving to Adodaroh, thanking the war chiefs, the clan mothers, the elders, the ancestors, the peace, and the people (or the confederacy). The song calmed Adodaroh and made him receptive. He accepted Ayonhwathah's wampum, and Ayonhwathah combed the snakes out of his hair,

Time Line

1680s
- The Haudenosaunee dominate much of the Northeast, extending their sway over other native peoples from western Maine to the Chesapeake Bay, from Kentucky to Michigan, and from southern Ontario to southwestern Quebec.

1722
- The Tuscarora are incorporated into the Haudenosaunee Confederacy, transforming the Five Nations into the Six Nations.

1779
- The Sullivan-Clinton campaign against the Haudenosaunee as a part of Revolutionary War military strategy destroys most Haudenosaunee villages, and the people of the confederacy face starvation and death in great numbers.

1780
- Through the 1840s, the newly formed U.S. government dispossesses the Haudenosaunee of most of their land through a combination of both legal and illegal treaties and purchases. Some Haudenosaunee people move to the Six Nations Reserve in Canada, splitting Haudenosaunee leadership, though most remain on their traditional—although dramatically reduced—lands in upstate New York.

1794
- **November 11**
  The Six Nations and the United States sign the Canandaigua Treaty, meant to create lasting peace and friendship between the two peoples.

calming his mind. The Peacemaker reshaped and straightened his twisted face and body. When Adodaroh was thus returned to his humanity, the Peacemaker formally brought him into the confederacy by designating him the Firekeeper at the center of the symbolic "great longhouse" of the confederacy and thus "first among equals." He and his successors (also called by the official title Adodaroh) would lead the fifty chiefs of the united Five Nations and wear a crown of antlers. With the inclusion of Adodaroh, the Great Law was established, and the Peacemaker taught it to all the members of the Haudenosaunee Confederacy.

The Thanksgiving Address has been translated into English by Haudenosaunee leaders for two reasons. First, because many Haudenosaunee people no longer speak

Ayonhwathah at the deathbed of his wife

(The Song of Hiawatha by Henry Wadsworth Longfellow [1807-82], Remington, Frederic [1861-1909] [after] / Private Collection / The Stapleton Collection / The Bridgeman Art Library International)

their traditional languages, it must be made accessible to them in order for them to maintain and transmit to their children their cultural and religious traditions. Second, the address has been made available to non-Haudenosaunee people by Haudenosaunee leaders so that others may learn about the central values of the Haudenosaunee people. It is hoped that this knowledge will lead to greater intercultural understanding.

About the Author

While the authorship of the Thanksgiving Address was possibly corporate—that is, the address was created and elaborated by the culture over time—rather than individual, the Haudenosaunee people associate it with the Peacemaker, the founding figure of the Haudenosaunee Confederacy. The story of the Peacemaker is so important to the Haudenosaunee and his given name so sacred that it is uttered only on ritual occasions. In everyday speech, he is called only "the Peacemaker." In order to respect Haudenosaunee values and practices, this convention is employed here as well.

According to Haudenosaunee tradition, the Peacemaker was a member of the Wendat (Huron), an Iroquoian-speaking group of nations whose lands were to the north of the Five Nations, on the shores of Lake Huron's Georgian Bay in present-day Ontario. It is said that the Peacemaker came into being in a special way. His mother, a virgin, found herself to be pregnant. Because of this, and because of a dream the young woman had, she knew that sacred powers were at work and that her child would be a boy who would grow up to accomplish extraordinary things. When her son reached manhood, he tried to unite his own warring people through his message of peace. In some versions of the story, his leadership was welcomed, and in others he was rejected. In all versions, he left his home in a white canoe and wandered southward on a mission of peace to the Five Nations, who were at war with one another. He traveled among them (in Mohawk versions from west to east and in Seneca versions from east to west), trying to spread his message, but he initially was not heard. Eventually, though, he was welcomed, and the Peacemaker continues to be revered among the Haudenosaunee as the founder of their nation.

Essential Quotes

"We have been given the duty to live in balance and harmony with each other and all living things."

"When we forget how to live in harmony, [the Enlightened Teachers] remind us of the way we were instructed to live as people."

"Of all the things we have named, it was not our intention to leave anything out. If something was forgotten, we leave it to each individual to send such greetings and thanks in their own way."

"Now our minds are one."

Explanation and Analysis of the Document

The Thanksgiving Address reproduced here is in English translation. All of the languages spoken by members of the Six Nations are part of the same language family, called the Iroquoian language group. The six languages are similar in some respects but quite different in others. For example, an Oneida speaker can understand the Mohawk language with some effort, and an Onondaga speaker can, with concentration, understand the Seneca language. The Cayuga language has much in common with both the Onondaga and Seneca languages, but it has other elements in common with the Tuscarora language. This version of the Thanksgiving Address is a short one in which some culturally specific details have been omitted in order to make it more accessible to non-Haudenosaunee readers.

The Thanksgiving Address can be properly recited in any of the six Haudenosaunee languages: Mohawk, Oneida, Onondaga, Cayuga, Seneca, or Tuscarora. Although it is traditionally recited orally at the opening and closing occasions of any gathering of Haudenosaunee people, it has been made available in abbreviated printed form for non-Haudenosaunee readers. While some recitations of the Thanksgiving Address can be quite brief, others can be rather lengthy. A recitation can take several minutes or several hours; the address is not read but memorized and spoken aloud. It is addressed to the people gathered together as well as to the sacred powers that are also profoundly present to the Haudenosaunee people. The Thanksgiving Address is deeply resonant for the people of the Six Nations because it expresses their reverence for the world in which they live. Recitation of the address contributes toward meeting their obligation to express their gratitude to all of the sacred powers that have sustained them as a people from ancient times up through the present day. It is understood that in the future the people must continue their struggle to remain in a proper and harmonious relationship with the sacred. The Thanksgiving Address reminds them of how they may do so.

The address is usually spoken aloud by a religious expert, called a Faithkeeper, who is knowledgeable about the particular order of this ritual statement. A Faithkeeper may incorporate some of his or her own words and expressions, but the form of the Thanksgiving Address must adhere to an invariable traditional structure. It is necessary, for example, to begin with thanking the sacred powers that exist on the earth. Next one must thank the sacred powers that exist in the sky. Last, one must thank sacred powers that exist beyond the sky. The Thanksgiving Address may also be recited by individuals, and some Haudenosaunee people recite it aloud every morning as they greet the day. When a Faithkeeper is addressing the people, at the end of each portion of the address he says, "Now our minds are one." The people respond, "Henh," which is an expression of support and assent meaning "It is true."

The structure of the Thanksgiving Address moves from the terrestrial to the celestial, from below to above. When "The Enlightened Teachers" are thanked for periodically coming to earth and reminding human beings how to live harmonious and balanced lives, this expression of gratitude occurs after the sun, moon, and stars are thanked. This is because when many Haudenosaunee think of Enlightened Teachers, they think of Handsome Lake (Ganeodiyo), the great Haudenosaunee visionary and religious leader, as a primary example. Handsome Lake died in 1815, and he is now considered to be residing in heaven. Although "heaven" is not an ancient Haudenosaunee concept, it was introduced into Haudenosaunee religious life by Handsome Lake's religious reforms at the turn of the nineteenth century.

Notably, at the end of the Thanksgiving Address, apologies are made for any potential omissions of gratitude, and each person is then asked to convey the appropriate thanks in his or her own way. This part of the address acknowledges the importance of individual responsibility in the Haudenosaunee community. Every person must act to ensure that the community continues to be in proper relation to all beings.

In the version of the address reproduced here, the concepts are simple and clear. Reference is made to the "cycles of life," emphasizing the Native American connectedness with the natural world. To survive in the natural world, it is necessary to maintain "balance and harmony." To achieve this balance and harmony, it is necessary to "bring our minds together as one." The address then goes on to acknowledge the power of natural phenomena. The earth is seen as the people's "Mother." The waters not only display great power but also quench thirst. Fish are thanked not only as a source of food but also for their role in keeping the waters clean. Food plants, too, are a source of strength, and medicinal herbs take away sickness. Trees provide shelter, shade, and fruit, and the tree is a symbol of peace and power. Birds and birdsong serve primarily an aesthetic purpose, reminding people of the beauty of the earth. The Four Winds refresh and purify the air, and the "Thunderers," conceived as grandfathers, announce the arrival of purifying and refreshing rain. The sun, regarded as a brother, brings the fires of life, and "Grandmother Moon" serves as the leader of women and governs the tides, marks the passage of time, and watches over the birth of children. The stars not only light the sky but also serve as guides for night travelers. Enlightened Teachers "remind us of the way we were instructed to live as people." Finally, thanks are given to the Creator, the "Great Spirit," who provides the gifts of creation.

Audience

Haudenosaunee people treasure the Thanksgiving Address, but it is not simply an historical artifact for them—it is an important contemporary practice. For the Haudenosaunee, it is a way to articulate their relationships with sacred powers in the same way their ancestors did. The Thanksgiving Address gives Haudenosaunee people the opportunity to remind themselves of (and to renew within themselves) harmonious relationships with the sacred powers in this world and beyond it. An expression of gratitude toward these sacred powers reminds the people of the importance of all of the beings of the cosmos. While the Faithkeeper memorizes and recites the Thanksgiving Address on suitable occasions, the community must also listen closely to the Faithkeeper's words. After each distinct portion of the address, the audience must assent to the Faithkeeper's statements by saying "Henh" in unison. Participating in the recitation of the address is a way to help create and reinforce community solidarity, as all of the people come together as one, in their words of assent and in their renewal of a conscious relationship of gratitude to all beings.

Impact

Despite the Great Law, the formation of the confederacy, and the pervasiveness of the Thanksgiving Address, peace did not always reign among the Haudenosaunee. In the late 1770s part of Revolutionary War military strategy was to divide the Haudenosaunee into "pro-English" and "pro-Yankee" nations and to destroy most Haudenosaunee villages. The so-called Sullivan-Clinton campaign of 1779, under the leadership of Major Generals John Sullivan and James Clinton, was a full-scale assault on the Haudenosaunee, and the people of the confederacy faced starvation and death in great numbers. On November 11, 1794, the Six Nations and the United States signed the Canandaigua Treaty, which was meant to create lasting peace and friendship between the two peoples. Nevertheless, from about 1780 until the 1840s, the U.S. government dispossessed the Haudenosaunee of most of their land through a combination of both legal and illegal treaties and purchases. Some Haudenosaunee people moved to the Six Nations Reserve in Canada, though most remain on their traditional—although dramatically reduced—lands in upstate New York.

Not all Haudenosaunee people still speak their traditional languages. Since the Thanksgiving Address is a tradition in every Haudenosaunee language, the address is especially highly valued as a pedagogical tool by those who are dedicated to linguistic revitalization, and it is often one of the first things to be taught in Haudenosaunee language revitalization classes. It is broadcast on some Native American radio stations daily; for instance, CKRZ-FM, a Six Nations community radio station in Ohsweken, Ontario, broadcasts a Cayuga language version of the Thanksgiving Address at six o'clock every morning. In some Haudenosaunee schools, it is recited over the public address system at the beginning of the school day. The Thanksgiving Address serves as the foundation of the entire curriculum at the Akwesasne Freedom School, a Mohawk Nation grammar school in Rooseveltown, New York.

Recently, there was a controversy regarding the broadcast of the Thanksgiving Address at the Salmon River Central School in Fort Covington, New York. Two-thirds of the students at the Salmon River Central School are Mohawk, and from 2002 to 2005 the address was recited twice a week over the school's public address system as well as at pep rallies and at lacrosse games. A non-Mohawk parent complained to the school district's superintendent on the ground that the Thanksgiving Address resembled a prayer and therefore might violate the First Amendment, which provides for the separation of church and state. The public address daily recitations were stopped in 2005, but the school auditorium was made available on Monday mornings and Friday afternoons for any students to gather voluntarily to recite the Thanksgiving Address. In response, a group of Mohawk parents filed a suit claiming that their rights under the Fourteenth Amendment, which provide for equal protection under the law, were violated. In 2007 a federal judge ruled that the Mohawk families' rights were not violated by the suspension of the daily recitation, because the school provided accommodations for voluntary recitation of the Thanksgiving Address. The judge pointedly refused to rule on whether the daily public recitation violated the First Amendment, noting that the courts are not qualified to determine what does or does not constitute prayer.

Further Reading

■ Books

Johansen, Bruce Elliott, and Barbara Alice Mann. *The Encyclopedia of the Haudenosaunee (Iroquois Confederacy)*. Westport, Conn.: Greenwood Publishing Group, 2000.

Lounsbury, Floyd G. "Iroquoian Languages." In *Handbook of North American Indians*. Vol. 15: *Northeast*, ed. Bruce G. Trigger. Washington, D.C.: Smithsonian Institution, 1978.

Parker, Arthur C. *The Constitution of the Five Nations*. Albany, N.Y.: New York State Museum, 1916.

Snow, Dean R. *The Iroquois*. Cambridge, Mass.: Blackwell Publishers, 1994.

Tooker, Elisabeth. "The League of the Iroquois: Its History, Politics, and Ritual." In *Handbook of the North American Indians*. Washington, D.C.: Smithsonian Institution, 1978.

■ Journals

Mann, Barbara A., and Jerry L. Fields. "A Sign in the Sky: Dating the League of the Haudenosaunee." *American Indian Culture and Research Journal* 21, no. 2 (1997): 105–163.

■ Web Sites

"The Peacemaker." Iroquois Indian Museum Web site.
http://www.iroquoismuseum.org/PEACEMAKER.htm

—Lisa J. M. Poirier

Questions for Further Study

1. In what way can a house structure—in this case, the longhouse—become, as the entry states, "a metaphor for the cultural and social values of the Haudenosaunee"? How might other types of structures—chalets, castles, split-level suburban homes, teepees, mobile homes—similarly become metaphors for cultural and social values?

2. What similarities, if any, do you see, between the Peacemaker and other religious leaders, such as the Buddha, Christ, Muhammad, or the Bab?

3. The actual name of the Peacemaker is uttered only on ritual occasions. Why do you think the Haudenosaunee maintain this practice? What value does the practice have for the people?

4. Another indigenous religious document associated with the Americas is the Hawaiian Kumulipo. Compare the two documents and draw a conclusion about how the sacredness of the text influenced beliefs about when and how often it should be recited.

5. What is your position on the dispute between Mohawks and non-Mohawks at the Salmon River Central School in Fort Covington, New York? Do you believe that recitation of the Thanksgiving Address violates the principle of separation of church and state? Explain your view.

Mohawk Thanksgiving Address

Greetings to the Natural World

The People

Today we have gathered and we see that the cycles of life continue. We have been given the duty to live in balance and harmony with each other and all living things. So now, we bring our minds together as one as we give greetings and thanks to each other as People.

Now our minds are one.

The Earth Mother

We are all thankful to our Mother, the Earth, for she gives us all that we need for life. She supports our feet as we walk about upon her. It gives us joy that she continues to care for us as she has from the beginning of time. To our Mother, we send greetings and thanks.

Now our minds are one.

The Waters

We give thanks to all the Waters of the world for quenching our thirst and providing us with strength. Water is life. We know its power in many forms—waterfalls and rain, mists and streams, rivers and oceans. With one mind, we send greetings and thanks to the spirit of Water.

Now our minds are one.

The Fish

We turn our minds to all the Fish life in the water. They were instructed to cleanse and purify the water. They also give themselves to us as food. We are grateful that we can still find pure water. So, we turn now to the Fish and send our greetings and thanks.

Now our minds are one.

The Plants

Now we turn toward the vast fields of Plant life. As far as the eye can see, the Plants grow, working many wonders. They sustain many life forms. With our minds gathered together, we give thanks and look forward to seeing Plant life for many generations to come.

Now our minds are one.

The Food Plants

With one mind, we turn to honor and thank all the Food Plants we harvest from the garden. Since the beginning of time, the grains, vegetables, beans and berries have helped the people survive. Many other living things draw strength from them too. We gather all the Plant Foods together as one and send them a greeting and thanks.

Now our minds are one.

The Medicine Herbs

Now we turn to all the Medicine Herbs of the world. From the beginning, they were instructed to take away sickness. They are always waiting and ready to heal us. We are happy there are still among us those special few who remember how to use these plants for healing. With one mind, we send greetings and thanks to the Medicines and to the keepers of the Medicines.

Now our minds are one.

The Animals

We gather our minds together to send greetings and thanks to all the Animal life in the world. They have many things to teach us as people. We see them near our homes and in the deep forests. We are glad they are still here and we hope that it will always be so.

Now our minds are one.

The Trees

We now turn our thoughts to the Trees. The Earth has many families of Trees who have their own instructions and uses. Some provide us with shelter and shade, others with fruit, beauty and other useful things. Many peoples of the world use a Tree as a symbol of peace and strength. With one mind, we greet and thank the Tree life.

Now our minds are one.

The Birds

We put our minds together as one and thank all the Birds who move and fly about over our heads. The Creator gave them beautiful songs. Each day they remind us to enjoy and appreciate life. The Eagle was chosen to be their leader. To all the Birds—from the smallest to the largest—we send our joyful greetings and thanks.

Now our minds are one.

The Four Winds

We are all thankful to the powers we know as the Four Winds. We hear their voices in the moving air as they refresh us and purify the air we breathe. They help to bring the change of seasons. From the four directions they come, bringing us messages and giving us strength. With one mind, we send our greetings and thanks to the Four Winds.

Now our minds are one.

The Thunderers

Now we turn to the west where our Grandfathers, the Thunder Beings, live. With lightning and thundering voices, they bring with them the water that renews life. We bring our minds together as one to send greetings and thanks to our Grandfathers, the Thunderers.

Now our minds are one.

The Sun

We now send greetings and thanks to our eldest Brother, the Sun. Each day without fail he travels the sky from east to west, bringing the light of a new day. He is the source of all the fires of life. With one mind, we send greetings and thanks to our Brother, the Sun.

Now our minds are one.

Grandmother Moon

We put our minds together and give thanks to our oldest Grandmother, the Moon, who lights the nighttime sky. She is the leader of women all over the world, and she governs the movement of the ocean tides. By her changing face we measure time, and it is the Moon who watches over the arrival of children here on Earth. With one mind, we send greetings and thanks to our Grandmother, the Moon.

Now our minds are one.

The Stars

We give thanks to the Stars who are spread across the sky like jewelry. We see them in the night, helping the Moon to light the darkness and bringing dew to the gardens and growing things. When we travel at night, they guide us home. With our minds gathered together as one, we send greetings and thanks to all the Stars.

Now our minds are one.

The Enlightened Teachers

We gather our minds to greet and thank the enlightened Teachers who have come to help throughout the ages. When we forget how to live in harmony, they remind us of the way we were instructed to live as people. With one mind, we send greetings and thanks to these caring Teachers.

Now our minds are one.

The Creator

Now we turn our thoughts to the Creator, or Great Spirit, and send greetings and thanks for all the gifts of Creation. Everything we need to live a good life is here on this Mother Earth. For all the love that is still around us, we gather our minds together as one and send our choicest words of greetings and thanks to the Creator.

Now our minds are one.

Closing Words

Document Text

We have now arrived at the place where we end our words. Of all the things we have named, it was not our intention to leave anything out. If something was forgotten, we leave it to each individual to send such greetings and thanks in their own way.

And now our minds are one.

The burning of Jan Hus for heresy
(The Burning of Jan Hus, from Chronik des Konstanzer Konzils by Ulrich von Richenthal / Deutsches Historisches Museum, Berlin, Germany / © DHM / The Bridgeman Art Library International)

Henricus Institoris and Jacobus Sprenger: *Malleus maleficarum*

1486

"Just as... the physician sees in a sick person certain things that the simple person does not notice, the demon sees things that no human sees naturally."

Overview

The *Malleus maleficarum*, popularly known as "The Hammer of Witches," is a seminal work in the history of witchcraft. It was written in 1486 by two Dominican inquisitors, Henricus Institoris and Jacobus Sprenger, who were in charge of seeking out and eradicating heretics, or people who held beliefs in contradiction to Catholic doctrine, in the region of Germany east of the Elbe River. In the course of their duties, Institoris and Sprenger were told by witnesses stories of individuals who worked harmful magic (in Latin, *maleficia*). The authors believed that these individuals obtained the power to do evil by entering into a pact with the Devil and his emissaries, demons who were sent to earth to wreak havoc among the Christian faithful.

The *Malleus maleficarum* is often referred to as a manual for inquisitors, but its original title, "Treatise about Workers of Harmful Magic," demonstrates that a manual was not the authors' intent. In fact, the long work is divided into three major sections, two of which address the reality and practice of harmful magic and only one of which deals with the process of prosecuting its practitioners. Book 1 is a theological justification, in which Institoris and Sprenger use authoritative texts to explain that demons can indeed cooperate with humans to produce harmful effects. They argue that God allows this to occur to test the virtuous and punish the sinful more severely. Book 2 is predominantly a compilation of popular beliefs about harmful magic that the authors gathered in their travels around Germany, complete with anecdotes. Book 3 is the only section that could be called a true handbook for inquisitors; it outlines the judicial process for trying and sentencing those people who engage in harmful magical activities.

Context

Henricus Institoris, with the help of Jacobus Sprenger, composed the *Malleus maleficarum* in a time of transition between the Middle Ages (ca. 500–1500) and the early-modern period (ca. 1500–1800). The European Late Middle Ages was a period when many began to question traditional authority, such as the monopoly the Roman Catholic Church held on interpreting the Bible and outlining religious doctrine. These concerns would be realized in early-modern Europe, when Martin Luther's criticisms of the Roman Catholic Church in 1517 sparked the Reformation. The subsequent troubled religious, social, and political environment helped to produce what have been called witch hunts, or sporadic persecution against perceived witches in certain parts of Europe, most notably the Germanic regions, between about 1550 and 1700.

Although the *Malleus maleficarum* clearly deals with what is now called witchcraft, it is more a product of the Middle Ages than the early-modern period. Institoris describes the harmful magic he discusses as "sorcery" and its practitioners as sorcerers or sorceresses. This terminology provides a clue to how Institoris thought of the people who, as he believed, colluded with the Devil. Sorcery, Institoris claims, was by its nature a rejection of Christianity. Sorcerers and sorceresses renounced the faith they were born and baptized into and switched their allegiance from God to the Devil. Sorcery was not just a case of harmful acts or magic practiced with the help of demons, as witchcraft would later be described, but a case where the orthodox Christian became heterodox.

Following orthodox Christianity in Europe in the age before the Reformation meant adhering to the doctrines of the Roman Church as headed by the pope, today known as Roman Catholicism. The heretic, or heterodox person, had been instructed in these beliefs but willfully rejected them. The eleventh and twelfth centuries saw an emergence of heretical ideas in western Europe, for reasons that scholars are still debating. Whatever their cause, the Church quickly realized the threat such unorthodox ideas posed to its authority. Heresy, the Church argued, was like a disease that could spread and infect the larger population and so needed to be eradicated. In the course of the thirteenth century, popes created the inquisitional office, appointing clerics as inquisitors to debate and, later, seek out and prosecute heretics.

The men who served as inquisitors were trained preachers, mostly members of the Dominican and Franciscan mendicant orders. The mendicants, or friars, unlike members of traditional monastic orders, who withdraw from the world to

Time Line

1413
- Followers of the condemned heretic John Wycliffe (d. 1384) march on London and are suppressed.

1415
- Jan Hus, a reformer from Bohemia, is condemned as a heretic and burned by the Roman Church's Council of Constance; this leads to a series of wars in Bohemia from 1420 to 1434.

CA. 1430
- Henricus Institoris is born in Schlettstadt, Germany.

CA. 1436
- Jacobus Sprenger is born in the Holy Roman Empire in Basel (in modern-day Switzerland).

1456
- Johannes Gutenberg prints his first Bible using moveable type, paving the way for the printing of Institoris's work as well as that of perceived heretics, like John Wycliffe's Bible and Martin Luther's treatises.

1476
- A shepherd named Hans Behem leads a peasant uprising in the German village of Niklashausen after having a vision of the Virgin Mary; Behem is executed as a heretic the same year.

1478
- The Spanish Inquisition is established to inquire into Jews and Muslims who had converted to Christianity to determine if they secretly retained their former faith.

1484
- **Spring**
  Pope Innocent VIII confirms Institoris and Sprenger as lead inquisitors of eastern Germany.
- **December 5**
  Pope Innocent VIII issues the papal bull *Summis desiderantes affectibus*, which condemns all heresy and sorcery in Germany and orders clerics and inquisitors to do all they could to eradicate enemies of the faith.

1484
- The *Malleus maleficarum* is published.

---

contemplate God, vowed to live like the apostles by wandering and preaching in cities, and so they were especially qualified to serve as inquisitors. Saint Dominic (ca. 1170–1221) was admired for his preaching against heretics in Spain and southern France, and the Dominicans subsequently became the pope's right-hand men in the war against heresy, taking charge as inquisitors in many regions of Europe. The inquisitor's job was to persuade heretics to return to the Christian fold. Those who were stubborn and refused to do so received capital punishment, while torture was used to persuade heretics to confess. Inquisitors functioned in a loose chain of command; it was not until the Spanish Inquisition was established in 1478 that there was any centralized bureaucracy. The fact that the pope personally confirmed Henricus Institoris and Jacobus Sprenger as inquisitors over a region of Germany demonstrates that there was no systematic local organization of inquisitors before that period and in other areas of Europe. The pope took further responsibility in personally overseeing their duties through a papal bull, or directive, issued in December 1484, *Summis desiderantes affectibus (Desiring with Supreme Ardor)*, in which he instructed that all local ecclesiastical authorities must assist Institoris and Sprenger in their duties.

Institoris and Sprenger, therefore, were products of the late medieval Roman Church's concern over heresy and its potential to draw others away from orthodox Christianity. By the late fifteenth century, this seemed to be a losing battle. England and Bohemia (in the modern-day Czech Republic), in particular, seemed to be on the verge of religious revolt. In England, John Wycliffe had gained followers, called Lollards, by criticizing corruption in the Church hierarchy and calling for the Bible to be translated from Latin into spoken languages. In Bohemia, Jan Hus was an intellectual who challenged some of the theological doctrines of the Roman Church. The condemnation of Hus resulted in fifteen years of war in Bohemia between his supporters, the Hussites, and various secular and clerical authorities, as religion and politics became intertwined. Furthermore, in southern Germany just ten years before Institoris and Sprenger wrote their treatise, a peasant boy named Hans Behem (or Böhm) instigated a religious revolt by claiming that the Virgin Mary had visited him and told him to preach against the sins of the clergy. Institoris, in particular, as a Dominican inquisitor aware of this history, was devoted to preventing the same type of turmoil in the area under his command. The *Malleus maleficarum*, written primarily by Institoris, details his experiences seeking heretics in eastern Germany.

It was not unusual that Institoris heard about harmful acts of magic in the course of his duties and saw its practitioners as heretics. What is unique, and where Institoris's discussion of sorcery differs from earlier texts, is that he steadfastly believed that all the stories he heard were true: that there were people who could transport themselves through the air, ate babies, and had secret rites with demons. Previous authors, influenced by a ninth-century tract called the Canon Episcopi, claimed that there were some women who imagined that they did such things but did not do so in reality. Institoris, in contrast, repeatedly argues that magic was truly practiced with the help of demons, allowing seemingly impossible acts to be manifested in the world. So while the *Malleus maleficarum* was composed within the context of the Late Middle Ages, it laid the foundation for what would become the early-modern conception of witchcraft.

About the Author

Henricus Institoris was born Heinrich Kraemer but preferred the Latin version of his name, by which he is now known. He was born about 1430 in the town of Schlettstadt in southwestern Germany (now part of France and named Sélestat). By 1458 he joined the Order of Preachers, also known as the Dominican Order, a mendicant monastic order founded by Saint Dominic in 1216. Institoris played a role in fighting against the supporters of the condemned heretic Jan Hus, called the Hussites, in Bohemia from 1468 to 1470. By 1478 he was university educated and had been appointed by Pope Sixtus IV as lead inquisitor of Upper Germany. In March 1482 he was arrested and brought to Rome on charges of theft. The incident had no lasting effect on his career, for in September of that same year he was appointed inquisitor of the diocese of Basel, and in 1484 he was confirmed, along with Jacobus Sprenger, as head inquisitor for all of Germany east of the Elbe River. In 1485 Institoris was involved in a witch trial in Innsbruck. The Innsbruck bishop's reluctance to take the accusations of harmful magic seriously perhaps persuaded Institoris to begin writing the *Malleus maleficarum*, which was published in 1486. His subsequent career was not illustrious. Institoris seems to have become embroiled in secular politics, which led to his being transferred from place to place. He wrote a few subsequent treatises, none of which was influential. He died in 1505 fighting the Hussites in Bohemia, the place where he had started his career combating heresy.

Jacobus Sprenger was from the town of Basel, born sometime between 1436 and 1438. Basel at the time was part of the Holy Roman Empire but ruled locally by the bishop, who had both secular and sacred authority. Sprenger joined the Dominicans as a young man. He went to obtain his doctorate in theology at the University of Cologne, becoming prior, or lead administrator, of the Dominicans in that town in 1471. In 1481 he became the inquisitor for the dioceses of Mainz, Trier, and Cologne in Germany. Sprenger was confirmed, along with Institoris, as lead inquisitor of eastern Germany in 1484. While the two men certainly would have known each other at this point and were engaged in the same mission, scholars think Sprenger was much less invested in the eradication of heresy than his colleague. Sprenger was more concerned with internal church reform and the promotion of the rosary, marked by prayers that use beads as a memory and counting device. While his name is on the *Malleus maleficarum*, it is generally believed that he was not a coauthor and only minimally edited parts of the work. He died in 1495 in Cologne, where he had retained some administrative and university positions during his tenure as inquisitor.

Time Line

1492 ■ Spain's King Ferdinand II of Aragon and Queen Isabella of Castile expel all Jews who will not convert to Christianity.

1495 ■ Jacobus Sprenger dies in Cologne, Germany.

1505 ■ Henricus Institoris dies in Bohemia.

Explanation and Analysis of the Document

The present excerpt is the beginning of book 2, the second expository part of the *Malleus maleficarum*. The excerpt explains how demons lure people into rejecting their faith and entering into pacts to do evil, as illustrated by a number of examples. The excerpt also discusses the types of sorcery believed to exist. Throughout, Institoris is concerned with making clear that sorcery is a threat and produces very real results. To counteract the argument that God, if he was all-powerful, would allow the Devil to work such evil in the world, Institoris emphasizes that sorcery occurs with God's permission.

Many scholars have used the *Malleus maleficarum* to argue that witches were almost always identified as women. The unreliable data from the witch hunts in the sixteenth and seventeenth centuries seems to support this view, in some regions of Europe, if not in others. The excerpt included here does often refer to female sorceresses. This trend of identification does not persist throughout this very long work, however, for Institoris does give examples of male sorcerers. But the first English translation of the *Malleus maleficarum* in the early twentieth century changed many Latin words from the masculine plural, suggesting a group that included men, to feminine and also used the feminized term "witch" rather than "sorcerer/sorceress." This excerpt, from a new translation of the work, provides more careful and precise word choices so that the text retains Institoris's original meaning.

♦ **On the Different Methods by Which Demons Allure and Entice the Innocent through Sorceresses to Increase This Form of Breaking the Faith**

Institoris opens this section with a discussion of how demons are able to tempt people in three different ways and why God allows this temptation to happen. The first reason for why people enter into pacts with the Devil is what he terms "exhaustion" over temporal, or earthly, losses. Institoris makes clear that the fault lies with the people who are lured in this way. God gave humans the strength to withstand such ruses, as anyone's own power is greater than that of the Devil's temptation. God therefore allows

Sorcerers presenting a child to the Devil

(Sorcerers presenting a child to the Devil, from 'Compendium Maleticarum' by Fr M Guaccius [1608] / Private Collection / The Stapleton Collection / The Bridgeman Art Library International)

this to happen so that people can prove their faith and not become lazy, thinking that God will always provide. Rather, the Christian has a responsibility to him- or herself and to God to maintain faith. Using a biblical passage, Institoris further suggests that God allows harmful magic as a tool to teach the faithful this lesson.

He proceeds to outline the way in which the Devil entices people through temporal losses, presenting it as a type of domino effect: A demon enters into a pact with one person, who becomes a sorceress; the demon uses that sorceress to inflict harm on another's person and property; the person who is suffering material losses through this sorcery has no choice but to turn to another sorceress for help; and, in doing so, the person submits to that sorceress and thus to the Devil. Institoris provides examples that demonstrate this process. At first the afflicted person is just asked to do some small things that would displease God, like not making a full confession of sins to a priest. These acts increase and serve to slowly draw the person deeper into rejection of Christianity. The cunning and subtlety of the Devil is therefore demonstrated, something that Institoris discusses in more depth later. This mode of temptation works best among respectable married women, Institoris claims, because they are the ones most concerned with material things and personal belongings.

Institoris then moves on to the next method that the Devil uses, that of luring women through physical attraction and sexual desire. Young girls, according to Institoris, are more concerned with "ambition and the pleasures of the body." The Devil is particularly set on tempting virgins, since it is a greater coup to get the "righteous" to renounce their faith. He therefore sets his sights on virgins and entices them through handsome young men. A sorceress functions as the intermediary, leading a young virgin to a meeting with a man who is really the Devil in disguise. Two of the examples in this section provide the information that if the maiden makes the sign of the cross, the Devil cannot appear. Although the author does not explain how this works, the presumption is that if a virgin crosses herself, it somehow builds a shell of holy protection, a barrier that the Devil cannot penetrate. Institoris's final ex-

Essential Quotes

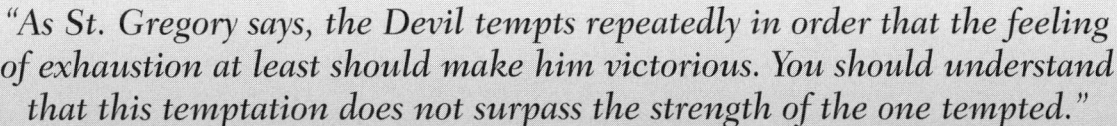

"As St. Gregory says, the Devil tempts repeatedly in order that the feeling of exhaustion at least should make him victorious. You should understand that this temptation does not surpass the strength of the one tempted."

"Thus, the demons use the sorceresses to afflict the neighbors of the sorceresses and the innocent with losses in temporal matters that are so great that as if under compulsion the neighbors must first beg for the help of the sorceresses and finally submit to their advice."

"Here it should be noted that since the Devil's intent and appetite are greater in tempting the good than the evil . . . he makes greater efforts to lead astray all the holiest virgins and girls."

"It should first be noticed that while the sorceresses appear in three kinds (those who harm but are unable to heal, those who cure and do not harm . . . and those who harm and heal) . . . among those who harm one kind is supreme, and those who belong to this kind are able to commit all the acts of sorcery, while the others practice only some each."

"For just as through signs the physician sees in a sick person certain things that the simple person does not notice, the demon sees things that no human sees naturally."

---

ample here is different, as it concerns a woman who had already ended (or decided to end) her virginity and was on her way to see her boyfriend to have sexual relations. In this case, the Devil stops her on her way and easily persuades her to become his "mistress." This example reinforces the point made earlier that the Devil more easily tempts those who are leaning toward "evil" acts, and it implicitly establishes that virginity is preferred by God and somehow holy.

Finally, Institoris presents the last way through which the Devil lures the faithful. Again, the goal is to entice young women, but this time nonvirgins. According to the text, many girls are persuaded to have sex on the promise of marriage but are then deserted by their lovers. The author suggests that such a young woman feels "disgraced" and ashamed. As a result, she is angry and vindictive and so employs a sorceress to retaliate and cast spells on her former lover or his new partner. The examples in this section describe two situations: one in which a woman vows that her former lover's new bride will be beset by ill health, which comes to pass, and another in which a woman successfully makes her former lover impotent so that he cannot consummate his new marriage. Institoris claims that this method of luring women toward sorcery for the sake of vengeance is the most prevalent of all. In making this assertion, Institoris again upholds the beliefs that virginity until marriage is preferred and that young women are more easily drawn into working for the Devil because of their frequent bad choices. Those who remain virgins are harder to lure and have the means to protect themselves, since their moral compass has not been corrupted by sexual pleasure.

♦ **There Follows a Discussion of the Method of Making a Sacrilegious Avowal**

The next chapter of book 2 moves on to discuss how, once one is tempted by the Devil or his demons, a formal pact in which the person vows loyalty to the Devil takes place. The form of this ritual differs, depending on which category of sorcery the person engages in. Institoris outlines three types of sorceresses: those who harm but do not heal, those who heal only, and those who both harm and heal. Those who are able to harm are further subdivided according to the evil effects they can produce, with one type "supreme" because they have totally surrendered themselves to evil. It is this group that, he claims, "regularly devour and consume babies of their own kind," like wolves; babies "of their own kind" means babies they gave birth to, although the author does state that such sorceresses kill other babies as well.

Institoris goes on to describe the innate evil of this type of sorceress by stating that they are the ones who want to—and are able to—produce the most harm in the world. He provides a long list of all of these sorceresses' abilities, which include inducing hailstorms, making people and animals sterile, transporting themselves from place to place through the air "in body or imagination," foreseeing events, and killing. Within this list, almost all of what have become popular beliefs about witches are present, outlined for the first time in one place. The author emphasizes that these sorceresses are real and exist—based on the account of the inquisitor Johannes Nider, who discussed them in his book *Formicarius*, or "Ant Hill" (ca. 1437)—and are currently present in northern Italy, where forty-one women were burned just the previous year. In order to preempt any arguments that the existence of such evil women shows that God is not omnipotent, Institoris takes care to mention that God allows these harmful acts through his "justice." Presumably Institoris is referring back to his argument in the first chapter of this book that God allows sorcery as a test of people's faith and a lesson to others.

Institoris finally moves on to discussing the actual ritual of vowing oneself in league with the Devil, stating that there are two types of rites. One is ceremonial and is done in the presence of witnesses. The individual renounces Christianity and then swears loyalty or homage to the Devil, promising to serve him and to persuade others to become his servants, too. In return, the individual, with the Devil's help, will be able to get all that he or she desires. This type of vow occurs when one sorcerer or sorceress brings another into the sect. Institoris's example includes a long digression about how one girl from Strasburg (or Strasbourg) was persuaded to make her avowal. In the course of this discussion he uses her story to show that sorceresses physically transported themselves from place to place and did not just do so in their imagination, contradicting the text of the Canon Episcopi. He then uses a report from another sorceress to show that the reason they kill and eat babies is to make concoctions from the baby's body that allow them to fly through the air and give them other powers. The second rite, a private ritual, merits only a paragraph. In this scenario, a demon appears personally to someone who is suffering and promises to heal the person or fix a problem if they follow his commands.

Having established the types of rituals, Institoris addresses why the act of homage takes place. There are two parts to the pledge: the vow in which a person rejects the Christian faith and the act of homage, or giving oneself over "body and soul" to the Devil. These acts do not have to be done at the same time, but both acts are necessary to "increase the offence against the majesty of God" and to secure the damnation of the person, which is the Devil's "greatest desire."

Separation of the vow and the act of homage is desirable for four reasons, according to Institoris: That way, demons can slowly entice a person into the act of homage by fulfilling a succession of small desires first; the Devil can test a person, seeing whether he or she will stay true to his or her rejection of the faith; if the person does not seem loyal, the Devil can then punish him or her harshly, since the formal act of homage has not taken place; and since demons can predict the future and know when someone will die, they have the patience to wait between securing these two aspects of the pledge.

In the final few paragraphs of this chapter, Institoris briefly discusses the powers that demons have, in particular why they are able to predict the future. Demons have "natural subtlety" or intellect, physical swiftness, and experience "with time and the revelations made by the spirits above." In other words, since demons are from the other world, they somehow have knowledge of how angels work and what God intends, even though they are barred from heaven proper. They can also predict what will happen after they use their powers, and they have heightened senses that allow them to foretell approaching death. Their cunning helps them to identify human intentions and have a better understanding of the revelations of the biblical prophets who gave clues to future events. The long example that follows this discussion simply demonstrates that a sorceress was able to predict that she would die soon. The next short example has little to do with the previous discussion but rather provides a moral lesson. A sorceress who was condemned to die thwarted the demons by making a full confession and went to her death happily because "she escaped the power of the demon." For her actions and intent, God would have given her forgiveness, thus rescuing her from the eternal fire if not the earthly physical one. The point is that God is merciful, even to those who have rejected him, if they are truly penitent.

Audience

The audience for the *Malleus maleficarum* is difficult to clearly ascertain, in part because each section of the source is very different. Book 2 was probably intended to be read by other inquisitors and preachers; the purpose seems to be to educate other inquisitors and preachers about how the Devil produces evil in the world and how to recognize it. In the opening of book 2, Institoris addresses his audience directly, instructing them, "You should understand that this temptation does not surpass the strength of the one tempted." Institoris is explaining to educated clergymen the Devil's process of temptation using an argument derived from Saint Gregory the Great, the pope at the turn of the seventh century. He also wants to give preachers the tools to explain this process to their parishioners, so that Christians can guard themselves against demons. He continues, "As for the divine permission, explain that God gives His permission." He is thus suggesting how other clerics can explain difficult theological concepts about the nature of God and evil to their Christian flock. So the intended audience for book 2 of the *Malleus maleficarum* was literate preachers who were grappling with demonic activity within their dioceses. In contrast, book 1 discusses complex theological issues regarding the nature of body and soul and the corporeality of demons, topics of most interest to learned, university-trained theologians and scholars. Book 3 consists of guidelines and protocol for inquisitorial inquiries and so is rather addressed to other inquisitors or clerics with specific responsibilities for prosecuting heretics.

Impact

German presses printed eight editions of the *Malleus maleficarum* in the first ten years after it was composed in 1486. Sixteen further printings occurred in France and Italy, the last in 1669. The *Malleus maleficarum* seems to have had little practical application as a handbook used by later inquisitors or influence in sparking widespread fears about witches, for the period of the witch hunts began a good century after the *Malleus maleficarum*'s publication. Written in Latin, it was not translated into modern languages until the early twentieth century, with the first English translation completed in 1928. It is of religious and historical importance because Institoris and Sprenger's work has subsequently become the foundational text for scholars examining the so-called witch hunts that occurred in the sixteenth and seventeenth centuries in Europe and up through the eighteenth century in the American colonies.

Further Reading

■ Books

Bailey, Michael D. *Magic and Superstition in Europe: A Concise History from Antiquity to the Present.* New York: Rowman & Littlefield, 2007.

Broedel, Hans Peter. *The "Malleus Maleficarum" and the Construction of Witchcraft: Theology and Popular Belief.* New York: Manchester University Press, 2003.

Levack, Brian P. *The Witch-Hunt in Early Modern Europe.* 2nd ed. New York: Longman, 1995.

MacKay, Christopher S., ed. and trans. "General Introduction." In *Malleus Maleficarum.* 2 vols. New York: Cambridge University Press, 2006.

Maxwell-Stuart, P. G. *Witchcraft: A History.* Charleston, S.C.: Tempus, 2000.

■ Web Sites

"The Witch Hunts (A.D. 1400–1800)." Women's History Resource Site Web page.
http://departments.kings.edu/womens_history/witch/index.html

—Janine Larmon Peterson

Questions for Further Study

1. Why do you think investigation into witchcraft in the Middle Ages and beyond tended to focus more on women than on men? (Note that *maleficarum* is the feminine form of the word.)

2. The introduction of printing by Johannes Gutenberg took place just thirty years before *Malleus maleficarum* was written. What impact do you think printing might have had on the promulgation of the document throughout the German-speaking world and beyond and hence on the fervor with which witches were hunted? Put differently, would witch hunting have been less prevalent had the printing press not yet been invented?

3. What impact did religious disputes in Europe during this time have on the concern with witches and witchcraft?

4. Read this document in conjunction with Gerald Gardner's *Book of Shadows.* How do you think Gardner would respond to the contents of *Malleus maleficarum*?

5. In the contemporary world, the attitude toward "witches" and "witchcraft" is generally one of much greater tolerance in comparison with the medieval world. Today, the average person is likely to think that a self-proclaimed witch is a harmless eccentric, witches are a staple of modern Halloween festivities, and from 1964 to 1972 a popular television comedy, *Bewitched*, featured a woman with powers of witchcraft. What, in your view, accounts for the difference? Why was witchcraft taken so seriously in the fifteenth century and apparently less so today?

Henricus Institoris and Jacobus Sprenger: *Malleus maleficarum*

On the Different Methods by Which Demons Allure and Entice the Innocent through Sorceresses to Increase This Form of Breaking the Faith

◆ **Chapter One**

THERE are three methods that the demons use more than the others to overturn the innocent through sorceresses and as a result of which that form of breach of the Faith is constantly increased. The first is the exhaustion that results from them relentlessly causing losses in temporal matters. As St. Gregory says, the Devil tempts repeatedly in order that the feeling of exhaustion at least should make him victorious. You should understand that this temptation does not surpass the strength of the one tempted. As for the divine permission, explain that God gives His permission so that humans will not grow sluggish through laziness. In token of this it is said, "The reason why God did not destroy these races was in order that he might educate Israel with them" (Judges 2). This passage is speaking of the neighboring Canaanite, Jebusite and other nations, and in the present day the Hussites and other heretics are given permission, so that they cannot be destroyed. Thus, the demons use the sorceresses to afflict the neighbors of the sorceresses and the innocent with losses in temporal matters that are so great that as if under compulsion the neighbors must first beg for the help of the sorceresses and finally submit to their advice.

Experience has often taught us this. We know an inn-keeper in the diocese of Augsburg who within one year had forty-four horses affected with sorcery, one after the other. Being afflicted with the feeling of exhaustion, his wife consulted sorceresses. By following their advice, which was clearly not wholesome, she rescued the other horses that he had subsequently bought since he was a haulier. When we were in the Office of the Inquisition, how many women complained to us that when they had consulted suspected sorceresses because of losses inflicted on cows though the deprivation of milk and on other domestic animals, they heard remedies offered on the condition that they were willing to make some promise to a spirit! When they asked what promise had to be made, the sorceresses answered that it was not much. The women just had to agree to follow the Master's instructions about certain observances during Divine Service in church or to keep silent about certain things when making Confession to priests. Here it should be noted that, as was discussed above, the infamous Contriver of a Thousand Deceits begins with a few trivial matters, like spitting on the ground or closing one's eyes at the Elevation of the Body of Christ, or uttering some unsalutary words. For instance, we know that when the priest greets the congregation during the solemn rites of the Mass by saying, "The Lord be with you," the woman who still survives because of the protection of the secular arm, always adds in the vernacular, "Kehr' mir die Zunge im Arsche um" ["Twirl your tongue in my ass"]. Other trivial acts are the uttering of similar words in Confession after Absolution has been granted or never making a full Confession, especially about mortal sins. In this way, they are gradually brought to the complete renunciation of the Faith and the sacrilegious avowal.

This method, as well as any similar one, is a practice used by sorceresses on respectable matrons, who are less given over to carnal vices and more greedy for earthly benefits. But for young women, who are more given over to ambition and the pleasures of the body, they practice a different method, making use of the desires of the flesh and pleasures of the body.

Here it should be noted that since the Devil's intent and appetite are greater in tempting the good than the evil (although from the point of view of those tempted he tempts the evil more than the good, that is, a greater ease in accepting the temptation of the Devil is found in the evil than is in the good), he makes greater efforts to lead astray all the holiest virgins and girls. Experience provides more than enough proof of this, and so does reason. Since he already owns the evil but not the good, he makes greater efforts to lead astray to his dominion the righteous, whom he does not own, than the evil whom he does, in the same way that an earthly prince rears up more against a man who derogates more from his rights than he does against others who do not oppose him.

Experience, in the town of Ravensburg, two women were burned to ashes, as will be explained below where the method followed by them in stirring up storms is discussed, and the one of them who was a bath keeper told the following story among the other things to which she confessed. She endured many injuries at the hands of the Devil, because she had to lead astray a certain devout maiden who was the daughter of a certain very rich man (there is no need to name him, since she is dead, it having been arranged by divine mercy that evil should not make her heart depraved) by inviting her on some holy day, so that the demon could engage in his sorts of conversation with her in the appearance of a young man. She added that although she had tried to do this very often, whenever she addressed the young woman, she would always protect herself with the Sign of the Holy Cross. No one doubts that this clearly resulted from the prompting of a holy angel in order to rout the works of the Devil.

There is another maiden in the diocese of Strasburg, and in confession to one of us she claimed that one Sunday, when she was walking around alone in her father's house, a certain old woman of that town came to visit her, and among the other dirty words that she uttered, she added at the end, that if the maiden wished, she would take her to a place where young men unknown to all the people of that town were staying. "After I agreed" the maiden said, "and followed her to the house, the old woman added, 'All right, we'll go upstairs to the upper room, where the young men are staying, but make sure that you don't protect yourself with the Sign of the Cross.' After I claimed that I would do this, she led the way, and while I followed up the stairs, I secretly protected myself with the Sign of the Cross. What happened then is that when we both stood in front of the room at the top of the stairs, with a fearsome expression and angry demeanor the old woman turned and looked at me, saying, 'Hey, curse you! Why did you cross yourself with the Sign of the Cross? In the name of the Devil, get out of here!' Thus, I returned home unharmed." From this story one can gather the cunning with which the Ancient Foe runs riot for the purpose of leading souls astray.

The bath keeper mentioned above who was burned to ashes claimed that she too had been led astray like this by an old woman, but her companion was led astray in a different way. This companion came upon a demon in the appearance of a human on a road, while she was intending to visit her boyfriend to fornicate. She was recognized by the incubus demon and he asked whether she recognized him. When she stated that she did not recognize him at all, he answered, "I am a demon, and if you wish, I will always be ready for your desire, and I won't abandon you in any dire straits." She agreed to this, and for the next eighteen years until the end of her life, she dedicated herself to those filthy acts of the Devil (with a complete renunciation of the Faith).

There is also a third method of alluring, by means of sadness and poverty. Young girls are sometimes corrupted by lovers with whom they have shamelessly copulated for the sake of marriage. The girls trust their lovers' promises, and then when they are rejected, they are disappointed in their every expectation and consider themselves to be disgraced in every regard. At this point, they turn to every sort of assistance offered by the Devil or plot vengeance by affecting with sorcery their lover or the woman to whom he has joined himself or else by subjecting themselves to all filthy acts. There is no counting the number of such young women, as experience unfortunately teaches, and, there is likewise no counting the number of sorceresses who rear up from among them.

Let us recount a few events among many. There is a place in the diocese of Brixen, and there a young man testified to such a case regarding his wife, who had been affected by sorcery directed against him. "I fell in love with a certain woman during my youth," he said, "and while she continually importuned me to join with her in marriage, I rejected her and took as my wife a woman from another territory. I nonetheless wished to please her for the sake of friendship and invited her to the wedding. She came, and when the other, respectable women were giving presents (offerings), the woman whom I had invited raised her hand and said in the hearing of the other women who were standing around, "There will be few healthy days that will you have after this one." Terrified, my bride asked the by-standers who this woman was who had made such threats to her, since she did not recognize her, having been brought for marriage, as I've already said, from another territory. The other women stated that she was a lax and promiscuous woman. In any case, the events that she foretold ensued, and in that order—a few days later she was affected by sorcery, so that she lost the use of all her limbs. More than ten years later, the effects of this sorcery can still be seen on her body today."

If it were necessary to insert the occurrences that were found in just the one town of that diocese, a whole book would have to be written. Those occurrences were written up and deposited with the Bishop of Brixen, and they are certainly both astonishing and unheard of, as the Bishop can attest.

Nor, we think, should another astonishing and unheard-of affair be passed over in silence. A certain high-born count of the land of Westrich within the territory of the diocese of Strasburg took as his wife a similarly high-born young woman, but he was unable to know her carnally until the third year after the celebration of the marriage, since, as the upshot of the matter proved, he was hindered by an impediment caused through sorcery. Being worried and not knowing what to do, he constantly invoked the Saints of God, and one day he happened to go to the city of Metz to finish some business. As he was walking through the streets and lanes of the city surrounded by his servants and family, he met a certain woman who had been his concubine many years before. When he saw her, the farthest thing from his mind were the acts of sorcery inflicted on him, and unexpectedly addressed her politely because of the old friendship they had formed, asking her how she was doing and how her health was. Seeing the piety of the count, she in turn earnestly asked about the health of his body and his situation. When he answered that everything was turning out prosperously for him, she was astonished and fell silent for a little while. Seeing her astonishment, the count spoke to her some more with polite words, inviting her to a dinner party. When she asked about the situation of his wife, she received a similar answer, to the effect that she was well in all regards, and when she then asked whether he had fathered children, the count said, "I have three male children. She's given birth to one each year." At this she was further amazed and fell silent for a while, and then the count said, "I ask you, my dear, tell me why you are asking so urgently. I don't doubt that you are glad for me on account of my good fortune." Then she said, "Truly I am, but curse that old woman who offered to affect your body with sorcery, so that you could hardly perform the carnal act with your wife! As a sign of this, the well in the middle of your courtyard has at its bottom a jar that contains certain objects for sorcery, and it was placed there so that you would have impotence in copulating for as long as the jar remained there. But now look! All the things that I have been rejoicing at are in vain" and so on. The count did not waste a minute. Returning home, he had the well emptied and found the jar. After burning everything, he suddenly recovered the power that he had lost. Next, the Countess re-invited all the noblewomen to a new wedding, stating that now she was the mistress of that castle and territory after having remained a maiden for so long. (Out of respect for the count, it would not be useful to mention the castle and territory by name. For right reason urges not only this but also that the essence of the deed should be revealed as a public indication of the repugnance felt for such a great crime.) From these facts are revealed the various methods followed by sorceresses for the increase of their lack of faith. For the woman mentioned above inflicted this act of sorcery on the count following the instructions of another sorceress after having been replaced by the count's wife, and this reason leads to countless effects caused through sorcery.

There Follows a Discussion of the Method of Making a Sacrilegious Avowal

♦ **Chapter Two**

The method of making the sacrilegious avowal in connection with an explicit agreement for faithfulness with the demons is varied, inasmuch as the sorceresses themselves engage in various practices in the infliction of acts of sorcery. To understand this, it should first be noticed that while the sorceresses appear in three kinds (those who harm but are unable to heal, those who cure and do not harm as a result of a particular agreement entered into with a demon, and those who harm and heal), as was discussed in Part One of the treatise, among those who harm one kind is supreme, and those who belong to this kind are able to commit all the acts of sorcery, while the others practice only some each. Hence, when the method by which the former make their avowal is described, a sufficient explanation of the other, lower varieties is given. It is they who, contrary to the tendency of human nature, indeed of all wild animals with the sole exception of wolves, regularly devour and consume babies of their own kind. This is the kind that is supreme in practicing acts of sorcery. For it is they who have a propensity for all other forms of harm. It is these sorceresses who stir up hailstorms and harmful winds with lightning, who cause sterility in humans and domestic animals, who offer to demons, as was explained above, or else kill the babies whom they do not devour. (This concerns babies who have not been reborn in the Font of Baptism; those that they devour have been reborn, as will be explained, but they do this only with God's permission.) They also know how to cast infants who are walking near water into it without anyone seeing, even within the sight of their parents; how to make horses go crazy under their riders; how to move from place to place through the air, either in body or imagination; how to change the attitude of judges and governmental authorities so that they cannot harm them; how to bring about silence for themselves and others during torture; how to instill great trembling in the hands and minds of those arresting them; how to reveal hidden things and to foretell certain future events on the basis of information from demons, (i.e., those events that have some natural cause; see the question as to whether demons can learn of future events in advance in *Pronouncements*, Bk. 2, Dist. 12 [actually, *Sent*. 2.7.2.2]); how to see absent things as if they were present; how to turn human minds to irregular love or hatred; on many occasions, how to kill someone they wish to with lightning, or to kill some humans and domestic animals; how to take away the force of procreation or the ability to copulate; how to kill infants in the mother's womb with only a touch on the outside; also on occasion how to affect humans and domestic animals with sorcery or inflict death upon them by sight alone without touch; and how to dedicate their own infants to demons. In short, when God's justice permits such things to happen, these sorceresses who belong to this supreme variety know how to commit all these baneful deeds, while the others know how to bring about only some of them. The reverse, however, is not the case. (It is, however, the common practice of them all to perform filthy carnal acts with demons.) Accordingly, from the method of making the avowal used by the sorcerers who belong to the supreme variety, one can also easily grasp the method of the other sorceresses.

There were such sorceresses thirty years ago within the territory of Savoy in the direction of the domain of Berne, as Nider recounts in his *Ant Hill*. Today, they are within the territory of Lombardy in the direction of the domain of the duke of Austria, where the inquisitor of Como, as was mentioned in the preceding part, had forty-one sorceresses burned to ashes in one year (the year of Our Lord '85), and he is still engaged in constant labor in the Inquisition.

There are two methods of making the avowal. One is a ceremonial way similar to a ceremonial vow. The other is a private one that can be made to a demon individually at any hour. The ceremonial one is carried out among them when the sorceresses come to a certain assembly on a fixed day and see the demon in the assumed guise of a human as he urges them to keep their faith to him, which would be accompanied by prosperity in temporal matters and longevity of life. The women who are in attendance commend to him the female novice who is to be accepted, and then, if the demon finds the female novice (or male disciple) ready to renounce the Most Christian Faith and Worship, and never to adore the "Distended Woman" (that is what they call the Most Blessed Virgin Mary) and Sacraments, then the demon holds out his hand and conversely the male disciple (or female novice) promises to follow those practices, pledging this by signature. After getting these promises, the demon immediately adds that they are not enough, and when the disciple asks what further ones must be made, the demon asks for homage, which contains the provision that the person will belong to him eternally in body and soul and be willing, to the best of his abilities, to turn any other people, of both sexes, into the demon's associates. He then adds that the person should make himself certain pastes out of the bones and limbs of children, especially those reborn with the Font of Baptism, and that with these pastes he would able to fulfill all his desires with the demon's assistance.

We inquisitors learned of this method through the testimony of experience in the town of Breisach in the diocese of Basel, receiving full information from a young woman who was a sorceress but converted. Her aunt, too, had been burned to ashes in the diocese of Strasburg, and the young woman stated that the method by which her aunt had originally attempted to lead her astray was as follows. One day she had to go upstairs with her aunt and enter a room at her command. There, she saw fifteen young men in green-colored garments after the fashion in which knights are accustomed to go about, and the aunt said to her, "Well, then! From among these young men I will hand over to you the one that you want, and he will take you as his bride." When the young woman said that she did not wish to have any of them, she was badly wounded and eventually gave in, indicating the method mentioned above. She also stated that she had been transported quite often over long stretches of the earth with her aunt at night, all the way from Strasburg to Cologne. It is this woman who gave rise to our promise in Question One to explain whether sorceresses really are moved in body from place to place by demons. (This promise was made because of the words of the Canon, where the sense of the text is that they do so only in the imagination, though sometimes they really are moved in body.) When she was asked whether they went about like this only in the imagination and fantasy, being deluded by the demons, she answered that they did so both ways. This is in fact the case, as will be explained below in connection with the method of being transported in location. She stated that greater losses are inflicted by midwives, since they must generally either kill babies or offer them to demons.

Document Text

She stated that she had also been severely beaten by the aunt because she had opened a covered jar and found the heads of very many babies inside. She also recounted many other stories, having first sworn an oath to tell the truth, as was fitting.

To her words about the way of making the avowal, unimpeachable corroboration is provided by the things that the aforementioned Johannes Nider, a notable Doctor who even in our days is famous for wondrous writings, recounted in his *Ant Hill* on the basis of the report of an inquisitor of the diocese of Autun, who conducted an inquisition in that diocese into many people accused of acts of sorcery and had them burned to ashes. Nider says, "From the account told to me by the inquisitor mentioned above I learned that in the Duchy of Lausanne certain sorcerers cooked and ate their own baby children. The method of learning this art was, as he said, that the sorcerers came to a certain gathering and by their work they saw the demon as if real in the assumed image of a human, and to him the disciple was obliged to give his word about renouncing Christianity, never worshipping the Eucharist and treading on the Cross when he could do so secretly."

Another illustration from Nider follows. There was also the common report (the story is from Judge Peter in Boltigen), that in the land of Berne thirteen babies were devoured by sorcerers, and for this reason public justice had blazed forth quite harshly against such parricides. When Peter asked a certain captured sorceress about the method by which they ate infants, she answered, "The method is this. We prey on babies, especially those not yet baptized, but also those baptized, particularly when they are not protected with the Sign of the Cross or prayers." (Notice, reader, that they prey on the unbaptized in particular at the instigation of the Devil, so that they should not be baptized.) It goes on: "With our ceremonies we kill them in their cribs or while they lie beside their parents, and while they are thought to have been squashed or to have died of something else, we steal them secretly from the tomb and boil them down in a caldron until all the flesh is made almost drinkable, the bones having been pulled out. From the more solid matter we make a paste suitable for our desires and arts and movements by flight, and from the more runny liquid we fill a container, for instance a bottle made out of a skin. Whoever drinks from this container is immediately rendered knowledgeable when a few ceremonies are added, and becomes the master of our sect."

Here is another method for the same purpose, one that is more distinct and clear. When a certain young man who had been arrested with his sorceress wife, and in the court of Berne was being held separately from her in a different tower, he said, "If I could receive forgiveness for my misdeeds, I would readily reveal all the things that I know about acts of sorcery. For I see I will have to die." When he had heard from the learned men standing around that he could receive complete forgiveness if he truly repented, he offered himself happily to death, and described the methods of the original tainting. "The procedure," he said, "by which I was led astray is this. It is first necessary that on Sunday, before the Holy Water is consecrated, the prospective disciple should enter a church with the masters and in their presence renounce Christ, the Faith in Him, Baptism and the whole Church, and then do homage to the masterling." (That is, to the little master. For this and nothing else is what they call the demon.)

Here it should be noted that this method agrees with the others already mentioned. It is no obstacle that sometimes the demon is present when the homage is done to him, and sometimes not. For he is working craftily in the latter case, perceiving the inclination of the prospective disciple, who, as a novice, will perhaps shrink from his presence through fear, though through his friends and acquaintances the demon easily guesses that the prospective disciple gives his assent. The reason why they call him the "masterling" even when he is absent is so that the prospective disciple will be struck with less terror as a result of his considering him to be small.

The following appears at the end. "He drinks from this skin, and once this is done, he immediately perceives that in his innards he conceives and retains pictures of our art concerning the fundamental rites of this sect. By this method," he said, "was I led astray. So was my wife, whom I believe to be so obstinate that she would rather endure the flames than be willing to confess to the smallest truth. But, alas, we are both guilty."

The truth was found to be exactly as the young man said. After confessing in advance, he was seen to die in great contrition. His wife, on the other hand, though convicted by witnesses, was unwilling to confess to any of the truth, either under torture or in death. Instead, when the fire had been prepared by the executioner, she cursed him with the vilest words and was in this way burned to ashes. From these facts their ceremonial way of making an avowal is clear.

The other method, the private one, is performed in various ways. Sometimes, a demon appears to men or to women who are trapped in some bodily or temporal affliction, sometimes addressing them visibly, sometimes using people as intermediaries. He promises that if they are willing to act in accordance with his advice, everything will turn out as they wish. As was discussed in Chapter One, he begins with small matters in order to lead them gradually to greater ones. Various deeds and events discovered by us in the Inquisition could be narrated in proof of this, but because this topic is not subject to difficulty, it is necessary to strive for brevity, though a further explanation is added.

For an explanation of the way they do homage a few things should be noticed

Regarding the fact that the Devil receives homage, a few things should be noted: for what reason and in what different ways he does this.

First, he does this fundamentally to increase the offence against the majesty of God by appropriating for himself a creature dedicated to God and to be more certain of the future damnation that is his greatest desire, but it has often been found by us that he accepted such homage for a certain number of years at the time of the avowal, though on some occasions he took the avowal only and postponed the homage for a certain number of years. Let us say that the avowal consists of a complete or partial renunciation of the Faith, this being complete when the Faith is renounced as a whole, as was discussed above, partial when as a result of the pact entered into the person has to follow certain ceremonial rituals contrary to the ordinances of the Church (for instance fasting on Sundays or eating meat on Fridays or concealing certain crimes in Confession or committing a similar crime). Let us say that homage consists of the handing over of body and soul.

As for why they follow such practices, we can cite four reasons from the point of view of the demon. As was explained in the second basic section of Part One of the treatise ("Whether demons are able to turn men's minds to hatred or love"), he cannot enter the inner thoughts of the heart, since this is appropriate for God alone, but comes to know them from conjectures (as will be explained below), and therefore if the infamous Wily Foe considers that it would be difficult to approach a female novice to secure her assent, he approaches her cajolingly, making few demands in order to bring her gradually to greater ones.

The second reason. Since it must be believed that there is a diversity among those who renounce the Faith, some doing so by mouth and not by heart, some by mouth and by heart, the Devil wishes to test whether she makes her avowal to him by heart as she does by mouth, assigning a certain number of years, so that in that time he may discover her intention on the basis of her works and behavior.

The third reason. If over such a course of time he recognizes that she is not very eager to carry out any crime at all and that she is now adhering to him by mouth but not by heart, and if he presumes that God's mercy will help her through the protection of a good angel, which the demon can test in respect to many things, then he undertakes to abandon her, and expose her to temporal afflictions so that in this way at least he may make profit from her despondency. The truth of this is obvious. If it is asked why it is that certain sorceresses are unwilling to confess to even the least truth under any torture, even the greatest, while others readily confess to their crimes after each list of questions, and also why it is that after they have confessed, they endeavor to do away with their lives by hanging themselves—for it can in fact be said that when divine compulsion through a holy angel does not co-operate in forcing the sorceress to confess the truth and in dispelling the spell of silence caused by sorcery, then whatever happens, whether this is silence or a confession of crimes, is done by the work of the demons—the first is the case with those whom the demon knows to have denied the Faith by mouth and by heart and to have done homage in the same way, since he is certain of their obstinacy, while, conversely, he abandons the others by not protecting them, because he knows that they are of no use to him at all. Experience has often taught us this in that it was made clear by their confessions that all those women whom we caused to be burned to ashes were involuntary in inflicting acts of sorcery. They did not say this in hopes of escaping, because the truth was clear from the blows and scourges inflicted on them by the demons when they did not comply with their wishes (they were very often seen with faces swollen and bruised), and, likewise, because after they have confessed their crimes under torture, they always contrive to end their lives by hanging themselves. The truth is grasped from our practice whereby guards are assigned every hour to watch for such things after they confess their crimes, though sometimes they have been found hanging from shoelaces or veils through the carelessness of the guards. As has been said, the Foe clearly brings this about to prevent them from gaining forgiveness through contrition or Sacramental Confession.

As for those whom he could never entice in their heart, he now endeavors, since it would have been very easy for them to find forgiveness with God, to bring them to despair through temporal shame and the horrible death, although by the Grace of God greater forgiveness, as the pious belief must be, resulted through true contrition and pure confession in instances where they were not voluntary in clinging to those filthy acts.

This is made clear by the things that happened barely three years ago in the towns of Hagenau and Ravensburg in the dioceses of Strasburg and Constance. In the first town, one hanged herself by a cheap veil that could be torn into strips. Another one (by the name of Walpurgis) was known for the sorcery of silence, instructing other women as to how they should bring about such silence with a first-born male child cooked up in an oven. More deeds and events are available, and similar accounts of others burned to ashes in the second town will be cited here and there in various passages.

There is a fourth reason why demons postpone receiving homage in the case of some sorceresses, but do not do so at all in the case of others. Since they can learn the length of a person's life more subtly than astrologers can, they have an easier time than astrologers do in either fixing in advance the end point of a life or in anticipating the natural end with one that is caused, in the manner already discussed.

These acts and deeds of sorceresses can be explained briefly, first by citing the demon's cleverness in such matters. In *The Nature of Demons*, Augustine gives seven reasons why contingent events in the future can be conjectured in a likely manner (not that the demons can know them as a certainty). The first is that they have a strong natural subtlety with regards to the workings of their intellect, and for this reason they understand causes even without running around as is necessary in our case. The second is that they know more things than we do because of their experience with time and the revelations made by the spirits above. Hence, on the basis of Isidore, the Doctors quite often affirm that the demons have excellent knowledge through three sorts of acuity (subtlety of nature, experience of time, and revelations from the spirits above). The fourth is their swiftness of movement, which results in their ability to foretell with miraculous swiftness in the west things that have happened in the east. The fifth is that since they can use their power to cause diseases, taint the breeze, and cause famine when God permits, they can likewise foretell these events. The sixth is that they can foretell a death more subtly through signs than a physician can by examining the urine and the pulse. For just as through signs the physician sees in a sick person certain things that the simple person does not notice, the demon sees things that no human sees naturally. The seventh is that on the basis of signs that derive from the intent of a human they conjecture the things that are or will be in the soul more cleverly than a wise man can. For they know what urges, and consequently what sort of works, are probably going to result. The eighth is that since they know the acts and writings of the prophets better than humans do, and many future events are determined by them, they can foretell many future events on this basis. . . . Hence, it is no wonder if a demon can know the natural length of a human's life. The situation is different, however, in the case of a death that has been caused. Such a death is what happens through the burning to ashes that the demon brings about in the end, when, as has been said, he finds the sorceresses not to be voluntary and he is apprehensive about their return and conversion, while others whom he knows to be voluntary he protects up to the time of their natural, as it were, death.

Let us give illustrations from either perspective that have been found or performed by us. In the diocese of Basel, a village situated above the Rhine called Oberweiler had a parish priest who was respectable in behavior but who held the view, or rather error, that there is no such thing as sorcery in the world, but only in the opinion of humans, who ascribe effects of this kind to womenfolk. God wished to cleanse him of his error in a way that would also reveal other activities on the part of demons in fixing a limit on sorceresses' lives in advance. When this priest wished to cross a bridge quickly to finish some business, he had an encounter with a certain old woman who was rude like him, and being unwilling to give way at the entryway to the bridge so that she could go first, he instead walked on rudely and accidentally knocked the old woman into the mud. Outraged at this, she burst out with insulting words, saying to him, "Father, you will not cross unharmed." He did not pay much attention to the words, but that night when he wanted to get up from bed, he felt that he had been affected by sorcery below the belt. The result was that when he wanted to visit the church, other people always had to hold him up with their arms. He remained in this condition for three years, under the domestic care of his mother by the flesh. After these three years, when the old woman, whom he had always suspected of inflicting the sorcery on him because of the insulting words with which she had threatened him, fell ill, it nonetheless happened that the sick woman sent for him to hear her confession. Though the priest rudely

Document Text

said she should confess to her master, the Devil, at the insistence of his mother he went to her home supported by the arms of two peasants. While he sat at the head of the bed in which the sorceress was lying, the two peasants wanted to hear from outside by the window—the room was situated at ground level—whether she would confess to the sorcery inflicted on the parish priest. Then, it happened that although during confession she made no mention of the sorcery that had been inflicted, after finishing confession she said, "Father, do you know who affected you with sorcery?" When he answered politely that he did not, she replied, "You suspect me, and rightly so. You should know that I inflicted it on you" (for the reason mentioned above). When he pressed her to free him, she said, "Look, the appointed time is coming and I have to die, but I will arrange things so that you will be made healthy a few days after my death." And so it turned out. For she died according to the limit set by the demon, and one night within the next thirty days the priest found himself entirely healthy. The name of the priest is Father Heflin, who is now in the diocese of Strasburg.

Something similar happened in the village of Bühl near the town of Gübwiller in the diocese of Basel. There was a certain woman, who was arrested and eventually burned to ashes, and for six years this woman had an incubus demon, in fact right beside her husband as he slept in bed—three times a week (on Sunday, Thursday and Tuesday) and on other, more holy nights. She had done homage to the Devil with the provision that after seven years she would be dedicated to him forever in body and soul. Nonetheless, God arranged things piously. For when she was arrested and condemned to the flames in the sixth year, she made a full and genuine confession and is believed to have received forgiveness from God. For she was very voluntary in dying, claiming that although she could have been set free, she preferred death so long as she escaped the power of the demon.

Glossary

Augustine	Saint Augustine of Hippo, a church father of the fourth/fifth centuries
Canaanite	a historical/biblical people who inhabited the region around modern-day Israel
Canon	Canon Episcopi, a ninth-century document on witchcraft
Eucharist	the sacrament of Holy Communion, in which, according to Catholicism, the body and blood of Christ, in the form of bread and wine, is consumed
Hussites	a Christian movement begun by Jan Hus in fifteenth-century Bohemia
Isidore	Saint Isidore, the archbishop of Seville, Spain, in the early seventh century
Jebusite	an early Canaanite tribe
Nider	Johannes Nider, a German theologian
Pronouncements	the University of Paris Pronouncements of 1398, written by academics to declare magic to be real and dangerous, in contradiction to church doctrine that magic is imaginary
Sign of the Cross	the ritual crossing of oneself by touching the forehead, the breast, and the shoulders to signify the cross on which Christ died
St. Gregory	a sixth-century church father

Martin Luther
(Library of Congress)

Martin Luther: Ninety-five Theses

1517

"Those preachers of indulgences are in error who say that by the pope's indulgences a man is freed from every penalty."

Overview

According to legend, on October 31, 1517, Martin Luther, a Catholic monk of the Augustinian order serving in Wittenberg, Germany, nailed a document containing ninety-five theses (points for discussion and debate) to the door of a chapel in Wittenberg. Luther's motive for this act was to provoke debate about what he regarded as errors in Roman Catholic Church teachings and practices and to correct abuses in the Church, particularly the practice of selling indulgences. The issues that Luther raised generated a much-wider debate, which in time split Western Christianity. The immediate outcome of that split was to be Lutheranism, a form of Protestant Christianity that enlisted millions of people with its appeal to freedom of conscience and freedom of speech.

Luther's *Ninety-five Theses on the Power and Efficacy of Indulgences*, commonly known simply as *Ninety-five Theses*, unintentionally sparked a powder keg that spawned the Protestant Reformation, the sixteenth-century movement that rejected many of the teachings of Catholicism and led to the formation of numerous Protestant denominations, including the Lutheran Church. The theses called for religious reform (note that the word *Protestant* is derived from "protest"), but in an age when religion and politics were often one and the same, their implications were also political. Religious wars erupted that were not to cease until the Peace of Westphalia in 1648. When the fighting stopped, Germany and Scandinavia were Lutheran. England continued to hold to Anglicanism, while Scotland joined fellow Calvinists in France, Switzerland, Holland, and elsewhere in Presbyterianism. Spain, Portugal, Italy, and most of France and Switzerland remained Roman Catholic.

Context

Martin Luther, an ordained Catholic priest with a doctorate in theology, joined the theology faculty at Wittenberg University, at the same time serving as a parish priest at Schlosskirche, or Castle Church, in Wittenberg. In the years that followed, Luther came to dispute many of the theological principles of Catholicism and concluded that the Church had gone astray by becoming worldly and corrupt. At the core of his reexamination of Catholicism was the issue of how a person achieved salvation in heaven. According to Church teaching, salvation could be achieved in part through good works, that is, by leading an exemplary life. This teaching was based on a theological principle called supererogation, which states that Jesus; his mother, Mary; and the Church's saints had performed a great many good works—far in excess of what was needed to achieve their own salvation—and these good works were stored as treasure in heaven. An ordinary person typically died with more sins than merits on his or her soul, so in effect the merits of Jesus, Mary, and the saints were used to cleanse the soul, allowing a person's soul to enter heaven. This is why a deceased person's living relatives and loved ones prayed and offered masses for the dead; prayers and masses were their supplication to God to transfer these stored-up merits to the deceased. This doctrine, then, was the foundation of the belief in good works as one path to salvation

Based on his reading of the Bible, particularly the book of Romans, Luther came to conclude that this view was erroneous. He insisted instead on the doctrine of justification by grace through faith, which is now usually phrased more simply as "justification through faith." According to this view, salvation in heaven is an unconditional gift of God's love and grace. A person receives it through faith alone and acceptance of Jesus Christ as the source of salvation; it cannot be "earned" through the performance of good works, for that would imply that a well-behaved, charitable atheist could be admitted to heaven. The doctrine of justification by faith became a central doctrine of the Protestant Reformation.

Luther's teachings about indulgences began to attract the attention of Church authorities. Catholic theology teaches that when a penitent confesses a sin to a priest and is given absolution (or forgiveness from God through the priest), the sin is forgiven; the person is then in a state of grace, and the person's soul can enter heaven. (The Catholic Church distinguishes between mortal sins, or severe sins that merit punishment in hell, and venial sins, or minor transgressions that by themselves do not preclude entrance to heaven.) According to the Church, however, the stain of sin is not fully taken away by the sacrament of penance, or confession. After death, a person's soul has to

Time Line

1483
- **November 10** Martin Luther is born in Eisleben, Germany.

1505
- **July 2** Luther is struck by lightning but lives and vows to become a monk.
- **July 17** Luther enters the Augustinian cloister at Erfurt.

1517
- **October 31** Luther, according to tradition, nails his *Ninety-five Theses* to the chapel door of Castle Church in Wittenberg.

1520
- **July 15** Pope Leo X issues a papal bull proclaiming forty-one of Luther's theses heretical.

1521
- **January 3** Luther is excommunicated from the Catholic Church.
- **April 18** At the Diet of Worms, Luther declares he cannot renounce his teachings on salvation.
- **May 25** Holy Roman Emperor Charles V issues the Edict of Worms, declaring Luther a wanted heretic.

1524
- The Peasants' War erupts; the war ends the following year.

1546
- **February 18** Luther dies at Eisleben.

1555
- **September 25** The Lutheran Church is officially recognized by the Holy Roman Empire in the Peace of Augsburg.

1618
- **May 23** The Thirty Years' War begins.

1648
- **October 24** The Thirty Years' War ends with the signing of the Peace of Westphalia.

---

spend time in purgatory, an intermediate state between this world and heaven. In purgatory, a word related to the word *purge* through the Latin word *purgare*, a person is shut out from God's presence, a form of punishment that enables the person to give satisfaction for past sins and become fit to enter heaven. An indulgence, which is typically in the form of a prayer or some other type of religious observance, earns the soul a reduction in the time spent in purgatory. Church teaching distinguishes between partial and plenary indulgences. A partial indulgence reduces the time spent in purgatory; a plenary indulgence remits all of the time the person's soul would otherwise have spent in purgatory.

In the sixteenth century the practice of granting indulgences was much abused. The Catholic Church often sold them by granting letters of indulgence (or what Luther called letters of pardon) to people who donated money to the Church. Among the worst offenders was Johann Tetzel, a Dominican friar who traveled about selling indulgences to raise funds for the renovation of Saint Peter's Basilica in Rome. Tetzel was reported to have often said, "As soon as the coin in the coffer rings, the soul from purgatory springs." Luther was deeply troubled by this practice, along with other indications that the Church had grown greedy and worldly, and he preached sermons against it. He objected to what he saw as Pope Leo X's greed and wealth, for the pope had struck a bargain with an ambitious German nobleman, Alfred of Mainz, who was trying to buy a bishopric and who took part in the Tetzel scheme in Germany as part of his payment to the pope for the position. Luther, meanwhile, feared that Catholics would neglect confession, absolution, and penance because they believed that buying indulgences would serve the same purpose—that, in effect, they would believe they could buy their way into heaven.

Put simply, conflict was brewing between Luther and the Church hierarchy. The growing dispute was not just with a faraway pope, for the Wittenberg church at which Luther served contained one of the largest collections of sacred relics in Europe, some seventeen thousand items at the time, including a purported twig from the burning bush of Moses and a fragment of bread from the Last Supper. The Wittenberg church had a special dispensation from the pope allowing it to sell indulgences to people who came to view the relics—and who paid a stipulated fee. The church hierarchy actually computed that a person who visited the relics on All Saints' Day (November 1) and paid the fee would have the time spent in purgatory reduced by 1,902,202 years and 270 days. Luther had had enough of this practice and was determined to provoke debate and public discussion about it. It was for this reason that he published his *Ninety-five Theses*.

About the Author

Luther was born on November 10, 1483, as Martin Luder (later Latinizing his name) in the town of Eisleben in what is now Germany. (At the time, Germany was a loose collection of independent states, each ruled by a noble, that

Luther nails his theses to the door of the Castle Church in Wittenberg.
(Library of Congress)

were part of the Holy Roman Empire.) Early in life, he was content to follow his family's wishes and enter the family copper business. But on July 2, 1505, his life was altered when, according to legend, he was knocked off his horse by a lightning bolt. Grateful that his life had been spared, he vowed to become a monk and entered the monastery of the Augustinian monks at Erfurt, where he devoted himself to an ascetic life of fasting, prayers, and pilgrimages.

In 1507 Luther was ordained as a Catholic priest. After earning bachelor's degrees in theology in 1508 and 1509 and a doctorate in theology in 1512, he joined the theology faculty at Wittenberg University. He also served as a parish priest at Castle Church in Wittenberg. On October 31, 1517, he purportedly nailed the *Ninety-five Theses* to the door of Castle Church, though many historians dispute that he actually nailed the document to the church door (a story started by a fellow theologian but never confirmed by others), believing instead that he sent it to a small number of bishops. Soon the theses were translated from Latin and, with the help of the recently invented printing press, distributed throughout Germany and then all of Europe. Luther's life was tumultuous after the publication of the *Ninety-five Theses*: He was excommunicated from the Catholic Church and branded a heretic and an outlaw. Eventually, he settled in Wittenberg, Germany. On June 13, 1525, he married Katharina von Bora, who in time gave birth to their three sons and three daughters.

In the final years of his life, Luther, who was often known to be rude, who had an irascible temper, and whose anti-Semitism modern Lutherans are quick to repudiate, continued to preach and write, publishing a German translation of the complete Bible in 1534 and numerous books and tracts. He engaged in disputes with various religious factions that, he believed, were advocating extreme views, among them the Baptists. In his final years, he suffered from health problems, and the death of one of his daughters in 1542 was a blow from which he never fully recovered. In early 1546 he was traveling to his birthplace, Eisleben, when he began complaining of chest pains. He died early on February 18, 1546, and on February 22 was laid to rest at Castle Church in Wittenberg.

Essential Quotes

> "Our Lord and Master Jesus Christ, when He said Poenitentiam agite, willed that the whole life of believers should be repentance."

> "The pope does not intend to remit, and cannot remit any penalties other than those which he has imposed either by his own authority or by that of the Canons."

> "Therefore those preachers of indulgences are in error who say that by the pope's indulgences a man is freed from every penalty, and saved."

> "Every true Christian, whether living or dead, has part in all the blessings of Christ and the Church; and this is granted him by God, even without letters of pardon."

> "But he who guards against the lust and license of the pardon-preachers, let him be blessed!"

Explanation and Analysis of the Document

Nailing a document such as the *Ninety-five Theses* to the door of Wittenberg's Castle Church was not a particularly unusual act in Martin Luther's day. The door served as a kind of billboard, and it was a common way to announce a meeting to discuss matters concerning Christendom and Christianity. It is uncertain whether Luther actually nailed the document to the church door or simply sent it to select bishops, including Albert of Mainz, the German nobleman who took part in the Tetzel scheme for selling indulgences. The document opens with an announcement that for the love of the truth and with a desire to bring truth to light, Doctor Martin Luther, professor of theology, planned to hold a meeting where the points he raised would be discussed. He invited all interested parties to attend or to send their arguments to him via letter to be included in the discussion.

♦ **Theses 1–9**

Luther first takes up the issue of repentance. He uses the Latin phrase *Poenitentiam agite*, which is generally translated as simply "repent," though sometimes it is translated as "do penance." The distinction was important to Luther, for it pointed to the difference between being truly penitent and simply performing outward acts of penance, such as sacramental penance—that is, receiving the sacrament of penance after confessing to a priest. He argues that true inward repentance consists of self-hatred caused by sin. A crucial thesis is number 5, which states: "The pope does not intend to remit, and cannot remit any penalties other than those which he has imposed either by his own authority or by that of the Canons." In other words, the pope (and by extension priests) can impose penalties on the faithful only for violation of the "Canons," that is, canon law or church law. Nor, as thesis 6 states, can the pope remit guilt except insofar as guilt has been remitted by God. Further, the portions of canon law that pertain to repentance can be imposed only on the living, not on the dead. In sum, Luther is making a clear distinction between the pope and God in matters of repentance and in the applicability of church law to penitents. Ultimately, this view would lead to the Protestant rejection of the Catholic Church's sacrament of penance, that is, confession of sins to a priest.

♦ **Theses 10–26**

In this group of theses, Luther turns to the theological concept of purgatory. He calls those priests who impose canonical penances on the dying "ignorant and wicked" and characterizes this practice as "tares," or weeds that are sown in a field of wheat or other grain—that is, an undesirable element. His use of this word is an allusion to Jesus's parable of the wheat and the tares in the Gospel of Matthew (13:24–30). Luther says that canonical penalties used to be imposed before penitents were given absolution (forgiveness) in the sacrament of penance, not after, as a test of their sincerity. Luther maintains that when people die, they are released from all earthly penalties as embodied in canon law. The penalty of purgatory is imposed not by earthly law but by the person's own fear, even despair, brought about by his or her sinfulness. Purgatory is a process by which souls increase in love and decrease their own fear as they become more assured of their own blessedness. Accordingly, when the pope remits all penalties in purgatory, he can remit only those that he himself has imposed—again, according to earthly or canon law. This line of argument leads to another crucial thesis, number 21: "Therefore those preachers of indulgences are in error who say that by the pope's indulgences a man is freed from every penalty, and saved." The pope can free souls only from earthly penalties. Luther goes on to argue that if the pope could remit all penalties, only the most perfect could gain entrance to heaven, meaning that most people are deceived by "that indiscriminate and high-sounding promise of release from penalty." The pope does not hold the keys to heaven, but he can intercede, that is, pray for the souls of the deceased.

♦ **Theses 27–38**

Luther at this point turns specifically to the practice of selling indulgences and, what amounts to the same thing, letters of pardon. He refers to Johann Tetzel's rhyme quoted earlier about the penny jingling or ringing in the coffer, noting that the practice of paying for indulgences is a mark of "avarice" and citing a central doctrine of Protestantism—that "the intercession of the Church is in the power of God alone." As a result of what Luther is laying out here, it can be said that, in general, Protestantism believes in a more personal relationship with God, in contrast to Catholicism, which traditionally saw the Church as a necessary mediator between people and God at a time when people in general could not read and, even if they could, had no copy of the Bible to read for themselves. Luther states that no one can know whether people wish to be bought out of purgatory. Pointing to the rarity of true contrition, Luther makes a bold statement in thesis 32: He says that people who depend on letters of pardon will be "condemned eternally" and that people should be cautious in believing that such letters from the pope will have any effect on a person's salvation. Letters of pardon are ineffective without true contrition; the soul cannot be bought out of purgatory by indulgences and "confessionalia," another term for letters of pardon. Luther contends that every Christian has a right to remission of guilt and to the blessings of Christ without letters of pardon.

♦ **Theses 39–55**

A common theme in this group of theses is the deleterious effect of the practice of selling indulgences and letters of pardon. Luther sees an inconsistency in the effort to preach true contrition while selling letters of pardon. True contrition actually loves penalties, but letters of pardon "relax" people and make them hate penalties. In several theses, Luther argues that the performance of good works and acts of charity are preferable to purchasing "apostolic" pardons, or pardons from the pope and the Church hierarchy. Money that is spent on indulgences and letters of pardon would be better spent by helping the poor and would be even better spent to meet the needs of one's own family. Indulgences and letters of pardon fail to make people better; instead, they only make them free from penalty, and spending money on them merits only God's "indignation." Luther is particularly concerned about the possibility that in purchasing indulgences, people will lose their "fear of God." It leads to a failure to emphasize the word of God in churches, which is far more significant than the effort to sell from the pulpit pardons and remissions from punishment. Luther alludes to his particular quarrel with the pope—that money gained from the selling of indulgences is being used for the church of Saint Peter in Rome at the expense of the German people. He even suggests boldly that it would be better for the pope to sell the church of Saint Peter and give the money to those from whom "hawkers" of indulgences take it.

♦ **Theses 56–80**

In this group of theses, Luther walks a fine line between condemnation of the pope—and, by extension, the entire Church hierarchy—and his recognition of the pope's authority. Indeed, the power of the pope became a key issue in the Protestant Reformation, one of the results of which was the growing belief among the laity that the hierarchy of bishops, archbishops, cardinals, and popes interfered with a person's individual relationship with God. As a result, many Protestant denominations explicitly disavow hierarchies and the mandated forms of worship they prescribe (such as the Catholic mass) in favor of scriptural reading and more personal forms of worship.

Thus, on the one hand, Luther acknowledges the power of the pope in the remission of penalties in certain cases. A person is "accursed" if he speaks against the validity of apostolic pardons. The pope has "graces" at his disposal, including the Gospel and gifts of healing. But while acknowledging the authority of the pope, Luther condemns practices that the pope condones and that lead to corruption, greed, and false doctrine. He discusses the "treasures" of the Church, arguing that the treasures consist of the keys of the Church and the Gospel, not material goods. Luther turns ironic when he says that not enough clerics recognize this supremacy of the Gospel, for the Gospel makes the last first and the first last, an allusion to Matthew 20:16: "So the last shall be first, and the first last." In other words, the emphasis on material things rather than the Gospel of Jesus inverts priorities and turns the Gospel into a tool used as a net to catch riches from men—again a biblical allusion, this time to Matthew 4:19 and Mark 1:17, where Jesus invites his apostles to follow him and be fishers of men. The core of Luther's view is contained in thesis 72: "But he who guards against the lust and license of the pardon-preachers, let him be blessed!"

♦ **Theses 81–95**

Much of the remainder of the document is taken up with questions that Luther believes the laity would put to Church authorities. If the pope has the power to remit time in purgatory through the sale of indulences, why does he not simply empty purgatory? Why does the practice of saying masses for the dead at the time of their death and on anniversaries of their death have to continue if indulgences can be purchased? Why do God and the pope allow sinners to buy others' way out of purgatory? Why does not the pope use his own riches to build his church in Rome? Why does the pope suspend pardons and indulgences that have not been paid for? Luther then goes on to call for discussion of these matters, believing that the Church should answer these questions. He concludes by urging the faithful to "be diligent in following Christ," confident that they can overcome tribulations and enter heaven.

Audience

The immediate audience for Luther's *Ninety-five Theses* included members of the local academic and ecclesiastical community. The document was also directed at preachers and others who supported the sale of indulgences. The burden of Luther's concern was for the Christian laity, but he was also concerned for the purity of the theology and practice of the Church. As word of the theses spread, knowledge of them extended to all orders of society, especially in northern Europe. For many reformers, including the French theologian John Calvin (who gave his name to Calvinism and is regarded as a spiritual force behind Presbyterianism), the German reformer Martin Bucer, and the French reformer Guillaume Farel, Luther's teachings, expressed in part in the *Ninety-five Theses*, gave them reasons for pressing ahead with ecclesiastical reform.

Impact

Luther himself expressed surprise at the firestorm the *Ninety-five Theses* set off. He once said, "I would never have thought that such a storm would rise from Rome over one simple scrap of paper." Luther could not have known the far-reaching impact his scrap of paper would have, for it launched the Protestant Reformation, breaking the hold of the Catholic Church on Europe.

The impact on his life and on the Catholic Church was almost immediate. In response to the publication of the theses, Pope Leo X ordered a prominent Italian theologian, Sylvester Mazzolini of Prierio (also known as Prierias), to investigate the dispute. Mazzolini concluded that Luther's teachings were opposed to the Church's doctrine on indulgences and branded Luther a heretic (that is, a dissenter from official teachings). The pope demanded that Luther submit to the pope's authority by recanting his heretical views. To that end he dispatched his representative to confront Luther at Augsburg, Germany, in October 1518. Over the next two years, the dispute grew more heated until the pope threatened to excommunicate Luther. In response, Luther burned the papal bull that contained the pope's warning. (A "bull" is an official papal letter, so called because it is sealed with a lead seal called a bulla.) On January 3, 1521, the pope issued a bull excommunicating Luther.

That same month, Charles V, the emperor of the Holy Roman Empire, convened the Diet of Worms, an assembly similar to a parliament and held in a small town on the Rhine River. Luther appeared before the diet. When he was asked whether he still believed his "errors," he replied the next day (April 18, 1521): "Unless I am convinced by the testimony of Scripture or by plain reason (for I believe in neither the pope nor in councils alone, for it is well-known, not only that they have erred, but also have contradicted themselves) . . . my conscience is captive to the Word of God. I cannot and will not recant, for it is neither safe nor honest to violate one's conscience."

According to legend, he then said, "I can do no other. Here I take my stand."

On May 25, 1521, Charles V issued the Edict of Worms, declaring Luther a heretic and an outlaw. He took refuge in Eisenach, where he lived for the next year under the protection of a German prince, occupying his time by translating the New Testament of the Bible into simple German that ordinary people could understand—another step in his efforts to free the faithful from the grip of Church authority. Groups from all over Europe sent him letters soliciting his comments on assorted matters of Church doctrine or seeking his support for their own reform movements.

But the impact of the "scrap of paper" extended far beyond Luther's own life. By the early 1520s, like-minded people in Europe were already calling themselves Lutherans, although Luther did not regard himself as the creator of a new religion and even urged his followers to call themselves Christians, not Lutherans. They rejected his advice, and today there are some sixty-six million Lutherans in the world. His conflicts with the Church helped spark the so-called Peasants' War of 1524–1525. At the time, Europe was in a state of upheaval. Since at least the fourteenth century, European peasants had been in rebellion against their landowning masters. They regarded Luther's challenge to the Church as an attack as well on the social and economic system that oppressed them. Accordingly, they believed that if they rose up in revolt, they would gain the support of Protestant reformers like Luther. Aiding the peasants were poor nobles who had no way to repay the debts they owed to the Catholic Church.

Initially, Luther supported the peasants, but he withdrew this support when the revolts turned bloody. Critics blamed Luther for the revolts, so he succumbed to increasing pressure to condemn the peasants, which he did, with characteristic vehemence, in 1525 in *Against the Murderous, Thieving Hordes of Peasants*—though his motivation, in part, was to lend his support to the German nobility who, like him, questioned the authority of the pope and offered him protection. The revolt was put down in 1525, though henchmen continued to ransack churches, abduct Church officials, and commit other atrocities.

The Peasants' War was only a harbinger of things to come. In the years and decades that followed, Catholicism and Protestantism formed the two sides in an ongoing debate that frequently erupted in warfare. Throughout the 1500s, tensions between Catholics and Protestants increased, turning violent in 1606 when Catholics and Protestants clashed in the German city of Donauwörth. Nations on the European continent, many of them—such as Spain and Italy—still Catholic, looked on the swelling influence of Protestant Germans with fear and distrust. In 1618 these tensions came to a head in the Thirty Years' War, a series of conflicts that embroiled most of Europe and led to the death of nearly a third of the German population before it ended with the signing of the Peace of Westphalia in 1648.

These kinds of religious conflicts continued. Protestant England was racked with religious dissension that led to armed insurrection, which ended when the Catholic king, Charles I, was beheaded by Protestant revolutionaries in 1649. The monarchy was restored in 1660, but Catholic-Protestant animosity continued, and in 1688 the Catholic James II fled England into exile, to be replaced by King William and Queen Mary, both Protestants. For decades English Protestants feared that James's Catholic heirs would return to reclaim the throne. Until the nineteenth century, Catholics (and Jews) in England were not allowed to attend universities or hold public office. In the largely Protestant United States, similar anti-Catholic prejudice was commonplace throughout the nineteenth century and well into the twentieth. Throughout the twentieth century, Catholics and Protestants in Northern Ireland died in bloody bombings and assassinations.

The Protestant Reformation in Europe had as its by-products bloodshed, conflict, and discrimination. Nevertheless, historians agree that the Reformation Luther and others launched made an important contribution to the development of Europe. The Reformation freed the nations of Europe from the grip the Catholic Church had on most aspects of life: government, education, scientific research, and publication of books, among others. The emphasis on personal belief rather than Church authority sparked a renewed interest in learning. This interest, in turn, fueled the rapid artistic, intellectual, and social advancement of Europe.

Further Reading

■ **Books**

Atkinson, James. *The Great Light: Luther and the Reformation.* Grand Rapids, Mich.: Eerdmans, 1968.

Bainton, Roland. *Here I Stand: A Life of Martin Luther.* London: Penguin, 2002.

Brecht, Martin. *Martin Luther,* trans. James L. Schaaf. 3 vols. Minneapolis, Minn.: Fortress Press, 1985–1993.

Ebeling, Gerhard. *Luther: An Introduction to His Thought.* Philadelphia: Fortress Press, 1970.

Questions for Further Study

1. What were the intersections between politics and religion in the context surrounding Luther's theses? What were the intersections between money and religion in the same context?

2. What were some of the Church abuses to which Luther objected? On what specific grounds did he object to them?

3. Luther's beliefs, and the actions he took on those beliefs, might seem almost tame today. He did not deny the existence of God, the divinity of Christ, or most other fundamental Church doctrines. Yet his actions attracted a great deal of attention from Rome, led to the Diet of Worms, and caused his excommunication from the Church. Why was the Church so troubled by the teachings of one priest in Germany?

4. Why do you think Catholics in Europe and North America were held in such suspicion in the centuries following the Protestant Reformation?

5. In the modern world, there are numerous Protestant denominations, among them Methodists, Baptists, Seventh-day Adventists, various Reformed churches, and Anabaptists (including the Amish, Mennonites, and Quakers). Additionally, there are numerous small sects, such as the Churches of Christ, the Zion Christian Church, and the Free Apostolic Church of Pentecost, among many others. What do you believe Luther would have thought about this proliferation of Protestant denominations and sects? What do you believe he would have thought about the prominence of nondenominational televangelists in the modern world?

Edwards, Mark U., Jr. *Luther's Last Battles: Politics and Polemics, 1531–46*. Ithaca, N.Y.: Cornell University Press, 1983.

Estep, William Roscoe. *Renaissance and Reformation*. Grand Rapids, Mich.: Eerdmans, 1986.

Kolb, Robert. *Martin Luther: Confessor of the Faith*. New York: Oxford University Press, 2009.

Krey, Philip D. W., and Peter D. S. Krey, eds. *Luther's Spirituality*. New York: Paulist Press, 2007.

Lohse, Bernhard. *Martin Luther: An Introduction to His Life and Work*. Philadelphia: Fortress Press, 1986.

Wilson, Derek. *Out of the Storm: The Life and Legacy of Martin Luther*. New York: St. Martin's Press, 2008.

■ Web Sites

Kreis, Steven. "Lectures on Early Modern European History—Lecture 3: The Protestant Reformation." History Guide Web site.
http://www.historyguide.org/earlymod/lecture3c.html.

"Martin Luther: The Reluctant Revolutionary." PBS Web site.
http://www.pbs.org/empires/martinluther.

—Andrew J. Waskey and Michael J. O'Neal

Martin Luther: Ninety-five Theses

Disputation of Doctor Martin Luther on the Power and Efficacy of Indulgences

October 31, 1517

Out of love for the truth and the desire to bring it to light, the following propositions will be discussed at Wittenberg, under the presidency of the Reverend Father Martin Luther, Master of Arts and of Sacred Theology, and Lecturer in Ordinary on the same at that place. Wherefore he requests that those who are unable to be present and debate orally with us, may do so by letter.

In the Name our Lord Jesus Christ. Amen.

1. Our Lord and Master Jesus Christ, when He said *Poenitentiam agite*, willed that the whole life of believers should be repentance.

2. This word cannot be understood to mean sacramental penance, i.e., confession and satisfaction, which is administered by the priests.

3. Yet it means not inward repentance only; nay, there is no inward repentance which does not outwardly work divers mortifications of the flesh.

4. The penalty [of sin], therefore, continues so long as hatred of self continues; for this is the true inward repentance, and continues until our entrance into the kingdom of heaven.

5. The pope does not intend to remit, and cannot remit any penalties other than those which he has imposed either by his own authority or by that of the Canons.

6. The pope cannot remit any guilt, except by declaring that it has been remitted by God and by assenting to God's remission; though, to be sure, he may grant remission in cases reserved to his judgment. If his right to grant remission in such cases were despised, the guilt would remain entirely unforgiven.

7. God remits guilt to no one whom He does not, at the same time, humble in all things and bring into subjection to His vicar, the priest.

8. The penitential canons are imposed only on the living, and, according to them, nothing should be imposed on the dying.

9. Therefore the Holy Spirit in the pope is kind to us, because in his decrees he always makes exception of the article of death and of necessity.

10. Ignorant and wicked are the doings of those priests who, in the case of the dying, reserve canonical penances for purgatory.

11. This changing of the canonical penalty to the penalty of purgatory is quite evidently one of the tares that were sown while the bishops slept.

12. In former times the canonical penalties were imposed not after, but before absolution, as tests of true contrition.

13. The dying are freed by death from all penalties; they are already dead to canonical rules, and have a right to be released from them.

14. The imperfect health [of soul], that is to say, the imperfect love, of the dying brings with it, of necessity, great fear; and the smaller the love, the greater is the fear.

15. This fear and horror is sufficient of itself alone (to say nothing of other things) to constitute the penalty of purgatory, since it is very near to the horror of despair.

16. Hell, purgatory, and heaven seem to differ as do despair, almost-despair, and the assurance of safety.

17. With souls in purgatory it seems necessary that horror should grow less and love increase.

18. It seems unproved, either by reason or Scripture, that they are outside the state of merit, that is to say, of increasing love.

19. Again, it seems unproved that they, or at least that all of them, are certain or assured of their own blessedness, though we may be quite certain of it.

20. Therefore by "full remission of all penalties" the pope means not actually "of all," but only of those imposed by himself.

21. Therefore those preachers of indulgences are in error who say that by the pope's indulgences a man is freed from every penalty, and saved;

22. Whereas he remits to souls in purgatory no penalty which, according to the canons, they would have had to pay in this life.

23. If it is at all possible to grant to any one the remission of all penalties whatsoever, it is certain that this remission can be granted only to the most perfect, that is, to the very fewest.

24. It must needs be, therefore, that the greater part of the people are deceived by that indiscriminate and high-sounding promise of release from penalty.

25. The power which the pope has, in a general way, over purgatory, is just like the power which any bishop or curate has, in a special way, within his own diocese or parish.

26. The pope does well when he grants remission to souls [in purgatory], not by the power of the keys (which he does not possess), but by way of intercession.

27. They preach only human doctrines who say that so soon as the penny jingles into the money-box, the soul flies out [of purgatory].

28. It is certain that when the penny jingles into the money-box, gain and avarice can be increased, but the result of the intercession of the Church is in the power of God alone.

29. Who knows whether all the souls in purgatory wish to be bought out of it, as in the legend of Sts. Severinus and Paschal.

30. No one is sure that his own contrition is sincere; much less that he has attained full remission.

31. Rare as is the man that is truly penitent, so rare is also the man who truly buys indulgences, i.e., such men are most rare.

32. They will be condemned eternally, together with their teachers, who believe themselves sure of their salvation because they have letters of pardon.

33. Men must be on their guard against those who say that the pope's pardons are that inestimable gift of God by which man is reconciled to Him;

34. For these "graces of pardon" concern only the penalties of sacramental satisfaction, and these are appointed by man.

35. They preach no Christian doctrine who teach that contrition is not necessary in those who intend to buy souls out of purgatory or to buy confessionalia.

36. Every truly repentant Christian has a right to full remission of penalty and guilt, even without letters of pardon.

37. Every true Christian, whether living or dead, has part in all the blessings of Christ and the Church; and this is granted him by God, even without letters of pardon.

38. Nevertheless, the remission and participation [in the blessings of the Church] which are granted by the pope are in no way to be despised, for they are, as I have said, the declaration of divine remission.

39. It is most difficult, even for the very keenest theologians, at one and the same time to commend to the people the abundance of pardons and [the need of] true contrition.

40. True contrition seeks and loves penalties, but liberal pardons only relax penalties and cause them to be hated, or at least, furnish an occasion [for hating them].

41. Apostolic pardons are to be preached with caution, lest the people may falsely think them preferable to other good works of love.

Document Text

42. Christians are to be taught that the pope does not intend the buying of pardons to be compared in any way to works of mercy.

43. Christians are to be taught that he who gives to the poor or lends to the needy does a better work than buying pardons;

44. Because love grows by works of love, and man becomes better; but by pardons man does not grow better, only more free from penalty.

45. Christians are to be taught that he who sees a man in need, and passes him by, and gives [his money] for pardons, purchases not the indulgences of the pope, but the indignation of God.

46. Christians are to be taught that unless they have more than they need, they are bound to keep back what is necessary for their own families, and by no means to squander it on pardons.

47. Christians are to be taught that the buying of pardons is a matter of free will, and not of commandment.

48. Christians are to be taught that the pope, in granting pardons, needs, and therefore desires, their devout prayer for him more than the money they bring.

49. Christians are to be taught that the pope's pardons are useful, if they do not put their trust in them; but altogether harmful, if through them they lose their fear of God.

50. Christians are to be taught that if the pope knew the exactions of the pardon-preachers, he would rather that St. Peter's church should go to ashes, than that it should be built up with the skin, flesh and bones of his sheep.

51. Christians are to be taught that it would be the pope's wish, as it is his duty, to give of his own money to very many of those from whom certain hawkers of pardons cajole money, even though the church of St. Peter might have to be sold.

52. The assurance of salvation by letters of pardon is vain, even though the commissary, nay, even though the pope himself, were to stake his soul upon it.

53. They are enemies of Christ and of the pope, who bid the Word of God be altogether silent in some Churches, in order that pardons may be preached in others.

54. Injury is done the Word of God when, in the same sermon, an equal or a longer time is spent on pardons than on this Word.

55. It must be the intention of the pope that if pardons, which are a very small thing, are celebrated with one bell, with single processions and ceremonies, then the Gospel, which is the very greatest thing, should be preached with a hundred bells, a hundred processions, a hundred ceremonies.

56. The "treasures of the Church," out of which the pope grants indulgences, are not sufficiently named or known among the people of Christ.

57. That they are not temporal treasures is certainly evident, for many of the vendors do not pour out such treasures so easily, but only gather them.

58. Nor are they the merits of Christ and the Saints, for even without the pope, these always work grace for the inner man and the cross, death, and hell for the outward man.

59. St. Lawrence said that the treasures of the Church were the Church's poor, but he spoke according to the usage of the word in his own time.

60. Without rashness we say that the keys of the Church, given by Christ's merit, are that treasure;

61. For it is clear that for the remission of penalties and of reserved cases, the power of the pope is of itself sufficient.

62. The true treasure of the Church is the Most Holy Gospel of the glory and the grace of God.

63. But this treasure is naturally most odious, for it makes the first to be last.

64. On the other hand, the treasure of indulgences is naturally most acceptable, for it makes the last to be first.

65. Therefore the treasures of the Gospel are nets with which they formerly were wont to fish for men of riches.

66. The treasures of the indulgences are nets with which they now fish for the riches of men.

67. The indulgences which the preachers cry as the "greatest graces" are known to be truly such, in so far as they promote gain.

68. Yet they are in truth the very smallest graces compared with the grace of God and the piety of the Cross.

69. Bishops and curates are bound to admit the commissaries of apostolic pardons, with all reverence.

70. But still more are they bound to strain all their eyes and attend with all their ears, lest these men preach their own dreams instead of the commission of the pope.

71. He who speaks against the truth of apostolic pardons, let him be anathema and accursed!

72. But he who guards against the lust and license of the pardon-preachers, let him be blessed!

73. The pope justly thunders against those who, by any art, contrive the injury of the traffic in pardons.

74. But much more does he intend to thunder against those who use the pretext of pardons to contrive the injury of holy love and truth.

75. To think the papal pardons so great that they could absolve a man even if he had committed an impossible sin and violated the Mother of God—this is madness.

76. We say, on the contrary, that the papal pardons are not able to remove the very least of venial sins, so far as its guilt is concerned.

77. It is said that even St. Peter, if he were now Pope, could not bestow greater graces; this is blasphemy against St. Peter and against the pope.

78. We say, on the contrary, that even the present pope, and any pope at all, has greater graces at his disposal; to wit, the Gospel, powers, gifts of healing, etc., as it is written in I. Corinthians xii.

79. To say that the cross, emblazoned with the papal arms, which is set up [by the preachers of indulgences], is of equal worth with the Cross of Christ, is blasphemy.

80. The bishops, curates and theologians who allow such talk to be spread among the people, will have an account to render.

81. This unbridled preaching of pardons makes it no easy matter, even for learned men, to rescue the reverence due to the pope from slander, or even from the shrewd questionings of the laity.

82. To wit:—"Why does not the pope empty purgatory, for the sake of holy love and of the dire need of the souls that are there, if he redeems an infinite number of souls for the sake of miserable money with which to build a Church? The former reasons would be most just; the latter is most trivial."

83. Again:—"Why are mortuary and anniversary masses for the dead continued, and why does he not return or permit the withdrawal of the endowments founded on their behalf, since it is wrong to pray for the redeemed?"

84. Again:—"What is this new piety of God and the pope, that for money they allow a man who is impious and their enemy to buy out of purgatory the pious soul of a friend of God, and do not rather, because of that pious and beloved soul's own need, free it for pure love's sake?"

85. Again:—"Why are the penitential canons long since in actual fact and through disuse abrogated and dead, now satisfied by the granting of indulgences, as though they were still alive and in force?"

86. Again:—"Why does not the pope, whose wealth is to-day greater than the riches of the richest, build just this one church of St. Peter with his own money, rather than with the money of poor believers?"

87. Again:—"What is it that the pope remits, and what participation does he grant to those who, by perfect contrition, have a right to full remission and participation?"

88. Again:—"What greater blessing could come to the Church than if the pope were to do a hundred times a day what he now does once, and

Document Text

bestow on every believer these remissions and participations?"

89. "Since the pope, by his pardons, seeks the salvation of souls rather than money, why does he suspend the indulgences and pardons granted heretofore, since these have equal efficacy?"

90. To repress these arguments and scruples of the laity by force alone, and not to resolve them by giving reasons, is to expose the Church and the pope to the ridicule of their enemies, and to make Christians unhappy.

91. If, therefore, pardons were preached according to the spirit and mind of the pope, all these doubts would be readily resolved; nay, they would not exist.

92. Away, then, with all those prophets who say to the people of Christ, "Peace, peace," and there is no peace!

93. Blessed be all those prophets who say to the people of Christ, "Cross, cross," and there is no cross!

94. Christians are to be exhorted that they be diligent in following Christ, their Head, through penalties, deaths, and hell;

95. And thus be confident of entering into heaven rather through many tribulations, than through the assurance of peace.

Glossary

Apostolic pardon	an indulgence, given by a priest, for the remission (releasing from guilt) of sins
commissary	in this context, the person responsible for executing a function of a superior
greater graces	as enumerated in 1 Corinthians 12:4–11
mortuary and anniversary masses	respectively, masses for the dead individually and for all those who have died in a given year
St. Lawrence	a bishop who was tortured and martyred in the third century, during the reign of the Roman emperor Valerian
St. Peter's church	the Catholic (that is, universal) Church
Sts. Severinus and Paschal	respectively, a French abbot of the sixth century, famed for his exercise of penance, and an Italian pope (Paschal I) of the eighth century who oversaw restoration of basilicas in Rome
tares that were sown	an allusion to the parable of Jesus given in Matthew 13:24–30
true contrition	repentance that includes the firm will never to sin again

Aleister Crowley
(AP/Wide World Photos)

THE KEY OF SOLOMON THE KING

ca. 1525

"I saw that all the writings and wisdom of this present age were vain and futile, and that no man was perfect."

Overview

The Key of Solomon the King (in Latin, Clavis Salomonis or Clavicula Salomonis) is a grimoire, a handbook for how to carry out various magical rituals through summoning demons. Grimoires are a common element of popular culture. They are often seen in popular literature, films, and television shows, but these portrayals rarely relate very closely to historical realities. Nevertheless, The Key of Solomon the King is the source of the common image of the grimoire, with its combination of demonic conjurations and spells based on the power of magical names. The grimoire is a genre almost as old as writing in ancient Egypt and Mesopotamia. The oldest magical handbooks had tremendous prestige, since they contained rituals for protecting and benefiting the king and the state. Over time the ritualists who used such books adapted them to the needs of a more popular audience. This trend increased as Near Eastern magic was received in the Greek and Roman worlds. Magic was mainly meant to benefit the individual at the expense of society through attacking business rivals, subverting the courts, seducing married women, and the like.

The Key of Solomon was composed in the early sixteenth century by an unknown humanist, probably an Italian priest. However, the magical way of thinking championed by the text was abandoned during the Scientific Revolution (beginning in the mid-sixteenth century) and, later, the Enlightenment, and the text fell into obscurity. The Key of Solomon assumed its historical importance in the late nineteenth century, when it was revived because it had been forgotten, to serve as the cornerstone of the modern occultist movement.

Context

The precise context of the original composition of The Key of Solomon the King cannot be recovered, since the author is unknown. The document claims to be by King Solomon, the son of David, but this an example of pseudepigraphy, the legitimatization of a religious or magical book by linking it to a culture hero of the distant past. Solomon, famous for his wisdom, was highly suitable for this purpose. Magical books circulating within Christian communities were attributed to Solomon as early as The Testament of Solomon in the first to third centuries, linked to myths about his use of demons and magic to build the original Jewish Temple. The tradition flourished in the late Byzantine Empire with such books as the fourteenth-century Magical Treatise of Solomon, the probable inspiration for The Key of Solomon. When Byzantine scholars fled the Turks in the years before the fall of Constantinople in 1453, they brought magical books to Italy along with the vast treasury of classical Greek literature. Magic claimed to be ancient wisdom that knew how to control the physical universe. Respected sources such as the Bible and works of the Greek philosophers agreed that magic is a real force in the world. The Renaissance humanists who revived ancient learning were not in a position to question their authorities on this point. What if Solomon really did build the Temple using spirits, and what if that feat could be repeated at will using rituals like those in The Key of Solomon? Or, less fantastically, what if the elements of the world were connected by occult sympathies and the forces of nature and the bodies of human beings could be controlled by knowledge of those sympathies (perhaps through talismanic or spiritual magic, such as is described in The Key of Solomon)? Giovanni Pico della Mirandola, a member of the Platonic Academy in Florence, went so far as to say that magic is the operative part of natural science—technology, in other words. On the other hand, could Christianity, Judaism, and Islam be united in a single religion based on magic and the new revelations it might make possible? The Key of Solomon was composed in about 1525 in this expectant atmosphere, which persisted through the so-called Rosicrucian Enlightenment of the early seventeenth century. But such hopes were never to be fulfilled in the development of science, though occult ideas certainly played their parts in activating the imagination of early scientists like Isaac Newton and Robert Boyle to make some of their discoveries. But, in general, magic was quickly forgotten by Western culture as the world was found to operate on different principles. The Key of Solomon was nevertheless quickly and widely circulated among magicians and translated into the vernacular languages, including English (by 1550) and modern Hebrew.

Time Line

100–300
- The pseudo-Solomonic magical literature tradition, including the *Testament of Solomon*, begins.

1300–1400
- Books of ceremonial magic like *The Magical Treatise of Solomon* are composed in the Byzantine Empire and disseminated to Western Europe.

CA. 1525
- *The Key of Solomon the King* is composed in Latin by an unknown Italian humanist.

CA. 1500–1572
- The British Library Sloane Ms. 3645 and Additional Ms. 36674, the oldest witnesses to *The Key of Solomon*, are produced; both are English versions.

CA. 1600
- The first published text of *The Key of Solomon*—the anonymous Latin text of the *Clavicula Salomonis filii David*—is produced, probably in Germany or the Netherlands.

CA. 1825
- The last known (French) manuscript of *The Key of Solomon* is written.

1854
- January 8 or 11
- S. L. MacGregor Mathers is born.

1885 OR 1886
- Mathers joins the Theosophical Society.

1888
- March 1
- Mathers helps to found the Hermetic Order of the Golden Dawn.

1889
- Mathers publishes *The Key of Solomon the King*.

1904
- Mathers, together with Aleister Crowley, publishes *Goetia: The Lesser Key of Solomon*.

1918
- November 5 or 20
- Mathers dies in Paris, reportedly of the influenza pandemic.

About the Author

Magical books began to be composed in Latin as interpretations rather than translations of Greek originals. *The Key of Solomon* is a magical book,, along with many other similar treatises, including *The Lesser Key of Solomon the King* (in Latin, *Clavicula Salomonis regis* or *Lemegeton clavicula Salomonis*), that were composed during the Italian Renaissance based on Greek grimoires brought by scholars from the Byzantine Empire. The authorship of *The Key of Solomon* as an element within this tradition is completely unknown. It was certainly someone with a humanistic education (trained in Greek). Probably most of the men (and there is no evidence that women participated in scholarly magic) who wrote magical books of this kind in sixteenth-century Italy were priests, whether in monastic life or teaching at universities.

The real importance of *The Key of Solomon*, however, came after it was forgotten by the world at large and then recalled to the mind of the occultist movement by the 1889 edition of S. L. Mathers. His published text became a foundational document of modern occultism. Mathers's choices in handling the unwieldy manuscript tradition, as well as his own transformations of the text, put his stamp on the well-known modern form of the book. Relatively little is known about Mathers's life, and it has not received a detailed scholarly study. Samuel Liddell MacGregor Mathers was born in 1854 as the son of a London clerk and advanced himself through membership in Masonic lodges and occultist societies. He made his mark as the cofounder and leader of the Hermetic Order of the Golden Dawn and occupied himself with editing obscure occultist literature (including *The Key of Solomon*) that even today is generally of interest to historians only in connection with its role in the occultist revival. Mathers seems to have lived largely from the patronage of his wealthy benefactors within the movement. Mathers gave himself the name MacGregor as well as the title Comte de Glenstrae as part of an elaborate fantasy deriving his ancestry from the Scottish nobility. (He purportedly was informed of this identity by spirits whom he "channeled"—perhaps coining the use of that term.) The Scottish connection was important because of his identity as a Freemason, as was the association of the grimoires he translated with Solomon, the mythical founder of Freemasonry. He died during the influenza epidemic of 1918, despite his claims to have partaken of the alchemical elixir of immortality.

Explanation and Analysis of the Document

The Key of Solomon the King begins with an introduction that establishes a pseudohistory for the text. It is purported to be a book written by the biblical King Solomon. After Solomon's death, his son Roboam (or Rehoboam) buried the manuscript with him. It was later discovered by the "Babylonian philosopher" Iohé Grevis, who reburied it after making a translation that became the source of the present text. This document uses several techniques to legitimize

Remains of King Solomon's palace at Megiddo, in modern-day Israel
(AP/Wide World Photos)

the text, beginning with the biblical authority of the figure of Solomon. Moreover, Solomon himself is said to have received the text as a revelation from God through an angel, likening it to the revelation of the law to Moses at Mount Sinai (mediated by an angel, according to Paul's Epistle to the Galatians 3:19). An angel also reveals the translation of the text to Iohé, who, as a Babylonian philosopher, may be compared to the Magi from the East who attended Jesus's birth (Gospel of Matthew 2:1). Aware that they were using translations, the learned magicians of the Renaissance had to invest the act of translation itself with the same authority as an original. Within the humanistic context of *The Key of Solomon*'s composition, this story credits the text not only with biblical authority but also with the authority of an ancient text, superior because "all the writings and wisdom of this present age were vain and futile." For Mathers, the modern editor of *The Key of Solomon*, the angelic revelation—especially the angelic translation that enables Iohé to see a (presumably) Hebrew text in his own language—authorized his own practice of channeling and automatic writing by which he communicated with his "secret masters."

While Roboam receives the manuscript of *The Key of Solomon* from his father, he does not actually gain knowledge of its secret teaching because, by his own admission, he lacks the learning to understand it. Once the text is translated, Iohé, in contrast, does have the required wisdom because he is a philosopher. He, in turn, swears to the angel to pass the text on only to other experts. Compare this to the dictate in Judaism that the esoteric secrets of theology can be discussed only with other rabbis who are already sages or the provision of the Hippocratic Oath that the teachings of medicine may be passed on only those who agree to keep them secret from nonphysicians. *The Key of Solomon* is an important precedent to the interest of modern occultism in initiation. The ancient model of initiation is well represented by ordinary Christianity, in which the Christian participates in the central rituals of the cult (such as baptism and the Eucharist) and thereafter is considered to be an initiated member of the community. *The Key of Solomon* anticipates and may even have contributed to the Rosicrucian belief of the early seventeenth century that an occult philosophy was handed down from master to pupil in secret lodges. (while Rosicrucianism began as a hoax to the effect that such a lodge was about to reveal its existence, the idea itself loomed large in the scholarly imagination of that era.) Such a chain of initiation from modern users of the *The Key of Solomon* back to Iohé is implied in the text. The purpose of the Golden Dawn was to formalize such initiation. Mathers accounted for his own initiation by fabricating a group of German Rosicrucian adepts who sup-

Essential Quotes

"I understood that in me was the knowledge of all creatures, both things which are in the heavens and things which are beneath the heavens; and I saw that all the writings and wisdom of this present age were vain and futile, and that no man was perfect."

"And when, therefore men had waited for a long time, there came unto the Sepulchre certain Babylonian Philosophers."

"The Prayer being finished, let the Exorcist lay his hand upon the Pentacles, while one of the Disciples shall hold open before him the Book wherein are written the prayers and conjurations proper for conquering, subduing, and reproving the Spirits."

"Behold the Symbols and Names of the Creator, which give unto ye for ever Terror and Fear. Obey then, by the virtue of these Holy Names, and by these Mysteries of Mysteries."

"ADONAI, YAH, HOA, EL, ELOHA, ELOHINU, ELOHIM, EHEIEH, MARON, KAPHU, ESCH, INNON, AVEN, AGLA, HAZOR, EMETH, YAII, ARARITHA, YOVA, HA-KABIR, MESSIACH, IONAH, MAL-KA, EREL, KUZU, MATZPATZ, EL SHADDAI; and by all the Holy Names of God which have been written with blood in the sign of an eternal alliance."

"And I most humbly entreat the possessor of this, by the Ineffable Name of God in four Letters, YOD, HE, VAU, HE, and by the Name ADONAI, and by all the other Most High and Holy Names of God, that he values this work as dearly as his own soul, and that he makes no foolish or ignorant man a partaker therein."

"HE who wisheth to apply himself unto so great and so difficult a Science should have his mind free from all business, and from all extraneous ideas of whatever nature they may be."

"In many operations it is necessary to make some sort of sacrifice unto the Demons, and in various ways. Sometimes white animals are sacrificed to the good Spirits and black to the evil."

posedly had initiated him as well as by his "psychic" communication with secret masters and spirits that validated him as "no unworthy person."

♦ Book I: Chapter V

This part of *The Key of Solomon* gives instructions for summoning demons ("Apostates from God" or "rebellious Spirits"). More than any other single text, this is the source of the most stereotypical image of the magician in popular culture, standing in a magic circle and summoning a fallen angel. In this case, the magician does not make a pact with the demon (an element of the classic German Faust legend) but intends to use the magical power of the demons to activate the talismans and other forms of magic made later in the text. This kind of formal ritual to invoke the sensible presence of a supernatural entity is generally known as ceremonial magic. While the stylized, even decadent, form such magic is given in *The Key of Solomon* is quite late, the basic concepts probably date back to Egyptian and Babylonian rituals to summon a divine presence into a cult statue used in religious worship and to Assyrian rituals to take divination from the spirits of the dead through necromancy. This ritual is part of a series of conjurations the magician can use to summon demons, each one graded with the use of increasing threats and magical power to compel the demon. This kind of conjuration was the ultimate goal of the magic practiced within Mather's Golden Dawn order, but no member except Mathers himself ever received a grade of initiation high enough to perform it.

The magician gains the power to conjure demons from two elements of the text: divine names and histriola, which retell traditional myths to use their sacred power in the magical operations of the magician. The demon is compelled by a large number of names of God in Hebrew and pseudo-Hebrew (EL, ELOHIM, EHEIEH, ELOAH VA-DAATH, and so on). Speaking these names gives the magician the divine power to command demons in the same way that God's speech has the power to create in Genesis. "TETRAGRAMMATON" is Greek for "four-lettered" and refers to the letters YHWH (Yahweh), that form the personal name of the Judeo-Christian god, often considered by magicians as too powerful to utter and which may be referred to only in periphrasis—that is, longer phrasing in place of a shorter form of expression. The text's "Holy Name of God EHEIEH, which is the root, trunk, source, and origin of all the other Divine Names," probably originated as a textual corruption of "Yahweh." Many other nonsensical names throughout the text, such as Iah and Iohé, are probably abbreviated or derived forms of "Yahweh." The magician also uses histriola from the sacred texts of the Bible, for example, Joseph's escape from his brothers, the story of Exodus, or the cherub's expulsion of Adam and Eve from the Garden of Eden. Histriola serve to bring the sacred power attributed to the Bible by its believers into the magical operations of the magician.

♦ Book I: Chapter X

The general instructions for conjuring demons are followed by rituals for achieving specific ends. In this case the magician wants the demon Almiras to make him invisible. Spells for invisibility go back to the magical handbooks that circulated in the Roman Empire. In general, they are supposed to protect the invisible person from detection by the authorities while committing crimes. They may have been sought after by professional criminals, the uncertainty of whose work made them seek out any psychological reassurance they could. Compare this with the escape of the apostle Peter from prison after an angel made him invisible to his guards (Acts 12:5–25). In *The Key of Solomon*, however, any context for the spell has been stripped away, leaving it an abstract exercise. Notice that as the purpose of the spell becomes more physically impossible, the text begins to supply reasons for why it will probably fail. Referring to the extensive astrological and ritual prescriptions the magician must follow to the letter, the author warns: "If thou lettest any of these things escape thee, or if thou despiseth them, never shalt thou be able to arrive at thy proposed end." Invisibility may also relate to the magician's desire to become godlike, insofar as invisibility is a divine attribute. This fed into Mather's conception of magic as the magician's tool of personal spiritual development.

♦ Book I: Chapter XV

In this ritual the magician creates an amulet (copying the text at the end of the section) on a piece of paper to carry on his person at all times. The spell imbues the amulet with power. This amulet is technically known as a victory charm. The purpose of such a charm is to grant the bearer of it success and advantage in any dealings he has with other people. If he is in a lawsuit, he will win it. If he makes a business transaction, he will profit from it. If he wants to seduce a woman, he will succeed. This is a very ancient form of magic, attested in magical texts from Mesopotamia as far back as the second millennium BCE. Most likely it is as old as cities. The kinds of interactions it governs are those had with strangers who can only be met with in cities, not in a village or tribal setting where one would interact only with the small of group of people known throughout one's life. The kinds of social interactions that the spell supposedly aids are those favored by boldness and self-confidence. A person using such a spell would be more likely to succeed in his endeavors because he is confident that he has magic working for him: It would give him a psychological boost. The manuscripts of *The Key of Solomon* contain a number of other victory spells that are more specifically aimed at seducing women, but Mathers excised these from the text because, for all his pretensions as a magician, he had an essentially prudish Victorian moral sensibility.

The form of the spell is highly simplified. One merely writes out the amulet (observing all of the complicated astrological and other technical injunctions enforced by the ritual) and carries it in a pocket. Victory spells can be far more elaborate. Sometimes they require the manufacture of a "voodoo doll" (which were used in European, not Afro-Caribbean, magic and for victory charms, not to attempt murder through magic) that might have to be buried under the victim's (a desired woman, a customer, or a judge, for instance) doorstep or somewhere else where he or she would walk over it. Procedures of that kind probably gave the magician the sense that he was accomplishing something effective, a function analogous to following the astrological and other ritual requirements in *The Key of Solomon*.

The talisman itself consists of a long list of magical names from a wide range of sources. The first set (SATOR, AREPO, TENET, OPERA, ROTAS) is a very common and very old (it has been discovered as graffiti in Pompeii) magical formula. Notice that the text has the uncanny property of reading the same backward and forward and if the words are placed one above the other, the columns of letters will read the same as the rows. Moreover, the text is an anagram of the phrase "*Pater noster*" (the first two words of the Lord's Prayer in Latin) plus A O (alpha and omega, the symbolic designation of Jesus in the book of Revelation). This, too, binds the biblical text into the magical spell. These words are followed by more variants on the tetragrammaton and by the names of the *sephiroth*, the ten mystical stages of creation within God in the Jewish mystical system of the Kabbalah. It ends with the names of biblical heroes, the three great patriarchs, and the three young Jews cast into the fiery furnace by the king of Babylon in the book of Daniel.

♦ **Book II: Prefatory Note**

While the first part of the book gave the detailed rituals of the magicians for conjuration and specific spells, the second deals with general preparations and conditions that pertain to all his rituals. The magician is again reminded to share his knowledge only with other experts and admonished that he must understand and be able to provide the astrological and other contexts for every spell. A prayer to the same effect is offered, in this case giving the names of the Hebrew letters of the tetragrammaton—YOD, HE, VAU, HE—but refraining from using it as a simple name, reemphasizing its power and mystery as the root of the magician's magic.

♦ **Book II: Chapter II**

This section describes the personal preparations of the magician. The later part prescribes his ritual purity and provides a prayer with the greatest variety of pseudo-Hebrew divine names yet seen. But the first three paragraphs are more interesting. The first requires the magician essentially to have an independent living so that he can devote himself entirely to his rituals. The second calls for him to use *The Key of Solomon* as a handbook, so that he must compose the entirety of any particular ritual he wants, using conjurations, prayers, astrological calculations, and so forth drawn from his understanding of the appropriate parts of the text and how they relate to each other. Finally, the third demands that he set aside a particular place dedicated to his magical operations. This is clearly Mathers's model for the Golden Dawn. He sought out and obtained patronage from wealthy students who maintained him so that he could devote himself full time to magic. His principal magical work was in devising specific manuals of instructions and graded rites of initiation for his students. He also constructed a special initiatory chamber in the London headquarters of the Golden Dawn, where he conducted his initiation rituals—something like a small theater where rituals were performed like plays with costumes and stage effects (figures appearing from trapdoors and the like). In this way Mathers at least gained the power of drama to elicit the emotions of his initiates, giving them cathartic and educative experiences.

♦ **Book II: Chapter XXII**

This final section of *The Key of Solomon* makes an interesting contrast to the remainder of the book. The text generally presents its rituals as akin to cabalistic theurgy, in which the magician commands the spirits by assuming the relative role of God through the use of divine names. But this last chapter entirely repudiates that conception, as well as the whole Judeo-Christian tradition, and reverts to the pagan practice of animal sacrifice to spirits—in the Christian view, the worst kind of idolatry and blasphemy. Nothing is done to resolve these contradictions, but perhaps the attraction of *The Key of Solomon* to modern occultism lies in that lack of resolution. Although animal sacrifice is rare in modern occultist practice (and certainly was not performed by the Golden Dawn), the popular image of occultism is just this: animal and even human sacrifice in the black mass that inverts Christianity. The inclusion of these last rituals makes magic simultaneously Christian and anti-Christian, scholarly and popular: a reconciliation of opposites. This inversion of tradition makes occultism a fitting symbol of the counterculture.

Audience

Mathers's 1889 edition of *The Key of Solomon* introduced the work to an entirely new audience. He primarily intended his text to serve for his own use in the creation of new rituals and for the edification of his small circle of devotees in the Golden Dawn as well as his larger Masonic/esoteric circles. *The Key of Solomon* was already famous among such groups, and he aimed to capitalize on their existing interest. But Mathers's book proved popular and took on a life of its own. It has been continuously in print in cheap and widely distributed copies and is now freely available on the Internet. It has become a common reference point for modern esotericism and a point of entry for anyone wishing to begin study within an esoteric tradition.

Impact

The impact of the original composition and eventual publication of *The Key of Solomon the King* was limited to a small network of magicians who were increasingly ignored by the modern world around them. In fact, only a single copy of the seventeenth-century publication of the Latin version of the text survives, now held by the University of Wisconsin at Madison. But the impact of Mathers's edition of *The Key of Solomon* has been foundational for the modern occultist movement. It is not going too far to say that Mathers's publishing output, together with that of his colleague and rival in the Golden Dawn, A. E. Waite, and his errant disciple, Aleister Crowley, is the backbone of modern occultism. The grimoires that they either edited or composed have promoted a new book-based magical tradition, quite different from the oral and manuscript traditions of earlier magicians. The most successful participant in this movement has been Gerald Gardner, the founder of the new and growing religion of Wicca. The rituals he devised for Wicca were principally based on his reading of *The Key of Solomon*. Mathers's *Key of Solomon* is also the basis of the work of many groups and individuals that practice more traditional ceremonial magic, such as the followers of Enochian magic and Chaos Magic. Mathers's work also lives on in a number of Rosicrucian orders of a spiritual or religious character, more than a magical character, such as Crowley's Thelema, and a dozen or so groups that still use some version of the Golden Dawn name.

In the nineteenth century a post-Romantic reaction set in against the industrial society and rationalist system of thought that had been created by the Enlightenment, the Scientific Revolution, and the ascendency of capitalism and democracy. There was little cohesion to the reaction against modernity because it often meant that individuals turned their backs on society or else organized innumerable small groups. One frequent theme, though, was the embrace of magic as the antithesis of modernity and the turning to occult lodges and esoteric schools. Mathers was originally a Mason and a member of Helena Blavatsky's Theosophical Society, which tried to replace modern Western culture by importing into nineteenth-century London an ersatz version of ancient Indian spirituality. It appealed to authority as an alternative to scientific rationalism and empiricism, submitting itself to secret masters who supposedly lived in the Himalayas and with whom Blavatsky was in psychic communication. Blavatsky associated esotericism with the most progressive political causes of the day, such as feminism and the end of British rule in India, and combined them with occult teachings like vegetarianism and antivivisection to produce a social movement that is now frequently described as the New Age.

Mathers and a few others (including women) broke away from the Theosophical Society in 1888 because they preferred the Western esoteric tradition (the past) over Indian lore (the exotic). They founded their own esoteric group: the Hermetic Order of the Golden Dawn. (Mathers was soon channeling his own secret masters.) Their practice consisted of various rituals devised by Mathers, based on his researches into older forms of magic, most important, *The Key of Solomon*. Mathers and his followers were trying to feed a spiritual hunger that they could not satisfy with modernity. This was the common ground between Mathers and his most famous disciple, the Nobel Prize–winning Irish poet William Butler Yeats. The work of the order consisted of a series of initiations into various grades, based on the study of esoteric texts and a university-style examinations system, capped by emotionally powerful ceremonies of Mathers's invention. The revival of a forgotten book like *The Key of Solomon* enabled the retreat from modernity into a private world of spiritual discipline that erased the common concerns of the everyday world.

Mathers's publications of grimoires also established a canon, with *The Key of Solomon the King* as it most prestigious volume, that is honored within modern occultism. In many circles, those books and those books alone are considered the bearer of occult tradition. *The Key of Solomon the King* in particular carries tremendous prestige and is preferred nearly as scripture over the wide range of far older and, by the usual logic of occultism, therefore potentially more authoritative magical handbooks that scholars have been busy publishing and translating into English, such as the Greek Magical Papyri (the first to the fifth centuries CE), the Babylonian series Maqlû (ca. 1000 BCE), the Egyptian Pyramid Texts (ca. 2500 BCE) or early Christian grimoires attributed to Solomon or the Virgin Mary. The existence of this manufactured canon, as much as methodological differences, creates a sharp cultural divide between practitioners and scholars of magic. The canon also imprints Mathers's approach to magic as a spiritual discipline similar to mysticism, rather than a practical art, on much modern occultism. He understood the spirits invoked in magic as somehow representing the higher self of the magician. The rituals of *The Key of Solomon* that he transformed into the initiations of the Golden Dawn were for him a kind of psychological exploration that can be compared to psychoanalysis and other modern schools of psychology developed at the same time as the Golden Dawn. Thanks to Mathers, modern magic is practiced as a tool of psychological inner development rather than a series of practical rituals meant to mediate the magician's encounter with the social world.

Further Reading

■ **Books**

Copenhaver, Brian P. "Magic." In *The Cambridge History of Science*. Vol. 3: *Early Modern Science*, ed. Katharine Park and Lorraine Daston. Cambridge, U.K.: Cambridge University Press, 2006.

Davies, Owen. *Grimoires: A History of Magic Books*. New York: Oxford University Press, 2009.

Duling, D. C., trans. "Testament of Solomon." In *The Old Testament Pseudepigrapha*. Vol. 1: *Apocalyptic Literature and Testaments (First to Third Century A.D.)*, ed. James H. Charlesworth. New York: Doubleday, 1983.

Frankfurter, David. "Narrating Power: The Theory and Practice of the Magical Histriola in Ritual Spells." In *Ancient Magic and Ritual Power*, ed. Marvin Meyer and Paul Mirecki. Boston: E. J. Brill, 2001.

Gilbert, Robert A. "Hermetic Order of the Golden Dawn." In *Dictionary of Gnosis and Western Esotericism*, ed. Wouter J. Hanegraaff. Boston: E. J. Brill, 2005.

Greenfield, Richard P. H. *Traditions of Belief in Late Byzantine Demonology*. Amsterdam: Adolf M. Hakkert, 1988.

Greenwood, Susan. *The Nature of Magic: An Anthropology of Consciousness*. New York: Berg, 2005.

Hanegraaff, Wouter J. "Magic V: 18th–20th Century." In his *Dictionary of Gnosis and Western Esotericism*. Leiden, Netherlands: E. J. Brill, 2005.

Harper, George Mills. *Yeats's Golden Dawn: The Influence of the Hermetic Order of the Golden Dawn on the Life and Art of W. B. Yeats*. London: Macmillan, 1974.

Howe, Ellic. *The Magicians of the Golden Dawn: A Documentary History of a Magical Order 1887–1923*. London: Routledge & Kegan Paul, 1972.

Mathers, S. Liddell MacGregor, trans. and ed. *The Key of Solomon the King (Clavicula Salomonis)*. 1889. Rpt. York Beach, Maine: Samuel Weiser, 1974.

Mathers, S. Liddell MacGregor, and Aleister Crowley, eds. and trans. *The Goetia: The Lesser Key of Solomon the King (Clavicula Salomonis Regis)* 1904. Rpt. Boston: Samuel Weiser, 1997.

Phillips, Richard L. *In Pursuit of Invisibility: Ritual Texts from Late Roman Egypt*. Durham, N.C.: American Society of Papyrologists, 2009.

van Egmond, Daniël. "Western Esoteric Schools in the Late Nineteenth and Early Twentieth Centuries." In *Gnosis and Hermeticism from Antiquity to Modern Times*, ed. Roelof van den Broek and Wouter J. Hanegraaf. Albany, N.Y.: State University of New York Press, 1998.

Waite, Arthur Edward. *The Book of Ceremonial Magic*. 1913. Rpt. New York: Cosimo, 2007.

Winkler, John J. *The Constraints of Desire: The Anthropology of Sex and Gender in Ancient Greece*. New York: Routledge, 1989.

■ **Journals**

Fishwick, Duncan. "On the Origin of the Rotas-Sator Square." *Harvard Theological Review* 57, no. 1 (January 1964): 39–53.

Mathiesen, Robert. "The Key of Solomon: Toward a Typology of the Manuscripts." *Societas Magica Newsletter* 17 (Spring 2007): 1–9.

Pease, Arthur Stanley. "Some Aspects of Invisibility." *Harvard Studies in Classical Philology* 53 (1942): 1–36.

■ **Web Sites**

Peterson, Joseph H. "The Key of Solomon the King." Esoteric Archives Web site.
http://www.esotericarchives.com/solomon/ksol.htm

—Bradley A. Skeen

Questions for Further Study

1. Explain how *The Key of Solomon the King* represents a blending of religion, science, and the occult. Why was this blending attractive during the Renaissance?

2. Why was *The Key of Solomon the King* attributed to King Solomon of the Old Testament?

3. *The Key of Solomon the King* was rediscovered during the occultist movement of the late nineteenth century. Why do you think occultism experienced a revival at this time? What needs did spiritualists, fortune-tellers, and others fulfill for people?

4. *The Key of Solomon the King* is similar to the Book of Enoch in two ways. Both are pseudepigraphical and both purport to pass along esoteric wisdom. Given these two basic similarities, compare the works and explain how they are otherwise similar, and how they differ.

5. *The Key of Solomon the King* belongs to the same category as several works, including the Gardnerian *Book of Shadows*, *Malleus maleficarum*, and *The Magus*. Select one of these other texts and compare it with *The Key*. How does each text embody the views of demonism, witchcraft, and magic?

THE KEY OF SOLOMON THE KING

Book 1

♦ Introduction

TREASURE Up, O my son Roboam! the wisdom of my words, seeing that I, Solomon, have received it from the Lord.

Then answered Roboam, and said: How have I deserved to follow the example of my father Solomon in such things, who hath been found worthy to receive the knowledge of all living things through the teaching of an Angel of God?

And Solomon said: Hear, O my son, and receive my sayings, and learn the wonders of God. For, on a certain night, when I laid me down to sleep, I called upon that most holy Name of God, IAH, and prayed for the Ineffable Wisdom, and when I was beginning to close mine eyes, the Angel of the Lord, even Homadiel, appeared unto me, spake many things courteously unto me, and said: Listen, O Solomon! thy prayer before the Most High is not in vain, and since thou hast asked neither for long life, nor for much riches, nor for the souls of thine enemies, but hast asked for thyself wisdom to perform justice. Thus saith the Lord: According to thy word have I given unto thee a wise and understanding heart, so that before thee was none like unto thee, nor ever shall arise.

And when I comprehended the speech which was made unto me, I understood that in me was the knowledge of all creatures, both things which are in the heavens and things which are beneath the heavens; and I saw that all the writings and wisdom of this present age were vain and futile, and that no man was perfect. And I composed a certain work wherein I rehearsed the secret of secrets, in which I have preserved them hidden, and I have also therein concealed all secrets whatsoever of magical arts of any masters; any secret or experiments, namely, of these sciences which is in any way worth being accomplished. Also I have written them in this Key, so that like as a key openeth a treasure-house, so this Key alone may open the knowledge and understanding of magical arts and sciences.

Therefore, O my son! thou mayest see every experiment of mine or of others, and let everything be properly prepared for them, as thou shalt see properly set down by me, both day and hour, and all things necessary for without this there will be but falsehood and vanity in this my work; wherein are hidden all secrets and mysteries which can be performed; and that which is set down concerning a single divination or a single experiment, that same I think concerning all things which are in the Universe, and which have been, and which shall be in future time.

Therefore, O my son Roboam, I command thee by the blessing which thou expectest from thy father, that thou shall make an Ivory Casket, and therein place, keep, and hide this my Key; and when I shall have passed away unto my fathers, I entreat thee to place the same in my sepulchre beside me, lest at another time it might fall into the hands of the wicked. And as Solomon commanded, so was it done.

And when, therefore men had waited for a long time, there came unto the Sepulchre certain Babylonian Philosophers; and when they had assembled they at once took counsel together that a certain number of men should renew the Sepulchre in his Solomon's honour; and when the Sepulchre was dug out and repaired the Ivory Casket was discovered, and therein was the Key of Secrets, which they took with joyful mind, and when they had opened it none among them could understand it on account of the obscurity of the words and their occult arrangement, and the hidden character of the sense and knowledge, for they were not worthy to possess this treasure.

Then, therefore, arose one among them, more worthy than the others, both in the sight of the gods, and by reason of his age, who was called Iohé Grevis, and said unto the others: Unless we shall come and ask the interpretation from the Lord, with tears and entreaties, we shall never arrive at the knowledge of it.

Therefore, when each of them had retired to his bed, Iohé indeed falling upon his face on the earth, began to weep, and striking his breast, said:

What have I deserved above others, seeing that so many men can neither understand nor interpret this knowledge, even though there were no secret thing in nature which the Lord hath hidden from me! Wherefore are these words so obscure? Wherefore am I so ignorant?

And then on his bended knees, stretching his hands to heaven, he said:

O God, the Creator of all, Thou Who knowest all things, Who gavest so great Wisdom unto Solomon the Son of David the King; grant unto me, I beseech Thee, O Holy Omnipotent and Ineffable Father, to receive the virtue of that wisdom, so that I may become worthy by Thine aid to attain unto the understanding of this Key of Secrets.

And immediately there appeared unto me, the Angel of the Lord, saying:

Do thou remember if the secrets of Solomon appear hidden and obscure unto thee, that the Lord hath wished it, so that such wisdom may not fall into the hands of wicked men; wherefore do thou promise unto me, that thou art not willing that so great wisdom should ever come to any living creature, and that which thou revealest unto any let them know that they must keep it unto themselves, otherwise the secrets are profaned and no effect can follow?

And Iohé answered: I promise unto thee that to none will I reveal them, save to the honour of the Lord, and with much discipline, unto penitent, secret, and faithful persons.

Then answered the Angel: Go and read the Key, and its words which were obscure throughout shall be manifest unto thee.

And after this the Angel ascended into Heaven in a Flame of Fire.

Then Iohé was glad, and labouring with a clear mind, understood that which the Angel of the Lord had said, and he saw that the Key of Solomon was changed, so that it appeared quite clear unto him plainly in all parts. And Iohé understood that this Work might fall into the hands of the ignorant, and he said: I conjure him into whose hands this secret may come, by the Power of the Creator, and His Wisdom, that in all things he may, desire, intend and perform, that this Treasure may come unto no unworthy person, nor may he manifest it unto any who is unwise, nor unto one who feareth not God. Because if he act otherwise, I pray God that he may never be worthy to attain unto the desired effect.

And so he deposited the Key, which Solomon preserved, in the Ivory Casket. But the Words of the Key are as follows, divided into two books, and shown in order. . . .

♦ **Chapter V: Prayers and Conjurations**
PRAYER. O LORD God, Holy Father, Almighty and Merciful One, Who hast created all things, Who knowest all things and can do all things, from Whom nothing is hidden, to Whom nothing is impossible; Thou Who knowest that we perform not these ceremonies to tempt Thy power, but that we may penetrate into the knowledge of hidden things; we pray Thee by Thy Sacred Mercy to cause and to permit that we may arrive at this understanding of secret things, of whatever nature they may be, by Thine aid, O Most Holy ADONAI, Whose Kingdom and Power shall have no end unto the Ages of the Ages. Amen.

The Prayer being finished, let the Exorcist lay his hand upon the Pentacles, while one of the Disciples shall hold open before him the Book wherein are written the prayers and conjurations proper for conquering, subduing, and reproving the Spirits. Then the Master, turning towards each Quarter of the Earth, and raising his eyes to Heaven, shall say:

O Lord, be Thou unto me a strong tower of refuge, from the sight and assaults of the Evil Spirits.

After which let him turn again towards the Four Quarters of the Earth, and towards each let him utter the following words:

Behold the Symbols and Names of the Creator, which give unto ye for ever Terror and Fear. Obey then, by the virtue of these Holy Names, and by these Mysteries of Mysteries.

After this he shall see the Spirits come from every side. But in case they are occupied in some other place, or that they cannot come, or that they are unwilling to come: then let him commence afresh to invoke them after the following manner, and let the Exorcist be assured that even were they bound with chains of iron, and with fire, they could not refrain from coming to accomplish his will.

THE CONJURATION. O ye Spirits, ye I conjure by the Power, Wisdom, and Virtue of the Spirit of God, by the uncreate Divine Knowledge, by the vast Mercy of God, by the Strength of God, by the Greatness of God, by the Unity of God; and by the Holy Name of God EHEIEH, which is the root, trunk, source, and origin of all the other Divine Names, whence they all draw their life and their virtue, which Adam having invoked, he acquired the knowledge of all created things.

I conjure ye by the Indivisible Name IOD, which marketh and expresseth the Simplicity and the Unity of the Nature Divine, which Abel having invoked, he deserved to escape from the hands of Cain his brother.

I conjure ye by the Name TETRAGRAMMATON ELOHIM, which expresseth and signifieth the Grandeur of so lofty a Majesty, that Noah having pronounced it, saved himself, and protected himself with his whole household from the Waters of the Deluge.

I conjure ye by the Name of God EL Strong and Wonderful, which denoteth the Mercy and Goodness of His Majesty Divine, which Abraham having invoked, he was found worthy to come forth from the Ur of the Chaldeans.

I conjure ye by the most powerful Name of ELOHIM GIBOR, which showeth forth the Strength of God, of a God All Powerful, Who punisheth the crimes of the wicked, Who seeketh out and chastiseth the iniquities of the fathers upon the children unto the third and fourth generation; which Isaac having invoked, he was found worthy to escape from the Sword of Abraham his father.

I conjure ye and I exorcise ye by the most holy Name of ELOAH VA-DAATH, which Jacob invoked when in great trouble, and was found worthy to bear the Name of Israel, which signifieth Vanquisher of God and he was delivered from the fury of Esau his brother.

I conjure ye by the most potent Name of EL ADONAI TZABAOTH, which is the God of Armies, ruling in the Heavens, which Joseph invoked, and was found worthy to escape from the hands of his Brethren.

I conjure ye by the most potent name of ELOHIM TZABAOTH, which expresseth piety, mercy, splendour, and knowledge of God, which Moses invoked, and he was found worthy to deliver the People Israel from Egypt, and from the servitude of Pharaoh.

I conjure ye by the most potent Name of SHADDAI, which signifieth doing good unto all; which Moses invoked, and having struck the Sea, it divided into two parts in the midst, on the right hand and on the left. I conjure ye by the most holy Name of EL CHAT, which is that of the Living God, through the virtue of which alliance with us, and redemption for us have been made; which Moses invoked and all the waters returned to their prior state and enveloped the Egyptians, so that not one of them escaped to carry the news into the Land of Mizraim.

Lastly, I conjure ye all, ye rebellious Spirits, by the most holy Name of God ADONAI MELEKH, which Joshua invoked, and stayed the course of the Sun in his presence, through the virtue of Methratton, its principal Image; and by the troops of Angels who cease not to cry day and night, QADOSCH, QADOSCH, QADOSCH, ADONAI ELOHIM TZABAOTH (that is, Holy, Holy, Holy, Lord God of Hosts, Heaven and Earth are full of Thy Glory); and by the Ten Angels who preside over the Ten Sephiroth, by whom God communicateth and extendeth His influence over lower things, which are KETHER, CHOKMAH, BINAH, GEDULAH, GEBURAH, TIPHERETH, NETZACH, HOD, YESOD, and MALKUTH.

I conjure ye anew, O Spirits, by all the Names of God, and by all His marvellous work; by the heavens; by the earth; by the sea; by the depth of the Abyss, and by that firmament which the very Spirit of God hath moved; by the sun and by the stars; by the waters and by the seas, and all which they contain; by the winds, the whirlwinds, and the tempests; by the virtue of all herbs, plants, and stones; by all which is in the heavens, upon the earth, and in all the Abysses of the Shades.

I conjure ye anew, and I powerfully urge ye, O Demons, in whatsoever part of the world ye may be, so that ye shall be unable to remain in air, fire, water, earth, or in any part of the universe, or in any pleasant place which may attract ye; but that ye come promptly to accomplish our desire, and all things that we demand from your obedience.

I conjure ye anew by the two Tables of the Law, by the five books of Moses, by the Seven Burning Lamps on the Candlestick of Gold before the face of the Throne of the Majesty of God, and by the Holy of Holies wherein the KOHEN HA-GADUL was alone permitted to enter, that is to say, the High-Priest.

I conjure ye by Him Who hath made the heavens and the earth, and Who hath measured those heavens in the hollow of His hand, and enclosed the earth with three of His fingers, Who is seated upon the Kerubim and upon the Seraphim; and by the Kerubim, which is called the Kerub, which God constituted and placed to guard the Tree of Life, armed with a flaming sword, after that Man had been driven out of Paradise.

I conjure ye anew, Apostates from God, by Him Who alone hath performed great wonders; by the Heavenly Jerusalem; and by the Most Holy Name of God in Four Letters, and by Him Who enlighteneth all things and shineth upon all things by his Venerable and Ineffable Name, EHEIEH ASHER EHEIEH; that ye come immediately to execute our desire, whatever it may be.

I conjure ye, and I command ye absolutely, O Demons, in whatsoever part of the Universe ye may be, by the virtue of all these Holy Names:—

ADONAI, YAH, HOA, EL, ELOHA, ELOHINU, ELOHIM, EHEIEH, MARON, KAPHU, ESCH, INNON, AVEN, AGLA, HAZOR, EMETH, YAII, ARARITHA, YOVA, HA-KABIR, MESSIACH, IONAH, MAL-KA, EREL, KUZU, MATZPATZ, EL SHADDAI; and by all the Holy Names of God which have been written with blood in the sign of an eternal alliance.

I conjure ye anew by these other Names of God, Most Holy and unknown, by the virtue of which Names ye tremble every day:—BARUC, BACURABON, PATACEL, ALCHEEGHEL, AQUACHAI, HOMORION, EHEIEH, ABBATON, CHEVON, CEBON, OYZROYMAS, CHAI, EHEIEH, ALBAMACHI, ORTAGU, NALE, ABELECH (or HE-

LECH), YEZE (or SECHEZZE); that ye come quickly and without any delay into our presence from every quarter and every climate of the world wherein ye may be, to execute all that we shall command ye in the Great Name of God. . . .

♦ Chapter X: Of the Experiment of Invisibility, and How It Should Be Performed

IF thou wishest to perform the Experiment of Invisibility, thou shalt follow the instructions for the same. If it be necessary to observe the day and the hour, thou shalt do as is said in their Chapters. But if thou needest not observe the day and the hour as marked in the Chapter thereon, thou shalt do as taught in the Chapter which precedeth it. If in the course of the experiment it be necessary to write anything, it should be done as is described in the Chapters pertaining thereto, with the proper pen, paper, and ink, or blood. But if the matter is to be accomplished by invocation, before thy conjurations, thou shalt say devoutly in thine heart:—

SCEABOLES, ARBARON, ELOHI, ELIMIGITH, HERENOBULCULE, METHE, BALUTH, TIMAYAL, VILLAQUIEL, TEVENI, YEVIE, FERETE, BACUHABA, GUVARIN; through Him by Whom ye have empire and power over men, ye must accomplish this work so that I may go and remain invisible.

And if it be necessary in this operation to trace a Circle, thou shalt do as is ordained in the Chapter concerning Circles; and if it be necessary to write characters, etc., thou shalt follow the instructions given in the respective Chapters.

This operation being thus prepared, if there be an especial Conjuration to perform, thou shalt repeat it in the proper manner; if not, thou shalt say the general Conjuration, at the end of which thou shalt add the following words:—

O thou ALMIRAS, Master of Invisibility, with thy Ministers CHEROG, MAITOR, TANGEDEM, TRANSIDIM, SUVANTOS, ABELAIOS, BORED, BELAMITH, CASTUMI, DABUEL; I conjure ye by Him Who maketh Earth and Heaven to tremble, Who is seated upon the Throne of His Majesty, that this operation may be perfectly accomplished according to my will, so that at whatsoever time it may please me, I may be able to be invisible.

I conjure thee anew, O ALMIRAS, Chief of Invisibility, both thee and thy Ministers, by Him through Whom all things have their being, and by SATURIEL, HARCHIEL, DANIEL, BENIEL, ASSIMONEM, that thou immediately comest hither with all thy Ministers, and achievest this operation, as thou knowest it ought to be accomplished, and that by the same operation thou render me invisible, so that none may be able to see me.

In order then to accomplish this aforesaid operation, thou must prepare all things necessary with requisite care and diligence, and put them in practice with all the general and particular ceremonies laid down for these experiments; and with all the conditions contained in our first and second Books. Thou shalt also in the same operations duly repeat the appropriate Conjurations, with all the solemnities marked in the respective Chapters. Thus shalt thou accomplish the experiment surely and without hindrance, and thus shalt thou find it true.

But, on the contrary, if thou lettest any of these things escape thee, or if thou despiseth them, never shalt thou be able to arrive at thy proposed end; as, for example, we enter not easily into a fenced city over its walls but through its gates. . . .

♦ Chapter XV: Of the Experiment of Seeking Favour and Love

IF thou wishest to perform the Experiment of seeking favour and love, observe in what manner the Experiment is to be carried out, and if it be dependent upon the day and the hour, perform it in the day and the hour required, as thou wilt find it in the Chapter concerning the hours; and if the Experiment be one that requireth writing, thou shalt write as it is said in the Chapter concerning the same; and if it be with penal bonds, pacts, and fumigations, then thou shalt cense with a fit perfume as is said in the Chapter concerning suffumigations; and if it be necessary to sprinkle it with water and hyssop, then let it be as in the Chapter concerning the same; similarly if such Experiment require characters, names, or the like, let such names be written as the Chapter concerning the writing of characters, and place the same in a clean place as hath been said. Then thou shalt repeat over it the following Oration:—

THE ORATION. O ADONAI, most Holy, Most Righteous, and most Mighty God, Who hast made all things through Thy Mercy and Righteousness wherewith Thou art filled, grant unto us that we may be found worthy that this Experiment may be found consecrated and perfect, so that the Light may issue from Thy Most Holy Seat, O ADONAI, which may obtain for us favour and love. Amen.

This being said, thou shalt place it in clean silk, and bury it for a day and a night at the junction of four cross-roads; and whensoever thou wishest to obtain any grace or favour from any, take it, having first properly consecrated it according to the rule, and place it in thy right hand, and seek thou what thou wilt it shall not be denied thee. But if thou doest not the Experiment carefully and rightly, assuredly thou shalt not succeed in any manner.

For obtaining grace and love write down the following words
SATOR, AREPO, TENET, OPERA, ROTAS, IAH, IAH, IAH, ENAM, IAH, IAH, IAH, KETHER, CHOKMAH, BINAH, GEDULAH, GEBURAH, TIPHERETH, NETZACH, HOD, YESOD, MAL-KUTH, ABRAHAM, ISAAC, JACOB, SHADRACH, MESHACH, ABEDNEGO, be ye all present in my aid and for whatsoever I shall desire to obtain.

Which words being properly written as above, thou shalt also find thy desire brought to pass.

Book II

♦ Prefatory Note

THIS Work of Solomon is divided into two books. In the first thou mayest see and know how to avoid errors in Experiments, Operations, and in the Spirits themselves. In the second thou art taught in what manner Magical Arts may be reduced to the proposed object and end.

It is for this reason that thou shouldest take great heed and care that this Key of Secrets fall not into the hands of the foolish, the stupid, and the ignorant. For he who is the possessor hereof, and who availeth himself hereof according to the ordinances herein contained, will not only be able to reduce the Magical Arts herein unto their proposed end, but will, even if he findeth certain errors herein, be able to correct them.

Any Art or Operation of this kind will not be able to attain its end, unless the Master of the Art, or Exorcist, shall have this Work completely in his power, that is to say, unless he thoroughly understand it, for without this he will never attain the effect of any operation.

For this reason I earnestly pray and conjure the person into whose hands this Key of Secrets may fall, neither to communicate it, nor to make any one a partaker in this knowledge, if he be not faithful, nor capable of keeping a secret, nor expert in the Arts. And I most humbly entreat the possessor of this, by the Ineffable Name of God in four Letters, YOD, HE, VAU, HE, and by the Name ADONAI, and by all the other Most High and Holy Names of God, that he values this work as dearly as his own soul, and that he makes no foolish or ignorant man a partaker therein. . . .

♦ Chapter II

IN WHAT MANNER THE MASTER OF THE ART SHOULD KEEP, RULE, AND GOVERN HIMSELF. HE who wisheth to apply himself unto so great and so difficult a Science should have his mind free from all business, and from all extraneous ideas of whatever nature they may be.

He should then thoroughly examine the Art or Operation which he should undertake, and write it regularly out on paper, particularly set aside for that purpose, with the appropriate conjurations and exorcisms. If there be anything to mark or write down, it should be performed in the manner specified regarding the paper, ink, and pen. He should also observe at what day and at what hour this Experiment should be undertaken, and what things are necessary to prepare for it, what should be added, and what can be dispensed with.

The which matters being prepared, it is necessary for thee to search out and arrange some fitting place wherein the Magical Art and its Experiments can be put in practice. All these things being thus arranged and disposed, let the Master of the Art go into a proper and fitting place, or into his Cabinet or Secret Chamber if it be convenient for the purpose, and he can there dispose and set in order the whole operation; or he can use any other convenient secret place for the purpose, provided that no one knoweth where it is, and that no man can see him when there.

After this he must strip himself entirely naked, and let him have a bath ready prepared, wherein is water exorcised, after the manner which we shall describe, so that he may bathe and purify himself therein from the crown of his head unto the sole of his foot, saying:—

O Lord ADONAI, Who hast formed me Thine unworthy servant in Thine Image and resemblance of vile and of abject earth; deign to bless and to sanctify this Water, so that it may be for the health and purification of my soul, and of my body, so that no foolishness or deceitfulness may therein in any way have place.

O Most Powerful and Ineffable God, Who madest Thy people pass dryshod through the Red Sea when they came up out of the Land of Egypt, grant unto me grace that I may be purified and regenerated from all my past sins by this Water, that so no uncleanness may appear upon me in Thy Presence.

After this thou shalt entirely immerse thyself in the Water, and thou shalt dry thyself with a towel of clean white linen, and then thou shalt put upon thy flesh the garments of pure white linen whereof we shall speak hereafter.

Document Text

Hereafter, for three days at least, thou shalt abstain from all idle, vain, and impure reasonings, and from every kind of impurity and sin, as will be shown in the Chapter of fast and of vigil. Each day shalt thou recite the following prayer, at least once in the morning, twice about noon, thrice in the afternoon, four times in the evening, and five times before lying down to sleep; this shalt thou do on the three ensuing days:—

THE PRAYER. HERACHIO, ASAC, ASACRO, BEDRIMULAEL, TILATH, ARABONAS, IERAHLEM, IDEODOC, ARCHARZEL, ZOPHIEL, BLAUTEL, BARACATA, EDONIEL, ELOHIM, EMAGRO, ABRAGATEH, SAMOEL, GEBURAHEL, CADATO, ERA, ELOHI, ACHSAH, EBMISHA, IMACHEDEL, DANIEL, DAMA, ELAMOS, IZACHEL, BAEL, SEGON, GEMON, DEMAS.

O Lord God, Who art seated upon the Heavens, and Who regardest the Abysses beneath, grant unto me Thy Grace I beseech Thee, so that what I conceive in my mind I may accomplish in my work, through Thee, O God, the Sovereign Ruler of all, Who livest and reignest unto the Ages of the Ages. Amen.

These three days having passed, thou must have all things in readiness, as hath been said, and after this a day appointed and set apart. It will be necessary for thee to wait for the hour in which thou shouldest commence the Operation; but when once it shall be commenced at this hour, thou shalt be able to continue it unto the end, seeing that it deriveth its force and virtue from its beginning, which extendeth to and spreadeth over the succeeding hours, so that the Master of the Art will be enabled to complete his work so as to arrive at the desired result. . . .

♦ Chapter XXII

CONCERNING SACRIFICES TO THE SPIRITS, AND HOW THEY SHOULD BE MADE. IN many operations it is necessary to make some sort of sacrifice unto the Demons, and in various ways. Sometimes white animals are sacrificed to the good Spirits and black to the evil. Such sacrifices consist of the blood and sometimes of the flesh.

They who sacrifice animals, of whatsoever kind they be, should select those which are virgin, as being more agreeable unto the Spirits, and rendering them more obedient.

When blood is to be sacrificed it should be drawn also from virgin quadrupeds or birds, but before offering the oblation, say:—

May this Sacrifice which we find it proper to offer unto ye, noble and lofty Beings, be agreeable and pleasing unto your desires; be ye ready to obey us, and ye shall receive greater ones.

Then perfume and sprinkle it according to the rules of Art.

Glossary

ADONAI	a commonly used Hebrew name for God, usually translated as "Lord" to suggest God's mastery
EL, ELOHIM, EHEIEH, ELOAH VA-DAATH . . .	various names for God, most derived from Hebrew or pseudo-Hebrew and some possibly corruptions of "Yahweh"
Esau	the son of Isaac and brother of Jacob, who was cheated of his birthright
five books of Moses	the Torah, or the first five books of the Old Testament (Genesis, Exodus, Leviticus, Numbers, Deuteronomy
Iohé Grevis	a putative Babylonian philosopher
Jacob	in the Old Testament, the son of Isaac and the father of the twelve tribes of Israel
Joseph	the favored son of Jacob in the Old Testament
Joshua	Moses' successor as leader of the Israelites, best remembered for having stayed the course of the sun
Kerubim . . . Seraphim	orders of angels
Land of Mizraim	the Hebrew name for Egypt
Methratton	an angel, possibly the one spoken of in Exodus 23:21

Document Text

When it is necessary, with all the proper Ceremonies, to make Sacrifices of fire, they should be made of wood which hath some quality referring especially unto the Spirits invoked; as juniper, or pine, unto the Spirits of Saturn; box, or oak, unto those of Jupiter; cornel, or cedar, unto those of Mars; laurel unto those of the Sun; myrtle unto those of Venus; hazel unto those of Mercury; and willow unto those of the Moon.

But when we make sacrifices of food and drink, everything necessary should be prepared without the Circle, and the meats should be covered with some fine clean cloth, and have also a clean white cloth spread beneath them; with new bread and good and sparkling wine, but in all things those which refer to the nature of the Planet. Animals, such as fowls or pigeons, should be roasted. Especially shouldest thou have a vessel of clear and pure fountain water, and before thou enterest into the Circle, thou shalt summon the Spirits by their proper Names, or at least those chief among them, saying:—

In whatsoever place ye may be, ye Spirits, who are invited to this feast, come ye and be ready to receive our offerings, presents, and sacrifices, and ye shall have hereafter yet more agreeable oblations.

Perfume the viands with sweet incense, and sprinkle them with exorcised water; then commence to conjure the Spirits until they shall come.

This is the manner of making sacrifices in all arts and operations wherein it is necessary, and acting thus, the Spirits will be prompt to serve thee.

Here endeth our Key, the which if thou thoroughly instillest into thy memory, thou shalt be able, if it pleaseth thee, even to fly with the wings of the wind. But if thou takest little heed hereof, and despiseth this Book, never shalt thou attain unto the desired end in any Magical experiment or operation whatsoever.

For in this Book is comprised all science of Magical Art, and it should be strictly kept by thee. And hereunto is the end of our Key, in the Name of God the righteous, the merciful, and the eternal, Who liveth and reigneth throughout the Ages. Amen.

Glossary

Moses	the leader and lawgiver of the Israelites, remembered primarily for having brought the Ten Commandments down from Mount Sinai
Noah	a good man whom God saved from the flood that destroyed humankind
oblation	an offering of worship
pass dryshod through the Red Sea . . .	a reference to the parting of the Red Sea by Moses
Pentacles	amulets
Roboam	presumably Solomon's son
Sephiroth	literally, "enumeration," or, in Jewish mysticism, the ten attributes or emanations through which God reveals himself
Seven Burning Lamps on the Candlestick of Gold . . .	probably a reference to the book of Revelation 1:12 but also referred to in various Old Testament books
two Tables of the Law	the Ten Commandments, written on two stone tablets

Paracelsus
(Paracelsus [1493-1541] [engraving] [b/w photo], French School, [17th century] / Bibliotheque Nationale, Paris, France / Giraudon / The Bridgeman Art Library International)

Paracelsus: Concerning the Nature of Things

1537

"By the art and industry of a skilled Spagyrist a man can be born."

Overview

Paracelsus was one of the most important figures in the intellectual history of the first half of the sixteenth century. He is as famous today as an alchemist as he is for being a pioneering physician. The document examined here, *Concerning the Nature of Things*, which he probably wrote in 1537 (but which was not published until 1572), gives an overview of his thought, which influenced the development of modern science as well as homeopathic medicine and various forms of occultism. It begins with a detailed exposition of perhaps Paracelsus's most bizarre and evocative idea, the creation of an artificial human being, or homunculus.

Paracelsus has ample scope in *Concerning the Nature of Things* to illustrate both his empiricism, born from his cantankerous, contrarian personality, and his transformation of alchemy, which he expands from the art of working with metals into a causative explanation for medicine, physiology, and the entire physical world. The traits he demonstrates of doubt and questioning for their own sake and the idea that human skill and powers of creativity have unlimited potential, helped to guide medicine and chemistry to their modern forms, laying down a foundation for the scientific method and the vast achievements of the natural sciences in succeeding centuries. But Paracelsus's influence was even greater on the development of the occult sciences, which have persisted as highly influential bodies of knowledge in the shadows of natural science and rationalism even into the twenty-first century. Paracelsus's ideas find echoes in later authors from Isaac Newton (1642–1727) to Hans Christian Andersen (1805–1875). His homunculus, in particular, plays a leading role in Johann Wolfgang von Goethe's *Faust* (1808) and is the prototype of Frankenstein's monster in the novel by Mary Shelley (1818).

Context

The popular stereotype of the Middle Ages is that it was a period of benighted superstition. But while the Scholastic philosophers (professors of philosophy and theology at the first universities) of that era saw the supernatural and natural realms married in the control of the natural world exercised by God and his angels, they were generally skeptical of the possibility of mere human beings practicing magic or witchcraft. It did not seem a rational part of nature. The humanism of the Renaissance period, however, regarded the ideas passed down from classical antiquity in a new, exalted way, and Scholastic skepticism gave way to a different attitude: The ancient Greeks and Romans had believed in magic, and so, the humanists thought, it must be true. The educated classes who made up churchmen, lawyers and judges, physicians, and university professors in the Renaissance era all embraced the reality of magic. One result of this credence unfolded in the so-called witch craze, in which hundreds of thousands of people were convicted and executed for practicing witchcraft all over Europe and the European colonies in the Americas as late as the end of the seventeenth century. Another result was widespread acceptance of the conviction that the human being can work wonders and that there is no limit to knowledge. Alchemy, astrology, magic, and the other occult sciences were suddenly respectable and worthy of the most serious attention of scholars from Marsilio Ficino (the leader of the Platonic Academy at Florence in the fifteenth century) to Isaac Newton.

Paracelsus was born into the height of Renaissance occultism, both chronologically and as the son of an alchemist. He trained with the abbot Trithemius, one of the leading occultists of the early sixteenth century. The young Paracelsus learned Trithemius's kabbalistic philosophy (based on the mysticism of the Jews of medieval Spain as mediated to Christian Europe by Ramon Lull and Johannes Reuchlin), which saw everything in the universe, both natural and supernatural, tied together by a network of occult sympathies. Action on earth could affect the heavens, and the whole universe could be read in any single part of it, if one understood the language of which nature was composed. The larger structure of the universe (the macrocosm) was recapitulated again and again in the human being and in every isolated piece of the universe (the microcosm). The universe was alive, and so every bit of it was part of the same living body. Moreover, the world could be interrogated through the intelligences that went to make it up: angels and demons.

Time Line

1494
- ca. May 1 Paracelsus is born at Einsiedeln in central Switzerland.

1515–1516
- Paracelsus studies at the University of Ferrara.

1516–1517
- Paracelsus studies with Trithemius.

1517–1524
- Paracelsus wanders across Europe working as a military surgeon.

1529
- Paracelsus publishes his first pamphlet on syphilis.

1536
- Paracelsus publishes his *Grossen Wundarznei* (Great Book of Surgery).

1537
- It is thought that Paracelsus wrote *Concerning the Nature of Things* at this time.

1537–1538
- Paracelsus is employed as the chief metallurgist at a mine complex near Villach.

1541
- September 24 Paracelsus dies in Salzburg.

1572
- *Concerning the Nature of Things* is published for the first time.

1589–1605
- The Swiss printer Jan Husser publishes a collection of Paracelsus's medical and occultist works in ten volumes.

Paracelsus was by his nature a revolutionary. He accepted traditional occultism, of which medicine now seemed to be part, only as a starting point on which he would build his own new system. In particular, he rebelled against the medical establishment of his day, which described itself as Hippocratic, in that it considered the ancient Greek medical writers like Hippocrates, Galen, and Celsus to be inerrant sources of medical wisdom that could not be criticized or added to. To those invested in the old order, Paracelsus was a dangerous crank; to those who wished to forge ahead to find the truth, he was a visionary leading the way. Paracelsus accepted the occult tradition as an alphabet, as it were, that one had to use to write his own story. Paracelsus's new occultism had one unique feature: It was based on practical experience. His work in mines and as a surgeon exposed the insufficiency of the received scholarly traditions of alchemy and medicine. He broke through barriers of class and intellectual chauvinism to mix the scholarly, abstract learning received from the ancients with the practical work being done by the relatively uneducated professional classes of surgeons and miners. If he saw something in his examination of the human body that contradicted Hippocratic medicine, he did not look for a way to make the observation fit the authority; he plainly said the authority was wrong, and he made his own new hypothesis. Paracelsus's confidence that he could understand and explain all of nature, and achieve anything he pleased based on that understanding, exemplified and forwarded the scientific exuberance of the modern world. Although in many ways what Paracelsus created is only a particular kind of occultism, his reliance on experience to guide him was an important first step in the direction of the scientific method. The revolution in Paracelsus's work is of the same kind as in the work of his contemporary, the astronomer Copernicus. They were both willing to modify ancient tradition based on modern observation.

About the Author

Paracelsus was born probably on May 1, 1491, certainly within a year of that date, at Einsiedeln in Switzerland. His birth name was Philippus Aureolus Theophrastus Bombastus von Hohenheim. The name *Paracelsus* seems to have been given to him later in life by academic colleagues, as it simultaneously served as a Greek translation of *Hohenheim* (with both terms referring to a hilltop) and signified that his medical science had moved beyond that of Celsus, a respected Roman physician. Paracelsus's father, Wilhelm Bombast von Hohenheim, was himself a physician and alchemist, and in his writing Paracelsus frequently acknowledges his father's early instruction of him in these fields. For a brief moment during the early sixteenth century, the proliferation of printed books made it possible for a single individual to gain expert knowledge across every field of learning, before the very growth of knowledge fueled by printing increased the amount of available information beyond any individual's grasp.

Like his more famous contemporaries Thomas More or Erasmus, Paracelsus had the benefit of a universal education (called *pansophia,* or "all learning," at the time). Paracelsus's most influential teacher was Trithemius, the abbot of Sponheim in southern Germany and a leading occultist in his own right. Paracelsus studied at the universities in Vienna and Ferrara but does not seem to have taken a degree. Nevertheless, he did not have any difficulty finding work as a physician, and he wandered around Europe between 1517 and 1524, supporting himself as a battlefield surgeon. Through the late 1520s his fame as a surgeon enabled him easily to find prestigious medical positions either in public health departments or on medical school faculties in Salzburg, Strasburg, and Basel. But almost as soon as he would get such a job, he would be driven out of it by the local medical establishment because of his relentless criticism of traditional Hippocratic medicine.

In the 1530s he did not hold any official appointments, but he traveled around Germany, writing, lecturing, and working in medicine in private practice. He continued to challenge traditional medicine, and he was equally critical of both Catholic and mainstream Protestant Christianity. He was repeatedly banned from cities as a heretic, and he was nearly executed on more than one occasion. In 1537–1538 Paracelsus also worked as the chief metallurgist at a mining complex near Villach, Austria, where he studied the occurrence of mineral deposits firsthand to further his alchemical knowledge. By 1538 his fame based on his writings and practice was, despite its controversial nature, beginning to win for him the patronage of Ferdinand, the viceroy of Austria, and of the new bishop of Salzburg, the city in which he died on September 24, 1541. Paracelsus produced a vast body of technical literature in almost every field of scholarly study, amounting to well over ten thousand pages. Most of it was too controversial to have been published in his lifetime, but the posthumous edition of his works (brought out in Basel after 1589) was among the most popular books of the seventeenth century.

Explanation and Analysis of the Document

Concerning the Nature of Things is a general statement of how Paracelsus's alchemical philosophy explains the natural world and allows the alchemist to manipulate that world. In each chapter he describes a practical alchemical experiment and shows how alchemy explains its result. The first chapter concerns the creation of a homunculus, the second describes the dissolution of gold in acids and its reprecipitation, and the third addresses various means of preventing natural products from spoiling.

♦ Book I: Concerning the Generation of Natural Things

In this book, Paracelsus states how he believes chemical change happens in nature (putrefaction) and then discusses how this knowledge could be used to artificially mimic the natural process, allowing the alchemist to create a homunculus, or artificial human being. Paracelsus realized that in the natural world there is a cycle of life, whereby what is alive dies, decomposes (putrefies), and then is brought back together into a new arrangement to become life once more. He believed that the heat produced by decomposition (which can be observed in the steam rising from a compost pile when it is turned over in the winter) was sufficient to foster life. He saw proof of this in the fact that eggs can be incubated and still bring forth a chick apart from the hen. But Paracelsus further asserts that if a chicken is burned to ashes and those ashes placed inside a *venter equinus*, or mare's womb (this is an alchemical term for horse manure),

Illustration from Goethe's Faust *of Mephistopheles creating a homunculus*
(Illustration from Goethe's 'Faust' depicting Mephistopheles creating a homunculus / Bibliotheque des Arts Decoratifs, Paris, France / Archives Charmet / The Bridgeman Art Library International)

and the whole thing allowed to rot, it will produce a living chicken. Finally, he says the same process can be used to create a human being. ("Spagyrist" is Paracelsus's preferred term for an alchemist, meaning someone who opens and collects the secrets of nature.)

Although it may seem that Paracelsus is departing from his empirical insistence on observation in asserting the validity of a process that he never successfully carried out, a weakness of his system is that he considers folk legends, Jewish beliefs, or any other knowledge rejected by establishment intellectuals as the equivalent of direct observation—he accepts that such knowledge must be true by virtue of its being rejected and despised. It is hard to know what sources Paracelsus had in mind when he was formulating his idea of the homunculus, but there are a number of kabbalistic legends that might have given him inspiration. For instance, he may have been influenced by the story of the Sabbath calf, wherein two rabbis intently study the kabbalah and thereby gain the godlike power to create with the divine name (*Yahweh*, which, in kabbalistic lore, God is said to have spoken to effect the Creation in Genesis). They use this power to make a calf, which they sacrifice to God and eat for their Sabbath meal. By the time they finish eating,

Essential Quotes

"For you must know that in this way men can be generated without natural father and mother; that is to say, not in the natural way from the woman, but by the art and industry of a skilled Spagyrist a man can be born."

"For Mercury is the spirit, Sulphur is the soul, and Salt is the body."

"As man can return to the womb of his mother, that is, to the earth from which the first man sprang, and thus can be born again anew at the last day, so also all metals can return to quick mercury."

"Though this may be of no profit to you, still it is a very wonderful thing."

"There is always one thing placed over against another—one water over against another, . . . one poison over against another, one metal over against another—and the same in many other matters."

"If ever so small a quantity of bread made from flour be put or fall into it, the whole honey is turned into ants, and perishes entirely."

however, they have forgotten what they have learned, and therefore they do not blasphemously challenge the unique position of God. Another basis for the ideas of Paracelsus perhaps may be found in the better-known story of the Golem, in which a rabbi is able to make an artificial man out of clay animated by the divine name: Since humanity may not usurp the divine power, the creature becomes dangerous and has to be destroyed by erasing the name written on its forehead, whereupon it returns to a pile of clay. Older alchemical texts also describe creating artificial life and are closer to Paracelsus's procedure in technical details, but Paracelsus tended to find spiritual meaning in the kabbalah, so most likely he is combining that tradition with more secular ones. It may be that in this passage Paracelsus is merely conducting a thought experiment to imagine how such processes could be carried out in the natural world as he understands it. Certainly he makes it clear that he never attempted the experiment he describes (though many of his supporters and detractors through the centuries have insisted otherwise).

Paracelsus believed that in the course of ordinary procreation, the semen is nurtured and heated in the womb and goes through the process of disassembly and reassembly (it "putrefies," in his terms) to produce an infant. He imagines that if a human being impregnated some other animal (like a sheep), the process, though considered illegal and heretical, would produce a normal human infant. All that is necessary, he maintains, is to provide an environment—the womb—in which the seed can grow, in the same way that a wheat seed grows into wheat in whatever soil it is sown. On the other hand, if the mother imagines or sees a bull, for example, at the time of conception, the force of her imagination might deform the fetus and produce a creature such as a minotaur. Paracelsus cites the Aristotelian idea of the spontaneous generation of simple animals like snakes and insects as well as monsters such as the basilisk from putrefying grain as evidence for his speculation. He goes on to explain monstrously deformed births by positing that in such cases the devil has attacked the mother through her imagination and so caused the deformity, which displeases God—the necessary result is stillbirth or quick postpartum death.

Paracelsus makes a long digression that demonstrates the medieval, as opposed to ancient or kabbalistic, elements that he incorporated into his philosophy. He endorses the common medieval idea that menstrual blood was the opposite of life-creating semen and therefore a deadly poison. It was commonly believed that even a look from the eyes of a menstruating woman could destroy a man. Paracelsus gives a more developed version of this legend in which droplets of menstrual blood that happen to fall on the ground spontaneously generate monstrous basilisks who take on this power of the deadly gaze.

For Paracelsus, it follows from the broader line of reasoning that an alchemist could make a homunculus, or artificial human being. The process Paracelsus envisions is to place human semen in a mare's "womb," let the seed heat through putrefaction for forty days, and then nourish the resultant living creature—not with human blood (as the placenta does) but rather with the arcanum of blood (that is, chemically preserved blood, as described in book 3)—until it is a fully developed infant, albeit of a tiny size. Once the homunculus has matured, it will be able to reveal to its creator all the secrets of nature, because "from such homunculi when they come to manhood are produced giants, pigmies, and other marvellous people, who are the instruments of great things . . . and know all secret and hidden matters." All the alchemist has done is to create artificially what nature does naturally. Paracelsus thus not only believes that such creatures—"children of the wood-sprites and the nymphs," who "are not like men, but like spirits"—exist but also knows how they are created. Moreover, he believes that since they do not have human souls, he can simulate their creation in a laboratory. Such artificial humans would have some virtuous superiority over the human being in that they have never come in contact with the poisonous blood Paracelsus associates with the human womb; it is because of this relative purity that they have access to knowledge and understanding that human beings do not.

Paracelsus then recapitulates his theory of metals, as a background element of his theory of everything. Metals are concocted of three elements, he says—mercury, salt, and sulfur—which correspond to the spirit, soul, and body of human beings. Metals grow in the earth like a fetus in a womb, with mercury being the "Mother of Metals," and each of the seven different metals is a stage of growth. The alchemist does nothing but hasten the natural transmutation of one metal into another. Paracelsus describes in some detail how metals can supposedly be changed from one to another. Any given metal, he thinks, can be, by a series of chemical reactions, brought back to mercury, which is the neutral matter from which all metals differentiate. If this mercury is then transformed back into a specific metal, the new metal will have the ability to "tinge" or change one particular metal only into a different one (such as silver into copper). If this process were to be continued, the mythical philosopher's stone would be produced—a substance with the power to change any metal into any other. The famous transformation into gold obviously would be the most important from a secular viewpoint, but Paracelsus reveals that this is not his viewpoint when he says, "As man can return to the womb of his mother, that is, to the earth from which the first man sprang, and thus can be born again anew at the last day, so also all metals can return to quick mercury." The life cycle of a metal, then, is analogous to the life of a human being, and the creation of the philosopher's stone is like the resurrection and salvation of the dead promised in Christianity.

In this chapter, Paracelsus is making an imaginative leap forward beyond any technology or theory of nature he could have comprehended, to the creation of artificial life in a laboratory, something that scientists are only today becoming able to attempt. At the same time, he is accepting the testimony of the kabbalah and of folk tradition simply on the grounds that they are bodies of knowledge rejected by the learned establishment. He imagines that once he has disproved the theories of conventional physicians and alchemists that whatever he cares to put in place of the refuted knowledge must be true, but really his work of proving what is true has just begun. Paracelsus stands at the cusp between magic and science.

♦ **Book II: Concerning the Growth of Natural Things**

Paracelsus starts this chapter by further explaining the experiment of the homunculus, though he quickly turns to description of alchemical experiments with gold. He describes the process that promotes natural change in the earth, which is manipulated in the creation of the homunculus and which results in effects as various as the growth of crops and the transmutation of metals. He asserts that the process of putrefying the seed is similar to the effect of rain fertilizing the earth. This claim reflects a confusion between the role of seed and rain in agriculture that is very ancient. But he goes on to observe that the conditions that best promote the growth of crops involve the repeated moistening and drying of the soil, the process that for him is equivalent to putrefaction. He claims that doing this artificially can make crops grow even in snow. He reasons that metals grow in this same way and that common minerals and metals like granite or lead can be led through periods of moistness and dryness by the alchemist to grow into "Sol and Luna" (almost certainly here meaning gold and silver). The alchemist is only artificially speeding up natural growth. He presents the growth of hair and nails on corpses as evidence that putrefaction causes growth. He next claims that Sol can be constantly increased so long as it is buried in the ground and "fertilized with fresh human urine and pigeon dung." Here it seems unlikely that Sol means gold; rather Paracelsus is referring to some substance that the alchemists believed contained the essence of gold.

Paracelsus extends his discussion to a process he no doubt carried out and that is still used by chemists today. Gold cannot be efficiently dissolved by any single acid, but it can be acted upon by a combination of nitric and hydrochloric acids that the alchemists called *aqua regis*, or royal water, since it could dissolve the king of metals. The process can be reversed by changing the pH of the water (as we now know) by diluting the acidic mixture with water, boiling off the acid, and adding more water repeatedly until the gold suddenly precipitates. For Paracelsus, the point was the repetition of the hydration and boiling, which he saw as related to the repeated watering and drying of plants already described. This repeated dilution of a solution to finally achieve a miraculous effect would, together with other Paracelsan ideas such as that the dose makes the poison, later become the foundation of homeopathic medicine.

Paracelsus ends the chapter by noting that a rock (but any object will do) can be coated in precipitated minerals if it is exposed to water having a high proportion of minerals in suspension, as springs near caves often do. He evidently did this inside a beaker (cucurbite), and he created a stone accretion in the shape of a beaker that kept its shape when the glass was broken away, which he considered a tremendous novelty. He again sees this as the same sort of repetitive putrefying process he has already described.

◆ **Book III: Concerning the Preservation of Natural Things**

In this chapter, Paracelsus describes the process of decay and how alchemy can prevent it. For Paracelsus, nature works like an Aristotelian syllogism: A thesis and its antithesis combine to form a new synthesis. Similarly, in nature the process that drives development is putrefaction. The alternation of the wet and the dry works a transformation leading through the steps of a process that creates something new. If that new thing is something useful to humans, it is called creation, but if instead the useful becomes useless, it is called decay. Once this is understood, Paracelsus thinks, the process of decay can be stopped by keeping things from mixing with their opposites. The science of alchemy can identify these opposites and thus allow human beings to keep them apart and use art to prevent the natural process of decay.

The text of this chapter, then, is a long list of examples of the preservation of various substances by keeping them from their opposites, which are inimical to them. Some of the examples are based on simple empirical observation: Mothballs made of camphor will keep moths away from cloth. Others are clearly based on observations that Paracelsus made but that he did not analyze or understand in sufficient detail to draw the correct conclusions. Therefore, he believed that when one discovered a half-eaten jar of honey swarming with ants, the honey had reacted with crumbs of bread left in the jar to transform the substance of the honey into ants. Why, one may ask, did he not observe the trail of ants leading from the honey pot to an anthill outside the kitchen window and conclude that the ants were simply raiding the honeypot from their home? As keen as Paracelsus was to overturn false traditions, he was not in the habit of examining and reexamining every new premise, proving it to be true by attempting to falsify it. Since, in the world as he perceived it, the spontaneous generation of ants from honey was a logical explanation of their presence there, the matter did not need to be investigated further.

This same habit leads to other faults of reasoning. It is indeed plain to see that coating an iron implement in oil prevents it from rusting. But why does Paracelsus insist that oil be made from the fat of a sow that had had its uterus removed prior to slaughter? He is no doubt depending on a chain of occult reasoning that would be difficult to reconstruct today. One clue may come from the fact that female farm animals frequently did have their uteruses removed, because it was believed that spaying made them fatten up for slaughter faster and on less feed. Perhaps therefore the fat from such an animal was viewed as superior to, or at least different from, the fat of intact animals. But this belief in turn arose from a mixture of observation, deductions, and unexamined premises that would baffle modern understanding.

Audience

In his lifetime, Paracelsus published only one significant book, a treatise on surgery in 1536. The greater part of his reputation came from the publication of pamphlets and broadsheets (posters that might contain the information equivalent of a half-dozen pages that were a popular medium in the sixteenth century), which mostly dealt with astrology, although he also wrote two widely circulated pamphlets on syphilis (a disease as devastating in the sixteenth century as AIDS was in the late twentieth and early twenty-first). It was not that he did not want to publish his huge corpus of writings on medicine, alchemy, astrology, and theology, but the same intellectual establishments that denied him long-term medical employment prevailed upon municipal governments to censor his writings and ban local printers from taking them on.

In his lifetime, then, Paracelsus's most important audience consisted of students and other physicians to whom he communicated his ideas in person, either in public lectures or privately. This spawned a Paracelsan movement of people ready to propagate his ideas after his death. The publication of Paracelsus's works accelerated after 1560, together with new works by his followers that were also published under the name Paracelsus. Eventually a complete collection of Paracelsus's original manuscripts came into the possession of the Swiss printer Jan Husser, who printed all of the medical and alchemical works between 1589 and 1605 in ten quarto volumes. This collection is the main basis of our knowledge of Paracelsus's works today. He wrote perhaps half that much more on theological topics, which to this day remain largely unpublished, with manuscripts scattered over numerous European libraries and museums. In the seventeenth century Paracelsus's works became a standard part of the medical curriculum and surpassed the Hippocratic corpus as the largest single sector of medical book publishing. A more rigorous application of the scientific method by Robert Boyle (1627–1691) and subsequent chemists in the eighteenth century superseded Paracelsus's alchemy with modern chemistry, and much the same occurred in medicine with discoveries like William Harvey's observation of the circulation of the blood (publication in 1628). By 1800 Paracelsus was dismissed as a relic of the past. Seen as a representative of prescientific ideas, his role in the history of science would not be rehabilitated until the twentieth century. This rejected status, however, gave Paracelsus a new celebrity among occultists who purposefully latched on to old "wisdom" in reaction against science and modernity.

Impact

For all its fumbling, Paracelsus's empirical method was an important step toward placing medicine on a scientific foundation, a process that would not be completed until the nineteenth century. He is justly revered as a founder of the scientific method and has earned the reward of having a lunar crater named after him. Paracelsus was also one of the first important intellectuals to write in the vernacular, in his case German, rather than in Latin, helping to legitimize that practice. Some of Paracelsus's incidental achievements that persist include the invention of laudanum (the ancestor of the modern family of opiate pain-management drugs) and the coining of the metallic name *zinc*.

Paracelsus's writings were a standard part of the medical curriculum throughout the seventeenth century, but, as Mary Shelley points out in her 1818 novel *Frankenstein*, they were already falling out of favor in the eighteenth century as more scientific textbooks became available. This fact does not stop Shelley's hero, Victor Frankenstein, from emulating Paracelsus even at the end of the eighteenth century, and it is clear that Shelley's inspiration for the creation of an artificial man came from Paracelsus's homunculus. Thus there is a direct link between Paracelsus and one of the most popular characters of modern literature and film. In James Whale's 1935 film, *The Bride of Frankenstein*, there is a scene in which several homunculi of a more definitely Paracelsan character are briefly shown.

In other literary contexts, Paracelsus was one of the inspirations for Goethe's *Faust*, not only as a model for the title character but also in the way his experiments are the genesis for the scene involving the creation of a homunculus. Paracelsus appears with some frequency as a figure in the work of other writers from Robert Browning to Jorge Luis Borges.

In 1796, about the same time Mary Shelley's famous story takes place, the Swiss country doctor Samuel Hahnemann, like Victor Frankenstein, turned to the already-discredited theories of Paracelsus, in his case to find a philosophical foundation for a healing theory now referred to as "homeopathic" medicine. Hahnemann began with Paracelsus's hypothesis that smaller doses of a medicine are more effective than larger ones. He extended this idea by diluting the medicine in water, then diluting a drop of that mixture in a large container of water and so on a hundred times or more until, as is now understood from modern chemistry, not a single molecule of the original medicine could be left in the solution, decreasing the dose size to nothing. An important part of the process was "succussing" each new container of diluted solution, meaning that he tapped it with a Bible, a nod to Paracelsus's belief in the magical power of language and in that book's particular arrangement of language. Hahnemann also borrowed Paracelsus's vitalism: the belief that the body is possessed of a mysterious life force, that disease is an imbalance in this force, and that medical treatment is the restoration of balance. This form of treatment with what many consider to be a placebo made some sense when Hip-

Questions for Further Study

1. Alchemy is generally regarded as a pseudoscience, yet the entry states that Paracelsus, an alchemist, laid groundwork that was important to the development of modern science and medicine. How could the practitioner of a pseudoscience accomplish that?

2. Paracelsus belongs to a line of thinkers that includes the authors of the Emerald Tablet and *The Key of Solomon the King,* Helena Blavatsky (*The Secret Doctrine*), Gerald Gardner (*Book of Shadows*), and others. Using these documents, trace a history of magic and the relationship between magic and religion in Western thinking.

3. This document almost demands comparison with Lucretius's similarly titled *On the Nature of Things.* How would you contrast the viewpoints of the two authors about "the nature of things"? Do they share any beliefs?

4. In the nineteenth century, the British poet Robert Browning wrote a dramatic monologue in which the speaker of the poem is Paracelsus, who says, "Truth is within ourselves; it takes no rise / From outward things, whate'er you may believe. / There is an inmost centre in us all, / Where truth abides in fullness; and around, / Wall upon wall, the gross flesh hems it in, / This perfect, clear perception—which is truth." How accurate do you think these lines are in reflecting the views of Paracelsus?

5. The entry notes that the work of Paracelsus was used for propaganda purposes by the regime in Nazi Germany before and during World War II. Why would the Nazis have found his views congenial, however unfairly?

pocratic doctors still used dangerous and ineffective treatments such as bloodletting, and, as Paracelsus himself found without quite realizing it, offering no treatment was better than giving harmful treatment. In the twenty-first century, homeopathy remains a popular alternative to scientific medicine.

Another notable impact Paracelsus has had in more recent times derives from the use made of his legacy before and during World War II by the German National Socialists. One faction of the Nazi movement was extremely interested in occultism, and they saw Paracelsianism as being a more legitimate expression of "Aryan" tradition than modern science. Paracelsus was treated as a hero by this movement, particularly by physicians interested in reviving discredited ideas of vitalism. Despite his interest in the Jewish kabbalah, Paracelsus exhibited the reflexive anti-Semitism that was all too common in the sixteenth century, and his views were appropriated and used to justify the even-more-malignant anti-Semitism of the Nazis. He was particularly venerated by the Nazi medical establishment that laid down the intellectual foundation of the Holocaust. His status as a Nazi "hero" was enshrined in the 1943 film *Paracelsus*, which was directed by G. W. Pabst under pressure from the Nazi propaganda minister Joseph Goebbels. Of course, the misuse made of Paracelsus's legacy does not brand him as a Nazi before Nazism, any more than homeopathy can be read back into his medical work.

Further Reading

■ Books

Debus, Allen G. *Man and Nature in the Renaissance*. Cambridge, U.K.: Cambridge University Press, 1978.

Newman, William. "The Homunculus and His Forebears: Wonders of Art and Nature." In *Natural Particulars: Nature and the Disciplines in Renaissance Europe*, ed. Anthony Grafton and Nancy Siraisi. Boston: MIT Press, 1999.

Pagel, Walter. *Paracelsus: An Introduction to Philosophical Medicine in the Era of the Renaissance*. Basel: S. Krager, 1958.

Paracelsus. *Four Treatises*, ed. Henry Sigerist. Baltimore: Johns Hopkins University Press, 1941.

Paracelsus. *The Hermetic and Alchemical Writings of Aureolus Philippus Theophrastus Bombast of Hoheneheim, Called Paracelsus*. Vol. 1: *Hermetic Chemistry*, trans. A. E. Waite. London: James Eliot 1894.

Paracelsus. *Selected Writings*, ed. Jolande Jacob. Princeton, N.J.: Princeton University Press, 1969.

Prachter, Henry M. *Magic into Science: The Story of Paracelsus*. New York: Henry Schuman, 1951.

Scholem, Gershom. *On the Kabbalah and Its Symbolism*. New York: Schocken, 1965.

Shelley, Mary. *The Annotated Frankenstein*, ed. Leonard Wolf. New York: Clarkson N. Potter, 1977.

Shumaker, Wayne. *The Occult Sciences in the Renaissance: A Study in Intellectual Patterns*. Berkeley: University of California Press, 1972.

Webster, Charles. *Paracelsus: Medicine, Magic, and Mission at the End of Time*. New Haven, Conn.: Yale University Press, 2008.

■ Journals

Johnston, Sheila. "Ideological Ambiguity in G. W. Pabst's *Paracelsus* (1943)." *Monatshefte* 83, no. 2 (1991): 104–126.

Timmermann, Carsten. "Constitutional Medicine, Neoromanticism, and the Politics of Anti-mechanism in Interwar Germany." *Bulletin of the History of Medicine* 75, no. 4 (2001): 717–739.

■ Web Sites

The Zurich Paracelsus Project Web site.
    http://www.paracelsus.uzh.ch/index.html

—Bradley A. Skeen

Paracelsus: Concerning the Nature of Things

Book I: Concerning the Generation of Natural Things

THE generation of all natural things is twofold: one which takes place by Nature without Art, the other which is brought about by Art, that is to say, by Alchemy, though, generally, it might be said that all things are generated from the earth by the help of putrefaction. For putrefaction is the highest grade, and the first initiative to generation. But putrefaction originates from a moist heat. For a constant moist heat produces putrefaction and transmutes all natural things from their first form and essence, as well as their force and efficacy, into something else. For as putrefaction in the bowels transmutes and reduces all foods into dung, so, also, without the belly, putrefaction in glass transmutes all things from one form to another, from one essence to another, from one colour to another, from one odour to another, from one virtue to another, from one force to another, from one set of properties to another, and, in a word, from one quality to another. For it is known and proved by daily experience that many good things which are healthful and a medicine, become, after their putrefaction, bad, unwholesome, and mere poison. So, on the other hand, many things are bad, unwholesome, poisonous, and hurtful, which after their putrefaction become good, lose all their evil effect, and make notable medicines. For putrefaction brings forth great effects, as we have a good example in the sacred gospel, where Christ says, "Unless a grain of wheat be cast forth into a field and putrefy, it cannot bear fruit a hundred fold." Hence it may be known that many things are multiplied by putrefaction so that they produce excellent fruit. For putrefaction is the change and death of all things, and the destruction of the first essence of all natural objects, from whence there issues forth for us regeneration and a new birth ten thousand times better than before.

Since, then, putrefaction is the first step and commencement of generation, it is in the highest degree necessary that we should thoroughly understand this process. But there are many kinds of putrefaction, and one produces its generation better than another, one more quickly than another. We have also said that what is moist and warm constitutes the first grade and the beginning of putrefaction, which procreates all things as a hen procreates her eggs. Wherefore by and in putrefaction everything becomes mucilaginous phlegm and living matter, whatever it eventually turns out to be. You see an example in eggs, wherein is mucilaginous moisture, which by continuous heat putrefies and is quickened into the living chicken, not only by the heat which comes from the hen, but by any similar heat. For by such a degree of heat eggs can be brought to maturity in glass, and by the heat of ashes, so that they become living birds. Any man, too, can bring the *egg* to maturity under his own arm and procreate the chicken as well as the hen. And here something more is to be noticed. If the living bird be burned to dust and ashes in a sealed cucurbite with the third degree of fire, and then, still shut up, be putrefied with the highest degree of putrefaction in a *venter equinus* so as to become a mucilaginous phlegm, then that phlegm can again be brought to maturity, and so, renovated and restored, can become a living bird, provided the phlegm be once more enclosed in its jar or receptacle. This is to revive the dead by regeneration and clarification, which is indeed a great and profound miracle of Nature. By this process all birds can be killed and again made to live, to be renovated and restored. This is the very greatest and highest miracle and mystery of God, which God has disclosed to mortal man. For you must know that in this way men can be generated without natural father and mother; that is to say, not in the natural way from the woman, but by the art and industry of a skilled Spagyrist a man can be born and grow, as will hereafter be described.

It is also possible to Nature that men should be born from animals, and this result has natural causes, but still it cannot be produced without heresy and impiety. If a man have connection with an animal, and that animal, like a woman, receives the seed of the man with appetite and lust into its womb, and shuts it up there, then the seed necessarily putrefies, and, through the continuous heat of the body, a man, and not an animal, is born from it. For always, whatever seed is sown, such a fruit is produced from it. If this were not so it would be against the light of Nature and contrary to philosophy. Whatever the seed is, such is the herb which springs from it. From the seed of an onion an onion springs up, not a rose, a nut, or a lettuce. So, too, from corn comes corn; from barley, barley; from oats, oats. Thus it is, too, with all other fruits which have seeds and are sown.

In like manner, it is possible, and not contrary to Nature, that from a woman and a man an irrational animal should be born. Neither on this account should the same judgment be passed on a woman as on a man, that is, she should not on this account be deemed heretical, as if she had acted contrary to Nature; but the result must be assigned to imagination. Imagination is very frequently the cause of this: and the imagination of a pregnant woman is so active that in conceiving seed into her body she can transmute the fœtus in different ways: since her interior stars are so strongly directed to the fœtus that they produce impression and influence. Wherefore an infant in the mother's womb is, during its formation, as much in the hand and under the will of the mother as clay in the hand of the potter, who from it forms and makes what he likes and whatever pleases him. So the pregnant mother forms the fruit in her own body according to her imagination, and as her stars are. Thus it often happens that from the seed of a man are begotten cattle or other horrible monsters, as the imagination of the mother was strongly directed towards the embryo.

But as you have already heard that many and various things are generated and quickened out of putrefaction, so you should know that from different herbs, by a process of putrefaction, animals are produced, as those who have experience of such matters are aware. Here, too, you should learn that such animals as are produced in and by putrefaction do all of them contain some poison and are venomous; but one contains far more and more potent virus than another, and one is in one form, another in another, as you see in the case of serpents, toads, frogs, basilisks, spiders, bees, ants, and many worms, such as canker-worms, in locusts, and other creatures, all of which are produced out of putrefaction. For many monsters are produced amongst animals. There are those monsters, too, which are not produced by putrefaction, but are made by art in the glass, as has been said, since they often appear in very wonderful form and horrible aspect; frequently, for instance, with many heads, many feet, or many tails, and of diverse colours; sometimes worms with fishes' tails or birds' wings, and other unwonted shapes, the like of which one had never before seen. It is not, therefore, only animals which have no parents, or are born from parents unlike themselves, that are called monsters, but those which are produced in other ways. Thus you see with regard to the basilisk, which is a monster above all others, and than which none is to be more dreaded, since a man can be killed by the very sight and appearance of it, for it possesses a poison more virulent than all others, with which nothing else in the world can be compared. This poison, by some unknown means, it carries in its eyes, and it is a poison that acts on the imagination, not altogether unlike a menstruous woman, who also carries poison in her eyes, in such a way that from her very glance the mirror becomes spotted and stained. So, too, if she looks at a wound or a sore, she affects it in a similar way, and prevents its cure. By her breath, too, as well as by her look, she affects many objects, rendering them corrupted and weak, and also by her touch. You see that if she handles wine during her monthly courses it soon turns and becomes thick. Vinegar which she handles perishes and becomes useless. Generous wine loses its potency. In like manner, amber, civet, musk, and other strongly smelling substances being carried and handled by such a woman lose their odour. Gold, corals, and many gems are deprived of their colour, just as the mirrors are affected in this way. But—to return to my proposal of writing about the basilisk—how it carries its poison in its eye. You must know that it gets that power and that poison from unclean women, as has been said above. For the basilisk is produced and grows from the chief impurity of a woman, namely, from the menstrual blood. So, too, from the blood of the semen; if it be placed in a glass receptacle and allowed to putrefy in horse dung, from that putrefaction a basilisk is produced. But who would be so bold and daring as to wish to produce it, even to take it and at once kill it, unless he had first clothed and protected himself with mirrors? I would persuade no one to do so, and wish to advise every one to be cautious. But, to go on with our treatise about monsters, know that monstous growths amongst animals, which are produced by other methods than propagation from those like themselves, rarely live long, especially near or amongst other animals, since by their engrafted nature, and by the divine arrangement, all monsters are hateful to animals duly begotten from their own likeness. So, too, monstrous human growths seldom live long. The more wonderful and worthy of regard they are, the sooner death comes upon them; so much so that scarcely any one of them exceeds the third day in the presence of human beings, unless it be at once carried into a secret place and segregated from all men. It should be known, forsooth, that God abhors monsters of this kind. They displease Him, and none of them can be saved when they do not bear the likeness of God. One can only conjecture that they are shapen by the Devil, and born for the service of the Devil rather than of God; since from no monster was any good work ever derived, but, on the contrary, evil and sin, and all kinds of diabolical craft. For as the executioner marks his sons when he cuts off their ears, gouges out their eyes, brands their cheeks, cuts off their fingers, hands, or head, so the Devil, too, marks his own sons, through the imagination of the mother, which they derive from her evil desires, lusts, and thoughts in conception. All men, therefore, should be avoided who have more or less than the usual numbers of any member, or have any member duplicated. For that is a presage of the Devil, and a certain sign of hidden wickedness and crafts.

But neither must we by any means forget the generation of homunculi. For there is some truth in this thing, although for a long time it was held in a most occult manner and with secrecy, while there was no little doubt and question among some of the old Philosophers, whether it was possible to Nature and Art, that a man should be begotten without the female body and the natural womb. I answer hereto, that this is in no way opposed to Spagyric Art and to Nature, nay, that it is perfectly possible. In order to accomplish it, you must proceed thus. Let the semen of a man putrefy by itself in a sealed cucurbite with the highest putrefaction of the *venter equinus* for forty days, or until it begins at last to live, move, and be agitated, which can easily be seen. After this time it will be in some degree like a human being, but, nevertheless, transparent and without body. If now, after this, it be every day nourished and fed cautiously and prudently with the arcanum of human blood, and kept for forty weeks in the perpetual and equal heat of a *venter equinus*, it becomes, thenceforth a true and living infant, having all the members of a child that is born from a woman, but much smaller. This we call a homunculus; and it should be afterwards educated with the greatest care and zeal, until it grows up and begins to display intelligence. Now, this is one of the greatest secrets which God has revealed to mortal and fallible man. It is a miracle and marvel of God, an arcanum above all arcana, and deserves to be kept secret until the last times, when there shall be nothing hidden, but all things shall be made manifest. And although up to this time it has not been known to men, it was, nevertheless, known to the wood-sprites and nymphs and giants long ago, because they themselves were sprung from this source; since from such homunculi when they come to manhood are produced giants, pigmies, and other marvellous people, who are the instruments of great things, who get great victories over their enemies, and know all secret and hidden matters. As by Art they acquire their life, by Art acquire their body, flesh, bones and blood, and are born by Art, therefore Art is incorporated in them and born with them, and there is no need for them to learn, but others are compelled to learn from them, since they are sprung from Art and live by it, as a rose or a flower in a garden, and are called the children of the wood-sprites and the nymphs, because in their virtue they are not like men, but like spirits.

Here, too, it would be necessary to speak about the generation of metals, but since we have written sufficiently of these in our book on The Generation of Metals, we will treat the matter very briefly here; and only in a short space point out what we there omitted. Know, then, that all the seven metals are born from a threefold matter, namely, Mercury, Sulphur, and Salt, but with distinct and peculiar colourings. In this way, Hermes truly said that all the seven metals were made and compounded of three substances, and in like manner also tinctures and the Philosophers' Stone. These three substances he names Spirit, Soul, and Body. But he did not point out how this was to be understood, or what he meant by it, though possibly he might also have known the three principles, but he makes no mention of them. I do not therefore say that he was in error, but that he was silent. Now, in order that these three distinct substances may be rightly understood, namely, spirit, soul, and body, it should be known that they signify nothing else than the three principles, Mercury, Sulphur, and Salt, from which all the seven metals are generated. For Mercury is the spirit, Sulphur is the soul, and Salt is the body. The metal between the spirit and the body, concerning which Hermes speaks, is the soul, which indeed is Sulphur. It unites those two contraries, the body and the spirit, and changes them into one essence. But it must not be understood that from any Mercury, and any Sulphur, and any Salt, these seven metals can be generated, or, in like manner, the Tincture or the Philosophers' Stone by the Art and the industry of the Alchemist in the fire; but all these seven metals must be generated in the mountains by the Archeus of the earth. The alchemist will more easily transmute metals than generate or make them. Nevertheless, live Mercury is the mother of all the seven metals, and deserves to be called the Mother of Metals. For it is an open metal and, as it were, contains in itself all the colours which it renders up from itself in the fire;

and so also, in an occult manner, it contains in itself all metals which 'without fire it does not yield up from itself. But the regeneration and renovation of metals takes place thus: As man can return to the womb of his mother, that is, to the earth from which the first man sprang, and thus can be born again anew at the last day, so also all metals can return to quick mercury, can become Mercury, and be regenerated and clarified by fire, if they remain for forty weeks in perpetual heat, like a child in its mother's womb. Now, they are born, however, not as common metals, but as metals which tinge: for if, as has been said, Luna is regenerated, it will afterwards tinge all metals to Luna. So gold tinges other metals to Sol, and in like manner it must be understood of all other metals. Now, when Hermes said that the soul was the only medium which joins the spirit to the body, he had no inadequate conception of the truth. And since Sulphur is that soul, and, like fire, it hastens on and prepares all things, it can also link together the spirit and the body, incorporate and unite them, so that a most noble body shall be produced. Yet it is not common combustible sulphur which is to be esteemed the soul of metals; but that soul is another combustible and corruptible body. It cannot, therefore, be burnt with any fire, since it is itself entirely fire, and, in truth, it is nothing but the Quintessence of Sulphur, which is extracted by the spirit of wine from Reverberated Sulphur, and is ruby coloured and clear as the ruby itself. This is indeed a mighty and excellent arcanum for transmuting white metals, and for coagulating quick mercury into fixed and approved gold. Hold this in commendation as a treasure for making you rich; and you should be contented with this secret alone in the transmutation of metals. Concerning the generation of minerals and semi-metals, no more need be known than we stated at the beginning concerning the metals, namely, that they are produced, in like manner, from those three principles, Mercury, Sulphur, and Salt, though not, like the metals, from these principles in their perfection, but from the more imperfect and weaker Mercury, Sulphur, and Salt, yet still with their distinct colours.

The generation of gems takes place by, and flows out from, the subtlety of the earth, from the clear and crystalline Mercury, Sulphur, and Salt, also according to their own distinct colours. The generation of common stones is from the subtlety of water, by the mucilaginous Mercury, Sulphur, and Salt. For all stones are produced by the mucilage of water, as also pebbles and sand are coagulated from the same source into stones. This is patent to the eyes: for every stone placed in water soon draws the mucilage to itself. If, now, that mucilaginous matter be taken from such stones and coagulated in a cucurbite, a stone will be produced of the same kind as would of itself be produced and coagulated in the water, but after a long period of time.

Book II: Concerning the Growth of Natural Things.

IT is clear enough, and well known to everybody, that all natural things grow and mature by warmth and moisture, as is plainly demonstrated by the rain followed up with sunshine. None can deny that the earth is rendered fruitful by the rain, and all must confess that every kind of fruit is ripened by the sun. Since, then, by the Divine institution, this is possible to Nature, who will deny or refuse to believe that man possesses this same power by a prudent and skilful pursuit of the Alchemical Art, so that he shall render the fruitless fruitful, the unripe ripe, and make all increase and grow? The Scripture says that God subjected all created things to man, and handed them over to him as if they were his own property, so that he might use them for his necessity, that he might have dominion over the fishes of the sea, the fowls of the air, and everything on the earth without exception. Wherefore man ought to rejoice because God has illuminated him and endowed him, so that all God's creatures are compelled to obey Him and to be subject to Him, especially all the earth, together with all things which are born, live, and move in it and upon it. Since, then, we see with our eyes, and are taught by daily experience, that the oftener and the more plentifully the rain moistens the earth, and the sun dries it again with its heat and glow, the sooner the fruits of the earth come forth and ripen, while all fruits increase and grow, whatever be the time of year, let none wonder that the alchemist, too, by manifold imbibitions and distillations, can produce the same effect. For what is rain but the imbibition of the earth? What are the heat and glow of the sun other than the sun's process of distillation, which again extracts the humidity? Wherefore I say that it is possible by such co-optation in the middle of winter to produce green herbs, flowers, and fruits, by means of earth and water, from seed and root. Now, if this takes place with herbs and flowers, it will take place in many other similar things too, as, for instance, in all minerals, the imperfect metals whereof can be ripened with mineral water by the industry and art of the skilled alchemist. So, too, can all marchasites, granites, zincs, arsenics, talcs, cachimiæ, bismuths, antimonies, etc., all of which carry with them immature Sol and Luna, be so ripened as to be made equal to the richest veins of gold and silver, only by such co-optation. So, also, the Elixir and Tinctures of metals are matured and perfected.

Since, therefore, humidity and warmth mature all things and make them grow, let none wonder that, after a long time, in the case of a criminal on the gibbet, the beard, hair, and nails grow; nor let this be taken for a sign of innocence, as the ignorant read it. It is only natural, and proceeds from natural causes. As long as there is moisture in the body, the nails, beard, and hair grow; and, what is more, in the case of a man buried in the earth itself, nails, beard, and hair grow up to the second year, or up to the time of the man's decay.

It should be known, too, that many substances grow and increase perpetually in size, weight, and virtue, both in water and on land, in each of which they remain good and effective, such, for example, as metals, marchasites, cachymiae, talcs, granites, antimony, bismuths, gems, pearls, corals, all stones and clays. So also it can be brought about that Sol shall grow and increase in weight and in body, if only it be buried in land looking east, and be constantly fertilised with fresh human urine and pigeons' dung.

It is also possible for gold to be so acted upon by the industry and art of the skilled alchemist that it will grow in a cucurbite with many wonderful branches and leaves, which experiment is very pleasant to behold, and full of marvels. The process is as follows: Let gold be calcined by means of aqua regis so that it becomes a chalky lime; which place in a cucurbite, pouring in good and fresh aqua regis and water of gradation so that it exceeds four fingers across. Extract it again with the third degree of fire until nothing more ascends. Again pour over it distilled water, and once more extract by distillation as before. Do this until you see the Sol rise in the glass and grow in the form of a tree with many branches and leaves. Thus there is produced from Sol a wonderful and beautiful shrub which alchemists call the Golden Herb, or the Philosophers' Tree. The process is the same with the other metals, save that the calcination may be different, and some other aqua fortis may have to be used. This I leave to your experience. If you are practised in Alchemy you will do what is right in these details.

Know also that any flint may be taken out of river water, placed in a cucurbite, and sprinkled with its own running water until the cucurbite is full. This may again be extracted by distillation, as long as a single drop ascends, until the stone be dry. Let the cucurbite be again filled with this water, and once more extracted. Repeat this until the cucurbite is filled with this stone. In this way, by means of Alchemy, in a few days you will see that a very large stone can be made, such as the Archeus of the waters could scarcely make in many years. If you afterwards break the cucurbite on a stone you will have a flint in the shape of the cucurbite, just as though it had been poured into the glass. Though this may be of no profit to you, still it is a very wonderful thing.

Book III: Concerning the Preservation of Natural Things

IN order that a thing may be preserved and defended from injury, it is necessary that first of all its enemy should be known, so that it may be shielded therefrom, and that it may not be hurt or corrupted by it, in its substance, virtue, force, or in any other way suffer loss. A good deal depends upon this, then, that the enemy of all natural things should be recognised; for who can guard himself against loss and adverse chance if he is ignorant of his enemy? Surely, no one. It is therefore necessary that such enemy should be known. There are many enemies; and it is just as necessary to know the bad as the good. Who, in fact, can know the good without a knowledge of the evil? No one. No one who has never been sick knows how great a treasure health is. Who knows what joy is, that was never sad or sorrowful? And who knows rightly about what God is, who knows nothing about the devil? Wherefore since God has made known to us the enemy of our soul, that is, the devil, He also points out to us the enemy of our life, that is, death, which is the enemy of our body, of our health, the enemy of medicine, and of all natural things. He has made known this enemy to us and also how and by what means we must escape him. For as there is no disease against which there has not been created and discovered a medicine which cures and drives it away, so there is always one thing placed over against another—one water over against another, one stone over against another, one mineral over against another, one poison over against another, one metal over against another—and the same in many other matters, all of which it is not necessary to recount here.

But it ought to be known how, and by what means, each several thing is preserved and guarded from loss: that many things, for instance, have to be kept for a long time in the earth. All roots, especially, remain for a long while in the earth fruitful and uncorrupted. In like manner, herbs and flowers and all fruits keep undecayed and green in water. So also many other fruits, and especially apples, can be preserved in water, and protected from every decay, until new apples are produced.

So also flesh and blood, which very soon putrefy and become rancid, can be kept in cold spring water; and not only so, but by the co-optation of renewed and fresh spring water they can be transmuted into a quintessence, and conserved for ever from decay and bad odour without any balsam. And not only does this process preserve flesh and blood, but (so to say) it preserves all other kinds of flesh and blood, and especially the body of man, from ail decay and from many diseases which arise from decay, better than the common mumia does. But in order that blood may be preserved of itself from decay and ill odour, and not as a quintessence; and in order, also, to protect other blood, as aforesaid, you must use this process: Let the blood be separated from its phlegm, which moves of itself, and is driven to the surface. Draw off this water by a dexterous inclination of the vessel, and add to the blood a sufficient quantity of the water of salt, which we teach you in our Chirurgia Magna how to make. This water at once mingles with the blood, and so conserves the blood that it never putrefies or grows rancid, but remains fresh and exceedingly red after many years, just as well as on the first day; which, indeed, is a great marvel. But if you do not know how to prepare this water, or have none at hand, pour on a sufficient quantity of the best and most excellent balsam, which produces the same effect. Now this blood is the Balsam of Balsams, and is called the Arcanum of Blood. It is of such great and wonderful virtue as would be incredible were we to mention it. Therefore you will keep this occult, as a great secret in medicine.

In the conservation of metals the first thing to learn is what are their enemies, so that they may be thereby the better kept from loss. The principal enemies of metals, then, are all strong waters; all aquae regiæ, all corrosives and salts, shew their hostility in this circumstance, that they mortify all metals, calcine them, corrupt them, and reduce them to nothing. Crude sulphur shews its hostility by its smoke; for by its smoke it takes away the colour and redness from Venus, and renders it white. From white metals, as Luna, Jupiter, Saturn, and Mars, it takes away their whiteness and reddens them, or induces in them a reddish colour. From gold it takes away the agreeable yellowness and golden tint, renders it black, and makes it as uncomely as possible.

Antimony shews its hostility in this: that it spoils all metals with which it is liquefied in the fire, and with which it is mixed; it deprives and robs them; moreover, like the sulphur, it robs metals of their genuine colour and substitutes another.

Quicksilver, on the other hand, exercises a hostile force upon the metals with which it is conjoined, in that it invades and dissolves them so that it makes an amalgam from them. Moreover, its smoke, which we call the soot of Mercury, makes all metals immalleable and fragile; it calcines them and whitens all red and gold coloured metals. It is the chief enemy of iron and steel, for if common mercury touches a steel rod, or if the rod be anointed with mercurial oil, it can afterwards be broken like glass and cut off. This is indeed a great secret and must be kept strictly occult. In the same way, too, the magnet should be guarded and kept from Mercury, for it exerts hostility on it as on Mars. For every magnet which common mercury touches, or which is anointed with mercurial oil, or only placed in Mercury, never afterwards attracts iron. Let no one be surprised at this; there is a natural cause for it, seeing that Mercury extracts the spirit of iron which the magnet holds latent in itself. Wherefore also the spirit of iron in the magnet attracts the body of Mars to itself; and this happens not only in the magnet but in all other natural things, so that the foreign spirit which is in an alien body, which is not of its own nature, always attracts a body agreeing with its own nature. This should be known not only of the magnet, but of all natural bodies, such as minerals, stones, herbs, roots, men, and animals.

After this it should be known that metals exercise hostility amongst each other, and mutually hate one another from their inborn nature; as you see in the case of Saturn, which is the principal enemy of Sol, from its congenital nature. It breaks up all the members of gold, renders it deformed, weak, and destroys and corrupts it even to the death, more than it does any other metal. It also hates tin, and is an enemy of all the metals, for it renders them degenerate, unmalleable, hard and unfit, if it be mixed with either of them in fire or flux.

Since, therefore, you have now heard about the enemies of the metals, learn, moreover, about their preservation and conservation, which guard the metals from all loss and corruption, and, in addition, strengthen them in their nature and virtue, while they graduate them more highly in colour. First, then, it ought to be known concerning gold that it cannot be better and more beautifully preserved than in boys' urine, in which has been dissolved sal ammoniac, or in the water of sal ammoniac alone. In these, with time, it acquires such a high grade of colour as cannot be surpassed. Silver cannot be better preserved and conserved than if it be boiled in common water or acetum in which have been dissolved tartar and salt. In this way any old silver, though blackened and stained, is renewed, if it is boiled thus. Of iron and steel the best and most useful conservative and preservative is fresh, not salted, lard from a gelded sow. This protects all iron and steel from rust if they are anointed therewith once every month. In like manner, if iron be liquefied with fixed arsenic, and occasionally reduced to a flux, it can be so renewed and fixed that, like silver, it never rusts. Copper can be conserved and preserved if only it be mixed with sublimated Mercury, or anointed with oil of salt, so that for the future it gives forth no vitriol or verdigris, nor does it become of a green colour.

Lead cannot be conserved better than in cold water, and in a damp place, such is its nature. But for the conservation of the magnet nothing is better than filings of iron or steel. If the magnet be placed in these, not only does not its force decrease, but it grows more and more every day.

As to the conservation of salts, and all those substances which are of a salt nature, and are comprised under the name of salt, of which there are more than a hundred, it is well to know that they must be kept in a warm and dry place, and guarded well from the air in wooden chests. They must not be placed on glass, stone, or metal. By these they are dissolved and turn into water and amalgam; but this does not occur in wood.

Moreover, you should learn the method of conserving certain waters and liquids by means of pressed herbs, roots, and other fruits and growing things, which easily absorb all mustiness and mould just as if a skin were wrapped around them. Let these waters, or other liquids, be placed in a glass vessel, narrow at the top and wider below. Let the vessel be filled to the top and then some drops of olive oil added, so that all the water or liquid may be covered. The oil will float at the top, and, in this way, will protect the liquid or the water a long time from mustiness or mould. No water or liquid, if it be covered with oil, can ever become mouldy or smell badly. In this way also two waters, two liquids, two wines, can be kept separately in one vessel, so that they shall not mix; and not only two, but three, four, five, or still more, if only oil be between them, for they are separated by the oil as by a wall, which does not suffer them to be conjoined and united. For oil and water are two contraries, and neither can mingle with the other. As the oil does not allow the waters to mix, so, on the other hand, the water prevents the oils from blending.

For the conservation and preservation of cloth and garments from moth, so that they may not eat them or settle in them, nothing is better than mastix, camphor, ambergris, or musk: but the best is civet, which not only preserves from moth, but drives away and puts to flight moths, with other worms, fleas, lice, and bugs.

All timbers can be conserved, as in buildings or bridges, so that they shall never decay, whether they be in water, under water, or out of the water, in the ground, under the ground, or out of the ground, whether exposed to rain or wind, air, snow, or ice, in summer or winter, and moreover, preventing them from decaying or worms breeding in them when felled. The method of conservation in this case is that grand arcanum against all putrefactions, and so remarkable a secret that no other can compare with it. It is none other than the oil of sulphur, the process for making which is as follows:—Let common yellow sulphur be pulverised and placed in a cucurbite. Over it pour as much aquafortis as will cover four fingers across. Abstract this by distillation three or four times, the last time until it is completely dry. Let the sulphur which remains at the bottom, and is of a dark reddish colour, be placed in marble or glass and easily dissolved into an oil. This is a great secret in the conservation of timber so that it may never decay and may be protected from worms. For if sulphur be prepared as aforesaid, and turned into an oil, it afterwards tinges the timber which has been anointed with it so that it can never be obliterated. Many other things, also, can be conserved and preserved from decay in this oil of sulphur, especially ropes and cables in ships and on the masts of ships, in chariots, fishing-nets, birdcatchers' and hunters' snares, and other like things which are being frequently used in water and rain, and would otherwise be liable to decay and break; so also with linen cloths and other similar things.

The conservation of potable things, too, should be noticed, under which we comprise wine, beer, hydromel, vinegar, and milk. If we wish to keep these five unharmed and in their virtue, it is necessary to know their chief enemy. This is none other than unclean women at the time of their monthly courses. They corrupt these things if they handle or have anything to do with them, if they look at them, or breathe on them. The wine is changed and becomes thick, beer and hydromel turn sour,

Document Text

vinegar is weakened and loses its acidity, milk also becomes sour and clotted.

This, therefore, should be well known before anything is said specially about the conservation of one of these things in particular. Moreover, the chief preservative of wine is sulphur and oil of sulphur, by means of which all wine can be preserved for a very long time, so that it neither thickens nor is in any way changed.

The means of conserving beer is by oil of garyophyllon, if a few drops of it are put in, so that one measure has two or three drops. Better still is the oil of benedicta garyophyllata, which preserves beer from acidity. The preservative for hydromel is the oil of sugar, which must be used in the same way as the oil of garyophyllon or the benedicta.

The preservative of vinegar is oil of ginger, and of milk the expressed oil of almonds. These two must be used as described above.

The preservative of cheese is the herb hypericon or perforata, which protects all cheeses from worms. If it be placed against the cheese and touches it, no worm is produced in it, and if some have been already produced, they die and drop out of the cheese.

Honey has no special preservative, only it must be protected from its enemy. Its chief enemy is bread. If ever so small a quantity of bread made from flour be put or fall into it, the whole honey is turned into ants, and perishes entirely.

Glossary

arcanum	a mystery or deep secret, or an elixir or secret remedy
Archeus	the vital life force
basilisks	legendary reptiles or serpents
benedicta garyophyllata	an herb
cachymiae	the plural form of a word referring to an imperfect metallic body, or immature ore of metal, that is neither saline nor metal but almost metallic
civet	a catlike mammal that secretes a musk used in perfumes, or the musk itself
cucurbite	a vessel or flask for distillation
garyophyllon	dried flower buds of the clove
Hermes	probably a reference to Hermes Trismegistus, a Greco-Egyptian god and putative author of a Gnostic text
homunculus	an artificial human

The god Tlaloc
(Tlaloc [stone], Toltec / Museo Nacional de Antropologia, Mexico City, Mexico / Photo: Michel Zabe / AZA INAH / The Bridgeman Art Library International)

RIG VEDA AMERICANUS

"O noble Chicomolotl, arise, awake . . . conduct us to the home of Tlaloc."

Overview

At the end of the fourteenth century, the Aztecs established themselves as the leading nation in the region of modern-day central Mexico. Their power grew over the next 150 years, until their empire extended from the Atlantic to the Pacific. The Aztecs were warriors who conquered neighboring nations, but they themselves believed in the overwhelming influence wielded by the gods on earth and its inhabitants. In order to appease the gods, the Aztecs built monumental temples, where they committed sacrifices; like most Mesoamerican gods, the Aztec gods fed on human blood.

The *Rig Veda Americanus* is a collection of hymns addressing the pantheon of Aztec gods and presenting a small fraction of their mythology. The Aztec religion is characterized by several peculiarities: It was not constructed at once but is a conglomeration that emerged over several centuries as taken from various religions and myths from Central American tribes and nations. The mythology is extremely mysterious and complex. The same gods have different names and attributes in varying circumstances; some of them appear often, while others are neglected in parts of the accounts. Moreover, their powers, functions, and places in the hierarchy vary from one explanation to another, depending on the particular city as well as the particular tribe. In many cases gods are interchanged with their human representatives, who function on earth.

Owing to the scarcity of sources, large parts of Aztec beliefs cannot be reconstructed. The Aztec religious system was catastrophic and cyclical, meaning that everything was doomed to perish after each cycle and had to be reborn again. Gods often had to give up their lives so that the sun and moon would continue their travel in the skies. Most gods, as well as the sun and the moon, required blood to function, supplied through human sacrifices. The Aztec religion has thus evoked polarized reactions of fear, horror, and fascination, in terms of both curiosity about the unknown and historical interest.

With the conquest of the Aztec Empire by the Spaniards in the early sixteenth century, the native rituals were stopped, and knowledge about them started to vanish. The invaders, shocked by the cruelty of the Aztec religion, tried to wipe out all remnants of their ceremonies and sacrifices. Many of the Aztec written codices were labeled as works of the devil and destroyed. Between 1540 and 1585 a Spanish priest, Bernardino de Sahagún, worked closely with educated Aztecs and compiled twelve books of information about their culture. They were copied by Sahagún and his helpers from the original Aztec works, which are now lost, or drawn up based on oral tradition. The *Rig Veda Americanus* is a portion of this work.

Context

Although the Mexica, as the Aztecs originally called themselves, appeared on the historical scene very late—they arrived in central Mexico probably around 1250 to 1270—the history of their religion and mythology begins long before then. Through the preceding centuries, the Aztecs accepted and incorporated into their own culture numerous elements of the religions and mythologies of the peoples who inhabited central Mexico before them. The adopted elements included various gods.

Archaeological excavations point to 1400 BCE as the time at which the oldest culture is known to have existed in Mexico. It is referred to as the culture of the Olmecs, who were the first to leave behind pyramids and well-developed towns. Around the first century CE, a huge town and religious center known as Teotihuacán developed in central Mexico, with over 120,000 inhabitants at the peak of its growth at the turn of the sixth century. In the years 600 to 750, the Coyotlatelco, a new sister culture to Teotihuacán, developed with a center in Tula Chico. When Teotihuacán was deserted, Tula Chico and later centers, such as Cacaxtl, Canton, and Teotenango, ensured the survival of the legacies of the region's earlier cultures.

By the time of the Aztecs' arrival, Teotihuacán was already in ruins, and its builders had passed into history. The Aztecs believed that Teotihuacán was a city of giants who had perished. In reality, little is known of the residents of Teotihuacán or their fate, but excavations have revealed the extent of the magnificent city's influence. Its relics indicate that some of the future Aztec gods were already worshipped

Time Line

CA. 1400 –400 BCE	■ The Olmec culture dominates in central Mexico.
CA. 100 –250 CE	■ Teotihuacán grows to cover an area of 12.5 square miles and encompass eighty-five thousand inhabitants.
CA. 500	■ The population of Teotihuacán reaches one hundred twenty thousand.
CA. 600 –750	■ The Coyotlatelco culture grows, and inhabitants desert Teotihuacán.
CA. 1165	■ The Mexica, to be known as the Aztecs, leave their fatherland of Aztlán.
CA. 1270	■ The Aztecs arrive in Mexico and settle in Chapultepec, ruled by the descendants of Toltecs; they begin to adopt Toltec civilization.
CA. 1280	■ The Aztecs are defeated by Culhuacán and forced to settle in Tizapán.
1323	■ Aztecs capture and kill the daughter of Achitometl, the Culhuacán chief.
1325	■ The Aztecs are driven out of Tizapán by the Culhuacán and settle on Lake Texcoco, where they build their new city-state of Tenochtitlán.
1473	■ The Aztecs establish full control over the Tenochtitlán region
1475 –1478	■ The Aztecs expand their rule west of the valley of Mexico.
1487	■ The ceremony of consecration is held for the Great Temple in Tenochtitlán.
1497 –1500	■ The Aztec Empire reaches the Pacific Ocean.

there. In particular, one of the most important figures of the ancient pantheon was Tlaloc, the god of rain. Alongside him, the people of Teotihuacán worshipped a god referred to as the "Old Fire God"—later called Huehueteotl by the Aztecs—and Quetzalcoatl (Feathered Serpent), who was identified sometimes as a god and sometimes as a human and was supposed to be a great helper of people. Relations between these gods and their perceived degrees of power are subjects of debate.

Between the years 650 and 900, Teotihuacán was the scene of an invasion of nomadic Chichimec people, who represented a far lower level of culture than the inhabitants of Teotihuacán. According to the legends, they were led by their own gods—in particular, by Mixcoatl (Cloud Serpent), who would become an Aztec deity of the hunt and also would be treated by the Aztecs as their special protector and leader. In the following centuries the Chichimeca assimilated to the local culture and slowly started improving it. By the end of the millennium they became known as Toltecs and probably built their main city in Tula, just west of Teotihuacán. There is no full agreement among scholars on these issues. According to some, the term *Chichimeca* was generally applied to savage (and often nomadic) incomers who invaded the civilized states of central Mexico, and when those invaders adopted and developed high culture they were referred to as *Toltecs*.

It is generally accepted that the Mexica left their homeland, an unidentified place known as Aztlán—the source of the term *Aztecs*, by which they would be known to history—in the mid-twelfth century and migrated south, where they reached the well-developed lands of the Toltecs. In 1217 the Aztecs were supposed to start a new fifty-two-year cycle, an event connected with fear but also great hope. Each ending of a cycle meant great tensions and possible changes in the universe and could mean the end of the Aztec people as a nation—or even the end of humanity.

About fifty years later the Aztecs moved on and arrived in central Mexico, where initially the group settled in Chapultepec, ruled by the descendants of Toltecs. Over the next cycle they adopted Toltec civilization. During that time they are thought to have been defeated by the Culhuacán state and forced to settle to the west in the unfriendly region of Tizapán. When, in 1323, they captured and sacrificed to their gods in a ritual offering the daughter of Achitometl, the Culhuacán chief, the Culhuacán drove them out of Tizapán, forcing them to settle on Lake Texcoco. It was there that the Aztecs built their new city-state of Tenochtitlán (the site of modern-day Mexico City) at the very end of the fourteenth century. The fifteenth century witnessed the gradual growth of Aztec power. Verging toward empire, the Aztecs suppressed neighboring states and formed an alliance with the towns of Texcoco and Tlacapán, which soon controlled territories between the two oceans.

Throughout this time, the Aztecs continued to cultivate their complex religion and mythology. Wars were often an excuse to acquire slaves and hostages who would be the next sacrifices to the Aztec gods. Such events as the great drought and famine of the mid-fifteenth century escalated the numbers of sacrifices, as the Aztecs sought to earn the gods' favors through the shedding of ever-more human blood. Around this time the Aztecs introduced "flower wars," military engagements of limited scale during which opposing communities could gauge each other's capacities, train younger combatants, and capture prisoners for sacrifice. The flower-war tactic allowed the Aztecs to challenge an enemy state without committing a great number of troops, which would potentially leave them vulnerable on other fronts. If the enemy found itself intimidated by the Aztecs' might, it would capitulate and become a vassal state; if the enemy asserted its independence, the Aztecs would force further and larger flower wars, until all-out war was waged or the enemy surrendered. The Aztecs' neighbors had little choice but to abide by the flower-war custom, which proved an effective means of conquest. The finishing of the Great Temple at Tenochtitlán, which was consecrated most probably in 1487, after its last reconstruction and enlargement during the reign of Ahuitzotl, was marked by the sacrifice of thousands of people; some scholars provide a number as high as eighty thousand, but most probably it was closer to a still-horrifying ten thousand.

Through the turn of the sixteenth century, the Aztec Empire was at the peak of its power. But in 1519 a group of Spaniards led by Hernán Cortés landed north of the Yucatán Peninsula and started their march inland, toward the Aztec capital. Despite their firearms, horses, and armor, the Europeans were outmatched in confrontation against the skillful and brave native warriors. Fortunately for the white invaders, however, they proved able to count on the many local tribes who were tired of the constant Aztec wars and the capture and sacrifice of their kinsfolk. Thousands of these subjugated American Indians helped Cortés in his venture, but even then the task was not easy. On November 18, 1519, Spaniards entered the island town of Tenochtitlán for the first time; half a year later, in June 1520, they were chased out of the capital, and the Aztec chief Montezuma (or Moctezuma II), who had surrendered to the Europeans, was slain by his own people. In the summer of 1521, Cortés returned, and after heavy fighting the Spaniards captured the city. The Aztec Empire came to an end.

It was in 1519 that several Spanish soldiers who accompanied Cortés in his campaign against the Aztecs entered an Aztec temple for the first time. As the chronicler of those events, Bernal Díaz del Castillo, recounts, they were amazed by the richness of some of the objects and figures of the gods, and at the same time they were stunned, shocked, and terrified by the signs and remnants of sacrifices that had taken place in the temple. Díaz del Castillo describes the floors, walls, and furniture as covered with blood—both fresh and old—and mentions seeing bones and skulls. He writes about Aztec priests with their bodies and hair covered in blood. The invaders were told by other American Indians about the tradition of human sacrifices to the blood-hungry gods of the Aztec people, but thus far they had not seen any testament of these practices.

Indeed, the outward signs of the Aztec religious sacrifices were so terrifying for Europeans that they instantly took

Time Line

1519
- **November 8** The expedition of Hernán Cortés, which landed in Mexico in the spring, reaches Tenochtitlán and enters the city for the first time.

1521
- **August 13** Cortés and his Spanish forces capture Tenochtitlán and effectively conquer the Aztec Empire.

1540–1585
- Bernardino de Sahagún compiles what will be known as the Florentine Codex, consisting of twelve books copied from the original Aztec codices or derived from oral tradition, with Aztec hymns included.

1890
- The American scholar Daniel G. Brinton translates the Florentine Codex hymns from the Nahuatl language into English and publishes them as *Rig Veda Americanus*.

them for Satan's work and decided to eliminate these religious practices and convert the Indians to Christianity. The Aztec codices, written in the native Nahuatl language, were illegible to the Spaniards; bearing in mind the evidence of the bloody sacrifices, the invaders destroyed what they believed to be the work of the black forces and the Devil. Many Aztec codices were lost, and only a few survive to this day.

The Spaniards robbed, destroyed, and killed; meanwhile they also started Christianizing missions among the American Indians. A number of European priests who arrived at the time of or after the Conquest started to teach the Indians. Some learned the Nahuatl language to be more effective in their mission, among them a Franciscan priest, Bernardino de Sahagún, who mastered both the language and the local culture. He worked with Indian students, primarily members of the elite, and recorded information concerning Indian culture, history, and religion, such that his writings, composed in Nahuatl, Spanish, and Latin, form a unique source. From 1540 to 1585, Sahagún compiled his main codex: Twelve books were copied by himself and his helpers from the original Aztec codices (now lost) or drawn up based on the oral tradition described to him by his Aztec helpers and students. Sahagún's work is kept in Florence, Italy, and Madrid, Spain. The most complete of his codices, the so-called Florentine Codex, is held by the Bibliotheca Medicea Laurenziana in Florence. The Aztec hymns, *Rig Veda Americanus*, form part of this codex.

Aztec codex illustration of prisoners of war sacrificed to the sun god
(Prisoners of War Sacrificed to the Sun God, from an Aztec Codex [post conquest, 1519] [vellum], Aztec / Bibliotheque Nationale, Paris, France / The Bridgeman Art Library International)

About the Author

The hymns found in *Rig Veda Americanus* were written down and preserved by a Spanish Franciscan priest, Bernardino de Sahagún. Sahagún studied at the University of Salamanca before joining the Franciscans, and in 1529 he was sent to the New World with twenty other friars. In America he was the guardian of one of the convents and from 1536 taught Latin at the Colegio de Santa Cruz in Tlatelolco. He learned and mastered the indigenous Aztec language of Nahuatl and devoted his time to missionary work with the Aztecs. This collection of hymns is a small part of his overall achievement. Interestingly, he left his documentation of the Aztec world in Nahuatl, which he probably knew best among his contemporaries. Together with a group of native Aztecs, mostly students of their elite schools, *calmecac*, he collected and described the history, culture, arts, and ceremonies of the Aztecs. Along with a few other writers, he left a documentary work of twelve volumes in the Nahuatl language, with glosses in Spanish and Latin. Sahagún died in 1590, having spent the last five years of his life in the Convent of San Francisco in Mexico.

Sahagún was the author of the transcriptions but obviously not the author of the hymns. His collaborators and helpers and the elite students, who probably did some of the writing themselves, also probably revealed these hymns to him. The selection, form, and phrasing would thus have been theirs, but the texts themselves were not. The ceremonial, sacrificial, and praise songs were at that time several centuries old, and each one had different roots and was considerably changed as time went by. As such, no individual or group can be pointed to as author of these hymns. It is equally difficult to date the hymns, as historians are not even sure which are of Aztec origin and which were inherited from the peoples who inhabited central Mexico before the Aztecs arrived. They might have been authored by priests, warriors, monarchs, teachers, or other members of the highest social groups and were likely an element of elite Aztec culture, inaccessible to the common people.

Essential Quotes

"Huitzilopochtli is first in rank, no one, no one is like unto him: not vainly do I sing (his praises) coming forth in the garb of our ancestors; I shine; I glitter."

"In Mexico the god appears; thy banner is unfolded in all directions, and no one weeps. / I, the god, have returned again, I have turned again to the place of abundance of blood-sacrifices; there when the day grows old, I am beheld as a god. / Thy work is that of a noble magician; truly thou hast made thyself to be of our flesh; thou hast made thyself, and who dare affront thee?"

"Hail to our mother, who caused the yellow flowers to blossom, who scattered the seeds of the maguey, as she came forth from Paradise. / . . . Hail to the goddess who shines in the thorn bush like a bright butterfly. / Ho! she is our mother, goddess of the earth, she supplies food in the desert to the wild beasts, and causes them to live."

"O noble Chicomolotl, arise, awake, leave us not unprotected on the way, conduct us to the home of Tlaloc. / Arise, awake, leave us not unprotected on the way, conduct us to the home of Tlaloc."

Explanation and Analysis of the Document

The modern understanding of Aztec culture and religion is based on Aztec art, archaeological and ethnological finds, and information derived from the few surviving codices. It is estimated that in today's Mexico over one million Indians speak the Nahuatl language but do not read ancient Aztec writing. Aztec religious culture, which was limited to the highest groups within the society, was largely lost. The Aztec religion was complex and had several levels of sophistication, being primitive for the common people and sophisticated—as based on readings of the movements of planets and observations of the universe—for the elites. They all shared a belief in the catastrophic character of the world and the need to pray to gods for their goodwill and help.

During a regular year, Aztecs celebrated more than twenty festivals devoted to the various gods and goddesses and their powers, performances, and deeds. Each was accompanied by dancing, singing, and very often ball games and sacrifices, along with the recitation of hymns—some of which may have accompanied the sacrifices. For the highest group of society, the priests and possibly the aristocracy, these hymns had meaning but also were a mystery. Like poetry, they could be interpreted in a number of ways, and often they remained as mysterious as the gods to whom they were addressed. For the common people, they were part of mysterious rituals that they did not understand but which were essential for their survival and the existence of their world.

The hymns examined here, preserved by the work of the Spaniard Sahagún, form the only coherent written collection of this type relevant to Aztec religious life and ceremonies. *Rig Veda Americanus* owes its name to the American archaeologist and ethnographer Daniel G. Brinton, who in 1890 translated the hymns from the Nahautl language into English. Stating that they reminded him of the Vedic Sanskrit hymns of the Rig Veda of ancient India, he titled them similarly; "Americanus" was added to distinguish them as hymns originating in America. This religious text comprises twenty hymns composed in honor and praise of various gods. In that they were composed by the Aztecs, they refer to the Aztec gods, understood in a narrow sense. That is, they appear to address primarily the indigenous Aztec gods, with minimal attention to those whom the Aztecs adopted and incorporated into their religion from their predecessors and neighbors in Mexico.

Written and passed on through the Aztec generations in archaic form, the ritual hymns of the *Rig Veda Americanus*, which differ in length and composition, are neither self-explanatory nor simple. The songs are ceremonial, not texts of creation or revelation. Thus, they do not discuss the forming of a certain religious system or talk of its attributes. They tell very little about the gods concerned and nothing about the Aztec religious system or their mythology in general. They praise various deities without explaining who they are. These sorts of details, then, are known only from other texts. It is practically beyond doubt that the high priests were the ones who knew and sang these hymns, most probably during religious ceremonies in praise of the relevant gods.

"The Hymn of Huitzilopochtli" addresses the most important Aztec god. Huitzilopochtli ("Hummingbird of the Left") is an Aztec ancestral tutelary deity, who came with them from their homeland and always gave them hope. The first verse decidedly points to him as being the most important of all gods in the Aztec pantheon. He was the one who helped the Aztecs defeat the Mixteca and the Picha-Huasteca, two nations living on the coasts of the Pacific Ocean and Gulf of Mexico, respectively. In times of need he used lightning as his weapon and is thus called the "Dart-Hurler" here. The last two verses appeal to two groups of society asked to join in the praise of Huitzilopochtli: the Amanteca, who were skilled artists, and the Pipiteca, who are believed to have been a social class. This hymn, according to Brinton, was sung from sunset to dawn at the celebration of Huitzilopochtli's feast in the fifteenth month of the Aztec calendar.

The second hymn, "The War Song of the Huitznahuac," recalls the deeds of Huitzilopochtli (as known from the rest of Sahagún's work, other codices, and archaeological excavations), when upon being born he destroyed his enemies. The Huitznahuac represent the enemies of Huitzilopochtli, the magicians who came from the south, whom he was to defeat. In memory of that mythical event, captive slaves were divided into two groups that fought each other. Those who were defeated were promptly put to death by their captors. This is without doubt a song praising the deeds of the god but also connects with the special ritual of sacrificing slaves captured in a struggle. In the verses of this hymn are reference to the enemies coming from the south, all in feathers—the stronger one was, the more decorative dress one would wear—and descending upon Huitzilopochtli.

The god who appears in the first line of "The Hymn of Tlaloc" is Tlaloc, who can be considered equal in power to Huitzilopochtli. The use of the first person in this and several of the ensuing hymns should be viewed from two perspectives. During the ceremony, when the hymn was sung, it was the god himself who was understood to be passing the message to the people—to both those who conducted the sacrifice and those who were sacrificed. Also, in the Mesoamerican religions, the god and the priest playing his role were often blurred and hard to separate. For the simple people, often it was the priest who was considered the god himself.

Otherwise referred to by the Aztecs as "He Who Is Made of Dirt," Tlaloc is a god of water, rain, thunder, and lightning. His goodwill and generosity were considered essential every year for the good crops collected by the inhabitants of Mexico; he was thus responsible for the well-being of the region's peoples. Festivals in honor of Tlaloc took place in the time of corn planting and were aimed at securing the god's favor for the coming crops. Sacrifices made in honor of him often constituted young children. The souls of those children who remained brave when they were sacrificed, according to Aztec beliefs, remained in heaven for four years and later return to Tlaloc's palace, which was to be paradise on earth. Most probably sacrifices were also connected with playing ball games, which had special meaning in Aztec religion. (Playing ball represented the clash of the earth and universe, while the movement of the ball was identified with the movement of earth, sun, and planets.) Since the capital of the Aztecs was on islands largely created in the middle of a lake, casting reeds is symbolic as well; it signifies the act of creation of earthly dwellings.

"Hymn to the Mother of the Gods" is praise and prayer in honor of the mother of all gods. In Aztec mythology there were many names used to denote this goddess, and often her presentation was actually dual female/male. Brinton refers to this goddess as Teteoinan (Mother of Gods), but Teteoitah (Father of Gods) also appears to be correct. Other male/female names for this god are Ometecuhtli/Omecihuatl and Tonacatecuhli/Tonacacihuatl. This hymn should be understood, however, in a broader context related to fertility and creation in nature. The mother goddess ensured good crops, in particular, of the maguey plant, which was used for producing cloth, building houses, and brewing alcoholic drinks; it was also widely used in Aztec medicine. Many of the Aztec gods came from other, older cultures and were intermixed in terms of their names, prerogatives, and presentation. In particular, this hymn features a simple reference to the mother of all creation, but all natives of Mexico could identify their own gods of creation with the wording of the praise in this hymn.

"Hymn to Chimalipan in Parturition" is a hymn devoted to the virgin mother of Huitzilopochtli. According to sources, she was divinely impregnated by the spirit of All-father, who descended on her in the form of a bunch of feathers. Coatepec (Serpent Mountain) is a name of a mountain near Tula where the goddess was understood to dwell.

The hero of the next hymn, Ixcoçauhqui (the Yellow Faced), also called Xiuhtecutli (Lord of Fire) or Huehueteotl (the Ancient God), is the Aztec god of fire. The hymn refers to his power in the Hall of Flames, his temple. He was the patron of dramatic sacrifices, such as when naked, bound prisoners were cast into fire; still alive, they were pulled out to have their hearts torn out and sacrificed to the terrible god. The last verse is a reference to those women (exemplified by one person) who were sacrificed to Ixcoçauhqui. This god also appears in other circumstances as Xiuhcoatl (Snake of Fire). According to one version, Xiuhcoatl himself served as a weapon for the main Aztec god, Huitzilopochtli, when he was born and had to fight against his siblings.

"Hymn of Mixcoatl" is probably one of the oldest hymns, sung to the god of the Chichimeca. It commemorates their travel from their mythic homelands of Chicomoztec and Tziuactitlan, during which Mixcoatl led and protected them. This guidance helped them in their search for a place to settle (with their packs, traveling nets, and all other belongings). Once they reached their destination—here signified by the ball ground, a place to play but also a sacred ground—they rejoiced, just like one of the most colorful birds they knew, the quetzal. This is a joyful and bloodless song praising an ancient god who had guided tribespeople's ventures in past times.

The next hymn addresses Xochipilli, also called Macuilxochitl, the god of flowers as well as love, music, singing, and dancing. He was responsible for the protection of all plants, and he was closely associated with Tlaloc, as vegetation depended on both of them. This song talks about Xochipilli, god of flowers, music, and happiness, turning to Tlaloc, god of rain, and Cinteotl, god of maize, to ask for a good and plentiful harvest.

"Hymn to Xochiquetzal" addresses the goddess Xochiquetzal (Precious Feather), who had under her patronage artists, painters, weavers, metal engravers, silversmiths, and goldsmiths. It is another hymn of joy and happiness, asking all to seek Tamoanchan, the Aztec paradise. Celebrations of this goddess took place in October and were connected with ritual baths—hence the "place by the water"—which cleansed the body and the soul. The next song, "Hymn to Amimitl," addresses an old Chichimec god of fishing. The verses appear to refer to the celebrations held in honor of this god, with the "four noble ones" signifying four dancers dressed in different colors.

Olontecutli, named in the next hymn, is difficult to identify and is definitely not one of the popular Aztec gods. Most probably he was a deity of the Otomi tribe, which fought against the Aztecs. The Otomi lived in Mexico before the arrival of the Aztecs but were gradually pushed out of central Mexico, though they were not exterminated; Nonoalco was probably the home of the Otomis. The hymn indicates that it praises the Otomis' god for his help against the Aztecs. Why this is found among the Aztec hymns is not clear. It is likely that it was central to Aztec ceremonial efforts to appease enemy gods before waging war; appeasing an enemy god could be as helpful as appeasing one's own gods.

The goddess named in "Hymn to Ayopechcatl" is also difficult to identify. The hymn points to her as being the goddess of childbearing and therefore having an important place in the Aztec pantheon and culture. But this very hymn appears to be the only existing reference to Ayopechcatl. "Hymn to Cihuacoatl" is offered to a goddess, referred to in the first line as Quilaztli, who is perceived as the mother of human beings; thus she has a very special place in human history. In contemporary mythology she was also called Tonan or Tonantzin. The hymn refers to her as the source of fertility but also protection. She is depicted bringing tools, wearing sacred Aztec symbols such as eagle feathers and painted with serpents' blood.

According to Sahagún, the next hymn was sung every eight years, when the Aztecs fasted on bread and water. The song refers to gods who have been praised in the earlier hymns. In the first line, the "flower in my heart" is the song itself. Tonan (Cihuacoatl) is the mother of humankind, while Tlazolteotl is the goddess of lascivious love; their passion has been satisfied. Cinteotl is the god of maize and fertility. The hymn praises fertility and birth using various poetic comparisons to singing birds and glorious flowers. In verse 8 the tone changes, as the flowers come to represent the flesh of young people who are sacrificed. The hymn thus represents a merging of the worlds of the living and the dead, of growth and death. The house of the ball player is none other than a tomb. It appears, then, that these verses constitute a direct reference to the Aztec conviction that life is possible only as a result of death—that sacrifice is needed for a new life to be born. Fasting, too, is indispensable, needed so that the world and the gods can survive. The last two verses seem not to be integral to the preceding subject matter in that Xochiquetzal, whose hymn appears earlier, is the patron of artists.

"Hymn of the High Priest of Xipe Totec" is a short hymn to the priest of one of the most powerful and intriguing of the Aztec gods. Known as the patron of love and goldsmiths, Xipe Totec was worshipped by priests through the sacrifice of human hearts in the first month of the calendar. After a sacrifice, the priest clothed himself in the skin of the person killed. Thus Xipe Totec was also called "our God without skin," and the ceremony probably symbolized reincarnation. Xipe Totec's festival was likely celebrated at night, which would explain the mention of Yoatzin, "the noble night-god."

The deity of the next hymn, the goddess Chicomecoatl (also called Chicomolotl), was far less cruel. Her name is translated as "seven guests," and she was responsible for nourishment. Her holiday was usually especially solemn and celebrated in mid-September. The tone of this verse is clear and does not leave much space for interpretation or mystery. "Hymn to Tezcatzoncatl Totochtin" is sung to the god responsible for pulque, a popular alcoholic drink that often proved poisonous. The hymn starts with a verse of lamentation, followed by a description of what happens to those who drink too much.

"The Hymn of Atlaua" is possibly the most mysterious, as the nature of the god Atlaua has never been described in any detail and remains a mystery. It is difficult to deduce much from the hymn itself, which possibly constitutes praise to a god who leads in war—as his name Atlaua probably derives from *atlatl*, an arrow-slinging device. Chalmecatl in this case is not a noun but means "beating a drum." Quilaztli (Cihuacoatl) is the mother of humankind. So the hymn can be understood as praising a god of war who controls arrows, possibly even becoming an arrow himself in certain situations.

"Hymn to Macuilxochitl" is another song devoted to Xochipilli, the goddess of love, flowers, and music. In it are found references to vegetation and the need for sacrifice and work to bring fruit and blossom. At the same time there is a reference to an omnipotent deity of the Aztecs, Tezcatlipoca (Smoking Mirror), without whose goodwill nothing could be achieved. In the last verse is a poetic reference to the god being considered a "mirror" (where in Nahuatl, Tezcatzintli is the proper name derived from *tezcatl*, which means "a mirror").

The last hymn of *Rig Veda Americanus*, "Hymn to Yacatecutli" is a song to the god of travelers. The song contains many ancient terms (such as Tzocotzontlan, Pipitlan, and Cholollan) that are difficult to understand and interpret. Brinton believes that this was a hymn of death, sung by those who were about to be sacrificed. The mentions of food and eating may be references to food given to sacrificial victims just before their death. The last verse indicates some kind of paradise, where those sacrificed would go "to where the sand begins" and find food and drink, of which there was always scarcity in Mexico.

Audience

It is practically impossible to describe precisely the audience for whom the hymns of the *Rig Veda Americanus* were written. They should be considered as composed for the gods, whom they address. They were meant to please and appease the gods and thus bring good fortune to the Aztecs. For the sect of the priests, who used them during ceremonies and when performing sacrifices, the hymns were essential tools of prayer—songs that were to be heard by the gods and appreciated and accepted along with ritual and sacrifice. For the ordinary people the hymns sounded like magic, words and songs that were beyond their understanding and comprehension but had a direct impact on their lives. If the prayers and the sacrifice were accepted by the gods, the following months would be prosperous, crops plentiful, and enemies defeated.

The descendants of the Aztecs still live in Mexico today, with about one million Mexicans able to speak the Nahuatl language. But with the conquest by the Spanish, the highest classes of the society were either exterminated or had to go into hiding (such as by pretending to be commoners), and thus the Aztec Empire, in particular, its high culture, science, and religion, ceased to exist. Today's Nahuatl speakers do not know written Nahuatl, nor can they understand the complex cultural code of the days of the empire. Thus, in modern times, the Aztec hymns are but historic texts for ethnographers, anthropologists, and students of religion.

Impact

The *Rig Veda Americanus* does not present a typical religious vision, statement of faith, or mystical revelation, but rather is a collection of hymns utilized by Aztec priests during festivals, religious ceremonies, and especially sacrifices. For the priests and possibly the Aztec aristocracy, then, they were a tool of worship. For those who witnessed the ceremonies or were deeply involved in and perhaps taken by the ritual (both figuratively and literally), these songs were beyond comprehension but constituted an integral part of the holy, powerful, mysterious religious ritual. The hymns must, in many cases, have put people, particularly the vic-

---

Questions for Further Study

1. The entry states that Aztec religious beliefs are characterized by "several peculiarities." What are some of these peculiarities? What cultural, historical, and perhaps even geographical factors may have contributed to the development of these peculiarities?

2. Many early cultures recognized gods that were associated with natural phenomena; the sun is a common example. List some of the gods the Aztecs worshipped that were connected with natural phenomena. Compare the Aztec pantheon of gods with that of another culture, such as the ancient Egyptians, as reflected in the "Great Hymn to the Aten." What similarities and differences do you find?

3. What circumstances do you think prompted a culture such as that of the Aztecs to engage in human sacrifice?

4. Why was Huitzilopochtli the most important god in the Aztec pantheon? Does it strike you as odd that the meaning of this god's name is "Hummingbird of the Left"?

5. The document is a collection of hymns. In what way do these hymns differ from the sorts of hymns that are sung in modern-day churches, particularly Catholic and Protestant churches, or the chanting that often accompanies Jewish worship? Does the singing serve a common purpose? Explain.

tims, into a certain hypnotic coma and terrified witnesses. Doubtless the impact of the hymns was much greater on the participants in the rituals than modern-day humans, outside of a religion centered on sacrifice, experience through the simple reading of poetry-like hymns. The importance and impact of the Aztec hymns died with those who composed and utilized them.

Further Reading

■ Books

Léon Portilla, Miguel. *Aztec Thought and Culture: A Study of the Ancient Nahuatl Mind*, trans. Jack E. Davis. Norman: University of Oklahoma Press, 1990.

Miller, Mary, and Karl Taube. *The Gods and Symbols of Ancient Mexico and the Maya: An Illustrated Dictionary of Mesoamerican Religion*. New York: Thames & Hudson, 1993.

Smith, Michael E. *The Aztecs*. 2nd ed. Malden, Mass.: Blackwell, 2003.

Townsend, Richard F. *The Aztecs*. 2nd ed. London: Thames & Hudson, 2000.

■ Web Sites

"Aztecs." History.com Web site.
  http://www.history.com/topics/aztecs

"The Mexica/Aztecs." Washington State University "Civilizations in America" Web site.
  http://www.wsu.edu/~dee/CIVAMRCA/AZTECS.HTM

—Jakub Basista

RIG VEDA AMERICANUS

The Hymn of Huitzilopochtli

1. Huitzilopochtli is first in rank, no one, no one is like unto him: not vainly do I sing (his praises) coming forth in the garb of our ancestors; I shine; I glitter.
2. He is a terror to the Mixteca; he alone destroyed the Picha-Huasteca, he conquered them.
3. The Dart-Hurler is an example to the city, as he sets to work. He who commands in battle is called the representative of my God.
4. When he shouts aloud he inspires great terror, the divine hurler, the god turning himself in the combat, the divine hurler, the god turning himself in the combat.
5. Amanteca, gather yourselves together with me in the house of war against your enemies, gather yourselves together with me.
6. Pipiteca, gather yourselves together with me in the house of war against your enemies, gather yourselves together with me.

The War Song of the Huitznahuac

1. What ho! my work is in the hall of arms, I listen to no mortal, nor can any put me to shame, I know none such, I am the Terror, I know none other, I am where war is, my work is said to be in the hall of arms, let no one curse my children.
2. Our adornment comes from out the south, it is varied in color as the clothing of the eagle.
3. Ho! ho! abundance of youths doubly clothed, arrayed in feathers, are my captives, I deliver them up, I deliver them up, my captives arrayed in feathers.
4. Ho! youths for the Huitznahuac, arrayed in feathers, these are my captives, I deliver them up, I deliver them up, arrayed in feathers, my captives.
5. Youths from the south, arrayed in feathers, my captives, I deliver them up, I deliver them up, arrayed in feathers, my captives.
6. The god enters, the Huitznahuac, he descends as an example, he shines forth, he shines forth, descending as an example.
7. Adorned like us he enters as a god, he descends as an example, he shines forth, he shines forth, descending as an example.

The Hymn of Tlaloc

1. In Mexico the god appears; thy banner is unfolded in all directions, and no one weeps.
2. I, the god, have returned again, I have turned again to the place of abundance of blood-sacrifices; there when the day grows old, I am beheld as a god.
3. Thy work is that of a noble magician; truly thou hast made thyself to be of our flesh; thou hast made thyself, and who dare affront thee?
4. Truly he who affronts me does not find himself well with me; my fathers took by the head the tigers and the serpents.
5. In Tlalocan, in the verdant house, they play at ball, they cast the reeds.
6. Go forth, go forth to where the clouds are spread abundantly, where the thick mist makes the cloudy house of Tlaloc.
7. There with strong voice I rise up and cry aloud.
8. Go ye forth to seek me, seek for the words which I have said, as I rise, a terrible one, and cry aloud.
9. After four years they shall go forth, not to be known, not to be numbered, they shall descend to the beautiful house, to unite together and know the doctrine.
10. Go forth, go forth to where the clouds are spread abundantly, where the thick mist makes the cloudy house of Tlaloc.

Hymn to the Mother of the Gods

1. Hail to our mother, who caused the yellow flowers to blossom, who scattered the seeds of the maguey, as she came forth from Paradise.
2. Hail to our mother, who poured forth flowers in abundance, who scattered the seeds of the maguey, as she came forth from Paradise.
3. Hail to our mother, who caused the yellow flowers to blossom, she who scattered the seeds of the maguey, as she came forth from Paradise.
4. Hail to our mother, who poured forth white flowers in abundance, who scattered the seeds of the maguey, as she came forth from Paradise.
5. Hail to the goddess who shines in the thorn bush like a bright butterfly.

Document Text

6. Ho! she is our mother, goddess of the earth, she supplies food in the desert to the wild beasts, and causes them to live.
7. Thus, thus, you see her to be an ever-fresh model of liberality toward all flesh.
8. And as you see the goddess of the earth do to the wild beasts, so also does she toward the green herbs and the fishes.

Hymn to Chimalipan in Parturition

1. Chimalipan was a virgin when she brought forth the adviser of battles; Chimalipan was a virgin when she brought forth the adviser of battles.
2. On the Coatepec was her labor; on the mountain he ripened into age; as he became a man truly the earth was shaken, even as he became a man.

Hymn to Ixcoçauhqui

1. In the Hall of Flames let me not put to shame my ancestors; descending there, let me not put you to shame.
2. I fasten a rope to the sacred tree, I twist it in eight folds, that by it I, a magician, may descend to the magical house.
3. Begin your song in the Hall of Flames; begin your song in the Hall of Flames; why does the magician not come forth? Why does he not rise up?
4. Let his subjects assist in the Hall of Flames; he appears, he appears, let his subjects assist.
5. Let the servants never cease the song in the Hall of Flames; let them rejoice greatly, let them dance wonderfully.
6. Call ye for the woman with abundant hair, whose care is the mist and the rain, call ye for her.

Hymn of Mixcoatl

1. I come forth from Chicomoztoc, only to you, my friends, to you, honored ones.
2. I come forth from Tziuactitlan, only to you my friends, only to you honored ones.
3. I sought, I sought, in all directions I sought with my pack; in all directions I sought with my pack.
4. I sought, I sought, in all directions I sought with my traveling net.
5. I took them in hand, I took them in hand; yes, I took them in hand; yes, I took them in hand.
6. In the ball ground I sang well and strong, like to the quetzal bird; I answered back to the god.

Hymn to Xochipilli

1. O friends, the quetzal bird sings, it sings its song at midnight to Cinteotl.
2. The god will surely hear my song by night, he will hear my song as the day begins to break.
3. I send forth the priests to the house of Tlaloc.
4. The priests to the house of Tlaloc do I send forth.
5. I shall go forth, I shall join myself unto them, I shall go where is Cinteotl, I shall follow the path to him.
6. The priests go forth to the house of Tlaloc, to the home of the gods of the plain.

Hymn to Xochiquetzal

1. I, Xochiquetzal, go forth willingly to the dancing place by the water, going forth to the houses in Tamoanchan.
2. Ye noble youths, ye priests who wept, seeking Xochiquetzal, go forth there where I am going.

Hymn to Amimitl

1. Join together your hands in the house, take hands in the sequent course, let them spread forth, spread forth in the hall of arrows. Join hands, join hands in the house, for this, for this have I come, have I come.
2. Yes, I have come, bringing four with me, yes I have come, four being with me.
3. Four noble ones, carefully selected, four noble ones, carefully selected, yes, four noble ones.
4. They personally appear before his face, they personally appear before his face, they personally appear before his face.

Hymn of Olontecutli

1. At Nonoalco he rules, at Nonoalco, Oho! Oho!
2. In the pine woods he prepares your destruction at Nonoalco, in the tuna woods, in the cacao woods he prepares your destruction.
3. I, dweller in the palace, shook them; I, Quetzalcoatl, shook them.

Document Text

4. There was a splendor of spears, a splendor of spears.
5. With my captain, with my courage, with my skill, the Mexicans were put to flight; even the Mexicans, with my courage, with my skill.
6. Go forth, ye shield bearers, put the Mexicans to flight with my courage, with my skill.

Hymn to Ayopechcatl

1. Truly in whatever house there is a lying-in, Ayopechcatl takes charge of the child.
2. Truly in whatever house there is a lying-in, Ayopechcatl takes charge of the child, there where it is weeping in the house.
3. Come along and cry out, cry out, cry out, you new comer, come along and cry out.
4. Come along and cry out, cry out, cry out, you little jewel, cry out.

Hymn to Cihuacoatl

1. Quilaztli, plumed with eagle feathers, with the crest of eagles, painted with serpents' blood, comes with her hoe, beating her drum, from Colhuacan.
2. She alone, who is our flesh, goddess of the fields and shrubs, is strong to support us.
3. With the hoe, with the hoe, with hands full, with the hoe, with hands full, the goddess of the fields is strong to support us.
4. With a broom in her hands the goddess of the fields strongly supports us.
5. Our mother is as twelve eagles, goddess of drum-beating, filling the fields of tzioac and maguey like our lord Mixcoatl.
6. She is our mother, a goddess of war, our mother, a goddess of war, an example and a companion from the home of our ancestors (Colhuacan).
7. She comes forth, she appears when war is waged, she protects us in war that we shall not be destroyed, an example and companion from the home of our ancestors.
8. She comes adorned in the ancient manner with the eagle crest, in the ancient manner with the eagle crest.

This is the Hymn which they sang every eight years when they fasted on bread and water

1. The flower in my heart blossoms and spreads abroad in the middle of the night.

Glossary

Amanteca	a group of skilled artists
Chalmecatl	literally, "beating a drum"
Coatepec	"Serpent Mountain," the name of a mountain near Tula where Huitzilopochtli's mother was thought to dwell
Huitznahuac	the enemies of Huitzilopochtli, magicians who came from the south
maguey	a plant used for producing cloth, building houses, and brewing alcoholic drinks and also widely used in medicine
Mixteca	or Mixtec, one of the important tribes that inhabited south-central Mexico
Picha-Huasteca	a tribe that lived along the coast of the Gulf of Mexico
Pipiteca	possibly the name of a social class
quetzal	a species of strikingly colorful bird
Quilaztli	or Cihuacoatl, the mother of humankind
Tlaloc	a god of water, rain, thunder, and lightning
Tlazolteotl	the goddess of lascivious love
Tonan	or Cihuacoatl, the mother of humankind
Xipe Totec	the patron of love and goldsmiths

2. Tonan has satisfied her passion, the goddess Tlazolteotl has satisfied her passion.
3. I, Cinteotl, was born in Paradise, I come from the place of flowers. I am the only flower, the new, the glorious one.
4. Cinteotl was born from the water; he came born as a mortal, as a youth, from the cerulean home of the fishes, a new, a glorious god.
5. He shone forth as the sun; his mother dwelt in the house of the dawn, varied in hue as the quechol bird, a new, a glorious flower.
6. I came forth on the earth, even to the market place like a mortal, even I, Quetzalcoatl, great and glorious.
7. Be ye happy under the flower-bush varied in hue as the quetzal bird; listen to the quechol singing to the gods; listen to the singing of the quechol along the river; hear its flute along the river in the house of the reeds.
8. Alas! would that my flowers would cease from dying; our flesh is as flowers, even as flowers in the place of flowers.
9. He plays at ball, he plays at ball, the servant of marvellous skill; he plays at ball, the precious servant; look at him; even the ruler of the nobles follows him to his house.
10. O youths! O youths! follow the example of your ancestors; make yourselves equal to them in the ball count; establish yourselves in your houses.
11. She goes to the mart, they carry Xochiquetzal to the mart; she speaks at Cholula; she startles my heart; she startles my heart; she has not finished, the priest knows her; where the merchants sell green jade earrings she is to be seen, in the place of wonders she is to be seen.
12. Sleep, sleep, sleep, I fold my hands to sleep, I, O woman, sleep.

Hymn of the High Priest of Xipe Totec

1. The nightly drinking, why should I oppose it? Go forth and array yourselves in the golden garments, clothe yourselves in the glittering vestments.
2. My god descended upon the water, into the beautiful glistening surface; he was as a lovely water cypress, as a beauteous green serpent; now I have left behind me my suffering.
3. I go forth, I go forth about to destroy, I, Yoatzin; my soul is in the cerulean water; I am seen in the golden water; I shall appear unto mortals; I shall strengthen them for the words of war!
4. My god appears as a mortal; O Yoatzin, thou art seen upon the mountains; I shall appear unto mortals; I shall strengthen them for the words of war.

Hymn to Chicomecoatl

1. O noble Chicomolotl, arise, awake, leave us not unprotected on the way, conduct us to the home of Tlaloc.
2. Arise, awake, leave us not unprotected on the way, conduct us to the home of Tlaloc.

Hymn to Tezcatzoncatl Totochtin

1. Alas! alas! alas! alas! alas! alas!
2. In the home of our ancestors this creature was a fearful thing.
3. In the temple of Tezcatzoncatl he aids those who cry to him, he gives them to drink; the god gives to drink to those who cry to him.
4. In the temple by the water-reeds the god aids those who call upon him, he gives them to drink; the god aids those who cry unto him.

The Hymn of Atlaua

1. I Chalmecatl, I Chalmecatl, I leave behind my sandals, I leave my sandles and my helmet.
2. Go ye forth and follow the goddess Quilaztli, follow her
3. I shall call upon thee to arise when among the shields, I shall call upon thee to arise.
4. I boast of my arrows, even my reed arrows, I boast of my arrows, not to be broken.
5. Arrayed in priestly garb, take the arrow in thy hand, for even now I shall arise and come forth like the quetzal bird.
6. Mighty is my god Atlaua; truly I shall arise and come forth like the quetzal bird.

Hymn to Macuilxochitl

1. Yes, I shall go there to-night, to the house of flowers; I shall exercise the priestly office to-night.
2. We labor in thy house, our mother, from dawn unto night, fulfilling the priestly office, laboring in the night.

3. A dreadful god is our god Tezcatlipoca, he is the only god, he will answer us.
4. His heart is in the Tezcatzontli; my god is not timid like a hare nor is he peaceable; I shall overturn, I shall penetrate the Mixcoatepec in Colhuacan.
5. I sing, I play on an instrument, I am the noble instrument, the mirror; I am he who lifts the mirror; I cry aloud, intoxicated with the wine of the tuna.

Hymn to Yacatecutli

1. I know not what is said, I know not what is said, what is said about Tzocotzontlan, I know not what is said about Tzocotzontlan.
2. I know not what is said of Pipitlan, what is said of Pipitlan, nor what is said of Cholollan, what of Pipitlan, of Pipitlan.
3. Now I seek our food, proceeding to eat it and to drink of the water, going to where the sand begins.
4. Now I go to my beautiful house, there to eat my food, and to drink of the water, going to where the sand begins.

Pope Paul III

(Portrait of Pope Paul III, c.1547 [oil on canvas], Titian [Tiziano Vecellio] [c.1488-1576] / Hermitage, St. Petersburg, Russia / Photo © AISA / The Bridgeman Art Library International)

Canons and Decrees of the Council of Trent

"If any one saith, that the sacraments of the New Law were not all instituted by Jesus Christ, . . . let him be anathema."

Overview

The beginning of the sixteenth century witnessed a fast and broad disintegration of the Roman Catholic Church in some parts of Europe. The process, initiated by Martin Luther in 1517, resulted in the birth of numerous sects and heresies among Luther's countless followers. Eight years after Luther put forth questions concerning the selling of indulgences (that is, partial remission of punishment for sin after death), the German-speaking regions of Europe broke away from the Catholic Church and converted to Lutheranism. The Church did not have a plan for opposing what came to be called the Reformation, which attracted numerous people daily. Attempts to isolate Luther and his followers failed. Instead of reuniting Christianity, papal actions brought no results. Political forces, in particular, the Holy Roman Emperor, were not successful either. For a long time suggestions that the Church should summon a council as its highest authority to solve the problem were ignored for religious and political reasons.

After several attempts to stop the spread of new ideas, Pope Paul III decided to summon a council, which met in Trent, Germany, in 1545. Proceedings were long, but the issues were delicate and difficult: how to reverse the process of people leaving the Catholic Church and avoid losing more and how to treat those who questioned the teachings of the Church, its traditions, and its authority. The Council of Trent debated for almost twenty years, with several breaks between sessions. One pope opened it, and a different one closed it. The most contentious problems raised at the council were connected with the question of doctrinal truths denied by the reformers and the practical issues of dealing with the crisis within the Church.

Writings documenting the progress of the sessions of the council form a fascinating collection of documents pointing to the arguments, fears, and doubts that must have been raised and discussed during the sessions. A final outcome of the council, in addition to the Canons and Decrees of the Sacred and Ecumenical Council of Trent, was the Tridentine Catechism, published in 1566, which provided the Church's official answer to those who questioned its right to draw on tradition and suppress opposition. The Council of Trent gave clear answers to all the doubts of various Protestants of the day. These answers grew out of the Church's conservatism and its traditions dating back to its founding. The Church upheld all its teachings and dogmas, with no amendments, and no attempt was made to reconcile with the reformers.

Context

In 1517 a German Augustinian monk, Martin Luther, issued his Ninety-five Theses, which, among other things, questioned the Catholic Church's practice of selling indulgences. This quasirebellion grew quickly, attracting followers and new ideas, and the Church was unable to suppress the movement. The unstable political situation in Europe and, more important, the development of printing helped disseminate Luther's ideas.

After unsuccessful attempts to force Luther to recant his views, the Church excommunicated him in 1521. Thanks to the numerous friends in Germany, Luther avoided prison and possibly being burned at the stake, and he continued to publish, translating the Bible into German, and to broaden his group of followers. In his writings he questioned not only the sale of indulgences but also Church tradition, the practice of various sacraments, and papal authority. His ideas spread quickly and stimulated rebellion against the Church and against the feudal system. Numerous priests, theologians, and self-proclaimed prophets started challenging the dogmas of the Church. Radical religious thinkers incited the poor, and a peasant rebellion known as the Peasants' War broke out in German territories. The rebellion was suppressed with extreme cruelty, and its leaders were tortured, executed, and burned at the stake. Yet the religious movement could not be stopped.

Soon other representatives of fresh religious ideas followed Luther, who worked on the improvement of his religion. Among them were Philipp Melanchton in German lands and Huldrych Zwingli and John Calvin in Switzerland. These men established their own religious congregations and questioned the authority of the Church of Rome. In 1525 Albert of Brandenburg, the grand master of the Teutonic Order

Time Line

1517
- **October 31** Martin Luther, a German Augustinian monk, publicly challenges the sale of indulgences in the Roman Catholic Church.

1520
- **June 15** Pope Leo X issues the bull Exsurge Domine ("Arise, O Lord"), condemning Luther's teachings.

1521
- **May 25** At a meeting in Worms, Charles V (the Holy Roman Emperor) proclaims the Edict of Worms, in which he condemns Martin Luther for heresy for not refuting his teachings.
- In accord with imperial edict, Luther's works are burned in the Belgian cities of Antwerp, Leuven, and Liège.

1522
- Huldrych Zwingli announces the founding of a new Christian religion in Switzerland. His ideas are more radical than Luther's.

1525
- Albert, Duke of Prussia and the Grand Master of the Teutonic Order, converts to Lutheranism, and Prussia becomes the first Lutheran state in Europe.
- A rebellion of peasants with a very strong religious motivation, known as the Peasants' War, breaks out in the German states. It is brutally suppressed, and its religious leaders are executed.

1527
- The Swedish king, Gustavus Vasa, makes Lutheranism the state religion.

1536
- John Calvin publishes his doctrines in *Institutio christianae religionis* ("Institutes of the Christian Religion") in Basel, Switzerland; the publication would be amended numerous times before its final edition in 1559.

1542
- The Sacrum Officium (popularly known as the Inquisition) for the guarding of the purity of the Roman Catholic faith is formed by Pope Paul III.

(an order formed to defend and expand the Roman Catholic faith), converted to Lutheranism, along with all of Prussia, and acquired the new title of Duke of Prussia. The order ceased to exist in Prussia, which was secularized and became the first Protestant state in Europe. Soon other states followed: Sweden in 1527, Denmark and Norway in 1536, and Scotland in 1560. In 1534 King Henry VIII of England, hitherto a faithful Roman Catholic rewarded by the pope with the title "Defender of the Faith," broke relations with Rome over a dispute to annul his marriage with Catherine of Aragon. England established its own national church.

Heresies were not new or unusual in the Church and, in fact, were part of Church history in antiquity, but up to this point the Church was able to control and suppress them. This time, though, the extent and dynamics of the protest were too broad to control, and the widespread use of printing made it impossible for the Church to confiscate and destroy new writings that questioned traditional Church teachings. The propagators of new faiths soon started to be called Protestants, while they themselves preferred to think of their actions as a reform of the Church. Hence, the movement is referred to as either the Reformation or Protestantism.

When analyzing the new religious movements of the sixteenth century, three aspects are of vital importance: the doctrinal demands of the reformers, the extent of the protest, and the reaction of the pope and of the Church to these events. There was no single doctrinal proposal among the reformers. Each of them read the Bible in a slightly different way and formed his own conclusions. But some of their dogmas were similar. All reformers decided to base their teachings solely on the Bible, rejecting the teaching and traditions of the Catholic Church. Based on their interpretation of the Bible, Luther and others questioned the meaning of the sacraments, maintaining that Jesus Christ established only two: baptism and the Eucharist. In effect five sacraments were refuted: penance (confession), confirmation, marriage, holy orders, and extreme unction (or the last rites). Other doctrinal differences followed, with considerable diversity among protesters themselves.

The religious protest found many followers throughout Europe, and all attempts to stop it proved futile. Some states chose to convert to new religions; others, like Spain and various Italian states, remained loyal to the Church. Poland-Lithuania effectively tolerated almost all old and new Christian denominations. Europe became a religiously vivid, diverse, and dynamic scene. If a certain state remained Roman Catholic, it often controlled the situation by using the new Sacrum Officium, more popularly known as the Inquisition, an institution formed by the pope to control the purity of religion. Protestants, labeled as heretics, were arrested, tortured, tried, and burned at the stake. Where the state was not able to control the situation, religious disputes turned into religious wars.

The initial reaction of the Church to Luther, backed by the Holy Roman Emperor, was simple and traditional. Those responsible for questioning the doctrines of the Church should be arrested, brought before a religious tribunal, and forced to recant their heresies. Their works were to be destroyed and put on a special list of prohibited texts. The way these individuals would be treated would depend on the examination of each case. Punishment could range from simple penance to prohibition against teaching and conferring sacraments to death at the stake. At no moment did the pope see a need for or possibility of debating Luther and the others. In the political situation of that time, such a policy was doomed to fail. The Roman See could neither stop reformation nor turn its tide.

Facing a deep crisis, the Church had to react. Discussions concerning potential action focused on two major possibilities: to undertake a decided reform of the existing Church and its teachings or stage a strong counterattack against the heresies. Several attempts were undertaken to summon a council, the highest authority of the Roman Catholic Church—in 1535 in Mantua or Verona and in 1538 in Vicenza—but they failed. Finally, in 1545 Pope Paul III announced the opening of the Council of Trent, whose duty was to work out a satisfactory and efficient answer to the situation that had developed in the preceding thirty years. That the council was to meet in a German town was not accidental. It was the proposal of many priests and politicians, who wanted the council to debate outside the influence of Rome, the pope, and the cardinals.

On December 13, 1545, the Council opened in Trent, in the Holy Roman Empire. Almost one hundred delegates were present. From the very beginning the council entered a discussion about what it should accomplish. Was it to be focused on the questions of faith and reform of the Church, as the Holy Roman Emperor wanted, or the question of unity of the Church and Protestants, according to the will of the pope? In the end, contrary to papal wishes, both issues were discussed simultaneously, and appropriate decisions were prepared. The council met in sessions, each of which usually ended with the formulation and acceptance of certain decrees accompanied by canons. The first four sessions were devoted solely to issues of dogma. From the fifth session on, the council discussed dogmatic problems along with the issue of the reform of the Church.

The eighth session decided on the transfer of the council to Bologna due to war between France and the Holy Roman Emperor. Since not all deputies agreed to move to Italy and some remained in Trent, the council was on the edge of being broken up. In the end Pope Paul III suspended the council in February 1548. It was the next pope, Julius III, who resumed the council in 1551, but for less than a year. Once again the war and the conflict between France and the Holy Roman Empire prevented the council from continuing its work. This time the council did not meet for almost ten years. Paul IV, who succeeded Julius III and Marcellus II, was dogmatic and did not understand the changes that were taking place around him. His strict measures against Protestants were not even respected in Catholic countries. The council did not meet during his rule.

It was Pius IV who finally resumed the council in January 1562 and brought it happily to an end. Again it met in Trent and only eight sessions were needed to terminate work in December 1563. During the twenty-fifth (and last)

Time Line

1545
- Pope Paul III summons the Church council to meet in Trent.
- **December 13, 1545** The Council is opened in Trent, where its first seven sessions take place, lasting until June 2, 1547; the next three are held in Bologna.

1548
- **December** Pope Paul issues a papal bull suspending the council.

1551
- **May 1** Sessions 11–16 of the council take place in Trent, lasting until April 28, 1552.

1560
- **December 3** Pope Pius IV issues a Bull for the Celebration of the Council.

1562
- **January 18** Sessions 17–25 of the council are held, lasting until December 4, 1563.

1564
- **January 22** Pope Pius IV approves the Canons and Decrees of the Council of Trent.

session all decrees and canons of the Council, starting with the ones prepared in 1546, were read and approved by all but one participant (over 250 cardinals, bishops, and other priests). The council was officially closed and its decrees were presented to the pope for approval. On January 22, 1564, the pope, Pius IV, officially approved the work of the council. The decrees and canons passed and approved during the twenty-five sessions over almost eighteen years became an official document of the Roman Catholic Church.

About the Author

The Canons and Decrees of the Sacred and Ecumenical Council of Trent, as the document is officially named, was prepared by the Roman Catholic Church. Even though historians know and are able to describe practically all participants of the council at various stages of its work, with their particular background and theological beliefs, the final document was presented by the Church as an entity. The passages, formulas, and doctrinal assertions were accepted by all participants present at a certain session. Moreover, the whole document was read and approved point by point

The Council of Trent, meeting on December 4, 1563
(The Council of Trent, 4th December 1563 [oil on canvas], Italian School, [16th century] / Louvre, Paris, France / Giraudon / The Bridgeman Art Library International)

in December 1563 by all those present at council (except for one person). Finally, in 1564, it was Pope Pius IV who approved without change the work of the council. Thus, to this day, the Canons and Decrees have been an official voice of the Roman Catholic Church presented by the See of Rome and the pope. In the sixteenth century Catholics believed that the documents were written by the Holy Ghost, who inspired and overlooked the works and writings of the highest Church authority. On the other hand, for the Protestants the same documents were authored by Antichrist, that is, the devil himself.

Explanation and Analysis of the Document

The entire Canons and Decrees of the Sacred and Ecumenical Council of Trent, at more than ninety thousand words and over three hundred pages, was an official answer of the Roman Catholic Church to the beliefs of the Protestants as well as an attempt to reform the Church itself. The results of the council are published in the form of twenty-five sessions, each of which either formally started, postponed, or resumed a session or formed decrees and canons approved by the participants. The decrees and canons are the essential part of the work of the council. Decrees state the official understanding of various issues of faith or issues connected with the Roman Catholic Church. Canons specify the situation or cases in which a certain person will be considered anathema—that is, he or she would be considered a heretic if making statements contrary to the canons.

The decrees and canons can be divided into two main groups: those referring to dogmatic issues, that is, to faith of the Church, and those referring to the reform of the Church as an institution. Both were important at the time of the council, but today only the dogmatic decrees are important and relevant. They still present the dogmatic stand of the Roman Catholic Church. Historians agree that the decrees about faith and its source and justification and the decrees about the sacraments that formed an answer to the Protestant challenge were the most important, and they are excerpted here.

♦ **Session the Third**

During the third session, the council passed a "Decree Touching the Symbol of Faith." The decree starts with an explanation of the situation of faith at that moment of history, referring to the dangers of various heresies. Next it states the Creed, which is the shortest and most essential summing up of the Roman Catholic faith, starting with the words "I believe in one God." The Creed is recited in the same form in the Church today. This decree confirmed the Nicene Creed from 325 CE.

Essential Quotes

> "This sacred and holy, ecumenical, and general Synod of Trent . . . considering the magnitude of the matters to be treated of . . . the extirpating of heresies, and the reforming of manners . . . exhorts . . . all and each above all things, to be strengthened in the Lord, and in the might of his power, in all things taking the shield of faith, wherewith they may be able to extinguish all the fiery darts of the most wicked one."

> "Truth and discipline are contained in the written books, and the unwritten traditions which, received by the Apostles from the mouth of Christ himself, or from the Apostles themselves, the Holy Ghost dictating, have come down even unto us, transmitted as it were from hand to hand."

> "If any one saith, that the sacraments of the New Law were not all instituted by Jesus Christ, our Lord; or, that they are more, or less, than seven, to wit, Baptism, Confirmation, the Eucharist, Penance, Extreme Unction, Order, and Matrimony; or even that any one of these seven is not truly and properly a sacrament; let him be anathema."

> "In the august sacrament of the holy Eucharist, after the consecration of the bread and wine, our Lord Jesus Christ, true God and man, is truly, really, and substantially contained under the species of those sensible things."

♦ **Session the Fourth**

The fourth session prepared a decree on canonical scriptures. The decree refers directly to the activity and beliefs of reformers. First, it was decided that the teachings and faith of the Church are not limited to the Bible but include the whole tradition and work of the Church since antiquity. Leaving no doubt about this issue are these words: "Truth and discipline are contained in the written books, and the unwritten traditions which, received by the Apostles from the mouth of Christ himself, or from the Apostles themselves, the Holy Ghost dictating, have come down even unto us, transmitted as it were from hand to hand." Of course, such a stand was questioned by practically all Protestants from Luther to his later followers.

The same decree indicates which books of the Bible are considered canonical. If this list is compared with those compiled by Protestants, small differences can be noted. Having listed all the canonical books of the Old and New Testament, the council decided that only one version of the Bible is acceptable in the public usage of the Church—the Latin Vulgate version. It is worth noticing that the decree omits all earlier versions, as well as the versions of various fragments of the Bible in the original languages in which they were written, leaving but one for the public use of the Church. The indication that it was the Latin Vulgate edition meant that Latin retained its position as the official language of the Church and of all its ceremonies.

Furthermore, the same decree states that no one is allowed to read and interpret the Bible on his own if those interpretations remain contrary to the interpretation of the Church. Printers are forbidden to print the Bible without the proper permission from Church authorities. For the time being nothing was stated about the private use of the Bible, in particular translations into vernacular languages. It was not until 1559 and 1564 that these translations of the Bible were put on the Church's index of forbidden books.

♦ **Session the Fifth**

The fifth session produced a decree on original sin. The issue was important, as it touched on changes proposed by Martin Luther and other Protestants, who claimed that through original sin Adam and his posterity became sinful and thus their free will could only cause them to sin. The council states that indeed people are infected by Adam's original sin, even newborn babies, who had no chance to sin, yet people may be and should be redeemed through baptism. Future sinning may be redeemed thanks to the sacrifice of Christ.

◆ **Session the Sixth**

During the sixth session, the council passed an essential decree—the one on justification—that was the consequence of the council's teaching about original sin. In this decree the council defines justification and walks the reader through the psychological process of justification. Unlike Protestants, the council maintains that under certain conditions, through Christ's sacrifice, and thanks to God's grace, justification is possible. The council stresses, though, that faith alone is not enough to acquire it and there is need for the sacraments. More specifically, chapters 1–9 stress the incapacity of every person to save him- or herself, at the same time confirming the need for cooperation of free will in order to start a new life. Baptism is required for justification. The next four chapters stress the role of obedience to the Ten Commandments in justification, thus denying predestination. Finally, the last three chapters state that grace is forfeited by all grievous sins and must be recovered through the sacrament of penance. Salvation will come as both a reward and a gift of God through the sacrifice of Christ.

◆ **Session the Seventh**

In the next session (the seventh), the council presented its teaching on the sacraments in thirteen canons. The first canon lists seven sacraments, which are and will be considered as such by the council and therefore by the Church. The following twelve canons outline the Church's teachings on the sacraments' character. In particular, the council says that they are necessary for salvation. Further, three of the sacraments—baptism, matrimony, and holy orders—may be given only once, for they leave an indelible mark on the soul and cannot be repeated. These teachings about sacraments grow out of the two previous sessions about the original sin and justification, but at the same time they are an answer to Protestants, who recognized only baptism and the Eucharist, removing all others from their churches. The Church rejected Protestants' views and retained all sacraments as instituted by Christ.

◆ **Session the Thirteenth**

The next session's work reprinted here is the thirteenth, which produced a decree on the sacrament of the Eucharist. Once again it was a theological issue undertaken by the council in reply to Protestant teachings. The council decidedly stated that there is real presence of Christ in the sacrament of the Eucharist and that transubstantiation was confirmed. In other words, contrary to Luther and his followers, the Church maintains that the Eucharist is an offering, during which bread and wine are changed into Christ's blood and flesh.

◆ **Session the Twenty-second**

Even though some time passed between various sessions, there was continuity in the approved decrees and canons. During the twenty-second session, the council approved the doctrine of the Holy Mass as a sacrifice. It is directly connected with the understanding of the Eucharist and confirms that the Holy Mass is understood as a sacrifice, with Christ's sacrifice being repeated at the altar. The following chapters refer to specific issues connected with this sacrifice.

◆ **Session the Twenty-fifth**

The final session—the twenty-fifth—put forward decrees and decisions referring to the changes instituted by Protestants. These are simple, doctrinal statements on purgatory, relics and their cult, the question of saints and their images, and finally indulgences and their sale. Thus the issue that prompted Luther to speak up in 1517 finds its solution here, with the sale of indulgences being prohibited. At the very end, the council confirmed the decision on the preparation of a list of prohibited books, which were considered heretical and forbidden.

Audience

The work of the council was addressed to two audiences—the members of the Roman Catholic Church and Protestants. In the case of the first group, the council confirmed its dogmas on issues of faith and presented a number of reforms of the Church as an institution. With regard to Protestants, the council refused to debate with them and consider their proposals and different interpretations of Church history, sacraments, and doctrinal matters. In all issues on which Protestants differed from the See of Rome, the council upheld its traditional stand, at the same time pronouncing heretics anathema.

Impact

The Canons and Decrees of the Sacred and Ecumenical Council of Trent were largely accepted and implemented in the Church, while the reform of the Church instituted by the council remained either a matter of controversy or a dead letter in many countries. Almost all Catholic monarchs and the Roman Catholic clerics of various countries accepted and approved the writings by the end of the century (France being an exception). Two years after the end of the last session and approval of the work of the council by Pius IV, a catechism based on the council was published in Rome: *Catechismus ex decreto concilii Tridentini ad parochos,* or "The Catechism from the Decrees of the Council of Trent for the Parish Priests." The doctrines of the council were approved by all Catholic theological schools. As such they reinforced application of Roman Catholic doctrine and are still in force in the twenty-first century.

Reform of the church met many obstacles in the traditions and customs of various countries. The residencies of bishops, visitations to parishes by bishops and priests, and the restructuring of priests' seminars were implemented at halting paces throughout Europe. The Mediterranean countries reacted faster, and Italy, Spain, and Portugal enacted reforms by the end of sixteenth century. Various German states, Bohemia, the Netherlands, France, and Poland reacted to the reform only in the seventeenth century. It should also be stressed that even in those countries that approved and accepted the work of the council, their implementation of it was not always complete. The reform of the Church implemented by the council was changed only four hundred years later by the Second Vatican Council in the twentieth century.

The council strengthened and consolidated the Roman Catholic Church. The decrees and canons precisely explained the doctrinal teaching of the Church and provided all priests with clear, unquestionable answers to all questions that had emerged in the preceding decades. What the council failed to do was to unite Christianity. The participants of the council never made a serious attempt to discuss the theological problems raised by Martin Luther, Huldrych Zwingli, John Calvin, and other reformers. All of their suggestions and theories were rejected, and they, along with their followers, were excluded from the Church.

Further Reading

■ Books

Delumeau, Jean, *Catholicism between Luther and Voltaire: A New View of the Counter-reformation*. London: Burns & Oates, 1977.

Jedin, Hubert. *A History of the Council of Trent,* trans. Ernest Graf. 2 vols. London: Thomas Nelson, 1957–1961.

McNally, Robert E. *Council of Trent, the Spiritual Exercises and the Catholic Reform*. Philadelphia: Fortress Press, 1970.

Schroeder, H. J., *Canons and Decrees of the Council of Trent*. St. Louis, Mo.: B. Herder, 1941.

■ Web Sites

"Council of Trent." Believe Religious Information Source Web site. http://mb-soft.com/believe/txs/trent.htm

"Council of Trent." New Advent Web site. http://www.newadvent.org/cathen/15030c.htm

—Jakub Basista

Questions for Further Study

1. The entry makes frequent reference to Martin Luther and his *Ninety-five Theses*. Read that entry and then make a list of five quotations from the theses that you think the Council of Trent found particularly objectionable.

2. The sixteenth century was a time of great religious turmoil in Europe, and that religious turmoil spread into politics. What impact did the Protestant Reformation have on Europe, and how did the Council of Trent try to respond?

3. At the Council of Trent, the Catholic Church seemed to "dig in its heels" on various matters of doctrine and Church practice. How do you think European history and the history of Christianity might have been different if the Catholic Church had adopted a more flexible attitude? Why do you think it refused to do so?

4. What impact, if any, do you think the Canons and Decrees still have in the twenty-first century?

5. In the sixteenth century, membership in a certain faith and adherence to its doctrines were matters of great moment to people, often leading to wars and persecution. In the twenty-first century, few people are likely to even pay attention to whether a person is, say, a Lutheran or a Catholic—and indeed, these and other churches engage in outreach to find common ground. What do you think has led to these changes in attitude toward religion?

Canons and Decrees of the Council of Trent

SESSION THE THIRD

Celebrated on the fourth day of the month of February, in the year 1546.

♦ DECREE TOUCHING THE SYMBOL OF FAITH.

In the Name of the Holy and Undivided Trinity, Father, and Son, and Holy Ghost.

This sacred and holy, ecumenical, and general Synod of Trent, . . . considering the magnitude of the matters to be treated of, especially of those comprised under the two heads, of the extirpating of heresies, and the reforming of manners, for the sake of which chiefly It is assembled, and recognizing with the apostles, that Its wrestling is not against flesh and blood, but against the spirits of wickedness in the high places, exhorts, with the same apostle, all and each above all things, to be strengthened in the Lord, and in the might of his power, in all things taking the shield of faith, wherewith they may be able to extinguish all the fiery darts of the most wicked one, and to take the helmet of salvation, with the sword of the spirit, which is the word of God. . . . For which cause, this council has thought good, that the Symbol of faith which the holy Roman Church makes use of . . . be expressed in the very same words in which it is read in all the churches. Which Symbol is as follows: I believe in one God, the Father Almighty, maker of heaven and earth, of all things visible and invisible; and in one Lord Jesus Christ, the only-begotten Son of God, and born of the Father before all ages; God of God, light of light, true God of true God; begotten, not made, consubstantial with the Father, by whom all things were made: who for us men, and for our salvation, came down from the heavens, and was incarnate by the Holy Ghost of the Virgin Mary, and was made man: crucified also for us under Pontius Pilate, he suffered and was buried; and he rose again on the third day, according to the Scriptures; and he ascended into heaven, sitteth at the right hand of the Father ; and again he will come with glory to judge the living and the dead; of whose kingdom there shall be no end: and in the Holy Ghost the Lord, and the giver of life, who proceedeth from the Father and the Son; who with the Father and the Son together is adored and glorified; who spoke by the prophets and one holy Catholic and Apostolic Church. I confess one baptism for the remission of sins; and I look for the resurrection of the dead, and the life of the world to come. Amen.

SESSION THE FOURTH

Celebrated on the eighth day of the month of April, in the year 1546.

♦ DECREE CONCERNING THE CANONICAL SCRIPTURES.

. . . Keeping this always in view, that, errors being removed, the purity itself of the Gospel be preserved in the Church; which (Gospel), before promised through the prophets in the holy Scriptures, our Lord Jesus Christ, the Son of God, first promulgated with His own mouth, and then commanded to be preached by His Apostles to every creature, as the fountain of all, both saving truth, and moral discipline; and seeing clearly that this truth and discipline are contained in the written books, and the unwritten traditions which, received by the Apostles from the mouth of Christ himself, or from the Apostles themselves, the Holy Ghost dictating, have come down even unto us, transmitted as it were from hand to hand; (the Synod) following the examples of the orthodox Fathers, receives and venerates with an equal affection of piety, and reverence, all the books both of the Old and of the New Testament—seeing that one God is the author of both—as also the said traditions, as well those appertaining to faith as to morals, as having been dictated, either by Christ's own word of mouth, or by the Holy Ghost, and preserved in the Catholic Church by a continuous succession. And it has thought it meet that a list of the sacred books be inserted in this decree, lest a doubt may arise in any one's mind, which are the books that are received by this Synod. They are as set down here below: of the Old Testament: the five books of Moses, to wit, Genesis, Exodus, Leviticus, Numbers, Deuteronomy; Josue, Judges, Ruth, four books of Kings, two of Paralipomenon, the first book of Esdras, and the second which is entitled Nehemias; Tobias, Judith, Esther, Job, the Davidical Psalter, consisting of a hundred and fifty psalms; the Proverbs, Ecclesias-

Document Text

tes, the Canticle of Canticles, Wisdom, Ecclesiasticus, Isaias, Jeremias, with Baruch; Ezechiel, Daniel; the twelve minor prophets, to wit, Osee, Joel, Amos, Abdias, Jonas, Micheas, Nahum, Habacuc, Sophonias, Aggaeus, Zacharias, Malachias; two books of the Machabees, the first and the second. Of the New Testament: the four Gospels, according to Matthew, Mark, Luke, and John; the Acts of the Apostles written by Luke the Evangelist; fourteen epistles of Paul the apostle, (one) to the Romans, two to the Corinthians, (one) to the Galatians, to the Ephesians, to the Philippians, to the Colossians, two to the Thessalonians, two to Timothy, (one) to Titus, to Philemon, to the Hebrews; two of Peter the apostle, three of John the apostle, one of the apostle James, one of Jude the apostle, and the Apocalypse of John the apostle. But if any one receive not, as sacred and canonical, the said books entire with all their parts, as they have been used to be read in the Catholic Church, and as they are contained in the old Latin vulgate edition; and knowingly and deliberately contemn the traditions aforesaid; let him be anathema. . . .

♦ **DECREE CONCERNING THE EDITION, AND THE USE, OF THE SACRED BOOKS.**

Moreover, the same sacred and holy Synod . . . ordains and declares, that the said old and vulgate edition, which, by the lengthened usage of so many years, has been approved of in the Church, be, in public lectures, disputations, sermons and expositions, held as authentic; and that no one is to dare, or presume to reject it under any pretext whatever.

Furthermore, in order to restrain petulant spirits, It decrees, that no one, relying on his own skill, shall, . . . wresting the sacred Scripture to his own senses, presume to interpret the said sacred Scripture contrary to that sense which holy mother Church . . . hath held and doth hold.

. . . And wishing, as is just, to impose a restraint, in this matter, also on printers, who now without restraint . . . print, without the license of ecclesiastical superiors, the said books of sacred Scripture, and the notes and comments upon them of all persons indifferently, with the press ofttimes unnamed, often even fictitious, and what is more grievous still, without the author's name . . . (this Synod) ordains and decrees, that, henceforth, the sacred Scripture, and especially the said old and vulgate edition, be printed in the most correct manner possible; and that it shall not be lawful for any one to print, or cause to be printed, any books whatever, on sacred matters, without the name of the author; nor to sell them in future, or even to keep them, unless they shall have been first examined, and approved of, by the Ordinary; under pain of the anathema and fine. . . .

SESSION THE FIFTH

Celebrated on the seventeenth day of the month of June, in the year 1546.

♦ **DECREE CONCERNING ORIGINAL SIN.**

. . . The sacred and holy, ecumenical and general Synod of Trent . . . ordains, confesses, and declares these things touching the said original sin:

1. If any one does not confess that the first man, Adam, when he had transgressed the commandment of God in Paradise, immediately lost the holiness and justice wherein he had been constituted; and that he incurred, through the offence of that prevarication, the wrath and indignation of God, and consequently death, with which God had previously threatened him, and, together with death, captivity under his power who thenceforth had the empire of death, that is to say, the devil, and that the entire Adam, through that offence of prevarication, was changed, in body and soul, for the worse; let him be anathema.

2. If any one asserts, that the prevarication of Adam injured himself alone, and not his posterity; and that the holiness and justice, received of God, which he lost, he lost for himself alone, and not for us also; or that he, being defiled by the sin of disobedience, has only transfused death, and pains of the body, into the whole human race, but not sin also, which is the death of the soul; let him be anathema. . . .

3. If any one asserts, that this sin of Adam . . . is taken away either by the powers of human nature, or by any other remedy than the merit of the one mediator, our Lord Jesus Christ, who hath reconciled us to God in his own blood, made unto us justice, sanctification, and redemption; or if he denies that the said merit of Jesus Christ is applied, both to adults and to infants, by the sacrament of baptism rightly administered in the form of the church; let him be anathema. . . .

4. If any one denies, that infants, newly born from their mothers' wombs, even though they be sprung from baptized parents, are to be baptized; or says that they are baptized indeed for the remission of sins, but that they derive nothing of original sin from Adam, which has need of being expiated by the laver of regeneration for the obtaining life everlasting, . . . let him be anathema. . . .

5. If any one denies, that, by the grace of our Lord Jesus Christ, which is conferred in baptism, the guilt of original sin is remitted . . . let him be anathema. . . .

SESSION THE SIXTH

Celebrated on the thirteenth day of the month of January, 1547.

♦ **DECREE ON JUSTIFICATION.**

. . . The sacred and holy, ecumenical and general Synod of Trent, lawfully assembled in the Holy Ghost . . . purposes, unto the praise and glory of Almighty God, the tranquillizing of the Church, and the salvation of souls, to expound to all the faithful of Christ the true and sound doctrine touching the said Justification, . . . most strictly forbidding that any henceforth presume to believe, preach, or teach, otherwise than as by this present decree is defined and declared.

CHAPTER I. On the Inability of Nature and of the Law to justify man.

. . . For the correct and sound understanding of the doctrine of Justification, it is necessary that each one recognize and confess, that, whereas all men had lost their innocence in the prevarication of Adam—having become unclean, and . . . were able to be liberated, or to arise, therefrom; although free will, attenuated as it was in its powers, and bent down, was by no means extinguished in them.

CHAPTER II. On the dispensation and mystery of Christ's advent.

. . . Him [Christ] God hath proposed as a propitiator, through faith in his blood, for our sins, and not for our sins only, but also for those of the whole world.

CHAPTER III. Who are justified through Christ.

But, though He died for all, yet do not all receive the benefit of His death, but those only unto whom the merit of His passion is communicated. For as in truth men, if they were not born propagated of the seed of Adam, would not be born unjust . . . if they were not born again in Christ, they never would be justified; seeing that, in that new birth, there is bestowed upon them, through the merit of His passion, the grace whereby they are made just. . . .

CHAPTER IV. A description is introduced of the Justification of the impious, and of the Manner thereof under the law of grace.

By which words, a description of the Justification of the impious is indicated, as being a translation, from that state wherein man is born a child of the first Adam, to the state of grace, and of the adoption of the sons of God, through the second Adam, Jesus Christ, our Saviour . . . unless a man be born again of water and the Holy Ghost, he cannot enter into the Kingdom of God.

CHAPTER V. On the necessity, in adults, of preparation for Justification, and whence it proceeds.

. . . In adults, the beginning of the said Justification is to be derived from the prevenient grace of God, through Jesus Christ, that is to say, from His vocation, whereby, without any merits existing on their parts, they are called; that so they, who by sins were alienated from God, may be disposed through His quickening and assisting grace, to convert themselves to their own justification, by freely assenting to and cooperating with that said grace: in such sort that, while God touches the heart of man by the illumination of the Holy Ghost, neither is man himself utterly without doing anything while he receives that inspiration, forasmuch as he is also able to reject it; yet is he not able, by his own free will, without the grace of God, to move himself unto justice in His sight. . . .

CHAPTER VI. The manner of Preparation.

. . . God justifies the impious by His grace, through the redemption that is in Christ Jesus; and when, understanding themselves to be sinners, they, by turning themselves, from the fear of divine justice whereby they are profitably agitated, to consider the mercy of God, are raised unto hope, confiding that God will be propitious to them for Christ's sake; and they begin to love Him as the fountain of all justice; and are therefore moved against sins by a certain hatred and detestation, to wit, by that penitence which must be performed before baptism: lastly, when they purpose to receive baptism, to begin a new life, and to keep the commandments of God. . . . Do penance, and be baptized every one of you in the name of Jesus Christ, for the remission of your sins, and you shall receive the gift of the Holy Ghost. . .

CHAPTER VII. What the justification of the impious is, and what are the causes thereof.

. . . Preparation, is followed by Justification itself, which is not remission of sins merely, but also the sanctification and renewal of the inward man, through the voluntary reception of the grace, and of the gifts, whereby man of unjust becomes just, and of an enemy a friend, that so he may be an heir according to hope of life everlasting. Of this Justification the causes are these: the final cause indeed is the glory of God and of Jesus Christ, and life everlasting; while the efficient cause is a merciful God who washes and sanctifies gratuitously, signing, and anointing with the holy Spirit of promise, who is the pledge of our inheritance; but the meritorious cause is His most beloved only-begotten, our Lord Jesus Christ. . . .

. . . It is most truly said, that Faith without works is dead and profitless; and, In Christ Jesus neither circumcision, availeth anything, nor uncircumcision, but faith which worketh by charity. . .

CHAPTER VIII. In what manner it is to be understood, that the impious is justified by faith, and gratuitously.

And whereas the Apostle saith, that man is justified by faith and freely, those words are to be understood in that sense which the perpetual consent of the Catholic Church hath held and expressed; to wit, that we are therefore said to be justified by faith, because faith is the beginning of human salvation, the foundation, and the root of all Justification; without which it is impossible to please God, and to come unto the fellowship of His sons: but we are therefore said to be justified freely, because that none of those things which precede justification . . . merit the grace itself of justification. . . .

CHAPTER IX. Against the vain confidence of Heretics.

But, although it is necessary to believe that sins neither are remitted, nor ever were remitted save gratuitously by the mercy of God for Christ's sake; yet is it not to be said, that sins are forgiven, or have been forgiven, to any one who boasts of his confidence and certainty of the remission of his sins, and rests on that alone; seeing that it may exist, yea does in our day exist, amongst heretics and schismatics. . . .

CHAPTER X. On the increase of Justification received.

Having, therefore, been thus justified, and made the friends and domestics of God, advancing from virtue to virtue, they are renewed, as the Apostle says, day by day; that is, by mortifying the members of their own flesh, and by presenting them as instruments of justice unto sanctification, they, through the observance of the commandments of God and of the Church, faith co-operating with good works, increase in that justice which they have received through the grace of Christ, and are still further justified. . .

CHAPTER XI. On keeping the Commandments, and on the necessity and possibility thereof.

But no one, how much soever justified, ought to think himself exempt from the observance of the commandments; no one ought to make use of that rash saying, one prohibited by the Fathers under an anathema, that the observance of the commandments of God is impossible for one that is justified. For God commands not impossibilities, but, by commanding, both admonishes thee to do what thou are able, and to pray for what thou art not able (to do), and aids thee that thou mayest be able. . . .

CHAPTER XII. That a rash presumptuousness in the matter of Predestination is to be avoided.

No one . . . ought so far to presume as regards the secret mystery of divine predestination, as to determine for certain that he is assuredly in the number of the predestinate; as if it were true, that he that is justified, either cannot sin any more, or, if he do sin, that he ought to promise himself an assured repentance; for except by special revelation, it cannot be known whom God hath chosen unto Himself.

CHAPTER XIII. On the gift of Perseverance.

. . . So also as regards the gift of perseverance, of which it is written, He that shall persevere to the end, he shall be saved. . . .

CHAPTER XIV. On the fallen, and their restoration.

As regards those who, by sin, have fallen from the received grace of Justification, they may be again justified, when, God exciting them, through the sacrament of Penance they shall have attained to the recovery, by the merit of Christ, of the grace lost: for this manner of Justification is of the fallen the reparation: which the holy Fathers have aptly called a second plank after the shipwreck of grace lost. For, on behalf of those who fall into sins after baptism, Christ Jesus instituted the sacrament of Penance, when He said, Receive ye the Holy Ghost, whose sins you shall forgive, they are forgiven them, and whose sins you shall retain, they are retained. . . .

CHAPTER XV. That, by every mortal sin, grace is lost, but not faith.

. . . It is to be maintained, that the received grace of Justification is lost, not only by infidelity whereby even faith itself is lost, but also by any other mortal sin whatever, though faith be not lost; thus defending the doctrine of the divine law, which excludes from the kingdom of God not only the unbelieving, but the faithful also (who are) fornicators, adulterers, effeminate, liers with mankind, thieves, covetous, drunkards, railers, extortioners, and all others who commit deadly sins; from which, with the help of divine grace, they can refrain, and on account of which they are separated from the grace of Christ.

CHAPTER XVI. On the fruit of Justification, that is, on the merit of good works, and on the nature of that merit.

Before men, therefore, who have been justified in this manner . . . are to be set the words of the Apostle: Abound in every good work, knowing that your labour is not in vain in the Lord; for God is not unjust, that he should forget your work, and the love which you have shown in his name; and, do not lose your confidence, which hath a great reward. And, for this cause, life eternal is to be proposed to those working well unto the end, and hoping in God, both as a grace mercifully promised to the sons of God through Jesus Christ, and as a reward which is according to the promise of God Himself, to be faithfully rendered to their good works and merits. . . .

SESSION THE SEVENTH

Celebrated on the third day of the month of March, 1547.

♦ DECREE ON THE SACRAMENTS.

For the completion of the salutary doctrine on Justification, which was promulgated with the unanimous consent of the Fathers in the last preceding Session, it hath seemed suitable to treat of the most holy Sacraments of the Church, through which all true justice either begins, or being begun is increased, or being lost is repaired. . . .

ON THE SACRAMENTS IN GENERAL.

CANON I. If any one saith, that the sacraments of the New Law were not all instituted by Jesus Christ, our Lord; or, that they are more, or less, than seven, to wit, Baptism, Confirmation, the Eucharist, Penance, Extreme Unction, Order, and Matrimony; or even that any one of these seven is not truly and properly a sacrament; let him be anathema.

CANON II. If any one saith, that these said sacraments of the New Law do not differ from the sacraments of the Old Law, save that the ceremonies are different, and different the outward rites; let him be anathema.

CANON III. If any one saith, that these seven sacraments are in such wise equal to each other, as that one is not in any way more worthy than another; let him be anathema.

CANON IV. If any one saith, that the sacraments of the New Law are not necessary unto salvation, but superfluous; and that, without them, or without the desire thereof, men obtain of God, through faith alone, the grace of justification;—though all (the sacraments) are not indeed necessary for every individual; let him be anathema.

CANON V. If any one saith, that these sacraments were instituted for the sake of nourishing faith alone; let him be anathema.

CANON VI. If any one saith, that the sacraments of the New Law do not contain the grace which they signify; or, that they do not confer that grace on those who do not place an obstacle thereunto; as though they were merely outward signs of grace or justice received through faith, and certain marks of the Christian profession, whereby believers are distinguished amongst men from unbelievers; let him be anathema.

CANON VII. If any one saith, that grace, as far as God's part is concerned, is not given through the said sacraments, always, and to all men, even though they receive them rightly, but (only) sometimes, and to some persons; let him be anathema.

CANON VIII. If any one saith, that by the said sacraments of the New Law grace is not conferred through the act performed, but that faith alone in the divine promise suffices for the obtaining of grace; let him be anathema.

CANON IX. If any one saith, that, in the three sacraments, Baptism, to wit, Confirmation, and Order, there is not imprinted in the soul a character, that is, a certain spiritual and indelible Sign, on account of which they cannot be repeated; let him be anathema.

CANON X. If any one saith, that all Christians have power to administer the word, and all the sacraments; let him be anathema.

CANON XI. If any one saith, that, in ministers, when they effect, and confer the sacraments, there is not required the intention at least of doing what the Church does; let him be anathema.

CANON XII. If any one saith, that a minister, being in mortal sin . . . neither effects, nor confers the sacrament; let him be anathema.

CANON XIII. If any one saith, that the received and approved rites of the Catholic Church, wont to be used in the solemn administration of the sacraments, may be contemned, or without sin be omitted at pleasure by the ministers, or be changed, by every pastor of the churches, into other new ones; let him be anathema.

SESSION THE THIRTEENTH

Being the third under the Sovereign Pontiff, Julius III., celebrated on the eleventh day of October, 1551.

♦ DECREE CONCERNING THE MOST HOLY SACRAMENT OF THE EUCHARIST.

. . . Wherefore, this sacred and holy Synod delivering here, on this venerable and divine sacrament of the Eucharist, that sound and genuine doctrine, which the Catholic Church, instructed by our Lord Jesus Christ Himself, and by His apostles, and taught by the Holy Ghost, who day by day brings to her mind all truth, has always retained, and will preserve even to the end of the world, forbids all the faithful of Christ, to presume to believe, teach, or preach henceforth concerning the holy Eucharist, otherwise than as is explained and defined in this present decree.

CHAPTER I. On the real presence of our Lord Jesus Christ in the most holy sacrament of the Eucharist.

In the first place, the holy Synod teaches, and openly and simply professes, that, in the august sacrament of the holy Eucharist, after the consecration of the bread and wine, our Lord Jesus Christ, true God and man, is truly, really, and substantially contained under the species of those sensible things. . . .

CHAPTER II. On the reason of the Institution of this most holy Sacrament.

Wherefore, our Saviour, when about to depart out of this world to the Father, instituted this Sacrament, in which He poured forth as it were the riches of His divine love towards man, making a remembrance of his wonderful works; and He commanded us, in the participation thereof, to venerate His memory, and to show forth his death until He come to judge the world. And He would also that this sacrement should be received as the spiritual food of souls, whereby may be fed and strengthened those who live with His life. . . .

CHAPTER III. On the excellency of the most holy Eucharist over the rest of the Sacraments.

The most holy Eucharist has indeed this in common with the rest of the sacraments, that it is a symbol of a sacred thing, and is a visible form of an invisible grace; but there is found in the Eucharist this excellent and peculiar thing, that the other sacraments have then first the power of sanctifying when one uses them, whereas in the Eucharist, before being used, there is the Author Himself of sanctity. . . .

CHAPTER IV. On Transubstantiation.

And because that Christ, our Redeemer, declared that which He offered under the species of bread to be truly His own body, therefore has it ever been a firm belief in the Church of God, and this holy Synod doth now declare it anew, that, by the consecration of the bread and of the wine, a conversion is made of the whole substance of the bread into the substance of the body of Christ our Lord, and of the whole substance of the wine into the substance of His blood; which conversion is, by the holy Catholic Church, suitably and properly called Transubstantiation.

CHAPTER V. On the cult and veneration to be shown to this most holy Sacrament.

. . . All the faithful of Christ may, according to the custom ever received in the Catholic Church, render in veneration the worship of latria, which is due to the true God, to this most holy sacrament. . . .

The holy Synod declares, moreover, that very piously and religiously was this custom introduced into the Church, that this sublime and venerable sacrament be, with special veneration and solemnity, celebrated, every year, on a certain day, and that a festival; and that it be borne reverently and with honor in processions through the streets, and public places. . . .

CHAPTER VI. On reserving the Sacrament of the sacred Eucharist, and bearing it to the Sick.

The custom of reserving the holy Eucharist in the sacrarium is so ancient, that even the age of the Council of Nicaea recognized that usage. Moreover, as to carrying the sacred Eucharist itself to the sick, and carefully reserving it for this purpose in churches, besides that it is exceedingly conformable to equity and reason, it is also found enjoined in numerous councils, and is a very ancient observance of the Catholic Church. Wherefore, this holy Synod ordains, that this salutary and necessary custom is to be by all means retained.

CHAPTER VII. On the preparation to be given that one may worthily receive the sacred Eucharist

If it is unbeseeming for any one to approach to any of the sacred functions, unless he approach holily; assuredly, the more the holiness and divinity of

Document Text

this heavenly sacrament are understood by a Christian, the more diligently ought he to give heed that he approach not to receive it but with great reverence and holiness. . . . Wherefore, he who would communicate, ought to recall to mind the precept of the Apostle; Let a man prove himself. Now ecclesiastical usage declares that necessary proof to be, that no one, conscious to himself of mortal sin, how contrite soever he may seem to himself, ought to approach to the sacred Eucharist without previous sacramental confession. This the holy Synod hath decreed is to be invariably observed by all Christians, even by those priests on whom it may be incumbent by their office to celebrate, provided the opportunity of a confessor do not fail them; but if, in an urgent necessity, a priest should celebrate without previous confession, let him confess as soon as possible.

CHAPTER VIII. On the use of this admirable Sacrament.

Now as to the use of this holy sacrament, our Fathers have rightly and wisely distinguished three ways of receiving it. For they have taught that some receive it sacramentally only, to wit sinners: others spiritually only, those to wit who eating in desire that heavenly bread which is set before them, are, by a lively faith which worketh by charity, made sensible of the fruit and usefulness thereof: whereas the third (class) receive it both sacramentally and spiritually, and these are they who so prove and prepare themselves beforehand, as to approach to this divine table clothed with the wedding garment. Now as to the reception of the sacrament, it was always the custom in the Church of God, that laymen should receive the communion from priests; but that priests when celebrating should communicate themselves; which custom, as coming down from an apostolical tradition, ought with justice and reason to be retained. . . .

SESSION THE TWENTY-SECOND

Being the sixth under the Sovereign Pontiff, Pius IV., celebrated on the seventeenth day of September, 1562.

♦ DOCTRINE ON THE SACRIFICE OF THE MASS.

. . . (The Synod) instructed by the illumination of the Holy Ghost, teaches, declares; and decrees what follows, to be preached to the faithful, on the subject of the Eucharist, considered as being a true and singular sacrifice.

CHAPTER I. On the institution of the most holy Sacrifice of the Mass.

. . . He offered up to God the Father His own body and blood under the species of bread and wine; and, under the symbols of those same things, He delivered (His own body and blood) to be received by His apostles, whom He then constituted priests of the New Testament; and by those words, Do this in commemoration

Glossary

Apostolic	descended from Christ's apostles, particularly Peter, the first leader of Christianity after Christ's death
Confirmation	the sacrament by which a person entering adulthood is confirmed in his or her faith
Council of Nicaea	a council of church fathers held in Nicaea in modern-day Turkey; the first such council was held in 325, the second in 787.
Eucharist	the sacrament of Holy Communion by which, according to Church doctrine, bread and wine are transformed into the body and blood of Christ
Extreme Unction	the anointing of the dead or dying, today called the Anointing of the Sick
heretics	those who believe in doctrines contrary to the orthodox doctrines of the Church
indulgence	a full or partial remission of punishment for sin granted to souls in Purgatory
John	the author of the New Testament book of Revelation
justification	the process of achieving eternal salvation
Latin vulgate	the fourth-century Latin version of the Bible
latria	adoration given to God

Document Text

of me, He commanded them and their successors in the priesthood, to offer (them); even as the Catholic Church has always understood and taught. . . .

CHAPTER II. That the Sacrifice of the Mass is propitiatory both for the living and the dead.

. . . The holy Synod teaches, that this sacrifice is truly propitiatory and that by means thereof this is effected, that we obtain mercy, and find grace in seasonable aid, if we draw nigh unto God, contrite and penitent, with a sincere heart and upright faith, with fear and reverence. For the Lord, appeased by the oblation thereof, and granting the grace and gift of penitence, forgives even heinous crimes and sins. . . .

CHAPTER III. On Masses in honour of the Saints.

And although the Church has been accustomed at times to celebrate, certain masses in honour and memory of the saints; not therefore, however, doth she teach that sacrifice is offered unto them, but unto God alone, who crowned them; whence neither is the priest wont to say, "I offer sacrifice to thee, Peter, or Paul;" but, giving thanks to God for their victories, he implores their patronage, that they may vouchsafe to intercede for us in heaven, whose memory we celebrate upon earth.

CHAPTER IV. On the Canon of the Mass.

And whereas it beseemeth, that holy things be administered in a holy manner, and of all holy things this sacrifice is the most holy; to the end that it might be worthily and reverently offered and received, the Catholic Church instituted, many years ago, the sacred Canon, so pure from every error, that nothing is contained therein which does not in the highest degree savour of a certain holiness and piety, and raise up unto God the minds of those that offer.

For it is composed, out of the very words of the Lord, the traditions of the apostles, and the pious institutions also of holy pontiffs.

CHAPTER V. On the solemn ceremonies of the Sacrifice of the Mass.

. . . Holy Mother Church instituted certain rites, to wit that certain things be pronounced in the mass in a low, and others in a louder, tone. She has likewise employed ceremonies, such as mystic benedictions, lights, incense, vestments, and many other things of this kind, derived from an apostolical discipline and tradition, whereby both the majesty of so great a sacrifice might be recommended, and the minds of the faithful be excited, by those visible signs of religion and piety, to the contemplation of those most sublime things which are hidden in this sacrifice.

CHAPTER VI. On Mass wherein the priest alone communicates.

The sacred and holy Synod would fain indeed that, at each mass, the faithful who are present should communicate, not only in spiritual desire, but also

Glossary

mortal sin	in Church doctrine, a serious sin that, if unforgiven by God through confession, merits eternal punishment in hell
New Law	the New Testament
Order	Holy Orders, the sacrament of entering the priesthood
Paul	an early convert to Christianity and author of thirteen epistles, or letters, in the New Testament
Peter	one of Christ's apostles and the first leader of the Christian Church
Pontius Pilate	the Roman prefect of Judaea who sentenced Jesus Christ to his death
Purgatory	in Church teaching, the place where souls go temporarily until they are fit to enter heaven
sacrament	a formal religious ceremony that confers grace on the participant
schismatics	those who promote a schism, or a divergent branch of a religion
species	here, the external elements of the Eucharist, that is, the bread and wine
vulgar	here, a reference to a vernacular native language (as opposed to Latin)

by the sacramental participation of the Eucharist, that thereby a more abundant fruit might be derived to them from this most holy sacrifice: but not therefore, if this be not always done, does It condemn, as private and unlawful, but approves of and therefore commends, those masses in which the priest alone communicates sacramentally; since those masses also ought to be considered as truly common; partly because the people communicate spiritually thereat; partly also because they are celebrated by a public minister of the Church, not for himself only, but for all the faithful, who belong to the body of Christ.

CHAPTER VII. On the water that is to be mixed with the wine to be offered in the chalice.

The holy Synod notices, in the next place, that it has been enjoined by the Church on priests, to mix water with the wine that is to be offered in the chalice; as well because it is believed that Christ the Lord did this, as also because from His side there came out blood and water; the memory of which mystery is renewed by this commixture; and, whereas in the apocalypse of blessed John, the peoples are called waters, the union of that faithful people with Christ their head is hereby represented.

CHAPTER VIII. On not celebrating the Mass every where in the vulgar tongue; the mysteries of the Mass to be explained to the people.

Although the mass contains great instruction for the faithful people, nevertheless, it has not seemed expedient to the Fathers, that it should be every where celebrated in the vulgar tongue. Wherefore, the ancient usage of each church, and the rite approved of by the holy Roman Church, the mother and mistress of all churches, being in each place retained; and, that the sheep of Christ may not suffer hunger, nor the little ones ask for bread, and there be none to break it unto them, the holy Synod charges pastors, and all who have the cure of souls, that they frequently, during the celebration of mass, expound either by themselves, or others, some portion of those things which are read at mass, and that, amongst the rest, they explain some mystery of this most holy sacrifice, especially on the Lord's days and festivals.

CHAPTER IX. Preliminary Remark on the following Canons.

And because that many errors are at this time disseminated and many things are taught and maintained by divers persons, in opposition to this ancient faith, which is based on the sacred Gospel, the traditions of the Apostles, and the doctrine of the holy Fathers; the sacred and holy Synod, after many and grave deliberations maturely had touching these matters, has resolved, with the unanimous consent of all the Fathers, to condemn, and to eliminate from holy Church, by means of the canons subjoined, whatsoever is opposed to this most pure faith and sacred doctrine. . . .

SESSION THE TWENTY-FIFTH

Begun on the third, and terminated on the fourth, day of December, 1563, being the ninth and last under the Sovereign Pontiff, Pius IV.

♦ DECREE CONCERNING PURGATORY.

. . . There is a Purgatory, and . . . the souls there detained are helped by the suffrages of the faithful, but principally by the acceptable sacrifice of the altar; the holy Synod enjoins on bishops that they diligently endeavour that the sound doctrine concerning Purgatory, transmitted by the holy Fathers and sacred councils, be believed, maintained, taught, and every where proclaimed by the faithful of Christ. But let the more difficult and subtle questions, and which tend not to edification, and from which for the most part there is no increase of piety, be excluded from popular discourses before the uneducated multitude. . . .

♦ ON THE INVOCATION, VENERATION, AND RELICS, OF SAINTS, AND ON SACRED IMAGES.

The holy Synod enjoins on all bishops, and others who sustain the office and charge of teaching, that, agreeably to the usage of the Catholic and Apostolic Church, received from the primitive times of the Christian religion, and agreeably to the consent of the holy Fathers, and to the decrees of sacred Councils, they especially instruct the faithful diligently concerning the intercession and invocation of saints; the honour (paid) to relics; and the legitimate use of images: teaching them, that the saints, who reign together with Christ, offer up their own prayers to God for men. . . . Also, that the holy bodies of holy martyrs, and of others now living with Christ . . . are to be venerated by the faithful; through which (bodies) many benefits are bestowed by God on men. . . .

On the fourth day of December.

♦ DECREE CONCERNING INDULGENCES.

. . . The power of conferring Indulgences was granted by Christ to the Church; and she has, even in the most ancient times, used the said power, delivered unto her of God. . . . The use of Indulgences, for the Christian people most salutary, and approved of by the authority of sacred Councils, is to be retained in the Church; and It condemns with anathema those who either assert, that they are useless; or who deny that there is in the Church the power of granting them. In granting them, however, It desires that, in accordance with the ancient and approved custom in the Church, moderation be observed; lest, by excessive facility, ecclesiastical discipline be enervated. And being desirous that the abuses which have crept therein, and by occasion of which this honourable name of Indulgences is blasphemed by heretics, be amended and corrected. . . .

♦ **ON THE INDEX OF BOOKS; ON THE CATECHISM, BREVIARY, AND MISSAL.**

The sacred and Holy Synod . . . commissioned certain chosen Fathers to consider what ought to be done touching various censures, and books either suspected or pernicious, and to report thereon to the said holy Synod; hearing now that the finishing hand has been put to that labour by those Fathers, which, however, by reason of the variety and multitude of books cannot be distinctly and conveniently judged of by the holy Synod; It enjoins that whatsoever has been by them done shall be laid before the most holy Roman Pontiff, that it may be by his judgment and authority terminated and made public.

Teresa of Ávila
(Teresa of Avila's Vision of a Dove, c.1614 [oil on panel], Rubens, Peter Paul [1577-1640] / Fitzwilliam Museum, University of Cambridge, UK / The Bridgeman Art Library International)

THE LIFE OF ST. TERESA OF JESUS

"All the things of God gave me great pleasure; and I was a prisoner to the things of the world."

Overview

The Life of St. Teresa of Jesus is the title customarily given to the autobiography of Teresa of Ávila. Begun around 1562 and revised a few years later at the urging of her confessors, both as a way to examine her spiritual development and to spread the story of God's work in her life, the book traces her religious experience from early childhood to the time of writing. As such it was both a defense of her orthodoxy and a testimony to the larger Catholic world. The Life of St. Teresa of Jesus deals with some of the writer's favorite themes, including the importance of strict observance in convents and monasteries and the value and satisfaction of mental prayer. She also records her own mystical experiences as well as the beginning of her reforming career. The book provides an excellent introduction to a study of this remarkable woman.

Context

Teresa of Ávila wrote at a time of great change for the Catholic Church. The century in which she lived marked not only the Protestant Reformation but also the culmination of generations of struggle to achieve Catholic Reform (the Catholic equivalent of the Protestant Reformation). It was also a time of cultural and political upheaval, as governments in Europe began the shift from personal expressions of a monarch's will to the larger, more powerful, and more intrusive bureaucracies associated with the modern world.

Within the Catholic Church, the Council of Trent (1545–1563) defined Catholic beliefs and codified a number of reforms, strengthening the church hierarchy to carry out further work. The movement to transform and strengthen the Catholic Church represented by Trent was led by a number of religious orders, some of them traditional institutions in the midst of reform and others entirely new organizations. The Society of Jesus (the Jesuits) represented one sixteenth-century attempt to transform a certain type of monasticism to meet the needs of the Catholic Church of the day. In contrast to the Jesuits, who sought to strengthen the Church by engaging the world, other religious orders, including Teresa's Discalced Carmelites, participated in Catholic Reform by a return to rigorous discipline in monastery or convent. Teresa's own life spanned the period in which the somewhat relaxed standards of traditional convents were brought into line with the more rigorous and demanding expectations of contemporary Catholicism.

The sixteenth century is often viewed as Spain's golden age. Under the rule of the Hapsburg monarchs, particularly the Holy Roman Emperor Charles V and his son King Philip II, Spain reached the apogee of its political power and influence. Spanish armies, bolstered by gold from the New World, controlled Spain and a vast empire in the Americas as well as the Low Countries and parts of Italy and frequently threatened France, while diplomacy and marriage extended the Spanish Hapsburg hegemony into other lands. Catholic Reform was furthered to a great extent by the efforts of various Spanish churchmen. Cardinal Ximénes de Cisneros, for instance, the adviser to the rulers Ferdinand II of Aragon and Isabella I of Castile, initiated a campaign of reform in the Spanish church that in many ways showed the way for the reforms of Trent. Saint Ignatius of Loyola, founder of the Society of Jesus, was also Spanish, as were many of his early followers. And, of course, the sixteenth century was the great age of Spanish literature, the time of Miguel de Cervantes, who wrote Don Quixote.

Teresa of Ávila, along with her associate and protégé Saint John of the Cross (Juan de Yepes Álverez), are truly representative figures of Spanish accomplishment in religious matters and the development of vernacular literature. John of the Cross, in particular, is considered one of the greatest Spanish poets, while his and Teresa's prose accounts of their religious experience made important contributions to the growth of Spanish as a vehicle for literature. Their combined efforts to reform the Carmelite Order by founding the branch known as the Discalced Carmelites not only were representative of reform efforts but also helped show the way to a more disciplined and effective Catholic Church.

When Teresa's confessors urged her to write an account of her spiritual pilgrimage, they may have been primarily interested in helping her track her religious experience and growth. However, as the leading figure in

Time Line

1534
- **August 15**
  The Society of Jesus (the Jesuits) is founded when Ignatius Loyola and six other students from the University of Paris meet in a crypt beneath the Church of Saint Denis and take a vow of poverty and chastity.

1536
- Teresa enrolls as a Carmelite in the Convent of the Incarnation at Ávila.

1542
- **June 24**
  John of the Cross is born.

1545
- **December 13**
  The Council of Trent holds its first session.

1562
- Teresa establishes the reformed Carmelite house of Saint Joseph at Ávila.

1563
- The pope gives formal approval for the Discalced Carmelites.
- **December 4**
  The Council of Trent concludes.

1565
- Teresa revises and completes her autobiography at the direction of her confessor.

1567
- Teresa is granted permission to establish reformed houses of Discalced Carmelites.

1568
- The first male house of Discalced Carmelites is established at Duruelo, Spain.

1569
- Teresa finishes a revised copy of her *Way of Perfection*, describing the method for making progress in the contemplative life.

1576
- The Carmelite Order and the Inquisition begin disciplinary proceedings against Teresa.

1577
- Teresa writes *The Interior Castle*.

---

attempts to reform the Carmelite Order, Teresa's beliefs and program were of wide interest. Her autobiography could provide evidence of her religious orthodoxy to nervous superiors as well as explain the reasons behind the changes Teresa hoped to make.

About the Author

The mystic and church reformer commonly known as Teresa of Ávila was born to a noble Castilian family in 1515 and given the name Teresa Sánchez de Cepeda Dávila y Ahumada. According to her own account, she was raised in a pious family, but her early attraction to religion disappeared during her teenage years when she was caught up in the normal interests of a girl of her time. It was a serious illness that finally drew her attention back to religion, and ultimately, despite some family opposition, she became a nun.

Teresa had been educated in a local Augustinian convent, but in following her vocation she chose to join the Carmelite Convent of the Incarnation in her native Ávila. Although the Carmelites were a contemplative order (focused on prayer), Teresa found their relaxed rules and the presence of frequent visitors a distraction. A second serious illness briefly spurred initial experiences of prayer, but eventually social life in the convent turned Teresa's thoughts from the serious contemplation that in later life she came to expect of nuns. Guilt over her own lack of devotion made her reluctant to pray beyond participation in the mandatory oral prayers of the community. Reflecting on this part of her life in her autobiography, Teresa blamed her own sinful nature but also the lack of skill of confessors who should have guided her along the right path. It was also this experience that led to her later zeal for stricter standards to reform the Carmelite Order.

Teresa's spiritual awakening occurred gradually. While she gave the primary credit to God's work, she identified the assistance of several able confessors, the help of various spiritual books, and her own experiments in prayer as important contributors to her new devotion. The real change for Teresa was leaving behind the simple vocal prayers of the community and turning to mental prayer. This mental prayer, beginning with an imagining of Jesus or of stories from the Bible, led by a series of steps to a special state of prayer—acquired contemplation. Beyond this highest level of mental prayer, God might choose to draw a devout person to a supernatural state of mystical experience. Undergoing such an experience set Teresa permanently on her path of devotion.

A desire for a more austere environment to stir contemplation led Teresa to take steps toward establishing a new kind of Carmelite house, one with an emphasis on rigorous discipline. With financial support from a local widow and practical support from her bishop, Teresa founded a reformed Carmelite House in Ávila in 1562. The Convent of Saint Joseph, with its small population and strict rules, soon attracted popular admiration. The following year Teresa received papal approval for the standards of her new foundation. It was the requirement that the nuns go barefoot ("discalced") that gave the name of Discalced Carmelites to reformed houses in the Order. In 1567 the head of the Carmelite order gave Teresa permission to establish a number of reformed convents.

At about the same time that Teresa received the official blessing to begin founding reformed houses, she met a Carmelite priest, John of the Cross. The young man was preparing to transfer to the much stricter Carthusian order; Teresa persuaded him to remain a Carmelite, and he became instrumental in helping her with her reforms. Theologically educated and a gifted writer (he is considered one of Spain's greatest poets), John of the Cross busied himself with starting male houses for Discalced Carmelites. These male houses would produce the confessors necessary for the continued growth of Teresa's convents.

Not everyone appreciated Teresa's reforms. There were many Carmelites who felt that her houses were too strict, and in 1577 they launched a counter-attack against the reform movement. Teresa not only faced formal charges from her own order but was also investigated by the Inquisition (a tribunal established to maintain Catholic orthodoxy)—probably on the basis of complaints made by her detractors. Teresa obeyed a command to stop traveling and to remain at a single house. John of the Cross refused a similar order and was imprisoned under particularly harsh conditions. Fortunately for Teresa, she had powerful supporters in the Church and in Spain's government who appreciated her reforming efforts. In 1579 all proceedings against Teresa and her reform efforts were dropped, and she returned to her active role until the time of her death in 1582.

For all her efforts in founding new religious houses, Teresa is remembered today as a mystic. She chronicled some of her experiences of God's presence as well as advice about how to pray in such writings as *The Interior Castle* and *The Way of Perfection*. Certainly her writings give evidence of her intelligence and something of her powerful personality, but they do not reflect the sense of humor for which she was known in her own day or her charm, which impressed many of her contemporaries. In 1614 Teresa was beatified by Pope Paul V, and in 1622 she was canonized by Pope Gregory XV. Today, Teresa's reputation is as high as ever. Her devotional works are frequently reprinted and easily available. In 1970 she became the first female to be named officially a Doctor of the Church—a title given to those individuals recognized for their contribution to theology or doctrine.

Explanation and Analysis of the Document

Teresa's autobiography tells the story of her life from her birth to the beginning of her career as a reformer of the Carmelite Order. It includes a description of her childhood, her vocation as a nun, years that she judged as spiritually wasted, her increasing experience of God's presence in prayer, and her desire to enact stricter discipline in her convent in order to facilitate spirituality. The section represented here tells of Teresa's early days as a

Time Line

1579	■ All actions against Teresa are ended.
1582	■ October 4 — Teresa dies at Alba de Tormes, Salamanca, Spain.
1614	■ April 24 — Teresa is beatified by Pope Paul V.
1622	■ March 12 — Teresa is canonized by Pope Gregory XV.

nun, when various temptations kept her from full devotion to God. It was this experience that drove her to push for high standards in convents.

♦ My Soul Was So Distracted by Many Vanities, That I Was Ashamed to Draw Near unto God

Teresa had previously related how she became a nun not out of a love for God but from fear of damnation. After a serious illness, a miraculous healing, and a profound spiritual experience, she drifted through many years in the convent, caught up in trivial sins and without any real devotion. At one time private, personal prayer had been an important part of her spiritual experience. Now, ashamed to approach God because of her attachment to various frivolous distractions, she gave up such prayers, limiting her communication with God to the vocal prayers required of every nun.

The distinction between vocal and mental prayer is very important in Teresa's thought. Vocal prayer—simply speaking a prayer aloud to God, the type of prayer used in religious services—represented to her only the bottom rung of a ladder leading to increasingly vital communication with God. Mental prayer meant fully setting one's mind on God, an exercise that could be accomplished in conjunction with verbal prayer. In fact, Teresa believed that combining the two disciplines was often the most effective way to achieve full contemplation of God, the goal of prayer, and a source of great of joy.

Teresa's careful analysis of her sins during this period, identifying not only actions but also motives, is typical of the sort of autobiography written at the request of a confessor. Just as a doctor would seek to isolate symptoms in order to diagnose an underlying disease, a skilled spiritual counselor would use such details to help an individual make spiritual progress.

♦ They Gave Me as Much Liberty as They Did to the Oldest Nuns . . . and Had Great Confidence in Me

Teresa's comments about lax religious houses are very typical of her written work and her public career. Examin-

John of the Cross
(St. John of the Cross, detail [engraving], French School, [16th century] / Bibliotheque Nationale, Paris, France / Giraudon / The Bridgeman Art Library International)

ing her own life, she believed she would have avoided many occasions for sin if the rules at the Convent of the Incarnation had been stricter. She recognized that for those who were truly good, the relaxed rules did little harm. However, for those not inclined to the good (like herself), stricter regulations were of great value. The particular regulation Teresa advocated was "enclosure"—limitations on visitors to religious houses (and limitations on the ability of members of houses to leave on personal business). According to Teresa, God had to do extra work to keep nuns in lax houses on the right track. She is careful to note here that the lack of strict enclosure had not led to serious public sins in her own house, a comment meant to avoid offending her superiors or fellow nuns.

But even after making the concession that laxity did not harm her own house, Teresa returns to her main theme, that of the great danger posed by weak standards in convents. She suggests that if parents are not concerned enough about their daughters' spiritual condition to keep them out of lax convents, they at least ought to consider potential scandals. A woman would be better off making a disadvantageous marriage or living unmarried at home (and possibly getting into trouble) than going to a lax convent, where she might fall into sin. This criticism would have been far more biting to Teresa's contemporaries than to modern readers,

since in Teresa's time nuns were believed to be spiritually superior to married women, and it was considered a disgrace for a woman to marry "beneath" her station. For Teresa to proclaim that a bad marriage was spiritually superior to life in a convent was a telling indictment of lax houses. Teresa makes clear that the common failings she identifies are not the fault of individual women, who learn only what they are taught, but instead a systemic failure that leads to so much corruption. In a final rhetorical jab at lax houses, she compares their teaching to that of Protestant heretics, who reverse good and bad.

This was not a problem restricted to nuns. Lax male houses face the same pitfalls. She describes a religious house without strict rules as a place where two roads run in opposite directions, one leading to God and the other to destruction— where the downward path is often the most crowded. According to Teresa, monks or nuns in lax houses who are serious about their vocation must often hide their devotion from their fellows in order to escape persecution. This corruption of the important institution of monasticism is diagnosed as one of the serious faults leading to contemporary turmoil in the Catholic Church.

The term *friar* is the technical name for a male member of certain religious orders such as the Carmelites. A monk is a member of an enclosed order, devoting his life to prayer or service within a monastery. A friar is a member of a non-enclosed order (called mendicant orders), taking similar monastic vows but devoting his life to service in the world (preaching, teaching, or serving a parish, for example). Although Teresa believed that Carmelite convents should be enclosed so as to encourage the nuns in their lives of devotion, she did not see a lack of enclosure as a threat to the mission of mendicant friars, such as Dominicans, Jesuits, or Carmelites. She personally benefited greatly from the spiritual guidance of mendicants from different orders. Carmelite friars would play an important role in Teresa's reforms by supplying confessors and spiritual directors for her reformed convents.

♦ **When I Began to Indulge in These Conversations, I Did Not Think . . . That My Soul Must Be Injured**

Teresa then returns to her own story. The social life she found to be such a source of spiritual distraction does, in fact, seem very ordinary and not obviously wicked when viewed from the outside, and so it is easy to overlook as an occasion for sin. She concedes that possibly it would not have been a problem for a better person.

Teresa began to question her mode of life in the convent after she experienced a vision of Jesus. Initially she was disturbed by what she had seen and made a few superficial changes. Before long, however, she began to question the experience. Unsure whether it was a genuine vision, she wondered if it had been her imagination or worse—a deception. In retrospect, Teresa believes she knew at some level that it was a genuine message from God but was unwilling to accept what God required of her, and so she carried on according to her custom. Not long afterward she had a

Essential Quotes

> "Oh, what utter ruin . . . where the rules of the Order are not kept; where the same monastery offers two roads: one of virtue and observance, the other of inobservance, and both equally frequented! I have spoken incorrectly: they are not equally frequented; for, on account of our sins, the way of the greatest imperfection is the most frequented; and because it is the broadest, it is also the most in favour."

> "This Dominican father, who was a very good man, fearing God, did me a very great service; for I confessed to him. He took upon himself the task of helping my soul in earnest, and of making me see the perilous state I was in."

> "All the things of God gave me great pleasure; and I was a prisoner to the things of the world. It seemed as if I wished to reconcile two contradictions, so much at variance one with another as are the life of the spirit and the joys and pleasures and amusements of sense."

> "I know no reason why it should not be lawful for him who is beginning to love and serve God in earnest to confide to another his joys and sorrows; for they who are given to prayer are thoroughly accustomed to both."

second vision, this time of a loathsome creature, a vision shared by several other nuns.

Teresa also records words of warning and advice she received from an older nun, a woman who happened to be a relative. Looking back, Teresa laments her own bad example in the past and hopes her words now promote positive change. By presenting the image of the elderly nun, described as a "strict observer of the rule," Teresa is putting herself in the context of traditional Carmelite practice. Other Carmelite nuns had promoted strict regulations and warned against laxity as well; Teresa here is doing nothing more than other good members of the order had done in the past.

♦ **I Had a Very Strong Desire to Further the Progress of Others: A Most Common Temptation**

Teresa continues her spiritual autobiography in a lengthy discussion that tells of her interaction with her father and then of his death. Her father's seriousness about his own spiritual life is contrasted with Teresa's lack of dedication. The married (though widowed) layman is more devoted to pious observance than the nun in the convent. The mention of the book Teresa shared with her father underscores a common theme in her writing. She valued the impact that religious texts made on her life and felt they were good for others also. This may point to one of Teresa's many motives for writing her autobiography—the desire to help others as she had been helped.

Although Teresa identifies several sins in her conduct at the time, her great fault was giving up prayer, a mistake that led to other sins, because when she prayed she sometimes recognized her faults and repented of them. By avoiding prayer, she avoided this accountability. Teresa recognized many barriers to prayer but urged devout people to overcome them and continue in their efforts. Recognizing her own feeble excuses as mistakes, the author concludes (and urges) that there is no valid excuse not to pray.

In an aside on her sickness, Teresa indicates that in later years she induced vomiting to relieve stomach ailments. Modern people, familiar with anorexia and bulimia, have questioned whether some mystics in the past had what would today be diagnosed as eating disorders. The recognized authority in the field, Caroline Walker Bynum, who studies women in a slightly earlier period than Teresa of Ávila, cautions against a too-easy identification of past practices and modern disease—body image had nothing to do with their practices, for instance. In Teresa's case, along with other grounds to discount a diagnosis of bulimia, the self-induced vomiting appears to have been a remedy for a medical problem.

One of the great changes within Catholicism during Teresa's time was a tremendous transformation in attitudes toward the appropriate frequency of receiving Communion. During the Middle Ages, laypeople ordinarily received the Eucharist only once a year, the so-called Easter duty. It was during the era of Catholic Reform that Church authorities began to promote the value of more frequent reception. Teresa, obviously a devout woman, speaks of being counseled to receive once every two weeks.

The "choir" Teresa mentions is not a singing group in the modern sense but the responsibility to join her fellow nuns at religious services in the church. The choir (or quire) was generally the space between where laypeople would sit in a church and the sanctuary (the site of the altar). In a convent, nuns would sit in the choir and sing their parts of the service. The association with singing led, of course, to the contemporary meaning of *choir*. Modern church designs differ, but in some churches the choir is still situated in the area that gave the singing group its name.

♦ **My Father Was Not the Only Person Whom I Prevailed upon to Practise Prayer**

Teresa continues to develop some of the same themes, intermingling stories of her father with her thoughts on prayer. Catholic theology differentiates between two kinds of sin—mortal and venial. Mortal sins are serious sins that can send a person to hell without the intervention of forgiveness applied through the sacraments of the Church. Venial sins are trivial failings that cannot damn a soul to hell but which do impair spiritual growth. Although the sacraments cause Christ's redemptive suffering to wipe away the stain of sin, freeing the soul from the danger of hell, sins still must have consequences. The Catholic Church teaches that satisfaction for sins can be made either in this life (through suffering and good works or in other ways) or after death in purgatory. Teresa's analysis of the seriousness of sins (mortal versus venial) is typical of a document intended for a confessor, where spiritual guidance depended on a very accurate understanding of the subject's spiritual state.

The concept of redemptive suffering was important to Teresa, as to most mystics and to all Catholics of Teresa's time. A previous mention of the Lord's taking pleasure in her suffering was not an indication that she believed in a sadistic deity but that her attitude toward her infirmities was making them redemptive. Suffering itself was not a spiritual blessing—suffering could be an opportunity to receive blessing by accepting it with the right attitude. Teresa here speaks of physical pain as a blessing. Particularly, she points out to her father that the pain in his shoulder is reminiscent of Christ's pain in carrying the cross. Armed with this image, he could identify with Jesus and accept the pain, allowing it to become a blessing. Teresa cites a priest who believed that her father had so purified himself in life that he went straight to heaven, not needing the suffering of purgatory to prepare himself.

♦ **This Dominican Father . . . Did Me A Very Great Service; for I Confessed to Him**

One of the spiritual turning points in Teresa's life was meeting her Dominican confessor. Teresa had already lamented the lack of spiritual guidance she had received from other confessors. Now, at last, she came into contact with a priest who had the training and insight to give her the spiritual direction she needed. This direction included the command to receive the Eucharist more frequently and to persevere in prayer. Teresa did return to her habits of prayer but did not immediately cease other sinful behaviors. This led to a long period of ambivalence and discomfort; still, having gone back to praying, Teresa never again abandoned the practice.

The quality of the experience in the confessional was one of the major features of Catholic Reform. Medieval Catholics had recognized the value of spiritual guidance by priests during confessions, but the general lack of preparation and education for clergy meant that most people in confessions simply listed their sins and received penances and absolution. It was during the sixteenth century that real progress began to be made in training priests to use the confessional to assist people in spiritual growth. Jesuits, in particular, were known for their skill in helping those in confession discover the underlying motives and causes of sin and for assisting people in moving forward in their religious lives. Teresa's concern with finding skilled confessors was very typical of her age.

♦ **O My God! If I Might, I Would Speak of the Occasions from Which God Delivered Me**

As Teresa takes stock once again of this era of her life toward the end of the chapter, she is particularly grateful that God allowed her to escape some of the trouble her sins deserved. If her fellow nuns had realized how barren her devotional life had been at a time when she was well respected in her convent, it would have prevented her from being a leader in reform later. In fact, she identifies God's method of working in her life as giving her blessings in response to her sins—the continual gifts of "consolation" were far more effective at working on her conscience than any punishment would have been. This apostrophe to God is typical of this sort of autobiographical literature, following the model of Saint Augustine's *Confessions*. Although Teresa would have read many similar passages in other works, she knew and appreciated Augustine's classic spiritual work first hand.

♦ **It Is a Great Evil for a Soul to Be Alone in the Midst of Such Great Dangers**

In calling for enclosed convents and strict rules and in citing the distraction of social demands in the convent, Teresa was not advocating a limit to human contact in religious houses. Teresa believed that good companions could only help in the life of prayer, particularly through offering accountability and advice. Previously she had described how devout friars and nuns were pressured into laxity by their communities and forced to hide their commitment to prayer and contemplation. Teresa envisions houses where, in contrast, those serious about their vocations would be able to speak out and encourage others. This, in essence, was the goal of Teresa's reforms. The stricter rules she championed were simply a means to create an environment where nuns (or friars) were free to encourage each other to greater devotion.

Teresa closes the chapter with an address to her confessor (and, by extension, her superiors), humbly asking for guidance and correction. Such a statement is conventional for this sort of document, which was written in part so that the spiritual director could guide the writer.

Audience

An autobiography like *The Life of St. Teresa of Jesus* is always intended for more than one audience. The first audience is the author and his or her confessor. It allows the writer to contemplate experiences of sin and grace in a new and deeper way and provides opportunities for a confessor to understand the person he is guiding. Second, such an autobiography is frequently intended to be evaluated by ecclesiastical authorities as a proof of orthodoxy. In this instance, one of the original copies was forwarded to spiritual superiors, who, having read it, were able to endorse Teresa's ministry. Later, when she was investigated for heresy, the Inquisition studied a copy of her manuscript. It is not known if her autobiography helped exonerate her, but the fact that the Spanish church allowed the work to circulate shows that the authorities found nothing offensive in it.

Finally, spiritual autobiographies were always written with at least a possible view toward a popular audience. Teresa herself found religious books to be an extremely important part of her growth in devotion, and she singled out Augustine's *Confessions* as particularly vital for her own spiritual development. Even though the initial purpose of writing was to satisfy a confessor and spiritual superiors, Teresa certainly wrote with the hope that one day her words could help others as others' words had helped her.

Impact

The Life of St. Teresa of Jesus satisfied those in authority over the author. Since this endorsement allowed her to continue her career as a reformer, it was an important success. However, more significant was the way in which the eventual reception of the book by a larger audience helped establish and maintain Teresa's reputation. Finally, the Spanish-language *Life* and her other vernacular writings were early contributions to the growth of Spanish literature. In modern times, twentieth-century Catholic historians, using the writings of Teresa and John of the Cross, have frequently made their form of mysticism the standard by which other Catholic mystics are judged. As a result, the spiritual experience of Teresa has, through her writing, become almost normative as a guide for Catholic devotion. Such judgments are subjective and unofficial. Officially, however, the naming of Teresa as a Doctor of the Church gives all her writing substantial authority within the Catholic Church.

Questions for Further Study

1. What impact did broader political events in the sixteenth century have on the life of Teresa? What impact did they have on her writing?

2. Why do you believe that Teresa was a proponent of rigorous discipline in monastic life? What purpose did such a life serve?

3. In the contemporary world, fewer and fewer women are adopting lives of prayer and meditation in a convent. In the sixteenth century, though, convent life was a reasonable option for many women. Why do you think this was so?

4. Why did Teresa write her autobiography? Do you find it surprising that a woman dedicated to a life of prayer and contemplation would write such a public document? Explain.

5. What impact did Teresa and her writings have on the history of Spanish literature?

Further Reading

■ Books

Clissold, Stephen. *St. Teresa of Avila*. New York: Seabury Press, 1982.

Dicken, E. W. Trueman. *The Crucible of Love: A Study of the Mysticism of St. Teresa of Jesus and St. John of the Cross*. New York: Sheed and Ward, 1963.

Medwick, Cathleen. *Teresa of Avila: The Progress of a Soul*. New York: Knopf, 1999.

Teresa of Ávila. *The Interior Castle*, trans. Kieran Kavanaugh and Otilio Rodriguez. New York: Paulist Press, 1979.

Williams, Rowan. *Teresa of Avila*. London: Geoffrey Chapman, 1991.

■ Web sites

Teresa of Ávila. *The Way of Perfection*. Christian Classics Ethereal Library Web site.
  http://www.ccel.org/ccel/teresa/way.html

—Raymond A. Powell

The Life of St. Teresa of Jesus

Chapter VII

♦ **Lukewarmness. The Loss of Grace. Inconvenience of Laxity in Religious Houses.**

1. So, then, going on from pastime to pastime, from vanity to vanity, from one occasion of sin to another, I began to expose myself exceedingly to the very greatest dangers: my soul was so distracted by many vanities, that I was ashamed to draw near unto God in an act of such special friendship as that of prayer. As my sins multiplied, I began to lose the pleasure and comfort I had in virtuous things: and that loss contributed to the abandonment of prayer. I see now most clearly, O my Lord, that this comfort departed from me because I had departed from Thee.

2. It was the most fearful delusion into which Satan could plunge me—to give up prayer under the pretence of humility. I began to be afraid of giving myself to prayer, because I saw myself so lost. I thought it would be better for me, seeing that in my wickedness I was one of the most wicked, to live like the multitude—to say the prayers which I was bound to say, and that vocally: not to practise mental prayer nor commune with God so much; for I deserved to be with the devils, and was deceiving those who were about me, because I made an outward show of goodness; and therefore the community in which I dwelt is not to be blamed; for with my cunning I so managed matters, that all had a good opinion of me; and yet I did not seek this deliberately by simulating devotion; for in all that relates to hypocrisy and ostentation—glory be to God!—I do not remember that I ever offended Him, so far as I know. The very first movements herein gave me such pain, that the devil would depart from me with loss, and the gain remained with me; and thus, accordingly, he never tempted me much in this way. Perhaps, however, if God had permitted Satan to tempt me as sharply herein as he tempted me in other things, I should have fallen also into this; but His Majesty has preserved me until now. May He be blessed for evermore! It was rather a heavy affliction to me that I should be thought so well of; for I knew my own secret.

3. The reason why they thought I was not so wicked was this: they saw that I, who was so young, and exposed to so many occasions of sin, withdrew myself so often into solitude for prayer, read much, spoke of God, that I liked to have His image painted in many places, to have an oratory of my own, and furnish it with objects of devotion, that I spoke ill of no one, and other things of the same kind in me which have the appearance of virtue. Yet all the while—I was so vain—I knew how to procure respect for myself by doing those things which in the world are usually regarded with respect.

4. In consequence of this, they gave me as much liberty as they did to the oldest nuns, and even more, and had great confidence in me; for as to taking any liberty for myself, or doing anything without leave—such as conversing through the door, or in secret, or by night—I do not think I could have brought myself to speak with anybody in the monastery in that way, and I never did it; for our Lord held me back. It seemed to me—for I considered many things carefully and of set purpose—that it would be a very evil deed on my part, wicked as I was, to risk the credit of so many nuns, who were all good—as if everything else I did was well done! In truth, the evil I did was not the result of deliberation, as this would have been, if I had done it, although it was too much so.

5. Therefore, I think that it did me much harm to be in a monastery not enclosed. The liberty which those who were good might have with advantage—they not being obliged to do more than they do, because they had not bound themselves to enclosure—would certainly have led me, who am wicked, straight to hell, if our Lord, by so many remedies and means of His most singular mercy, had not delivered me out of that danger—and it is, I believe, the very greatest danger—namely, a monastery of women unenclosed—yea, more, I think it is, for those who will be wicked, a road to hell, rather than a help to their weakness. This is not to be understood of my monastery; for there are so many there who in the utmost sincerity, and

in great perfection, serve our Lord, so that His Majesty, according to His goodness, cannot but be gracious unto them; neither is it one of those which are most open for all religious observances are kept in it; and I am speaking only of others which I have seen and known.

6. I am exceedingly sorry for these houses, because our Lord must of necessity send His special inspirations not merely once, but many times, if the nuns therein are to be saved, seeing that the honours and amusements of the world are allowed among them, and the obligations of their state are so ill-understood. God grant they may not count that to be virtue which is sin, as I did so often! It is very difficult to make people understand this; it is necessary our Lord Himself should take the matter seriously into His own hands.

7. If parents would take my advice, now that they are at no pains to place their daughters where they may walk in the way of salvation without incurring a greater risk than they would do if they were left in the world, let them look at least at that which concerns their good name. Let them marry them to persons of a much lower degree, rather than place them in monasteries of this kind, unless they be of extremely good inclinations, and God grant that these inclinations may come to good! or let them keep them at home. If they will be wicked at home, their evil life can be hidden only for a short time; but in monasteries it can be hidden long, and, in the end, it is our Lord that discovers it. They injure not only themselves, but all the nuns also. And all the while the poor things are not in fault; for they walk in the way that is shown them. Many of them are to be pitied; for they wished to withdraw from the world, and, thinking to escape from the dangers of it, and that they were going to serve our Lord, have found themselves in ten worlds at once, without knowing what to do, or how to help themselves. Youth and sensuality and the devil invite them and incline them to follow certain ways which are of the essence of worldliness. They see these ways, so to speak, considered as safe there.

8. Now, these seem to me to be in some degree like those wretched heretics who will make themselves blind, and who will consider that which they do to be good, and so believe, but without really believing; for they have within themselves something that tells them it is wrong.

9. Oh, what utter ruin! utter ruin of religious persons—I am not speaking now more of women than of men—where the rules of the Order are not kept; where the same monastery offers two roads: one of virtue and observance, the other of inobservance, and both equally frequented! I have spoken incorrectly: they are not equally frequented; for, on account of our sins, the way of the greatest imperfection is the most frequented; and because it is the broadest, it is also the most in favour. The way of religious observance is so little used, that the friar and the nun who would really begin to follow their vocation thoroughly have reason to fear the members of their communities more than all the devils together. They must be more cautious, and dissemble more, when they would speak of that friendship with God which they desire to have, than when they would speak of those friendships and affections which the devil arranges in monasteries. I know not why we are astonished that the Church is in so much trouble, when we see those, who ought to be an example of every virtue to others, so disfigure the work which the spirit of the Saints departed wrought in their Orders. May it please His Divine Majesty to apply a remedy to this, as He sees it to be needful! Amen.

10. So, then, when I began to indulge in these conversations, I did not think, seeing they were customary, that my soul must be injured and dissipated, as I afterwards found it must be, by such conversations. I thought that, as receiving visits was so common in many monasteries, no more harm would befall me thereby than befell others, whom I knew to be good. I did not observe that they were much better than I was, and that an act which was perilous for me was not so perilous for them; and yet I have no doubt there was some danger in it, were it nothing else but a waste of time.

11. I was once with a person—it was at the very beginning of my acquaintance with her when our Lord was pleased to show me that these friendships were not good for me: to warn me also, and in my blindness, which was so great, to give me light. Christ stood before me, stern and grave, giving me to understand what in my conduct was offensive to Him. I saw Him with the eyes of the soul more distinctly than I could have seen Him with the eyes of the body. The vision made so deep an

impression upon me, that, though it is more than twenty-six years ago, I seem to see Him present even now. I was greatly astonished and disturbed, and I resolved not to see that person again.

12. It did me much harm that I did not then know it was possible to see anything otherwise than with the eyes of the body; so did Satan too, in that he helped me to think so: he made me understand it to be impossible, and suggested that I had imagined the vision—that it might be Satan himself—and other suppositions of that kind. For all this, the impression remained with me that the vision was from God, and not an imagination; but, as it was not to my liking, I forced myself to lie to myself; and as I did not dare to discuss the matter with any one, and as great importunity was used, I went back to my former conversation with the same person, and with others also, at different times; for I was assured that there was no harm in seeing such a person, and that I gained, instead of losing, reputation by doing so. I spent many years in this pestilent amusement; for it never appeared to me, when I was engaged in it, to be so bad as it really was, though at times I saw clearly it was not good. But no one caused me the same distraction which that person did of whom I am speaking; and that was because I had a great affection for her.

13. At another time, when I was with that person, we saw, both of us, and others who were present also saw, something like a great toad crawling towards us, more rapidly than such a creature is in the habit of crawling. I cannot understand how a reptile of that kind could, in the middle of the day, have come forth from that place; it never had done so before, but the impression it made on me was such, that I think it must have had a meaning; neither have I ever forgotten it. Oh, the greatness of God! with what care and tenderness didst Thou warn me in every way! and how little I profited by those warnings!

14. There was in that house a nun, who was related to me, now grown old, a great servant of God, and a strict observer of the rule. She too warned me from time to time; but I not only did not listen to her, but was even offended, thinking she was scandalized without cause. I have mentioned this in order that my wickedness and the great goodness of God might be understood, and to show how much I deserved hell for ingratitude so great, and, moreover, if it should be our Lord's will and pleasure that any nun at any time should read this, that she might take warning by me. I beseech them all, for the love of our Lord, to flee from such recreations as these.

15. May His Majesty grant I may undeceive some one of the many I led astray when I told them there was no harm in these things, and assured them there was no such great danger therein. I did so because I was blind myself; for I would not deliberately lead them astray. By the bad example I set before them—I spoke of this before—I was the occasion of much evil, not thinking I was doing so much harm.

16. In those early days, when I was ill, and before I knew how to be of use to myself, I had a very strong desire to further the progress of others: a most common temptation of beginners. With me, however, it had good results. Loving my father so much, I longed to see him in the possession of that good which I seemed to derive myself from prayer. I thought that in this life there could not be a greater good than prayer; and by roundabout ways, as well as I could, I contrived make him enter upon it; I gave him books for that end. As he was so good—I said so before—this exercise took such a hold upon him, that in five or six years, I think it was, he made so great a progress that I used to praise our Lord for it. It was a very great consolation to me. He had most grievous trials of diverse kinds; and he bore them all with the greatest resignation. He came often to see me; for it was a comfort to him to speak of the things of God.

17. And now that I had become so dissipated, and had ceased to pray, and yet saw that he still thought I was what I used to be, I could not endure it, and so undeceived him. I had been a year and more without praying, thinking it an act of greater humility to abstain. This—I shall speak of it again—was the greatest temptation I ever had, because it very nearly wrought my utter ruin; for, when I used to pray, if I offended God one day, on the following days I would recollect myself, and withdraw farther from the occasions of sin.

18. When that blessed man, having that good opinion of me, came to visit me, it pained me

to see him so deceived as to think that I used to pray to God as before. So I told him that I did not pray; but I did not tell him why. I put my infirmities forward as an excuse; for though I had recovered from that which was so troublesome, I have always been weak, even very much so; and though my infirmities are somewhat less troublesome now than they were, they still afflict me in many ways; specially, I have been suffering for twenty years from sickness every morning, so that I could not take any food till past mid-day, and even occasionally not till later; and now, since my Communions have become more frequent, it is at night, before I lie down to rest, that the sickness occurs, and with greater pain; for I have to bring it on with a feather, or other means. If I do not bring it on, I suffer more; and thus I am never, I believe, free from great pain, which is sometimes very acute, especially about the heart; though the fainting-fits are now but of rare occurrence. I am also, these eight years past, free from the paralysis, and from other infirmities of fever, which I had so often. These afflictions I now regard so lightly, that I am even glad of them, believing that our Lord in some degree takes His pleasure in them.

19. My father believed me when I gave him that for a reason, as he never told a lie himself; neither should I have done so, considering the relation we were in. I told him, in order to be the more easily believed, that it was much for me to be able to attend in choir, though I saw clearly that this was no excuse whatever; neither, however, was it a sufficient reason for giving up a practice which does not require, of necessity, bodily strength, but only love and a habit thereof; yet our Lord always furnishes an opportunity for it, if we but seek it. I say always; for though there may be times, as in illness, and from other causes, when we cannot be much alone, yet it never can be but there must be opportunities when our strength is sufficient for the purpose; and in sickness itself, and amidst other hindrances, true prayer consists, when the soul loves, in offering up its burden, and in thinking of Him for Whom it suffers, and in the resignation of the will, and in a thousand ways which then present themselves. It is under these circumstances that love exerts itself for it is not necessarily prayer when we are alone; and neither is it not prayer when we are not.

20. With a little care, we may find great blessings on those occasions when our Lord, by means of afflictions, deprives us of time for prayer; and so I found it when I had a good conscience. But my father, having that opinion of me which he had, and because of the love he bore me, believed all I told him; moreover, he was sorry for me; and as he had now risen to great heights of prayer himself, he never remained with me long; for when he had seen me, he went his way, saying that he was wasting his time. As I was wasting it in other vanities, I cared little about this.

21. My father was not the only person whom I prevailed upon to practise prayer, though I was walking in vanity myself. When I saw persons fond of reciting their prayers, I showed them how to make a meditation, and helped them and gave them books; for from the time I began myself to pray, as I said before, I always had a desire that others should serve God. I thought, now that I did not myself serve our Lord according to the light I had, that the knowledge His Majesty had given me ought not to be lost, and that others should serve Him for me. I say this in order to explain the great blindness I was in: going to ruin myself, and labouring to save others.

22. At this time, that illness befell my father of which he died; it lasted some days. I went to nurse him, being more sick in spirit than he was in body, owing to my many vanities—though not, so far as I know, to the extent of being in mortal sin—through the whole of that wretched time of which I am speaking; for, if I knew myself to be in mortal sin, I would not have continued in it on any account. I suffered much myself during his illness. I believe I rendered him some service in return for what he had suffered in mine. Though I was very ill, I did violence to myself; and though in losing him I was to lose all the comfort and good of my life—he was all this to me—I was so courageous, that I never betrayed my sorrows, concealing them till he was dead, as if I felt none at all. It seemed as if my very soul were wrenched when I saw him at the point of death—my love for him was so deep.

23. It was a matter for which we ought to praise our Lord—the death that he died, and the desire he had to die; so also was the advice he gave us after the last anointing, how he charged us to recom-

mend him to God, and to pray for mercy for him, how he bade us serve God always, and consider how all things come to an end. He told us with tears how sorry he was that he had not served Him himself; for he wished he was a friar—I mean, that he had been one in the Strictest Order that is. I have a most assured conviction that our Lord, some fifteen days before, had revealed to him he was not to live; for up to that time, though very ill, he did not think so; but now, though he was somewhat better, and the physicians said so, he gave no heed to them, but employed himself in the ordering of his soul.

24. His chief suffering consisted in a most acute pain of the shoulders, which never left him: it was so sharp at times, that it put him into great torture. I said to him, that as he had so great a devotion to our Lord carrying His cross on His shoulders, he should now think that His Majesty wished him to feel somewhat of that pain which He then suffered Himself. This so comforted him, that I do not think I heard him complain afterwards.

25. He remained three days without consciousness; but on the day he died, our Lord restored him so completely, that we were astonished: he preserved his understanding to the last; for in the middle of the creed, which he repeated himself, he died. He lay there like an angel—such he seemed to me, if I may say so, both in soul and disposition: he was very good.

26. I know not why I have said this, unless it be for the purpose of showing how much the more I am to be blamed for my wickedness; for after seeing such a death, and knowing what his life had been, I, in order to be in any wise like unto such a father, ought to have grown better. His confessor, a most learned Dominican, used to say that he had no doubt he went straight to heaven. He had heard his confession for some years, and spoke with praise of the purity of his conscience.

27. This Dominican father, who was a very good man, fearing God, did me a very great service; for I confessed to him. He took upon himself the task of helping my soul in earnest, and of making me see the perilous state I was in. He sent me to Communion once a fortnight; and I, by degrees beginning to speak to him, told him about my prayer. He charged me never to omit it: that, anyhow, it could not do me anything but good. I began to return to it—though I did not cut off the occasions of sin—and never afterwards gave it up. My life became most wretched, because I learned in prayer more and more of my faults. On one side, God was calling me; on the other, I was following the world. All the things of God gave me great pleasure; and I was a prisoner to the things of the world. It seemed as if I wished to reconcile two contradictions, so much at variance one with another as are the life of the spirit and the joys and pleasures and amusements of sense.

28. I suffered much in prayer; for the spirit was slave, and not master; and so I was not able to shut myself up within myself—that was my whole method of prayer—without shutting up with me a thousand vanities at the same time. I spent many years in this way; and I am now astonished that any one could have borne it without abandoning either the one or the other. I know well that it was not in my power then to give up prayer, because He held me in His hand Who sought me that He might show me greater mercies.

29. O my God! if I might, I would speak of the occasions from which God delivered me, and how I threw myself into them again; and of the risks I ran of losing utterly my good name, from which He delivered me. I did things to show what I was; and our Lord hid the evil, and revealed some little virtue—if so be I had any—and made it great in the eyes of all, so that they always held me in much honour. For although my follies came occasionally into light, people would not believe it when they saw other things, which they thought good. The reason is, that He Who knoweth all things saw it was necessary it should be so, in order that I might have some credit given me by those to whom in after years I was to speak of His service. His supreme munificence regarded not my great sins, but rather the desires I frequently had to please Him, and the pain I felt because I had not the strength to bring those desires to good effect.

30. O Lord of my soul! how shall I be able to magnify the graces which Thou, in those years, didst bestow upon me? Oh, how, at the very time that I offended Thee most, Thou didst prepare me in a moment, by a most profound compunction, to taste of the sweetness of Thy consolations and mercies!

Document Text

In truth, O my King, Thou didst administer to me the most delicate and painful chastisement it was possible for me to bear; for Thou knewest well what would have given me the most pain. Thou didst chastise my sins with great consolations. I do not believe I am saying foolish things, though it may well be that I am beside myself whenever I call to mind my ingratitude and my wickedness.

31. It was more painful for me, in the state I was in, to receive graces, when I had fallen into grievous faults, than it would have been to receive chastisement; for one of those faults, I am sure, used to bring me low, shame and distress me, more than many diseases, together with many heavy trials, could have done. For, as to the latter, I saw that I deserved them; and it seemed to me that by them I was making some reparation for my sins, though it was but slight, for my sins are so many. But when I see myself receive graces anew, after being so ungrateful for those already received, that is to me—and, I believe, to all who have any knowledge or love of God—a fearful kind of torment. We may see how true this is by considering what a virtuous mind must be. Hence my tears and vexation when I reflected on what I felt, seeing myself in a condition to fall at every moment, though my resolutions and desires then—I am speaking of that time—were strong.

32. It is a great evil for a soul to be alone in the midst of such great dangers; it seems to me that if I had had any one with whom I could have spoken of all this, it might have helped me not to fall. I might, at least, have been ashamed before him—and yet I was not ashamed before God.

33. For this reason, I would advise those who give themselves to prayer, particularly at first, to form friendships; and converse familiarly, with others who are doing the same thing. It is a matter of the last importance, even if it lead only to helping one another by prayer: how much more, seeing that it has led to much greater gain! Now, if in their intercourse one with another, and in the indulgence of human affections even not of the best kind, men seek friends with whom they may refresh themselves, and for the purpose of having greater satisfaction in speaking of their empty joys, I know no reason why it should not be lawful for him who is beginning to love and serve God in earnest to confide to another his joys and sorrows; for they who are given to prayer are thoroughly accustomed to both.

34. For if that friendship with God which he desires be real, let him not be afraid of vain-glory; and if the first movements thereof assail him, he will escape from it with merit; and I believe that he who will discuss the matter with this intention will profit both himself and those who hear him, and thus will derive more light for his own understanding, as well as for the instruction of his friends. He who in discussing his method of prayer falls into vain-glory will do so also when he hears Mass devoutly, if he is seen of men, and in doing other good works, which must be done under pain of being no Christian; and yet these things must not be omitted through fear of vain-glory.

35. Moreover, it is a most important matter for those souls who are not strong in virtue; for they have so many people, enemies as well as friends, to urge them the wrong way, that I do not see how this point is capable of exaggeration. It seems to me that Satan has employed this artifice—and it is of the greatest service to him—namely, that men who really wish to love and please God should hide the fact, while others, at his suggestion, make open show of their malicious dispositions; and this is so common, that it seems a matter of boasting now, and the offences committed against God are thus published abroad.

Glossary

Communion	the sacrament of the Eucharist, based on the belief that the consecrated bread and wine are the body and blood of Christ
Dominican	a member of an order of poor friars founded in thirteenth-century France
vanity	something that is empty or without value

36. I do not know whether the things I am saying are foolish or not. If they be so, your reverence will strike them out. I entreat you to help my simplicity by adding a good deal to this, because the things that relate to the service of God are so feebly managed, that it is necessary for those who would serve Him to join shoulder to shoulder, if they are to advance at all; for it is considered safe to live amidst the vanities and pleasures of the world, and few there be who regard them with unfavourable eyes. But if any one begins to give himself up to the service of God, there are so many to find fault with him, that it becomes necessary for him to seek companions, in order that he may find protection among them till he grows strong enough not to feel what he may be made to suffer. If he does not, he will find himself in great straits.

37. This, I believe, must have been the reason why some of the Saints withdrew into the desert. And it is a kind of humility in man not to trust to himself, but to believe that God will help him in his relations with those with whom he converses; and charity grows by being diffused; and there are a thousand blessings herein which I would not dare to speak of, if I had not known by experience the great importance of it. It is very true that I am the most wicked and the basest of all who are born of women; but I believe that he who, humbling himself, though strong, yet trusteth not in himself, and believeth another who in this matter has had experience, will lose nothing. Of myself I may say that, if our Lord had not revealed to me this truth, and given me the opportunity of speaking very frequently to persons given to prayer, I should have gone on falling and rising till I tumbled into hell. I had many friends to help me to fall; but as to rising again, I was so much left to myself, that I wonder now I was not always on the ground. I praise God for His mercy; for it was He only Who stretched out His hand to me. May He be blessed for ever! Amen.

Spanish Jews taking refuge in the Atlas Mountains in the fifteenth century
(Spanish Jews taking refuge in the Atlas Mountains, illustration by Michelet c.1900 (colour litho), Bombled, Louis (1862-1927) / Private Collection / Archives Charmet / The Bridgeman Art Library International)

Shulchan Arukh

ca. 1570

"A person should dress differently than he does on weekdays so he will remember that it is the Sabbath."

Overview

The Shulchan Arukh, literally translated as "The Set Table," is a compilation of Jewish legal codes. Written in the sixteenth century, it represents the first codification of Jewish law that is universally accepted by religiously observant Jews. It encompasses laws observed by both Ashkenazic Jews, those with German and eastern European roots, and Sephardic Jews, those with Spanish and Middle Eastern roots. Rabbi Yosef Karo composed the work in an effort to provide an authoritative legal text that would help to guide Jews in properly observing religious obligations. Although he composed the text before subdivisions of Judaism existed, the Shulchan Arukh persists as the most important document for Orthodox Jews. Its text expounds upon the legal code, and its importance indicates the significance of religious laws in the lives of observant Jews.

The Shulchan Arukh is divided into four volumes. The first, Orakh Hayyim, contains laws pertaining to the Sabbath, the synagogue, prayer, and holidays. The second volume, Yoreh De'ah, describes the laws of charity, kosher dietary restrictions, religious conversion, and sexual purity. The third volume, Even Ha-Ezer, discusses Jewish marriage and divorce. Finally, the fourth volume, Koshen Mishpat, covers laws pertaining to finances and Jewish legal systems. All contemporary Orthodox rabbis are expected to be well versed in the text. The Shulchan Arukh is written in Hebrew; rabbinical students are expected not only to be able to read the text but also to offer interpretation of it. Indeed, although the Shulchan Arukh provides a listing of laws, it is the rabbinical interpretation of the laws that brings them to life for religiously observant Jews. The text is largely inaccessible to those who cannot read Hebrew. This forces individuals who are interested in the laws to seek rabbinical interpretation.

The Shulchan Arukh's endurance speaks to its universal appeal. Contemporary Orthodox Jews still uphold the same laws that Rabbi Karo codified in the sixteenth century. Certainly, he could not have anticipated the development of the automobile, computer, cell phone, or Internet. However, through continuous rabbinic interpretation, the Shulchan Arukh continues to serve as a guide in the fast-paced contemporary world.

Context

Jews in the Middle Ages (ca. 500–1450) found themselves for the first time in competition with other monotheistic religions. Both Islam and Christianity claim to have roots in Judaism but to have superseded Judaism with subsequent revelations and prophets. This led to times of great oppression for Jews. With the endorsement of Christianity by the emperor Constantine I as a legal religion in 313 CE, it quickly became the favored religion of the Roman Empire. Jews were heavily persecuted by the Romans, and Jewish communities were controlled by severe restrictions that perpetuated the idea of Jews' inferior status.

As Jews were forced out of various European countries, Judaism became a religion of exile. Jews were driven out of England in 1290, expelled from France in 1394, and barred from numerous districts of Germany, Italy, and the Balkan Peninsula between 1350 and 1450. In 1478, Ferdinand II of Aragon and Isabella I of Castile began the Spanish Inquisition with the intent to establish and maintain Catholicism in Spain. Out of this came the 1492 Alhambra Decree, also called the Edict of Expulsion, which drove more than two hundred thousand Jews out of Spain. Prior to the decree, Spain had boasted the largest Jewish settlement in Europe. Not until December 16, 1968, after 476 years, would the Spanish government finally revoke the Alhambra Decree.

Most of the Jews fleeing Spain resettled in the new Slavic kingdoms, which promoted a slightly higher degree of religious tolerance. The Jews who dared to remain in Spain and Portugal were referred to as Marranos—literally, "pigs." Although an estimated one hundred thousand to two hundred thousand Iberian Jews converted to Christianity to avoid persecution, their conversion was still suspect. Small-scale hate crimes were perpetrated against them, and they were also blamed for a plague in Portugal. For this reason, from April 19 to 21, 1506, a mob rioted and killed more than five thousand Jews in Portugal, an occurrence known as the Easter Massacre.

One of the most impressive features of medieval Judaism was that the scattered groups of Jews managed to main-

Time Line

1478 — The Spanish Inquisition is instituted by Ferdinand II and Isabella I.

1488 — Yosef Karo is born in Toledo, Spain.

1492 — **March 31** The Alhambra Decree, also known as the Edict of Expulsion, is issued, causing Karo and his family to flee to Portugal.

1493 — Sicily announces that Jews are no longer welcome within its border.

1497 — King Manuel I forces the expulsion of Jews from Portugal. Karo and his family flee to Bulgaria.

1506 — **April 19–21** A mob kills more than five thousand Jews in Portugal during the Easter Massacre.

1516 — The first Jewish ghetto is established in Venice, prefiguring the forced ghettoization of Jews throughout much of Europe.

1522 — Karo begins *Beit Yosef*, his most extensive and thorough collection of commentary on Jewish law.

1535 — Karo immigrates to Palestine.

1546 — Karo's mentor, Rabbi Yaakov Beirav, dies. Karo is appointed as his successor and serves as the head of the Beit Din (Rabbinical Court) of Safed, Palestine.

1560 — Karo begins condensing and codifying the *Beit Yosef* to create the Shulchan Arukh.

CA. 1570 — Karo completes the Shulchan Arukh.

CA. 1571 — Rabbi Moses Isserles appends Ashkenazic commentary, the Mappah, to the Shulchan Arukh.

---

tain a relatively high degree of uniformity. These Jews accepted the same sacred books, engaged in the same rituals, and recited nearly identical prayers. That said, two main cultural groups of Jews emerged during this time. The Ashkenazic Jews lived in the Christian European lands and are generally considered to be those with German and eastern European roots. The Sephardic Jews are those with Spanish and Middle Eastern roots. Although these two groups differed socially, linguistically, and culturally, their religious observances remained quite similar, in large part owing to their shared canon of literature.

Many Jews moved to the Slavic kingdoms in search of religious tolerance and more equitable employment. As the influence of Catholicism began to spread into this area, many Jews felt pressure either to convert to Christianity or to relocate once more. There were movements that attempted to convert Jews to Christianity through writings and religious disputations. Eventually these movements were deemed ineffective, and in certain locations Jews were forced to live in walled ghettos. The first Jewish ghetto was established in 1516 in Venice, Italy. This model of ghettoization established the foundation for segregated living for Jews throughout much of Europe. When they were outside of the ghettos, Jews were forced to wear badges that identified them as Jewish. In many regions, local governments forced Jews to wear a *Judenhut*—literally, a "Jew hat"—a yellow conelike hat that distinguished them from non-Jews.

Rabbi Yosef Karo and his writings were a product of this time. Along with his family, he experienced forced exiles at a young age. Although he escaped much of the violence of this period, he was very much aware of the plight of his Jewish contemporaries. As his career advanced and his religious authority increased, his sense of responsibility to oppressed Jews grew. His attempt to codify Jewish law in the Shulchan Arukh represented a desire to standardize the Jewish experience for a dispersed people. Although he was living in a time of great animosity toward Judaism, he upheld Judaism as a worthy lifestyle full of religious truth.

About the Author

Yosef (or Joseph) ben Ephraim Karo was born in 1488 in Toledo, Spain. Only four years after his birth, in 1492, the Alhambra Decree was issued in Spain, forcing most Jews to flee the country or convert to Christianity. Karo and his family left Toledo that year and subsequently settled in Portugal. That nation, however, did not afford his family the protection they sought; Jews were expelled from Portugal in 1497, just five years after Karo's family arrived. They fled to Nicopolis (now Nikopol), Bulgaria, where Karo remained through his youth.

Karo began his religious studies with his father, Ephraim, who was a well-known scholar of the Talmud, a compilation of rabbinic discussions pertaining to Jewish law, ethics, philosophy, and customs. He continued his studies in Adrianople (now Edirne), Turkey, between 1520 and 1522 and immigrated in 1535 to Palestine. He surrounded himself with scholarship, which is apparent even in his marital record; he was widowed three times, and each of his wives was the daughter of a prominent Talmudic scholar. Immersed in study and scholarship, Karo remained in Safed, Palestine, until his death in 1575 at the age of eighty-seven.

From a young age, Karo experienced mystical visions and dreams. He believed them to be messages from God, which motivated him to study intensively. He was greatly influenced by the Portuguese mystic Solomon Molcho (ca. 1500–1532) and Rabbi Yaakov Beirav (1474–1546). Upon Beirav's death, Karo was appointed as the head of the Safed Beit Din, the central rabbinical court for Palestine. This meant that Karo had the ultimate say in Jewish legal decisions and issues. For this reason, his influence has been likened to that of Moses ben Maimon, or Maimonides (1135–1204), who is considered the preeminent medieval Jewish philosopher and Torah scholar.

Only three of Karo's works reached publication during his lifetime—his commentary *Beit Yosef*, the Shulchan Arukh, and a commentary on Maimonides' *Mishneh Torah*, titled *Kesef Mishneh*. Posthumously, six additional commentaries of Karo's would be published between 1598 and 1799. He remains best known for authoring the Shulchan Arukh, a text that despite its age remains surprisingly pertinent and applicable in the modern world.

Explanation and Analysis of the Document

This excerpt from the Shulchan Arukh comes from the first volume, Orakh Hayyim, which covers laws about the Sabbath, the synagogue, prayer, and Jewish holidays. The selected chapters discuss some of the Sabbath laws that observant Jews uphold. The Sabbath begins at nightfall on Friday and lasts until three stars can be seen in the sky on Saturday. Some of these laws may seem unfamiliar or even extreme; not all Jews follow these laws, but Orthodox Jews base their Sabbath observance largely on the laws found in these chapters. For Orthodoxy, the Sabbath is considered the most important religious holiday, a time to focus on God, spirituality, family, friends, and rest.

♦ Chapter 17: Preparations for the Sabbath

Observing the Sabbath requires preparation. In order to ensure that the Sabbath is work free and truly dedicated to rest, any work that must be completed is done before sundown on Friday night. Such necessary tasks include bathing, cleaning, setting the table, and food preparation. Karo reminds readers that even if they employ servants, they should still take an active part in Sabbath preparations, an injunction that forces individuals to take ownership and accountability for their Sabbath experience. As the sun sets, a candle is lit, typically by the matriarch of the home. Although observant Jews now use electricity, the candle lighting is still richly symbolic, representing not only the need for light in darkness but also the commencement of the Sabbath.

Time Line

1575
- Karo dies in Safed.

1577
- The first Hebrew printing press is established in Safed, Palestine.

♦ Chapter 22: Fire and Food Preparation on the Sabbath

Jews are forbidden to kindle a fire on the Sabbath. When Karo wrote this text, he was thinking of fire in terms of a burning source of heat and light. But modern commentators have taken this further to include creating a spark or igniting something; thus, since a car's engine is ignited by sparks, driving a car on the Sabbath is forbidden. In terms of electricity, if lights are turned on before the Sabbath, they may remain on. However, once the Sabbath has begun, lights should not be switched on or off. To accommodate this, many Sabbath-observant Jews set their lights on timers or sensors. Some groups dispute this, stating that if one's actions result in lights turning on, in however delayed a fashion, the individual has still kindled a fire through physical movement. Therefore, these groups choose to leave their lights switched on throughout the duration of the Sabbath.

Another significant impact of the injunction not to kindle fire pertains to cooking and food preparation. Since the observant are not permitted to cook with fire or any heated device, food preparation for the Sabbath is different from on other weekdays. Often food is prepared in advance and eaten at room temperature or chilled. One popular option is *cholent*, a rich stew that cooks for a long time at a low temperature. In this way, the food can be cooked in a slow-cooker or an oven set at a low temperature that is turned on before the beginning of the Sabbath.

Karo explains some interesting particularities in this chapter. He admonishes readers not to separate inedible material from food, but rather to separate the food from the nonfood item. This dictum ties into the idea that things should be done differently on the Sabbath in order to create mindfulness about the day. While it is a normal impulse to pluck something from food when it does not belong there, removing the food from the item requires a greater degree of conscious behavior. Along similar lines, salt and spices may be ground in nonstandard ways, and food may be cut with a knife but not passed through a grater. These methods force the cook to be aware of the difference of the Sabbath day.

♦ Chapter 23: Care of the Body and Clothing on the Sabbath

This chapter discusses the restrictions on bathing and clothing during the Sabbath. One of the most important elements of this chapter is the idea that "a person should dress differently than he does on weekdays so he will remember that it is the Sabbath." For some groups of Hasidim—one movement or subgroup of Orthodox Jews—men

Jewish scholars, including Yosef Karo (far left) sitting at the table of Moses ben Maimon, known as Maimonides
(Savants at the Table of Maimonides, from a Passover Haggadah (colour litho), Hungarian School, (20th Century) / Private Collection / Archives Charmet / The Bridgeman Art Library International)

wear a black satin caftan or long silk jacket on the Sabbath. Some wear a large round fur hat, called a *shtreimel*. Others wear black slip-on shoes so that they do not have to knot their shoelaces. Often these shoes are coupled with white knee socks that are worn with black knickers. Some also wear a *gartel*, or a belt that signifies the division of the lower and upper body, as is prescribed elsewhere in the Shulchan Arukh. This is done to create a separation between the heart and genitalia during prayer; the idea is that the *gartel* helps to control man's animal instincts and helps the individual focus on the heart and brain. Some Hasidim wear a *gartel* as part of their daily attire, while others wear one only during prayer. Although dress varies between groups of Orthodox Jews, the idea of dressing nicely for the Sabbath and not in daily work clothes is prevalent. As with other practices, this change in dress helps to signify that the Sabbath differs from other days.

Karo recognizes that clothing is so much a part of daily life that it can be overlooked during the Sabbath. For this reason, typical clothing-maintenance behavior is discouraged. Laundry and ironing should not be done, which falls in line with work prohibitions. Likewise, clothing should not be spot-cleaned. Although it is permissible to rub the hand or fingers over clothing, rubbing with the intention of cleaning is not permitted. Clothes also should be folded in a nonstandard way to remind the individual that the Sabbath is different from a normal weekday.

♦ **Chapter 24: Animals, Children, and the Sick on the Sabbath**

Karo is sensitive to the fact that even though Jews should rest during the Sabbath, they still have other commitments. They are permitted to feed their animals if the animals depend on them for food. Likewise, if a pregnant woman goes into labor, both the mother and newborn should be adequately cared for, even if this means breaking Sabbath laws to ensure their survival.

Observant Jews uphold the principle that saving a human life supersedes religious law. This idea is referred to as *pikuach nefesh*. Thus, Sabbath laws may be temporarily abandoned in emergency situations or in cases of caring for the sick or dying. This means, for example, that a telephone may be used to call for help, or an ambulance or car may be driven to the hospital. Likewise, although one should not begin an elective medical treatment on the Sabbath, if medical treatment is begun during the week and must extend into the Sabbath, it is permitted. *Pikuach nefesh* should not be used as an excuse to ignore Sabbath laws; it is a safety measure and should not become a common occurrence.

♦ **Chapter 25: Constructive Activities on the Sabbath**

Constructive activities, or actions that create something, are forbidden on the Sabbath. Although it is easy to say that work is forbidden, Karo's explanation of what is included in this demonstrates that it is not always clear what consti-

Essential Quotes

> "In honor of the Sabbath, . . . a candle must be lit to illuminate the house; if there is a woman in the household, she does this for everyone."

> "A person should dress differently than he does on weekdays so he will remember that it is the Sabbath."

> "Anything necessary must be done if there is a possibility that it will save or prolong someone's life. In such cases, the necessary Sabbath violations may be done by anyone."

> "It is Biblically forbidden to move things from a private domain to a public domain or vice versa."

tutes construction. He elaborates his description of work to include the gathering, planting, or watering of plants, breaking things, widening openings, making or assembling items, and chopping wood. His attention to these actions indicates that they had at some point come into question among observant Jews. Many of these prohibitions do not affect contemporary Jews, as most are based in agrarian circumstances. The inclusion of these specific prohibitions, however, is interpreted to include contemporary work situations that Karo could not have anticipated.

◆ Chapter 26: Other Activities on the Sabbath

In this chapter, Karo presents a list of miscellaneous activities that are forbidden on the Sabbath. They include playing musical instruments, gossiping, reading secular documents, engaging in monetary transactions, planning for activities that are forbidden during the Sabbath, making loans, gambling, arresting, punishing, marrying, divorcing, and making financial offerings. Many of these activities center on money; accordingly, observant Jews do not conduct any financial transactions during the Sabbath. For this reason, unlike in many Christian churches, no collection plate is passed around during Jewish services. Any contribution to the synagogue or other groups is made during the week. Likewise, all shopping, money lending or collecting, and other financial transactions are completed on weekdays.

While Karo discourages running and idle talk during the Sabbath, he encourages walks and social conversation, as the Sabbath centers on spending time with friends and family. Outside of religious services, Jews usually spend the day eating together, enjoying leisurely walks, chatting, or reading. After a busy week, many find this quiet time with family to be a much-needed break from work and stress.

◆ Chapter 27: Things That Must Not Be Handled on the Sabbath

It is forbidden to carry things outside the home during the Sabbath. Karo details the various ways in which items should not be handled or moved, including broken utensils, large quantities of food, and water. These prohibitions are linked to the idea of resting during the Sabbath. Even though carrying large quantities of food from one home to another is not work that is typically done during the week, it is considered work during the Sabbath unless it is for religious purposes or for guests. The same is true for water, although most contemporary Jews no longer have to draw water from an outside source. They are permitted to use water freely in their homes as long as it is not used in excess.

Although this chapter may seem outdated for contemporary Jews, the concept of not carrying on the Sabbath remains very important. As one can imagine, these laws are considered by many as among the most difficult to uphold. Observant Jews do not carry anything outside of the home during the Sabbath, including house keys, medicine, books, purses, wallets, and many other things. For this reason, prayer shawls and prayer books are kept at the synagogue. Doors are often left unlocked; or in some communities the key is integrated into a belt, in which case the key functions to hold the belt closed and is therefore considered to be part of the belt. Hence, the wearer is not carrying the key as a separate item.

♦ **Chapter 28: Moving Things from One Domain to Another on the Sabbath**

This chapter details the difference between public and private domains. Although Karo details the measurements of specific realms, a rule of thumb is that whatever is inside one's home is considered private. Once the house is exited, the area becomes public. For this reason, if a newspaper were to be delivered to the driveway during the Sabbath, it would be forbidden to pick it up and move it inside. However, if a letter came through a mail slot installed in the front door, it would be within the private area and could be picked up off the floor and moved to a table.

Karo is very specific about what constitutes certain domains, likely because of questions that were posed to him in the rabbinical court. When individuals and communities were uncertain about what constituted a region, they asked their rabbis. Karo explains that a partition must be able to withstand a normal wind—in other words, it has to be stable enough to really be considered a partition. Likewise, a partition cannot have large gaps and must be continuous. When considering the prohibition of carrying items outside the private domain, it becomes apparent why it is so important to understand what is included in the private and public realms. The specifics offered here by Karo help to illuminate how particular the understanding of each domain is.

♦ **Chapter 29: Restrictions on Private Domains; Combining Private Domains**

One way that the prohibition of carrying items is negotiated is through the creation of an *eruv*, a symbolic fence or border that a community creates around itself. It must be at least twelve square feet and create a continuous border; the perimeter may constitute row homes, natural bodies of water, land formations, or telephone and electrical wires. Where a continuous border fails, Orthodox communities erect something that looks similar to a doorway using two poles and wire or fishing line. The constructed *eruv* increases the size of the private sphere to include areas of the public realm. Within the *eruv*, observant Jews may carry items, push baby strollers or wheelchairs, and engage in a greater degree of social interaction outside of the home during the Sabbath.

Most cities with larger Jewish populations have established an *eruv*, although not all observant Jews utilize it, as some believe it is not a valid interpretation of Jewish law. Karo asserts that neighbors may create an *eruv* by connecting their two private domains. Some observant Jews object to an *eruv*'s being extended to include additional properties. This is done by symbolically renting the land from the city, and more often than not, the non-Jews who live within such an *eruv* are unaware of its existence.

Audience

The original audience for the Shulchan Arukh was learned Jews. In the age when it was written, literacy rates were low—perhaps between 20 and 30 percent among Jews in their own dialects, while the Hebrew literacy rate was perhaps between 5 and 10 percent. Thus, few other than rabbis and Jewish scholars, who would have also been experts in Jewish law, and who were responsible for disseminating and interpreting information for fellow Jews in their area, would have been able to read Karo's text.

Jews have long considered themselves a diasporic people. A *diaspora* is formed when a group of people who share a common culture or identity are scattered and form new pockets of their ethnic or cultural group within other nations. The Jewish diaspora began in 586 BCE with the Babylonian sacking of Jersualem and destruction of the First Temple, which brought the Kingdom of Judah to an end. As related in the Hebrew Bible, the First Temple was built in 957 BCE by King Solomon and had been the sole location for Jewish sacrifice. After the Babylonian conquest, the Jews emigrated, and the realm now referred to as ancient Israel eventually ceased to exist, rendering Jews a people without a country. After settling across Europe and the Middle East, they remained a distinct religious, ethnic, and cultural group within their new homelands. During the Middle Ages, forced Jewish exiles continued. Not until 1948 would the modern State of Israel be founded to create a safe haven for the Jewish people.

Karo's attempt to codify Jewish law represents an important step in the broader effort to maintain a unified cultural and ethnic identity for a group of people living in different lands, speaking different languages, and experiencing and assimilating to different cultures. In turning to authoritative works like the Shulchan Arukh for guidance, Jews sought to combat the ethical perils of assimilation and remained surprisingly similar despite geographic dispersion. Even now, the text remains paramount for observant Jews worldwide.

Impact

The enduring impact and authority of the Shulchan Arukh are astounding, especially when one considers that the Shulchan Arukh was compiled by Karo and is not considered divinely mandated. Karo's audience was vastly different from contemporary Orthodoxy, and the questions and problems that he addresses are also significantly different from those faced in modern times. Nonetheless, few documents have had and continue to have such a profound influence upon observant Jews.

The strength of Karo's writing rests in his sound logic. He attacks questions by referring to other texts in the Jewish canon, such that his approach can be likewise extended to address contemporary situations and concerns. Orthodox Jews have thus chosen to continue to accept Karo's interpretation of laws, even if their life circumstances are very different from those of Karo's original audience. For example, while it may be easier for contemporary Jews to avoid drawing water on the Sabbath, it is certainly more difficult to be unable to spark a car's ignition to drive to services on the Sabbath. Jews in Karo's time also walked to the synagogue, of course, but they were based in smaller towns and did not have to grapple with the transportation issues present in a commuter culture.

Karo's text has also evolved with time. In 1571, Rabbi Moses ben Israel Isserles, who was situated in Kraków, Poland, and was attentive to the needs and questions of Ashkenazic Jewry, published commentary on and additions to the Shulchan Arukh. Known as the Mappah (Tablecloth), his commentary helped to illuminate Karo's Sephardic text for a larger audience. This was particularly important for the text when the first Hebrew printing press was established in 1577 in Safed, Palestine. The existence of the Mappah, which is traditionally appended to the Shulchan Arukh, helped to increase the circulation of Karo's work within both Sephardic and Ashkenazic readerships.

The most significant impact of the Shulchan Arukh has been its role in helping to standardize the Jewish experience. Even with the creation of the State of Israel, Jews remained scattered throughout the world. This text continues to help unify them and create certain similarities in religious observance and practice. Although Jews in Israel, Ethiopia, Poland, and the United States all have different life experiences, certain aspects of their religious observance are quite similar. They may dress differently and speak different languages, but their local religious authorities consult and interpret the same Hebrew texts.

It is difficult to say whether Jews could have survived the forced exiles they endured without such a strong canon of texts. Even as Jews began to rebuild after the Holocaust, they still turned to the Shulchan Arukh for guidance. Contemporary liberal Jewry largely rejects the laws found in the Shulchan Arukh. Still, though they may consider the laws outdated, they remain heavily indebted to Rabbi Karo and his text for the survival of Judaism and the Jewish people. Without Karo's work, contemporary Orthodox Judaism as currently practiced would be inconceivable. The Shulchan Arukh has proved itself a critical component of the canon of Judaic texts, giving the Jewish people the roots they needed to survive and overcome even the most dire and distressing circumstances.

Further Reading

■ Books

Gurock, Jeffrey S. *Orthodox Jews in America*. Bloomington: Indiana University Press, 2009.

Heschel, Abraham Joshua. *The Sabbath: Its Meaning for Modern Man*. New York: Farrar, Straus & Giroux, 1975.

Mintz, Jerome. *Hasidic People: A Place in the New World*. Cambridge, Mass.: Harvard University Press, 1998.

Poll, Solomon. *The Hasidic Community of Williamsburg: A Study in the Sociology of Religion*. New Brunswick, N.J.: Transaction, 2006.

Wolfson, Ron. *Shabbat: The Family Guide to Preparing for and Welcoming the Sabbath*. Woodstock, Vt.: Jewish Lights, 2002.

Questions for Further Study

1. In what way, if any, does the Shulchan Arukh serve the same function in Judaism that the Hadith serve in Islam? (See the entry on the Sahih al-Bukhari for comparison.)

2. Why do you think this document is titled with words that mean "the Set Table"? What "table" is being "set"?

3. To a non-Jew, it might appear that traditional Judaism has an enormous number of laws and rules that Jews are expected to follow—and perhaps some Jews would agree. What is your response to this apparent rule-bound nature of Judaism—in contrast to a religion such as Japanese Shinto (see the entry on the Yengishiki)? What purposes do these laws serve?

4. With regard to observance of the Sabbath, can you think of another example of a modern technological development that the author could not have anticipated and how observant Jews might handle that matter? What might Karo have said, for example, about checking e-mails or dealing with a frozen water pipe that has burst? Would any type of television watching be acceptable?

5. Liberal contemporary Jews tend not to observe many of the laws in the Shulchan Arukh. Nevertheless, they acknowledge the text's value. What is this value, and why would Jews who do not follow its laws continue to recognize that value?

■ Web Sites

"Shabbat: An Island in Time." Chabad.org Web site.
    http://www.chabad.org/generic_cdo/aid/253215/jewish/Shabbat.htm

"Shabbat Shalom." Orthodox Union Web site.
    http://www.ou.org/shabbat_shalom

"Shulchan Aruch." Torah.org Web site.
    http://www.torah.org/advanced/shulchan-aruch/

—Amy Milligan

Shulchan Arukh

Chapter 17: Preparations for the Sabbath

In honor of the Sabbath, a person should bake bread and prepare extra food (including meat, wine, and delicacies) and special utensils before the Sabbath. He should wash clothes on Thursday, bathe or wash and cut his nails (and hair, if necessary) on Friday afternoon, and dress in good clothes. He should straighten out the house, set the table and make the beds before the Sabbath; the table should remain set throughout the Sabbath. Even if he has many servants, he should get up early on Friday and personally make some of the preparations for the Sabbath. Close to nightfall, he should ask the members of his household whether they have made their preparations. A person should plan to spend the Sabbath in a place where he is expected or can arrive in time to prepare.

A person should not eat an unusually large meal on Friday (except at a religious celebration), or even a regular weekday meal during the last quarter of the day; some people even fast every Friday. A person who voluntarily fasts on Friday should specify that he will eat immediately after the evening service; but if he is fasting because of a bad dream or a public fast, he should fast until after dark.

A person should not do regular work or study intensively on Friday afternoon; but work done in preparation for the Sabbath, such as washing clothes, preparing utensils, and cutting the hair are permitted. It is customary in Jewish communities to signal or announce the arrival of the Sabbath half an hour or an hour in advance, so that people can stop working and complete their preparations.

A candle must be lit to illuminate the house; if there is a woman in the household, she does this for everyone. It is customary to light several candles, especially on the table. They may be lit early if the Sabbath is accepted early. When the candles are lit, the blessing "…Who commanded us to light a Sabbath candle" is recited. It is customary not to derive benefit from the light before reciting the blessing, but benefit must be derived from it afterward. Candles whose light is used on the Sabbath must be able to burn steadily and should be treated with respect.

The Sabbath begins when it gets dark. For 13 minutes after sunset it is uncertain whether it is dark yet, and things that are rabbinically forbidden on the Sabbath may be done then if they are needed for the Sabbath or for a religious purpose. Some say that a person should begin observing the Sabbath somewhat before dark; but he should not begin it more than 1¼ hours before sunset. A person accepts the Sabbath by beginning the evening prayers; and a woman who lights candles accepts the Sabbath by doing so unless she stipulates otherwise. A person who has accepted the Sabbath early, or who is still observing it after dark on Saturday night, may ask others who are not observing it to do work for him, and may benefit from their work. . . .

Chapter 22: Fire and Food Preparation on the Sabbath

A person should not engage in activities that require close attention by the light of a fire if there are grounds for suspecting that he may adjust the fire. Taking fuel from a fire, even if the fuel is not yet burning, is forbidden. Any action that may cause a fire to burn more intensively is forbidden, and so is any action that may cause a fire to be extinguished unless there is danger that the fire may spread out of control or unless the action has no immediate effect. When there is danger to life or to public safety, a Jew is allowed to extinguish a fire.

It is forbidden to separate inferior material from food; but it is permitted to separate food from inferior material, or one type of food from another, if the separation is done by hand and for immediate consumption. Separation of food from its natural covering should be done only by hand or in a nonstandard way. Straining a liquid is permitted only if it is clear or at the time of drinking, but it is permitted to pour off the top layer of a liquid. Squeezing juice from fruit whose juice is commonly drunk is forbidden unless it is squeezed directly into food, but juice that comes out by itself is permitted if it began to come out before the Sabbath. Squeezing liquid out of food in order to eat the food is permitted. Ingredients may be added to food even if they cause it to change color. A person should not deliberately crush ice or salt to extract water from it, but he may allow it to melt or dissolve in water, and he may break through ice to reach the water under it. Small quantities of salt water may be made, provided it is not strong. Large quantities of food should not be salted unless it is to be eaten within a short time. A person may grind spices or salt in a nonstandard way, or crumble bread, or chop food up finely with a knife, but not with a grater, and fruits or vegetables may be chopped only for immediate consumption. A honeycomb may be removed from a beehive if it was detached or crushed before the Sabbath. It is forbidden to mix large quantities of roasted grain with water, and if it has been ground, it should be mixed with water only in a nonstandard way; and it is forbidden to mix finely divided substances with liquid so that they become a single mass. It is permitted to wash utensils that may be needed on the Sabbath, but they must not be washed with a substance that dissolves or that smooths their surface.

Cooking is forbidden. Cooking in the sun is permitted, but cooking in something that was heated by the sun or by a fire is forbidden. Heating solid food that has already been fully cooked is permitted, provided it is done in an indirect way, but food that contains a significant amount of liquid must not be heated if it has become cold, and additional cooking of partly cooked food, or cooking food that was previously baked or roasted, is forbidden. Adding uncooked spices or condiments to food that is still cooking is also forbidden, and soaking food to make it edible is forbidden. Some foods cook more easily than others, and should not be put even into hot water even if it is in a pot that is no longer [hot] or has not been on the fire. Foods or liquids may be warmed near a fire, but only in a place where they can never become hot. Food that has not been completely cooked should not be stirred even after it has been removed from the fire.

Chapter 23: Care of the Body and Clothing on the Sabbath

It is permitted to warm the body at a fire or to put warm objects on it. It is forbidden to wash in warm water even if the body is not all washed at once; but washing only parts of the body in water that was warmed before the Sabbath, washing in cold water after warming the body, and washing in an outdoor hot spring, are permitted. In particular, ritual immersion is permitted. It is forbidden to enter a hot bathhouse on the Sabbath, or to use a bathhouse after the Sabbath if it was heated on the Sabbath. It is permitted to walk in a public domain even if the body is wet, but this should not be done after washing until the water has dried. It is forbidden to wash with a depilatory or with a substance that dissolves or melts. It is forbidden to rub the body with liquids that are usually used for medicinal purposes, or to massage it normally, or to scrub it except to remove dirt. A person must not cut his hair or nails or remove growths from his body.

It is forbidden to wash clothes, or to shake water or dirt out of them or pick things off them whose presence is objectionable. It is forbidden to fold clothes along their original creases, or to remove them from a tight clothespress, or to rub them in order to clean them, but it is permitted to wipe them or scrape them as long as this has no other effect on the clothes or the dirt or on the cleaning instrument. It is permitted to dry or wipe something with a cloth, provided this does not make the cloth very wet or very dirty, which may lead to washing it or squeezing liquid out of it, and provided the cloth does not become stained. For important purposes, a person may wade through water even though his clothes get wet. He may walk in wet clothes, but after taking them off he must not handle them or spread them out to dry.

It is forbidden to carry anything outside a private domain that is not a garment or an ornament, or wear a garment or ornament that is likely to fall off or be taken off; but nowadays we are lenient about many types of ornaments. Wearing garments outside a private domain is permitted even if they are worn only to protect the body, and things worn for medical purposes are permitted. It is forbidden to go barefoot if this is not customary, and a person should dress differently than he does on weekdays so he will remember that it is the Sabbath. If wearing something is permitted, it can be removed in a public domain provided it is not carried; but if attaching something to the clothes and wearing them in a public domain is forbidden, a person should not attach it to his clothes even in a private domain, and similarly for most types of ornaments.

Chapter 24: Animals, Children, and the Sick on the Sabbath

It is forbidden to capture an animal unless it might injure people. It is forbidden to kill an animal or cause it to bleed unless it is dangerous or is chasing someone. It is permitted to alleviate an animal's suffering, but other types of care for a sick animal are forbidden, and it is forbidden to help an animal give birth.

It is forbidden to make any use of an animal; but an animal is allowed to carry things that are attached to it securely and are needed to protect it or are normally used to protect animals of that type. An animal that belongs to a Jew is not allowed to do work on the Sabbath, but is allowed to eat food that is attached to the ground. It is permitted to give food to animals that depend on people for their food.

A Jewish woman who is giving birth is treated like a person whose life is in danger; anything necessary must be done for her, but things that involve violations of the Sabbath should be done in a nonstandard way if possible. This applies from the time she goes into labor until three days after she gives birth; for the next four days, things that violate the Sabbath may be done for her only if she says that she needs them; and for the next 23 days she is treated like a sick person whose life is not in danger.

Anything necessary must be done for a newborn child if there is any chance that it will live. A boy who is definitely viable and who was born normally is circumcised on the Sabbath if it is definitely the eighth day after his birth, but the circumcision should be done only by an experienced person. Everything necessary for the circumcision may be done by Jews if it could not have been done before the Sabbath, and rabbinically forbidden things may be done by non-Jews in any case. A child must not be allowed to become accustomed to violating religious laws; his father must stop him from violating Biblical laws, and must teach him to observe all the laws when he becomes old enough.

Anything necessary must be done if there is a possibility that it will save or prolong someone's life. In such cases, the necessary Sabbath violations may be done by anyone; they must not be done in a nonstandard way, or by a non-Jew, or minimized, unless this involves no delay, and it is permitted to benefit from doing them. For illnesses that involve no danger to life, but that affect the whole body or require bedrest, or for care of small children, things that involve violation of the Sabbath may be done by a non-Jew, and things that involve only purely rabbinical prohibitions may be done even by a Jew. Treatment of minor illnesses, even by a non-Jew, is forbidden because it might lead to preparing medications on the Sabbath; many things that are usually eaten, drunk, or applied to the body for medical purposes are therefore forbidden. However, medical procedures that are begun during the week may be continued on the Sabbath.

Chapter 25: Constructive Activities on the Sabbath

Making or removing a partition a handsbreadth wide, even if it is temporary, is forbidden if it is a roof or is a wall that serves a religious purpose, but if a handsbreadth of such a wall or roof already existed before the Sabbath, temporary addition to it is permitted. Temporary partitions are permitted if the surrounded space is less than a handsbreadth or if there is no need for that space, but the walls should not be put up before the roof.

Breaking or opening an unbroken utensil, or deliberately widening an opening, is forbidden, but removing or opening attached pieces is permitted provided they are not permanently attached and the intent is only to get access to the contents, not to create an opening or to use the pieces. Temporarily opening or closing even a permanent structure is permitted when it is done with objects that are used for that purpose, such as doors, shutters, and locks. Making holes in the ground (or in an object attached to the ground), or smoothing them out, is forbidden.

Making, assembling, or fixing a utensil is forbidden unless the parts are loose, or the utensil is made from edible material, or the repair is done in a nonstandard way.

It is forbidden to tie or untie a permanent knot. It is permitted to tighten or loosen a drawstring, but it is forbidden to tighten or loosen even temporary stitching, to paste objects together or to separate pasted objects.

It is forbidden to gather plants or natural objects from the place where they originated or to assemble them into a single object. It is forbidden to reshape a deformable substance or to soften a hard substance. It is forbidden to make or destroy even temporary markings, or to make a surface suitable for marking.

It is forbidden to drop seeds in a place where they may grow, or to spill water in a place where plants may benefit from it, or to soak seeds in water. Cut plants may be put in water so they will not wilt, but not if they may open. It is forbidden to detach parts from a plant that has taken root, even in an object that is not attached to the ground, and even if the parts are no longer alive; and it is forbidden to take such an object off the ground or put it on the ground.

It is forbidden to make any direct use of any part of a tree that is more than three handsbreadths above the ground—for example, to climb it, move it, put something on it or lean something against it. It is permitted to make use of other types of plants, provided this does not detach them from the ground, but edible parts of such plants should not be handled.

Chapter 26: Other Activities on the Sabbath

A person should not run or take long steps, but walks are permitted, and a person may run to fulfill a Commandment or to do something enjoyable. It is forbidden to swim in a non-enclosed pool, or to float objects on the water, but it is permitted to enter a ship that is grounded or tied up.

It is forbidden to play a musical instrument or to make non-musical sounds with an instrument. It is permitted to set a clock before the Sabbath to strike the hours. A person should not engage excessively in idle talk, but enjoyable conversation is permitted. Commercial public announcements are forbidden.

It is permitted to read a letter that has just arrived if its contents might be urgent, but a person should not look at other secular documents. Children should not be taught new things, but reviewing is permitted. Mental calculations about things that have not yet been completed are forbidden unless they are for religious purposes. It is permitted to specify numbers of objects that are to be acquired, but not to measure or to specify quantities or prices, except for religious purposes.

A person should not be paid for doing things on the Sabbath, but may be paid for doing things in a period that includes the Sabbath. It is forbidden to prepare to go outside the Sabbath boundary immediately after the Sabbath except for religious purposes or to prevent loss, but it is permitted to prepare to do other things immediately after the Sabbath. It is forbidden to discuss plans for doing things after the Sabbath that are forbidden on the Sabbath. It is forbidden to make an agreement to do work or business after the Sabbath, but it is permitted to ask someone to do things after the Sabbath that could also be done on the Sabbath.

A person must not inspect his property, and should not even think about his affairs. It is permitted to borrow something for a short period, and to leave a security deposit, but longer-term loans should not be made or repaid. It is forbidden to play games of chance for profit, and things should not be divided by casting lots.

It is forbidden to arrest, judge, or punish, to marry or divorce (except on a deathbed), to sanctify or redeem, to inspect a first-born for blemishes, or to set aside offerings. It is permitted to release a person from a vow that interferes with observance of the Sabbath, and for a husband to annul a wife's vow. It is permitted to annul community bans, or to impose bans involving matters related to the Sabbath.

Chapter 27: Things That Must Not Be Handled on the Sabbath

It is forbidden to handle utensils whose use is forbidden or that are never used even on weekdays except for specific purposes that are not permitted on the Sabbath. Utensils that are usually used for purposes that are forbidden on the Sabbath may be used for permissible purposes, or may be moved if their place is needed, but otherwise they must not be handled. Other types of utensils and their parts may be handled whenever there is a reason for doing so, even if they are very large or heavy. Books, food, or utensils containing them may be handled even for no reason. Non-manufactured objects such as rocks must not be handled even for purposes of use unless they were set aside before the Sabbath for regular use or were made part of a utensil. Repulsive objects may be handled if it is necessary to dispose of them. Animals may be helped to move, but may not be lifted.

If a utensil breaks, even on the Sabbath, the pieces may be handled if they are still usable or if it would be dangerous not to remove them, but if they were discarded by their owner they must not be handled. It is forbidden to handle food that was put away by its owner before the Sabbath because it was not yet fit to eat, or food that did not exist or was not available when the Sabbath began. Similarly, a utensil that was intentionally made forbidden (for example, a lamp that was lit) when the Sabbath began must not be handled even after it becomes permitted (for example, after the lamp goes out).

Even when it is forbidden to handle an object, it is permitted to touch it or to handle things that are in contact with it even if this causes it to move. If an object that it is forbidden to handle is put on top of a permissible object that belongs to the same person with the intent that it remain there for the Sabbath, handling the permissible object becomes forbidden unless more important permissible objects are also on top of it before the Sabbath; but if there was no such intent, the permissible object may be moved so as to cause the forbidden object to fall off it, or it may be removed with the forbidden object still on it if its place is needed. A utensil must not be put where forbidden objects will fall on it on the Sabbath unless it was put there before the Sabbath; but it is permitted to cover a forbidden object with a utensil.

Large quantities of food should not be moved unless the space is needed for religious purposes or the food is needed for guests. Food should not be transported in a standard way unless it is needed for guests, and very large quantities of water should not be drawn.

Chapter 28: Moving Things from One Domain to Another on the Sabbath

A region at least four by four handsbreadths in horizontal size and at least ten handsbreadths high that is surrounded by partitions or adjacent regions having a combined height difference (from it) of at least ten handsbreadths is called a private domain. Even a portable object can be a private domain, and smaller regions adjacent to a private domain, as well as the space above it, are regarded as belonging to it.

An unroofed region at least 16 cubits wide that is open at both ends and is used for public passage is called a public domain. Portions of such a region, or regions adjacent to it, that differ from it in height by more than three handsbreadths are not regarded as part of [it] unless they are between nine and ten handsbreadths high and are used by the public, and the space ten or more handsbreadths above it is also not regarded as part of it.

A region of size at least four by four handsbreadths that is roofed or is not used for public passage (for example, if it is partly surrounded by partitions, or differs in height from the adjacent regions by between three and ten handsbreadths), even if it is adjacent to a public domain, is called a KARMELIS. A smaller region adjacent to a KARMELIS is also regarded as a KARMELIS unless it is ten or more handsbreadths above it.

A small region adjacent to a public domain that differs from it in height by between three and ten handsbreadths is called a MEKOM PETUR. The space ten or more handsbreadths above a public domain or KARMELIS is also called a MEKOM PETUR.

It is Biblically forbidden to move things from a private domain to a public domain or vice versa, and it is rabbinically forbidden to move things personally from either of them to a KARMELIS or vice versa.

It is Biblically forbidden to move things more than four cubits in a public domain, and rabbinically forbidden to do so in a KARMELIS, even if the moving is done only a little at a time.

To be valid, a partition must be able to withstand an ordinary wind and must come within three handsbreadths of the ground. It can be composed even of movable objects or of tied animals. It must not have a gap wider than ten cubits or a gap used by the public, and a majority of it must not consist of gaps three handsbreadths or more wide. A gap covered by a lintel that has two vertical pieces under it, forming an "entrance shape," is not regarded as a gap, but opinions differ as to whether this is effective in an uninhabited area or for a gap more than ten cubits wide.

Chapter 29: Restrictions on Private Domains; Combining Private Domains

It is rabbinically forbidden to move things more than four cubits in an unroofed private domain that is more than 100 cubits long or more than 5000 square cubits in area that is not used for residential purposes; and it is permitted to move things between such a domain and a KARMELIS.

It is rabbinically forbidden to move things more than four cubits in a courtyard or alley that is surrounded by partitions on only three sides; to make it permissible, the custom is to construct an "entrance shape" on the open side. These methods are effective even for a courtyard or alley that is open at both ends; but converting a public domain into a private domain requires doors that can be closed.

If a private domain such as a courtyard is shared by people who eat separately in permanent homes, things may be moved freely within the shared domain, but it is rabbinically forbidden to move things between the homes, or between them and the shared domain, unless the people "combine" by contributing to a common collection of food, called an ERUV CHATZEROS. Two groups of people may make a common ERUV if their domains are connected.

Similarly, when several courtyards are adjacent to the same alley, it is rabbinically forbidden to move things between the courtyards and the alley unless the residents in the courtyards form a "partnership" by contributing to a common collection of food. When an alley forms a partnership, the individual courtyards need not combine.

If someone who must participate in an ERUV or partnership did not do so, he may instead verbally annul his claim to a share in the common domain; but if he is a non-Jew, the others must rent his share from him for a token amount before they can make an ERUV.

When the food used for an ERUV or partnership is collected, the blessing "...Who commanded us about an ERUV" is recited.

Glossary

cubit	a unit of measurement based on the length of the forearm
eruv chatzeros	literally, "joining of courtyards" or "mixed courtyards"